THE PRINCETON COMPANION
TO JEWISH STUDIES

The Princeton Companion to Jewish Studies

EDITED BY

LEORA BATNITZKY

EVE KRAKOWSKI

STEVEN WEITZMAN

PRINCETON UNIVERSITY PRESS
PRINCETON & OXFORD

Copyright © 2025 by Princeton University Press

Princeton University Press is committed to the protection of copyright and the intellectual property our authors entrust to us. Copyright promotes the progress and integrity of knowledge created by humans. By engaging with an authorized copy of this work, you are supporting creators and the global exchange of ideas. As this work is protected by copyright, any reproduction or distribution of it in any form for any purpose requires permission; permission requests should be sent to permissions@press.princeton.edu. Ingestion of any IP for any AI purposes is strictly prohibited.

Published by Princeton University Press
41 William Street, Princeton, New Jersey 08540
99 Banbury Road, Oxford OX2 6JX

press.princeton.edu

GPSR Authorized Representative: Easy Access System Europe - Mustamäe tee 50, 10621 Tallinn, Estonia, gpsr.requests@easproject.com

All Rights Reserved

Library of Congress Control Number: 2025937766

ISBN 9780691215198
ISBN (e-book) 9780691220826

British Library Cataloging-in-Publication Data is available

Editorial: Fred Appel, James Collier
Production Editorial: Elizabeth Byrd
Jacket: Haley Jin Mee Chung
Production: Erin Suydam
Publicity: William Pagdatoon
Copyeditor: Gail Naron Chalew

Jacket Credit: Zoonar GmbH / Alamy Stock Photo

Printed in the United States of America

10 9 8 7 6 5 4 3 2 1

CONTENTS

Introduction	1
PART 1: RETHINKING THE PAST	13
1.1 ANTIQUITY AND ITS LEGACIES	15
1 Scripture—Naphtali S. Meshel	15
2 From Israel to the Jews—Sylvie Honigman	37
3 The Rabbis—Moulie Vidas	55
1.2 MEDIEVAL LIVES	80
4 The Jewish Community—Marina Rustow	80
5 Everyday Judaism—Elisheva Baumgarten	119
6 Difference and Violence—Magda Teter	139
7 Piety and Knowledge—Maoz Kahana	162
1.3. MODERNITIES	184
8 Citizenship—Julie E. Cooper	184
9 Colonialism—Ethan B. Katz	208
10 Catastrophe—Mark Roseman	231
11 Culture—Olga Litvak	253

PART 2. IDEAS AND EXPRESSION — 271

12 God and the Sacred—Sarit Kattan Gribetz — 273

13 Philosophy—Yonatan Y. Brafman — 293

14 Lived Religion—Rachel B. Gross — 312

15 Language—Sarah Bunin Benor — 331

16 Literature—Shachar Pinsker — 350

17 Music—Edwin Seroussi — 368

18 Visual Culture—Maya Balakirsky Katz — 397

19 Yiddish—Anna Shternshis — 414

PART 3. INTERACTIONS AND IDENTITY — 433

20 Sociology—Ilana M. Horwitz — 435

21 Anthropology—Michal Kravel-Tovi — 455

22 Law—Suzanne Last Stone — 474

23 Race—Bruce Haynes — 487

24 Gender—Laura Levitt — 505

25 Mizrahi Culture—Lital Levy — 518

26 Israel Studies—Jonathan Marc Gribetz — 541

Acknowledgments 559

Index 561

Introduction

NAVIGATING A KNOWLEDGE EXPLOSION

Leora Batnitzky, Eve Krakowski, and Steven Weitzman

THIS BOOK is intended as an opening into the field of Jewish Studies for readers who want to learn more about the questions it is asking and the insights it is generating. It is not an introduction to the Jews or Judaism or Jewish history. Its subject is the academic study of the Jews, an interdisciplinary field that brings together historical research and the study of philosophy, language, culture, behavior, social organization, and personal experience.

Scholarship has long been important in Jewish culture, but academic Jewish Studies represents a distinctly modern kind of study and knowledge different from earlier modes. Individual scholars in the field may be religious in their personal lives, but the field itself is not religious in orientation. Its goal is to understand Jewishness as a particular strand of human experience. In contrast to other modes of Jewish study, academic Jewish Studies is not a religious undertaking, a way of relating to God or Torah, but an intellectual enterprise driven by curiosity about the world. The field is "critical" in relation to its subjects, which does not mean that it is hostile to them, but rather that it takes a skeptical approach to knowledge about them, constantly questioning what can be learned from its sources, questioning the findings of earlier scholars, and interrogating its own premises and methods. This is how scholars in other fields, humanistic and scientific, pursue the truth. Academic Jewish Studies embraces this same approach in its quest for a deeper understanding of Jewish sources, history, and culture.

As this volume demonstrates, the subjects that scholars of Jewish Studies explore and the methods they use to do so are rich and diverse, but they all revolve around fundamental questions about Jews, Judaism, and Jewishness—distinct but at times related phenomena. Among the questions asked by scholars of Jewish Studies are the following: Who are the Jews? How do they differ from and relate to other peoples and cultures? Where do Jews come from, and what is their history? How have Jews influenced and been influenced by their assorted and at times divergent historical, political, and cultural environments? What do Jewish texts mean, and how does one make sense of them? What kinds of ideas and values have been central to Jewish traditions? How have these ideas and values changed and been expressed in different times and places? How have ordinary Jews lived their daily lives in the different worlds that they have inhabited? What kinds of languages, cultures, music, art, literature, and thought have Jews drawn from and produced? What is the role of law in Jewish life? Ritual? Family? Institutions? In one way or another, these are all questions about who Jews are, why they think and act as they do, and how they fit into the world.

To answer these questions, Jewish Studies draws on the disciplines and methods of the modern academy—critical historical research, anthropology, literary studies, philosophy, and sociology, among others—to illuminate the past and present of Jewish life, thought, and expression. The goal of such methods is to gain a better understanding of human experience through the careful observation and analysis of evidence, as well as through self-reflective examination of one's own assumptions, biases, and motivations. Such study is limited in what it can conclude, because it is confined by the available evidence; scholars interpret that evidence in different ways and can reach very different conclusions, and the field is always in the process of correcting and revising itself. And yet, Jewish Studies has succeeded in making many discoveries, big and small, and it has grown more nuanced, capacious, and sophisticated in its analyses. It is fair to say that we know more today about Jewish life past and present than ever before, with much yet to learn.

Jewish Studies originated in nineteenth-century Germany. The field has evolved significantly since its beginning, but it is still shaped by its origins and early history. In the context of European debates about Jewish emancipation, the initial main aim of Jewish Studies was to insist that Judaism and the Jewish people were worthy of academic study. Jews in Europe at the time faced hostility and discrimination from the Christian majority, but the Enlightenment and its belief in the power of reason to solve any problem had also penetrated Jewish intellectual culture in Europe. Early practitioners of what was then called *Wis-*

senschaft des Judentums and is now known as academic Jewish Studies brought this faith in reason to the study of the Jewish people. They adapted the methods of academic study at the time—the study of history, language, texts, and philosophy—and applied them to Jews with the hope of both overthrowing the shackles imposed by traditional modes of Jewish scholarship and helping the Jewish people develop and progress. They called what they did "science" (*Wissenschaft*)—not science in the sense that it is practiced today in the physical or life sciences but science in the sense of a rigorous, critical, evidence- and fact-based approach to research.

In the two centuries since the rise of academic Jewish Studies, the field has faced many challenges. The rise of Nazism proved especially devastating, first denying Jewish scholars access to universities, forcing many into exile, and slaughtering those who remained in Europe; it also brought to a tragic end some 750 institutions of European Jewish learning. But by this time academic study of the Jewish people had migrated to new contexts—to the United States; to mandatory Palestine, which saw the establishment of the Hebrew University in 1925; and even to the Soviet Union. The field took root in these new contexts. Academia today faces many challenges—declining interest in and funding for humanities-based scholarship, too few employment opportunities for scholars, disinterest or even suspicion in the broader community, and a movement to boycott Israeli academic institutions. Nonetheless, Jewish Studies has not only survived but also thrived, especially when granted sufficient resources.

In Israel, Jewish Studies research today is pursued in several universities at a very high level of specialization and benefits from the support of institutions that include a National Library housing some five million volumes. In the United States, in addition to Jewish institutions such as the Jewish Theological Seminary and Hebrew Union College, many major research universities and smaller liberal arts colleges across the country are home to Jewish Studies programs. The Association for Jewish Studies, based in North America and the largest learned society in the field of Jewish Studies, counts upward of two thousand members. The academic study of Judaism also flourishes in parts of Europe, most especially—and inspiringly—in Germany, where Jewish scholars and scholarship were previously devastated by the Holocaust.

The field in terms of its membership has also become increasingly diverse, now encompassing male, female, and transgender scholars, as well as scholars from both religious and secular backgrounds. Although the majority of scholars identity as Jewish, Jewish Studies also draws non-Jews, including a small number of Muslim scholars in Arab countries. Jewish Studies is still centered in

Israel, the United States, and Western Europe, but scholars can be found in many other contexts as well—in Latin America, South Africa, and even mainland China. The Russian invasion of Ukraine in 2023, which threatened Jewish-related archives and museums, made people elsewhere aware of how much Jewish Studies research has continued there in fields like Yiddish studies, Holocaust studies, and Jewish music studies. The digital revolution—the rise of the internet, the digitization of archives, and the use of computing tools for research and teaching—has transformed the creation and dissemination of knowledge.

Thanks in part to these technological advances, Jewish Studies—like every other field of academic research in the last few decades—has undergone a knowledge explosion, a proliferation of new information, and an expansion of new ways of managing and interpreting it. Reference works published as recently as a decade ago now feel out of date as information continues to flow in through new discoveries and scholars think about the data in new ways. What counts as worth studying has been increasingly broadened—first to include the perspectives of women and now encompassing children, the poor, and those with disabilities: This increasing breadth and variety are only matched by the field's expanded power to assemble and analyze large amounts of data from archaeology, new archival research, and the digital humanities.

Research has also made its way into less familiar realms. Today, one of the most vital subfields of Jewish Studies is the study of Jewish life in contexts once deemed too peripheral to focus on, such as North Africa, Yemen, and India. Even the most seemingly familiar of Jewish Studies subjects—the Bible, the Talmud, canonical Jewish thinkers of the Middle Ages and modernity—are unleashing new waves of study as they are read in new ways and placed in new historical and cultural contexts.

Jewish Studies today is no longer driven by the same defensiveness with which the field began. It does not need to justify its existence as in the nineteenth century, nor to defend Jews from the prejudices and forms of persecution that prevailed when the field originated. Still, like all fields in the humanities and social sciences, research in Jewish Studies continues to be driven by pressing contemporary concerns. Anti-Jewish prejudice was one of the reasons for the development of Jewish Studies in the first place, and its recent resurgence on college campuses is refocusing the field even in the short time it has taken to construct this volume. In the United States during the first half of the twentieth century, Jewish Studies was largely confined to Jewish institutions. Today it is based in non-Jewish universities, private and public, and in many of those places, it is organized in a way meant to help integrate scholars into other fields. (In many U.S. universities, Jewish Studies is a program rather than a department—that is, it does not operate as a separate unit, but brings together faculty whose primary academic home is some other department.) The desire to integrate into mainstream academia remains a driving impulse of the field to this very day.

This volume aims to offer readers an engaging picture of Jewish Studies and its insights in the early twenty-first century—to convey how the understanding of the Jewish past has changed in recent decades and to introduce the many other disciplines that are being used to understand Jewish culture and society both past and present. Jewish Studies is so capacious that we do not claim to offer a complete or definitive overview of the field. Our goal is to give a sense of its intellectual diversity and to offer readers a readable entry point into some of the many different pathways of knowledge that recent scholars have been pursuing. What follows are a series of doorways into different areas of research from across the expanse of Jewish Studies: These brief chapters aim to share what scholars in this field are focused on, what questions they are asking, and how they go about addressing those questions.

How This Book Is Organized

All research is collaborative. Even the most solitary forms of library research depend on scholars cooperating with each other to provide the feedback and critique necessary to improve and validate each other's findings, as well as to publish the journals and other channels through which new insights and knowledge are disseminated. Scholarship, in its quest for truth, must remain open to different perspectives and embrace debate and difference of interpretation. To give a true sense of the field, we felt it was important for this book to mirror these qualities—both the collaborative spirit of research and its intellectual diversity.

Rather than presuming to represent the field ourselves, we commissioned scholars from a range of disciplines to offer snapshots of their fields of research, along with a brief bibliography at the end of each chapter for those who want to learn more. We sought to coordinate the efforts of the contributors by bringing them together in small Zoom working groups to share their work and exchange feedback—that was our attempt at promoting collaboration. At the same time, we sought to stay true to the field's diversity by encouraging scholars to frame their chapters as they saw fit. One example of this diversity is scholars' use of different methods for rendering words in Hebrew and other Jewish languages into English. We have smoothed out some of the inconsistences, but not all of them, out of respect for the norms of different subfields. Such is our approach for deeper methodological differences as well.

Part of what we want to introduce in this book is the intellectual variety within Jewish Studies—how different disciplines approach the challenge of introducing their subfields, how they organize their presentation, what questions they highlight, and what insights they emphasize.

Part 1: Rethinking the Past

The anchoring field of Jewish Studies today, the subfield populated by the largest number of scholars, is the study of Jewish history, and the first half of the book is devoted to current scholarship in subfields of the study of the past. This is not itself a history—if one is interested in Jewish history, there are many books on the subject (including *The Jews: A History,* cowritten by one of us). What we offer here is chronologically arranged but is more eclectic in approach. Some chapters are focused on sources such as the Bible or rabbinic texts, and others are organized around a particular theme or historical change. We are also very mindful that significant areas of historical research are not represented in this book. Unable to accommodate it all within a single volume, our goal was to offer samples of the research.

Two fields represented in this first half of the volume—biblical studies and Holocaust studies—have a complex relationship to Jewish Studies. The field of biblical studies is older than Jewish Studies, and Jewish biblical scholars are greatly outnumbered by Christian scholars interested in the Hebrew Bible/Old Testament as a founding document in Christian tradition. Holocaust studies, to the extent that it focuses on the perpetrators of the Holocaust, is not focused on the Jews per se. But both biblical studies and Holocaust studies obviously intersect with Jewish Studies, so we decided to include them. Although we have not presumed to try to cover all of Jewish history, the chapters do move chronologically from the earliest origins of Jewish culture into the modern Jewish experience. Part 1 captures how much this enormously vital area of research as practiced today differs in its focus from the historical research produced by earlier generations of scholars. Readers interested in how the study of history has changed within Jewish Studies will find the chapters that focus on medieval Jewish history particularly illuminating.

Parts 2 and 3: Ideas and Expression,
and Interactions and Identity

History is not the only lens through which scholars have sought to understand Jews. This book's second half is devoted to research coming from other perspectives. Here, too, we make no claim to being comprehensive. The chapters in parts 2 and 3, however, make clear that Jewish Studies is a genuinely interdisciplinary field and one that has grown increasingly expansive in how it thinks about its subject.

Part 2 surveys scholarship focused on "ideas and expression." By "ideas," we mean important religious beliefs and concepts together with philosophy, the use of the intellect to explore life's purpose, questions of ethics and justice, and the relationship between revelation and reason. "Expression" encompasses language, ritual, material culture, literature, music, and visual culture—the processes and media through which Jews express imagination and emotion.

We were not able to include every kind of research that might be encompassed within these categories. Jewish folklore studies, the effort to document and analyze storytelling and popular culture among large groups of people, was once a very robust subfield and played an impotant role in the formation of Jewish Studies; however, this kind of research has gone into decline as the study of folklore in general has declined, although it continues to be part of the study of Jewish anthropology. On the upswing is the study of Jewish digital culture—how Jews use new technologies and social media to express themselves. That kind of research is so new that we were not able to digest and incorporate it, but it has grown increasingly important over the last two decades. The same is true for the impact of digital humanities on the practice of research in Jewish Studies; the increased accessibility of texts and art because of digitization, the construction of large databases, and the invention of new technological tools for the management and analysis of "big data."[1] These developments, now further empowered by AI-expanded capabilities, are a driver of the knowledge explosion underway, and this volume does not pretend to keep up with it all.

What we have tried to do is give a sense of the diversity of *interpretive* approaches that scholars today are bringing to the study of Jewish culture. At the core of this study is the act of close reading—the careful study of language, texts, and art in search of meaning. Thus, this section of the book stresses the continued importance of such interpretation to the field of Jewish Studies. As scholars know well, the humanities, although always facing one challenge or another, have been in a state of acute crisis since the 2010s, losing student engagement and university support. Jewish Studies is by no means insulated from this trend. One of our goals with part 2 is to assert the continued vitality of humanities-driven—and humanity-driven—Jewish Studies research.

The third part of the book, focused on "interactions and identity," moves beyond the humanities into anthropology, sociology, the study of law, identity, and politics. The Association for Jewish Studies, the largest learned society in this academic field, is largely centered on history and the humanities, but there also exist scholarly organizations like the Association for the Social Scientific Study of Jewry that draw on social-scientific fields to shed light on Jewish life. One of our goals in part 3 is to call attention to this kind of research. The concept of "identity" is double-edged, referring both to what distinguishes a person from others and to what connects one to others. Some chapters in this section focus on different dimensions of Jewish identity and what distinguishes Jews from each other, but they also explore the intersectional dimensions of Jewish identity; how Jewishness is inflected by gender, racial identity, and economics. In contrast to much of the research surveyed in part 1, which is focused on the Jewish past, the research explored in part 3 often concentrates on the Jewish present. We include chapters that think aloud about the challenges of such study to better understand aspects of Jewish life that are inexhaustibly variable and endlessly changing.

Because it was our goal to cover the field of Jewish Studies in a single, manageable volume, we had to make difficult decisions about what to include and thus what to exclude, and we are very mindful of all that we have left out. In addition to fields such as folklore studies and digital Jewish culture, there has been an explosion of relevant research in population genetics, the analysis of DNA evidence to study Jewish origins and ancestry, migration, and mating practices. Such research goes back to the early twentieth century but has taken off since the late 1990s, especially since completion of the Human Genome project. We have not been in a position to include it here or to include the vast amount of effort invested into genealogical research, a field distinguished by the important role played by hobbyists. Another entire field that did not make it into this survey is the study of Jewish education. Education is an essential part of any culture, and that is especially true for Jewish culture, which has placed great emphasis on study as a religiously and socially important endeavor since antiquity. Although the study of Jewish education itself is another relatively new field of academic research, intensifying in recent decades and growing increasingly capacious in what it counts as education, it too exceeded what we could accommodate within a single volume.[2]

We also acknowledge the North American bias of this book. We endeavored to include scholars from other regions, but we focused on scholars and scholarship that we thought would be of interest to English-language readers. We acknowledge falling short in conveying the global and multilanguage character of Jewish Studies scholarship, which includes research from the Soviet Union and Russia and the countries in the Soviet Bloc that came into their own after its collapse; Latin American Jewish Studies; the study of Jewish life in Africa and East Asia; and the study of anti-Jewish hatred in its many manifestations.

This last topic became newly central to the field following the Hamas attack on October 7, 2023, and the surge in anti-Jewish and anti-Zionist animus that followed in 2023 and 2024, precipitating new centers and academic positions in the field of antisemitism studies. To be sure, antisemitism had long been a central focus of Jewish Studies, especially as it related to the Holocaust, and there had existed centers for antisemitism research at Yale, Indiana University, and a few other places in North America, Israel, and Europe. Yet, scholars in the United States, feeling well integrated into American society, tended to treat it as a subject of historical inquiry, as part of the Jewish past; research that focused on contemporary antisemitism was rare. Although there were indications that antisemitism had been ticking upward globally since at least the mid-2010s, the field was to a large degree caught off-guard by the vitriol and violence of the last two years; it is still adapting, and we do not know where the field is headed.

That brings us to something else that we were not able to convey: the politics of the field and the way it is affected by politics. We finished this book at an extremely fraught moment. The Hamas attack, followed by Israel's war in Gaza and the worldwide public condemnation it unleashed, affected Israeli colleagues in very direct ways and created new institutional pressures within Israel and from abroad. Anti-Israel protests, distinct from but intersecting with a global uptick in antisemitism, changed the landscape for Jewish Studies in the United States and Europe—creating feelings of isolation, stigmatization, moral conflict, outrage, and stress among many scholars. Jewish Studies has never been insulated from politics and political conflicts, including rifts over Zionism, but the current situation goes beyond anything in living memory in terms of the numbers of scholars it affects, the rifts it has created with colleagues, and its impact on the positioning of Jewish Studies within universities.

This era of crisis, trauma, misunderstanding, and misrepresentation also underscores the importance of Jewish Studies as a counter to anti-Jewish hostility and discrimination, as well as its ability to challenge unfounded generalizations and simple binaries. While it is our hope that this volume reaches scholars, students, and other learners who are Jewish and are curious about what they can learn about their history, culture, and identity from academic research, we also very much want this book to reach learners who are not Jewish, believing as we do that Jewish Studies has insights to offer to anyone seeking to better understand what it means to be human.

We recognize that, just as the nineteenth-century European scholars who founded Jewish Studies were not as objective as they imagined themselves to be, it is likely future generations will see limitations in the perpective of today's scholars. But the questioning of scholarly objectivity does not mean that scholarship should abandon the pursuit of knowledge and truth based on evidence and arguments, rather than ideology. The integration of Jewish Studies within universities was a step forward in the struggle to make academia more encompassing of human experience, and the field has been able to make distinctive contributions to the study of minorities, among other subjects. Nothing that has happened in this era argues for knowing less about the Jews; it argues for knowing more. Indeed, the proliferation of competing ideologies that we are now experiencing only shows why universities have an obligation to be spaces dedicated to the pursuits of knowledge and truth above all, even when those findings are inconvenient for certain ideologies or points of view.

These are the beliefs that have sustained us in producing this volume, but its ultimate lessons will depend on you, the reader. If you are a scholar of Jewish Studies, the book offers a crash course in other subfields that may be unfamiliar. If you are a scholar from outside Jewish Studies, you may find it interesting to compare what is happening in this field to developments in your own area of specialty. If you are a reader being introduced to the field for the first time, you will encounter many of the fruits of contemporary Jewish Studies and get a sense of how many different pathways to knowledge coexist within the field. Whatever motivates you to learn more about Jewish Studies, each chapter ends with a brief bibliography of additional readings that can lead you further into the topic.

Two centuries of academic Jewish Studies inspire both pride and humility. The pride arises from all the insight and knowledge that scholars have generated and from the role that scholarship has played in sustaining the vitality of Jewish culture. The humility comes from knowing how much we don't know and from having to accept that scholarship has not had the transformative impact that the field's founders envisioned for it and that it is too often seen as irrelevant beyond academia. We will consider this book to be successful if it is able to open up

Jewish Studies as it exists today and help readers navigate its subfields—but even more so, if it is able to convey why this knowledge is worth pursuing and how much more remains to be discovered.

Notes

1. For a survey of this kind of research, see Heidi Campbell, *Digital Judaism: Jewish Negotiations with Digital Media and Culture* (Routledge, 2015).

2. See, for example, Ari Kelman, *Jewish Education* (Rutgers University Press, 2024).

PART 1

Rethinking the Past

1.1 Antiquity and Its Legacies

1

Scripture

Naphtali S. Meshel,
Hebrew University of Jerusalem

THE HEBREW Bible is an anthology of works composed and compiled over the course of roughly a millennium in the Southern Levant and among Judeans in Babylonian exile mostly in a language now called "Biblical Hebrew" (sections of Ezra–Nehemiah and of Daniel are in Aramaic).

The early Jewish designations of the Hebrew Bible were *kitvei ha-qodesh-* ("holy writings")—a term that points to its perception as a collection (cf. Greek *ta biblia*, "books," the source of our English word "Bible")—and *mikra* ("reading" || Aramaic *kera*). Today the term "Tanakh" has become current as an acronym for *Torah* ("Instruction"), *Nevi'im* ("Prophets"), and *Ketuvim* ("Writings")— these were the three major sections of the Hebrew Bible in medieval Jewish manuscripts and printed editions.

The (Jewish) Tanakh is generally coextensive with the (Christian) Old Testament, although the Tanakh does not include the Old Testament Apocrypha and a few minor additions included in some Christian Bibles, and the Tanakh and the Old Testament differ in their subdivisions and the internal order of their books.[1] The difference between them is primarily one of perspective: whether the Hebrew Bible, the Tanakh, is Scripture that is holy writ, or only part of Scripture along with the New Testament. In this chapter, the term "Bible" and its derivatives (biblical, postbiblical) occasionally serve as shorthand for the Hebrew Bible.

Very little is known about the processes by which some books comprising the Hebrew Bible came to be perceived as "biblical" and were included, while others considered "apocryphal" were excluded. These processes seem to have been gradual—first the Torah, then the Prophets, and finally the other Writings were canonized. It is possible that, in some stages, the process of canonization was one of collection, not selection.

This chapter explores the contents of the Hebrew Bible from two complementary perspectives: first, in terms of the forms and functions of the texts in the Hebrew Bible within the ancient Israelite cultures that produced them, and second, in terms of the role of the Hebrew Bible as a formative document of Jewish life. Each section highlights both significant continuities and important discontinuities between the Hebrew Bible as a repository of ancient Israelite texts and the Hebrew Bible as Jewish Scripture.

Although the incorporation of a chapter on the Hebrew Bible in a volume dedicated to Jewish Studies seems self-evident, it also highlights two major tensions. The first is between "Jewish" and "biblical," because the Hebrew Bible is not, strictly speaking, a Jewish composition. There is continuity between the pre-Hellenistic ancient Israelite cultures that produced the lion's share of the texts included in the Hebrew Bible and later Judaism(s) and Jewish cultures that inherited and reshaped these texts. Nevertheless, it is helpful to keep in mind that the English term "Judaism" (from the Greek *Ioudaismos*, cf. Hebrew *Yehuda*, "Judah/Judea") and the adjective "Jewish" usually refer to the cultures and religious beliefs that characterized Jews from the Hellenistic period onward, rather than to ancient Israelites in the Northern Kingdom of Israel (tenth to eighth centuries BCE), in the Southern Kingdom of Judah (destroyed in 586 BCE), in Babylonian Exile (sixth century BCE), and in the Persian province of Yehud (late sixth century to late fourth century BCE).

The second tension pertains to incorporating biblical studies, a field of knowledge that in modernity has its origins in Christian scholarship within a Western European academic setting, into the study of the Jews.

A telling example is the relative dating of the Pentateuch's various components in nineteenth-century scholarship, as epitomized in Julius Wellhausen's *Prolegomena zur Geschichte Israels*.[2] This influential historical-philological study was informed by a Hegelian conception of dialectical historical patterns and by a supersessionist agenda, imagining that the various strata of the Pentateuch reflected predictable stages in the evolution of the religious experience. Thus, early forms of "Yahwistic" religion were portrayed positively as expressions of a spontaneous religious experience close in spirit to the prophets. In contrast, meticulous, "parochial" laws were considered a degraded descendant of these ancient forms of religion, and the texts that contained them—such as Leviticus—were therefore considered to be of a late date. Priestly legalism was thus viewed as an unfortunate step in the direction of Pharisaic Jewish (and, ultimately, Catholic) religiosity, contrasting starkly with the kind of grassroots religious vivacity reflected in the earlier Pentateuchal texts—and in the early Jesus movement and ultimately in Protestant thought.

As a counterreaction to Wellhausen, scholars such as Yehezkel Kaufmann posited that Priestly legalism was not a late and fossilized form of Israelite religion but rather was pre-exilic in origin. Now that the dust has settled, a more balanced view has emerged. Yet, some Jewish thinkers—and not only those within Orthodox or fundamentalist circles—have remained suspicious of "higher criticism," which Solomon Schechter famously dubbed "higher anti-Semitism."[3]

The Texts of the Hebrew Bible

When considering the Hebrew Bible, it is helpful to remember that it constitutes a kind of anthology composed of texts written in different time periods and in slightly divergent dialects of Hebrew. These differences are masked by a standardization of the spelling and grammatical forms superimposed on the Bible by later scribes. We do not have biblical texts in the form that they were originally composed; they have been passed down over many generations and that long history of copying and recopying has changed the form and content of the Bible in significant ways.

Most known ancient Near Eastern writings (some of which had a long transmission history in antiquity) were discovered anew and deciphered in the last few centuries—including a small corpus of Canaanite inscriptions. Biblical texts, in contrast, have survived down to modernity through a process of continuous transmission. They reflect long and often intertwined processes of composition, editing, and copying—the earliest stages of this process, which may have been oral, are largely undocumented—first in the Northern and Southern Kingdoms and then among Judeans in Babylonian Exile and in the Persian province of Yehud. Later, the texts were copied and edited in Jewish, Christian, and (in the case of the Pentateuch) Samaritan communities in the Hellenistic and Roman periods, and then through the Middle Ages down to the modern era. The earliest surviving complete manuscript of the Hebrew Bible in the original language(s) dates from roughly 1000 CE, reflecting what is known as the Masoretic text of the Hebrew Bible. The Masoretic branch of the text began to crystallize around the turn of the Common Era, as shown by some but by no means all the Dead Sea scrolls (ca. 250 BCE–135 CE), and it became increasingly fixed and meticulously preserved in the Middle Ages. The "Hebrew Bible" as a concept is thus broader and more inclusive than the specific form that this collection took in the Masoretic text, which came to be accepted as authoritative Scripture in Jewish communities.

Over the course of these many centuries, biblical texts underwent many changes created by editing, the addition of comments, and errors or intentional alterations. Editorial decisions made in the early periods led to the production of more than one edition of some works. For example, a shorter version of Jeremiah, circulating in Palestine and in Alexandria, served as the basis for the Greek translation of Jeremiah found in the Septuagint, the early Greek translation of the Hebrew Bible. Moreover, scribes added comments for clarification, word borders were marked systematically, and passages were divided into verses (the chapter divisions currently used are late medieval). The ancient Hebrew ("Canaanite") alphabet gave way to the Aramaic alphabet, writing conventions changed, and the need for clarification occasioned the gradual insertion of vowels and cantillation marks designating musical phrases that reflected specific understandings of the text's syntax. Copyists occasionally erred or altered the text intentionally in order to adapt it to changing religious and ideological contexts. For instance, the phrase "sons of God/El" found in ancient copies of Deut 32:8, which originally alluded to a myth about a senior deity apportioning the world among his descendants, was "improved" to "sons of Israel," obscuring its mythological overtones.

Such alterations became rarer already in Late Antiquity, but even in minute forms these changes were powerful tools in forging the meanings of the biblical texts. For example, by a subtle maneuver that from a graphic perspective would involve merely removing one dot and relocating another, Qohelet's (Kohelet's) skepticism about the difference between humans and beasts in the afterlife ("Who knows whether the human spirit ascends and the animal spirit descends downward to the earth?" Kohelet 3:21) was transformed into the grammatically implausible but less heterodox, "Who knows the human spirit that ascends upward, and the animal spirit that descends (it) downward?" As a result, when reading from a medieval or modern copy of the Hebrew Bible, one is studying neither an ancient Israelite work, nor an early Jewish text, nor a medieval book, but rather a multilayered archaeological textual site.

Historical Contexts

Like the relationship between Israelite cultures and their Jewish and Christian successors, that between Israelite cultures and their ancient Near Eastern predecessors and contemporaries was characterized by both continuity and discontinuity. Ancient Israelite culture emerged and evolved on the outskirts of the great empires of the second and first millennia BCE—Egypt, Assyria, and Babylonia—and within the sphere of influence of Hittite and Aegean (including Philistine) cultures. It developed in political, economic, and cultural conversation with these "foreign" powers and with local cultures with which it shared linguistic, territorial, cultural and religious commonalities. These contacts, referenced in many biblical passages, are reflected in archaeological finds and a large body of inscriptions. They are also reflected in the literature(s) of these diverse cultures.

These literatures of neighboring cultures circulated in Canaan before, during and after the first millennium BCE, and local Israelite scribes and poets were exposed to them both directly and indirectly. The shared heritage of Israelite religion and other Levantine cultures is reflected in thematic, stylistic, and verbal similarities between hymns, proverbs, mythologies, and cultic texts in the Bible and parallel texts composed in Ugarit (late second millennium BCE), a language akin to Biblical Hebrew; for example, the mythologies about Baal. The influences of the literatures of the great empires to the east (Babylonian and Assyrian) and to the southwest (Egyptian) and the shared heritages with those cultures are also evident in biblical works. For example, the flood narrative(s) in Genesis 6–9 echo Mesopotamian versions of the myth, and the laws of the Covenant Code in Exodus 22–24 parallel law collections from Mesopotamia. Further, the concept and phrasing of the covenant between YHWH and Israel, particularly in Deuteronomy, could be described as an Israelite appropriation of the styles and conceptual worlds of Assyrian vassal treaties. A very small number of biblical texts have been found to be adaptations of known works in other languages, such as Prov 22:17–23:11, which is an adaptation (but not a direct translation) of the Egyptian teachings of Amenemope. It is therefore evident that in form and contents biblical works follow well-trod paths known from other ancient Near Eastern literatures in mythology, poetry, wisdom literature, ritual texts, and, to some extent, prophecy.

In contrast, the ancient Israelite scribes and poets, even though they were active in provincial literary circles far from the cultural centers of the great empires, were distinctively innovative and creative in developing uniquely new forms of literary expression that were to have a lasting impact on diverse cultures inheriting the biblical traditions through Jewish, Christian, and Islamic conduits. Prominent among these forms of literature is a distinct type of historiography in which God enters into covenantal relations with individuals, the Patriarchs, and with their descendants—the Israelites as a whole. This kind of writing, often called "salvation history," includes the Torah and the stories of the Israelite leaders who followed Moses.

Monolatry and Monotheism

The demand for the exclusive worship of a single deity (monolatry) and the conceptualization of this deity as the only God (monotheism) were to have a lasting effect on the course of the history of religion. Early biblical texts suggest an evolution from territorial exclusivity (1 Sam 26:19) to a more general portrayal of YHWH as a jealous God (Exod 20:1–5); only at a later stage did YHWH come to be perceived as the only true God, a claim most eloquently expressed in Deutero-Isaiah in chapters that form part of an early Persian-era appendix to the prophetic Book of Isaiah (chapters 40–66). It is difficult to pinpoint when monotheism was introduced within ancient Israelite religion, but the rhetoric of passages in Deutero-Isaiah (late sixth century BCE) seems to suggest that it was new (Isa 40:17–25; 44).

The radical claim that all other gods are false is distinct from the tendency to identify all members of the pantheon with one major deity, which is found in other religious writings in the ancient Near East and beyond. The innovation in biblical monotheism is thus not primarily a matter of one versus many gods, as the dichotomy monotheism/polytheism might imply. Rather, the depiction of a deity without a family or a lifecycle, together with the distinction between true and false gods, forms a radical break with contemporary theologies. (The distinction between true and false gods finds precedent in the religious reforms of Pharaoh Akhenaten in mid-fourteenth century BCE.)

The Bible as History: "Maximalism" and "Minimalism"

With respect to the Bible's value as a historical source, one might speak in broad terms of two points on a scholarly spectrum: a "maximalist" school that attributes large sections of the Hebrew Bible to a period before the Neo-Babylonian conquests in the Levant (late seventh/early sixth century BCE) and a "minimalist" school that considers the vast majority of the Hebrew Bible, if not its entirety, to be a product of Persian-era scribal schools. The maximalist and minimalist schools are tied to datings of the text because original manuscripts are lacking and explicit chronologies derived from the texts (e.g., from their titles) are not always helpful. As a result, many biblical writings are datable only by means of linguistic analysis and direct and oblique references to historical events, on which the conclusions of scholars differ. The stakes are high and the historical (and occasionally political) ramifications multifaceted.

A particularly vexed issue within biblical scholarship is the question of whether or not there existed a unified Judean kingdom under David and Solomon. There is extra-biblical evidence to support the Bible's claim that the Israelites split into two kingdoms after Solomon's death, but scholars do not agree on whether there was a unified kingdom before this time, because they assess the historical validity of the relevant biblical texts (1-2 Samuel and 1 Kings) differently.

Contents and Composition

Torah

The Torah ("instruction") comprises a more or less continuous narrative beginning with Creation (Genesis 1) and concluding with the death of Moses (Deuteronomy 34). Within this span, it narrates the call of Abram/Abraham, the growth of Israel from a single family to a people, the exodus from Egypt and lawgiving in the wilderness, Moses's last words summarizing this history and lawgiving, and preparations for entering Canaan. Despite the overarching narrative framework, the early names of the Pentateuch (Hebrew *Torah* = Aramaic *oraita*, lit. "instruction," Greek *ho nómos*, "The Law") highlight the prescriptive rather than the narrative aspects of the work. Strictly speaking, well over half of the Pentateuch is not narrative. This is so because its authors and compilers intertwined law and historiography in a way that is unparalleled in ancient literature, embedding extensive speeches voiced by YHWH and Moses throughout the work (Exodus 20–Numbers 36; Deuteronomy 1–33). The historiography thus serves as something of a framework for the legal sections.

Strictly speaking, the Torah is coextensive with the Pentateuch, or the "five Books of Moses," although in later Jewish writings "Torah" may also denote a much wider body of literature and even sacred knowledge writ large. The term "Pentateuch" reflects the division of the Torah into five sections. Although many scholars agree that the fivefold division was superimposed on the Torah in a later period, the division came to be accepted by Jews already in antiquity. The early names of these five books are suggestive of their contents—Genesis ("beginning"), Exodus ("emigration," Leviticus (= *torat kohanim*, "Instruction to the Levites"), Numbers (= *chummash happequdim*, "the five accountings," referring to the censuses mentioned in this tome), and Deuteronomy (= *mishneh torah*, "repetition of the instruction"). Since the Middle Ages, in Hebrew they are named after a distinctive word occurring in the opening verse of each—*Bereshit* ("in the beginning"), *Shemot* ("names"), *Vayikra* ("and he called"), *Bemidbar* ("in the wilderness"), and *Devarim* ("words"), respectively.

Many parts of the Torah were composed later than texts found later in the Hebrew Bible—for example, a song found in Judges 5 is considered one of the most ancient texts in the Bible. Nevertheless, the Torah comprises the first of the three sections of the Tanakh for at least three interrelated reasons: (1) It was the first section to reach a more or less closed form; (2) its narrative begins with the earliest times, concluding when the Former Prophets begin, and (3) its acceptance as divinely revealed law bestowed upon it a unique status among ancient Israelite writings, within a tradition that is strongly praxis oriented.

By modern classifications, the Pentateuch combines a wide variety of genres and textual types, including poetry (e.g., Exodus 15; Deuteronomy 32), law (e.g., Exodus 22–24; Deuteronomy 12–26), architectural and ritual instructions (e.g., Exodus 26; Leviticus 1–5), oration (Numbers 24; Deuteronomy 1–4), and genealogical and other lists (Genesis 36; Numbers 26). These are embedded within a prose narrative related from the perspective of an omniscient narrator. This narrator is not to be confused with the deity and protagonist YHWH, who later came to be perceived as the author of the Pentateuch in Jewish sources.

Continuity and discontinuity between ancient Israelite and early Jewish cultures can be demonstrated from the perspective of the centrality or peripherality of certain pentateuchal traditions. Some traditions central to early Jewish art, literature, liturgy, and ideology, such as the stories of Adam and Eve (Genesis 2–3) and the Binding of Isaac (Genesis 22), were hardly ever referenced in ancient Israelite literature. (For the sake of comparison, the tradition about Sodom and its destruction, which figures less prominently in later Jewish sources, is alluded to in no less than a dozen biblical passages). At the same time, major conceptual categories of what would become Judaism—the concept of YHWH as creator overseeing history, the election of Israel, covenants, monolatry, and the importance of revelation and lawgiving at Sinai/Horeb—were developed as central themes in the Pentateuch.

Most of the Torah's laws relate to the construction of the sanctuary and its cult, as well as the closely interrelated systems of sacrifice and of ritual pollution and purification required for its maintenance, to ensure YHWH's continued presence among the Israelites.The sanctuary and its sacrificial cult became central in Jewish life, both in practice and as conceptual templates for legal categories and conceptions of sacredness. After the discontinuation of actual sacrifices in 70 CE following the destruction of the Temple, the sacrificial cult continued to serve as a model for the study of Torah, even as Torah study was depicted as a substitute for sacrifice. Thus, Torah study, which had become already in antiquity a model for the ideal (literate, elite) Jewish way of life, began with a child's initiation into the study of the sacrificial passages in Leviticus, and the interaction with and interpretation of the Bible remained closely aligned in early Jewish minds with the devotion expressed through participation in the Temple cult.

COMPOSITION OF THE TORAH

The composition and formation of the Torah are among the most tangled issues in modern biblical scholarship. There is a broad consensus that the Pentateuch is a composite work formed over the course of many centuries, and a rather broad consensus about some of the details of its textual history, primarily that Priestly and non-Priestly materials can be distinguished. There is also a broad consensus that the laws of Deuteronomy that call for the abolition of previous forms of sacrificial worship by which YHWH could be worshiped "anywhere" (Deut 12:13) and mandate that YHWH be worshiped only in a single legitimate location,are related to the story about King Josiah in 2 Kgs 22–23. According to Kings, the finding of a scroll (or so-called finding if the scroll was in fac a contemporary pious fraud) instigated a violent, royally sanctioned religious reform (622 BCE), in which the Jerusalem Temple was declared the only legitimate place for sacrificial worship and traditional sites of worship were destroyed. Parts of Deuteronomy were therefore dated to the late seventh century BCE (though this conclusion has come under some criticism), and other parts of the Pentateuch were dated relative to it. Archaeological evidence for a "centralization of worship" has surfaced in recent years at the Judean site of Lachish, but it appears that an attempt at centralization was carried out nearly a century before the "Josianic Reform," in the times of his great-grandfather King Hezekiah.

The single most influential theory about the formation of the Pentateuch—the broad contours of which can be said to have stood the test of time, despite many revisions and important reservations—is the Documentary Hypothesis presented in Wellhausen's *Prolegomena,* published in 1885. In its classic formulation, this theory posits the existence of four distinct documents—J, E, P, and D—each combining law and narrative, and each reflecting a different version of the turn of events from primordial times, through the enslavement in Egypt, the Exodus, the sojourn in the wilderness, and continuing (at least) down to the death of Moses. Two—the Yahwistic (J) and Priestly (P) documents—were produced in Judea in the ninth to eighth and sixth to fifth centuries BCE, respectively (all dates in this context are tentative); the Elohistic document (E) originated in the Northern Kingdom of Israel in the ninth to eighth century BCE; and the Deuteronomic document (D), which contains northern elements and was acquainted with the content of E, was composed in the late seventh century BCE in Judea. These documents were interwoven, in a process that probably began in the early Persian era, into a single continuous text (consider the indiscriminate citations from "the Torah of Moses" in Nehemiah 8–9). The editors seem to have been guided by a desire to preserve as much of these ancient documents as possible, even at the expense of clarity and consistency. Careful attention to contradictions, redundancies, non sequiturs, and divergent presuppositions in the interwoven text allows one to unravel the four-ply cord that now constitutes the Pentateuch and to study the terminology, theology, and ideology of each document.

For example, the story of the flood (Genesis 6–9) combines two incompatible narrative lines. In one, the deluge, a response to humanity's evils, lasted forty days. Impure animals were taken to an ark in pairs, but pure species came in sevens, allowing Noah to offer an appeasing sacrifice to YHWH upon exiting the ark. The deity is consistently referred to by his private name, YHWH, which is also known to Noah (Gen 9:26), thereby enabling Noah to sacrifice to him: Making an offering to "God" without specifying his name would be like sending an envelope addressed to "Dad" without including a full address. That the deity's name is known by the characters from the earliest times led to naming this document J (for Jahwist, the spelling of Yahwist according the German scholars like Wellhausen).

In contrast, in the Priestly narrative strand (P), as a response to the corruption of all living beings, the flood lasted longer than a year. This version is adamant in insisting that the pure animals too came in pairs: Although whole "families" (Gen 8:19) of animals came out of the ark after the waters subsided (a fact consistent with the longer duration of the deluge in this strand), Noah offers none of them as sacrifices. This is consistent both with P's story of the deluge, in which no "spare" pure specimens were saved in the first place, and with its larger narrative arc. Further, in P, sacrificial service to YHWH is unthinkable before Sinai (when God's name was revealed, according to P). This dovetails with the fact that in P's deluge narrative, the deity is termed simply "god." Noah does not know his personal name, which will be revealed only in the days of Moses in P, and so no offerings are made to him.

Although the Documentary Hypothesis offers a compelling explanation for the many inconsistencies in the Pentateuch, it does not always apply as neatly as it does in the deluge story; therefore, in response to its shortcomings, "Neo-Documentarians" have honed and modified the theory. Most concede that the Documentary Hypothesis alone cannot account for all the complexities, tensions, and contradictions within the Pentateuch, and they argue that each document has a long prehistory. Others have proposed a wide variety of alternatives, according to which a much looser collection of diverse traditions was compiled by editors (or a series of editors), who left their mark on smaller collections as they crystallized into larger ones. None of these alternatives has gained the wide currency that the Documentary Hypothesis once held.

Regardless of their position on the Torah's textual history, many scholars would concede that the pentateuchal text as it stands has taken on new meanings as a result of the combination of diverse and even conflicting traditions. As a result, they endorse a harmonistic approach that attributes theological and literary value to the final form of the text while still conceding that it is the result of a long and complex history.

Traditional Jewish readings of the Torah are based on a very different set of presuppositions from those that guide the critical, text-historical approaches discussed here. In Late Antiquity the pentateuchal text (and, to a great extent, the biblical text in general) was assumed to be free of error or internal contradiction, in accordance with its divine origin. It was also assumed to be enigmatic, containing encoded messages that would speak directly to the circumstances of a present-day reader. As a result, traditional Jewish thinkers have rarely incorporated the insights of the text-historical study of the Pentateuch into their theologies.[4] Nevertheless, endorsement of text-historical methodologies and theories is theoretically and historically distinct from denial of the Pentateuch's divine origin, associated specifically with Baruch Spinoza, a seventeenth century Jewish philosopher who challenged the traditional view of the Bible as a divinely composed and inerrant revelation. Some avid proponents of the Documentary Hypothesis from the nineteenth century until modern times have considered the diverse documents to be discrete but intertwined divine

Prophets

NEVI'IM RISHONIM (FORMER PROPHETS)

The biblical section titled Prophets is subdivided into *Nevi'im Rishonim* (Former Prophets) and *Nevi'im Aharonim* (Latter Prophets). The first section, comprising the books of Joshua through Kings, is a continuous historiographic narrative that begins precisely where the Pentateuch ended—with the death of Moses on the eve of the Israelites' entry into the land of Canaan.

The narrative tells of the conquest of Canaan (book of Joshua), battles and border skirmishes of the Israelite tribes led by local charismatic leaders (Judges), the early failed kingdom of Saul, David's rise to the throne and related intrigues, and the intrigues of his potential successors (Samuel). The book of Kings tells of the construction of the Jerusalem Temple by David's son Solomon, who ultimately failed to establish a stable unified kingdom. Soon after Solomon's death, the kingdom split into the larger and stronger Northern Kingdom and the smaller kingdom of Judea, which was nevertheless characterized by a greater degree of dynastic stability: except for Queen Athalia, a single dynasty ruled Judah for nearly four hundred years. Kings relates the rise and fall of these two kingdoms until their ultimate incorporation into the Assyrian and Babylonian Empires, respectively.

This overall narrative thread, on which are strung diverse ancient traditions—traditions about local judges like Deborah and Barak (Judges 5) or narratives about Elijah and Elisha—reflects a distinctive ideology, language, and political outlook that echo the Deuteronomic document (D). Scholars therefore refer to the narrative that runs from the end of Moses' life in Deuteronomy to the Babylonian Exile in 2 Kings as the "Deuteronomistic History" (DtrH). Among the telltale signs of the "Deuteronomist" writer/editor are the severe condemnation of any sacrificial worship of YHWH outside the Jerusalem Temple after its construction, setting David as a model for the ideal king to which all others are frequently compared, and the belief that the king's conduct determines the fate of the kingdom.

Most Judean kings are therefore judged harshly for not living up to the standards of David. The Northern Kingdom, with its royally sanctioned sites of worship at Bethel and at Dan, was perceived by the (pro-Judean) authors of

Kings as fundamentally illegitimate. Even the most adamantly Yahwistic northern kings such as Jehu were condemned for tolerating worship of YHWH in sites that the Deuteronomistic History terms "high places." Their transgressions eventually led to the destruction of the Northern Kingdom of Israel by Tiglathpileser (745 BCE) and Shalmanesser (721 BCE) and to the two-stage destruction of Judea at the hands of Nebuchadnezzar (in 597 and 586 BCE).

Scholars hypothesize that the Deuteronomistic History appeared in two "editions." The first, composed shortly before the untimely death of King Josiah in the battle of Carchemish (605 BCE), ended on a high note, with the successful reign of this king. The materials in 2 Kgs 23:16–25 thus appear supplementary and reflect a degree of despair. Nevertheless, the final edition offers a bit of encouragement at the end: King Jehoiachin (exiled in 597 BCE), who had been held in the custody of King Nebuchadnezzar (a fact mirrored in Babylonian sources), is restored four years later to a degree of dignity in Babylon by Nebuchadnezzar's successor in 561 BCE.

Some of the foundational principles of later Jewish cultures can be traced back to Deuteronomistic historiography—the major importance of David (second only to God in the number of mentions in the entire Hebrew Bible), the centrality of Jerusalem and its Temple, and the concept of exile. Conversely, other basic tenets, such as the idea of the *mitzvot* (commandments) deriving from the Torah of Moses, the revelation and covenant, and the election of Abraham, Isaac, and Jacob, figure very little in Nevi'im Rishonim (and in the Prophets in general): They appear mostly in passages that for other reasons are considered by many scholars to be editorial supplements to the early materials that constitute the bulk of the Former Prophets.

NEVI'IM AHARONIM (LATTER PROPHETS)

The second section of the Prophets consists almost exclusively of prophetic orations, although Jonah and sections of Isaiah contain narrative, and Jeremiah intertwines narrative and prophecy. The term *navi'*—prophet—probably reflects the concept that the person is "called" (cf. English, "to have a calling"), and it came to denote a large variety of very disparate and at times overlapping roles. There may be some truth in the dichotomy that distinguishes between the earlier forms of prophesying and "classical" prophecy: the former included divination (Hos 4:12), collective ecstatic practices (1 Sam 10:5), or miracle working (2 Kgs 6:6), and the latter engendered the (oral or scribal) production of the literary works eventually collected in Isaiah, Jeremiah, Ezekiel, and most of the Twelve

Minor Prophets (Hosea, Joel, Amos, Obadiah, Jonah, Micah, Nahum, Habakkuk, Zephaniah, Haggai, Zechariah, and Malachi). Nevertheless, studies of the institution of prophecy, its varieties, the social role of the *navi'* or bands of *nevi'im*, questions of gender (female prophets are known as well as male ones), social class, literacy, and relations with royal, scribal, and priestly circles have revealed how variegated the role of a prophet was in both early and late periods.

The *navi'* could play a wide range of social roles, from a local "prophet errant" with a small band of followers in parts of the Northern Kingdom (primarily but not exclusively in "early" prophecy, cf. Elisha) to a widely respected authority visited by elders of the community of Judean exiles (Ezek 14:1, 20:1; ca. 590 BCE). The prophets originated from a broad spectrum of ancient Israelite society—from priestly, literate elites (Ezek 1:1–3) to simple folk (Amos 1), including disinherited, illiterate priests (Jeremiah). Some appear to have held close ties to the royal court (the prophetess Huldah, 2 Kgs 23) and may even have had a formal or semiformal appointment in the court (Nathan, 1 Samuel 12; 1 Kings 1); others seem to have been at odds with political authorities or even social outcasts (Elijah, Jeremiah). Some voiced prophecies directed toward nations far and wide (Ezekiel, Amos), whereas the prophecies of others are limited to Israel and Judea (Hosea). The worldview of prophets ranged from what in modern terms might be termed as strongly militant and nationalist to what one might term defeatist (Jer 38:4). What is common to all these widely divergent figures is the perception that they were "called" not necessarily to predict the future but rather to serve as God's mouthpiece—to be a medium for conveying God's thoughts, plans, and messages to humans and to serve as a vehicle in bringing those same thoughts, plans, and messages to fruition through the very act of pronouncing them, as in speech acts.

Prophecy in the ancient Near East was in no way limited to ancient Israel. Nevertheless, the breadth of the corpus comprising their orations and the centrality of *nevi'im* in biblical narratives are not paralleled in the surviving literatures of neighboring cultures (a curious and partial exception is the prophecy of "Balaam son of Beor," in an inscription discovered in 1967 in Jordan , cf. Numbers 22–24).The composition of extended orations—or at least their textual transmission among followers who deemed them worthy of preservation—seems to be a distinctive feature of ancient Israelite prophetic and scribal circles.

A fundamental attitude of early Jewish readers toward the Hebrew Bible writ large is best exemplified by their reading of prophetic passages: these texts were read not (or not primarily) as the words of ancient authors directed at those authors' contemporaries within their political and cultural contexts. Rather,

SCRIPTURE 29

readers conceived these texts as containing an encoded message directed specifically at their own days. For example, for the author of the text Pesher Habakkuk, a commentary on the book of Habakkuk discovered among the Dead Sea Scrolls, the "Chaldeans" of Habakkuk 1 are explained as a code-name for the Romans (*Kitiyim*, 1QpHab 2.11–12). Similarly, for the author of Pesher Nahum, also found among the Dead Sea Srolls, the "lion" mentioned in Nahum in an Assyrian context is understood as a reference to "Demeterius, King of the Greeks" (4QpNah 3, 1.1–2).

MESSIANISM

It is in the Latter Prophets that the concept of eschatology—in the sense of the end of historical time—was developed. The concept of a divinely sent leader, a scion of David who will bring about salvation, figures prominently in many prophecies (Isaiah 11; Ezek 34:23–24, 37:15–28), allthough the term "messiah" (from *mashiah*, "anointed") appears only twice (Isa 45:1 and Hab 3:13). This concept would have a lasting impact on Jewish thought in antiquity and, of course, in Christianity.

Within Jewish tradition, the biblical prophets were often viewed primarily as gadflies calling for repentance. This image is key in many biblical prophetic texts such as Jeremiah, but it is important to keep in mind that at least two major prophetic figures—Isaiah, late seventh century BCE, and Ezekiel, early sixth century BCE—portray their missions in very different and rather sinister terms, namely, as instruments to misguide their audiences, leading toward their imminent destruction (Isaiah 6; Ezekiel 2–4). In modern Jewish contexts, the message of Israel's prophets, broadly speaking, has come to be associated specifically with the universalist and utopian visions of prophecies like Isa 2:2–4 (4: "nation shall not lift up sword against nation") and 11:6–9 (6: "the wolf shall dwell with the lamb"), rather than with the strongly particularistic visions of other prophets (Micah 4:5: "All the nations may walk in the name of their gods, but we will walk in the name of the LORD our God for ever and ever") or the dystopian prophecies of Ezekiel.

The Writings (= Hagiographa, Ketuvim)

The third and most eclectic section of the Hebrew Bible is named *Ketuvim* (written [things, pl.] = "writings"). Although it is of mixed provenance—it contains texts that are among the earliest in the Hebrew Bible (e.g., Psalm 68) alongside early postexilic works (Psalm 144, possibly the Book of Job) and very late materials (Daniel 9–12)—it came to be recognized as a closed collection late in the history of the formation of the Hebrew Bible. It comprises writings that were not included in the other sections, either because their texts were considered less divinely inspired than prophecy (e.g., Job) or their composition was completed at a late date (e.g., Daniel), after those sections were already perceived as closed. The order of the Ketuvim varies greatly in different manuscripts and editions of the Hebrew Bible.

Very prominent among the nonpentateuchal and nonprophetic Writings is a collection of psalms, which number (at least) 150. Their titles, some of which contain attributions to their alleged authors or performers, tend to be late additions and vary greatly between the Masoretic text and the Septuagint. As the triadic formula "The Torah of Moses, the Prophets, and David," attested at Qumran (4QMMT = 4Q397) suggests, the Psalms in their entirety came to be associated with David very early on—either as author or as the subject of the psalms. They include poetry in a variety of subgenres, such as personal and communal laments (Psalms 88, 79), personal and communal hymns of praise (Psalms 145, 117), and historiographic resumes (Psalm 105). Some seem to preserve hints of their original functions, from sacrificial liturgy (Psalm 100) to royal weddings (Psalm 45).

Based on such hints and on the ways in which psalms and psalm-like materials are embedded in biblical (and late Second Temple) narratives, elaborate theories aimed at tracing the original social contexts of these diverse genres have been developed. However, a great many psalms comprise mixtures of these diverse poetic forms, and an overly rigorous application of genre distinctions tends to obscure the creativity, innovation, and relative freedom of expression evidenced in these ancient Israelite poems. Like the rest of biblical poetry, the psalms often deploy a literary form referred to by scholars as *parallelismus membrorum*, where the second half of a line is meant to balance out the first half of the line, creating the kind of regularity and structure that meter and rhyme do in English.

The gradual crystallization of individual psalms into small collections, and of those collections into larger collections now comprising the Book of Psalms, resulted in the occasional preservation of the same psalm in more than one subcollection (e.g., Psalms 14 and 53); it also left traces in the titles of some subgroups, such as the psalms associated with the sons of Korah (Psalms 42–49, 84–88) and Asaph (Psalms 73–83), which perhaps were composed or performed by musicians belonging to Levite family-guilds bearing those names (Num 26:9–11; Neh 12:46).

The Book of Psalms was eventually divided into five "books," each concluding with a doxology (a phrase of praise, 41:14, 72:18–19, 89:53, 106:48, 150:1–16). Given that the doxologies are found in the same locations in the Septuagint (the Greek translation made in the third to second century BCE), they are probably the earliest evidence—however indirect and uncertain—of the Pentateuch's division into precisely five "books"—that is, if the division of the Psalms into five books, which lacks an intrinsic textual motivation, was modeled after an earlier paradigm.

The Ketuvim also include wisdom literature. This is a loose term that includes collections of short, pithy, and sometimes riddle-like or even contradictory apothegms (Prov 10–12, 24:23–24), and longer narrativized reflections on divine justice (Job, perhaps composed in the early postexilic period) and on the value of life (Kohelet, ca. fourth century BCE), as well as poetry like the panegyric to the ideal woman (Proverbs 31, ca. fourth century BCE), who is at once a flesh-and-blood wife, mother, sage, and entrepreneur and at the same time Wisdom personified.

Like comparable works in Egypt and in Mesopotamia, much of Israelite wisdom literature, which often takes the form of a parent instructing a son, is characterized by its elaborate use of ambiguity and double meanings, condensing numerous and occasionally contradictory meanings into a single linguistic sequence. Thus, Prov 19:18 (which refers to corporal punishment) could be read either as a warning against excessive use of the rod in the process of education or, alternatively, as encouraging a parent to ignore whining and to keep up the beating.

Job and Kohelet, which may be considered iconoclastic because these books question the traditional assumption of just divine retribution, take the convention of double-edged wording a step further. These works are ambiguous through and through, simultaneously supporting a pietistic reading and serving as an indictment of God (Job) or an agnostic and anti-pietistic treatise (Qohelet). The use of this technique could be viewed as a form of subversive writing in the face of intellectual persecution, as a reflection of the authors' doubts about the nature of God, or as expressing a religious experience that encapsulates the tension between diametrically opposite understandings of the workings of YHWH.

In Jewish manuscripts and editions of the Hebrew Bible, a subsection of "Five Scrolls" is located within Ketuvim, comprising a subunit of their own. These five scrolls are Qohelet, Lamentations, Esther, Song of Songs, and Ruth. Even though they differ greatly from one another in origin, form, and contents, these

32   CHAPTER 1

scrolls share a common afterlife whereby each came to be incorporated into Jewish liturgy on an occasion associated either directly or indirectly with the contents of the book.

Lamentations consists of five postexilic laments over the fall of Jerusalem, four of which are acrostic poems following the order of the Hebrew alphabet. A lament about the fate of a city, Lamentations is unusual among biblical and ancient Near Eastern texts, the closest *comparanda* being Sumerian city-laments. Early Jewish traditions attributed it to the Prophet Jeremiah (introduction to Lamentations in the Septuagint, cf. BT Bava Batra 14b), and in the Alexandrian Jewish tradition—and hence some Christian Bibles—it is located immediately after Jeremiah. In the Jewish liturgical tradition, it is read on the Ninth of Av, a fast day commemorating the destruction of the Temple.

The Book of Esther, the only book in the Hebrew Bible of which no fragments have been found among the Dead Sea Scrolls, is one of the latest texts to have been included in the Hebrew Bible. It is a novella set in and around the Persian (Achaemenid) palace in Susa in the days of a king named Ahasuerus (the correlation between the book of Esther's Ahasuerus and a historical figure is not entirely clear). The author, who appears to have been well acquainted with the Joseph narratives (Genesis 37–50), tells of the near-destruction of the Jews throughout the Achaemenid Empire and of a denouement that led to their salvation and to the establishment of the festival of Purim, during which this scroll is to be read annually.

Song of Songs stands out as atypical within the biblical corpus both thematically, as erotic poetry, and linguistically: It often reflects a (provincial?) dialect with affinities to Mishnaic Hebrew, and it has a higher percentage of *hapax legomena* (words occurring only once in the Hebrew Bible) than any other biblical book. It is difficult to ascertain when the Song of Songs was compiled, when it came to be attributed to King Solomon, when it came to be understood as a reflection of the dynamics of human–divine relationships, and how it came to be perceived as part of Scripture—although some of these processes may be interrelated. Song of Songs is more of an anthology than a unified work. The poems in it revel in double entendre, playfully carrying multiple figurative and literal meanings. Because heterosexual erotic imagery as a reflection of the relation between YHWH and Israel is found in other ancient works (Hosea 2), the evocative carnal imagery of Song of Songs lends itself to a theological interpretation: It is possible that parts of Song of Songs were intended to reflect both carnal and theological yearnings from the outset.

The book of Daniel, which might have been more at home in the Prophets, was probably composed too late to be included there, because parts of its final chapters are among the very latest texts incorporated into the Hebrew Bible (ca. 165 BCE). Its first half (1–6) consists of narratives about the figure of the wise Daniel, a Joseph-like character who rises from servitude to greatness in a foreign court; it is set in early postexilic times. The second half comprises the apocalyptic visions of this character—revelations mediated by an angel (e.g., 10:5–9) containing highly evocative visions of imminent catastrophe leading to a new world order. Many of the predictions (expressed in allegorical terms) placed in the mouth of the sixth-century BCE Daniel are accurate to the letter, because they were composed after the events occurred and were disguised as predictions made by an ancient authority (on pseudepigraphy, see chapter 2).

The gap between the date of Daniel (the character and alleged author of the predictions) and Daniel (the book) results in a fascinating process of textual hermeneutics: In 9:2, the character is portrayed "examining the scrolls" of Jeremiah's prophecy (Jer 29:1, 10), which predict the salvation within "70 years" from the Babylonian exile (586 BCE); this would be near the end of the sixth century BCE.

Writing from a vantage point of many centuries later and realizing that Jeremiah's prediction had not been fulfilled after 70 years in any ordinary understanding of the term "year," the author of Daniel updated the prophecy by imagining an angel revealing to Daniel that the "70 years" in Jeremiah's prediction actually meant 70 sequences of 7 years—that is, 490 years. This would render the predicted salvation an imminent event from the perspective of the author's contemporary audiences.[5]

Although interpretations and reappropriations of earlier biblical materials in later biblical texts are quite common, Daniel 9 is evidence of a very specific process that would eventually become the epitome of Jewish engagement in the biblical texts. In addition to the assumption that the text speaks to the reader's own times, it exemplifies close attention to the smallest components of the text, attention to both the written form and the oral pronunciation, and the use of non-intuitive hermeneutic techniques.

Also included in the Writings are two Persian-era historiographic works, Chronicles and the (unified) book of Ezra–Nehemiah. Chronicles begins with a summary of genealogies from Adam onward, some apparently extending into the Hellenistic era. From the death of Saul, Chronicles tells the history of Judah and Israel, drawing heavily from the Deuteronomic History as a source: texts in

Classical Biblical Hebrew were "translated" into the more contemporary Late Biblical Hebrew characteristic of the Persian era (2 Sam 23:13–16 || 1 Chron 11:15–18). Sections perceived as problematic or irrelevant were reworked or omitted. Thus, David was placed on an even higher pedestal than in the Deuteronomistic History: whereas 2 Sam 5:21 has David and his men carry away the Philistine idols, in 1 Chron 14:12, David has them burnt, and the unflattering narrative about David and Bathsheba related in 1 Samuel 12 was omitted from Chronicles. The centrality of the Temple was highlighted, and historical narratives were systematically adjusted to align with Chronicles' theology, according to which divine punishment follows forewarning.

The narrative of Ezra–Nehemiah picks up precisely where Chronicles ends, with the edict of Cyrus (536 BCE) permitting and even encouraging Judean exiles to return to Judea and rebuild the Temple in Jerusalem (2 Chron 36:22–23 || Ezra 1:1–3). Nevertheless, Ezra–Nehemiah develops and puts forth a distinctive ideology that has left a strong and lasting mark on later Jewish cultures. Its exclusivist ideology regarding the lack of participation in the Jerusalem cult by the non-Judean neighboring communities (e.g., communities in Samaria) (Ezra 4:3) contrasts with Chronicles' depiction of the entirety of Israel as God's people, including the inhabitants of the territories of the former Northern Kingdom of Israel (see 1 Chron 4:42–43 regarding Israelites "abroad"). The book of Ruth, a novella about a resourceful young Moabite woman in Judea that is also included in the Writings, is possibly a contemporary reaction to Ezra–Nehamiah's emphatically exclusivist view on intermarriage.

The Bible's account of the beginning of the world is mysterious, never explaining what happened before God created the heaven and the earth. What happens after the last event recorded in Chronicles, Ezra and Nehemiah is also unclear, but we know that the Judeans who inherited the Bible from their Israelite ancestors did manage to survive, and it was they who laid the ground for the emergence of the people known as the Jews in the following centuries.

Biblical Interpretation

Returning to the tension between continuity and discontinuity in terms of the Bible and Judaism, it is important to emphasize that there is no clear-cut division between the formation of the Hebrew Bible and its interpretation, or between its "history of composition" and "reception history." The earliest forms of biblical interpretation are found within the Bible itself, and the degree of fluidity that characterized some of the biblical texts around the turn of the Common

SCRIPTURE   35

Era meant that the final forms of the text are themselves stratified compositions in which older strata, interpretive comments, and additions are deceptively and indistinguishably woven into a single textual sequence.

The study of Jewish biblical interpretation has emerged into a subfield of Jewish Studies in its own right. The Torah and other biblical texts went on to play a central role in Jewish religious life in the context of communal worship in the synagogue; as a result, there emerged many kinds of Jewish biblical interpretation, ranging from midrash to mystical interpretations and to the rise during the medieval period of a kind of interpretation known as *peshat*, a new grammatically informed approach to the text. The history of Jewish biblical interpretation, including modern Jewish engagement with secular biblical scholarship, far exceeds what can be covered in a brief chapter, but it extends throughout Jewish history. One of the main goals of biblical studies as a part of Jewish Studies is to explore the Bible's roles in Jewish thought and imagination.

Recommended Readings

Alter, Robert. *The Art of Biblical Narrative* (Basic Books, 2011).

Berlin, Adele, and Marc Brettler. *The Jewish Study Bible* (Oxford University Press, 2004).

Douglas, Mary. *Leviticus as Literature* (Oxford University Press, 1999).

Fishbane, Michael. *Biblical Interpretation in Ancient Israel* (Oxford University Press, 1985).

Freedman, David Noel. *Anchor Bible Dictionary* (Yale University Press, 1992).

Japhet, Sara. *The Ideology of the Book of Chronicles and Its Place in Biblical Thought* (Penn State Press, 2009).

Kugel, James L. *The Bible as It Was* (Harvard University Press, 1997).

Levenson, Jon. *Sinai and Zion: An Entry into the Jewish Bible* (HarperOne, 1987).

Mulder, M. J. *Mikra: Text, Translation, Reading, and Interpretation of the Hebrew Bible in Ancient Judaism, Christianity, and Islam* (Fortress, 1988).

Sommer, Benjamin. *Jewish Concepts of Scripture* (New York University Press, 2012).

Notes

1. In contrast to the Masoretic tripartite division, Jewish communities in the Greek-speaking world subdivided the Bible into four sections, and this order was accepted and preserved in many Christian Bibles: (1) the Pentateuch, (2) the historical books, (3) the poetical and wisdom books, and (4) the prophetic books. For example, Daniel and Ruth, which are found in Writings in the Tanakh, are found in the prophetic books and the historical books, respectively, in many editions of the Old Testament.

2. G. Reimer, 1883; Engl. *Prolegomena to the History of Israel: With a Reprint of the Article Israel from the "Encyclopaedia Britannica"* (A & C Black, 1885).

3. See "Higher Criticism—Higher Anti-Semitism," in *Seminary Addresses and Other Papers* (Ark, 1915), 35–39.

4. A noted exception is Rabbi Joseph B. Soloveichik's study of the creation stories of P and J in *The Lonely Man of Faith* (Doubleday, 1965), though it does not adopt text-historical methods.

5. The cue might have been the word *shana*, "year," taken as a homograph for "repeat." The justification for reading "70" twice is not arbitrary: the exegetical technique is hinted at in the angel's instruction to pay attention to the "vision," as well as the "spoken word" (9:23).

2

From Israel to the Jews

Sylvie Honigman, Tel Aviv University

THE WAY we divide time into periods and how we name things condition what we say about these matters. When to place the dividing line between the "history of Israel" and the "birth of Judaism" and how to define the nature of this shift are not straightforward. First, there is the matter of chronology: Some books about early Judaism start with Hellenistic times, the period following Alexander the Great's conquest of the Persian Empire (332–24 BCE). This leaves out the Persian era and sees early Judaism as beginning when a potentially unfamiliar Near Eastern society encountered Greek culture. Moreover, it upholds the once-prevailing view that Alexander's conquest was a watershed in the history of the eastern Mediterranean, a view that originated in modern colonialism and negates the achievements of pre-Hellenistic societies. More specifically, this starting point downplays the centrality of the Jerusalem Temple in early Judaism while highlighting Hellenization and the emergence of the Greek-speaking Jewish diaspora, two factors deemed crucial to understanding the origins of Christianity. In contrast, an alternative periodization favored by some Jewish scholars delineates time according to the history of the Jerusalem Temple: The "Second Temple Period" starts in Persian times (550–332 BCE) when it was rebuilt and ends with its destruction during the Great Revolt against Rome in 67–74 CE. This narrative emphasizes Jewish continuity while downplaying the impact that the successive empires—Persian, Hellenistic, and Roman—had not only on daily life but also on cultural and religious matters in Judea.

Likewise, nomenclature is a bone of contention. The literal meaning of *Yehudim* in Hebrew and *Ioudaioi* in Greek is "inhabitants of Yehud/Judea," and scholars disagree about how to translate this phrase in modern languages: Should it be "Jews" or "Judeans"? Certain scholars deem the term "Jews" problematic, because it evokes a minority persecuted through the ages because of its religion. Its use has indeed led certain scholars to overemphasize religious factors in historical explanations regarding "Jews." Other scholars instead opt for the term "Judeans," which denotes ethnicity, thereby emphasizing their willingness to investigate those inhabitants as they would any other people. Ethnicity is a flexible matter, and each ethnic group selects certain traits such as language, religion, and physical features that it holds as defining. We may define *Yehudim/Ioudaioi* as an ethnic group for which religion was a prominent defining criterion, while stressing that religious aspects are always entangled in political, social, and economic features.

This issue is further complicated by the factor of time. Originally, what we call "religion" was not perceived as a separate aspect of life. Symptomatically, no ancient Mediterranean languages (including ancient Hebrew and Greek) had words that we might translate as "religion." This changed gradually between the second century BCE and the second century CE, at different paces in the diverse societies across the Mediterranean. Furthermore, ethnic identity is not static, and the defining features of a given ethnic group change according to time and place as the group adjusts to changing conditions. A vexed question, therefore, is to pinpoint when "Judeans" became "Jews"; that is, when the religious component of their identity became an exclusive defining factor for themselves and for others in their homeland and in diaspora communities.

The birth of Judaism is rooted in the progressive emergence of a new corpus of texts following the promulgation in Persian times of the Pentateuch and of collections of prophetic texts. Likewise, new bodily practices, which gradually came to form a coherent system, responded to the centralization of the sacrificial cult in the Jerusalem Temple even as the formation of diasporas made it impossible for numerous people to attend this cult. Moreover, the incorporation of Judea into successive imperial settings—Persian, Hellenistic, and Roman—and the related cross-cultural circulation of ideas and texts are key to understanding how the Judeans of the time shaped their texts, culture, and religion.

The historical narrative presented in this chapter runs from the Persian period—acknowledging its immense, multifaceted impact on the subsequent development of Judaism—to the revolt of Bar Kochba in 135 CE, after which the Romans banned *Jews* from their homeland Judea. It treats "Judeans" as a "normal" people—hence, the lowercase "temple"—and for each time period, political history and social and cultural developments serve to contextualize literary production and religious innovations.

The Persian Era (550–333 BCE)

Under the Persian Achaemenid Empire, populations deported to Mesopotamia by the Babylonians and Assyrians gradually returned to their ancestral lands. Part of the deported Judeans, however, remained in place. In subsequent centuries, groups of Judeans from Babylonia were resettled on the Mediterranean (as in Asia Minor under the Seleucids) and in this way contributed to the development of Mediterranean diasporas. Moreover, sporadic evidence hints at continued links between Judeans in Babylonia and Judea, and there was presumably some continuity between these early settlements and the intellectual centers that later produced the Babylonian Talmud.

In Judea, the Babylonians had moved the administrative capital to Mitzpah, and although the land was never deserted as the book of Ezra-Nehemiah claims, local social structures were utterly disrupted. It seems that the capital was relocated in Jerusalem in the mid-fifth century BCE at the instigation of the Judeans themselves, following the reactivation of a cultic center on the site of the ruined Temple there. This new start illustrates the power of religious memory.

The new temple differed from its predecessor in status and function. In the monarchic period, the Jerusalem Temple was a royal institution: Its divine dweller was the dynasty's patron, and the kings financed its cult. In contrast, the new Temple became the center of popular piety, and the Judean population as a whole came to endorse duties and related privileges (divine protection) usually reserved to the king and priests. In particular, the cult was financed through direct taxes on the people, as the book of Nehemiah emphasizes, and purity rules were gradually extended to nonpriests. This explains the rising prominence of food taboos and additional bodily practices from Hellenistic times onward. At the same time, the ideological longing for a king persisted. Although Persian kings were fully acknowledged—biblical texts affirm that Cyrus the Great owed his kingship to Yahweh—there emerged the notion of divine kingship, whose imaginative power was later to shape apocalyptic literature and messianism.

Like the Jerusalem Temple, the Judean god also changed identity, shifting from a territorial deity ruling over a specific kingdom in the monarchic period to being a god governing the whole world. This transition responded both to the ideology of the Achaemenid kings—claiming that they ruled over a universal empire—and to the geographical dispersion of the Judeans. Judean settlements are attested in Egypt in addition to Judea and Babylonia, and in the absence of a Judean king, the deterritorialization of their collective patron-deity was instrumental to their continued ethnic cohesion.

At first, these settlements built their own shrines. In early Persian times, alongside Jerusalem, temples dedicated to "Yaho" operated on Mount Gerizim (Samaria); in Elephantine (Upper Egypt), where Judean mercenaries at the service of the Persians were settled; and in Idumea, a region bordering Judea to the south. By late Persian times, however, the sacrificial cult was centralized in the Jerusalem Temple. Nonetheless, its coexistence with the Mount Gerizim temple continued down to early Hasmonean times, and when the Temple altar in Jerusalem was desecrated under Antiochus IV, a Jerusalem high priest fled to Egypt and founded an alternative temple at Leontopolis.

The relationship between Judea and Samaria in Persian times warrants consideration. Samaria was a far wealthier region than Judea. During this era, the city of Samaria continued to serve as its political and administrative center; its social structures, including priestly ones, remained in place, and as archaeological finds revealed, the Yahwistic temple of Mount Gerizim was rebuilt slightly earlier than the Jerusalem one. Moreover, it seems that the priestly personnel of the two temples intermarried. These elements raise questions about what is arguably the most important legacy of Persian times to Judaism: the development of several textual corpora, including the Torah (Pentateuch) and collections of prophecies attributed to various prophets. A much-debated issue today is whether the Masoretic and Samaritan Pentateuchs were composed as separate corpora from the outset or originated in collaborative work between scribes affiliated with the two Temples. Indeed, in Deuteronomy the "place that Yahweh will chose as his residence" is nowhere identified. Its precise location therefore—Jerusalem or Mount Gerizim—was a matter of oral exegesis, suggesting a deliberate compromise. In Judea, it was the conjunction of "Torah and Prophets" that identified this chosen place as Jerusalem. Whatever the case, "Torah and Prophets" became a set phrase in Judea, showing that these corpora had acquired an authoritative status at a time when the "Bible" did not exist. This development spawned the need for interpretation and commentary, an enterprise that to this day remains a central aspect of Judaism.

Early Hellenistic Times (333–175 BCE)

Rise of the High Priest

Alexander's conquest of the Persian Empire and the period of the Diadochi, Alexander's generals (333–301 BCE), brought massive disruptions. The city of Samaria was destroyed and repopulated with Greek settlers, and archaeology reveals wide-scale destruction in rural areas in Judea. These troubled times had major consequences. First, the protracted wars between the Diadochi disrupted the imperial government, and high priests in various places took over the powers previously held by governors to keep local administrations running. A coin minted in the name of "Yohanan Ha-Cohen" ("John the [high] priest") in Judea documents the first high priest to combine administrative, economic, and religious functions. Under Persian rule, as Ezra-Nehemiah shows, a governor had the upper hand, including over the nonritual activities of the Temple, whereas the high priest had limited, cultic responsibilities. The last governor of Judea disappeared shortly after Alexander's conquest. The subsequent history of the Jerusalem high priesthood was far from linear, however, and the extent of their powers fluctuated according to ever-changing geopolitical circumstances.

The Judean Community of Egypt: The Origins of the Synagogue

Meanwhile, the destruction of rural settlements led numerous villagers to migrate to Egypt. Greek papyri from the Fayum, a rural region in Middle Egypt, document the recent settlement there of numerous groups of *Ioudaioi* alongside immigrants from all around the Mediterranean. Third-century papyri show that those labeled as *Ioudaioi* came from both Judea and Samaria, suggesting that their respective populations did not yet form distinct ethnoreligious groups. Moreover, literary sources suggest the early formation of a Judean community in Alexandria, which was to become the most flourishing Greek-speaking Judean/Jewish community of the Mediterranean. Part of its brilliant literary production was eventually preserved by Christians, primarily the earliest translation of the Bible into Greek (the Septuagint) and the works of Philo of Alexandria.

The communities of Ptolemaic Egypt devised innovative solutions to pursue religious life. "Houses of prayer" (*proseuche*) are attested from the reign of Ptolemy III (246–222 BCE) in inscriptions and papyri. They represented a new kind of Judean religious institution whose very name advertised a nonsacrificial form of worship, providing evidence that Jerusalem's monopoly over sacrifices was accepted by commoners. *Proseuches* soon spread to other places across the Mediterranean together with Judean-Egyptian merchants.

Material Culture

Archaeological remains show that material culture in early Hellenistic Judea was poor, and foreign imports were notably absent. This was in sharp contrast with neighboring societies, including Samaria, Marisa (the capital of Idumea), and the coastal cities, where wealthy families imported goods from the Mediterranean and endorsed various aspects of the Greek way of life.

Scholars disagree about how to interpret this contrast. Those foregrounding "Jewish" religious exceptionalism attribute the absence of imported goods in early Hellenistic Judea to concerns for purity rules. Other scholars object that the earliest evidence of purity rules affecting material culture dates to the late second century BCE. Therefore, they attribute the lack of imports in the third century to lingering economic factors. The Persians had imposed an exclusive agricultural orientation on Judea so it could feed their troops; this prevented the region's urban and commercial development. Up to Hasmonean times, the city of Jerusalem was restricted to the City of David, and its tiny population essentially comprised Temple personnel and their families.

This picture has important implications when it comes to understanding how the Judean literature of early Hellenistic times was produced. Contrary to what scholars used to believe, literary activity then was intense, variegated, and innovative, raising the question of who composed the works. In the modern imagination, a temple is a shrine of conservatism, and therefore certain scholars have sought to ascribe the new literary genres that emerged at the time to alternative, newly formed elites. However, the dearth of urban life, and poor material culture argue against the idea of Judean society having diversified elites in early Hellenistic times. Furthermore, the decipherment of literary works composed in Babylonian and Egyptian temples in Hellenistic times has revealed that these centers of learning retained their intellectual vitality long after Alexander's conquest. Comparative data support the view that, like in Babylonia and Egypt, the scribal schools linked to the Jerusalem Temple were eager to appropriate the most advanced intellectual and literary tools of their time to keep their received traditions updated and thus ensure that the conceptual basis framing their world remained relevant. To this end, they borrowed both from Greek culture and from other temple cultures.

Interpreting "Torah and Prophets"

The compilation of "Torah and Prophets" provided a comprehensive worldview combining a foundational historical narrative starting from the creation of the world; the description of a social organization—from which the king is notably absent, as suits the postexilic political reality; a list of appropriate means of communication with the divine, such as rites and festivals; and morals providing tenets for understanding the divine will and hence the meaning of history

FROM ISRAEL TO THE JEWS   43

(such as divine retribution and salvation). To a large extent, the acknowledgment of "Torah and Prophets" as being authoritative delineated the ethnic boundary between Judeans and non-Judeans.

The corpora's authoritative status entailed the need for interpretation. Multiple details in the texts, such as ritual prescriptions in Leviticus, were deliberately left incomplete or obscure, because the compilers acknowledged the organic interplay between the written words and their oral, collective interpretation in scribal schools. The remarkable fluidity of the Pentateuch and prophetic books before their canonization in Late Antiquity was first revealed by the publication of the Dead Sea Scrolls. Although the scrolls themselves are dated between ca. 100 BCE and ca. 70 CE, a substantial proportion are copies of texts composed at earlier dates. They have played a key role in our understanding of ancient Judean scribal practices in Hellenistic and early Roman times.

Textual fluidity is a shared feature of biblical and biblically inspired works composed in Hebrew, Greek, and Aramaic and took two basic forms. First, the texts themselves were modified. Each time a text was copied, the scribe adjusted its wording to the oral exegesis carried out in his own school; the works—particularly, the prophetic books—also were expanded with new additions. The three modern, canonical forms of the Pentateuch (Masoretic, Samaritan, and Greek Septuagint) are a legacy of this scribal culture, and the Dead Sea Scrolls contain Hebrew prototypes of all three.

Second, the contents of one or several texts were entirely reshaped to generate an entirely new work, the product of which modern scholars used to call the "Rewritten Bible." The earliest example of this method is the Books of Chronicles composed in the late fourth century BCE, which for the first time created a complete linear historical narrative running from the creation of Adam to the end of monarchy and the proclamation of the return from exile by King Cyrus of Persia. Likewise, the book of Jubilees (attested through Dead Sea Scroll fragments and today preserved in Ge'ez translation in the language of the Ethiopian Church) divides history into periods of fifty years; the Temple Scroll (attested only in the Dead Sea Scrolls) rearranges biblical laws uttered by God in the first person according to a spatial logic, from the Temple through the city to the land; and the Letter of Aristeas composed in Alexandria relates the (totally legendary) origins of the Septuagint while also reshaping the Exodus story according to Alexandrian literary taste and the religious needs of Alexandrian Judeans. According to this version, King Ptolemy II had the Torah translated by seventy elders ("Septuagint" in Greek means "seventy") for his library. Because this new pharoah was so benevolent, the new

Israelites remained in Egypt and received their Torah in Alexandria, rather than on Mount Sinai.

Engagement with the Pentateuch also involved the engagement of foreign intellectual traditions. The Book of the Watchers—originally composed in Aramaic and eventually incorporated through Ge'ez translation in the Ethiopian Book of Enoch—includes an original story of creation combining Genesis and Babylonian and Syrian-Phoenician myths (such as the myth of Fallen Angels). In Alexandria, Demetrius the Chronographer wrote an early biblical commentary in Greek, gathering chronological data from the Septuagint Pentateuch and Kings to build a scientific timeline. He also clarified textual difficulties, using the exegetical methods worked out by the commentators of the Homeric epics in the Alexandrian library. In the second century BCE, Aristobulus wrote an allegorical commentary of the Pentateuch by adapting the allegorical readings of Homer devised by Greek philosophical schools. This merging between the Pentateuch and Greek philosophy culminated in the work of Philo of Alexandria in the early first century CE. In Judea, the Dead Sea Scrolls have revealed the existence of commentaries that apply to the Hebrew Bible interpretive methods similar to those used by Greek scholars to interpret Homer.

Alongside the reshaping of authoritative texts, new compositions were attributed to authoritative figures of old, a device labeled "pseudepigraphy" aimed at enhancing the status of the works in question. Prominent examples include the "Testament literature," such as the Testaments of the Twelve Patriarchs, and the Psalms of Solomon.

Textual fluidity had a counterpoint in the variety of collective and individual rites, such as prayers and abstinence from certain foods, whose performance was perceived as being organically correlated to the notion of "Torah." In Hellenistic and early Roman times, this plurality of texts and practices defined multiple Judean sub-identities, which progressively extended from the sole learned elites of the priestly and scribal schools to the wider Judean population. Even though the ancient Judean historian Josephus mentions the Pharisees, Sadducees, and Essenes for the first time in the days of the Hasmonean Dynasty, their emergence must be situated in social and cultural practices harking back to late Persian and early Hellenistic times.

The Emergence of New Literary Genres

The Judean scribes' receptiveness to foreign ideas is also noted in several new literary genres. First, Kohelet and the Wisdom of Ben Sira represent a new form of sapiential literature combining an innovative identification between "Wisdom" and "Torah," as well as between themes borrowed from Demotic (Egyptian) wisdom literature and an eclectic form of Greek philosophy originating in Alexandrian schools. Second, the Astronomical Book and Book of the Watchers (both documented through Aramaic fragments in the Dead Sea Scrolls and today comprising the Ethiopian Book of Enoch) are the earliest examples of apocalyptic literature. They depict otherworldly journeys guided by angels, in which ancestor Enoch received revelations of hidden knowledge, elements echoing scientific lore, and a conception about the transmission of knowledge originating in Babylonian priestly culture.

Late Hellenistic and Herodian Times (175–4 BCE)

Although the eastern Mediterranean had been under Greco-Macedonian rule since 333 BCE, Hellenistic imperial cultures only started to have a meaningful impact on Judean society and culture in the second century BCE. In 198 BCE, Seleucid King Antiochus III conquered southern Syria, taking it from the Ptolemies; thereafter, influences from both dynasties intermingled.

The Maccabean Crisis (175–141 BCE)

The Maccabean crisis illustrates how members of the Judean priestly elite used Greek social models to gain the support of the imperial overlords and, hence, power at home. In 175 BCE, a certain Jason ousted High Priest Onias III, transforming Jerusalem into a city of a Greek type. To secure King Antiochus IV's agreement to his reforms, he promised to increase the tribute rate paid to the imperial administration. Jason's moves ushered in a period of political and social instability, with one usurpation following another. Internal fights provoked Antiochus IV into storming Jerusalem in 168 BCE to crush what from the imperial standpoint was a rebellion. In accordance with the rules of revolt suppression at the time, wide-scale massacre and plundering ensued, and the Judeans lost their political autonomy. Military settlers were installed on confiscated lands and assigned control over the Judeans' communal institutions, including the Jerusalem Temple. From the Judeans' viewpoint, the settlers desecrated the Temple when they performed their own rites and erected a cultic statue within its precinct. Moreover, it seems that some Judeans tried to perform traditional rites, such as the reading of the Torah and circumcision of babies; these deeds were interpreted as signs of resistance by the royal troops and were met with harsh repression. The Judeans eventually recovered their temple under

Antiochus IV's successor, and as Seleucid power collapsed during intra-dynastic struggles, two Maccabean brothers (Jonathan and Simon) successively negotiated their appointment as high priests. Simon eventually established the Hasmonean dynasty in 141 BCE.

The exploits of the Maccabees are well known, because they are commemorated in the Hanukkah festival. Their historicity is disputed however. Our main literary sources (1 and 2 Maccabees) were composed in early Hasmonean times, and their accounts were the result of a twofold distortion. The books' primary motivation was political: As usurpers, the first Hasmoneans were in dire need of a legitimizing narrative. The Maccabean books supplied just that, painting the Maccabees (their ancestors) as the sole heroes of a struggle for independence against the wicked Seleucids. In addition, Judean collective memory subjectively reinterpreted Antiochus IV's military suppression as a religious persecution, and the Hasmoneans appropriated this memory for their own needs, enshrining it in festivals of a new kind.

The Hasmonean Dynasty Up to the Roman Conquest (141–63 BCE)

The Hasmoneans devised an original political model, ruling as both high priests and kings simultaneously. Moreover, they shaped their kingship through a creative combination of Judean and Greco-Macedonian elements. Although they used symbols borrowed from the Ptolemaic and Seleucid dynasties—the cornucopia and the anchor—on their coins, the Hasmoneans refrained from representing their own effigies: This departure from accepted Hellenistic practice signaled the new prohibition within Judean society of depicting living beings. By claiming the "re-inauguration" (*hanukkah*) of the Temple during the Maccabean crisis as a deed of their own making, the Hasmoneans posed as heirs to David and Solomon. In line with Ptolemaic and Seleucid precedents, Salome Alexandra became queen at the death of her husband Alexander Jannaeus (76–67 BCE). As a woman, however, she was barred from the high priesthood and appointed her elder son in her stead.

This merging of Judean and Greek elements also brought new religious institutions. Under the Hasmoneans, the festivals of Passover, Pentecost (Shavuot), and Tabernacles (Sukkot) developed into mass pilgrimages inspired by the Panhellenic festivals that thrived in the Hellenistic East. However, the pilgrimages were centered on the Jerusalem Temple, not sportive games. As they drew people from outside Judea, these pilgrimages strengthened ties between

FROM ISRAEL TO THE JEWS 47

Jerusalem and diaspora communities while enhancing the Hasmoneans' geopolitical position.

TERRITORIAL EXPANSIONS (112/111–76 BCE) AND THE INVENTION OF CONVERSION

Given the collapse of Seleucid power in the region, the Hasmoneans considerably expanded their kingdom while implementing a new policy of territorial control. In Galilee, vast rural tracts were abandoned by their villagers during the Seleucid internecine wars in the 150s BCE, and populations from Judea started resettling there after a short gap in time, paving the way for Hasmonean conquest. This migratory flux radically modified the ethnic composition of Galilee, creating the multicultural society in which Jesus and his earliest followers were to appear.

Elsewhere, the Hasmoneans opted for a policy of integration, which was at odds with the Seleucids' ruling culture that accommodated multiculturalism. Integration meant the violent destruction of what could not be integrated. In Marisa (Idumea) and Jamnia on the coast, archaeological finds show the deliberate destruction of local shrines and cultic statues. In Samaria, the temple of Mount Gerizim was destroyed by John Hyrcanus, presumably both to eliminate the threat of a rival high priest and to ensure the primacy of Jerusalem as a religious center: This second aim failed, and the Samaritans eventually became a separate ethnoreligious group.

While efforts to absorb new populations could provoke conflict and violence, the Idumeans and Itureans (based in Galilee) were successfully incorporated by forcing or inducing them to accept circumcision, a step that may have been facilitated by preexisting cultural affinities. Aramaic ostraca from fourth-century Idumea (late Persian times) attest the existence of a temple of Yaho there, and the intermingling of Idumean, Arabic, and Hebrew names, sometimes within the same family, suggests intermarriages. Moreover, Idumeans and Itureans already practiced circumcision, although Hasmonean historiography falsely claimed the opposite (Josephus, *Antiquities* 13.257–58, 318). This policy of circumcision has been interpreted as a functional political arrangement that in practice allowed these populations greater freedom of action. Nonetheless, it reflected a conceptual shift in the definition of Judean identity. From being a purely genealogical matter whereby incorporation was possible only through marriage, it evolved a new mode based on ritual action. This form of conversion constitutes the earliest known landmark in the shift from "Judeanness" to

"Jewishness." Similarly, the books of Judith, Esther, and 2 Maccabees composed in Hasmonean times raise the possibility for individuals to become *Ioudaioi* by acknowledging the god of the Judeans and being circumcised. The integration of the Idumeans seems to have been effective; indeed, King Herod the Great, who succeeded the Hasmoneans, reigning from 37 to 4 BCE, was the son of an Idumean aristocrat and a Judean mother.

Domestic Affairs: Support and Opposition, Pharisees and Sadducees

Under the Hasmoneans, political tensions shifted from struggles for power between members of the priestly elite to popular opposition. This evolution may have been inherent to the constitution of an autonomous Judean state and was presumably also facilitated by the demographic growth of Jerusalem and the periodic gatherings of crowds during pilgrimages. According to Josephus, one celebration of the Festival of Tabernacles turned into a riot against Alexander Jannaeus, prefiguring a pattern that became recurrent in Roman times.

Josephus, our main source of information for this period, mentions what he calls the three "schools" (Sadducees, Pharisees, and Essenes) for the first time in his account of John Hyrcanus's rule (135–105 BCE). Unfortunately, the Greek word *hairesis* that Josephus uses connotes the three Greek philosophical schools, and this distorting analogy hampers our understanding of the nature of the three Judean groups.

Josephus lumped together two very different social and religious developments. The Pharisees and Sadducees, who vied for political and religious influence with the Hasmonean rulers, were presumably rooted in the pre-Hasmonean scribal schools. We perceive the existence of those scribal schools through their diverging textual exegeses, whereas our literary sources on the Pharisees and Sadducees (Gospels, Acts, Josephus, and Mishnah) focus on their diverging beliefs—for example, about life after death and resurrection—and ritual observances. In social terms, Josephus suggests that the Sadducees belonged to priestly families closely linked to the Temple; in contrast, the Pharisees' leaders also included those who were not priests, and the emergence of a nonpriestly religious leadership in these years is a crucial innovation. Although the Pharisees are rightly seen as the ancestors of the rabbis who devised the halakhic system of the Mishnah, they also are harbingers of the numerous nonpriestly religious leaders of Roman times, such as Jesus.

Sectarianism: The Essenes and the Dead Sea Scrolls

Whereas Pharisees and Sadducees lived at the core of Judean society, the Essenes are considered to be a sect, although recent reappraisals show that this labeling is only partially correct. Essenes mostly formed rural communities, but some did live in Jerusalem. Altogether, they were never entirely secluded from the rest of society and eventually took an active part in the Great Revolt of 67–74 CE.

Sectarianism was both a social and religious phenomenon. Although the Qumran sectarian texts suggest that the leaders of the movement were priests who opposed the Hasmoneans and (in their mind, temporarily) severed ties with the Jerusalem Temple, rank-and-file members were of humble social origins. Judean society was made up of extended families, meaning that adult brothers and cousins lived together in the same villages. Sectarianism, in contrast, recomposes new social groups out of individual trajectories, and therefore its growth in Judea is a token of major social and economic disruptions compelling people to abandon their villages. Membership in a sectarian community supplied as much an economic and social safety net, as well as religious and emotional support during periods of crisis and stress.

The community that lived in Qumran from about 100 BCE until the Great Revolt has been identified as Essene, but the relationship between this settlement and the Dead Sea Scrolls that were discovered in eleven caves in the vicinity of the site is still debated. According to the prevailing theory, the manuscripts were deposited in the caves by the inhabitants of Qumran, presumably shortly before destruction of the settlement, and may be considered its library. However, despite the discovery of writing material in Qumran, the variety of scribal habits observed in the scrolls suggests that a high proportion were copied elsewhere.

According to scholarly estimations, the Dead Sea Scroll fragments belong to between 900 and 1,000 manuscripts. In addition to biblical texts and their commentaries, the collection includes a wide range of works. Some were subsequently transmitted as apocrypha and pseudepigrapha, whereas others—including collections of prayers and hymns; liturgical, legal, and calendrical texts; eschatological and sapiential works; and "Community Rules"—reveal the beliefs and practices of a previously unknown Judean community.

Given the widely agreed assumption that the collection belonged to a single library, the eclectic nature of the corpus is a witness to the multifaceted cultural and religious life of the time. For instance, the collection included different versions of the Pentateuchal books side by side, and even though its owners had a predilection for works endorsing the solar calendar of 364 days (such as the Astronomical Book, Jubilees, and sectarian literature), they nonetheless coexisted with works following the calendar used in the Jerusalem Temple. This example is particularly telling, because calendars determined when festivals were celebrated and therefore differences between a solar and a lunar calendar meant differences in how and when to worship God. Moreover, although most of the texts are in Hebrew, the library also contained works in Aramaic and Greek; instances of Babylonian lore (in astronomy) and Alexandrian techniques of Homeric commentaries in the commentaries on prophets (*pesher*) are additional evidence that the library owners were connected to the outside world.

This is the intellectual and religious setting in which we must read the so-called Community Rules, a small corpus of works that regulated the life of the assorted sectarian community, which called itself *Yahad* ("Community"). New members underwent a long and complex procedure of admission, and communal life was governed by strict rules, features definitively pointing to a sect. At the same time, certain details in the Rules themselves suggest that there was a gap between the strict, ideal way of life laid out in them and actual practice.

Qumran's sectarian literature casts an invaluable light on the religious history of Judea. Numerous beliefs and concepts held by the Dead Sea Scroll sect were also shared by Jesus's followers, and these scrolls thus enable us to better situate the origins of Christianity in this complex landscape. Likewise, the Dead Sea Scroll sect exemplifies a highly consequential paradox: While imagining the reform of the Jerusalem cult that would enable them to resume worship there, the sect leaders devised a religious system that could do without the existing Temple.

The Cultural Impact of Empire

The rise of the Hasmoneans and the birth of sectarianism were rooted in the political, social, and economic conditions that were largely shaped by the Hellenistic imperial setting. The impact of the Greco-Macedonian dynasties' ruling culture on Judean society was also cognitive, and it was prompted by the very instruments of imperial domination that introduced abstract thinking into daily life. Although coinage was nothing new in the eastern Mediterranean, the Greco-Macedonians introduced key changes in its use. They imposed the use of bronze coinage (a base metal) to pay taxes, while decoupling the nominal value of the coins from their actual worth in metal: Whereas the worth of silver coins was determined by their weight in precious metal, that of bronze coins

FROM ISRAEL TO THE JEWS 51

became fiduciary, meaning arbitrary, and hence an abstract value. Likewise, for the first time in the Mediterranean, the Seleucids introduced a linear, autonomous system of reckoning time: The Seleucid calendar started in 311 BCE and continued to count in years, regardless of the life cycles of successive kings. In contrast, in the traditional system, a new era began with each new reign.

These innovations generated a new understanding of history. Most importantly, the present was both historicized and perceived as distinct from the past. For the first time under the Hasmoneans, new festivals were instituted—such as Hanukkah—that explicitly commemorated events of recent memory, and the stories used to explain their origins were similar to and perhaps modeled on Greek historiography (1 and 2 Maccabees). These new festivals were strikingly different from the traditional ones of Passover, Pentecost, Tabernacles, and the New Year, which each commemorated mythical events of cosmic significance and were tied to cyclical moments of the agricultural year, not to any specific date in the past.

The Seleucid invention of linear time also spawned an imaginative projection into the future. The future was likewise historicized, as it were, and eschatological literature began to compute the end of time. Apocalyptic literature in the second century BCE underwent a major shift, engaging in a reflection about the meaning of history, past, present, and future. The earliest example of this shift is the book of Daniel, which responded to the traumatic events of Antiochus IV's days and had a major influence on subsequent apocalyptic literatures: Jewish, Christian, and Parthian-Persian. The historicization of the future was also a powerful vector of messianism, because the end of days would usher in the Kingdom of God. The disintegration of the Seleucid Empire in the late second century could only accelerate these beliefs; subsequently, messianic expectations played a prominent role in the Judean rebellions that occurred during the early Roman Empire.

The Roman Empire

On the eve of the Roman conquest (63 BCE), most of the constitutive elements of Judaism and early Christianity were in place. Ever since the promulgation of "Torah and Prophets" and the centralization of sacrifices in Jerusalem in Persian times, the Judeans had been developing original forms of worship. When we consider together the Judean-Egyptian "houses of prayer," the Pharisees' legal traditions, the movements like the Essenes and Jesus's followers breaking away from the Temple, and the Samaritans surviving the destruction of their temple on Mount Gerizim, we may readily understand how Judaism was ultimately able to cope with the destruction of the Jerusalem Temple by the Romans in 70 CE. Although the trauma of this loss was immense, its practical religious implications were ultimately minor. Appropriate responses had already been worked out beforehand, enabling Judaism as a system to promptly adjust to the new reality. That said, the Roman imperial authorities contributed yet one more crucial element to Judaism: They finally transformed the Judeans into a deterritorialized, religious minority; that is, into "Jews." This shift may be traced through several major conflicts against the Romans, some in the diaspora, others in Judea.

The first episode focuses on Alexandria, where growing tensions between Greek citizens and the Judean community over its status in the city descended into violence in 38 CE; numerous Judeans were massacred, and their "houses of prayer" were desecrated. In the ensuing settlement of 41 CE (according to a papyrus), Emperor Claudius defined the rights of each side. Crucially, according to Josephus, Claudius promulgated this edict for the entire empire, thereby defining the status of all Judean communities dwelling in Greek cities. Thus, Claudius treated the Judeans/Jews as a single minority group throughout the Roman Empire.

Provincial revolts against the Romans were frequent, but in Judea one such revolt escalated into a conflict of historical impact. Vespasian, the Roman general who led the early operations against the rebels, became emperor in 69 CE, and he and his son Titus used their campaign in Judea to bolster their legitimacy. This led them to paint the rebels in negative terms, anexploiting clichés that had widespread currency in Rome about what Romans saw as the Judeans/Jews' irrational religious behavior. This self-serving propaganda certainly influenced the decision to destroy the Jerusalem Temple, which was an unusually harsh punishment.

After the Jewish revolt, which led to the destruction of the Second Temple, Vespasian contrived additional punishments. After the temple of Capitoline Jupiter in Rome was destroyed by a fire in 69 CE, to finance its rebuilding Vespasian imposed a special tax on all Judeans throughout the empire, not only the crushed rebels in Judea and Galilee. The payment of the "Jewish tax" is documented by papyri and ostraca in Egypt, and in addition to casting opprobrium on entire communities, it constituted a substantial economic burden.

Social humiliation and economic burdens led to coordinated Judean revolts in 115–17 CE, as Trajan's campaign in Mesopotamia reduced the army's presence in the Mediterranean. The main foci were Cyprus, Egypt, and Cyrenaica (Libya), but there may have been troubles in Judea as well. The revolts had messianic undertones, and the rebels deliberately targeted pagan temples in their attacks. Greek inscriptions in Egypt and Libya bear witness to the wide-scale destruction that they wrought.

The suppression of the revolts was merciless. All Judean communal existence in Egypt was wiped out, annihilating the most brilliant Mediterranean diaspora in antiquity. When Jewish life resumed in Egypt after a gap of several decades, it was on entirely new grounds.

The Revolt of Bar Kochba (132–35 CE)

A new revolt erupted in Judea in 132 CE, triggered by Emperor Hadrian's decision to create a Roman colony, Aelia Capitolina, on the site of Jerusalem. The rebels acknowledged Simon Bar Kochba ("Son of the Star") as their leader, and the legends they overstruck on Roman coins to create their own coinage proclaimed the beginning of a messianic era.

Thanks in part to a system of hideouts excavated in the Judean desert, the rebels were able to hold nine Roman legions in check for more than three years. Afterward, Hadrian banned Jews from Jerusalem entirely and built the colony of Aelia Capitolina, including a temple to Capitoline Jupiter on the site of the former Judean Temple. Moreover, he changed the name of the province from Judea to Syria Palestine, wiping out the very memory of the Judeans from their homeland. The center of Jewish life in the region finally shifted to the Galilee, where it eventually reorganized on a new basis.

From "Judeans" to "Jews" and Christians

The shift from Judean-ness to Jewishness and Judaism—that is, from ethnic to religious identity—was gradual, and it is pointless to try and pinpoint a pivotal moment when "Judeans" became "Jews." More usefully, we may stress the part played by political decisions in this process, from the Hasmoneans integrating conquered populations by means of circumcision to Roman imperial policies.

Questions remain regarding the extent to which this shift was endorsed by the Judeans/Jews themselves or whether it was primarily the viewpoint of outsiders—especially the Roman authorities. Meanwhile, whereas Jesus's followers eventually endorsed the Roman ideology, opening Judaism to all Gentiles and endorsing wide-ranging changes in Jewish practices, the rest of the Jews incorporated peoplehood into the core of their religious identity, blurring the lines between the two in another way.

Recommended Readings

Adams, Sean A. *Greek Genres and Jewish Authors: Negotiating Literary Culture in the Greco-Roman Era* (Baylor University Press, 2020).

Brooke, George J., Philip R. Davies, and Philip R. Callaway. *The Complete World of the Dead Sea Scrolls* (Thames & Hudson, 2011).

Carlson Hasler, Laura. *Archival Historiography in Jewish Antiquity* (Oxford University Press, 2020).

Goodman, Martin. *Rome and Jerusalem: The Clash of Ancient Civilizations* (Knopf, 2007).

Henze, Matthias, and Rodney A. Werline, eds. *Early Judaism and Its Modern Interpreters* (Society of Biblical Literature, 2020).

Mélèze Modrzejewski, Joseph. *The Jews of Egypt: From Rameses II to Emperor Hadrian* (Princeton University Press, 1997).

Mirguet, Françoise. *An Early History of Compassion: Emotion and Imagination in Hellenistic Judaism* (Cambridge University Press, 2017).

Schäfer, Peter. *The History of the Jews in the Greco-Roman World: The Jews of Palestine from Alexander the Great to the Arab Conquest* (Routledge, 2003).

Schwartz, Seth. *The Ancient Jews: From Alexander to Muhammad* (Cambridge University Press, 2014).

3

The Rabbis

Moulie Vidas, Princeton University

THIS CHAPTER centers on a group of ancient teachers and scholars who came to be obsessed with words and their significance. The term they used most often to refer to themselves is "sages" or "wise ones" (*hakhamim*), emphasizing intellectual virtue; they are still known by that name in Hebrew, with honorific additions: "our sages of blessed memory." In English, they are conventionally called "the Rabbis," which draws a continuous line between these ancient sages and modern Jewish clerics and signals their foundational role with the definite article and capitalization (compare the American "Founding Fathers"). Still, as scholars have emphasized, the Rabbis of antiquity are not really like modern rabbis, who interact with their publics in synagogue services and rituals like weddings and funerals; the sages, in contrast, did not work in synagogues and focused on scholarship and on teaching their students. But like other intellectuals in antiquity, they perceived what they were teaching not simply as information but also as knowledge with transformative potential for their students' lives.

For much of its early history, the term "rabbi" did not indicate a specific profession or group affiliation. The earliest texts in which this term is documented as addressing an individual are the New Testament gospels, which have Jesus's disciple address him as "rabbi"; it is true that, like the sages, Jesus was a Jewish teacher.[1] But epigraphic evidence suggests that the title, which literally means "my master," was used to honor a broad range of people. In part, this lack of specificity attests to the loose structure of the community of sages in its early history; yet it also tells us something about its ambition. The ancient Jewish world was populated with groups that identified with functional or ideological specificity: "scribes," "priests," "Pharisees," and "Sadducees." It is likely that the sages emerged from some of these groups. They share a great deal with the Pharisees—who were remembered for insisting, like the sages, on the importance of traditions even if they are not recorded in Scripture—and with the scribes, the teachers and interpreters of the Torah. If the "wise ones" deliberately chose to present themselves in less specific terms, it may have been to signal a departure from sectarian identification and to support their claim—only ostensibly ecumenical—that they were the rightful teachers of Israel as a whole.[2]

The Rabbinic Transformation of Judaism

The sages are often presented in modern scholarship as revolutionary innovators. This presentation stands in tension with traditionalist aspects of rabbinic rhetoric. A well-known passage from tractate Avot (1:1), for example, presents the sages as the most recent links in an unbroken tradition of teaching that goes back to the revelation to Moses at Sinai, a claim to continuity and authority that was championed by the sages' defenders in polemical contexts from the Middle Ages on. But this traditionalist rhetoric is only part of the story. It is not only the case that there are passages in rabbinic literature, often celebrated by modern readers, that make extraordinary claims of discontinuity with the past—the Talmud, for example, tells us that the same Moses, at the same moment of Sinaitic revelation, time-traveled to Rabbi Akiba's lesson but could not understand a thing (Menahot 29b). It is also that pervasive rhetorical practices throughout the corpus, such as the deliberate departure from biblical terminology, the attribution of teachings to successive generations of sages, and even the fact that biblical verses are quoted and interpreted rather than paraphrased or rewritten (as we find them in other ancient Jewish texts), all show that, even though the sages claimed to have inherited Moses's authority, they also indicated that something fundamental has changed.

The destruction of the Temple of Jerusalem by the Romans in 70 CE provided the historical framework and cause for this rabbinic transformation. Judaism, like all religions in antiquity, centered on animal sacrifices, but after the destruction of the Temple the sages—this narrative goes—placed at its center the study and observance of *torah*, defined expansively as a body of texts and norms that stems from the Pentateuch but also includes the sages' own teachings. This connection between the destruction and the new rabbinic model is reflected already in rabbinic texts that interpret scriptural references to the Temple cult as referring to Torah study (e.g., Sifre Deut §48) or statements like "from the day the Temple was destroyed, the Holy One, blessed be he, has only the four cubits of halakhah" (Berakhot 8a).[3]

This model, the story goes, introduced new configurations of leadership and authority. If the priests' authority rested on heredity and genealogical distinction, the sages based their own on knowledge of the Torah: one rabbinic teaching states that a *mamzer*, a descendant of an illegitimate union, who is a disciple of the sages, takes precedence over a high priest who is an ignoramus (Mishnah Horayot 3:8). Statements such as a "sage is superior to a prophet" or that "from the day the Temple was destroyed, prophecy was taken from the prophets and given to the sages" (Bava Batra 12a) supported the idea that the sages transformed a "culture based on direct divine revelations to one based on their study and reinterpretation."[4] The pervasive citation of multiple opinions throughout the corpus and texts such as the story of the Oven of Akhnai (Bava Metsiʻa 59b), in which Rabbi Eliezer's opinion is rejected despite the fact that God intervenes to side with him, were used to argue that the sages replaced the definite and singular divine voice with rational argumentation.[5]

The destruction of the Temple was also associated with the sages' introduction of a new Jewish politics. A talmudic story tells how during the Great Revolt against Rome, shortly before the destruction, Rabban Yohanan ben Zakkai tricked the rebels and escaped the besieged city to strike a deal with the Romans that would ensure the future of rabbinic learning (Gittin 56a–b). Although few scholars would claim that this story accurately reports the events in the first century CE, it has played an important role in attributing to the sages a political vision that has endured throughout Jewish history. Some condemned the sages for transforming the virile nation of warriors reflected in the Bible into the passive nation of scholars reflected in the Talmud; others praised them for a diasporic alternative to nationalistic militarism that has proved essential for Jewish survival.[6]

Much in this story of transformation is true, and as we have seen, it is partially reflected in the way the sages presented themselves. At the same time, certain versions of this narrative miss the mark, especially when they portray the sages in a way that appeals to modern tastes. Far from doing away with the "primitive" practice of animal sacrifices, the sages worked hard to develop new approaches to the cult in all its bloody details. Rather than producing a "rational" world that avoided the supernatural, the sages interacted with angels and demons, ghosts, and magical practices. Rabbinic "pluralism" did not work like its modern counterpart, and the sages were certainly not inclusive. Hierarchies of heredity and genealogical purity persisted and expanded even as the merit of

Torah ascended. And alongside the diasporic vision, we find new types of ethnic exclusivism.[7]

Furthermore, the story of rabbinic transformation has often left out the rich world of ancient Jewish culture and experiences that the sages and, consequently, Jewish tradition forgot, erased, and marginalized. We have a broader picture thanks to Christians who transmitted a different set of Jewish writings, and thanks to modern discoveries of texts, documents, and monuments. Considering this evidence means we cannot contrast "Biblical Israel" with "Rabbinic Judaism" as if one followed the other. Terms, ideas, and practices that had been associated exclusively with the sages—ritualized Torah study, biblical interpretation, legal innovation, and synagogue liturgies—had a longer history that went beyond what was included in the Bible but that predated the sages. The recognition that alternative visions of Jewish culture persisted even during the rabbinic period highlights the peculiarity of the sages, undermines narratives of inevitable evolution, and helps us appreciate better how rabbinic ideas were shaped in a diverse landscape in which competing visions existed.

Although earlier accounts that attributed to the sages a pivotal role in ancient Jewish history assumed that they had power and influence in their own time, the consideration of ancient Jewish evidence outside rabbinic texts has contributed to a reevaluation of the sages' role in Jewish society. Palestinian synagogues and burial sites in Late Antiquity, as well as Babylonian Jewish magic bowls, present a picture in which the sages are marginal. Even rabbinic sources sometimes present Jews as operating independently, or even at odds with the sages, not as their obedient flock. Thus, it is incorrect to claim that the sages stepped into the position of leadership for Jews immediately after the destruction of the Temple, or to suggest that the sages' authority was uniformly accepted. For much of their early history, they were an elite but relatively loosely organized and marginal group with limited influence, in some instances until the early Middle Ages. This reevaluation has raised the question of how and when the sages came to be organized institutionally and to exert influence or authority on the Jewish population more broadly.

Rather than positing a single linear process, scholars have focused on different developments, contexts, and types of evidence. A moderate degree of institutionalization, for example, is apparent in the third and fourth century CE, probably under the influence of the Patriarchate, a well-resourced and connected familial institution of patrons to at least a segment of the sages. Significant evidence of their broader influence comes from later antiquity and the early Middle Ages. It includes, for example, the earliest material evidence we have for a rabbinic text: the seventh-century monumental synagogue inscription from Rehov, which resembles a passage from the Jerusalem Talmud about rabbinic agricultural laws and the boundaries of Jewish settlement in the Land of Israel.[8]

The story of rabbinic transformation is often told as a story internal to Judaism, as if, apart from the impact of the Temple's destruction, it could have taken place in any historical context. But even some of this story's most ostensibly "internal" subplots—the cessation of prophecy and the replacement of sacrifice—are found in traditions across the Greco-Roman world. In part, the insularity of the narrative reflects the insular orientation of rabbinic texts. Although they feature some discussion of the Roman holidays, much of the corpus seems to operate in its own internal world. More recent scholarship has insisted that we must explain the ways in which the sages, their texts, and their ideas are a product of their place and time. Studies have investigated how the rise of the sages as a particular kind of elite conformed with distinctive social structures of the Roman and Sasanian Empires;[9] how their seemingly internal study of Torah may be illuminated by Greek, Roman, and Persian traditions;[10] and how, even though Christianity and Christians are mentioned nowhere by name in rabbinic literature, the engagement with Christians—sometimes the polemical production of difference, sometimes a shared journey through similar terrain—considerably shaped the sages' world.[11]

Rabbinic Literature

Rabbinic literature is one of the most expansive corpora surviving in any language from antiquity. Its production, along with the development of a curriculum around it that has dominated Jewish education since the Middle Ages, constitutes the sages' most important contribution to Jewish culture. Today, this corpus may be accessed as a series of free-standing written works, but this mode of transmission is fundamentally different from how the rabbinic tradition was accessed in antiquity.

Until the early Middle Ages, rabbinic texts circulated predominantly in oral form. Written records of the sages' words figure only rarely in the detailed picture we have of the culture of rabbinic study. Orality may have functioned to distinguish the teachings of the sages from written Scripture or to emphasize the importance of the master–disciple relationship. It was also deployed in polemical contexts, such as against Christianity, to argue that the "Oral Torah" was given to Moses in addition to the "Written Torah," so that God could tell the true

Israel from those who relied only on Scripture. Orality does not mean that rabbinic texts could not be transmitted in fixed form—we find ample discussions in the corpus of the precise wording of orally transmitted texts—but it did mean that they were accessed primarily through performances that allowed varying degrees of flexibility. It also means that our own encounter with these texts as words on the page (or screen) misses a great deal of their original presentation, which included facial expression and hand gestures, as well as answers to questions from the audience.[12] We still know very little about the process by which rabbinic texts were committed to writing or the extent to which they were transformed in the process.

Relatedly, although we find the sages' words in discrete works—the Mishnah, the Talmuds, the Midrashim—these works are not single-voiced and uniform compositions, but rather compilations or anthologies that drew from a large body of rabbinic teachings. These teachings are the basic building blocks of rabbinic text, and they consist of rulings on the law, exegetical comments on Scripture or other teachings, short stories, and descriptive statements about the world. They may be attributed to a sage ("Rabbi so-and-so said . . .") or transmitted anonymously. The compilations also present an anonymous framework that weaves these teachings together, sometimes with short connectors and at other times with substantial argumentative narration. The same teaching may appear in several compilations, sometimes with significant variations.

When the sages commented on rabbinic teachings, they focused on individual teachings, rather than on the compilations in which they were embedded. When modern approaches emerged, this orientation persisted because scholars viewed compilations primarily as archives of the teachings included in them. A statement attributed to Rabbi Meir, a second-century Palestinian sage, was seen as reflecting the position of Rabbi Meir, whether it was recorded in the Tosefta, a third-century compilation from Palestine, or in the later Babylonian Talmud. In the latter part of the twentieth century, following the work of Jacob Neusner, scholars took the opposite approach. They felt that, given that different compilations present different accounts of the sages' teachings, compilers must have changed or even composed the teachings they were presenting, rather than only transmitting them verbatim. Under this approach, a teaching presented in the Babylonian Talmud, no matter whether it is attributed to a second-century sage from the Galilee or a fifth-century sage from Mesopotamia, represents first and foremost, or even exclusively, the fifth–sixth-century compilers of the Talmud. In its most distinctive expression, this approach resulted in attempts to reconstruct Judaism as presented by each compilation: the "Judaism of the Mishnah," "the Judaism of the Tosefta," and so forth.

Scholarship today has moved from both approaches. It recognizes that our compilations are not transparent windows and that all the teachings we encounter in them have gone through various processes of composition that reflect different literary, ideological, and cultural factors. The variety of such processes and motives means we cannot reduce them to a singular moment or agency. The compilations themselves present contradictions, redundancies, and a diversity of terminology and premises that undermine the idea that they even intended to deliver a systematic vision. Comparative analysis of the compilations also suggests that we can find patterns among teachings attributed to sages from the same period even if they are preserved in different compilations.[13] We should be aware of how an approach that looks at the Mishnah and the Talmud as distinct and self-contained objects may anachronistically project to antiquity the transmission of rabbinic texts in bound books.

Manuscripts of rabbinic literature—the earliest are fragments found in the Cairo Geniza—present variations ranging from small variants in spelling or formulation, to major structural differences. Although classical models of textual criticism construed such variations as "corruptions" of the original work, whether erroneous or deliberate, scholars of rabbinic literature have shown that such models are not apt for rabbinic texts. Manuscripts may vary because they stem from different oral performances; alternative arrangements may represent the composition of an alternative compilation; and even additions and adaptations that we can securely attribute to medieval scribes should be understood as attesting to the vitality of rabbinic scholarship.[14] Another set of questions emerges when we consider medieval manuscripts on their own, rather than merely as witnesses to ancient works. Who produced these manuscripts and for what purpose? What can we learn from the material form of these manuscripts— their sizes, layouts, divisions into units, and so on, or from their history of ownership? Although such questions have been raised before, they are only now coming to the center of the field.

Mishnaic Literature and Halakhah

The earliest surviving rabbinic compilation is the Mishnah. It was compiled around 200 CE, but some aspects of the text go further back. It is not only that, as its name suggests, it is a "recitation," *mishnah*, of the tradition, presenting or claiming to present the teachings of earlier generations. It is also the case, scholars have shown, that it preserves sequences of teachings that had already circulated in long-form structures before the Mishnah was composed. Because none of these sequences survive independently, it is difficult to assess their scope and nature. Some take the fact that we have no compilation earlier than the Mishnah as an indication that it was the first large-scale gathering of rabbinic teachings, the earliest attempt to present, or construct, the rabbinic tradition as an interconnected conversation. Others contend that the Mishnah's composition was a relatively conservative enterprise, consisting mostly of patching together existing materials and introducing occasional reformulations. And there are many opinions in between.[15]

At the very least, the Mishnah was distinct in its reception. The sages consult other *mishnayot*, other "recitations" of the tradition, but refer to the Mishnah as "our Mishnah." It did not immediately attain the legal authority it would have later, but the Mishnah did become the curricular baseline. Traditional Jewish historiography divides the rabbinic period into two: the "tannaitic period" (associated with the rabbis known as the Tannaim), which concludes with the Mishnah, and the "amoraic period" (associated with the Amoraim) that follows. This unique status of the Mishnah is owed to the agents who promulgated it. Already in antiquity, the Mishnah was associated with Judah the Patriarch, who was not only a brilliant sage but also the head of a dynasty that exerted its considerable resources to centralize the community of sages in the early third century CE. We find other indications of a modest degree of institutionalization from that period: the expression *beit midrash*, "study house," was used to refer to a building, presumably permanent, rather than to a study session; and we have the first references to rabbinic "appointments," the assignment of a role and responsibility to a sage by another sage or group of sages with greater authority. The promulgation of the Mishnah constituted a standardization of the curriculum that was part of that effort of centralization.[16]

The Mishnah consists of sixty tractates divided into six "orders," which are organized thematically. The order of Nashim ("women"), for example, includes mostly tractates addressing family law but also those addressing the tangential issue of vows. At the same time, we find mnemonic, formal, or associative patterns of organization: Within each order, tractates are sorted by length; and within the tractates, teachings addressing different subjects may appear together because they are attributed to the same sage or because they share formal characteristics.

Although no "Mishnah" survives other than the one associated with the patriarch Judah, we have a wealth of tannaitic teachings in other compilations that allow us to consider both alternative perspectives and the distinctiveness of the Mishnah's approach. The most important comparative evidence comes from a compilation called the Tosefta. The name means "the supplement," and its purpose seems to be to "supplement" the Mishnah by collecting teachings not included in it. Even though the Tosefta was compiled after the Mishnah, we find a variety of relationships between the discrete teachings included in the Tosefta and those in the Mishnah. Some Tosefta teachings present commentary on the Mishnah's teachings, but there are also cases where the Tosefta presents teachings that are earlier than those we find in the Mishnah or even teachings that served as a source for the Mishnah. Tannaitic teachings in the Tosefta and other compilations often differ from the Mishnah in ways small and large, allowing us both to appreciate the diversity of tannaitic teachings and in turn to understand better the particularities of the Mishnah itself.[17]

The primary subject of the Mishnah and the Tosefta is halakhah, a term that is often translated as "law" because it covers normative questions of behavior. Yet halakhah is not identical to "law" in the modern western sense. It certainly addresses issues we may put under the rubric of law, such as tort and criminal law, marriage and divorce, and so forth. Yet, it also addresses questions that we may put in the category of ritual, such as liturgy to procedures concerning the Temple sacrifices. And even though halakhah often speaks in legal language of prohibitions and permissions, obligations and exemptions, it also includes other types of normativity, such as local customs and supererogation.[18]

The halakhah we find in the Mishnah represents an unprecedented development. It has its origins, to be sure, in a long and dynamic tradition that we can trace from the earliest layers of the Hebrew Bible through the Second Temple period. But what we find in the Mishnah is different in scope and resolution. The idea of the Sabbath, for example, figures prominently in the Hebrew Bible and subsequent ancient Jewish texts; yet the prohibition on labor is expressed in Scripture only briefly and with a handful of examples (see especially Exodus 16), and it is only somewhat elaborated on in other pre-rabbinic Jewish literature. In the Mishnah, this prohibition is the subject of two lengthy tractates (Shabbat and 'Eruvin), presenting a "totally new statement."[19] It is not just that the Mishnah presents a departure from Scripture but also that it does not even attempt to support halakhah with Scripture. This is most striking in those cases where the Mishnah's teachings do straightforwardly stem from the Bible but do not mention the Bible—although we do find appeals to biblical verses here and there. This absence of consistent biblical grounding is evident also in the fact that the Mishnah is organized not around the Bible but rather its own thematic categories.

Although the centrality of halakhah means that the Mishnah addresses questions of practice, it is far from a practical guide. The Mishnah often offers several answers to a given question without offering a key on how to decide among them. It presents detailed discussions of the sacrificial laws, even though the Temple and its sacrifices were a distant memory by the time of its compilation. Although even these discussions have been interpreted as addressing practical concerns, they more likely reflect the sages' emphasis on intellectual engagement and their aim to draw an authoritative, analytical, and complete picture of what they considered to be knowledge about the observance of Torah. The same aim is apparent in the regular treatment of cases that are liminal or unusual, sometimes in the extreme. One discussion in tractate Karetot, for example, addresses various cases where a man becomes liable for multiple transgressions in a single instance of unintentional sexual intercourse because the woman was related to him in several ways; one such case posits that the woman was the man's daughter, his sister, his brother's widow, and his uncle's current wife—and that she also happened to be menstruating at the time.

The sages construct halakhah as a system, with principles and concepts underlying the treatment of each subject, as well as cutting across different realms. Conflicting claims in a property dispute are compared to cases where a husband and a wife have conflicting claims about the latter's virginity at the time of their marriage (Ketubbot 2); the earlier mentioned discussion in tractate Karetot compares the multiple liabilities incurred by sexual intercourse to multiple liabilities incurred by Sabbath transgression. Although the Mishnah generally speaks in terms of concrete cases rather than concepts, it invites its students to discover such concepts on their own by showing them how different cases result in different rulings. More explicit conceptualization is found in the Talmuds (Babylonian and Jerusalem).[20]

Halakhic discussions often develop through their own internal logic and the interpretation of earlier rabbinic statements. Yet scholarship has shown that they can be interrogated productively from the perspective of cultural studies. The requirement for attentiveness and self-examination in the discussions of purity laws, for example, shapes a particular kind of self-awareness. Different notions of space inform the way the sages debate the 'eruv, the fictional space that allows for carrying items on the Sabbath; ideas about animality and humanity undergird laws regulating damages caused by animals; and the halakhic discourse of sexual identities beyond male and female demonstrates a careful and rich construction of gender.[21]

The Example of the Shema

The Shema consists of the recitation, twice a day, of certain portions from the Pentateuch. It is named after the opening verse of these portions ("Hear O Israel, Our Lord Is One," Deut 6:4). Although the ritual does not appear in the Bible, it is not simply a rabbinic invention but rather a development of practices and ideas that can be traced in ancient Jewish texts predating the sages.[22] The opening of the Mishnah (Berakhot 1:1) discusses the obligation to recite the Shema in the evening. It is not clear how much we can make of the fact that this discussion is at "the beginning" of the Mishnah: There is evidence for alternative arrangements of the tractates, and in any event linear readings may not be applicable in the case of rabbinic textuality. Still, this discussion of the Shema can serve as a good example of the characteristics of rabbinic texts and how modern scholars read them:

> From what time do they recite the Shema in the evening? From the time the priests enter [their homes] to eat their priests' share, until the end of the first watch; the words of Rabbi Eliezer. And the sages say: Until midnight. Rabban Gamaliel says: Until the dawn comes up.
>
> It once happened that his sons came [home late] from the drinking-house. They said to him: We have not recited the Shema. He said to them: If dawn has not yet come up, you are [still] obligated to recite.
>
> And not only in this case, but in all cases in which the sages have ruled "until midnight," the obligation extends until the dawn comes up. The burning of the fatty pieces and limbs—their obligation extends until the rise of dawn. And all those [sacrifices] that must be eaten on the same day—their obligation extends until the rise of dawn. If so, why did the sages say, "Until midnight?" In order to keep a person at a distance from transgression.

A few things about this passage are typical of mishnaic literature. It jumps into the details of the ritual without any introduction and assumes a great deal of knowledge; for example, that the priests may only go in to eat their priests' share in the evening because they only attain the state of purity required for the consumption of consecrated food after the sun has set. Considering the orality of rabbinic texts allows us to recognize that the primary form of encountering the Mishnah would have been in lessons, in which students could ask questions and teachers could offer introductions and clarifications.

Like other passages in the Mishnah, this discussion is interested in limits and the liminal, asking when, exactly, "evening" begins and ends. It does not offer biblical or, for the most part, any other support for its rulings. And it presents a mix of attributed and anonymous voices. The first position, which tells us when the obligation begins, is presented anonymously and uncontested, almost as if in the voice of the Mishnah itself (although in the Tosefta, the same opinion appears contested by Meir). With respect to the night's end, we hear in the Mishnah the position of the majority, "the sages," and the dissenting opinions of Rabban Gamaliel and Rabbi Eliezer. The final part of the excerpt expands the discussion from consideration of the Shema to a general rule about nightly obligations, specifically those relating to sacrifices—showing the principles governing multiple realms of halakhah.

This section on the sacrifices is not, however, as systematic as it may appear, and it reveals this unit's complex history of composition. Subjecting the passage to text and source criticism, a recent study has shown that it was imported into this passage from another text, which addressed the Paschal sacrifices. This transposition caused various inconsistencies, including the implication that reciting the Shema later than its statutory time constitutes a "transgression," an implication that is contradicted already in the next unit in the Mishnah ("one who reads from this point on has not lost out," Mishnah Berakhot 1:2).[23] Still, as it stands now, the discussion of sacrifices may serve a broader literary function. This chapter in the Mishnah as a whole presents an artful literary design unified by a thematic interest in the contrast between night and day that is mobilized, in the chapter's conclusion, to symbolize the world before and after Israel's redemption. The references to the sacrifices and the priests in the opening of the chapter may serve in this context to make the absence of the Temple present.

Our passage also features a story about Rabban Gamaliel's drunken sons. This story raises a set of questions about the mood and motives of its characters. The sons' inebriated entrance late into the night after a wedding party contrasts, perhaps, with the orderly entrance of the priests in the beginning of the night. Or perhaps it is meant to anticipate a story in the next chapter of the Mishnah about how Rabban Gamaliel himself insisted on reciting the Shema on the first night of his marriage, even though bridegrooms are not required to do so (Berakhot 2:5).[24] That this story is about Rabban Gamaliel and his *sons* is not incidental. The Mishnah rules that women (as well as enslaved people and minors) are exempt from reciting the Shema (Berakhot 3:3), and it is in part through a reading of the Shema passages that the sages derived the argument that made Torah study a masculine realm. One recent study has posited that the daily examination associated with the laws of menstrual purity provided a feminine counterpart to the masculine daily rituals of the Shema recitation and that

through this ritual differentiation the sages produced distinct gendered temporalities and even selves.[25]

Midrash

Even as much of mishnaic literature is independent of the Bible either substantively or rhetorically, the sages of the tannaitic period also developed a rich
discourse of biblical interpretation, midrash. Although the interpretation of
Scripture is now seen as one of the sages' main occupations, scholars have
shown that midrash only developed in the second half of the second century
CE.[26] Midrashic teachings are found in all rabbinic compilations, but especially
in the midrashim, which are traditionally divided into two groups. The halakhic midrashim were produced around the time of the Mishnah in the third
century and present teachings attributed to tannaitic-era sages. The name "halakhic" reflects the focus of these midrashim on the halakhic sections of the
Pentateuch (there is no tannaitic midrashic compilation for the book of Genesis, which has few laws), but these works do contain a lot of non-halakhic
materials. A second group of midrashim, featuring amoraic-era sages, are called
the aggadic midrashim because they concentrate almost exclusively on non-
halakhic matters; the earliest of these compilations, such as Genesis Rabbah
and Leviticus Rabbah, are dated to the fifth century. Amoraic halakhic midrash
appears in the Talmuds.

Modern assessments of midrash have ranged from Abraham Geiger's statement that it presents a "turbid" sense of interpretation, to a celebration of the
sages as the brilliant forerunners of twentieth-century literary theory.[27] Because
midrash rarely states its own principles and ideas of interpretation, scholarship
has focused on reconstructing the sages' hermeneutics through analysis of midrashic practice and terminology. The central question for midrash is not "what
is said" in Scripture but "why" something is said.[28] It tends to assign specific
meanings to phrases, word choices, or linguistic features that other readers may
view as inessential to the sense of the text. A relatively simple example comes
from the same first chapter of Mishnah Berakhot from which we read earlier:

THE HOUSE OF SHAMMAI SAY: In the evening, all people must recline to
recite [the Shema], and in the morning, they must stand [to recite it], as
it is said, *when you lie down and when you rise* (Deut 6:7).

BUT THE HOUSE OF HILLEL SAY: All people may recite it in their own way,
as it is said, *and as you go on your way* (Deut 6:7).

> If this be so, why is it stated, *when you lie down and when you arise?* [It means] at the time when people normally lie down and at the time when people normally arise.

The Houses of Shammai and Hillel—groups of sages tracing themselves to the first-century CE founding figures Hillel and Shammai—each argue that their position is supported by the same verses: "Keep these words that I am commanding you today in your heart. Recite them to your children and talk about them as you sit at home and as you go on your way, as you lie down and as you rise" (Deut 6:7). In its context in the Bible, the verses instruct the people to recite God's commandments to one's children and discuss them frequently and everywhere. The sages, however, took it to require a specific liturgical recitation: They read the phrase, "as you sit at home and as you go on your way, as you lie down and as you rise," not as a metonymic description for "frequently and everywhere" but as instructions on how the recitation is to be performed. The House of Shammai argued that "as you lie down and as you rise" is an instruction to recline in the evening recitation and to stand up in the morning recitation. The House of Hillel took the phrase "walk on your way" as an instruction that one may recite the Shema in one's own way (i.e., manner). Finally, we also hear an explanation on how, from the position of the House of Hillel, we can account for the words used to support the position of the House of the Shammai: The phrase "as you lie down and as you rise" refers to the times in which people lie down and rise; that is, the evening and the morning.

Although the derivation of significance from textual details is characteristic of midrash broadly, we find diversity in its application. The tradition remembers a dispute between two prominent second-century sages Akiba and Ishmael. Akiba derived legal significance from repetitions or prepositions. Ishmael is said to have responded, in several instances, that "the Torah spoke in the language of mankind": much like human authors, the Torah may use repetition for rhetorical effect, rather than to introduce a particular referent. The Talmuds already conceived of this dispute as forming two different schools of scriptural exegesis, and modern scholars have discovered that tannaitic–era midrashic compilations align with this division: They presented different methods of interpretation, terminology, and prosopography that can be associated with Ishmael and Akiba, respectively. The *Mekhilta de-Rabbi Ishmael*, for example, is the Ishmaelean compilation of commentary on the book of Exodus, whereas the *Mekhilta de-Rabbi Simeon b. Yohai* is its Akiban counterpart.[29]

THE RABBIS 69

Midrash approaches Scripture as a unity: Every verse, indeed every word, in Scripture can illuminate another, regardless of the biblical book in which it is found. The sages often juxtaposed verses or parts of verses from different contexts to produce new meanings, stories, and laws.[30] I offer one intricate example, this time from the amoraic compilation of Genesis Rabbah, in a series of comments on the creation of humankind:

> *And God said let us make a human being* (Gen 1:26). R. Yohanan opened,
> *Behind and before you formed me* (Pss 139:5). R. Yohanan said: If a
> person is worthy, he benefits from two worlds, as it was said, *Behind
> and before you formed me*; if not, he will have to account for himself, as
> it was said, *and you lay your hand upon me* (Pss 139:5).
> SAID R. JEREMIAH BEN ELEAZAR: At the time the Holy One, blessed be
> He, created the first human being, he created him an androgyne, for it
> was said, *male and female he created them* (Gen 5:2).
> SAID R. SAMUEL B. R. NAHMAN: At the time the Holy One, blessed be,
> created the first human being, he created him of two faces, and he
> sawed him and made him one back here and one back there.
> THEY RESPONDED TO HIM: But it was written, *then he took one of his ribs*
> [*tzal'otav*]? He said to them, [it means one] of his sides, just as you say, *and
> for the side* [*tzela*] *of the tabernacle* (Exod 26:20). (Genesis Rabbah 8:1)

Rabbi Yohanan "opens" the homily on Gen 1:26 by quoting Pss 139:5. "Open" is a technical term in such homilies, introducing an unconnected verse that, sometimes after a long suspenseful negotiation, will illuminate the verse at hand. Psalm 139 is concerned with God's complete knowledge of the speaker: "You know when I sit down and when I rise up . . . even before a word is on my tongue, O Lord, you know it completely" (vv.2, 4). V.5 quoted in the midrash similarly emphasizes God's complete mastery of the human being: "Behind and before you formed me and you lay your hand upon me." But in Genesis Rabbah, it is taken to provide specific details about the creation of humankind.

For Rabbi Yohanan, the verse points to the freedom that is given to human beings when they were created and to the consequences of that freedom in terms of divine reward and punishment. He reads "behind" (also, "after") and "before" as saying that righteous people receive rewards both before the final judgment, in this world, and after it, in the world to come. The second half of the verse, "and you lay your hand upon me," refers to God's punishment of those who transgress. We then hear two additional teachings. Rabbi Jeremiah tells us that the first person was created with both male and female sexual organs.

He supports his claim with Gen 5:2, which reports that God created both the male and female and called them "Adam," taken here to be the name of a specific individual, rather than the species. Rabbi Samuel similarly says that Adam was created two-faced. God then sawed the two-faced creature into two persons: Adam and Eve. Although Pss 139:5 is not quoted here, it stands behind these teachings as well: God formed Adam "before" and "behind"—that is, with a male side and a female side—and then he "laid his hand upon him," slicing the creature into two. The midrash proceeds with an anonymous objection to Samuel's sawing story—the verse says that Eve was created out of Adam's rib, not as one of Adam's sides. However, the sage replies ingeniously—using another verse, Exod 26:20—that the word Genesis uses here, *tzela*, can mean not only rib but also "side"—confirming that Eve was created by separating Adam's feminine side from his masculine one.

The story produced through this juxtaposition of verses from Genesis and the psalm resolves an apparent inconsistency. In Gen 1:26–27, God creates humankind, male and female, on the sixth day of creation, after all the animals had been created; in Genesis 2, in contrast, God first creates Adam, then the animals, and only then Eve—who is created out of Adam's rib. The sages do not call out this contradiction but use it as an opportunity to tell a new story: God created Adam, male and female in one, and then sawed Adam into Adam and Eve.

There is more to the story, however. Ancient Greek authors knew of a story of primordial androgynes cut into two by the gods; in Plato's *Symposium*, Aristophanes uses this story to explain heterosexuality. The story was also known, and condemned, by Philo of Alexandria. In reading the story into the Bible, the sages were using the repertoire of myths in their society. Thus, what we see in these comments in Genesis Rabbah shows how the sages took an apparent contradiction in Scripture as an opportunity to tell a new story, inspired by their contemporary culture, through reading particular details of the text and juxtaposing it with another set of verses—and as they were doing so, they also argued that the first human being was beyond the gender binary.

The Talmuds

Several generations after the promulgation of the Mishnah, commentary on rabbinic teachings became a major occupation for the sages. The two massive compilations that present this commentary are called "Talmud." The Palestinian Talmud or Yerushalmi was compiled in Tiberias and includes teachings attributed to sages up to the second half of the fourth century. The Babylonian

Talmud or Bavli was compiled in what is now Iraq and includes teachings attributed to sages up to the late fifth century; many scholars, however, posit that it had a particularly complex and protracted process of crystallization and composition that may have continued through the seventh century CE.[31]

Although the Talmuds share a great deal in structure and even in content, there are differences between them, both in the specific traditions they present and in their general characteristics. For example, the Bavli is significantly longer than the Yerushalmi, and it includes more large-scale dialectical structures that attempt to sustain each conflicting claim. But the most significant difference between these compilations is their reception. It was the Bavli that became the authoritative source of Jewish law and the central text in the rabbinic curriculum, whereas the Yerushalmi has been relatively neglected. If you could ask Pirqoy ben Baboy, a ninth-century champion of the Babylonian academies, he would say that the Bavli's authority reflects its inherent superiority over the Yerushalmi. More recent accounts suggest that the Bavli's hegemony may have resulted from the increasing power of the Babylonian academies, which were located right in the seat of Abbasid government in Baghdad.[32]

Although the Talmuds, especially the Bavli, include a variety of materials, they are primarily interpretive texts. Their discussions are organized around the Mishnah, although some of their points of departure may be other tannaitic or amoraic teachings or Scripture. In both Talmuds but especially in the Bavli, we find commentary on rabbinic teachings that shares some of the fundamental characteristics of midrashic commentary on Scripture, including reading teachings intertextually and deriving meaning from features that are marked as apparently redundant. Yet we also find scholarly techniques that seldom appear in the rabbinic study of Scripture, such as discussion of textual variants, textual criticism, and reconstructing the approaches of individual sages from their teachings.[33]

The Talmuds often present alternative and opposing perspectives to the Mishnah, not just by juxtaposing or confronting the Mishnah with alternative tannaitic teachings but also by undermining the authority, claims, and logic of mishnaic literature. If the Mishnah's lack of regular appeal to Scripture is a deliberate claim to independent authority, then the Talmuds undermine that claim by frequently asking for and presenting the biblical origins of mishnaic rulings. And if the anonymity of much of the Mishnah gives the impression that the "tradition is speaking for itself" or that the teaching stems from the majority of the sages, then the Talmuds undermine that impression by frequently identifying anonymous teachings as belonging to individual sages.

72 CHAPTER 3

In its commentary on the Mishnah's passage on the Shema evening recitation, for example, the Bavli highlights the scriptural source of the Shema recitation in Deuteronomy. In addition, it explains that the Mishnah begins with the evening rather than morning recitation much like the opening of the Bible, "and there was evening and there was morning, the first day" (Gen 1:5), thereby connecting the opening passages of the written and oral Torah. In both Talmuds, the Mishnah is confronted with a series of alternative teachings on the timing of the evening recitation, which are themselves subjected to various kinds of interpretation. The Yerushalmi, for example, first points out that according to the version of this *mishnah* or recitation attributed to Rabbi Hiyya, the obligation begins at "the time people enter to eat their bread on Sabbath eves," rather than "the time the priests enter to eat their priest's due," and that an additional tannaitic teaching has it that both positions are "close to being identical." The Talmud asks how they could be so similar, when they ostensibly point to different times, and it quotes an interpretation by the amoraic sage Rabbi Yose that Rabbi Hiyya's recitation refers specifically to people in small villages, who go home earlier from work because they are worried about wild beasts. The Yerushalmi also discusses a textual variant, according to which the Mishnah mentions paschal lambs, and it suggests that the now common version, which omits this reference, stems from Rabbi Eliezer's position.

Talmudic discussions often go far beyond their departure points, employing various mishnaic and midrashic texts, back-and-forth arguments, and stories on a large range of topics. These sources are woven into *sugyot* (sing. *sugya*), literary units that are sometimes tightly organized around a narrative of inquiry and at other times present looser associations. Consider, for example, the incredible range of just the first five folios of the Bavli's commentary on the Mishnah's passage on the Shema, which we saw earlier. They present discussions of God's nightly mournful roar, reasons one should not go into ruins, King David's sleeping habits, the hierarchy between the angels Michael and Gabriel, and the merits of suffering. When the Yerushalmi gets to the story of Rabban Gamaliel's sons coming back from the wedding, it presents a wide-ranging discussion on the question of whether sages may instruct halakhah that goes against the majority interpretation of their peers, adducing various other examples from the tannaitic corpus. Much of talmudic scholarship in the twentieth century was dedicated to establishing the *sugya* as a carefully designed literary composition with a clear structure and even an agenda. Studies of literary design other than the *sugya*— whole chapters, tractates, or repetition across the Talmud—have also detected formal and ideological patterns in what at first seems associative or eclectic.[34]

THE RABBIS 73

With respect to the Bavli, this question of literary art and the manipulation of sources has been linked particularly with the anonymous layer. For many scholars, this layer's distinct style, concepts, and terminology indicate that it is a later composition; others have argued that these stylistic differences are not straightforward chronological indicators, but rather part of a deliberate literary design.[35] Because it is the anonymous material that structures discussions and comments on the different sources, it has had enormous influence on the history of Judaism. We saw earlier, for example, that rabbinic texts explain the exemption of women from the Shema recitation by associating it with Torah study. But the anonymous Bavli instead understands that exemption as resulting from a mishnaic rule that women are exempt from "positive timebound commandments" (Berakhot 20b), an interpretation that has been central to discussions of the role of women in Judaism.[36]

All rabbinic texts are the result of creative textual processes, in which teachings were reformulated or given new meaning as they were embedded in new contexts, but such processes are particularly visible in the Talmuds. This is in part because the Talmuds present more explicitly their interpretation of rabbinic teachings and in part because we can often trace developments and textual adaptation by comparing the tannaitic corpus with the Talmuds. I offer another example relating to the Shema. The discussion begins with a passage from the Mishnah that addresses how different activities interact with the Amidah prayer, the central mandatory prayer in the rabbinic liturgical system:

> A person may not sit down for a haircut near the time of the afternoon service, unless he has already prayed, nor enter a bath-house. ... But if they started [such activities], they do not need to stop. They must stop [such activities] to recite the Shema, but they need not stop for the [Amidah] Prayer. (Shabbat 1:2)

The conclusion of this passage is formulated a bit oddly. It would have been simpler to say something like "If they started, they do not need to stop, except for the recitation of the Shema," rather than stating first that there is no need to stop, then that one must stop for the Shema, and then repeat the point that one need not stop for the Amidah. The last sentence seems like it came from somewhere else, and perhaps it did. The Bavli's response to this issue assumes that, like Scripture, the Mishnah is so precisely composed that what seems like a repetition must be introducing a different subject: "But he [the sage formulating this passage in the Mishnah] taught [already] in the beginning that "they do not need to stop"? The ending [of the teaching] refers to Torah study" (Bavli, Shabbat 11a),

Because the Mishnah already taught in the beginning of the passage that one need not stop activities like getting a haircut or bathing for the Amidah, referred to in the text as the Prayer, the Bavli posits that the final clause, "They must stop to recite the Shema, but they need not stop for the Prayer" refers to a different subject: Torah study. It is as if the Mishnah said, "And with respect to Torah study: they stop it for the recitation of the Shema, but not for the Prayer." This interpretation of the Mishnah not only suggests a reason for the seemingly odd formulation, but also allows for the discussion of a cultural tension by posing a conflict between two religious activities: the liturgical activity of reciting the Shema and the scholastic activity of Torah study.

We can trace this opposition and its significance by looking at the parallel discussion in the Yerushalmi (Shabbat 1:23a–b), which also discusses whether one must interrupt Torah study for liturgical rituals:

> R. YOHANAN [SAID] IN THE NAME OF R. SIMEON B. YOHAI: "Those like us who are engaged [constantly] in the study of Torah do not stop it even for the recitation of the Shema."
>
> R. Yohanan said about himself, "Those like us who are not engaged [constantly] in the study of Torah [must] stop [it] even for the [Amidah] Prayer."

Rabbi Yohanan first quotes Rabbi Simeon's teaching that people like him, such as those who are constantly engaged in the study of Torah, need not stop it even for the recitation of the Shema (let alone the Amidah). Next, Rabbi Yohanan says "about himself" that because people like him are not occupied with Torah as much, they must stop their study even for the lesser Amidah (let alone the Shema). This statement seems ironic or hyperbolically humble—Rabbi Yohanan was, after all, the foremost scholar of his generation. The next stage in the talmudic discussion interprets these teachings not as applying to different people, but as representing two different approaches:

> R. YOHANAN [TAUGHT ACCORDING] TO HIS OWN OPINION, FOR R. YOHANAN SAID: "Oh that we might [be able] to pray all day long! Why? Prayer never loses its value."
>
> R. SIMEON B. YOHAI [TAUGHT ACCORDING] TO HIS OWN OPINION, FOR R. SIMEON B. YOHAI SAID: "Had I been at Mount Sinai when the Torah was given to Israel, I would have asked God to give man two mouths, one to toil in Torah, and one to use for all his other needs."

To show how these sages' positions about the Shema represent their different approaches more broadly, the Talmud cites other statements attributed to them.

It quotes Rabbi Yohanan's statement that he wished it was possible to "pray all day" to demonstrate that he had a positive inclination toward prayer, thereby implying that it was this inclination that led him to rule that one should stop Torah study for prayer. Next, it quotes Rabbi Simeon's statement that he wished the granting of the Torah came with two mouths, so that he would never need to stop studying. This sentiment, the Talmud argues, is also reflected in his ruling that one should not stop studying even for the Shema.

The effect of this interpretation is to expand the discussion on the Shema into a broad opposition between the scholastic and the liturgical. A closer look at Rabbi Simeon's teaching reveals both the interpretive work the Talmud does through mere placement and the astonishing nature of the resulting argument. In the tannaitic compilation *Sifre Deuteronomy* (§42), we find Rabbi Simeon arguing for a total commitment to Torah study, as opposed to the worldly pursuit of material gain or even sustenance. The statement attributed to Rabbi Simeon in our passage in the Talmud, read outside its current context, may be making the same point. It presents a dichotomy between Torah-related speech—on the one hand, and all other kinds of speech—including, say, conducting business—on the other hand. One might think that liturgy, and especially the Shema recitation—which is, after all, a recitation of passages from the Torah that the sages traditionally construed as an instance of Torah study—would fall into the category of Torah-related speech. And yet the Talmud, by using this teaching to explain Rabbi Simeon's position on the Shema and the prayer, puts these rituals in the opposite category, that is, with all other speech. Although the Talmud later offers a different explanation for Rabbi Simeon's position, it never retracts this dichotomy. This passage reflects the intensification of scholastic ideology among the sages—the idea that Torah study alone is a sacred activity and anything else, including even prayer, is akin to the mundane. But although this ideology became increasingly dominant as the rabbinic movement developed, we can see in passages like this that it had to be argued against competing notions that championed other kinds of piety—based on ritual, social justice, and "holy men" of the kind we find in other late ancient traditions—which were equally Jewish and even rabbinic.

————

Much of this chapter has concerned the sages' engagement with words. We have seen how quoting, interpreting, and composing texts allowed for their preservation and revision, as well as the inclusion of conflicting claims. These features are not unique to rabbinic culture, but by identifying Torah study with this particular model of textual engagement and placing it as the highest value, the sages made it uniquely central to their vision for Jewish culture. We also saw how for all its richness and apparent diversity this world of words kept many voices out. In the centuries that followed, some of these exclusions were contested, even or indeed because the rabbinic tradition remained central to Jewish life. The Hasidic movement centered prayer and embodied piety at the expense of study and scholastic virtue; modern Jewish Studies offers a vision of Jewish textual scholarship that is often at odds with that of the sages; and Torah study today is by no means an exclusively masculine realm (though it continues to be in some quarters). But even as these oppositions abolished some of the hierarchies originally promoted by the rabbinic tradition, reconfigured its values, and challenged its claims to authority, they also, in some sense, joined the conversation it has shaped—building another story in the messy house of study. It is this capacity for continuity, change, and contradiction that has made the sages' model both enduring and seductive.

Recommended Readings

Balberg, Mira. *Purity, Body, and Self in Early Rabbinic Literature* (University of California Press, 2014).

Boyarin, Daniel. *Border Lines: The Partition of Judeo-Christianity* (University of Pennsylvania Press, 2004).

Boyarin, Daniel. *Carnal Israel: Reading Sex in Talmudic Culture* (University of California Press, 1993).

Gross, Simcha. *Babylonian Jews and Sasanian Imperialism in Late Antiquity* (Cambridge University Press, 2024).

Halbertal, Moshe. *People of the Book: Canon, Meaning, Authority* (Harvard University Press, 1997).

Hayes, Christine. *What's Divine about Divine Law? Early Perspectives* (Princeton University Press, 2015).

Lapin, Hayim. *Rabbis as Romans: The Rabbinic Movement in Palestine, 100–400 CE* (Oxford University Press, 2012).

Rosen Zvi, Ishay. *Between Midrash and Mishnah* (Hebrew; Lamda, 2020; Engl., University of California Press, forthcoming).

Rubenstein, Jeffrey L. *The Culture of the Babylonian Talmud* (Johns Hopkins University Press, 2003).

Schäfer, Peter. *The Jewish Jesus: How Judaism and Christianity Shaped Each Other* (Princeton University Press, 2012).

Schwartz, Seth. *Imperialism and Jewish Society: 200 B.C.E. to 640 C.E.* (Princeton University Press, 2001).

THE RABBIS 77

Notes

1. See, e.g., Mark 9:5.

2. See Shaye Cohen, *The Significance of Yavneh and Other Essays in Jewish Hellenism* (Mohr Siebeck, 2010), 44–70, 227–43; Daniel Boyarin, *Border Lines: The Partition of Judaeo-Christianity* (University of Pennsylvania Press, 2004), 174.

3. This is a reference to the Babylonian Talmud. For discussion of the two Talmuds, Babylonian and Palestinian, see section, "The Talmuds." References to the Palestinian Talmud are indicated. Talmudic references without such notations are to the Bablylonian Talmud.

4. Michael Fishbane, *The Garments of Torah* (Indiana University Press, 1989), 65.

5. Menahem Fisch, *Rational Rabbis: Science and Talmud Culture* (Indiana University Press, 1997).

6. Compare the account by Berdyczewski, as recounted in Jacob Golomb, *Nietzsche and Zion* (Cornell University Press, 2004), 118–19, with the pro-diaspora view of the same story in Jonathan and Daniel Boyarin, *Powers of Diaspora: Two Essays on the Relevance of Jewish Culture* (University of Minnesota, 2002), 50–52.

7. Mira Balberg, *Blood for Thought: The Reinvention of Sacrifice in Early Rabbinic Literature* (University of California Press, 2017); Gideon Bohak, *Ancient Jewish Magic: A History* (University of Cambridge Press, 2008); Mika Ahuvia, *On My Right Michael, on My left Gabriel: Angels in Ancient Jewish Culture* (University of California Press, 2021); Martha Himmelfarb, *Ancestry and Merit in Ancient Judaism* (University of Pennsylvania Press, 2006); Adi Ophir and Ishay Rosen Zvi, *Goy: Israel's Multiple Others and the Birth of the Gentile* (Oxford University Press, 2018).

8. Catherine Hezser, *The Social Structure of the Rabbinic Movement in Roman Palestine* (Mohr Siebeck, 1997); Seth Schwartz, *Imperialism and Jewish Society: 200 B.C.E. to 640 C.E.* (Princeton University Press, 2001); Ra'anan Boustan, "Afterword: Rabbinization and the Persistence of Diversity in Jewish Culture in Late Antiquity," in *Diversity and Rabbinization: Jewish Texts and Societies between 400 and 1000 CE*, ed. G. McDowell et al. (Open Book, 2021).

9. Hayim Lapin, *Rabbis as Romans: The Rabbinic Movement in Palestine, 100–400 CE* (Oxford University Press, 2012); Simcha Gross, *Babylonian Jews and Sasanian Imperialism in Late Antiquity* (Cambridge University Press, 2024).

10. Yakir Paz, *From Scribes to Scholars: Rabbinic Biblical Exegesis in Light of the Homeric Commentaries* (Mohr Siebeck, 2022); Shai Secunda, *The Iranian Talmud: Reading the Bavli in Its Sasanian Context* (University of Pennsylvania Press, 2014); Yair Furstenberg, "The Rabbinic Movement from Pharisees to Provincial Jurists," *Journal for the Study of Judaism* 55 (2023): 1–43.

11. Boyarin, *Border Lines*; Peter Schäfer, *The Jewish Jesus: How Judaism and Christianity Shaped Each Other* (Princeton University Press, 2012); Michal Bar-Asher Siegal, *Jewish-Christian Dialogues on Scripture in Late Antiquity* (Cambridge University Press, 2019).

12. On orality, see Martin Jaffee, *Torah in the Mouth: Writing and Oral Tradition in Palestinian Judaism 200 BCE–400 CE* (Oxford University Press, 2001); David Stern, "The Publication and Early Transmission of the Mishnah," in *What Is The Mishnah? The State of the Question*, ed. S. J. D. Cohen (Harvard University Press, 2022), 444–70.

78   CHAPTER 3

13. For a statement of Neusner's theory, see, e.g., Jacob Neusner, *The Documentary Foundation of Rabbinic Culture* (Scholars, 1989). For critiques, see Shaye Cohen, *The Synoptic Problem in Rabbinic Literature* (Brown Judaic Studies, 2000).

14. Peter Schäfer, "Research into Rabbinic Literature: An Attempt to Define the *Status Quaestionis*," *Journal of Jewish Studies* 37 (1986): 139–52. Most of the work on textual variation is in Hebrew by scholars such as Jacob N. Epstein, E. S. Rosenthal, and Shamma Friedman.

15. Yair Furstenberg, "The Literary Evolution of the Mishnah," in *What Is the Mishnah?* 98–125.

16. Hayim Lapin, "Institutionalization, 'Orthodoxy', and Hierarchy," in *The Routledge Handbook of Jews and Judaism in Late Antiquity*, ed. C. Hezser (Routledge, 2024), 154–67.

17. Judith Hauptman, *Rereading the Mishnah: A New Approach to Ancient Jewish Texts* (Mohr Siebeck, 2005), providing a good account of scholarship while also forwarding a claim that even as a compilation, the Tosefta precedes our version of the Mishnah.

18. Rafael Neis, "The Seduction of Law: Rethinking Legal Studies in Jewish Studies," *Jewish Quarterly Review* 109 (2019): 119–38.

19. Shaye Cohen, "Shabbat: Introduction," in *Oxford Annotated Mishnah* (Oxford University Press, 2021), 370. On halakhah in the context of earlier Jewish texts, see Aharon Shemesh, *Halakha in the Making* (University of California Press, 2009); Vered Noam, "The Emergence of Rabbinic Culture from the Perspective of Qumran," *Journal of Ancient Judaism* 6 (2015): 253–74.

20. Leib Moscovitz, *Talmudic Reasoning: From Casuistics to Conceptualization* (Mohr Siebeck, 2002); Elizabeth S. Alexander, *Transmitting Mishnah: The Shaping Influence of Oral Tradition* (Cambridge University Press, 2006).

21. Mira Balberg, *Purity, Body, and Self in Early Rabbinic Literature* (University of California Press, 2014); Charlotte Fonrobert, "Neighborhood as Ritual Space: The Case of the Rabbinic Eruv," *Archiv für Religionsgeschichte* 10 (2008): 239–58; Beth Berkovitz, *Animals and Animality in the Babylonian Talmud* (Cambridge University Press, 2018); Max Strassfeld, *Trans Talmud: Androgynes and Eunuchs in Rabbinic Literature* (University of California Press, 2022).

22. Sarit Kattan Gribetz, "The Shema in the Second Temple Period: A Reconsideration," *Journal of Ancient Judaism* 6 (2015): 58–84.

23. Shelomo Naeh, "The Eating of Paschal Lambs Is Not Recited" [Hebrew] *Te'uda* 31 (2021), 251–76.

24. These observations are based in part on Avraham Walfish, *Mishnaic Tapestries: Tractate Berakhot* [Hebrew] (Herzog College, 2018), and Moshe Simon-Shoshan, *Stories of the Law: Narrative Discourse and the Construction of Authority in the Mishnah* (Oxford University Press, 2012).

25. Sarit Kattan Gribetz, *Time and Difference in Rabbinic Judaism* (Princeton University Press, 2020).

26. Paul Mandel, *The Origins of Midrash: From Teaching to Text* (Brill, 2017); Azzan Yadin-Israel, *Scripture and Tradition: Rabbi Aqiva and the Triumph of Midrash* (University of Pennsylvania Press, 2015).

27. On Geiger, see Jay Harris, *How Do We Know This? Midrash and the Fragmentation of Modern Judaism* (SUNY Press, 1995), 162; for the latter position, see Susan Handelman, *The*

THE RABBIS 79

Slayers of Moses: The Emergence of Rabbinic Interpretation in Modern Literary Theory (SUNY Press, 1992).

28. Ishay Rosen Zvi, *Between Mishnah and Midrash* (University of California Press, forthcoming).

29. Menahem Kahana, "The Halakhic Midrashim," in *The Literature of the Sages II,* ed. S. Safrai et al. (Van Gorcum, 2006), 3–105; Azzan Yadin-Israel, "Concepts of Scripture in the Schools of Rabbi Akiva and Rabbi Ishmael," in *Jewish Concepts of Scripture: A Comparative Perspective*, ed. B. Sommer (NYU Press, 2012), 47–63.

30. Daniel Boyarin, *Intertextuality and the Reading of Midrash* (Indiana University Press, 1991).

31. On dating the Yerushalmi, see Uzi Leibner, "Settlement Patterns in the Eastern Galilee: Implication regarding the Transformation of Rabbinic Culture in Late Antiquity," in *Jewish Identities in Antiquity*, ed. I. L. Levine and D. R. Schwartz (Mohr Siebeck, 2009), 269–95; on the Bavli, see Simcha Gross, "Editorial Material in the Babylonian Talmud and Its Sasanian Context," *AJS Review* 47 (2023): 51–76.

32. David Kraemer, *History of the Talmud* (Cambridge University Press, 2019).

33. Moulie Vidas, *The Rise of Talmud* (Oxford University Press, 2025).

34. On the Talmuds' literary history, see Kraemer, *History of the Talmud*; on the function of stories within *sugyot*, see Jeffrey Rubenstein, *Talmudic Stories: Narrative Art, Composition, and Culture* (Johns Hopkins, 1999). For a study of a whole tractate, see Mira Wasserman, *Jews, Gentiles, and Other Animals: The Talmud after the Humanities* (University of Pennsylvania Press, 2017).

35. Moulie Vidas, *Tradition and the Formation of the Talmud* (Princeton University Press, 2014).

36. Elizabeth Shanks Alexander, *Gender and Timebound Commitments in Judaism* (Cambridge University Press, 2013).

1.2 Medieval Lives

4

The Jewish Community

Marina Rustow, Princeton University

READERS MAKING their way into scholarship in Jewish Studies will soon notice the frequent appearance of the phrase "the Jewish community," with varying degrees of specification—for instance, "the Jewish community of Mainz," "the Jewish community of Fusṭāṭ," "the Jewish communities of medieval Ashkenaz," or "the Jewish communities of the medieval Islamic world." Just as frequently, scholars refer to the "Jewish community" without qualification. Community seems to be a pervasive concept in the study of premodern Jews and Judaism, but its potentially baffling presence is rarely explained. Is it a habit of modern scholars, or is the concept present in premodern sources?

The answer is both. Medieval Jewish collectivities did indeed often write about themselves as communities in more than an ordinary sense of the term— not merely as an aggregation of individuals but also as an entity with common interests and even a common destiny—and they developed the administrative capacity to serve those interests. Modern scholars, for their part, have written of the Jewish community as a self-governing entity that appointed its own officers; a juridical power that promulgated laws and statutes and expected or even coerced Jews to follow them; an administrative body that made claims on revenue from its members and redistributed it; and a collectivity to which states granted autonomy.

Some modern scholars have even described the premodern Jewish community as a "state within a state." But what precisely might this mean? Was it a formal organization with legal and administrative institutions or a self-constituted group in which membership was voluntary? The tension between these two poles pervades scholarship on Jewish communities in the medieval and early modern periods. There are no easy answers to these questions, because the degree to which Jewish community officials exercised jurisdiction over their members was often subject to contestation and dependent on the actual states in which Jews lived.

Most twentieth-century scholarship on premodern Jewish communities took for granted their authority and centrality in the lives of Jews. But a growing consensus now holds that they possessed legal autonomy only in certain matters; that they were self-governing only in some domains; that individual Jews and even groups of Jews could, and very often did, seek legal redress and pursue rights outside communal institutions—and, perhaps paradoxically, that the sources of Jewish communal authority often lay outside the community itself. In the last several decades, scholarship on medieval and early modern Jews has taken a more minimal approach to what precisely the existence of an organized Jewish community implied for individual Jews.

An increasing number of sources have likewise come to light demonstrating that very few Jewish communities—and perhaps none at all—possessed robust means of enforcing their own laws and statutes; instead, communal officials maintained alliances with state officials for just that reason. (In older scholarship, the state was often called "the non-Jewish [or Christian, or Muslim] government," betraying the belief that Jewish self-government was its equivalent.) Qualifying these older theories of Jewish legal autonomy and self-governance remains a promising area of research. Doing so persuasively depends not just on tracking the workings of power and institutions but also on finding sources that offer glimpses of those workings in real time. In the twentieth century, scholars of the Jewish past focused disproportionately on the male elite and their writings. More recent phenomenological approaches balance these older views by paying attention to women, non-elites, daily life, and institutional structures outside the Jewish community. If the old theories of communal autonomy tended to overstate the clarity and inviolability of the boundaries between Jews and others, more recent views see those boundaries as porous, easily traversed, situation-dependent and sometimes nonexistent.

That said, although old assumptions about Jewish communal autonomy have undergone significant revision and qualification, it would be premature to do away entirely with the notion of "the Jewish community." On the contrary, many Jewish sources use terms that translate as "community," including *qahal* and *qehilla* in Hebrew, *qahala* in Aramaic, *jamā'a* in Judeo-Arabic, and *kehile* in Yiddish.[1] Being part of a community, benefiting from its institutions, and relying on them in need were all facts that conditioned premodern Jewish life.

Scholarship has, then, persisted in discussing "the Jewish community" not merely out of inertia but also because invoking the concept in discussing the Jewish past can serve a good purpose so long as one explains it clearly, rigorously examining how the sources use it.

In ordinary English parlance, some communities are comprised of people who happen to come together by virtue of where they live, whereas others share common interests or labels of self-identification—they are communities of place, interest, and category. All three types recur in this chapter. That said, I do not use "community" as a synonym for "subculture" or "minority." Although this usage has become widespread in contemporary English, it entails considerable analytical loss and risks, including objectifying the group in question, presuming its unity, referring to it euphemistically, or claiming to speak for it. This is one reason among many others why the decision to refer to "the Jewish community" in scholarship about the past should be made advisedly and justified explicitly.

This chapter accordingly discusses "the Jewish community" as both a historical fact and the object of a historiographic tradition. The first section explores the actor's category: How do premodern sources—whether written by Jews or non-Jews—conceive of Jewish collectivities? The second section turns to modern scholarship: What did the giants of Jewish historiography in the twentieth century assume about organized Jewish communities, and how have more recent scholars qualified or dismantled those assumptions?

Jewish Communities in the Sources

Medieval and early modern authors writing in Hebrew deployed biblical terms perforce, but not always with the same meaning as the Bible. These authors' quotidian experience and postbiblical circumstances played a role in filling biblical terms with new meaning.

The ancient Hebrew lexeme that described the collectivity was *q-h-l*, a root meaning to assemble or gather. The verb was used intransitively and transitively depending on the form: The Israelites assemble (*va-yiqqahalu*, Josh 18:1, 22:12; cf. Esther 9:15), Moses and Aaron assemble the Israelites (*va-yaqhilu*, Num 20:10), and God orders them to do so (*haqhel*, Num 20:8, Deut 31:12). At one crucial juncture, in the episode of the golden calf, the Israelites assemble *against* Moses and Aaron (*va-yiqqahalu 'al*, Num 16:3, 20:2; cf. Exod 32:1). Each of these verb forms implies physical assembly—gathering together into a group—and in each context, it is for some finite purpose.

Two Hebrew nouns derive from the same root: *qahal* and *qehilla*. Both mean "community," but they are used with slightly different nuances.

Qahal

A *qahal* is a gathering, assembly, convocation, or congregation. It is always large in number but can be more or less comprehensive: It can comprise all Israelites, as in a passage requiring "the congregation of the assembly" (*qehal ʿedah*) to perform the paschal sacrifice (Exod 12:6); it can comprise a subgroup of Israelites, as when the book of Ezra calls the Judeans of Persia "the congregation of the exiles" (*qehal ha-gola,* Ezra 10:8); or it can be a gathering of non-Israelites, as when the prophet Jeremiah delivers the message that God is "rousing and leading an assemblage of nations (*qehal goyim*) against Babylon" (Jer 50:9). It often implies a temporary gathering or a community of category coming together for some finite purpose.

But to be a *qahal* can imply more than merely a physical gathering or a finite assembly of people who can see each other face to face. When God blesses Jacob, he tells him to be fruitful and multiply so that an "assembly of nations" (*qehal goyim*) will descend from him (Gen 35:11); when Isaac blesses Jacob, he tells him to be "fertile and numerous, so that you become an assembly of peoples" (*qehal ʿammim,* Gen 28:3). A *qahal* can then be something akin to what the political scientist Benedict Anderson calls an "imagined community," entailing solidarity with people one does not know personally by virtue of belonging to some shared social grouping.[2] Likewise, "coming into the congregation of the Lord" (*qehal YHWH,* Deut 23:4) means becoming an Israelite in a specific sense: joining a collectivity with shared institutions. This sense of a people possessing institutions (whether in the past, present, or future) is also reflected in the extrabiblical ancient Jewish texts preserved at Qumran.

In rabbinic texts, there is a shift in nuance from the biblical *qahal* in which membership is categorical to one in which it is voluntary—from the Israelites as a community of assembly and category to one of interest. This new usage implies a shift from peoplehood in the ancient sense to a collectivity bound by custom and law, a nuance that reflects the rabbis' own self-conception as the arbiters of communal practice and belonging. Thus, the Mishnah, the earliest stratum of rabbinic texts, interprets the verse from Deuteronomy about "coming into the congregation of the Lord" (*qehal YHWH*) specifically to mean marrying an Israelite woman (mYad. 4:4; cf. bBer. 28a).

Interestingly, however, medieval usages of *qahal* and related terms reflect not just the rabbinic meanings of the term but also the biblical ones. Thus, medieval texts use the term *qahal* to refer to communities of place, category, and interest. In documents from the Cairo Geniza, which provide an unparalleled store of everyday usage from around the Mediterranean basin, the term *qahal* appears primarily when the Jewish community of one locale is addressing its counterpart somewhere else. Thus the word *qahal* describes the Jewish communities of the Egyptian towns and cities of Alexandria, Ashmūm, Bilbays, Damietta, Damsīs, Fusṭāṭ, al-Maḥalla, and Minyat Ziftā, and Jewish communities outside Egypt including (moving more or less counterclockwise around the Mediterranean) Nájera (in Castille), Fez, Tlemcen, Qayrawān, al-Mahdiyya, Siracusa, Gaza, Ascalon, Jerusalem, Tyre, Damascus, Jubayl, Tripoli, and Aleppo.[3] There are also references in geniza letters to the "holy community of the land of Yavan," meaning Byzantium.[4] In each of these uses, the word *qahal* means "a group of Jews in a specific place." This suggests that when Jews around the Mediterranean were writing in Hebrew, they often fell back on the biblical meaning of *qahal* as a community of place, in keeping with the tendency of medieval epistolary Hebrew to draw not only on biblical words but also on biblical concepts. But how inclusive was the community of category? When did it include all Jews everywhere, in a particular region, or within a circumscribed place like a town or city? The ambiguity is inherent to any premodern society in which slow travel and communication prevented people from being in two places at once. While premodern Jews were spread across a vast geographic expanse, they maintained contact with each other through letters; sometimes their officials and leaders were the authors of those letters or read them aloud publicly. They may have come together as a community only when their leaders represented them publicly to Jews in other places. Tellingly, one document refers to "the community of [Jewish] foreigners,"[5] a subgroup within a Jewish community but not a separate congregation—implying something akin to the biblical meaning of *qahal* as a grouping without institutional valence.

Some medieval sources, however, suggest that Jews thought of a *qahal* not only as a community of place but also as an organized collectivity in a formal sense—a community of category and interest at once, with the accompanying notion that membership implied partaking of organizational resources and services. One early eleventh-century geniza document, written in a typical mixture of Arabic and Hebrew, refers seemingly redundantly to "the *qahal* of the Syro-Palestinian congregation of Fusṭāṭ" (*qehal kanīsat al-shāmiyyīn bi-miṣr*).[6] Given that a congregation (*kanīsa*) is already a gathering of people, *qahal* here

THE JEWISH COMMUNITY 85

seems to have an administrative connotation; the phrase can be understood as "the administrative structure of the Syro-Palestinian congregation of Fusṭāṭ." Similarly, a fifteenth-century document from Fusṭāṭ refers to the *negid qehal yisra'el*, "the head of the community of Jews," meaning the head of a social organization comprising the Jews.[7] Natan b. Yeḥi'el of Rome (d. 1106), author of a dictionary of Hebrew called the *Arukh*, defines the word *qahal* by offering the example of a second-century confraternity of Jews, "the sacred community of Jerusalem" (in Aramaic, *qehala qadisha di-rushalayim*) that was voluntary in membership and observed specific practices, including service, prayer, text study, ritual purity, and piety.[8] This suggests that he was thinking of a *qahal* both as an organized institutional grouping, like his counterparts in Islamic lands, and as a voluntary grouping, in keeping with the Mishnah.

In medieval parlance, then, a *qahal* could be a community of place (a collectivity by virtue of physical proximity), a community of category (Jews as distinct from others or a distinct group of Jews), or a formal community with a leadership structure, an organizational chart, a standard set of procedures, and practices of legal document production. Sometimes, it meant more than one of these things at the same time. In addition, *qahal* in the sense of an "imagined community" of Jews everywhere at all times may have filtered into everyday use, as when a thirteenth-century Jewish legal scribe in Egypt used the biblical phrase "the congregation of the Lord" (*qehal YHWH*) in the rabbinic sense of "the Jewish people" but with a twist, meaning only those descended from Jews, excluding those who had opted in via conversion.[9] Communities of descent include not just those physically present but also the dead and distant and were therefore, by definition, imagined.

Qehilla

The related noun *qehilla* also means assembly and can refer to either a temporary gathering or an abstract category. This word appears only twice in the Hebrew Bible—in one case as a concrete gathering, when Nehemiah says that he "raised a large crowd (*qehilla gedola*) against" the Jewish nobles and prefects (Neh 5:7), and in the other, as an abstract one, when the law of Moses is called "the heritage of the congregation of Jacob" (*qehillat ya'aqov*, Deut 33:4), implying a community that transcends time and place.

In medieval Hebrew, *qehilla* retained this ambiguity. It was the usual word for a congregation centered around a house of worship—a concrete, purposive gathering—and could also describe the Jewish population of a town, a meaning

86   CHAPTER 4

as often expressed with the word *qahal*. But interestingly, when geniza documents use *qehilla* in the plural (*qehillot*), it is often accompanied by "all" or "every," suggesting that like *qahal*, it had a categorical level pointing to the Jewish collectivity in the abstract. Thus, eleventh-century Jewish communal leaders in Palestine refer to "all the communities (*qehillot*) of Israel,"[10] "all the communities (*qehillot*) of our Jewish brethren,"[11] "all the communities (*qehillot*) of Israel in their multitudes,"[12] and "the communities (*qehillot*) of Egypt, ... the people of the Talmud and the people of the Bible" (Rabbanites and Qaraites).[13] When leaders wanted to express an abstract, categorical sense of Jewish collectivity, they reached for the term *qehilla* more often than *qahal*, where *qahal* also referred to the group of leaders who led the *qehilla*. Elia Levita (1469–1549), a German-speaking Jewish scholar and author of a Hebrew dictionary, suggests that the distinction between *qahal* and *qehilla* had by his era become standardized: A *qahal* is "a gathering of Jews living in a single city," whereas a *qehilla* is the entire Jewry of that city. One speaks of "the *qehilla* of Padova or Venice," he wrote, whereas the *qahal* of Padova or Venice would be a smaller subset of its Jews.[14]

Qehilla could likewise imply a group of concrete communities that added up to an abstract community. Thus, a tenth-century letter from Kiev refers to the "holy communities (*qehillot*) that are dispersed to every corner" of the globe[15]; a twelfth-century Jew from Byzantium refers to "all communities of Jews" (*kol qehillot yisra'el*)[16]; another twelfth-century Byzantine Jew writes of "all the communities (*qehillot*) of the land of Edom"[17]; and an undated letter from an Egyptian Jewish woman sojourning (unhappily) in Byzantium refers to "the people of the communities of Byzantium" (*qehillot Romania*).[18] This plural sense of *qehillot* implied a diasporic model of community as networks of groups, not networks of individuals.

Beyond these Hebrew terms, in the Islamic world—where most medieval Jews lived—many Arabic terms described Jewish collectivities, among them *qawm* (group or faction), *jamā'a* (group), and *ṭā'ifa* (group or faction).[19] In everyday Arabic writings—as opposed to prescriptive and narrative sources—there was no fixed technical term for "the Jewish community." Theoretical writings tended to use *ahl al-dhimma*, "people under a pact of protection," or *milla*, "religious group," but in administrative and legal documents, the terms were more fluid and generic. Thus an early eleventh-century Fatimid government decree from Egypt uses *qawm, jamā'a*, and *ṭā'ifa* alike to refer to both specific Jewish congregations and the wider Jewish community,[20] as does a late twelfth-century Ayyubid investiture for the leader of a Jewish community in Syria[21] and a pair of thirteenth-century legal queries from Jews to Muslim jurisconsults.[22] All these documents reflect how state officials or legal experts saw Jewish collectivities after Jews had asked them to confirm their privileges; the Arabic terms seem to convey the same range of meanings as the Hebrew terms *qahal* and *qehilla* and reflect Jews' self-conception.

Interestingly, documents drawn up for individual members of the Jewish community in state and legal institutions, such as tax receipts and legal deeds, do not refer to Jews as members of a community. Instead, they use the straightforward Arabic term *yahūdī* (pl. *yahūd,* Jew or Jews). Likewise, they describe Jews as hailing not from the Jewish community of a particular place but from the place itself; for example, in a petition to a high Ayyubid official around 1200 from a Jewish petitioner "from the port of Alexandria" (*min ahl thaghr al-Iskandariyya*)[23] and an eleventh-century request for tax exemption for a petitioner descended from Khaybarī Jews and hailing from Baghdad (*khaybarī baghdādī*).[24] Neither document describes its petitioner as coming from a Jewish community in the sense of *qahal, qehilla,* or any of the Arabic terms mentioned earlier.

It seems, then, that when Jews asked the state to focus on collective administration and communal leadership, they became a community in the eyes of state officials. But in everyday contexts, Muslim legal and state venues treated Jews as individuals. This mirrored a flexibility of legal venues: Jews could seek redress from communal or non-Jewish legal courts and could petition either communal or state officials for charity, rights, privileges, or legal mediation, depending on which strategy they thought best served their interests. In professional contexts, Jews did not always speak of Jews to other Jews as members of the Jewish community: in 1156, when several Jewish traders in Aden wrote to inform a Jewish colleague in Fusṭāṭ of the death of the latter's son-in-law and of another trader in a shipwreck en route to Kollam on the southwest coast of India, they describe them as "two of our colleagues from 'Aden" (*ithnayn min aṣḥābinā min ahl 'adan*).[25]

Sometimes, then, Jews were members of a *qahal*; sometimes they were merely individuals. Jewish communities were neither merely the stuff of wishful epistolary invocations nor all-encompassing organizations that governed Jews' lives from the cradle to the grave. Instead, they were alternative and simultaneous forms of identification that Jews could invoke depending on the circumstances.

MULTILEVEL ADMINISTRATION IN THE ISLAMIC WORLD

The actor's category as reflected in self-descriptions tells us how certain community leaders and members thought of the community when they were consciously invoking it. But the ontological reality of the Jewish community had more to do with institutional structures.

Jews in the Islamic world developed a robust administrative structure or, rather, overlapping administrative structures that were mostly cooperative and sometimes competed in hostile ways. Before 1000, the Babylonian *ge'onim*, the heads of the rabbinic academies (*yeshivot*) in Abbasid Iraq (in lower Iraq and then, by the late ninth century, in Baghdad) claimed jurisdiction over the Jews of Iraq and western Iran. But their relationship with Jewish communities farther away is unclear. They received students from abroad and sent legal responsa to Jewish communities outside Iraq, but they had little to do with the daily administration of communities outside their immediate jurisdiction.[26] In addition, the Jewish exilarch (Aramaic *resh galuta*) in Iraq ran his own academy in the shadow of one of the ge'onim.[27] Despite very limited evidence to that effect, modern historians have styled him the caliph's designated official in representing the Jewish community to the Abbasid caliphs, but his authority seems to have been mainly symbolic. Most of this picture is inferred from the responsa, legal monographs, and other writings of the ge'onim themselves, as well as from Arabic chronicles and compendia.

Starting in the early tenth century, the fragmentation of the Abbasid caliphate sparked a westward migration from Iraq, Iran, and Central Asia. Jews who moved to Mediterranean communities such as Fusṭāṭ, Qayrawān (in today's Tunisia), and Palermo (under Islamic rule until the late eleventh century) brought their fealty to the ge'onim with them. Geniza documents start to fill the informational void around 950, especially letters that the ge'onim sent to Mediterranean communities, and vice versa, as well as communal and mercantile correspondence from Jews in Syria, Palestine, Egypt, Ifrīqiya (central North Africa, home to the important Jewish community of Qayrawān), and Sicily. These sources show Jewish communities around the Mediterranean maintaining multiple levels of institutions and administration: the two yeshivot in Baghdad; a yeshiva in Jerusalem, which relocated briefly to Tyre in the 1070s and then to Damascus; and relatively independent Jewish communities elsewhere with their own hierarchies of local administration.

We have the most detailed information from Fusṭāṭ (Old Cairo), but it must be borne in mind that Fusṭāṭ was not representative of all Jewish communities:

THE JEWISH COMMUNITY 89

Egypt was an economic powerhouse at the hinge of the Mediterranean and Indian Ocean trades, centralized along the axis of the Nile, with a relatively large Jewish population for which disproportionately abundant sources happen to have survived. After 969, a succession of polities—the Fatimid caliphate (909–1171), the Ayyubid sultanate (1171–1250), and the Mamluk sultanate (1250–1517)—ruled Egypt from Egypt itself, putting its Jewish communities close to the court and bureaucracy. Fusṭāṭ's Jewish community may then have been more centralized than most. All the same, even Egypt's functional and well-articulated Jewish community, with its multitiered administrative system, was linked to Jewish institutions in Palestine, Syria, Iraq, Sicily, and Ifrīqiya.[28]

Egypt's Jewish communities consisted of not one but three Jewish groups. Two groups comprised rabbinic Jews who followed the teachings of the Babylonian and Palestinian Talmuds, the main rabbinic compilations from Late Antiquity, and the ge'onim of Iraq and Palestine, respectively. The term used for these groups in English-language scholarship is Rabbanites, derived from the Arabic rabbāniyyūn, which itself derives from the Hebrew plural for rabbi, rabbanim. Geniza sources refer to a Rabbanite "synagogue of the Iraqis" (kanīsat al-'irāqiyyīn) and a "synagogue of the Syrians" (kanīsat al-shāmiyyīn) in Fusṭāṭ.[29] Congregational loyalties did not necessarily reflect one's geographic origins. Westward migrants from Iraq and Iran in the tenth and eleventh centuries had helped create the commercial and social networks that allowed the Iraqi ge'onim to cultivate followers not only outside their immediate geographic orbit but also in Palestine, despite the presence of a yeshiva there with its own loyalists both locally and in Egypt. The third group were the Qaraites, who did not feel compelled to follow rabbinic teachings at all. Qaraites were full participants in the broader Jewish communal structure and ran their own academic institution in Jerusalem, an intellectual powerhouse of theology, philosophy, law, biblical exegesis, and Hebrew linguistics.

All three groups worked in concert at various levels of communal administration. Many of the legal documents from the Palestinian synagogue of Fusṭāṭ reflect a hybrid of Jewish scholastic (as well as non-Jewish) traditions. Legal scribes tended to draw up their documents with whatever formulae worked, rather than using the wording of documents to police the boundaries between groups—with the exception of some marriage and divorce documents.[30] Each group may or may not have run its own judicial institutions; this is less clear, because most surviving legal documents came from the Palestinian Rabbanite synagogue of Fusṭāṭ, in addition to a few dozen from a Qaraite geniza in Cairo; no Iraqi geniza survived in Fusṭāṭ or elsewhere. Our information is asymmetrical.

But there is enough of it to demonstrate that in practice, many Jews maintained loyalty to one or more of these institutions and schools of thought. A complex arrangement of scholastic authority—as well as the structure of religious law in the Islamic world—left the field open to competition among the groups, and this was a defining feature of Jewish communities in the tenth through thirteenth centuries and perhaps later. Where a Jewish man chose to study, if he pursued higher learning, did not necessarily determine where he attended synagogue, what kind of court scribe he asked to draw up his legal deeds, or where he sent donations. (Geniza letters suggest that the yeshivot in Iraq and Palestine each had a geographically expansive network of donors.) Some Qaraites, while attending their own houses of worship and feeling no obligation to study rabbinic literature (although many did), donated money to the Rabbanite yeshivot and used rabbinical courts; some Rabbanite Jews studied at the Palestinian and Babylonian yeshivot alike, donated money to them, and sought honorific titles from them—often from more than one—while also marrying Qaraites. The Jews documented in the geniza seem not to have sensed a contradiction in any of this. In the 1020s, the Qaraites even became the key kingmakers not just in the Jewish community of Egypt but also in Rabbanite politics in Jerusalem.

The complexity of these overlapping layers of Jewish communal administration made sense in a social world structured by complex webs of both asymmetrical and symmetrical reciprocal relationships among individuals. It also mirrored the way Jews sometimes identified as a part of a *qahal* and sometimes as individuals, depending on the context and their strategies.

Over the course of the eleventh century, the tripartite Jewish community of Egypt developed a more streamlined and centralized structure. This, too, was a response to the immediate environment. In the 1060s, the Jewish community established an office of leadership as a way of managing the Fatimid court and bureaucracy more effectively: the *ra'īs al-yahūd* (Arabic for "head of the Jews"), similar to the Coptic patriarch.[31] But even at its most streamlined, the Jewish community of Egypt was not structured like a smooth pyramid, with a single point of contact between it and state officials. Other courtiers, wealthy merchants, family dynasties, and respected scholars also played a part in supporting the *ra'īs al-yahūd* or curtailing his authority. Jewish communal leaders depended on multiple sources of power both inside and outside the Jewish community. And this upper echelon of communal power did not participate in all mundane, quotidian matters—as in the early 1100s, when congregants in Bilbays in the Nile delta voted unanimously in favor of rebuilding their synagogue after an earthquake, rebranding it to the local governor as a home renovation,[32] or in

THE JEWISH COMMUNITY 91

the early thirteenth century when the two synagogues in Alexandria came together to choose a new judge.[33] Even during crises such as the Crusader conquest of Jerusalem in 1099, multiple Jewish leaders coordinated among various communities; for example, a group of Rabbanite leaders in Fusṭāṭ and Cairo wrote to their counterparts in Ascalon to manage the ransoming of Jewish captives and books from the Franks,[34] and one year later, the Qaraite Jews of Ascalon wrote to the Qaraites and Rabbanites of Fusṭāṭ seeking help managing refugees and ransom payments.[35]

Among the other services that a well-organized Jewish community such as that of Fusṭāṭ provided was the provision of charity to destitute members—and even to people from outside the community who joined it for the purpose of receiving charity, to judge by the number of Jews on Fusṭāṭ charity distribution lists who are called al-ger, "the convert."[36] Such communities may even have excelled in relief for the poor, to judge by the remark of a Coptic bishop in the early 1230s, who admonished his well-to-do coreligionists for their indifference in the face of the Ayyubid corvée by comparing them invidiously to Jews who, "as is their custom, came together, the richer vouching for the poorer so that none of them suffered the trials our community did."[37] Dozens of charity lists from twelfth-century Fusṭāṭ attest to regular distributions of bread and wheat, the collection of funds, and a system for managing them.[38]

The Jewish court system likewise provided access to notarial services and mediation. Jewish legal scribes were best equipped to draw up documents of hoary Jewish pedigree, such as ketubbot (marriage contracts) or gittin (bills of divorce). Yet Jews also contracted debts and business partnerships in Jewish courts, even though their enforcement power was limited. Thousands of Jewish court documents survive for business transactions, suggesting that Jews regarded them as more than just legal instruments. Since documents drawn up by Muslim notaries were equally available and easier for state authorities to enforce, enforcement may have been precisely what they were trying to avoid.

Jewish officials could attempt to broker compromises or mediate conflicts while inflicting minimal public humiliation. Litigants' demands for new legal instruments also drove the expansion of the Jewish court system, as did scribes' willingness to meet those demands by domesticating non-Jewish legal instruments; for instance, by borrowing Muslim notaries' legal formulae and transcribing them wholesale in Judeo-Arabic or, in one case, translating a snippet of an Islamic marriage contract into Aramaic.[39]

Despite the fact that the various polities of the Islamic world did not explicitly grant or guarantee Jewish communities the right to run their own legal systems,

Jewish scribes produced robust quantities of legal documents, building on earlier Jewish legal practice and the prestige of having a legal tradition in the Islamicate environment.[40] The state granted the community its imprimatur, instead, in a more limited sense: Jewish leaders procured government decrees of investiture when they needed to expand their toolkit for resolving internal communal conflicts. Investitures and other types of rescripts—all of them granted in response to Jews' petitions—helped Jewish leaders lay the groundwork for intervention by law enforcement when they needed access to coercive powers that they themselves did not possess. Theoretically, appealing to state authorities for investitures and other kinds of decrees could open the door to state intervention in communal affairs, but that rarely stopped leaders from turning to the state to shore up their own authority.[41]

This suggests a fundamental paradox at the heart of Jewish communal organization: From the point of view of community leaders, state support strengthened their autonomy. Thus, the community's self-governance depended, in practice, on privileges granted from outside the community.

The same was true for the Jewish communities of medieval Ashkenaz, a cultural zone spanning England, northern France, and the Rhine valley—even though they operated in a different environment characterized not by cities with cosmopolitan elites and capillary state infrastructures but by small towns under less centralized rule. The town was an important unit of local administration; a legacy of Roman law in Europe was the legal construct of the corporation, which made collectivities legally more than the sum of their parts and allowed them to exercise rights. This body of theoretical law expanded in the law schools of twelfth-century Bologna and gave legal structure to the communes in northern and central Italy and eventually also in the German lands. Citizens in communes swore to protect each other from the arbitrary impositions of the nobility and the clergy, sometimes with the help of charters that they purchased from the monarch or church. Jewish communities of medieval Latin Europe also negotiated the right to live in towns from their local bishops, lords, and monarchs.

The internal definition of Jewish communities responded to this environment. Jewish communities in Ashkenaz were subject to legal definition as communities in part by virtue of their male members' status as burghers or municipal citizens, and their right to use the local Christian legal courts also derived from their status as burghers, even as they retained the option of turning to Jewish courts. But if a Jewish man wished to become the leader of a commune, in theory, he had to leave the *qahal*, because the operative assumption was that he

THE JEWISH COMMUNITY   93

could not participate in both organizations. This was different from how Jewish communal leaders gained authority in the Islamicate world—and in Christian Iberia—where they often held positions in government bureaucracies or at the courts of rulers, which gave them easier access to enforcement mechanisms over Jewish community members.

Despite these limitations, the *qahal* in some Christian-ruled territories enjoyed a robust legal character precisely by analogy with organized Christian municipalities. Jewish communities in Ashkenaz modeled themselves after their Christian counterparts, for instance by issuing *taqqanot* (statutes). In the thirteenth century, at Speyer, Worms, and elsewhere, Jewish community leaders (*rashei ha-qahal*) formed councils, and some community councils (*ṭuvey ha-'ir*) of twelfth- and thirteenth-century Ashkenaz employed community seals, just as the municipal councils did.[42] The Jews of Crete—under Venetian rule starting in the thirteenth century—also formed a supracommunal council that issued *taqqanot* (rabbinic decrees).[43]

As in the Muslim-ruled world, then, so too in the Christian-ruled world did the organization of the Jewish community and its authority over its members follow the logic of what Ivan Marcus has called "inward acculturation": Jews built institutions to distinguish themselves from the ambient society often by using legal and administrative concepts and means borrowed from that society.[44] The development of juridical and administrative forms of corporate Jewish identity must have reinforced Jews' sense of belonging not just to a specific community of coreligionists but also to a general, abstract group. But despite robust evidence for Jewish communal solidarity in the medieval period in certain circumstances, that solidarity was not as absolute as later scholarship made it out to be. Corporate institutions like guilds, confraternities, and communes were not nearly as pervasive in medieval Europe as later believed, nor did they possess the robust legal powers later attributed to them until the fourteenth and fifteenth centuries.[45]

That period was also one of disruption in the Jewish communities of Europe: Numerous Western and Central European polities expelled their Jewish populations during this period, among them England in 1290, Hungary in 1360, France in 1394, Austria in 1421, various German principalities in the fifteenth and sixteenth centuries, the Iberian kingdoms in 1492–98, and the Papal States in 1593. That raises the question of the continuity between medieval and early modern Jewish communal organization—a promising area of research that this chapter cannot address in detail.

EARLY MODERN CENTRALIZATION

The period between 1300 and 1600 was a watershed in the lives of Jewish communities in Europe, North Africa, and the Eastern Mediterranean. Forced migrations led Jews to establish new centers or expand existing ones, especially in the Polish-Lithuanian Commonwealth, Northern Italy, and the Ottoman Empire.

In some areas, Jewish communities developed a supracommunal level of governance. The most important example of this was the Council of Four Lands in Poland and Ukraine and the Council of Lithuania in the sixteenth to eighteenth centuries, which coordinated and mediated among the legal decisions and institutional structures of hundreds of local communities, represented them to the Polish state, and collected and redistributed communal taxes. After 1592, Jews in the Polish-Lithuanian Commonwealth were exempt from the jurisdiction of the Catholic Church unless they lived on church-owned estates, and this gave the *qehillot* more authority over their members. This juridical autonomy remained a fact of Jewish life until the Polish parliament (the Sejm) abolished it in 1764—even as some church officials attempted to encroach on those privileges and some Jewish community officials invited church officials to adjudicate conflicts within the community.[46]

But the overall effect of the councils was greater autonomy and centralization. They also expanded their recordkeeping in concert with the proliferation of Eastern European documentation more broadly.[47] Some Jewish communities in Europe had already begun keeping records in registers or notebooks, but in the sixteenth century, the genre of the communal register (*pinqas qehilla* or *pinqas qahal*) expanded to include communal customs, ordinances, and fiscal accounts. Not all these forms of recordkeeping came into being for internal purposes: Some satisfied the demands of state authorities. Nonetheless, as the administrative level of communal governance grew, the genre of the *pinqas* became standardized across a surprisingly broad geographic area. It also assumed a cultural function, as exemplified by a Lithuanian scribe around 1800 who wrote a panegyric to the *pinqas* itself on its opening pages.[48] This kind of recordkeeping and its standardization contributed to the development of Jewish solidarity on a large scale—strengthening Jewishness as a community of category or an "imagined community."

Some modern scholars argue that the Jewish communities of early modern Eastern Europe were not just more centralized than their medieval counterparts but also more autonomous. The roots of that autonomy were clearly medieval, but at least one consensus holds that Jewish autonomy attained its "most articulated expression" in the Polish-Lithuanian Commonwealth in the sixteenth to eighteenth centuries, a consensus that strikingly echoes the judgment of early modern Jewish communities themselves.[49] Still other historians have described that sense of solidarity and even "chosenness" as a cultural outlook or *mentalité* of Eastern European Jews.[50] But the fact remains that the councils—and other Jewish collectivities—possessed institutional and legal privileges on the sufferance of state, church, or local authorities. Their autonomy inevitably had limits when they came into conflict with the state or even with communities outside their jurisdiction. Indeed, over the course of the eighteenth century, the absolutist governments of Europe "saw the exercise of autonomy by corporate entities as an impediment to their power" and attempted to restrict the scope of Jewish communal authority to matters of Jewish ritual law.[51] This happened in Poland, as well as Prussia, where in the eighteenth century, the erosion of communal leadership and external interference by the state led to a complete "dissolution of Jewish autonomy by an autocratic state."[52]

In the Ottoman Empire, the reconstitution of Jewish communal life took a form almost diametrically opposed to that of the Polish-Lithuanian Commonwealth. In the Ottoman Empire, Jewish communities were more fragmented, which impeded their capacity to represent themselves before the state as a unified body. One reason for this fragmentation was that the communities had been flooded by refugees from Christian Europe, leading to the erasure of local customs and communal authority structures. Another cause was disruptive state policies. In the late fifteenth century, the Iberian Peninsula and the extra-Iberian territories of the Aragonese Crown had housed the largest Jewish communities in the world; most ended up in the Ottoman Empire, and this led to the eventual domination of Iberian Jewish (Sefaradi) communities over local Jewish communities.[53] At the same time, as the Ottomans conquered more territory, especially after the conquest of Constantinople in 1453, they applied a policy of forced population transfer (*sürgün*) to the conquered territories, a policy that applied increasingly to Jewish communities once exiles began arriving from Iberia and elsewhere.[54] Forced resettlement created new Jewish communities, destroyed old ones, and placed Jews of different geographic origins and customs side by side in the same towns and cities. These microcommunities competed in adjudicating legal conflicts and collecting (and redirecting) communal funds. In practice, individual community members often fell under the direct jurisdiction of the Ottoman state.[55] Thus, whereas communal solidarity developed apace among the Jewish communities of the Polish-Lithuanian Commonwealth, those of the Ottoman Empire became more divided. The consensus is now that Ottoman Jewish communities outside Istanbul had no centralized or supracommunal institutions before the Ottoman Empire's establishment of the post of *hahambaşı* (chief rabbi) in 1835.[56]

If the Jews of the Polish-Lithuanian Commonwealth and the Ottoman Empire occupied opposite ends of the spectrum of early modern communal organization, those of the Dutch Republic were at its midpoint. Starting in the 1590s, the Netherlands became a major new center of Jewish life. Unlike the Republic of Venice after 1516 and the Papal States after 1555, the Dutch Republic never restricted Jews to residence in ghettos; instead, they lived in mixed neighborhoods.[57] Membership in the Jewish communities of the Dutch Republic was voluntary, just as membership in the Calvinist Church was. The communities were heterogeneous: In Amsterdam, there was a cosmopolitan Sefaradi community that was well networked with Jews in Hamburg, the Ottoman Empire, the Caribbean, New York, and London (Jews had been readmitted to England in 1656), as well as with crypto-Jews living in Spanish territories. The Ashkenazi community of Amsterdam, established in 1639, split into two when Polish Jewish refugees from the Khmelnytsky pogroms of 1648 established a community of their own (they rejoined the main Ashkenazi community in 1673).[58] Moreover, there were forces of decentralization at work in the political structures of the Dutch Republic, a complex warren of local political arrangements. So even though Dutch law defined Jews as a nation (*natie*)—allowing them a pyramidal structure with leaders at its apex who negotiated with the state about taxes, public order, and security—in practice, the Jewish communities' main partners in negotiation were municipal councils, and this fact tended to preclude supracommunal organization.[59]

At the same time, there were strong forces encouraging solidarity among the Jews of the Dutch Republic. They not only adopted the "nation" nomenclature, referring to themselves as a *naçao* in Portuguese and *nación* in Spanish; the "nation" also managed internal matters such as education and care for the poor. As Yosef Kaplan has persuasively argued, it also rigorously policed its members' religious observance and moral behavior through public reprimands, threats, and humiliation.[60] The Jewish community was in effect an oligarchy, run with disciplinary zeal by "a social elite with great power, which sought to govern the Jewish communities in a centralized and often autocratic manner."[61] Most members of the community were immigrants or New Christians returning to Judaism, and they tended to prefer "the Jewish communal framework to a hard life of isolation in a foreign country."[62]

The Dutch Republic's Jews were, then, less centralized than Poland's but developed communal governance structures that were more robust than those in the Ottoman Empire. Interestingly, when in the late nineteenth century Dutch politics bifurcated into royalists and republicans, the Jewish oligarchy supported the House of Orange, judging traditional structures of sovereign patronage the best means of sustaining their authority over the community.[63] Sovereign patronage proved, however, to be a double-edged sword: As Jews' late medieval experience had abundantly demonstrated, grants of communal autonomy could be revoked. Those bearing the brunt of communal discipline might have had good reason to prefer living in a republic.[64]

One essential factor in the structure of communal governance, then, was state politics itself. More important than the degree to which a polity granted Jews residency for theological reasons, or allowed them to pay for the privilege with their taxes, was how centralized the state was and whether it governed Jews collectively or as individuals.

The rights and privileges of Jews as communities versus Jews as individuals was a question that began increasingly to concern nation-states as well—and as it did, it also concerned historians of the Jewish community. It is to their scholarship that this chapter now turns.

The Jewish Community in Historiography

With the disruption and demise of traditional forms of Jewish communal organization, historians began to write about it from across the watershed. A historiographic consensus held the medieval Jewish community to be the great shaper and organizer of Jewish life, both collective and individual. Likewise, scholars almost universally understood medieval and early modern states to have treated their Jewish subjects at least in part as collective groups defined by their Jewishness. One reason for this was an assumption about what made the medieval era distinct from the modern: privileges granted to collectivities and corporations, as opposed to rights held by individuals.

Thus, on the threshold of modernity, the corporate structure of European society appeared to the supporters of republican revolution as the main obstacle impeding both individual liberty and broader kinds of solidarity, such as that of all Frenchmen. In late December 1789, a delegate to the National Assembly of France, the Comte Stanislas de Clermont-Tonnerre (1747–92), stated before the Assembly, "We must refuse everything to the Jews as a nation and accord everything to Jews as individuals," on the reasoning that "the presumed status of every man resident in a country is to be a citizen."[65] According to this logic, one could not be both a citizen of a nation-state and a member of an organized Jewish community—a putative impossibility that denied Jews a right they had actually possessed in medieval communes. The modern democratic nation-state thus deprived Jews of some long-established rights and required Jewish collectivities to make compromises. On the heels of the French Revolution, the Jewish community of Alsace-Lorraine saw these impositions clearly and rejected the offer of citizenship, not wishing to dismantle their communal organizations. The Sephardi Jews of Bordeaux, by contrast, long accustomed to operating in a cosmopolitan mode, embraced it. But eventually even the Jews of Alsace succumbed to the arguments of Clermont-Tonnerre.

Matters unfolded differently in the German Confederation, where Jews achieved full citizenship only with the unification of 1870. The long wait for rights, which came piecemeal and unevenly, made Central European Jews all the more eager to relegate "medieval" treatment to the past. One of them was a Prussian by the name of Heinrich Graetz (1817–91), among the earliest historians of the Jewish community. Graetz's magnum opus, an eleven-volume comprehensive history of the Jews published in 1853–70, recounted Jewish history as, on the one hand, a triumph of rabbinic scholarship and rationalist thought and, on the other, an unremitting series of oppressive measures imposed on Jews by their non-Jewish overlords, especially Christian rulers north of the Alps. Much twentieth-century scholarship emphasized the centrality of the medieval Jewish community and its autonomous organization as a reaction against Graetz and his belief that modern citizenship would be better for Jews than premodern communal autonomy.

There was some intellectual context to this. Debates over rights, collectivities, and community extended well beyond Jewish historians. The influential writings of *fin de siècle* legal theorists and sociologists set in motion broader currents to which historians reacted. In 1868, the legal historian Otto Gierke (1841–1921) pioneered the study of community as a middle ground between democratic and hieratic rule and between the individual and public law.[66] The sociologist Ferdinand Tönnies (1855–1936), in his *Gemeinschaft und Gesellschaft*, published in 1887 (with six subsequent editions up to 1935), divided societies into those based on *Gemeinschaft* (community)—face-to-face relations, tradition, and religion—and those based on *Gesellschaft* (society, in both the general and organizational senses)—mediated impersonal relations, cosmopolitan worldviews, and organizational complexity. Premodernity was characterized by *Gemeinschaft* and modernity by *Gesellschaft*. Some of the work of the Alsatian Jewish sociologist Émile Durkheim (1858–1917) was a response to Tönnies, exploring the nature of solidarity in each type of society. But the most important modification of Tönnies came from Max Weber (1864–1920), a sociologist, economist, and legal historian (and a thinker of exceptional insight and complexity) who in his magnum opus, *Wirtschaft und Gesellschaft* (published posthumously in 1921–22), broke open Tönnies's schema by reformulating *Gemeinschaft* and *Gesellschaft* not as historical phases, one superseding the other, but as qualities (or "types") intermixed in every society to varying degrees. It was only natural that historians in the late nineteenth and early twentieth centuries examining Jewish sources suffused by invocations of *qahal* and *qehilla* would see the nature of community, communal life, social organization, and legal autonomy as central questions. Community had become a subject with a distinguished theoretical pedigree.

Diasporic Social History: Simon Dubnow and Salo Baron

Although historians after Graetz to some extent partook of the same theoretical background as he, their approaches to medieval Jewish communities were remarkably different. The next opus magnum of Jewish history after Graetz came from a Russian Jew, Simon Dubnow (1860–1941), whose comprehensive, ten-volume history of the Jewish people (first published in German translation in 1925–29, followed closely by the Russian original and a Hebrew translation) emerged organically out of the background of Eastern European Jewish communitarianism. Whereas Graetz came from a bourgeois world riven by the dilemmas of emancipation and assimilation, Dubnow grew up in the Pale of Settlement, in the shtetl of Mscislaŭ (now in Belarus): He came of age under the May Laws of 1882 and the subsequent years during which the czarist state restricted Jewish settlement, migration, land tenure, real-estate ownership, enrollment in educational institutions, and eventually also their practice of the professions, dwelling in cities, participation in local elections, and holding local office. Under such circumstances, Jewish collective life was, in fact, largely autonomous, if highly restricted. Against Graetz, Dubnow stressed that Jews "have not only 'thought and suffered,'" rejecting Graetz's twin focus on Jewish intellectual activity and victimhood; they have, he argued, "in all possible circumstances proceeded to build their life as a separate social unit." For Dubnow, the autonomous Jewish community was a fact of daily life.

In his political activism, it was also a point of ideology: Dubnow believed that Jews should live in self-governing communities and be accorded autonomy as a national minority. He rejected calls for a Jewish state in Palestine along with other secularist-socialist Jews of the period because of his belief that territorial Zionism was an opiate of the Jewish masses. But he was nonetheless inclined to see Jewish history as revolving around the autonomous Jewish community— and to see that community as having a continuous history, a matter not just of self-defense in a hostile environment but also of archival record. The Jewish community was, Dubnow argued, a permanent feature of Jewish history that was, in turn, "a vivid expression of nationalism, not merely of a religious group among other nations." Dubnow took for granted that Jews were a nation, regardless of whether they possessed a state. "This continuously living nation has always and everywhere defended the autonomous existence not only of its social life but also of all the areas of its culture."[67]

Against this background, it is easier to understand what drove Salo Wittmayer Baron (1895–1989) to write monumental works that sidestepped ideological nationalism—republican and Jewish alike.[68] Baron was an Austro-Hungarian Jew who between 1917 and 1923 completed three doctorates—in philosophy, political science, and law—and a rabbinical degree; then, in 1927, he emigrated to the United States, where he spent the rest of his life. Graetz's work, and to a lesser extent Dubnow's, had motivated Baron to write a comprehensive Jewish history. Yet he had serious reservations about Graetz's treatment of Jews as the passive victims of their own history and about Dubnow's treatment of their history in isolation from everyone else's. Both Graetz and Dubnow tended toward "internalist" explanations in Jewish history, which for Baron were analytically flawed because they cherrypicked among causal factors. Baron's predecessors had seen, for instance, the medieval European legal restrictions against Jews as motivated by anti-Jewish animus, but Baron instead considered how the medieval church and European states alike competed for jurisdiction over the subjects they ruled: it was precisely that competition that led them not only to curtail Jewish rights but also occasionally to expand them.[69] From an inner-Jewish point of view, curtailment was bad, expansion good; from Baron's point of view, they were both effects of larger causes.

Baron's *Jewish Community*, like Dubnow's *World History of the Jewish People*, was a study of Jewish self-governance. But whereas Dubnow's throughline was the Jewish "nation," Baron's was the synagogue. The difference was emblematic of Baron's ambivalence toward Jewish nationalism not on principle but as the sole basis for Jewish solidarity. In the book's first chapter, Baron describes late nineteenth-century Jewish nationalism as a movement to turn the traditional religious community (*Religionsgenossenschaft*) into "an all-embracing *Volksgemeinde* [national or ethnic community]."[70] In other words, Zionism—both the political and cultural varieties—was not an organic outgrowth of Jewish religious belonging but an attempt to eradicate it and replace it with secular-nationalist solidarity. Baron cites Tönnies in the footnote to this sentence, but the ideas owe as much to Weber's attempts to explain the basis of social solidarity.

Indeed, Baron shared an interest in organizations with Weber and other exponents of classical German sociology. He described the premodern Jewish community as possessing the character of a "state within the state" or else as having "partly replaced the missing state"—thus turning the derogatory characterization of the Jewish community by various polemicists, from revolutionary France to the late Russian Empire, into a value-neutral description.[71] The Jewish community was, Baron argued, oligarchical, but it was also effective—not as an "inner expression of the soul of the Jewish nation," as Dubnow had romantically had it, but as an organization.

To explain the organizational persistence of the Jewish community, Baron pointed to both Jewish law and state law. This was typical of his equal attention not only to the internal and external dynamics of Jewish history but also to legal history. Instead of Graetz's eternal conflict between the interests of the state and those of the Jewish community, Baron emphasized that their aims were sometimes aligned, at least in premodern contexts in which membership in the Jewish community was obligatory. Under modern conditions of the separation of church and state, membership in synagogues was voluntary—which was why it was sometimes anemic by comparison with premodernity. But given that there was no turning back the tide of modernity, and modern conditions allowed for a Jewish community based only on voluntary membership, the modern Jewish community was very much alive and well; it just functioned through the synagogue.

Baron thus emphasized the trade-offs that modernity had required of Jews. One implication was his pervasive cautioning against a misplaced faith in nation-states—Jewish or otherwise. His criticism of Jewish nationalism emerged not from antinationalism per se but from a more comprehensively critical stance toward modernity. Thus, whereas earlier assessments had implicitly accepted the dissolution of the organized Jewish community as an inevitable consequence of full legal equality, for Baron, it was merely the latest challenge forcing the Jewish community to evolve new organizational strategies: "Recognition of the Jewish community by public law" since the American and French Revolutions, he wrote, had "played an enormous role in the diversification of the new communal types."[72] Where the quid pro quo that had dissolved the Jewish community in exchange for citizen's rights had appeared to nineteenth-century Jews like Graetz as part of the enlightenment-era march of progress, Baron focused instead on what had been lost—and how it was then rebuilt.

Baron's focus on the Jewish community did not, then, emerge from nostalgia for the premodern past or from a romantic idealization of the medieval period. His most famous line, published at the end of a 1928 essay in a popular Jewish magazine, was a call "to break with the lachrymose theory of *pre-revolutionary woe*" (my emphasis).[73] Some subsequent historians interpreted this line as a caution against all lachrymose conceptions of Jewish history. But Baron objected at least as strongly to Jews' decidedly non-lachrymose embrace of the modern democratic nation-state, because—like any other form of political organization—the democratic nation-state was not an unalloyed good. The revolutions gave individual Jews equal rights but denied Jewish communities authority over their members in education, law, taxation, and social services.

Baer: Community and Commune

Baron's contemporary Yitzhak (Fritz) Baer (1888–1980) took a nearly opposite approach to the premodern Jewish community from Baron's. Baer was born and educated in Prussia six decades after Graetz and two decades after Jews in Germany had achieved legal equality. On the one hand, Baer shared Baron's focus on the history of the Jewish community and his skepticism about the supposedly unalloyed good of political emancipation. On the other, instead of striving for social integration in Germany, Baer emigrated to Palestine after serving as a soldier of the German Reich in the Great War.

Baer's Jewish nationalism deeply conditioned his view of premodern Jewish history. Like Baron, Baer saw the Jewish community as a statelet taking responsibility not just for prayer, ritual, and charity but also for political and economic matters. Baer described Jewish communal autonomy as robust but refused to understand it as deriving from alliances with the state. On the contrary, in a still much-cited article published in Hebrew in 1950, he argued that the Jewish community was not only autonomous but also virtually impermeable to outside interference. He attributed its autonomy to a quasi-mystical force: the spontaneously democratic character of its social organization. It was not Jewish communal organization that created Jewish communal solidarity for Baer but the other way round: The Jewish community was the institutionalized manifestation of a primordial national solidarity. The *qehilla,* Baer held, was the most enduring expression of Jewish authenticity because it was a form of "participatory government strengthened by its resistance to outside forces."[74]

Baer further argued that the Jewish *qehilla* had existed in its authentic, uncorrupted form in only two contexts: ancient Palestine and medieval Ashkenaz.[75] Jews had developed democratic institutions before the Romans had, he argued, and only in Ashkenaz had the Jewish community preserved the seeds of democratic organization and carried them into the new millennium. "After the disintegration of the national structure in the Land of Israel" in the first century CE, Baer wrote, "the local *qehilla* remained—until the period of the Jewish enlightenment in the eighteenth century—the only political expression of the invisible national community of Israel."[76]

The link Baer drew between Jewish solidarity and spontaneous democracy closely mirrored how he saw the Christian communes of medieval Europe. But his strictly internalist analysis did not allow him to see Jewish political organization as partaking of the legal structure of the communes. Quite the contrary: He argued that the *qehilla* took from the European environment "only those elements which help[ed] it realize its immanent goals and consciously define them."[77] Thus Baer read medieval Ashkenazi legal responsa as reflecting an autonomous community performing "certain functions found only later in the Christian city."[78] This forced him to launch a strained argument against the medieval historian Henri Pirenne, who had identified these urban institutions as the cause of Europe's commercial growth beginning in the late tenth century. Baer argued, in response, that Pirenne's evidence in fact derived from twelfth-century sources and that the earliest evidence of communes in Europe was the Jewish *qehilla*.

Baer also claimed that the self-sufficient and autonomous communities found in Ashkenaz scarcely existed in the Islamic world. He painted the *ge'onim* and exilarchs of Iraq as ruling hieratically, eroding the self-reliant, democratic character of the Jewish community and stifling its creativity. The only exception he allowed was the Jewish community of the Land of Israel, which he argued had preserved and renewed the democratic form of the *qehilla*. The passage is strikingly devoid of argumentation: "*One must recognize* that the *natural* venue for creating and renewing autonomous communal organization was the Land of Israel with its long-established communities" (my emphases). Despite the availability of evidence to the contrary, Baer asserted, "It is difficult to find any material reference to an autonomous communal administration in the Geniza documents of the geonic period" (for Baer, from 640 to 1040 CE). He acknowledged that Fusṭāṭ was a "community of merchants" with "a special tradition of commercial law" that was "reminiscent of contemporary European cities"; yet, it paled in comparison with "the Christian city and the Jewish *qehilla* in Europe"— for Baer, Fusṭāṭ was an urban island in a sea of Islamicate autocracy. The idea that the cities of medieval Christian Europe were more complex and better developed economically than those of the medieval Islamic world was far-fetched even in 1950. Admittedly, the economic history of the medieval Islamicate world was a field that began to flourish only after 1960. But even the first monograph on Jewish self-government in medieval Europe, published by Louis Finkelstein in 1924, had recognized the vast differences between the cosmopolitan and technologically sophisticated Jewish communities of the Islamicate world and those of the largely agrarian world north of the Alps, where "even so great a potentate as Charlemagne had been unable to write his name."[79]

Reading Baer on the *qehilla* is like stepping through a historiosophic looking glass: The Red Queen is nationalism, and she is very, very large; the Red King is romanticism, and he's telling you that what you know about Jewish history is a figment of his imagination. Much has been written about Baer's internalist reading of Jewish history, his Neoplatonic (or Hegelian) belief in a mystical force driving Jews toward their "national destiny," and about his pitting the pure mystics and martyrs of medieval Ashkenaz against the corrupt, assimilating rationalist philosophers of medieval Christian Iberia.[80] But if Baer's gnostic-nationalist reading of Jewish communal history is well understood, its roots in German fin-de-siècle thought have received less attention. It was Elka Klein who first realized that the star witness in the case for Baer as a German fin-de-siècle thinker is Otto Gierke, the legal historian who argued that the legal traditions of the Roman Empire, on the one hand, and of the German lands, on the other, were diametrically opposed. Guenther Roth has described Gierke as drawing an "invidious contrast between 'cold-blooded' Roman law and 'communal' Germanic law"; between Roman "authoritarian" associations (*Herrschaftsverbände*) and Germanic "egalitarian" cooperatives or mutual benefit societies (*Genossenschaften*); between Roman law's supposedly "rigid, cold-hearted, and egoistic individualism" and Germanic law's "embodiment of a warm-hearted spirit of folk community."[81] The dichotomy that Gierke applied to Germanic and Roman law was what Baer applied to the Jewish communities of the medieval world: Palestine and Ashkenaz were home to warm-hearted, authentic folk communities, whereas Christian Iberia and the Islamic world had inherited the rigidity and authoritarianism of Rome. The terrible irony—or tragedy—of Baer's worldview is that he clung to it even long after National Socialist jurists had declared the superiority of "German" over "Roman" law, denouncing the latter as "in some unspecified way a product of the Jewish mind."[82] Yet surprisingly, the debate over which historical Jewish communities had developed "democratic" or "hieratic" governance persisted for many decades after Baer, albeit without addressing the origins of those dichotomies, let alone the nefarious purposes to which they had been deployed.[83]

Goitein and Katz: The Social History of Jewish Communities

An important riposte to Baer came from Shelomo Dov Goitein (1900–85), who around 1947 had begun deciphering, translating, and interpreting thousands of geniza documents, most of them from the Fatimid and Ayyubid periods (969–1250). The scale of his geniza research was staggering, and three generations later, an entire field is still building on it, sifting through it and refining its conclusions. Goitein was born in Bavaria, emigrated to Palestine in 1923, conducted ethnographic fieldwork among Jews in and from Yemen in the 1930s and 1940s, then shifted his focus to the geniza, and moved permanently to the United States in 1957. Goitein's origins in anthropology conditioned his approach to what he found in the geniza, but so did his deep immersion in Jewish history and deep erudition in semitic philology.

The second volume of Goitein's five-volume synthesis, *A Mediterranean Society*, is devoted to the Jewish communities of Fusṭāṭ and elsewhere; their various overlapping offices of leadership; and their legal, educational, and charity systems. The documents he identified offered the finest-grained picture to date of how premodern Jewish communities actually operated. Echoing Baron, Goitein dubbed the Jewish community a "state not only within a Muslim state, but also beyond its confines."[84] And refuting Baer, Goitein denied that the Jewish communities of the Islamic world were governed hieratically from afar. The independent Jewish communities that he studied operated, he argued, outside the direct control of either the Palestinian and Iraqi *ge 'onim* or the *negidim*. But in extending Baer's vision of an autonomous Jewish community to the one sphere from which Baer had claimed it was missing—the Islamic world— Goitein implicitly accepted Baer's model of organic, democratic communities. After all, Goitein argued, there was no theoretical or legal basis for such Jewish communities in Jewish or Islamic law, neither of which recognizes "public bodies as legal personalities," as Roman law does. The implication was that if "the *qahal* or *jamā 'a,* as the Jewish local community was called in Hebrew and Arabic, respectively, does appear as such in [geniza] documents," it must have been a spontaneous development.[85] This sounds remarkably like Baer. Jewish communal organization in the Islamicate world may have had a different etiology from that of medieval Ashkenaz, but for Goitein, it was no less corporative, autonomous, or democratic.

In a lengthy review essay, Haim Hillel Ben-Sasson took Goitein to task for his use of the term "democratic," criticizing it as anachronistic and substantively unwarranted.[86] He was equally critical of Goitein's depiction of the Fatimid Mediterranean as economically laissez-faire. But in retrospect, Baer was one reason Goitein wrote about the Jewish community within an internalist frame of reference, even though the geniza offers ample reason to question it.[87] Goitein was absolutely correct to see the headship of the Jews and the ga'onate as organic offices of Jewish communal leadership, not the impositions of the caliphs. But the internalist approach caused him to overlook evidence of how integral state officials were to the authority of Jewish communal leaders.[88]

Then again, most historians of the Jewish community took an internalist approach before the end of the twentieth century, with the notable exception of Baron. Paradoxically, this was true even of most social historians, despite their avowed commitment to writing history from the ground up. No brief survey of them would be complete without Jacob Katz (1904–88), who was born in the Austro-Hungarian village of Magyargencs and emigrated to Palestine in 1936. Katz's focus was the Jewish communities of Central and Eastern Europe, seen through the lens of a midcentury iteration of sociology that valued abstraction over contingent detail and groups over individuals. Although his work focused on how European Jews experienced the ruptures of modernity, what we would now call "early modernity" held an explanatory key in his work, and he was one of the first historians of Jewish communities to drill into the period between 1600 and 1800 as a discrete and significant one.[89] Katz's work on the social history of Jewish law (halakha) was unparalleled, including its drive to limit Jews' contact with non-Jews.[90] At the same time, that very focus on halakha led him to overestimate the legal monopoly that Jewish communities exercised over their members and their separation from non-Jews in practice.[91] Katz held the halakha to be the great shaper of collective and individual Jewish life in Central and Eastern Europe, and the rupture Jews faced with the encroachments of absolutist governments and modern nation-states to be profound.[92] (Compare Baron on the flexibility and innovations of modern Jewish communities.) It is an open question whether Katz could have written similarly of Jewish communities in other parts of the world: Jews' experiences in Italy, southwestern France, the Netherlands, and the Ottoman Empire were markedly different from what he described. Historians of the Jews of Central and Eastern Europe have also subjected his work to extensive revision.[93]

Breaking the Paradigm of Communal Autonomy

Up until the end of the twentieth century, the history of medieval and early modern Jews continued to be written with reference to an autonomous community or communities. From one perspective, this was understandable: the recurrence of an organized Jewish community over long stretches of time and space helped render Jewish history coherent and comprehensible. Yet, as Jewish history expanded as an academic field, historians no longer seemed to be talking about the same community, and their deepening immersion in the histories of the broader societies they studied inevitably brought increasing dissent from the old internalist models. Today Jewish historiography has shifted decisively away from the explicitly and implicitly inward-looking studies of the twentieth century. The field has not only survived this challenge but also thrived because of it. The objects of study in some cases remain Jewish communities and their organizational structures, but without the assumed *cordon sanitaire* between Jews and the rest of society.

The type of sources that survived from medieval Latin Europe may have made the consensus about communal autonomy endure longer in studies of Ashkenaz than in studies based on everyday writings from the Cairo Geniza. But by the turn of the millennium, scholarship on Jews in Christian Europe had begun to view even the intimately Jewish realms of piety and ritual as inseparable from Christian practices.[94] One of the first theoretical statements to this effect came from Ivan Marcus in his study of Jewish life-cycle rituals in medieval Ashkenaz, in which he found striking parallels with those of Christians. For Marcus, not only were Jewish practices statements of deeply held Jewish beliefs; they were also legible to the societies in which Jews lived and were often polemics against them.[95] Elisheva Baumgarten has made the case for replacing Marcus's model of "inward acculturation" with "appropriation" to shift the emphasis to "a flexible repertoire of practices and discourses rather than a fixed and stable set of beliefs, values, and institutions."[96]

Even more remarkable is how precipitously the consensus on the autonomy of medieval Jewish communities in Christian Iberia has come undone. Baer cast a long shadow, having made his career on a two-volume study of the Jews in medieval Spain in which he argued in especially strong terms for an autonomous Jewish community with exceptional powers of enforcement.[97] In a 2005 article calling on scholarship to set aside its overriding concern with dynamics of tolerance and persecution, Jonathan Ray pointed out that studies focused on *groups*—their contacts, their status, and the extent to which they borrowed from each other—may be valuable for intellectual and cultural history but were flawed for social history.[98] But the most extensive call for the banishment of the concept of Jewish communal autonomy came from Elka Klein's study of the Jewish community of twelfth- and thirteenth-century Barcelona. Klein argued on behalf of "the porousness of what once seemed an insurmountable barrier" between the Jewish community and royal power, because the Jewish community cannot be understood if it "is seen as an isolated and sui generis institution, accepting outside interference only against its will."[99] Rather, communal power was a function of royal power. Previous studies had acknowledged that royal involvement played some role in communal autonomy; Baron had "recognized variations in [the] degree" of Jewish communal autonomy depending on how acutely the rulers needed Jewish taxes, while for Baer, taxation bought Jews rights as a community in "struggle with the government." But both had nonetheless taken autonomy "to be the natural state of Jewish communities."[100] So long as historians held rulers to be guilty of fiscal rapaciousness or unremitting oppression, Jewish communities would appear to be the sole dynamic element in the equation.

Klein's model also allowed for a more nuanced reading of rabbinic sources. Where rabbinic responsa and communal ordinances condemned Jews for turning to non-Jewish courts of law, Baer had understood the recourse to Christian or Muslim legal institutions as a betrayal of communal solidarity. In contrast, Klein noted that "a startling number" of these responsa "end with the conclusion that the case in question was ... [a] legitimate use of the courts."[101] She concluded that medieval rabbinic scholars were "far less hesitant" than modern ones "to recognize the utility" of royal courts for individuals seeking justice and for communities seeking to bolster their own autonomy.[102] Even one of Baer's key sources, the Jewish jurist Shelomo Ibn Adret, justified having participated in "a complicated and bitter royal prosecution" by noting the procedural advantages of royal over Jewish courts: "The laws of the kingdom only deal with knowledge of the truth. If we did not rely on them, but only on biblical provisions relative to the Sanhedrin, the world would be destroyed."[103] Instead, Klein argued that communal autonomy should be studied from multiple perspectives, weighing the interests of the counts and the kings, as well as those of Jewish leaders.

Klein argued, furthermore, for a distinction between "autonomy by default," a result of "lordly impotence or indifference," and "autonomy by design," in which lords actively granted the community its powers.[104] The maximal version of Jewish communal autonomy—which Baer had falsely generalized—was often the result of autonomy by design and was virtually impossible to achieve without the state's granting of powers. What Baer had seen as autonomy was, in other words, an effect of drawing the analytical frame around the Jewish community without considering the wider arena of politics and power. In that wider frame, Jewish communal rights might seem to be nothing but royal support for a minority oligarchy.

This was also the view of Uriel Simonsohn, who arrived at it via a different path: examining Jewish sources from the eastern Islamic world and comparing them with Christian responsa in Syriac.[105] Between the seventh and twelfth centuries, Simonsohn argued, condemnations of those seeking justice outside Jewish or Christian institutions typically came from the very same communal leaders—such as ge'onim, patriarchs, and bishops—who then turned around and violated their own principles by appealing to institutions outside the community to shore up their own power. When community members went outside the system of communal justice, they posed a threat to the power of communal leaders, who condemned them for it; when communal leaders did so, the result was strengthened power over the community. Conversely, for the anonymous *dhimmī* masses, communal autonomy could be a serious impediment to their interests rather than a protective envelope.

One of the implications of Simonsohn's work was the need to study those very anonymous community members—and not just the ones who happened to be male elites. Studying women's legal strategies in medieval Egypt led Oded Zinger to the conclusion that women faced disproportionate challenges in defending their rights in rabbinical courts without the backing of a male protector such as a father, husband, uncle, or brother, let alone when they went up against their spouses or male kin; without their backing, they were more likely to threaten to turn to state-run tribunals.[106] My own work argued in parallel that Fatimid and Ayyubid state tribunals were, in principle, delighted to handle cases from the powerless and that the rulers and the architects of their policy saw protecting the powerless as part of their *raison d'être,* both out of considerations of political legitimacy and because they genuinely believed that protecting the powerless was an ethical imperative.[107]

Taking Jewish communal autonomy and the authority of Jewish leaders for granted, then, has concealed as much as it revealed about the inner workings of the Jewish community itself. Premodern Jewish history was not a zero-sum game between the community and the state but could be better understood in terms of interests that often aligned across religious boundaries. The more scholarship considered sources from beyond the male and/or rabbinic elites, the more communal autonomy has come to seem as but one small domain of the medieval and early modern Jewish experience.

Should one tentatively conclude from this turn away from collectivities that the individual is the new, most important unit in premodern Jewish society? No. Freed from the old assumptions, one can also ask what attracted Jewish litigants not just to non-Jewish courts but also to Jewish ones. Eve Krakowski has argued that Jewish courts were "convenient, low-risk forums for dispute resolution,"[108] and Jews turned to them not just because of hard legal and economic power but because of a form of soft capital that was particularly valuable in premodern societies: legal expertise. This accounts for the simultaneous development of multiple systems of religious law in the Islamic world—Rabbanite, Qaraite, Melkite, West Syrian, East Syrian, Zoroastrian, Sunnī, Imāmī, and Ismāʿīlī alike (not an exhaustive list).[109] Doing away with the old model of communal autonomy need not, then, entail doing away with the study of groups. It should, rather, drive us to study more of them.

My profound thanks to Yaacob Dweck for reading a draft of this chapter and suggesting numerous improvements. I take full responsibility for the omissions and errors that remain.

Recommended Readings

Baron, Salo W. "Ghetto and Emancipation: Shall We Revise the Traditional View?" *Menorah Journal* 14 (1928): 515–26.

Baron, Salo W. *The Jewish Community: Its History and Structure to the American Revolution,* 3 vols. (Jewish Publication Society of America, 1942).

Cohen, Mark R. *Jewish Self-Government in Medieval Egypt: The Origins of the Office of the Head of the Jews, ca. 1065–1126* (Princeton University Press, 1981).

Frenkel, Miriam. *"The Compassionate and Benevolent": Jewish Ruling Elites in the Medieval Islamicate World: Alexandria as a Case Study* (De Gruyter, 2020).

Goitein, S. D. *A Mediterranean Society: The Jewish Communities of the Arab World as Portrayed in the Documents of the Cairo Geniza,* 6 vols. (University of California Press, 1967–93).

Hacker, Joseph R. "The Rise of Ottoman Jewry," in *The Cambridge History of Judaism: Volume VII, The Early Modern World, 1500–1815,* ed. J. Karp and A. Sutcliffe (Cambridge University Press, 2018), 77–112.

Kaplan, Yosef. "Discipline, Dissent, and Communal Authority in the Western Sephardic Diaspora," in *The Cambridge History of Judaism: Volume VII, The Early Modern World, 1500–1815,* ed. J. Karp and A. Sutcliffe (Cambridge University Press, 2018), 378–406.

Klein, Elka. *Jews, Christian Society, and Royal Power in Medieval Barcelona* (University of Michigan Press, 2006).

Maciejko, Paweł. *The Mixed Multitude: Jacob Frank and the Frankist Movement, 1755–1816* (University of Pennsylvania Press, 2011).

Rosman, Moshe. "'The Authority of the Council of Four Lands outside Poland-Lithuania," in *Social and Cultural Boundaries in Pre-Modern Poland, Polin: Studies in Polish Jewry* 22 (2007): 201–27.

Ruderman, David B. *Early Modern Jewry: A New Cultural History* (Princeton University Press, 2010).

Rustow, Marina. "The Genizah and Jewish Communal History," in *"From a Sacred Source": Genizah Studies in Honour of Professor Stefan C. Reif*, ed. B. Outhwaite and S. Bhayro (Brill, 2011), 289–317.

Rustow, Marina. *Heresy and the Politics of Community: The Jews of the Fatimid Caliphate* (Cornell University Press, 2008).

Woolf, Jeffrey R., *The Fabric of Religious Life in Medieval Ashkenaz (1000–1300): Creating Sacred Communities* (Brill, 2015).

Zinger, Oded. *Living with the Law: Gender and Community among the Jews of Medieval Egypt* (University of Pennsylvania Press, 2023)

Notes

1. There are other Hebrew terms, including *'edah* and *ṣibbur*, that this chapter does not cover in the interests of space.

2. Benedict Anderson, *Imagined Communities: Reflections on the Origin and Spread of Nationalism* (rev. and expanded edition, Verso, 2006).

3. For Geniza fragments, see the Princeton Geniza Project database online. On the Jewish community of Alexandria, see Miriam Frenkel, "The Compassionate and Benevolent": Jewish Ruling Elites in the Medieval Islamicate World: Alexandria as a Case Study (De Gruyter, 2020). The communities cited here appear in Bodl. MS heb. d 68/101; ENA 2804.11; T-S 13J27.1; T-S 13J9.17; T-S 13J26.16; ENA NS 18.2; Bodl. MS heb. d 77/12; ENA 1822a.52; T-S 13J19.6; T-S 13J16.8; T-S NS 323.31 + T-S 12.532; T-S 8J31.2; T-S 8J31.2; T-S 24.6; T-S NS 308.122; T-S 24.6; Bodl. MS heb. d 79/36; T-S 20.149; PER H94; T-S 13J19.15; T-S 13J18.24; ENA 4020.48; T-S 32.10; ENA 4010.47; T-S 16.121; T-S 8J41.4.

4. T-S 16.251.

5. JRL Series B 4351.

6. T-S 10J28.18.

7. T-S 8J23.11. The *nagid* in question is Yosef Khalīfa, one of the last *negidim* of Egypt before the Ottomans abolished the office.

8. Jeffrey R. Woolf, *The Fabric of Religious Life in Medieval Ashkenaz (1000–1300): Creating Sacred Communities* (Brill, 2015), 29–30.

9. T-S 13J3.26, line 6.

10. T-S 13J23.4.

11. ENA 4020.23.

12. T-S 13J23.4.

13. T-S 16.347.

14. Elia Levita, *Sefer ha-Tishbi* (1541), s.v. *qahal*. Thanks to Yaacob Dweck for suggesting this source.

15. T-S 20.122.

112   CHAPTER 4

16. T-S 10J9.14.

17. F 1908.44EE + F 1908.44FF.

18. T-S 13J11.4.

19. The Arabic word *ṭā 'ifa* is usually translated as "party" or "sect," but in medieval documentary sources it is used for the Jewish community as a whole and for segments of it (such as the Rabbanites and Qaraites), often without implying any invidious distinctions or conflicts among the segments. See Marina Rustow, *Heresy and the Politics of Community: The Jews of the Fatimid Caliphate* (Cornell University Press, 2008), xxviii, n. 18.

20. T-S 13J7.29.

21. T-S Ar.38.93. This document also uses a nearly Hobbesian homology in comparing the Jewish community to a body and its leader to a head: "You are a guide for the community as is the head for the body: If one is healthy, so is the other; if one is corrupt, so is the other."

22. T-S Ar.41.105 and T-S AS 182.291.

23. CUL Or.1081 1.2.

24. T-S K25.214.

25. PER H161. S. D. Goitein and Mordechai Akiva Friedman, *India Traders of the Middle Ages: Documents from the Cairo Geniza ('India Book')* (Brill, 2008) 533 translate *aṣḥāb* as "coreligionists," but the plain sense of the word is companions or colleagues, and it appears frequently in business letters in the sense of "fellow traders" rather than necessarily "fellow Jews." See Roxani Eleni Margariti, "Aṣḥābunā al-tujjār—Our Associates, the Merchants: Non-Jewish Business Partners of the Cairo Geniza's India Traders," in *Jews, Christians and Muslims in Medieval and Early Modern Times: A Festschrift in Honor of Mark R. Cohen*, ed. A. Franklin et al. (Brill, 2014), 40–58.

26. This is one of the main arguments of Menahem Ben-Sasson, *The Emergence of the Local Jewish Community in the Muslim World: Qayrawan, 800–1057* [Hebrew] (Magnes Press, 1997).

27. Robert Brody, *The Geonim of Babylonia and the Shaping of Medieval Jewish Culture* (Yale University Press, 1998), 41, 60–61, 73–74.

28. Cf. Rustow, *Heresy*, 3.

29. Syria (*al-shām*) was the Arabic term for the entire eastern Mediterranean littoral between the Red Sea and Anatolia, and in Judeo-Arabic, Jews used this term interchangeably with the Hebrew term "the Land of Israel" (*ereṣ yisra'el*). Modern scholarship has therefore translated *kanīsat al-shāmiyyīn* as the Palestinian-rite synagogue to highlight this group's relationship to the yeshiva of the Land of Israel and, by extension, the Palestinian Talmud, but the Syrian-rite synagogue would be an equally valid translation.

30. Judith Olszowy-Schlanger, "La lettre du divorce caraïte et sa place dans les relations entre caraïtes et rabbanites au moyen age: Une étude de manuscrits de la Geniza du Caire," *Revue des études juives* 155 (1996): 337–62, and "Karaite Ketubbot from the Cairo Geniza and the Origins of the Karaite Legal Formulae Tradition" [Hebrew] *Te'uda* 15 (1999): 127–44; Mordechai Akiva Friedman, "On the Relationship of the Karaite and the Palestinian Rabbanite Marriage Contracts from the Geniza" [Hebrew] *Te'uda* 15 (1999): 145–57; Olszowy-Schlanger, *Karaite Marriage Documents from the Cairo Geniza: Legal Tradition and Community Life in*

Mediaeval Egypt and Palestine (Brill, 1998), and "Karaite Legal Documents," in *Karaite Judaism: A Guide to Its History and Literary Sources*, ed. M. Polliack (Brill, 2003), 255–74; Rustow, *Heresy*, chap. 10.

31. Mark R. Cohen, *Jewish Self-Government in Medieval Egypt: The Origins of the Office of the Head of the Jews, ca. 1065–1126* (Princeton University Press, 1981). In addition to the community's leadership, another area ripe for further exploration is its finances, for which the starting points should be Moshe Gil, *Documents of the Jewish Pious Foundations from the Cairo Geniza* (Brill, 1976) and Mark R. Cohen, *Poverty and Charity in the Jewish Community of Medieval Egypt* (Princeton University Press, 2006).

32. T-S Ar.18(2).4.

33. T-S 13J21.30.

34. T-S AS 146.3 + DK 242 (alt: XXI).

35. T-S 10J5.6 + T-S 20.113. See most recently Brendan G. Goldman, *The Camps of the Uncircumcised: The Cairo Geniza and the Jews of the Latin Kingdom of Jerusalem, 1098–1291* (University of Pennsylvania Press, forthcoming).

36. There are dozens of appearances for *al-ger* (and a few for *ha-ger*) in the corpus of charity lists published in Mark R. Cohen, *The Voice of the Poor in the Middle Ages: An Anthology of Documents from the Cairo Geniza* (Princeton University Press, 2005).

37. Severus b. al-Muqaffaʿ, *Kitāb siyar al-abāʾ al-baṭārika* (History of the Patriarchs of the Egyptian Church), Bibliothèque Nationale de France, MS arabe 302, f. 171r, cited in Tamer el-Leithy, "Coptic Culture and Conversion in Medieval Cairo, 1293–1524 A.D." (PhD diss., Princeton University, 2005), 45.

38. Cohen, *Voice of the Poor*, and *Poverty and Charity*.

39. Eve Krakowski and Marina Rustow, "Formula as Content: Medieval Jewish Institutions, the Cairo Geniza, and the New Diplomatics," *Jewish Social Studies* 20 (2014), 111–46.

40. Eve Krakowski, *Coming of Age in Medieval Egypt: Female Adolescence, Jewish Law, and Ordinary Culture* (Princeton University Press, 2018); see the later discussion.

41. Rustow, *The Lost Archive: Traces of a Caliphate in a Cairo Synagogue* (Princeton University Press, 2020), chap. 9; and below, n. 110.

42. Alfred Haverkamp, *Jews in the Medieval German Kingdom*, trans. Christoph Cluse (Trier University Library, 2015), https://ubt.opus.hbz-nrw.de/opus45-ubtr/frontdoor/deliver /index/docId/671/file/Jews_German_Kingdom.pdf (accessed December 10, 2024), 37.

43. Elia Capsali, *Taqqanot Qandiya u-zikhronoteha (Statuta Iudaeorum Candiae eorumque Memorabilia)*, ed. E. Artom and U. Cassuto (Mekize Nirdamim, 1943); Rena N. Lauer, *Colonial Justice and the Jews of Venetian Crete* (University of Pennsylvania Press, 2019), 28–29; and the literature cited there at 213, n. 22.

44. Ivan G. Marcus, *Rituals of Childhood: Jewish Acculturation in Medieval Europe* (Yale University Press, 1998) and "A Jewish–Christian Symbiosis: The Culture of Early Ashkenaz," in *The Cultures of the Jews: A New History*, ed. David Biale (Schocken, 2002).

45. B. Chevalier, *Les Bonnes Villes de France du XIVe au XVIe siècle* (Aubier Montaigne, 1982), 76–83.

46. Paweł Maciejko, *The Mixed Multitude: Jacob Frank and the Frankist Movement, 1755–1816* (University of Pennsylvania Press, 2011).

47. This was also true outside Eastern Europe, where Jewish recordkeeping was modeled after non-Jewish notarial practice, as in Rome and Metz. Elisheva Carlebach, "The Early Modern Jewish Community and Its Institutions," in *The Cambridge History of Judaism: Volume VII, The Early Modern World, 1500–1815*, ed. J. Karp and A. Sutcliffe (Cambridge University Press, 2018), 168–98 (178, and the references there).

48. Adam Teller, "The East European Pinkas Kahal: Form and Function," *Polin: Studies in Polish Jewry* 34 (2022), 87–98 (88).

49. Moshe Rosman, "The Authority of the Council of Four Lands outside Poland-Lithuania," in *Social and Cultural Boundaries in Pre-Modern Poland, Polin: Studies in Polish Jewry* 22 (2007): 83–108.

50. Gershon David Hundert, *Jews in Poland-Lithuania in the Eighteenth Century: A Genealogy of Modernity* (University of California Press, 2004).

51. Carlebach, "Early Modern Jewish Community," 194.

52. Carlebach, "Early Modern Jewish Community," 194. See especially Baron, "Ghetto and Emancipation: Shall We Revise the Traditional View?" *Menorah Journal* 14 (1928): 515–26.

53. Joseph R. Hacker, "The Rise of Ottoman Jewry," in *Cambridge History of Judaism, Volume VII, The Early Modern World, 1500–1815*, ed. J. Karp and A. Sutcliffe (Cambridge University Press, 2018), 77–112 (79–81).

54. Hacker, "Rise of Ottoman Jewry," 81–83.

55. Hacker, "Rise of Ottoman Jewry," 86–88.

56. Joseph Hacker, "The 'Chief Rabbinate' in the Ottoman Empire in the 15th and 16th Century" [Hebrew] *Zion* 49 (1984): 225–63, and "Rise of Ottoman Jewry," 95; Yaron Ayalon, "Rethinking Rabbinical Leadership in Ottoman Jewish Communities," *Jewish Quarterly Review* 107 (2017): 323–53.

57. Bart T. Wallet and Irene E. Zwiep, "Locals: Jews in the Early Modern Dutch Republic," in *Cambridge History of Judaism, Volume VII, The Early Modern World, 1500–1815*, ed. J. Karp and A. Sutcliffe (Cambridge University Press, 2018), 894–922.

58. Wallet and Zwiep, "Locals," 901.

59. Wallet and Zwiep, "Locals," 916.

60. Yosef Kaplan, "Discipline, Dissent, and Communal Authority in the Western Sephardic Diaspora," in *Cambridge History of Judaism, Volume VII, The Early Modern World, 1500–1815*, ed. J. Karp and A. Sutcliffe (Cambridge University Press, 2018), 378–406 (401).

61. Kaplan, "Discipline, Dissent, and Communal Authority," 379.

62. Kaplan, "Discipline, Dissent, and Communal Authority," 404.

63. Wallet and Zwiep, "Locals," 916.

64. On the preference for sovereign patronage, see Yosef Hayim Yerushalmi, *The Lisbon Massacre of 1506 and the Royal Image in the "Shebet Yehudah"* (Hebrew Union College Annual Supplements, 1976), and "Servants of Kings and Not Servants of Servants: Some Aspects of the Political History of the Jews," in *The Faith of Fallen Jews: Yosef Hayim Yerushalmi and the Writing of Jewish History,* ed. D. N. Myers and A. Kaye (Brandeis University Press, 2014), 245–76; Marina Rustow, "La notion d'Alliance royale et Yerushalmi pour maître," in S. A. Goldberg, *L'histoire et la mémoire de l'histoire. Hommage à Yosef Hayim Yerushalmi*, ed. S. A. Goldberg (Albin Michel, 2012), 57–69; Lois C. Dubin, "Yosef Hayim Yerushalmi, the Royal Alliance, and Jewish Political Theory," *Jewish History* 28 (2014): 51–81.

THE JEWISH COMMUNITY   115

65. On the long history of quoting this passage in Jewish historiography, see David Sorkin, "The Count Stanislas de Clermont-Tonnerre's 'To the Jews as a Nation . . .': The Career of a Quotation," *Jacob Katz Memorial Lecture* 2012 (Leo Baeck Institute, 2012).

66. Elka Klein, *Jews, Christian Society, and Royal Power in Medieval Barcelona* (University of Michigan Press, 2006), 18–19; Gierke, *Das Deutsche Genossenschaftsrecht*, 4 vols. (Weidmann, 1868), and *Community in Historical Perspective*, ed. A. Black (Cambridge University Press, 1990).

67. Dubnow, *History of the Jews: From the Beginning to Early Christianity*, Eng. trans. from Russian, 4th rev. ed., 5 vols. (New York, 1967), 1:26.

68. Salo W. Baron, *A Social and Religious History of the Jews* (published in 3 volumes in 1937; expanded into 18 volumes, published 1957–80), and *The Jewish Community: Its History and Structure to the American Revolution*, 3 vols. (Jewish Publication Society of America, 1942). See also his "An Historical Critique of the Jewish Community," *Jewish Education* 8, no. 1 (September 1935): 2–8.

69. Salo W. Baron, "'Plenitude of Apostolic Powers' and Medieval 'Jewish Serfdom,'" in *Yitzhak F. Baer Jubilee Volume* [Hebrew] (Jerusalem, 1960), 102–24; repr. in *Ancient and Medieval Jewish History: Essays*, ed. L. A. Feldman (Rutgers University Press, 1972), 284–307; "Medieval Nationalism and Jewish Serfdom," *Studies and Essays in Honor of Abraham A. Neuman* (Philadelphia, 1962), 17–48, repr. in Baron, *Ancient and Medieval Jewish History*, 308–22.

70. Baron, *Jewish Community*, 1:7.

71. "With the disappearance of corporative organization from western society, little room was left for the old, segregated Jewish corporate body. Leaders of the emancipatory movement, Jewish and non-Jewish, long agreed that the establishment of a general equality of rights and the incorporation of Jewish citizens into the national majorities was to be accompanied by the destruction of the former Jewish 'state within the state.'" Baron, *Jewish Community*, 1:8, and cf. 2:358; *Social and Religious History* (1937), 1:12; *Social and Religious History*, 2nd ed., 18 vols. (Columbia University Press, 1962–83), 2:87–88. See also Hannah Arendt, *The Origins of Totalitarianism* (Meridian Books, 1958), 33–34.

72. Baron, *Jewish Community*, 1:21.

73. Baron, "Ghetto and Emancipation," 526.

74. Yitzhak Baer, "The Origins of the Organisation of the Jewish Community in the Middle Ages" [Hebrew] *Zion* 15 (1950): 1–41; Engl. in Yitzhak Baer, "The Origins of Jewish Communal Organization in the Middle Ages," in *Binah: Studies in Jewish History*, vol. I, ed. J. Dan (Bloomsbury, 1988), 59–82 (quotation on 67).

75. Baer, "Origins."

76. Baer, "Origins" [Eng.], 60.

77. Baer, "Origins" [Eng.], 74.

78. Baer, "Origins" [Eng.], 74.

79. Finkelstein, *Jewish Self-Government in the Middle Ages* (Jewish Theological Seminary of America, 1924), 3. Views of Charlemagne's literacy and the broader meanings of literate practices in the Carolingian era have evolved since Finkelstein wrote those lines.

80. See notably Isaiah Sonne, "On Baer and His Philosophy of Jewish History," *Jewish Social Studies* 9 (1947), 61–80; this article is a review of Baer's *History of the Jews in Christian Spain*.

81. Guenther Roth in Max Weber, *Economy and Society: An Outline of Interpretive Sociology*, ed. G. Roth and C. Wittich (University of California Press, 1978), 60 n. 24; 752 n. 177.

82. Roth in Weber, *Economy and Society*, 752 n. 177.

83. For a related and analogous dichotomy and its ideological weight in the historiography of medieval communes and city-states, see Chris Wickham, *Sleepwalking into a New World: The Emergence of Italian City Communes in the Twelfth Century* (Princeton University Press, 2015), chap. 1, and Patrick Lantschner, "City States in the Later Medieval Mediterranean World," *Past & Present* 254 (2022): 3–49.

84. Goitein, *A Mediterranean Society: The Jewish Communities of the Arab World as Portrayed in the Documents of the Cairo Geniza*, 6 vols. (University of California Press, 1967–93), 2:403.

85. Goitein, *Mediterranean Society*, 2:42.

86. Haim Hillel Ben-Sasson, "New Paths into the 'Genizah Land': Review Essay of S. D. Goitein's *A Mediterranean Society*, Vols. I–II" [Hebrew] *Zion* 41 (1976): 1–46.

87. Goitein does not discuss Baer explicitly. See Mark R. Cohen, "Jewish Communal Organization in Medieval Egypt: Research, Results and Prospects," in *Judaeo-Arabic Studies: Proceedings of the Founding Conference of the Society for Judaeo-Arabic Studies*, ed. N. Golb (Harwood Academic Publishers, 1997), 73–86.

88. For some of that evidence, see Rustow, *Lost Archive*, chap. 9; "At the Limits of Communal Autonomy: Jewish Bids for Intervention from the Mamluk State," *Mamlūk Studies Review* 9 (2009): 133–60; "The Genizah and Jewish Communal History," in *"From a Sacred Source": Genizah Studies in Honour of Professor Stefan C. Reif*, ed. B. Outhwaite and S. Bhayro (Brill, 2011), 302–8; and "The Legal Status of dimmī-s in the Fatimid East: A View from the Palace in Cairo," in *The Legal Status of dimmī-s in the Islamic West (Second/Eighth–Ninth/ Fifteenth Centuries)*, ed. M. Fierro and J. Tolan (Brepols, 2013), 307–32.

89. Bernard Dov Cooperman, "Afterword: Tradition and Crisis and the Study of Early Modern Jewish History," in *Tradition and Crisis: Jewish Society at the End of the Middle Ages*, ed. Jacob Katz and trans. B. D. Cooperman (Syracuse University Press, 2000; orig. Hebrew ed. 1958), 238, and cf. Karp and Sutcliffe, "Introduction," in *Cambridge History of Judaism, Volume VII, The Early Modern World, 1500–1815*, ed. J. Karp and A. Sutcliffe (Cambridge University Press, 2018), 2.

90. Katz, *Tradition and Crisis*, and *Exclusiveness and Tolerance: Studies in Jewish-Gentile Relations in Medieval and Modern Times* (Behrman House, 1961).

91. See, for example, the opening of Katz's chapter "The Form and Structure of the Kehila," in *Tradition and Crisis*, 65: "The fact that Jews were segregated from the rest of society—both by state law and of their own volition—meant that the majority of their individual and group needs had to be provided from within their own community. The Jews were forced to create institutions with the ability and authority to carry out the various necessary social functions. The most common and most basic of these institutions was the *kehila* (plural: *kehilot*; communal organization), which united within itself and bound together all of the permanent residents of a given locale.... The formation of a *kehila* was a social act intended to articulate the religious and cultural ties that linked individual Jews to one another. Organization was, in the first place, imposed on the Jews by their common and parallel needs. But the *kehila* that they created was based upon Talmudic law and implied explicit or implicit acceptance of the valid-

ity of that law. In this sense, the *kehila* derived from the attachment of its members to the shared Jewish tradition."

92. See, e.g., *Tradition and Crisis*, 216, where he attributes to the *qehilla* "functions such as the collection of promissory notes and the liquidation of bankruptcy holdings" and highlights the crisis Jews faced when state bureaucracies took over those functions. For a different view of the extent of Jewish engagement in non-Jewish legal forums, see Tamar Menashe, "The Imperial Supreme Court and Jews in Cross-Confessional Legal Cultures in Germany, 1495–1690" (PhD diss., Columbia University, 2022).

93. See, notably, Adam Teller, "Tradition and Crisis? Eighteenth-Century Critiques of the Polish-Lithuanian Rabbinate," *Jewish Social Studies* 17 (2011), 1–39; Hundert, *Jews in Poland-Lithuania*, chap. 5.

94. See, e.g., Haym Soloveitchik, *Jews and the Wine Trade in Medieval Europe: Principles and Pressures* (Liverpool University Press, 2024; original edition in Hebrew, Am Oved, 2003).

95. See Marcus, *Rituals of Childhood*.

96. Elisheva Baumgarten, "Appropriation and Differentiation: Jewish Identity in Medieval Ashkenaz," *AJS Review* 42 (2018): 39–63, *Mothers and Children: Jewish Family Life in Medieval Europe* (Princeton University Press, 2004), and *Practicing Piety in Medieval Ashkenaz: Men, Women and Everyday Religious Observance* (University of Pennsylvania Press, 2014).

97. Yitzhak Baer, *A History of the Jews in Christian Spain*, 2 vols., trans. Louis Schoffman (Jewish Publication Society of America, 1959–61; repr., 1992), originally published in Hebrew in 1945.

98. Jonathan Ray, "Beyond Tolerance and Persecution: Reassessing Our Approach to Medieval Convivencia," *Jewish Social Studies* 11 (2005): 1–18. Cf. Elisheva Baumgarten, "Introduction: Money Matters: Individuals, Communities and Everyday Economic Interactions between Jews and Christians in Medieval Europe," *Medieval Encounters* 27 (2021), 293–307: "Scholarship to date has tended to approach" Jewish economic history "from a communal perspective, discussing the activities of Jews as an organized group rather than as individuals, and emphasizing collective norms, legislation, ideologies, and policies. In such studies, the status of Jews as a tolerated religious minority was the point of departure and religious difference was paramount. While these perspectives were undoubtedly a defining feature of medieval Jewish life, a top-down communal perspective is just one facet, albeit an important one, of the economic activities of medieval Jews. In addition, most studies focused on moments of change, tension, and crisis, rather than on the ongoing roles of Jews both within their communities and in interaction with their Christian neighbors" (293).

99. Klein, *Jews, Christian Society, and Royal Power*, 2.

100. Klein, *Jews, Christian Society, and Royal Power*, 21.

101. Klein, *Jews, Christian Society, and Royal Power*, 153–54.

102. Klein, *Jews, Christian Society, and Royal Power*, 154.

103. Klein, *Jews, Christian Society, and Royal Power*, 154.

104. Klein, *Jews, Christian Society, and Royal Power*, 24–25; see also 45–50.

105. Uriel I. Simonsohn, "Communal Boundaries Reconsidered: Jews and Christians Appealing to Muslim Authorities in the Medieval Near East," *Jewish Studies Quarterly* 14 (2007):

328–63, and *A Common Justice: The Legal Allegiances of Christians and Jews under Early Islam* (University of Pennsylvania Press, 2011).

106. Oded Zinger, *Living with the Law: Gender and Community among the Jews of Medieval Egypt* (University of Pennsylvania Press, 2023), esp. 133–39.

107. Rustow, *Lost Archive,* chap. 8.

108. Krakowski, *Coming of Age,* 80; cf. Goldberg, *Trade and Institutions,* 162–63; 355–57.

109. Krakowski, *Coming of Age,* chap. 2, esp. 81–93.

5

Everyday Judaism

Elisheva Baumgarten,
Hebrew University of Jerusalem

JEWS HAVE LIVED in Europe for millennia, with evidence of Jewish communities in southern Europe dating to as early as the end of the Second Temple period (1 CE). In the centuries that followed, particularly after 800 CE, Jews moved northward, westward, and eastward, becoming a constant presence across the continent throughout the medieval period. Jewish communities were founded and expanded and then, in many places, expelled or annihilated during the fourteenth and fifteenth centuries, the end of the medieval period. These medieval Jews are best known for the significant centers of Jewish life and learning they established, their writings that survived and still play a central role in Jewish and western culture, and their history of integration and subsequent alienation and expulsion.

Beginnings

A Hundred Years of Historiography
(Mid-Nineteenth to Mid-Twentieth Century)

Since its inception in the nineteenth century, the field of Jewish Studies, and particularly the study of the history of European Jewry, has been subject to shifting areas of emphasis. In what follows, I present a review of some of these trends, focusing on how scholars have approached the topic of "everyday Judaism." By everyday Judaism, I mean their interest in the daily lives of most of the Jews in those communities—those who were not erudite and often left no written record. Central to this review of past and current scholarship is the way the importance of the everyday was assessed in various historical accounts, as well as the changing understandings of what the "everyday" consisted of and how this has been analyzed in conjunction not only with Jewish practice and records but also in relation to the lives of the Christian population among whom medieval Jews in Europe lived.

Throughout this chapter, I outline some of the questions that have guided scholarship to date and point to possible future directions. Although I focus on the ways scholars have studied the Jews of medieval Ashkenaz, my concluding remarks reference, albeit briefly, other medieval diasporas as well, underlining their differences, similarities, and future challenges.

A History of the Jews?

For nineteenth-century Jewish Studies scholars, everyday life was far removed from their definitions of history. Occupied with justifying how Jews had a national history without a land or a country for so many centuries, they dismissed the everyday practices of the Jewish communities as having little import. National definitions and identity were burning matters during this period, and the scholars of Jewish Studies, like all scholars in all periods, were deeply rooted in the ideological and political debates of their time. Heinrich Graetz (1817–91), in his opus magnus, the *History of the Jews,* expressed his basic understanding of medieval Jewish history, primarily in Ashkenazic lands, with the following description:

> The Jews of Europe had no history, in the proper sense of the word, until a conjunction of fortunate circumstances enabled them to develop their powers, and to produce certain works whereby they wrested the pre-eminence from their brethren in the East. Until then there are only chronicles of martyrdom at the hands of the victorious Church, monotonously repeated with but little variation in all countries. "Dispersed and scattered throughout the world," says a celebrated author of this period, "the Jews, though subject to the Roman yoke, nevertheless live in accordance with their own laws." The only point of interest is the manner in which the Jews settled in the European states, and lived unmolested, in friendly intercourse with their neighbors, until Christianity gradually encompassed them, and deprived them of the very breath of life. (3: 35–38)

In the volume Graetz produced about the Middle Ages, the focus was on spiritual writings pertaining to halakhah and philosophy produced by the great medieval thinkers: Rashi, R. Tam, the Tosafists, and others in Ashkenaz; in Iberia, figures such as Nachmanides and Even Ezra; and in North Africa, the *ge'onim* and Maimonides. Graetz's perception of the relationship between these aspects of Jewish thought and the lives of everyday Jews was almost entirely limited to the relationship between the political powers and the Jews subjected to them—more specifically, to crises or to moments that led to crises over time. The highlights of Jewish existence were those that took place within the Jewish community, namely the learned contributions of the great scholars to Jewish culture, both of their time and of the generations that followed, and Christianity was the implacable enemy that eventually suffocated Jewish life. On the whole, Graetz's account tells of the spiritually powerful, of those who left their mark in writings that survived. Underlying this approach was the assumption that what was written in the different treatises, commentaries, and tractates was, in fact, adhered to and that these were not just guidelines but also a trustworthy account of practice.

Graetz's approach was typical of some but not all of his contemporaries. Other scholars writing around the same time or later in the century, after Jewish Studies had become more firmly entrenched, presented Jewish life in medieval Europe differently. Adolf Berliner (1833–1915), for example, writing a few decades later in Germany, wrote a short treatise that examined the everyday affairs of medieval Jews, virtually ignoring events such as the Crusades, attacks on the communities, or expulsions and showing far more interest in pastimes and leisure activities.[1] This was an outlier, however, because in his other work Berliner tended to follow Graetz in the importance he attributed to medieval Jewish scholarship. One of Berliner's goals in this short composition was clearly contemporary. In his sketch of medieval German life, he sought to demonstrate how Jews were a distinct and contained cultural entity while also being proud participants in local culture. One can read, between the lines of his book, pointed messages to his readers regarding both the importance of preserving a discrete way of life and his pride, as a German Jew, in the fact that his ancestors were part and parcel of the German past.

Writing at roughly the same time as Berliner were Moritz Güdemann (1835–1918), a Viennese rabbi and scholar, and Israel Abrahams (1858–1925), a British scholar. Güdemann wrote a three-volume book that was organized chronologically and thematically, with some chapters treating medieval Hebrew compositions, their authors, and contents and others focusing on everyday practices.[2] He was among the first to explicitly examine how medieval Jewish institutions and trends could and should be understood in relation to their non-Jewish milieu. He firmly believed that only by studying those who were not the leaders of the community, "the rank and file," could one understand some of the signature features of medieval Jewish life. His colleague, Israel Abrahams, who expressed his obligation to both Berliner and Güdemann, set out in his *Jewish Life in the Middle Ages*[3] to synthetically present everyday Jewish life; like Berliner, he ignored key events of the period, and like Güdemann, he claimed that medieval Jews were deeply enmeshed in medieval Christian institutions and beliefs, as manifested in the home, on the street, and in the synagogue. The cardinal uniqueness of Jewish distinctiveness was, in his eyes, the synagogue; yet, as he stated, "The Synagogue was the centre of life, but it was not the custodian of thought. If Judaism ever came to exercise a tyranny over the Jewish mind, it did so not in the Middle Ages at all, but in the middle of the sixteenth century" (xvii). In Abrahams's view, their community of religious practice is what set Jews apart, whereas culturally and intellectually, they were full participants in European life.

A combination of these approaches prevailed in late ninteteenth- and early twentieth-century Europe. They were further developed in the mid-twentieth century by Salo W. Baron (1895–1989), who rejected the "lachrymose narrative" of crisis for the Jewish Middle Ages and sought to write as broad a social and religious history of the Jews as he could.[4] However, all these studies, that of Baron included, were still not able to fully integrate the new schools of social thought pertaining to social history being developed in France during the interwar and pre–World War II period as part of the Annales School. Moreover, in keeping with their times, and except for some short comments or asides, their books focus almost entirely on men, rather than women and children, and the history of male everyday Judaism. This remained the case up to the end of the twentieth century.

During this same period, other scholars who had left Europe and emigrated to what was to become the State of Israel developed a new approach to Jewish history. For them, this history—especially the history of Jews in the diaspora and the way it was to be understood—was an issue of utmost importance. Steeped in the European methods and historical training of the time, they founded, first in Jerusalem and then elsewhere, what became known as the Jerusalem School of history, whose luminaries included Ben Zion Dinur (1884–1973), Yitzhak Baer (1888–1980), and Haim Hillel Ben Sasson (1914–77). The interests of the Jerusalem School, from the early years of the State of Israel into the 1970s, revolved around several key points that were aligned with their beliefs. The first was that Jews, in whatever locality and time period, had more in common with each other than with their neighbors. They thus stressed continuity, rather than change, and transmission from one place to another, rather than disruption, and sought to strengthen the pan-Jewish aspects of the historical past. Animosity toward Jews was an organizing element of the narrative, and any suggested affinity between Jews and their surroundings was easily refuted by employing the lachrymose narrative Baron opposed as the defining story of *galut* (exile).

The Holocaust reinforced this approach, underlining the vivacity and creativity of the Jews within their community alongside a trail of destruction and hatred on the part of Christian society. The events of the twentieth century were often "read back" into medieval Europe, with little distinction between times and ideologies, in the interest of defining the trajectory of antisemitism and the reason for the persisting hatred of Jews across the centuries.

A second key point had to do with communal organization. As the nascent Israeli society was developing, the ways Jewish societies had historically been organized came to be considered of utmost importance. According to the vision of the Jerusalemite historians, leaders most often had the last word, the community was unified, and Jews felt closest to their coreligionists and to the traditions of their fathers. These emphases led them all the way back to Graetz and to the cultural authorities throughout the generations, even though they were, of course, well aware of the scholarship that had been produced in the intervening years and were also in conversation with Baron and his students. Many studies produced during these years thus focused on communal mechanisms and leaders, and all posited shared norms and ideals among Jews, wherever they were, rather than local varieties.

It was not until the 1980s and 1990s that new approaches began to shake the field and change it yet again. Central in this transformation was the work of Jacob Katz (1904–98), who began writing in the 1960s but whose work became more and more central over time. Katz was focused on explaining the transition from the medieval era to the modern one; as a result, his work did little to sever the connection between all Jews and all periods that was characteristic of the work of the Jerusalem School, at least when discussing the periods of Jewish history preceding modernity. At the same time, in the context of the study of the medieval period, he daringly suggested that Jews were far more entangled in local Christian life than previously assumed.[5] Katz, who also had training in sociology, was one of the first scholars of his generation to focus on the everyday. Although he brought the idea of social history to the forefront of those studying medieval Jews, his students in Israel, with a few notable exceptions, remained focused on halakhic sources, and Katz himself relied on the history of halakhah as a standard for understanding daily life throughout his career. His most influential contribution remains the attention he drew to the daily interactions between Jews and Christians and to the extent to which the two communities were in constant contact with each other.

Methods and Periodization

Much as Jewish life in the Middle Ages was lived alongside Christian neighbors, so too developments in the way medieval Jews were studied were directly related to developments in the study of history at large. Graetz, Berliner, Güdemann, and Abrahams, as well as the Jerusalem School historians, were perplexed by questions related to nationalism; the first Zionist historians lived during a period when Marxism and that of the French Annales School were transforming the study of history. By the end of the twentieth century, social history had become a central tenet of all historical studies, and questions relating to childhood, gender, women's lives, and deviance became popular avenues of historical inquiry. Methods from the fields of sociology, already promoted by Jacob Katz, were enhanced by anthropological theory, narrative approaches, political science, and gender studies. Ritual was a key area of inquiry, leading scholars to question how rituals reflected Jewish familiarity with their Christian neighbors. These methods brought a new awareness to the many facets of everyday life as the site of routine, as well as of disruption. Language also served as an indicator of a divide, with scholars in Israel focusing on Hebrew sources and those outside the country focusing on sources in a variety of local vernaculars and Latin. Because members of the younger generation worldwide were not as proficient in languages as their teachers—Israelis and Americans did not know Latin and European languages as well as their teachers did, and Europeans did not know Hebrew as well as their teachers—language became a central factor in training and analysis.

In Israel, the creation of departments of Jewish history alongside of but independent from those of history, also changed the trajectory of their academic approach. For a time, Israeli historians were determined to create a distinct Jewish timeline for the Middle Ages, rather than relying on traditional divisions—early Middle Ages until roughly 1000, High Middle Ages until the late thirteenth century, and late Middle Ages until the invention of print and Reformation, etc. Some began the Middle Ages with the completion of the Babylonian Talmud or the rise of Islam (sixth or seventh century); others ended the

Jewish Middle Ages with the expulsion from Spain (1492) or even as late as the French Revolution. Over time, arguments relating to periodization have become less prevalent, whereas questions relating to current methods have become more pronounced, as detailed next.

Jews, Christians, and Everyday Life

The various methods applied to the study of Jews and the medieval sources that emerged from them elicited different answers regarding the nature of Jewish everyday life during the medieval period. No matter the methodology, however, one aspect that appears in all of them is halakhah. Since Late Antiquity and the onset of rabbinic Judaism, Jewish everyday life was conceptualized through the lens of halakhah: It thus consisted of a list of ongoing practices Jews observed from early in the morning until late at night. Because these actions were religious mandates, their study and that of the logic bolstering them were entrenched in Jewish texts, propelled by an internal logic. A major source of information on this topic was a huge body of literature known as responsa that was penned by medieval rabbinic scholars. Indeed, one of the key topics during the decades in which social history became more and more prominent as a field at large was the discussion of how and why the responsa literature was useful for the study of social history. One answer was its unintentional insight into details about everyday situations. Another was that the questions and responses reflected actual occurrences, thus revealing much about the practices and deviations from the norm of Jewish communities.

Although much valuable research emerged from this direction of inquiry, it had two main shortcomings. The first was that the nature of rabbinic responsa, which was aligned with halakhic requirements, positioned the discussion within a diachronic trajectory starting with the Bible, if there were biblical foundations for the matter at hand, and then surveying discussions of this matter from Late Antiquity until medieval times. Changes over time were sometimes explained by local circumstances, but the main thrust of the discussion was contained within the framework of Jewish life. Any "external influences" noted were usually quickly appropriated and "Judaized." The rabbinic logic and the effort it required overtook any other voices that could have been hiding within the source material. The vast extent of the rabbinic texts also served to sideline other sources found in archives, chronicles, and other documents that most often were neither produced by Jews nor written in Hebrew. The second shortcoming was the underlying assumption held by many of these scholars that the halakhic discussions were accurate reflections of reality and that halakhic language was embedded in the way medieval Jews thought about these everyday situations.

Was this, in fact, the case? Were all members of the Jewish communities of the Middle Ages dedicated observers of halakhah? What was the relationship between the community at large and the rabbis who penned the responsa or even between those who turned to them with questions? In some instances, it seemed as if the rabbis were playing "catch up," justifying local practices after they became widespread or fighting battles against practices they felt needed to be curbed. In other cases, they were changing ancient mandates in ways that at first glance prove difficult to understand. When historians made halakhic writings one of the mainstays of history, these issues gained great importance.

This focus on responsa and other halakhic texts also meant that scholars were attempting to learn about the daily lives of Jews by reading writings in Hebrew, at a time when these lives were in fact lived in entirely different languages, such as Middle High German, Old French, or other local vernaculars. Moreover, this emphasis left little room for considerations of external sources written in the vernacular or in Latin, penned not by theologians but by local leaders and bureaucracy, even though this corpus contained a wealth of information about Jewish daily life. It was not until the mid-1970s in Germany that scholars, such as Arye Maimon (1903–88), Alfred Haverkamp (1937–2021), and, later, those at the Arye Maimon Institute under Haverkamp's leadership, began to access these sources, housed in local archives but not considered since before the Holocaust. In France, Berhard Blumenkranz (1913–89) and Gerard Nahon (1931–2018) were doing similar work with regard to French Jews. These administrative, legal, and theological discussions in Latin and local languages allowed a better understanding of the legal status of Jews, a topic that complemented the Jerusalem School's interest in community structures. It also allowed more extensive study of the economic lives of Jews. This topic had been studied in the context of halakhic responsa concerning financial interactions between Jews, and between Jews and Christians, including, to some extent, Jewish ideology concerning such interactions. Although the legal and economic aspects of Jewish medieval life had been previously touched on, the increased interest in the archival material constituted a major breakthrough for social historians because it enabled a familiarity with and understanding of multiple individuals, rather than just communal leaders. It must be noted, however, that even these sources tended to focus predominantly on the privileged members of society.

Over the past thirty years or so, the types of sources medieval historians use have continued to expand and now include material culture, art, codicology, and archaeology, as well as narrative and literary texts that were not frequently consulted by earlier historians. Furthermore, rather than studying these various sources in isolation, from the turn of the twenty-first century there has been increasing interest in combining them—a trend aligning with the methods and studies in the field of medieval history at large.

Alongside the expansion of the sources used to study the lives of medieval Jews, a central factor in recent historiography is the shift in ideologies underlying conceptions of Jewish relations with their Christian rulers, neighbors, and environment. Medieval history was punctuated by Christian persecution of and attacks on the Jews, as well as persistent Jewish–Christian religious tensions and animosity. Thus, the chronology of Jewish life in Europe can be told as a progression from attacks on the Rhineland communities during the First Crusade; to host and blood libel accusations from the mid-twelfth century onward; to public debates concerning the Talmud and Jewish faith in the thirteenth century; and to expulsion from England, repeated expulsions from France, and then from all over Europe following well-poisoning accusations in the mid-fourteenth century. As described, many scholars made these events and waves of violence the strongholds of their narratives.

Yet, even during times of crisis, patterns of interaction and reaction were not monolithic. Recent scholarship has emphasized the idea that understanding local dynamics is key for assessing the consequences of different occurrences. Why was the Jewish community from one town or region expelled, whereas another was not? How did local factors influence outcomes? Moreover, ideologies, beliefs, and courses of actions are the specific products of specific times and places, and Jews lived alongside their Christian neighbors in these same times and places.

This complexity was less discernible in more traditional historiography when reading theological and ideological sources, often written in the respective holy tongues, Hebrew for Jews or Latin for Christians, and expressed in stark theological terms. Even these bodies of literature, however, prompted questions about the interaction between Jews and Christians while still underlining ideological divides. Thus, both in nineteenth-century writings and in more recent scholarship, the Tosafist dialectic commentaries were compared to medieval scholasticism, and scholars of Christian biblical exegesis noted the Hebrew knowledge acquired by twelfth-century Hebraist scholars and the ideas they themselves adapted from their Jewish neighbors. Often, differences were accentuated, and a more general zeitgeist was called on to explain similarity; yet, such explanations have been increasingly called into question, with scholars seeking to explain parallels and shared ideas using a more detailed on-the-ground analysis.

Scholars have often noted the familiarity of Jews with Christian life and ideas and of Christians with their Jewish neighbors. Intellectual historians have also frequently remarked on the comparison that medieval learned men made when rebuking their students and congregants, comparing them to their Christian or Jewish counterparts. Whether discussing literacy, noise made in churches or synagogues, or the way members of the other religion treated their wives, there was no doubt that medieval Jews were well aware of what was happening among their Christian neighbors, beyond just what could be observed on the street, and that Christians were familiar with their Jewish neighbors and their customs as well. Yet much of this similarity and familiarity was subdued by political tensions, attacks on Jewish communities, and, above all, vitriolic rhetoric. Texts containing polemics and exhortative speech against the other religion abound.

The Jews of Europe and European Jews

It was only in the 1980s and 1990s as social history and the everyday became more central that scholars started intensively seeking the dialogue and connections between the texts on either side of the religious boundaries. From a position arguing that there were parallels but direct connections were hard to find, scholars began to anticipate the shared world of ideas and practices within which medieval Jews and Christians lived. This led to the understanding that medieval Jews felt at home in medieval Europe and displayed loyalty and pride in their local environs, even during decades when religious tensions and animosity were increasing. Interest in explaining the facets of medieval life shared by Jews and Christians also grew, and the question of how Jews were "influenced" and became aware of prevailing norms became pressing.

Over the past quarter-century, different ideas and terms have been used to explain how the Jews were embedded within their local Christian surroundings yet still retained their distinct identity. Each theory carries with it a different understanding of the degrees of separation between Jews and their neighbors.[6] "Inward acculturation" suggested by Ivan Marcus (b. 1941) was one way of expressing the integration of Christian ideas within Jewish culture, suggesting that Jews internalized and adapted ideas from their surroundings, often with a tendency to engage in polemics with the very idea they were adopting.[7] Israel Yuval (b. 1949) focused even more on the polemic that ensued when ideas and beliefs were shared.[8] More recently, terms such as "entanglement," "appropriation," and "adaptation" have been used to express the ways Jews adapted and adopted elements from Christian culture and made them an inherent part of Jewish practice, including explanations and prooftexts from the Bible, the Talmud, and other Jewish works that were often reinterpreted for this purpose.

In addition to many of the ideological issues that pertained to relationships between Jews and Christians, social history—and, with it, an interest in everyday life—became a central avenue of inquiry as binaries began to be challenged philosophically. Rather than either/or scenarios, scholars became interested in spectrums and in hybridity. This further enforced the decentering of what had previously been considered of import—namely, moments of crisis and change— rather than ongoing, repetitive everyday life. This was accompanied by a shift in the perception of the kind of historical actors considered worthy of scrutiny. Additional categories in play were gendered history, spatial studies, and material culture.

The reevaluation of binary categories led to fascinating reexaminations of medieval sources pertaining to Jews and their Christian neighbors. Daily repetitive practices fit well with the history of halakhah but less so with the stark definitions of medieval Jews as either insiders or not, as citizens or outcasts, or as believers or heretics. The prevailing narrative both among Jewish Studies scholars and those of medieval Christendom had contrasting foci, much as the medieval people themselves did, between church and synagogue. Contrasts were also drawn between public and private spaces, between home and street, between the laity and elite. Recent research has begun to question the extent to which the distance between these different binaries was in fact as great as was suggested. In what follows, I address some of these binaries, although by no means in an exhaustive manner, drawing out the continuum between extremities. The first, and most important, pair is that of synagogue and church.

Synagogue and Church

These public spaces served as the respective locus of worship for members of each religion and, in the medieval period, occupied a place of utmost importance—constituting a declaration of belief and of belonging socially, culturally, and administratively. Medieval Christian neighborhoods were organized around their local churches, as well as around their professions and political alliances. Each circle of belonging included a possible ecclesiastic affiliation. Larger Jewish communities also had more than one house of worship, but generally the Jews living within an urban center, or its periphery, all gathered around one synagogue. Both synagogue and church also included other functional spaces. Churches often had an adjacent cemetery, a treasury and crypt for relics, and a courtyard where marriage ceremonies and other rituals took place. Synagogues often included a ritual bath, along with a *tanzhaus* (dancehall) for weddings and sometimes a bakery as well.

Undoubtedly, the services in each of these spaces were geared toward members of the respective religion. Yet, sources that describe everyday life suggest that Jews entered churches and Christians entered synagogues daily. They did so not only for business reasons but also as neighbors and friends, as potential converts (especially to Christianity), as workers, and as missionaries. This meant that they were familiar with each other's symbols and artifacts, an issue that could also lead to misunderstandings, and with the functions of each building. They often followed the same trends; for example, Christians held all baptisms, except for emergency ones, in the church, and medieval Ashkenazic Jews moved all circumcision ceremonies to the synagogue. Similarly, when marriage became a sacrament in the twelfth century, Christian nuptials moved to the churchyard. So, too, were Jewish couples then wed in the synagogue courtyard.

At the same time, some ritual spaces were distinct and dissimilar. For example, as noted earlier, Christian dead were buried in the church; the Jewish dead, however, following ancient traditions, were buried outside city limits. The ritual in each space was in a distinct language and tradition, despite certain similarities. Despite these divergences, recent scholarship has begun to realize the extent to which ideas and beliefs were incorporated by members of the other religion, most prominently by Jews as members of a minority group. Scholars have suggested that it was this minority status that led Jews to take their example from the dominant majority.

Elites and Non-Elites: Social and Cultural Distinctions

Because most of the medieval sources were written by learned and powerful elites, much of the research has focused on men from these categories. For those studying medieval Christians, these were church authorities, leaders, and administrators. For those studying Jews, these were first and foremost the rabbis. Because medieval Jewish communities were quite small, it was easy to conflate the rabbinic and financial elite with the entire community. This led to the assumption, perhaps also partly due to self-perception, that Jews most closely resembled the urban bourgeoisie.

EVERYDAY JUDAISM   131

It is only in recent years that there has been a growing awareness of the Jewish poor, artisan class, and professional groups. Furthermore, from sources such as court records comes the understanding that Jews and Christians associated across multiple social boundaries and tended to cooperate along lines of gender, class, and profession. Silk makers lent and borrowed money from silk makers, and casketmakers did the same. The richer Jews associated with royal and governing powers, whereas the poorer ones did their business with itinerants. Questions of class allow a better understanding of those who belonged to the Jewish community, beyond the elite, and demonstrate the complexity of those who were part of different communities.

Jewish Space and Christian Space

Questions of class and local politics also have implications when investigating the spaces where Jews lived. Although scholars have always stressed the fact that medieval Jews did not reside in ghettos because they were an innovation of the early modern period, much research has emphasized the existence of a Jewish street or quarter (*rue de juifs* or *judengasse*). Evidence from France, Germany, and England demonstrates, however, that although the Jews lived close to each other and in proximity to the synagogue, they were far from being the only inhabitants of these streets or buildings, which they often shared with non-Jewish neighbors. Thus, understanding Jewish homes is a necessity. Evidence indicates that, rather than being total strangers to each other, Christians were frequently in Jewish homes and Jews were in Christian homes. They entered these spaces as part of everyday commerce, because many aspects of business were conducted within the house, often on its first floor. They also entered each other's homes as neighbors, as medical practitioners, and, in the case of Jewish homes, as servants and wet nurses working within the house.

Everyday relations forged allies and adversaries, sometimes aligned by gender and sometimes by profession, with class playing a role in these relationships. This is particularly evident in texts relating to the legal system. The picture arising from court records is that Jews and Christians often associated with each other based on their occupations and social status. This proves important when addressing moneylending, which has been seen as a major occupation for medieval Jews. Although many Jews offered loans to people with whom they were not familiar, many others—far more than was understood in earlier scholarship—in fact did business, including credit exchange, with Christian business partners or fellow craftspeople. Their Christian counterparts also lent to and borrowed from Jews, indicating that these activities were part of run-of-the-mill commerce rather than "usurious" by definition. That the church authorities or royal magistrates, seeking to profit both spiritually and fiscally, condemned these activities, does not mean that the ordinary exchanges of credit that were at the foundation of medieval economics did not persist.

This is an excellent example of how studying the quotidian casts new light on topics previously addressed from a theological or ideological point of view. When this latter view was the focus, the definition of usury seemed all-encompassing. When examining the quotidian, it seems exactly that—more ordinary. Extending credit was a regular feature of medieval life for members of all religions, and Christians, like Jews, engaged in this practice.

Courts are another example of spaces that had been characterized as separate for Jews and Christians. Indeed, responsa literature suggests that Jews took other Jews to court exclusively within the community. Yet, Jews and Christians litigated against each other in local Christian courts, as evident in court records that discuss loans and reveal the extent to which Jews were regulars in Christian courts. This leads to two important understandings of medieval Jewish life. First, despite the tensions with neighboring Christians and local authorities, and indeed the demand that Jews look out for each other in times of calamity, Jews had plenty of disagreements among themselves and with their neighbors that were dealt with routinely and were not a cause for panic or crisis.

Second, the examination of local court records reveals a Jewish presence in local courts not only when issues arose between Jews and Christians but also when Jews had disagreements with each other. This has led to a reassessment of the correct way to interpret ideological discussions found within halakhic writings that condemned any Jew who brought another Jew to be judged in a non-Jewish court. Jews' continued presence in Christian courts and their familiarity with the ways Christian courts were run have important implications for research on the conflicts between Jews documented in the responsa literature. It also accounts for the seepage of local ideas and values into the Hebrew sources, explaining new notions of justice and law in ways unconsidered in the past. This is an area that is just starting to be investigated and can offer an in-depth comparison between communities across Europe, as well as those of the Islamic world.

Above all, this everyday approach has dissipated many binaries concerning space and ritual while fostering the growing understanding that even if economic affairs and religious practice are separated in the extant sources, Jews and Christians in fact performed religious rituals and belonged to their respective communities while also doing business, exchanging recipes, and buying daily commodities with and from each other. Although one can heuristically separate these different modes of practice, they coexisted in medieval life, much as they do today. This understanding is particularly evident in my two final examples, that of material culture and gender studies.

The turn to material culture in recent years allows a new moment of reflection about everyday life. Most medieval objects have not survived. Those that have, like many of the textual sources, tend to represent the elite and the extraordinary. An unusual vessel, piece of cloth, or lavishly illuminated manuscript may reveal the techniques used to make them or the genesis of the materials they were made from, but they are far from mundane. These highly valued and expertly crafted objects were likely used by only the wealthiest members of society and often only for special occasions. Furthermore, given that religion was one of the most prominent features of medieval society, if not the most valuable, these objects often served religious purposes. To some extent then, material objects such as these unusual ones are indicative of the gulf between the lives of Jews and Christians. Jews had no objects similar to Christian reliquaries, for example, and where Christian objects were adorned with crosses and saints' images, the Jews perforce made use of other symbols.

Despite these distinctions, Jews and Christians frequented the same markets and did business with the same craftspeople. They had access to the same imports and exports and had the same materials available to them, even if they chose to use them differently. For example, Jewish scribes used the same parchment used by their Christian counterparts, as well as the same quills and ink. When a Jew wanted a manuscript to be decorated, he usually took it to a local atelier where Christian artists and Jewish scribes cooperated to produce the desired outcome, often using shared models adapted to Jewish needs. This is not to say that Jewish or Christian ideology and beliefs were not central in this encounter, but rather that they were entangled with each other on multiple levels.

To take a more mundane example, when Jews went to the market to buy vegetables, they would have encountered local produce coated in tallow, a common method of preservation. Tallow was, however, a non-kosher substance, so Jews would have bought the produce and then simply washed it off. Non-Jewish servants and wet nurses may have brought tallow into the Jewish home, using it to prepare food that Jews who cared about keeping kosher would have avoided, as well as other household needs. A cheap and widely available substance, tallow was also used in making candles. However, despite (or perhaps because of) its ubiquity, it was forbidden, already in Late Antiquity, to use tallow as a source for Shabbat candles. Material culture thus provides a prime example of the ways Jewish life was shaped by local markets and standards while also being guided by ancient practices and customs, handed down from generation to generation and reinterpreted over time.

Gender studies provides a different perspective. The ways that societal expectations and roles were distributed and practiced by medieval women and men has, for the past few decades, been an exciting avenue of research. Here one often discovers that, despite the differences between religions—for example, the option of celibacy available to Christian men and women versus the Jewish adherence to family life—gender attitudes were shared by both communities, and Jews often adopted whatever the current attitude toward women's activities was in Christian society, whether in religious issues or related to market roles. Thus, family economics were organized in similar ways, as were attitudes about women performing men's traditional roles.

Comparisons: Looking East, South, and Ahead

This chapter has focused on the social history of the Jews of medieval northern and central Europe. Many of the issues raised here are central avenues of inquiry for other medieval Jewish diasporas under Christianity; for example, the Jews of Provence, Iberia, Italy, Eastern Europe, or Byzantium or alternatively for Jews who lived under Islam, from Muslim Spain to Yemen. Each of these diasporas has its own history and its own historiography, yet many of the same questions and basic issues are evident in this scholarship, albeit with different approaches. Broadly stated, all scholars seek ways to present the distinctiveness of the Jews alongside their embeddedness in their local surroundings. The ways in which these studies and their conclusions are reached have much to do with surviving sources and with their overarching approach. For example, far fewer sources survive for Eastern Europe before the fourteenth century or for Byzantium.

In general, scholars have seen Jews as better integrated and accepted under Islam, where, like Christians, Jews had a distinct status as *dhimmi*. This was especially evident in Goitein's magnum opus on the Jews as a part of Mediterranean culture, and recent scholarship has underlined both the distinctiveness of Jews and their integration.[9] As a result of this approach, some of the pairs of terms presented earlier, particularly those related to space and religious observance, have been explored with different emphases.[10] Especially in the fields of economic and legal history, the Jews under Islam have been examined and presented as far more integrated into their local economies. Iberia has been explored as part of both Muslim and Christian culture, and for the Jews living under Christianity, the expulsion of 1492 has led to a narrative that often looks back, seeking affirmations for eventual historical events long before they took place.[11] The Jews of Provence and Italy during the High Middle Ages have also often been overlooked or assumed to be very similar to those in northern Europe or Spain, despite the unique circumstances in these geographies.[12] More research on the Jews of medieval Italy and Provence is required to address new questions that have yet to be integrated.

Studies of the early modern period have both followed the medieval contours and charted a path of their own.[13] In those places where Jews were not expelled in Western and Central Europe, Jewish daily life became markedly rural, because they were compelled and chose to live outside the urban centers. This has ramifications for both the surviving sources and the conduct of communal aspects of Jewish ritual. Religious developments among Christians—first and foremost, the Protestant Reformation—also influenced Jewish daily and religious life.[14] In contrast, communities that during the medieval period were smaller, such as those of Central and Eastern Europe, grew larger during the following centuries, and old practices and norms were adopted and changed over time.[15] As for Jews under Islam, with the rise of the Ottoman Empire that encompassed large areas of Jewish life under Islam, work on continuity and change is still an avenue for future research.

Future Directions

Although it is impossible to predict what trends will become prevalent in future research, let me point out three possible directions, which are not mutually exclusive and, in fact, can be pursued together in different ways.

1. One of the issues emphasized throughout this chapter is the importance of religious practice for the understanding of Jewish life. Yet, a comparison between the historiography of medieval European Jews— particularly but not limited to Ashkenazi Jews—and that of other diasporas, most notedly those under Islam, indicates that this is not the only narrative through which one can study their history. Those who study the texts from the Cairo Geniza, for example, often view the Jews of Egypt as part of a "Mediterranean society" rather than a distinct social and religious community. It seems the time is ripe for scholars of

medieval Ashkenaz to learn from those who study Jews in the Islamic world how to approach the Jews of Europe as just one more sector of European society while retaining their distinction as a religious minority. How was a Jewish merchant different from his Christian colleagues? It is also time for those studying the Jews of Islam to further probe the religious identities and their implications for Jews under Islam.

2. Being Jewish was a marked category in everyday Jewish life. Although recent research has indicated that sometimes Jews were part of other local groups, be they craft related or related to the locality itself, scholars have assumed that a Jew's first order of identification was his or her religion. Scholars of women have questioned whether this was true of women in the same way it was true of men. Whatever the answer to this query may be, this kind of identification, the assumption that a Jew was distinct and not comparable to non-Jews, has led scholars studying Christian Europe, when researching local events, to dismiss evidence about local Jews as irrelevant or atypical. Much as historians of medieval Jews have learned to integrate their historical subjects within the environments in which they lived (local politics, identities, and events), so too it is time for the Jews to be integrated in pan-European studies, especially but not only in the context of social history.

3. Scholars of everyday Jewish life have tended to focus on times of relative calm and the everyday interactions between Jews and between Jews and their neighbors. Everyday life continued during crises, even when it sometimes ended in violence and persecution. In contrast, scholars who have focused on theology and politics have often emphasized crises and moments of disaster. A new approach that integrates between the people undergoing the crises, the driving elite forces involved in them, and the ebbing and waning of tensions is now needed. If the first decades of the twenty-first century have taught us anything, it is that life goes on even in the midst of catastrophe and that everyday life continues to exist even while deep hatreds such as antisemitism persist, at times latent and at other times more active.

As this chapter is being written, some of these latent sentiments, subdued since the Holocaust, are once again rising to the surface. As the next decades unfold, the concerns of scholars and of the communities they belong to will certainly find their way into the histories that will be written about medieval Jews.

EVERYDAY JUDAISM 137

Recommended Readings

Abrahams, Israel. *Jewish Life in the Middle Ages* (Jewish Publication Society, repr. 1993).

Berger, David. "A Generation of Scholarship on Jewish-Christian Interaction in the Medieval World," *Tradition: A Journal of Orthodox Jewish Thought* 38, no. 2 (2004): 4–14.

Berliner, Abraham, and Ismar Elbogen. *Aus dem Leben der Juden Deutschlands im Mittelalter* (Schocken, 1937).

Graetz, Heinrich. *History of the Jews,* Vol. 3 (Perlego, 2013).

Güdemann, Moritz. *Geschichte des Erziehungswesens und der Cultur der Abendländischen Juden, Während des Mittelalters und der Neueren Zeit* (Philo, 1966).

Haverkamp, Alfred, ed. *Geschichte der Juden im Mittelalter von der Nordsee bis zu den Südalpen: Kommentiertes Kartenwerk* (Hahnsche Buchhandlung, 2002).

Katz, Jacob. *Exclusiveness and Tolerance: Studies in Jewish-Gentile Relations in Medieval and Modern Times* (Behrman, 1961).

Marcus, Ivan G. "Israeli Medieval Jewish Historiography: From Nationalist Positivism to New Cultural and Social Histories." *Jewish Studies Quarterly* 17 (2010): 244–85.

Myers, David N. *Re-Inventing the Jewish Past: European Jewish Intellectuals and the Zionist Return to History* (Oxford University Press, 1995).

Peters, Edward. "Review of '*Settlement, Assimilation, Distinctive Identity': A Century of Historians and Historiography of Medieval German Jewry, 1902–2002, by Christoph Cluse*," *Jewish Quarterly Review* 97 (2007): 237–79.

Yuval, Israel Jacob. *Two Nations in Your Womb: Perceptions of Jews and Christians in Late Antiquity* (University of California Press, 2006).

Notes

1. Abraham Berliner, *Aus dem Leben der deutschen Juden im Mittelalter: zugleich ein Beitrag für deutsche Culturgeschichte* (Poppelauer, 1900).

2. Moritz Güdemann, *Geschichte des Erziehungswesens und der Cultur der Juden in Deutschland während des XIV und XV Jahrhunderts: Volume 3, Geschichte des Erziehungswesens und der Cultur der abendländischen Juden während des Mittelalters und der neueren Zeit* (Hölder, 1888).

3. Repr. Jewish Publication Society, 1993.

4. Salon W. Baron, *Social and Religious History of the Jews* (13 vols., Columbia University Press, 1952–93).

5. Jacob Katz, *Exclusiveness and Tolerance: Studies in Jewish-Gentile Relations in Medieval and Modern Times* (Behrman House, 1961).

6. For one review of these theories, see David Berger, "A Generation of Scholarship on Jewish-Christian Interaction in the Medieval World," *Tradition: A Journal of Orthodox Jewish Thought* 38, no. 2 (2004): 4–14. See also Elisheva Baumgarten, "Appropriation and Differentiation: Jewish Identity in Medieval Ashkenaz," *AJS Review* 42 (2018): 39–63.

7. Ivan G. Marcus, *Rituals of Childhood: Jewish Acculturation in Medieval Europe* (Yale University Press, 1996).

8. Israel Jacob Yuval, *Two Nations in Your Womb: Perceptions of Jews and Christians in Late Antiquity* (University of California Press, 2006).

9. Mark R. Cohen, *Under Crescent and Cross: The Jews in the Middle Ages* (Princeton University Press, 2008); S. D. Goitein and Paula Sanders, *A Mediterranean Society: The Jewish Communities of the Arab World as Portrayed in the Documents of the Cairo Geniza* (University of California Press, 1967).

10. A nice example of these different approaches can be seen in the essays published in Cohen's honor: Mark R. Cohen and A. E. Franklin, ed., *Jews, Christians, and Muslims in Medieval and Early Modern Times: A Festschrift in Honor of Mark R. Cohen* (Brill, 2014).

11. For an opposing approach and a survey of scholarship, see Mark D. Meyerson, *A Jewish Renaissance in Fifteenth-Century Spain* (Princeton University Press, 2004).

12. Recent work on Provence has focused more on intellectual exchange than everyday life; see Ram Ben-Shalom, *The Jews of Provence and Languedoc*, trans. Shmuel Sermoneta-Gertel (Liverpool University Press, 2024). Work on Italy has been more concentrated on the early Middle Ages; see, for example, Robert Bonfil and Ahimaaz ben Paltiel, *History and Folklore in a Medieval Jewish Chronicle: The Family Chronicle of Ahima'az Ben Paltiel* (Brill, 2009); or on the Renaissance, see Robert Bonfil, *Jewish Life in Renaissance Italy* (University of California Press, 1994). More work on the High Middle Ages is a desideratum.

13. David B. Ruderman, *Early Modern Jewry: A New Cultural History* (Princeton University Press, 2010).

14. For one example of some of these changes, see Debra Kaplan, *Beyond Expulsion: Jews, Christians, and Reformation Strasbourg* (Stanford University Press, 2011).

15. See studies by Moshe Rosman, Magda Teter, and Adam Teller, among others. For example, Teter's *Blood Libel: On the Trail of an Antisemitic Myth* (Harvard University Press, 2020) is a good example of both continuity and change in the context of antisemitism. It is hard to point to one study that provides a similar overview of continuity and change for social history.

6

Difference and Violence

Magda Teter, Fordham University

MODERN HISTORIOGRAPHY, Jewish and non-Jewish, emerged in the nineteenth century in an era of nation-building and a search for a new collective identity in the wake of the political transformations that followed the French Revolution. These nineteenth-century historians laid the foundations for national historiographies, set the contours of scholarly research, and defined questions that would reverberate for decades, if not centuries, to come. Given that most of the work of these nineteenth- and early twentieth-century historians focused on the premodern past, they shaped, with their questions and framing, our understanding and scholarship of the premodern period. But for modern Jewish historiography, the context for its rise includes another pertinent factor—anti-Jewish violence and exclusion, making them central motifs addressed by historians of the Jewish past. Although scholars in the last several decades have rethought some of the categories set by the early historians, the new scholarship nonetheless bears the marks these earlier questions even as it tries to reshape our understanding of the past for our times.

Violence, Antisemitism, and the Beginning of Jewish Historiography

The first group of scholars formally devoted to the study of Jewish history and culture emerged in the early nineteenth century in the immediate aftermath of Napoleon's fall and during the ensuing anti-Jewish violence. At the time "the prospects" of political equality for Jews were "rapidly receding," and in the summer of 1819, violent anti-Jewish attacks, known as the HEP HEP riots, erupted across German lands.[1] Dispirited, some Jews converted to Christianity, but a number of Jewish intellectuals decided to respond to this crisis by looking for ways to "unite" Jews as a people and to "preserve our Jewishness." Fearing that "in the future, we, as individuals, will not be able to continue to live as Jews, or at least not in the way we would like to," a group of seven young Jewish men formed in Berlin the Verein für Cultur und Wissenschaft der Juden, a society devoted to academic studies of Jewish history and culture, later known as the Wissenschaft des Judentums.[2] They embraced "a scientific" approach to the study of Judaism and Jewish history and were committed to "the dissemination of clear, objective knowledge" and "purely scholarly" (*reinwissenschaflitche*) activities.[3]

Anti-Jewish violence, exclusion, and a battle for equal rights were thus at the forefront of the concerns of the scholars involved in Wissenschaft des Judentums.[4] Eduard Gans, one of the founders of the Verein für Cultur und Wissenschaft der Juden, remarked, "It was toward the end of 1819 that we met for the first time. In many cities of the German fatherland dreadful scenes occurred that made some people suspect an unanticipated return to the Middle Ages. We came together to help discuss, when necessary, how best to escape the deeply rooted damage."[5] Gans's statement reveals his and his colleague's view of the premodern era, the Middle Ages, as a woeful and violent time. And while the field of Jewish studies was maturing during the nineteenth century, modern anti-Jewish hostility gradually developed into a fully articulated political movement that came to be known as antisemitism.

A glance at the topics covered by the early scholarly Jewish journals in Europe and the United States makes clear the role that modern antisemitism played in shaping the narrative of both premodern and modern Jewish history. In 1909, Ludwig Philippson, a rabbi and scholar, observed, "Antisemitism dominates directly and indirectly the whole history of the Jewish community in the last quarter of the nineteenth century," and he devoted a significant section of his multivolume history of Jews to the history of modern antisemitism.[6]

Modern nationalism and anti-Jewish animosity also colored the way Jews of the past came to be seen—or ignored—by non-Jewish scholars. In the national histories written by Christians, Jews did not register at all—Jews were not part of what was in the nineteenth century considered a nation. By the time these modern national historians were writing, Jews were no longer seen as neighbors and compatriots but rather regarded as foreigners, "Orientals," or even "Asiatics."[7] The German historian Heinrich von Treitschke would call them in 1880 "German-speaking Orientals."[8]

DIFFERENCE AND VIOLENCE 141

Responding to what he saw as the Christian denial of Jewish history, the Jewish historian Heinrich Graetz embarked on the task of writing a multivolume *History of the Jews*, the first volume of which was published in 1853.[9] It is hard to overstate the extent to which Graetz's work shaped the field and subsequent generations of historians who embraced or rejected his framing of Jewish history. His influence was so significant that Simon Dubnow, a later prominent historian of Jews, called Graetz "the first architect of [Jewish] historiography."[10]

The most explicit articulation of Graetz's vision of Jewish history is in the introduction to the fourth volume of his *History of the Jews*.[11] Graetz saw Jewish history as seventeen centuries of "unprecedented suffering, uninterrupted martyrdom, a constantly aggravated degradation and humiliation unparalleled in history—but also by mental activity, unremitting intellectual effort, and indefatigable research."[12] He evoked a striking pair of imageries: a "subjugated Judah with the pilgrim staff in hand, the pilgrim pack upon the back, with mournful eye addressed toward heaven, surrounded by prison walls, implements of torture and red-hot branding irons" and "the same figure with earnestness of the thinker upon his placid brow, with the air of the scholar . . . seated in a hall of learning, which is filled with a colossal library in all the languages spoken by man and on all branches of divine and human lore." One represented for Graetz "the external history" (*die äußere Geschichte*), a history of suffering; the other, "the inner history" (*die innere Geschichte*), a "literary history of the knowledge of God." Graetz saw Jewish history as a contrasting binary of "studying and wandering, thinking and enduring, learning and suffering."

Graetz celebrated the intellectual accomplishments of the Jewish people, idealized the culture of Jews in Islamic lands and Spain, and despised the obscurantism that characterized Jews in Christian Europe, especially the Kabbalah.[13] The "physical dimensions" of Jewish history encompassed, for Graetz, "the fate of the Jews among the nations to which they were driven by their persecutors or carried by their own wanderings; the manner in which individuals combined to form communities," and how these communities connected with others. In his conceptualization of Jewish history as consisting of clashing "external" and "inner" elements, the "inner" remained protected. Jews, despite being swept by the "maelstrom of history," retained "their style and character unaltered amid the rushing flood of nations."[14]

Simon Dubnow would—at least initially—accept Graetz's dichotomy and would speak of an essence of Judaism and of the Jewish people. In an essay outlining the contours of Jewish history, published first in Odessa in 1896, Dubnow reiterated that in the medieval period "to think and to suffer became the watchword of the whole nation."[15] Persecution was especially the hallmark of Jewish life under Christendom, and Dubnow contrasted it with the vibrancy of Jewish life and intellectual achievements under Islam. He extolled "the vivifying magic of young Arab culture" and juxtaposed it to Christian rule that was characterized by "barbarism" and "shrouded in impenetrable darkness."[16] In Christendom, he claimed, Jews never reached the "breadth" of "spiritual development of the Jews of Arabic Spain."[17] "Their circumstances were too grievous," their "horizon was as contracted as the streets of the Jewries in which they were penned."

For Dubnow, the Crusades were the turning point in Jewish history in Europe. They began a "calamitous epoch" marked by "a sad deterioration in civil and spiritual life of German Jews"[18]; this was a period of "torture," "the horrors—the rivers of blood, the groans of massacred communities, the serried ranks of martyrs, the ever-haunting fear of the morrow," and the degeneration of Judaism. Facing the dangers, Jews "held fast to its precious relics, clung to the pillars of its religion," and "withdrew from the outer world."[19] They devoted themselves to the study of the Talmud, turning it into "scholastic pedantry." They produced books of devotion with "harrowing outcries" and "prayerful lamentations"—unlike the works of Abraham ibn Ezra or Maimonides who explored philosophy and science, or of Solomon ibn Gabirol or Judah Halevi who wrote poetry. Elsewhere, Dubnow reiterated, "The condition of the Jews in northern France and in Germany were most unfavorable to the development of research in any branch of secular learning, and it was natural that the Hebrew scholars, living in the midst of suffering and hardship, should bury themselves in their religious literature and trust to finding courage and consolation therein, since there was none to be found elsewhere."[20] This "suffering, humiliation, and poverty" not only "darkened the lives of the German Jews" but also "shrank" their "mental vision" to "the narrowness of their ghetto street." According to Dubnow, the medieval Jewish community was not only persecuted but also insular and isolated in what he termed anachronistically as "ghettos," where they were living in undignified conditions. The home and the synagogue, he argued, "were the sole spots on earth where the persecuted and condemned Jew could find rest from his tribulations, and where he might feel himself a man once more, in possession of his soul."[21]

In an expressive passage worth quoting at length, Dubnow vividly rendered what he imagined was Jewish life in medieval Christian Europe and what he believed was the true Jewish spirit:

They were shut up in their cramped Jewries, huddled in wretched cabins, which were clustered about the dilapidated synagogue in a shamefaced way.

DIFFERENCE AND VIOLENCE   143

What gigantic misery, what boundless suffering dumbly borne, was concealed in those crumbling, curse-laden dwellings! And yet, how resplendent they were with spiritual light, what exalted virtues, what lofty heroism they harbored! In those gloomy, tumbledown Jew houses, intellectual endeavor was at white heat. The torch of faith blazed clear in them, and on the pure domestic hearth played a gentle flame. In the abject, dishonored son of the ghetto was hidden an intellectual giant. In his nerveless body, bent double by suffering, and enveloped in the shabby old cloak still further disfigured by the yellow circle, dwelt the soul of a thinker. The son of the ghetto might have worn his badge with pride, for in truth it was a medal of distinction awarded by the papal Church to the Jews, for dauntlessness and courage. The awkward, puny Jew in his way was stronger and braver than a German knight, armed cap-a-pie, for he was penetrated by the faith that "moves mountains."[22]

Later in life, Dubnow rejected this approach as "one-sided," acknowledging, "It is becoming clear that in the course of thousands of years the nation not only 'thought and suffered' but also molded its own life as a distinct social unit under every condition possible."[23] Even so, Dubnow's and Graetz's early works shaped the collective memory of Jewish suffering in medieval Christian lands among the modern reading public. For both Dubnow and Graetz, the medieval period did not end until the Enlightenment. Only then, both argued, did Jews emerge from their dens and begin to breathe the fresh air again. As Dubnow put it, "In the sunny days of mankind's history, in which reason, justice, and philanthropic instinct had the upper hand, the Jews steadfastly made common cause with the other nations. Hand in hand with them, they trod the path leading to perfection."[24] The myth of the medieval period as "the Dark Ages" was very much embraced by Jewish historians.

Challenging the Paradigm

In the interwar period, the paradigm established by Graetz and Dubnow was challenged. In 1928, in a pathbreaking and succinct essay titled "Ghetto and Emancipation," Salo Wittmayer Baron, a young scholar who had just recently arrived in the United States from East-Central Europe, confronted the "habit of thinking" about Jewish history shaped by both Dubnow and Graetz that had drawn a sharp contrast between the medieval "dark ages" and the modern era of progress that has grown out of the Enlightenment ideals.[25] Jews, Baron argued, had more rights than many Christians in medieval Europe; they were relatively "well off"; they could "move freely from place to place with few exceptions"; and they enjoyed "full autonomy." Baron acknowledged violence and persecution in the premodern era, but he noted that violence did not diminish "after Emancipation"—that is, after Jews acquired citizenship rights in the modern era. His examples of anti-Jewish violence from the early modern period, which he described the period of "the deepest decline," were even more compelling.

Although the key point of his essay was to demonstrate that "it is clear that Emancipation has not brought the Golden Age," the most remembered, most repeated, and most misunderstood phrase was the last sentence of the article: "Surely it is time to break with the lachrymose theory of pre-Revolutionary woe, and to adopt a view more in accord with historic truth."[26] Many scholars latched onto the idea of breaking "with the lachrymose theory of pre-Revolutionary woe" but failed to pay attention to the last words calling for an adoption of "a view more in accord with historic truth."[27]

Baron was not denying suffering and persecution. In the 1928 article, he still accepted the idea of cultural separateness between Jews and non-Jews, though he argued that "social exclusion from the Gentile world was hardly a calamity." With time, however, he developed a more subtle understanding of the premodern Jewish past, describing, for example, the Jewish communal experience within a larger social and political context. Baron never abandoned—even after the Holocaust—his commitment to show a nuanced history of the Jewish people that also underscored its inspiring beauty. For example, in 1958, in a discussion about the relations between Israel and the Jewish diaspora, Baron reiterated his call to "abandon" the lachrymose conception of Jewish history. It was both inaccurate "from the point of view of historical truth" and not "congenial to our generation, a generation not of ghetto Jews, but of Jews living a young life, who are free and active in various countries."[28] Baron argued that there was "much greatness in Jewish history, creative greatness," and this is what the new generation of Jews needed.

During the interwar decades, across the ocean in Oxford, the British Jewish historian Cecil Roth also wanted "to break with" the earlier Jewish historiography that tended to overstress "the traditional tale of woe."[29] In his 1932 essay published in the Italian journal *La Rassegna Mensile di Israel* titled "The Most Persecuted People?" Roth aimed to complicate the notions of Jewish suffering and martyrdom and to challenge the idea that all violence from which Jews suffered was automatically antisemitic.[30] Episodes of "Jewish martyrdom," Roth argued, were very often episodes of "general history" in which Jews were caught in larger events.[31] The "tribulations" Jews experienced were not as "exceptional as is generally supposed."[32] But he admitted, "They were certainly exceptional in a degree," in that Jews were "a distinct ethnic group and an unpopular religious minority," urban residents "who suffered disproportionately during domestic disturbances," people of "substance" with houses "worth sacking." It was no surprise, Roth wrote, that "at any time of civil or political unrest; on every occasion when a town was taken by storm; at every period of pestilence or misfortune, when a scapegoat seemed necessary; whenever religious passions were stirred to a more than ordinary extent—in all such cases an attack upon the Jew was a foregone conclusion." Still, despite those acts of violence, the relations between Jews and Christians "were generally intimate," and Jewish culture was very much embedded in the local surroundings.[33] But when Roth focused on persecution, he sounded very much like the early Wissenschaft des Judenthums scholar Leopold Zunz.[34]

Yet, the call to move away from "the lachrymose conception of Jewish history" pertained only to the history of Jews in Christian Europe, and its fruits began to be seen in the years after World War II. The history of Jews in Islamicate lands that had typically been focused on intellectual achievements and contrasted with persecution under Christian rule saw the opposite trend in the aftermath of the creation of the State of Israel and the mass forced migrations of Jews from Arab lands.

Post-Holocaust Reconfiguration

After World War II, despite—or perhaps because of—the greatest catastrophe in Jewish history, scholars tended to shy away from studying persecution of Jews; they continued to explore Jewish history along the program outlined by Baron and Roth, with new questions being asked of familiar sources and new methodological approaches emerging. Baron noted in 1959 that both in Israel and in the United States it was "difficult to find young scholars to study the Jewish history of the Nazi period."[35] Scholars admitted that it was "an important subject" but did not wish to devote their time to it. According to Baron, neither Israel nor the United States had—by 1959—given "us an artistic-literary account of the Holocaust, the greatest disaster in the whole of Jewish history." He understood it to be "a symptom of a new feeling, a new approach." Baron noted that there was more interest in the fighters of the ghetto than the millions of silent martyrs and contrasted it with the martyr stories left to posterity by the Crusade chroniclers.[36]

But this shift in focus and interest was likely not a form of escapism. The new approach to Jewish history focused on the "perseverance" and "survival" of Jews, rather than moments of defeat and destruction. Although this approach might have served the emotional needs of the Jewish population, the recent mass murder of Jews in Europe also provided a new angle to see past persecutions. Cecil Roth noted that "the indescribable horrors of the decade of Nazi domination" put Jews' medieval and early modern suffering in perspective.[37] "The martyrdom of the Jews" in the premodern period was "paradise" in comparison to the Nazi period, he submitted.

This new perspective, along with new questions about how Jews lived and survived, resulted in studies about the workings of Jewish communities, the Jews' legal status, and Jewish art and material culture; there also appeared publications of different primary sources, including those related to past persecutions, and translations of Hebrew and Yiddish works.[38]

A breakthrough in the historiography of Jews in Christian Europe came from a book by the Hungarian-born Israeli scholar Jacob Katz, *Exclusiveness and Tolerance: Studies in Jewish-Gentile Relations in Medieval and Modern Times,* which was published in English in 1961 by Oxford University Press.[39] The book, as Katz would later describe it, "presented the attitude of Jews to their Christian environment over the ages and demonstrated that traditional Judaism upheld neither absolute religious tolerance nor a universalist code of morality."[40] Katz showed that it was not just Christians who promulgated restrictions on Jewish–Christian interactions; the rabbis also sought to prevent such close contacts and regulated them in Jewish law (the halakhah) rooted in rabbinic writings from the Graeco-Roman period. Even though rigorous application of "segregation" between Jews and non-Jews was not possible, there was an internal Jewish impetus for such separation.

The book was groundbreaking and controversial, initially arousing Katz's fears that if published, it "might provide ammunition for the enemies of the Jewish people."[41] Until then, scholars writing about Jewish–Christian relations had focused predominantly on the *Christian* attitudes toward Jews and the Christian laws regulating Jewish–Christian interaction, which were considered part and parcel of Christian "anti-Jewish" persecution and fit the narrative of Jewish history as a history of suffering and persecution. But Jewish views of Christianity had remained taboo. The idea that Jews themselves sought, as Katz put it, religious "segregation" echoed centuries-old Christian suspicions about Jewish anti-Christian attitudes and antisemitic ideas of Jewish clannishness.[42]

DIFFERENCE AND VIOLENCE 147

Despite Katz's fears, the book was received largely positively, and Katz went on to publish other works on the topic, notably *Shabbes Goy* about the common phenomenon of non-Jews serving Jews on the Sabbath and Jewish holidays—another controversial idea in a book containing in its title the word "goy," which some considered derogatory.[43] Katz's books were examples of the new non-apologetic approach to studying Jewish attitudes toward non-Jews, especially toward Christians.

Perhaps it was the new postwar environment or a new sense of confidence in a Jewish state that allowed for this new approach. As Davin N. Myers remarked, early Zionist historians, "feeling at home" in Israel, ... "could now remove the residue of apologia that they saw [had] blanketed over Jewish scholarship."[44]

The 1960s brought another major shift, which was bound to leave an imprint on the historiography of Jewish life in medieval Christian Europe—this change, however, occurred not in scholarship but in the official attitudes of the Catholic Church toward Jews. In October 1965, the "Declaration on the Relation of the Church to Non-Christian Religions," known as *Nostra Aetate,* was promulgated by the Second Vatican Council. It was the fruit of years-long advocacy and calls to reckon with Christian roots of antisemitism in the aftermath of World War II. Although the document mentioned other religions—Hinduism, Buddhism, and Islam—its significance for Jewish–Catholic relations was revolutionary. The declaration changed the Catholic Church's teachings about Jews, departing from the doctrine of Jewish deicide and explicitly acknowledging that "the Church's main-stay and pillars, as well as most of the early disciples who proclaimed Christ's Gospel to the world, sprang from the Jewish people."[45] One of the impacts of *Nostra Aetate* on Jewish–Christian relations was a careful reexamination of church teachings about Jews in history. As Israel Yuval, an Israeli scholar of medieval Jewish history, remarked, "The Christian–Jewish debate that started nineteen hundred years ago, in our day, came to a conciliatory end."[46]

This increasing openness inspired Jewish Studies scholars to move beyond "the apologetic spirit" that had dominated any previous attempt at "self-examination" meant to address questions of Jewish attitudes toward Christians. If the nineteenth-century German Jewish historians meekly and apologetically acknowledged the existence of Jewish anti-Christian sentiments, in the decades after World War II it became clear that nothing could justify a genocide like that committed by the Nazis, no matter what Jews may have historically felt about Christians. Thus, after Katz's studies on Jewish attitudes toward Christians, the path was now open to other scholars who, in the spirit of the new postwar academic freedom, wanted to delve even more deeply into the Jewish side of Jewish–Christian relations, including Jewish anti-Christian polemic. Israel Yuval would later credit the creation of the State of Israel and *Nostra Aetate* for this change and argue that the new generation of scholars, now living in "a postpolemical age," could publicly engage with topics that "were once discussed in whispers in private chambers or known only to a chosen few."[47]

In 1977 Daniel Lasker published a book on Jewish philosophical polemic against Christianity in the Middle Ages, exploring Jewish arguments against key Christian dogmas: the Trinity, incarnation, transubstantiation, and virgin birth.[48] Two years later, in 1979, David Berger published a bilingual English–Hebrew, annotated edition of *Niẓaḥon Vetus*, or the book of old polemic, offering assertive Jewish "refutations of Christian interpretations of the Bible," including the New Testament.[49]

But even more importantly, Jewish scholars began to treat Christian sources—even the polemical ones—with less suspicion and used them to inform their studies of Jewish society and culture. This new approach challenged earlier interpretations of Jewish history and revolutionized the field. For example, one of Salo Baron's students, Yosef Hayim Yerushalmi—in his study of *Practica inquisitionis heretice pravitatis*, an inquisitorial manual written by Bernard Gui, a Dominican inquisitor in thirteenth-century France—demonstrated that the authenticity of Jewish "prayers translated in the Practica" was "unimpeachable."[50] Later, Robert Chazan reinterpreted the dynamic of the Barcelona debate of 1263 by methodically examining Christian sources, their production, and content, alongside the Hebrew account written by the Jewish participant Moses Nahmanides.[51] Chazan gave more weight to the Latin accounts than previous scholars had while raising questions about the plausibility of the descriptions found in the Hebrew account. His book elicited a lengthy review by David Berger in which he defended Nahmanides's account against Chazan's skepticism.[52]

This more holistic look at both Jewish and Christian sources resulted in new discoveries and revolutionary reinterpretations of Jewish–Christian boundaries and distinctions, at times leading to controversies. Israel Yuval explored what he called the "dialogism" of Jewish and Christian worlds, jettisoning the idea of the "authenticity of Judaism," what Yitzhak Baer called "immanence" or what Simon Dubnow saw as the "soul" of Jewish culture. Yuval suggested that in "Ashkenazi Jewry, previously considered a bastion of closure and loyalty to its internal religious tradition, there developed a profound affinity, albeit one mixed with hatred, with its sister religion, Christianity."[53] Yuval embraced a "dialogic" approach that presented "Jewish life in Christian Europe as involving the absorption and internalization of many values of the environment, along with its body language, ceremonies, and holy time."[54]

In his book, *Two Nations in Your Womb*, for example, Yuval showed that the Christian legend *Vindicta Salvatoris* (The Vengeance of the Savior) had a close parallel in talmudic stories; he also claimed that Passover and Easter rituals and symbolism are linked not because, as some had earlier thought, Easter had roots in Passover but because they developed as polemical responses to each other after the destruction of the Jerusalem Temple, with each side emphasizing the validity of its own story of redemption. Yuval argued that the *Dayyenu* prayer of gratitude to God, included in the Passover Hagaddah, was a Jewish *response* to the Christian prayer *Improperia*, the reproaches chanted on Good Friday that accused Jews of being ungrateful. According to Yuval, the prayer *Dayyenu* "should be seen as part of the Jewish–Christian dialogue and a response to the Christian accusations of the ingratitude of the Jews."[55] The discussion of "the bread of affliction" in the Hagaddah, Yuval contended, was aimed at "the liturgical use of Jesus's words concerning the bread of the Last Supper"; the paschal lamb was a parallel to Jesus as *agnus dei*; and the *maror* at the Passover seder a parallel to the bitter herbs (of the Passover seder), which "were read as a symbol of the torment and suffering of the Savior," a likely reference to the myrrh offered to Jesus mixed with wine during crucifixion.[56] According to Yuval, Judaism and Christianity do not have a mother–daughter relationship, but rather, they are siblings—competing with and feeling threatened by each other. They share a common language but, Yuval stressed, "This common language should not mislead us into thinking it constituted any sort of closeness between the religions. To the contrary: hostility and rivalry demand a common language for formulating diametrically opposed positions, because conflicting conceptual messages can only be conveyed through symbols understood by both sides."[57] The "postpolemical" era allowed scholars to look dispassionately at *mutual* hostilities.

Indeed, in recent decades, scholars have shown that Ashkenazi Jews—those previously seen as deeply insular and almost impervious to Christian influences—were, in fact, culturally integrated within Christian societies and deeply familiar with Christian symbols and meanings. That familiarity, however, did not mean "assimilation." Rather, it suggested Jews' ability to retain a distinct identity while absorbing Christian motifs into Jewish practices, sometimes with polemical intentions. In his study of Jewish rituals of childhood, Ivan

Marcus called this process "an inward acculturation."[58] Marcus showed how medieval Jews "made sense of their world" and how they "ritualized" metaphors engaging deeply with the dominant Christian environment.[59] Marcus applied anthropological tools to medieval Jewish society and culture and explored the meanings imbued in medieval Ashkenazi rituals as "a public symbolic expression reflected in collective action."[60] What he found were newly developed rituals that absorbed Christian metaphors but with the purpose of denying their power—the rituals Ashkenazi Jews developed were therefore polemical. He claimed that the rituals surrounding the initiation of a child into the study of the Torah—in which young boys ate sweet cakes decorated with verses of Scripture and licked Hebrew letters written in honey off tablets—symbolized "the idea of eating God's words" and effectively transformed "the central liturgical mystery of the church, the Eucharist," which had become sanctioned in the doctrine of transubstantiation.[61] Marcus argued that this ritual played on the proclamation found in the Gospel of John (1:1) that Jesus was "the Word" and, thus, "the Jewish ceremony proclaims that the Torah is the word of God and symbolically creates an equivalent to the central ritual of the Mass."

Other scholars confirmed this pattern. The omnipresence of the Christian Marian cult is an example. Ephraim Shoham-Steiner showed the many "subtle ways" in which Jews in medieval Christian Europe had to "contend" with the "formidable" challenge of this cult and its "appealing and persuasive aspects," such as "motherly love and the role of charity and compassion it advocated."[62] Jews then, Shoham-Steiner argued, "came up with a variety of tools in their attempt to deflect the power of the virgin and her cult. One such way was the internal empowerment of Jewish female figures, such as the prophetess Miriam and other Jewish female figures." Marc Michael Epstein, too, showed the influence of Marian imagery on medieval haggadot, noting the adaptation of the image of the holy family in the Golden Haggadah.[63] Recently, Karen Blough has identified the adaptation of Marian iconography in the Darmstadt Haggadah, in which one of the most impressive full-page illuminations features a woman, dressed in blue and depicted in a way reminiscent of Mary, holding not the baby Jesus but a book symbolizing the Torah.[64] Similarly, Ivan Marcus pointed to deployment of the visual vocabulary of Madonna and a Child to illustrate the rituals of initiation to the Torah study. In the *Leipzig Maḥzor*, for example, the teacher with the boy about to be taught the Torah is shown in a way echoing Mary holding baby Jesus.[65] The most ubiquitous aspects of Christian devotion, scholars have shown, were symbolically adapted and then replaced with images, rituals, and representations related to the Torah. This process shows not only familiarity with the meaning of Christian devotion but also a tension between attraction and rejection.

This expansion of tools to include anthropological and comparative lenses has led even to the reevaluation of the much-studied chronicles of the Crusades. Early historians viewed the Crusade chronicles and post-Crusade liturgical and penitential poems, *selihot* and *kinot*, as evidence of the insularity and isolation of Ashkenazi Jews from their Christian neighbors. In contrast, in recent decades, historians have demonstrated not only Jews' awareness of the presence of Christian beliefs in their virulent anti-Christian rhetoric but also argued that some of the descriptions of the events portrayed echo, as Jeremy Cohen has argued, "the idiom of Christian culture."[66] According to Cohen, even these chronicles of violence demonstrate that "Ashkenazi Jews involved themselves in the culture and religious traditions" of the Christian world.[67]

Cohen applied the tools of literary analysis and postmodern theories that see historical texts as narratives that do not necessarily recount what exactly happened but rather what "was believed" to have happened.[68] Cohen explored the chronicles as works of literature composed in the Christian milieu and not as works that only chronicle events. He noted both the uncanny rhetorical resemblance of Rachel of Mainz, a mother who slaughtered her children to prevent forced conversions, to the Virgin Mary, Jesus's mother, and polemical echoes between Rachel and Mary. For example, the chronicler's statement that Rachel "the mother stretched out her arms to receive their blood in her sleeves instead of the cultic chalice of blood," functions as a polemical counterpoint to the imagery of Mary collecting Jesus's blood into a chalice at the crucifixion.[69] Cohen, like Ivan Marcus, Ephraim Shoham-Steiner, and Israel Yuval, has revealed the adaptation and inversion of Christian rituals and beliefs in medieval Jewish literary works and practices; thus, he demonstrates not Jewish insularity in medieval northern Europe as earlier historians had assumed but closeness between the two cultures, as well as deep and sophisticated cultural exchange even in works that seem to say more about enmity than proximity.

Jews in Islamicate Lands: Myths and Counter-Myths

The traditional view of the history of Jews in Islamicate lands was, as we have seen, not lachrymose. Rather, it focused on achievements in poetry and philosophy, political influence, and the splendor of court culture. It therefore required a revision on its own—in the opposite direction. That revision came from within Zionist historiography, its adumbrations palpable already in Yitzhak

Baer's scathing review, published in 1938 in the scholarly journal *Zion*, of the first edition of Salo Baron's *Social and Religious History of the Jews*.[70] Although Baron did note that "Islam was by no means friendly to Judaism" and acknowledged "much animosity between the two groups," overall, he did not question the narrative of Jewish cultural accomplishments in Islamicate lands and saw Jewish history under Islam as a "great period of achievement."[71] Baer, who was writing this review in the midst of the violent Arab revolt in Palestine that started in 1936, objected to what he called Baron's "optimistic" view of Jewish experience under Islam that was "somewhat distorted" and in need of revision.[72] According to Baer, "Islamic conquerors" brought with them the "subjugation of Jews" (*ha-shibud shel 'am Yisrael*).[73] What Baron called achievements were not so, Baer countered: "The greatness of the Jews in commerce and in the service of the kings and in political leadership is the greatness of exiles and slaves." He doubted that "the dependence on the courts of the Arab capital in Baghdad" was truly the source of these intellectual achievements. Baer also disagreed that the extolled philosophy and poetry were representative of "the immanent forces" within Jewish history and whether they could be taken as signs of happiness and prosperity in *galut* (in exile). Baer ended the section of the review mentioning Maimonides's "Epistle on Forced Conversion" (*iggeret ha-shemad*) and his "Epistle to Yemen"—both pointing to the violence and persecution of Jews in Islamicate lands and not a golden age.[74] Thus emerged what Marc Cohen called "the counter-myth" of Jewish experience in Islamicate lands. It was strengthened in the aftermath of the forced migrations of Jews from the Arab lands to Israel in the 1950s and 1960s.

In a subtle intervention, already in the 1930s and the 1940s, Bernard Lewis published articles and primary sources about Jews in Islamicate lands, in Hebrew and in English, to address different audiences while challenging these same stereotypes.[75] But, it would not be until the 1980s and 1990s, perhaps influenced by the peace agreements in the Middle East and better access to the archives, that scholars would return to reevaluate the history of Jews under Islam and complicate both "the myth" and "the counter-myth."[76] In 1984 Bernard Lewis published a poignantly titled book *Jews of Islam*, in which he presented a "more balanced paradigm of interfaith relations" in Islamicate lands and argued for the adoption of the term "Judaeo-Islamic" to parallel the much more popular term "Judaeo-Christian." He began his book by demolishing the two persistent myths of Islam popularized by Edward Gibbon and symbolized by an image of a "fanatical" Arab warrior in the desert, holding a sword in one hand and the Qur'an in another. Lewis was not the only one undercutting the "neo-lachrymose" approach to Jewish history under Islam. His contemporary, S. D. Goitein, an Arabicist and a scholar of the Geniza documents, also provided a much more nuanced approach.[77] Finally, Mark Cohen offered a comparative lens through which to view the life of Jews "under Crescent and Cross."[78]

Rethinking Violence

Anti-Jewish violence in the medieval period has been studied predominantly from the perspective of massacres, such as during the Crusades, the Black Death, or anti-Jewish libels. The history of Jews in the Iberian Peninsula, in contrast, had been mired with the myth of *convivencia*, a peaceful coexistence between Christians, Jews, and Muslims that had been valorized and idealized in western scholarship pining to find models to overcome interreligious divisions. David Nirenberg's book *Communities of Violence* challenged some of these notions, arguing that "violence was a central and systemic aspect of the coexistence of majority and minorities" in the Middle Ages, and that "*convivencia* was predicated upon violence" and "not its peaceful antithesis."[79] Multireligious societies, as Nirenberg noted in the preface to the second edition of *Communities of Violence*, had the concurrent potential for both "coexistence and violent intolerance."[80] Nirenberg did not see tolerance and violence as mutually exclusive; instead, he saw a need to perceive "both these phenomena at once, rather than dismissing the importance of the one or the other. From this point of view neither histories of pluralism that ignore its failures, nor histories of persecution that overlook long periods of effective coexistence, are satisfactory." Nirenberg drew attention to ritualized enactments of violence, such as the symbolic stoning of a Jewish quarter during Holy Week, which annually reminded Jews of their precarious outsider status yet paradoxically allowed for "coexistence" for the rest of the year.[81] Violence and tolerance, coexistence and intolerance were thus "interdependent" not exclusive forces.[82] Nirenberg's work, much like the work by Jeremy Cohen, Israel Yuval, and Ivan Marcus, highlighted that intimacy and proximity do not guarantee harmonious and mutually respectful relations.[83]

Nirenberg redefined the framework not only of *convivencia* but also of the traditional "lachrymose" narrative of Jewish history that had emphasized eruptions of "cataclysmic" violence, such as the Crusades, the mid-fourteenth-century massacres during the bubonic plague, or a catastrophic wave of slaughters in Castile 1391, typically flattening them under a rubric of decontextualized anti-Jewish violence. He explored "the functions and meanings" of such violence, noting their political contexts and their uses and highlighting the relationship between these "cataclysmic" outbreaks with "systemic," "everyday functional violence of a relatively stable society."[84] Both episodic and everyday forms of violence were "part of the same violent mechanisms by which the Christian majority articulated the terms of coexistence and made it possible"; "both were meant as much to reinforce the social order of this multireligious community as to shatter it."[85] Nirenberg's *Communities of Violence* included discussions of other targets of mass violence and persecution—religious and social minorities, such as Muslims, beggars, and lepers—thus avoiding singling out Jews while, at the same time, pointing to impulses behind specifically anti-Jewish violence. Nirenberg argued that, without such contextualization, violence "resists interpretation."[86] Yet, this contextualization meant that violent persecution could "no longer be reduced to that of a simple measurement of hatred."

Rethinking Persecution by Widening the Lens

In trying to widen the lens to include other groups and to contextualize Jewish experiences, Nirenberg was echoing Salo Baron. In his 1928 seminal essay "Ghetto and Emancipation," Baron widened the analytical lens to compare Jews' legal position in the premodern period to that of other social groups—nobility, clergy, urban dwellers, and enserfed peasants—thereby providing a new perspective on the Jewish experience. Baron noted that toward the end of the premodern era, Jews' status was "on the average lower than those of their urban Christian neighbors, yet even then they belonged to the privileged minority which included nobles, clergy, and urban citizenry." This was because Jews "had fewer duties and more rights than the great bulk of the population—the enormous mass of peasants, the great majority of whom were little more than appurtenances of the soil on which they were born."[87]

More recently, other scholars have also been rethinking more sustained waves of mass violence and persecutions, such as expulsions of Jews and violent attacks related to the charge of well poisoning. Tzafrir Barzilay, for example, building on the work of David Nirenberg's *Communities of Violence*, explored "well-poisoning accusations within a range of local phenomena," as well as broader "environmental, demographic, and economic crises."[88] Using local archival records, such as of criminal trials and property transfers, alongside chronicles and official correspondence, Barzilay offered an anatomy of the well-poisoning myth; he mapped out "how and why medieval people and institutions accepted, adopted, and spread well-poisoning accusations" leading to outbreaks of mass violence against different minorities, including Jews, and to major transformations within European Christian societies.

Rowan Dorin took a similar approach in his study of expulsions, whereas Robert Chazan sought to reconsider the conception of Jews as perpetual refugees.[89] Dorin argued that "medieval expulsions of Jews cannot be fully understood without taking into account the wider association of usury and expulsion" in medieval "rhetoric and practice."[90] He noted, "From the beginning of the thirteenth century to the middle of the fourteenth, every major European polity that ordered the expulsion of its Jewish community also ordered the expulsion of foreign Christian usurers." He found that the map of expulsions of Jews overlapped with the map of expulsions of Christians engaged in moneylending. The comparative approach allowed Dorin to unpack the meaning of the expulsions and, like Nirenberg, move beyond "anti-Jewish hatred," "religious divides," or "purity" as common explanations.[91] Dorin's No Return thus placed expulsions in a very specific medieval context, underscored the novelty of the policies, and showed that this practice was not aimed uniquely at Jews; he concluded that, even though anti-Jewish sentiments and rhetoric might have played a role in the policies, they were not the prime and only motivators. The expulsion of Jews, some of whom may have engaged in lending, was a byproduct of the anxiety about moneylenders and their exclusion. Dorin's work challenged exile as a Jewish condition and the image articulated by Heinrich Graetz and emblazoned in Jewish memory of "a subjugated Judah with the pilgrim staff in hand, the pilgrim pack upon the back, with mournful eye addressed toward heaven, surrounded by prison walls, implements of torture and red-hot branding irons."

Dorin explicitly confronted the pernicious stereotypical association of Jews with moneylending, arguing that although only "a minority of Jews" made moneylending "the core of their business affairs," Jews were frequently assumed to have had "a near monopoly" on lending.[92] Indeed, the "very existence" of "Christian professional moneylenders is largely forgotten," and the narrative is so pervasive "that even some distinguished modern scholars have effaced medieval records of Christian moneylenders by mistakenly assuming that these concerned Jews." Dorin, Nirenberg, and Barzilay were so effective in challenging stereotypes and deeply entrenched narratives because they examined archival records not simply by looking only for materials concerning Jews—or, as might be the case of scholars uninterested in Jewish history, by skipping over them—but by examining them holistically. This allowed them to widen the lens and helped, as Salo Baron insisted, "break with the lachrymose theory of pre-Revolutionary woe, and to adopt a view more in accord with historic truth."[93]

———

As the story told in this chapter shows, Jewish historiography has changed dramatically from its earliest years and, along with it, so has our understanding of Jewish suffering and anti-Jewish animus and violence. In its earliest years, Jewish scholars defined the Jewish experience in the Middle Ages in terms of suffering, oppression, and insularity; they saw the outbreaks of violence as a continuum that connected the destruction of the Temple in Jerusalem with the Kishinev pogrom of 1903.[94] In contrast, today, historians would no longer place the Kishinev pogrom of 1903 next to the Crusades or Black Death. Although—contrary to another myth—they do not deny suffering and persecution as part of the Jewish historical experience, they offer new explanations and interpretations of anti-Jewish animus and violence. Without reducing anti-Jewish sentiments and actions to anti-Jewish hatred, they instead take into consideration local political and social dynamics, as well as the treatment of other minority groups, to make sense of these outbreaks and daily experiences. Thus today, our understanding of anti-Jewish hostility and violence is much more nuanced than when modern Jewish Studies first emerged. Jewish history includes "lachrymose" aspects, but they can no longer be seen as decontextualized expressions of antisemitism as "the longest hatred of Jews."

Recommended Readings

Baron, Salo Wittmayer. "Ghetto and Emancipation," *Menorah Journal* 14 (1928): 515–26.

Barzilay, Tzafrir. *Poisoned Wells: Accusations, Persecution, and Minorities in Medieval Europe, 1321–1422* (University of Pennsylvania Press, 2022).

Brenner, Michael. *Prophets of the Past: Interpreters of Jewish History* (Princeton University Press, 2010).

Cohen, Mark R. *Under Crescent and Cross: The Jews in the Middle Ages* (Princeton University Press, 1994.

Dorin, Rowan. *No Return: Jews, Christian Usurers, and the Spread of Mass Expulsion in Medieval Europe* (Princeton University Press, 2023).

Dubnow, Simon. *An Outline of Jewish History* (3 vols., Max N. Maisel, 1929).

Graetz, Heinrich. *The Structure of Jewish History, and Other Essays*, transl Ismar Schorsch (JTS/Ktav, 1975).

Katz, Jacob. *Exclusiveness and Tolerance: Studies in Jewish-Gentile Relations in Medieval and Modern Times* (Oxford University Press, 1961).

Marcus, Ivan G. *Rituals of Childhood: Jewish Culture and Accultaration in the Middle Ages* (Yale University Press, 1996).

Myers, David N. *Re-Inventing the Jewish Past : European Jewish Intellectuals and the Zionist Return to History* (Oxford University Press, 1995).

Nirenberg, David. *Communities of Violence: Persecution of Minorities in the Middle Ages* (Princeton University Press, 1996).

Schorsch, Ismar. *Leopold Zunz: Creativity in Adversity* (University of Pennsylvania Press, 2017).

Shoham-Steiner, Ephraim. "The Virgin Mary, Miriam, and Jewish Reactions to Marian Devotion in the High Middle Ages," *AJS Review* 37 (2013): 75–91.

Yerushalmi, Yosef Hayim. "The Inquisition and the Jews of France in the Time of Bernard Gui," *Harvard Theological Review* 63 (1970): 317–76.

Yuval, Israel Jacob. *Two Nations in Your Womb: Perceptions of Jews and Christians in Late Antiquity and the Middle Ages* (University of California Press, 2006).

Zunz, Leopold. *The Sufferings of the Jews during the Middle Ages,* transl.Albert Löwy and George Alexander Kohut (Bloch, 1907).

Notes

1. Ismar Schorsch, *Leopold Zunz: Creativity in Adversity* (University of Pennsylvania Press, 2017), 29–30.

2. Joel Abraham List, "A Society for the Preservation of the Jewish People (1819)," in *The Jew in the Modern World*, ed. Paul Mendes-Flohr and Yehuda Reinharz (Oxford University Press, 1995), 236–37. On the founding of the society, see Schorsch, *Leopold Zunz*, chap. 2.

3. *Entwurf von Statuten des Vereins für Cultur und Wissenschaft der Juden* (Ferd. Nietack, 1822), 6. Sections published in English in Mendes-Flohr and Reinharz, *Jew in the Modern World*, 238–39.

4. Quoted in Michael Brenner, *Prophets of the Past: Interpreters of Jewish History* (Princeton University Press, 2010), 29.

5. Quoted in Brenner, *Prophets of the Past*, 29.

6. Brenner, *Prophets of the Past*, 80.

7. On the process of the de-Europeanization of Jews, see Magda Teter, *Christian Supremacy: Reckoning with the Roots of Antisemitism and Racism* (Princeton University Press, 2023).

8. Heinrich von Treitschke, *Ein Wort über unser Judentum* (Reimer, 1880), 5.

9. Heinrich Graetz, *Geschichte der Juden: von den ältesten Zeiten bis auf die Gegenwart: Aus den Quellen Neu Bearbeitet* (O. Leiner, 1853). Graetz's work provoked a virulent response from Heinrich von Treitschke; *Ein Wort*, 6–16.

10. Simon Dubnow, "Cedars of Lebanon: A New Conception of Jewish History," *Commentary* (March, 1946).

11. Graetz, *Geschichte der Juden*, 4:1–9; Engl. trans. by Ismar Schorsch in Heinrich Graetz, *The Structure of Jewish History, and Other Essays* (JTS/Ktav, 1975), 125–32.

12. The English follows Schorsch's translation. The following passages come from Graetz, *Geschichte der Juden*, 4:1–2; Graetz, *Structure of Jewish History*, 125–26.

158   CHAPTER 6

13. Graetz, *Structure of Jewish History*.

14. Introduction to Vol. 5, in Graetz, *Structure of Jewish History*, 135.

15. Simon Dubnow, *Jewish History: An Essay in the Philosophy of History* (Jewish Publication Society, 1903), 19 and 116. The essay was later republished in Simon Dubnow, *Nationalism and History: Essays on Old and New Judaism* (Jewish Publication Society, 1958), 256–324; quote is on pp. 262 and 299.

16. Dubnow, *Jewish History*, 102 and 108; *Nationalism and History*, 294 and 296.

17. Dubnow, *Jewish History*, 120–21; *Nationalism and History*, 300–301.

18. Simon Dubnow, *An Outline of Jewish History* (3 vols.; Max N. Maisel, 1929), 3:88, 96.

19. Dubnow, *Jewish History*, 120–21; *Nationalism and History*, 300–301.

20. Dubnow, *Outline of Jewish History*, 3: 94–95.

21. Dubnow, *Outline of Jewish History*, 3:133.

22. Dubnow, *Jewish History*, 126–27; *Nationalism and History*, 303.

23. Dubnow, "New Conception."

24. Dubnow, *Jewish History*, 181; *Nationalism and History*, 323.

25. Salo Wittmayer Baron, "Ghetto and Emancipation," *Menorah Journal* 14 (1928): 515–26.

26. Baron, "Ghetto and Emancipation," 526.

27. On the misunderstanding of Baron's essay, see David Engel, "Crisis and Lachrymosity: On Salo Baron, Neobaronianism, and the Study of Modern European Jewish History," *Jewish History* 20 (2006): 243–64. For an example of the characterization of Baron's idea as "opposition to the lachrymose conception," see Adam Teller, "Revisiting Baron's 'Lachrymose Conception': The Meanings of Violence in Jewish History," *AJS Review* 38 (2014): 431–39.

28. Salo W. Baron, "The Dialogue between Israel and the Diaspora," in *The Jerusalem Ideological Conference*, ed. Nathan Rotenstreich et al. (World Zionist Organization, 1959), 239. See also Magda Teter, "The Pandemic, Antisemitism, and the Lachrymose Conception of Jewish History," *Jewish Social Studies* 26 (2020), 20–32.

29. Cecil Roth, *A Short History of the Jewish People 1600 B.C.–A.D. 1935* (MacMillan, 1936), vii.

30. Cecil Roth, "Il Popolo Più Perseguitato?" *La Rassegna Mensile di Israel* 7/3 (1932): 83–92.

31. Roth, "Il Popolo Più Perseguitato?" 85.

32. Roth, *Short History,* 190.

33. Roth, *Short History*, 214.

34. Compare for example, Roth, *Short History*, chap. 20, "Expulsion and Persecution," with Leopold Zunz, *The Sufferings of the Jews during the Middle Ages* (Bloch, 1907).

35. Baron, "Dialogue," 239.

36. Baron, "Dialogue," 239.

37. Cecil Roth, *A Short History of the Jewish People* (East and West Library, 1948), vi.

38. See, for example, Abraham Meir Habermann, ed., *Sefer Gezerot Ashkenaz Ve-Tsarfat: Divre Zikhronot Mi-Bene Ha-Dorot Shebi-Tekufat Mas`E Ha-Tselav U-Mivhar Piyutehem* (Mosad ha-Rav Kook, 1945); Israel Halpern, ed., *Pinkas Va`Ad Arb`a Aratzot* (Jerusalem: Mosad Bialik, 1945); N. M. Gelber, "The Sephardic Community in Vienna," *Jewish Social Studies* 10, no. 4 (1948); Wladyslaw Pociecha, "Ezofowicz, Rabinkowicz Michel," in *Polski Slownik Biograficzny*, ed. Wladyslaw Konopczynski (Akademia Umiejetnosci, 1948); Guido Kisch, *The Jews in Medieval Germany: A Study of Their Legal and Social Status* (University of

Chicago Press, 1949); Moses Maimonides, *The Code of Maimonides. Uniform Title: Mishneh Torah* (Yale University Press, 1949); Roth Cecil, "Leone Da Modena and His English Correspondents," *Transactions (Jewish Historical Society of England)* 17 (1951); Selig Schachnowitz, *Avraham Ben Avraham: Sipur Histori* (Hotsa'at Netsa'h, 1951); Uriel Acosta, *Das "Exemplar Humane Vitae" Des Uriel Da Costa* (Aarau, 1952); Salo Wittmayer Baron, *A Social and Religious History of the Jews* (18 vols.; Columbia University Press, 1952–83); Franz Kobler, *Letters of Jews through the Ages: From Biblical Times to the Middle of the Eighteenth Century* (Ararat, 1952); Israel Halpern, ed., *Bet Israel Be-Polin* (Youth Department of the Zionist Organization, 1953); Salomon Maimon, *Autobiography* (East and West Library, 1954); Shmuel Ettinger, "The Legal and Social Status of Jews in the Ukraine from the 15th to the 17th Centuries" [Hebrew] *Zion* 20 (1955), 128–52; Solomon Bennett Freehof, *The Responsa Literature* (Jewish Publication Society, 1955); Leo W. Schwarz and Salo Wittmayer Baron, *Great Ages and Ideas of the Jewish People* (Modern Library, 1956); Hayyim Hillel Ben-Sasson, *Hagut Ve-Hanhagah: Hashkafotehem Ha-Ḥevratiyot Shel Yehudei Polin Be-Shilhe Yeme Ha-Beynayim* (Mosad Bialik, 1959); Joseph Gutmann, "When the Kingdom Comes, Messianic Themes in Medieval Jewish Art," *Art Journal* 27 (1967): 168–75.

39. Jacob Katz, *Exclusiveness and Tolerance: Studies in Jewish-Gentile Relations in Medieval and Modern Times* (Oxford University Press, 1961).

40. Jacob Katz, *With My Own Eyes: The Autobiography of a Historian* (University Press of New England, 1995), 147.

41. Katz, *With My Own Eyes*, 20, 147.

42. Katz, *Exclusiveness and Tolerance*, chap. 4, "Social and Religious Segregation," 37–47.

43. Orig. Hebrew; Jacob Katz, *Goi Shel Shabat* (Merkaz Zalman Shazar, 1983); Jacob Katz, *The "Shabbes Goy": A Study in Halakhic Flexibility* (Jewish Publication Society, 1992).

44. David N. Myers, *Re-Inventing the Jewish Past: European Jewish Intellectuals and the Zionist Return to History* (Oxford University Press, 1995), 6.

45. English online at New Advent Library. On the history of *Nostra Aetate*, see John Connelly, *From Enemy to Brother: The Revolution in Catholic Teaching on the Jews, 1933–1965* (Harvard University Press, 2012).

46. Israel Jacob Yuval, *Two Nations in Your Womb: Perceptions of Jews and Christians in Late Antiquity and the Middle Ages* (University of California Press, 2006), 20.

47. Yuval, *Two Nations*, 21.

48. Daniel J. Lasker, *Jewish Philosophical Polemics against Christianity in the Middle Ages* (Ktav, 1977). See also Ḥasdai Crescas and Daniel J. Lasker, *The Refutation of the Christian Principles* (SUNY Press, 1992); Daniel J. Lasker and Sarah Stroumsa, *The Polemic of Nestor the Priest: Qissat Mujadalat Al-Usquf and Sefer Nestor Ha-Komer* (Ben-Zvi Institute, 1996); and, most recently, Daniel J. Lasker, "Jewish Anti-Christian Polemics in Islamic Countries and the Unchanging Nature of the Jewish Critique of Christianity," in *Religious and Intellectual Diversity in the Islamicate World and Beyond: Essays in Honor of Sarah Stroumsa*, ed. Omer Michaelis and Sabine Schmidtke (Brill, 2024). A second edition of *Jewish Philosophical Polemics* was published in 2007.

49. David Berger, *The Jewish-Christian Debate in the High Middle Ages: A Critical Edition of the Nitsahon Vetus with an Introduction, Translation, and Commentary*, Vol. 4 (Jewish Publication Society, 1979), 11.

50. Yosef Hayim Yerushalmi, "The Inquisition and the Jews of France in the Time of Bernard Gui," *Harvard Theological Review* 63 (1970): 317–76, quote on 360.

51. Robert Chazan, *Barcelona and Beyond: The Disputation of 1263 and Its Aftermath* (University of California Press, 1992).

52. David Berger, "The Barcelona Disputation," review of *Barcelona and Beyond: The Disputation of 1263 and Its Aftermath,* by Robert Chazan, *AJS Review* 20 (1995): 379–88.

53. Israel Yuval, "Vengeance and Damnation, Blood and Defamation: From Jewish Martyrdom to Blood Libel Accusations" [Hebrew] *Zion* 48 (1993), 33–90.

54. Yuval, *Two Nations,* 24.

55. Yuval, *Two Nations,* 71; the book appeared earlier in Hebrew (Alma Am Oved, 2000). Yuval's 1993 article "Vengeance and Damnation" became a building block for the book and elicited a backlash from scholars.

56. Yuval, *Two Nations,* chap. 2, esp. 72–76. For the reference to myrrh, see Mark 15:23; Matthew 27:34 refers to "wine mixed with gall."

57. Yuval, *Two Nations,* 33.

58. Ivan G. Marcus, *Rituals of Childhood: Jewish Culture and Acculturation in the Middle Ages* (Yale University Press, 1996); and "A Jewish-Christian Symbiosis: The Culture of Early Ashkenaz," in *Cultures of the Jews: A New History,* ed. David Biale (Schocken, 2002), 448–516.

59. Marcus, *Rituals of Childhood,* 4–5.

60. Marcus, *Rituals of Childhood,* 5.

61. Marcus, "A Jewish-Christian Symbiosis," 492.

62. Ephraim Shoham-Steiner, "The Virgin Mary, Miriam, and Jewish Reactions to Marian Devotion in the High Middle Ages," *AJS Review* 37 (2013): 77.

63. Marc Michael Epstein, *The Medieval Haggadah: Art, Narrative, and Religious Imagination* (Yale University Press, 2010), 197–98, 248.

64. Karen Blough, "Adoption, Adaptation, and Subversion of Christian Motifs in the First Darmstadt Haggadah," *Journal of the Early Book Society for the Study of Manuscripts and Printing History* 23 (online, 2020).

65. Marcus, *Rituals of Childhood,* 15; "A Jewish-Christian Symbiosis," 492.

66. Jeremy Cohen, *Sanctifying the Name of God: Jewish Martyrs and Jewish Memories of the First Crusade* (University of Pennsylvania Press, 2006), 41.

67. Cohen, *Sanctifying the Name of God,* 56.

68. Cohen, *Sanctifying the Name of God,* see chap. 2, esp. 43–50.

69. Cohen, *Sanctifying the Name of God,* chap. 6, quote on p. 121.

70. Yitzhak Baer, "'A Social and Religious History of the Jews': Comments on S. Baron's New Book" [Hebrew] *Zion* 3 (1938): 277–99; henceforth, "Review of Baron's SRHJ."

71. Baron, *Social and Religious History* 1: 307–8.

72. For a recent study of the revolt, see Oren Kessler, *Palestine 1936: The Great Revolt and the Roots of the Middle East Conflict* (Rowman & Littlefield, 2023).

73. Baer, "Review of Baron's SRHJ," 288–89.

74. Baer, "Review of Baron's SRHJ," 288–89.

75. *The Jews of Islam* (Princeton University Press, 2014), xiii–xiv.

DIFFERENCE AND VIOLENCE   161

76. Mark Cohen, "Islam and the Jews: Myth, Counter-Myth, History," in *Jews among Muslims: Communities in the Precolonial Middle East*, ed. Shlomo Deshen and Walter P. Zenner (Palgrave Macmillan UK, 1996).

77. See for example, S. D. Goitein, *Jews and Arabs: Their Contacts through the Ages* (Schocken, 1955), and his multivolume work based on the Geniza that began to be published in 1967: *A Mediterranean Society: The Jewish Communities of the Arab World as Portrayed in the Documents of the Cairo Geniza* (6 vols.; University of California Press, 1967–1993).

78. Mark R. Cohen, *Under Crescent and Cross: The Jews in the Middle Ages* (Princeton University Press, 1994).

79. Nirenberg, *Communities of Violence: Persecution of Minorities in the Middle Ages* (Princeton University Press, 1996), 245.

80. Nirenberg, *Communities of Violence*, ix.

81. Nirenberg, *Communities of Violence*, chap. 7.

82. Nirenberg, *Communities of Violence*, 7.

83. Jeremy Cohen, *The Friars and the Jews: A Study in the Development of Medieval Anti-Judaism* (Cornell University Press, 1982); Marcus, *Rituals of Childhood*; Yuval, *Two Nations*.

84. Nirenberg, *Communities of Violence*, 231.

85. Nirenberg, *Communities of Violence*, 245.

86. Nirenberg, *Communities of Violence*, 68.

87. Baron, "Ghetto and Emancipation," 517.

88. Tzafrir Barzilay, *Poisoned Wells: Accusations, Persecution, and Minorities in Medieval Europe, 1321–1422* (University of Pennsylvania Press, 2022), 2–3.

89. Rowan Dorin, *No Return: Jews, Christian Usurers, and the Spread of Mass Expulsion in Medieval Europe* (Princeton University Press, 2023); Robert Chazan, *Refugees or Migrants: Pre-Modern Jewish Population Movement* (Yale University Press, 2018).

90. Dorin, *No Return*, 4.

91. For example, Dorin, *No Return*, 5.

92. Dorin, *No Return*, 9–10.

93. Baron, "Ghetto and Emancipation," 526.

94. See, for example, the editor's preface in Zunz, *Suffering of the Jews*.

7

Piety and Knowledge

Maoz Kahana, Tel Aviv University

The Heritage of the First Millennium

Torah Study

In the beginning was the Talmud, and its words were nearly all. Since the second century CE and perhaps even earlier, Jews have woven together book with desire. This desire, sparked by the commandment obligating the study of Torah ("Talmud Torah"), served as a democratic directive that challenged traditional priestly authority, inviting every qualified individual to pursue comprehensive knowledge. Unlike the quest for divine revelation or the affirmation of dogma found in Gnostic circles and ecclesiastical synods, and unlike the apocalyptic interpretations of scriptures as sought by Jewish ascetics in the Judean desert and the early church fathers, Talmud Torah was designed as a distinct, more ambiguous call.

In this sense, what does "Torah" mean?

Torah emerges not only as a book but also as a profound idea, with the idea being essentially greater than any book. The idea is "thou shalt ponder therein day and night" (Josh 1:8, TB Menachot 99:2), encapsulating a longing imbued with *eros*—a complete immersion in divine wisdom. The book, as becomes clear, extends beyond the biblical Torah (engaged in by both Judean desert sects and early Christians): It has centered, since the sixth to eight centuries CE, on the Talmud. Yet, the commandment and the longing it inspires transcend, by their very nature, any single text, fostering the creation of new interpretations across the generations.

The permanent pondering commanded by the Torah inspires expectations and passions greater than the text or the commandments, and the divine text, as an embodiment of the transcendental idea, becomes an expectation for God: divine in its essence, rich and sophisticated in its ways of expression, with guid-

PIETY AND KNOWLEDGE   163

ance for precise normative performance (halakhah) while simultaneously mirroring the divine and the wondrous nature of the word and the world. Can a single text survive all such desires? In other words, what are the several paradigms of Talmud Torah that have been generated by Jewish scholarly cultures across the millennia? Which books might emerge from this internal logic, the pondering act, and how?

The Talmud and Its Limitless Edges

What, then, is the Talmud? Its foundation lies in the *mishnayot*—a collection of concise legal texts with a poetic tone, compiled in the Land of Israel during the second and third centuries, spanning sixty tractates. These texts, along with similar collections from around the same time, fueled sophisticated scholarly discussions in study centers (*yeshivot*) across the Land of Israel and Babylon from the third to the end of the sixth century. The culmination of these debates led to the creation of two Talmuds: the Jerusalem Talmud (the Yerushalmi, edited in the Land of Israel) and the Babylonian Talmud (the Bavli, debated and edited in several areas of today's Iraq). The latter gained primacy, partly because of the sustained cultural and economic influence of the Jewish community in its region of origin, under Sassanian rule that, after the seventh-century Arab conquest, became a central hub of the Muslim caliphate. These talmudic texts were the cornerstone documents of this learned culture, whose leaders—the Geonim, heads of two esteemed academies—held supreme authority in the Jewish world toward the end of the first millennium CE.

Beyond its sociological aspects, the Talmud's phenomenology is remarkable. It is a monumental collective work spanning hundreds of years, with hundreds of contributors whose voices are embedded in it. This structured talmudic discourse was orally transmitted for longer than five centuries. Its style of discourse is equally unique: Despite the lengthy editing process, the Talmud retained an argumentative dialogic nature that is integral to the text to the extent that it invites, and even compels, diligent readers to continue its narrative threads. In this sense, the Talmud was crafted in the complex and unique format of an "unfinished book" by design. This concept continued from the manuscript era into the age of print, even as dense columns of commentary surrounded its pages. Many Talmud commentators (such as the medieval Rashi and the Tosafists, followed by their multitude of successors) throughout the second millennium continued to expand on the conceptual framework the Talmud laid over Jewish life.[1] The Talmud's "flawed"—dialogic and thus unfinished—nature can be seen as a key factor in its unparalleled intellectual dominance among learned Jewish communities for the next millennium. In an era when the Ecclesia leaned toward dogma, the Synagoga sanctified the Hebrew letter and word, emerging from biblical texts to midrashic and talmudic realms to create a multifaceted interpretive culture that sparked a multigenerational choir.[2]

The Babylonian era did not last forever. The dawn of the second millennium witnessed the rise of new Jewish centers in Andalusia, the Mediterranean coast, and Central Europe. This geographical and cultural shift gave rise to novel literary genres. This chapter explores four such genres: two from the Middle Ages and two from the early modern era. These arose alongside the enduring power of talmudic culture and scholarship, which continued to evolve simultaneously.

Beyond the Talmud: Mysticism and Reason
Intertwined in the Middle Ages

Jewish philosophy and Kabbalah emerged as distinct genres in the Middle Ages, evolving independently from the realms of talmudic literature. The former is exemplified by Maimonides' *Guide for the Perplexed*, a twelfth-century work from Egypt, whereas the Zohar, a thirteenth-century Spanish compilation, stands as a seminal example of the latter. Earlier scholarship often depicted these three libraries as competing one with another. Kabbalah was seen as a semi-heretical gnosis, a rebellion against the legalistic and "formal" religion embodied by the Talmud. Jewish philosophy, conversely, was perceived as adversarial to both, championing a rational, universally reasoned future steeped in Aristotelianism. Contemporary research, however, portrays a different picture. This discussion explores the unique characteristics of each domain and their interrelationships, starting with Kabbalah and philosophical literature, moving to halakhah, and culminating with a return to the Talmud.

Gershom Scholem originally attributed the Zohar's authorship to the kabbalist R. Moses de Leon (d. circa 1305), placing this pivotal esoteric text within the cultural and historical milieu of thirteenth-century Spain. Recent scholarship has challenged this assertion. For instance, Yehuda Liebes proposed that the Zohar was the collective work of several authors, with de Leon as a significant contributor.[3] This theory of collaborative authorship highlights the Zohar's diverse voices, aligning it more closely with talmudic culture.[4] Liebes also noted the Zohar's covert dialogue with contemporary Christianity, the predominant faith in medieval Spain, and identified traces of pseudo-Clementine literature from early Judeo-Christian sects in the Zoharic literature more than a millennium after its emergence. Ronit Meroz and Daniel Abrams further complicated the Zohar's origins. Through philological analysis of numerous manuscripts, they argued that the Zohar is not the work of two generations (R. Moses de Leon and a student, as Scholem suggested) but a vast tapestry of fragments. Some predate de Leon, whereas others postdate him, challenging the conventional understanding of the Zohar as a singular coherent text. Instead, it is now seen as a dynamic corpus, evolving over centuries and encompassing influences ranging from late antique materials[5] and pseudo-Clementine texts,[6] to writings from eleventh-century Israel and fourteenth-century Spanish court culture.[7] The role of printers in Mantua and Cremona in editing the text has also gained prominence in recent scholarship.[8]

Recent trends in Zohar research have also diminished the once clear distinction between "esoteric" and "normative" knowledge. Israel Ta-Shma's groundbreaking study,[9] for example, uses references to halakhah and custom within Zoharic literature as a means to infer its location of composition and the identities of its authors. Ta-Shma posits that the Zohar's halakhic elements, which are heavily influenced by Maimonidean thought, indicate a thirteenth-century Spanish origin. In contrast, the customs reflected in the text suggest connections to an earlier period and to Ashkenazi traditions. He attributes the "Ashkenaz" components of the Zohar to R. Judah from Girundi (d. 1263). Ta-Shma's Ashkenazi Zohar hypothesis has elicited sharp criticism.[10] Nevertheless, his focus on integrating halakhah and custom, intertwined in Zoharic literature, has challenged the long-standing rigid dichotomy between *nomos* and *gnosis* in scholarly discourse. Other researchers have explored the Zohar's midrashic aspects, illuminating from a literary perspective its continuity with the homiletic literature (Midrash) from the talmudic era and beyond.[11]

Conversely, the works of Yehuda Liebes and Moshe Idel have shed light on the mythical elements deeply embedded in this homiletic literature, dating from the early first millennium. This perspective diverges from the Wissenschaft des Judentums approach, which portrayed the Talmud as a rational compilation of semi-philosophical beliefs, reflecting dominant nineteenth-century German trends.[12] In contrast, the detailed analyses by Liebes and Idel have revealed the mythic potency in the talmudic and midrashic conceptions of God and the divine. Their work posits that the talmudic era might represent the pinnacle of Jewish myth, whereas the systematic Ten Sefirot, integral to interpreting Zoharic literature, embodies a form of medieval rationalization (!) of these earlier, enigmatic rabbinic myths.[13]

In summary, research scholarship has established that the Zohar is inherently talmudic in nature, as evident in its diversity of voices, writing times, locations, editing processes, and engagement with the world of halakhah and law. Similarly, the Talmud is increasingly perceived as Zoharic, with a renewed emphasis on its hidden traditions. This reunion between Zoharic literature and the Talmud is noteworthy, because the Zohar, like the Talmud, is characterized as an unfinished, multilayered, and polyphonic paradigm characterized by an ongoing dialogue.

Regarding philosophy, the "rational rival" of esoteric literature, research has highlighted esoteric elements in the *Guide for the Perplexed*[14] and in its unique reception history: Access was often restricted to those deeply familiar with the Talmud and subsequent halakhic literature.[15] Interestingly, the most enduring and influential adaptations of this philosophical genre may reside within Zoharic literature itself. A comprehensive philological examination shows that medieval Zoharic layers incorporated concepts, terms, and arguments from the *Guide* into their framework, legitimizing them while simultaneously constraining their scope within a more sophisticated structure.[16] Reflecting—not merely consciously—this complexity, early modern readers of the *Guide* frequently integrated its teachings with Kabbalistic streams, buoyed by the widely accepted belief in the Renaissance era that "Kabbalah and philosophy are theologically synonymous, merely articulated in two languages."[17] Thus, one might expect a set of texts that express the same ideas in different formats, which may point to their source of inspiration as divine.

Embodied Wisdom: Bodily Paths to the Sublime

Alongside recontextualizing Zoharic literature in time and space, there has been a reevaluation of its role within the broader Kabbalistic heritage spanning the first and second millennia. Moshe Idel, in a series of groundbreaking studies, highlighted the lasting impact of a distinct Kabbalistic stream: the prophetic-ecstatic Kabbalah developed by R. Abraham Abulafia (d. 1291). Emerging concurrently with the Zohar in Spain,[18] this form of Kabbalah is characterized by its experiential emphasis and its techniques such as measured breathing and the meditative use of letter sounds, in contrast to the interpretive-theosophical nature of Zoharic Kabbalah. Idel demonstrated this stream's enduring influence on various mystical movements, ranging from the sixteenth-century Safed Kabbalists to Sabbateanism and Hasidism in subsequent centuries. The study of these streams and their diverse Kabbalistic syntheses has significantly expanded, offering a broad panorama of Kabbalistic possibilities beyond a singular Zoharic "canon." Research into ecstatic Kabbalah has also revived interest in its earlier sources, including the Hekhalot literature. Originating in Late Antiquity, this esoteric body of work describes heavenly ascents, angelic hierarchies, and the knowledge of heavenly realms. Although it was initially overshadowed by talmudic literature, recent studies reveal its significant resurgence across generations, notably in non-Zoharic Kabbalistic movements such as the Ashkenazi Hasidim and ecstatic Kabbalah, as well as in eighteenth-century mysticism; for example, the personal magical practices of Israel Ba'al Shem Tov.[19]

The influence of ecstatic Kabbalah and the Hekhalot literature reemphasizes Kabbalah's experiential-visionary aspects and operative magical practices, beyond its conventional theological perception. This suggests an intriguing link between piety and scholarship, where the absorption of the sublime is cultivated not only through the mind (thought) and heart (understanding) but also through the body and its limbs (breath, sight). This tradition intersects with studies of a unique Egyptian pious circle, descendants of Maimonides and their disciples, who integrated study and prayer with physical practices, partly influenced by Islamic-Sufi traditions.[20]

Similarly, research into ecstatic Kabbalah, akin to contemporary studies of the Zohar, has challenged the traditional dichotomy between rationality and mysticism in the Middle Ages and beyond. Abraham Abulafia's mystical journey to prophecy, involving a deep study of Maimonides, underscores this point. Modern research highlights the *Guide*'s multifaceted impact. It influenced the Christian-majority society and appealed to both rational and mystical inclinations: In its Latin translations, the *Guide* was used at around the same time by the scholastic Thomas Aquinas and in the mystical writings of Meister Eckhart.[21]

Jews and Christians: Hebraica Veritas

The *Guide for the Perplexed* was not the only Jewish work in the Christian libraries of the late medieval period and beyond. The critique of the church by humanists, both before and after the Reformation, along with Renaissance thought, imbued the ancient life of the "Hebrews" with new relevance as a source for Christian renewal. Similarly, esoteric texts like those of Jewish Kabbalah, considered part of *prisca theologia*—an ancient and universal hidden truth—gained increased significance. A pivotal development in this intellectual trend was the advent of Christian Kabbalah: Christian engagement with Jewish Kabbalah during the Renaissance spawned a multitude of works, establishing a vibrant research field. Yehuda Liebes and Judith Weiss published the first Hebrew editions of Latin works by Christian kabbalists such as Egidio da Viterbo and Guillaume Postel.[22] This scholarly endeavor has enriched the study of a corpus in which Jewish Kabbalah is a significant facet of the Christian Renaissance.[23] One crucial insight from this research raises a new question: Even though Christian Kabbalah was founded on "ancient" Jewish Kabbalah, what was its reciprocal impact on medieval and early modern Jewish Kabbalah?[24]

Toward the end of the Middle Ages, the merging of Jewish writings with Christian scholarship was on the rise. In the intellectual milieu of the Renaissance, the "Jewish letter" took on renewed importance for the "Christian spirit" in various fields. Hermetic philosophers revitalized ancient texts ascribed to Hermes Trismegistus, finding parallels in the concealed truths of Jewish Kabbalistic doctrine. Soon thereafter, emerging political science viewed the ancient "Hebrew Republic" as a model for contemporary political thought, advocating for the revival and reconstruction of its alleged principles.[25] Concurrently, humanist philologists examined a range of ancient sources to address issues fundamental to the interpretation, refinement, and historical critique of the Christian truths they possessed.[26] Inquiries such as the exact date of Jesus's crucifixion according to the Hebrew calendar of the first century, the accuracy of Jerome's fourth-century Vulgate translation, and the shape of the matzah at the historical Last Supper (round or square?[27]) were all introspective questions relevant to Christianity's self-understanding. *Hebraica veritas*, the Jewish truth, thus acted as an intellectual conduit linking distinct cultures of learning from that era.

The Early Modern Period: Two Safedian Revolutions

The Middle Ages were notable for introducing two distinct scholarly vocabularies to rabbinic scholarship: the philosophical, influenced by Aristotle, and the Kabbalistic, with a Neoplatonic orientation. In contrast, the Renaissance is characterized by the fusion of these vocabularies and the concurrent expansion of the Hebrew printed book into new realms of popular knowledge. This expansion introduced scholarly writing in history, science, and Greco-Roman mythology to the public domain of rabbinic Hebrew readers.[28] (Further discussion of this latter topic is beyond the scope of this chapter.)

The sixteenth century witnessed two seminal scholarly revolutions that would profoundly shape Jewish modernity and its scholarship for centuries to come. Both emerged from the quaint town of Safed in the Galilee and radiated out to Jewish communities throughout Europe and the Ottoman Empire. These movements fostered new methodologies of study and avenues for creative expression. Our exploration begins with Lurianic Kabbalah and proceeds to Rabbi Joseph Caro's formulation of the normative canon.

Spiritual Pursuit in Tangible Galilee

Rabbi Isaac Luria, known as the Ari (d. 1572), resided in Safed for less than two years. His literary legacy is confined to just three short poems, designed for recitation during Sabbath meals. In the years that followed, under his influence, his disciples in Safed authored thousands of pages of intricate Kabbalistic doctrines. Even before Luria, Safed was a hub for various Kabbalistic circles, with Rabbi Moses Cordovero (the Ramak, d. 1570) leading one of the most notable ones. Collectively, these groups formed what is now acknowledged as Safed Kabbalah. During the sixteenth century, this movement significantly elevated and sanctified the Zohar, which had been largely confined within the cultural bounds of Sephardic Judaism, until its widespread diffusion was catalyzed by the intellectual upheaval after the expulsion of Jews from Iberian territories. From the perspective of reception history, it was Safed Kabbalah that canonized the Iberian Zohar for subsequent generations. At the same time, Safed Kabbalah was distinguished by its own creative vitality, presenting rabbinic Hebrew readers with vivid portrayals of detailed celestial domains never known before.

Contrasting with the long-standing Jewish scholarly tradition focused on the written letter and diverging from the Shulchan Arukh of the same era that melded a universe of words,[29] contemporary scholarship accentuates the decisive role that the Galilean landscape played in nurturing Safed Kabbalah. The Kabbalists of Safed immersed themselves in both the physical and spiritual terrains of Galilee, believed to be the fountainhead of Zoharic literature. Through mystical practices—such as seeking spontaneous utterances amid the natural environs of Galilee or performing meditative unifications (*yihudim*) at the physical graves of Zoharic luminaries—they endeavored to tap into the tangible landscape to unlock the esoteric wisdom chronicled in the Zohar. These pursuits were directed toward literary ends: to interpret and systematize the disparate sections of the Zohar into a coherent anthology (as accomplished by the Ramak in his multivolume work *Or Yakar*) and to forge a trailblazing hermeneutic for contemporary Zoharic exposition (as pioneered by the Ari).

The material and visual elements that shaped the celestial secrets within Lurianic Kabbalah have led research scholarship to pay attention to the professional-alchemical syntax in the writings of Rabbi Hayyim Vital. As a disciple of the Ari and a skilled silversmith and goldsmith, Vital's oeuvre reflects a distinctive integration of craftsmanship vocabulary and theories into the Lurianic conceptualization of the cosmos.[30] Subsequent research has revealed the profound influence of Vital's medical education on Lurianic Kabbalah, particularly his engagement with the integrative and holistic tendencies of sixteenth-century Ottoman medicine, as Tamari detailed. Medical discourse of that era, especially regarding pregnancy and nursing, deeply informed the foundational terms of Lurianic Kabbalah.[31]

Zohar and Eros

Embodying its medieval heritage, Zoharic literature was distinguished by a creative glow—an *ars poetica* preoccupied with the nature of creativity, which scholars have termed "eros," representing the vigor and creative power of life.[32] In the Zoharic age, this creativity was primarily channeled into interpreting established halakhic details.[33] Yet, the Lurianic syntax that emerged, which was dominant for the next three centuries, transformed Kabbalistic language into a medium for crafting rituals—from the creation of the Kabbalat Shabbat service to issuing new, precise guidelines for birth and death ceremonies and even for extreme practices like flagellation.[34] This celestial scholarship produced a potent performative syntax, reshaping various facets of Jewish thought and practice in the modern era across prayer, liturgy, poetry, theology, ritual, and halakhah. The interplay between this innovative ritualistic creativity and the more conventional halakhic structures is explored in research as "Kabbalah and halakhah," with significant contributions to this discourse.[35] However, this interplay might serve as an optical illusion, because these frictions are just the surface of a more extensive creative process in which the Lurianic vocabulary in the Baroque period evolved into an all-encompassing conceptual framework. This framework enabled the creation of new rituals and the nuanced interpretation, "correction," and refinement of traditional practices. It also facilitated the incorporation of daily secular practices, such as drinking coffee or smoking tobacco, into a sacred cosmic enterprise.[36] This Lurianic paradigm also served as an intellectual key to unlocking an array of new realms—from history[37] to the exploration of cultural and natural landscapes[38] to the depths of the individual's soul, as highlighted in some branches of eighteenth-century Hasidism.[39]

Most of the adaptations of the Lurianic school to nomian practice were found in the majority groups of Jewish society,[40] but some of the more creative ones were designed by members of the Hasidic circle of Nathan of Gaza.[41] The Hasidic turn by the disciples of the Ba'al Shem Tov in the late eighteenth century can be seen equally as an additional emphasis within this long-lasting Lurianic syntax and as its refinement and narrowing for the sake of a more direct, less mediated connection with the divine.[42]

This ritual language is characterized by significant popular power. However, the Lurianic ethos also shaped the Zoharic eros concurrently into more elitist study paths. In the eighteenth century, *kloyzen* (from the German *Klaus*)—closed study groups dealing intensively with talmudic and Lurianic texts—spread throughout Europe. They often served as an elitist breeding ground for non-consensus strands in rabbinic scholarship, such as scientific investigation and Sabbatean theology that flourished in these academic bubbles and served as a cultural bridge to such inclinations in the contemporary scholarly world.[43]

I already mentioned the physical or ritual-performative manifestations of the Zoharic and post-Zoharic kabbalistic ethos and the more theoretical, theosophical formations, but the Zoharic eros was also carved into a third path—a personal one. In this path the revered figure of Rabbi Shimon bar Yochai (the all-encompassing sage who stands at the center of Zoharic literature) served as a source for personal imitation and, at times, for the claim of soul transmigration (*gilgul*) to later sages. The personal identification with Rabbi Shimon bar Yochai is prominent in the writings of the Ramak and the Ari, and in parallel in the creation of Rabbi Joseph Caro's *Magid Meisharim*, written in the guise of Zoharic language. In subsequent generations, this mimesis is evident in a long line of creators from the Sabbatean prophet Nathan of Gaza to the Kabbalist Rabbi Naftali Bacharach and up to Rabbi Moshe Chaim Luzzatto (in works such as *Zohar Tinyana* and *Tikunim Hadashim*). Creative mimesis of this kind can even be found in the writings of the twentieth-century kabbalist Rabbi Yehuda Leib Ashlag.

The combination of the various studies that surveyed parts of these phenomena[44] allows us to observe how, alongside the textual scholarship that flourished at that time, the individual self served as a ground for experience and investigation. Since Montaigne, the self has been a fundamental component in early modern culture. In our field, in particular, the mimetic identification with the soul of an ancient sage—not only Rabbi Shimon bar Yochai but also prophets like Ezekiel and Jeremiah, as occurred at the beginning of Hasidism, and with the Ari himself in other cases—provided both support and impetus for unbounded creativity. To summarize: The personal study room of the rabbi or the generic *beit midrash* (house of study) were not the only places of shaping Jewish learning culture in the early modern era. The closed European *kloyzen*, the open fields of Galilee, and the agency of the individual-mimetic self represent different ends of a network of sites where knowledge was created and acquired.[45]

All this occurred simultaneously with another Safed revolution.

A Universe Made of Words

Rabbi Joseph Caro (d. 1575) introduced his monumental legal works *Beit Yosef* and the Shulchan Arukh to his readers of his time and to the Jewish world. These multivolume texts, completed in the city of Safed and printed in Venice from the 1550s to the 1560s, reflected the innovations of the sixteenth-century commercial printing industry. Recent studies have emphasized how this industry influenced Caro's vision for his work and its universal scope.[46] The innovation of printing was just one of the many factors that fostered the creation of comprehensive and universal knowledge during this period. Other research has situated the Shulchan Arukh within its intellectual environment, given the advent of censorship after the Council of Trent in Europe and the establishment of the centralized judicial authority, the Shaykh al-Islam, in the Ottoman Empire.[47] Further studies have delved into the mystical and cosmological aspects of Rabbi Joseph Caro's thoughts, which were particularly influenced by the Zohar, and his utopian concepts of knowledge, law, and canon. In this view, the meticulous organization of legal sources in *Beit Yosef* materializes a utopian vision of a cosmological Kabbalistic unification (*yihudim*), achieved by harmonizing diverse legal sources within a singular framework. The private, inner life of Rabbi Joseph Caro, a Kabbalist who experienced significant spiritual tension as evidenced in his diary *Magid Meisharim*, played a crucial role in his legislative work.[48]

After the expulsion from Spain in 1492, Jewish traditions from various regions converged and clashed in new territories. *Beit Yosef* and the Shulchan Arukh provided both settled and displaced Jewish communities a new home (*bayit*), an extensive legal canon that integrated the halakhic cultures of Ashkenazim and Sephardim from diverse cultural regions into a single, universal legal system: "one law for all Israel."[49] The Safedian movement profoundly influenced the Jewish scholarly world for centuries.

A Labyrinth Emerges: Complexities of a Legal Canon

Rabbi Joseph Caro bequeathed an extensive literary-halakhic universe to his disciples: *Kesef Mishneh* (his commentary on Maimonides' code of law), *Beit Yosef*, and Shulchan Arukh are multivolume works, abundant in details. These

PIETY AND KNOWLEDGE 173

three texts overlap in halakhic content and were composed during concurrent periods. Over the centuries the intricate details of Rabbi Caro's writings have gained canonical status. This exceptional halakhic authority, however, as often occurs, sharply exposed the fissures within this grand structure—the ambiguities, challenges, inconsistencies, and even blatant contradictions among these works and within the texts themselves.

Proficient in the Jewish-Spanish tradition of general principles and decision-making rules, Rabbi Caro authored *Klaley Hagmara*, a treatise on resolving ambiguities among talmudic opinions. However, he left no systematic method for solving such complexities in his own texts. How are we to decide between two contradictory opinions (typically under the heading "Some say") presented side by side in the Shulchan Arukh? About two thousand (!) such "unclosed" places stand out in the book, resembling unconnected edges that testify to the utopian hubris described in the previous paragraph—the unification of all legal sources—and, simultaneously, to its limitations.[50]

The contradictions and inherent ambiguities in the legal corpus are not merely problems: They also represent rich intellectual opportunities for many commentators (often referred to as *nosey-hakelim*) and decisors (like the expansive "responsa literature" makers) in subsequent centuries. These scholars used the gaps within the canon as a maneuvering tool, providing them with interpretive space and dynamism to meet their needs as "clients" of this new literary universe.[51] In this sense, the incomprehensible complexity of this legal universe was and still is an important part of the relevance of *Beit Yosef* and the Shulchan Arukh as dynamic knowledge resources rich in possibilities.

The pioneer in navigating this universe was Rabbi Moses Isserles (d. 1572) of the Krakow community. His systematic glosses to *Beit Yosef* and the Shulchan Arukh offered their readers an "Ashkenazi" correction to the "Sephardic" tendency evident in the cultural biases of Rabbi Caro, a native of Spain who lived since the expulsion in the Ottoman lands. The sizable urban Jewish communities of Poland, whose voice Isserles expressed, formed the backdrop of the rabbinic authority that he expressed. In response, his scholarly-halakhic enterprise sought to express the deep loyalty of the urban community of Polish Jews to the cultural heritage it revered, which encompassed community customs, as well as knowledge and methodology: the Central European ethos established by the French Tosafists and the German Ashkenazi decisors of the Middle Ages. Yet, a deeper look into the glosses of Isserles reveals that many of the materials he raised against Caro are taken from *Beit Yosef* itself, which includes a wealth of Sephardic opinions! Against Caro's prominent aspiration to close or at least tighten the legal panorama, Isserles stands out in opening this panorama using opinions pushed to the margins—from Ashkenazi and Sephardi sources alike. Editions of the Shulchan Arukh since 1580 have been printed with the words of Caro and Isserles intertwined—and the result is a rich and unfinished legal paradigm, speaking in more than one voice.[52]

This dynamic legal paradigm opened avenues for varied and diverse interpretations and applications. For instance, *Knesset Hagedolah*, authored by Rabbi Haim Benveniste (d. 1663) in Izmir, sought to augment the legal corpus by diligently documenting additional halakhic materials that were not previously included. This "informative"-oriented Sephardic approach continued in the writings of Sephardic scholars such as Rabbi Chaim Yosef David Azulai, known as Hida (d. 1806), and its influence can be traced up to Rabbi Ovadia Yosef (d. 2013) in our time. However, as early as the seventeenth century yeshivot in Poland used the Shulchan Arukh in a very different way: In these yeshivas it replaced the Talmud as the source text for student inquiry and debate.

The Infinite Nomian Fractal: Jewish Legal Traditions and the Quest for Infinite Wisdom

The term *pilpul* collectively referred to various study methods that were not confined to a singular, "realistic" (interpretive or halakhic) result from the talmudic text but rather aimed to evolve and enhance it into new philosophical and theoretical horizons. Pilpul was a powerful demonstration of intellectual vigor and brilliantly showcased a blend of independent innovation born from rigid structural demands for interpretation. In Spain a distinctive method of pilpul was developed in the yeshiva of Rabbi Isaac Canpanton (d. 1463), employing terms from Aristotelian logic (through the mediation of Averroes) as a tool for a sophisticated interpretation of talmudic topics well beyond the existing text. In Ashkenaz in the sixteenth century, pilpul techniques that used a collection of hypothetical assumptions refined the basic talmudic topic into stunning and virtuosic structures. This aesthetic technique played a central part in the daily yeshiva curriculum in Ashkenaz, its social structure, and enhancing the status of the rabbi—the head of the yeshiva—who demonstrated his power using pilpul but was simultaneously challenged by his adept students who could offer their independently conceived, sophisticated solutions to the topic within a discussion framework unencumbered by past interpretive traditions.[53] This unprecedented *hidush* (Torah innovation) granted a supreme value and a coveted scholarly passion to this environment.

PIETY AND KNOWLEDGE   175

A hundred and fifty years later, in Polish territories, books like *Sefer Meirat Einayim* (by Rabbi Joshua Falk, d. 1614) and *Siftei Cohen* (by Rabbi Shabtai Cohen, d. 1663) offered to historical scholarship the literary fruits of a turning point in which the complex text of the Shulchan Arukh became a new locus for the yeshiva students' pilpul—incisive study that probed words and concepts, continually yielding innovative insights for fresh legal determinations.[54] This new cultural trend swiftly added dense layers of additional interpretation to the Shulchan Arukh, refashioning what may have seemed as a closed canon of decisive halakhah back into an open text meant for discussion, rather than precise guidance. Many such layers later found their way to printed versions of the Shulchan Arukh, surrounding its words (placed at the heart and center of each page), while raising questions resulting from its text and questioning its rulings. In this context, Rabbi Jonathan Eybeschutz (d. 1764) made a fascinating claim:

> Everything was inscribed by the hand of God through them [Rabbis Caro and Isserles]. For many difficulties that the later commentators have questioned about [the Shulchan Aruch] and resolved in sharp and profound ways. And likewise, they [Caro and Isserles] included in the sweetness and brevity of their tongue many unknown laws. And there is no doubt that they did not intend to include all of that [unknown laws] ... only the spirit of God fluttered in their midst for their tongue to be directed without the writer's intention.[55]

Thus, according to Eybeschutz, the Shulchan Arukh, perceived as the collaborative work of Rabbis Caro and Isserles, was not intended by its authors to encompass all the interpretations that have been attributed to it. The authoritative legitimacy granted to these myriad innovations is rooted in the insight that the true authors of the Shulchan Arukh are not merely the human scribes but God. At this moment the Shulchan Arukh became revered as a text of almost biblical stature, its divine inspiration enabling its words to flourish beyond any specific intent.

The passage of time is mirrored in the creative genre of , *ha-kelim*, the commentators of the Shulchan Arukh. A conceptual shift, evident in the nineteenth century, led to the distillation of themes from the Talmud and the Shulchan Arukh, enabling them to transcend their somewhat "material" concreteness and the confines of their textual context and propelling them into a realm of abstract thought. The novel conceptual turn inspired such projects to draw on a variety of texts to forge increasingly theoretical and analytical constructs. Pioneers of this intellectual movement are exemplified by works such as *Ketzot Hachoshen*, which provides a conceptual interpretation of the Choshen Mishpat section of the Shulchan Arukh, and *Minhat Hinukh*, ostensibly a nineteenth-century commentary on the thirteenth-century *Sefer Hahinukh*, which presents a halakhic-conceptual mindset in an innovative literary form, reflecting similar intellectual endeavors.[56] The apex of this conceptual turn can be seen manifested in the influential writings of Rabbi Chaim Soloveitchik of Brisk (d. 1918) on Maimonides' *Mishneh Torah*. Rabbi Aryeh Leib Heller (d. 1812, author of *Ketzot Hachoshen*) captured this innovative approach with an allusion to the Zohar, suggesting that scholarly Torah innovations allow humankind to create "new heavens and new earths" (based on Isa 65:17) perhaps even when they may not align with the "initial" divine intention. Subsequently, scholars drew parallels between this scholarly school and the Kantian concept of *a priori*, where halakhic ideas exist autonomously, independent of their physical manifestations.[57]

Meanwhile, contrasting with this enchanted celestial creativity, there were those who yearned for a more grounded orientation. By the mid-eighteenth century a pendulum movement initiated a paradigmatic return to the ancient "sea of the Talmud." In this robust movement, which initially challenged venerable halakhic traditions, key figures, such as Rabbi Yechezkel Landau of Prague and Rabbi Eliyahu Kremer, the Vilna Gaon, advocated for a uniquely Jewish *sola scriptura* approach: a direct derivation of law from the Talmud itself. Other scholars sought more direct, unmediated interpretations of talmudic discussions, bypassing its traditional exegetes.[58] Soon after, this deconstructive process marginalized not just the authority of *nosey ha-kelim* but also the decisions of the Shulchan Arukh itself, shifting the cultural focus from this sixteenth-century canon toward the potency of original texts manifested by ancient sources. In this climate, the Talmud, like the Leviathan from the depths of the sea, re-emerged from the vast ocean of interpretations, unsettling the stability of its intermediaries who had navigated a millennium of extensive interpretive labor and wealth.

Such a dynamic phase confronts us with enduring tensions filled with possibilities and questions, marking the essence of a living culture. This insight presents an opportune moment to pause our exploration and reflect, and so impart the sense of a perpetual scholarly quest that is endless by its very nature.

To Conclude

In the middle of the nineteenth century, it was possible to observe various forms of folk societies in Jewish communities in thousands of small towns (*shtetlach*) from Eastern Europe to the Balkans. Hevrat Tehilim (psalm societies) convened for the communal recitation of Psalms, and Hevrat Mishniot gathered for the study of the Mishnah. Societies dedicated to Talmud study emerged alongside Ein Yaakov societies, which focused on compiling talmudic legends, and Chayei Adam societies centered around a popular halakhic codex published in the early nineteenth century. Women also established numerous women's societies, where they predominantly discussed legends or recited Psalms together.[59] Consequently, Talmud Torah was characterized by broader, more diverse, and notably more popular engagement than the sophisticated intellectual movements explored in our earlier discussions. Before engaging in their daily routines, elderly Jews committed to recite Hok LeYisrael (a compilation of verses, mishnayot, and Zoharic passages organized according to the weekly Torah portion) each morning. Others convened beside the warmth of a stove on winter Shabbatot to delve into the weekly Torah portion through *Or Hachaim* (Rabbi Haim ben Atar's Kabbalistic commentary on the Pentateuch). This enduring cycle of recitation and spiritual enthusiasm markedly differed from the conceptual innovations reviewed here, showcasing a deeply rooted, communal religious life seemingly far removed from abstract intellectual discourse.

Yet between these contrasting poles, strong connections indeed existed: Or Hachaim, for example, ultimately showcased the potential of Lurianic Kabbalah to offer a framework for an original, profound interpretation of the Pentateuch in the eighteenth century. "Ein Yaakov" was merely a folk adaptation of the Babylonian Talmud legends, yet the Talmud itself continued to be a subject of both folk and elitist study. Similarly, the Chayei Adam societies and the hundreds of Mishnah Berurah societies that emerged following the publication of this popular halakhic work at the end of the nineteenth century ultimately provided the most updated interpretations for the Shulchan Arukh, aiming (both in their respective times) to assimilate all their predecessor *nosey ha-kelim* into an additional "final" ruling framework. These popular trends were thus inherently linked both to the annual cycle, as manifested in the ancient ritual of weekly Torah readings, and to the evolution of new literary vocabularies, spanning a millennium, as discussed here.

This chapter has offered a bird's-eye view of the gradual creation of three literary universes, each distinct yet interconnected. The first, talmudic literature, unfolds in a fractal-like manner, continuously expanding its exploration of the Jewish world and its many facets. Zoharic literature, the second, aims to capture the glow of the upper worlds, in between the revealed and the concealed. Lastly, halakhic literature, with the Shulchan Arukh and *Beit Yosef* at its heart, turns to subjects—individuals and communities—for the precise execution of Jewish law.

Talmudic and Zoharic literature are collective works by nature. Their multiplicity of voices was inherent to their ongoing vitality. The canon of law created by Rabbi Yosef Caro began its journey with a utopian aspiration to make the transition from multiplicity to unity. Yet it too eventually mirrored the complexities of the universes that preceded it. Divine inspiration, simultaneously, flows from the Pentateuch through the Talmud and Zohar, infusing at the end the halakhic writings with esoteric motivations and a celestial load.

These literary traditions have deeply influenced Jewish culture, becoming foundational texts for scholarly study and spawning countless interpretations and imitations. Over the millennia, these literary universes have been shaped and explored across multiple settings and through diverse methods: from the solitude of personal study rooms to vibrant discussions in crowded study halls. Scholars meticulously analyze talmudic terms but may also engage with texts in tangible earthly realms, such as the righteous tombs in the Galilee. With mind and heart, body, and even breath (as exemplified in Abulafia's practice), they might seek the cosmic echoes that resonate within the letters.

My sincere thanks go to Yakov Z. Mayer, Yehuda Targin, and Daniel Goldman whose attention, wisdom, and substantial contributions have greatly enriched this chapter, which. also interweaves with the philosophical tapestry woven by my late friend Rabbi Adin Steinsaltz (1937–2020). May these words serve as threads lifting his soul ever higher.

Recommended Readings

Abrams, Daniel. *Kabbalistic Manuscripts and Textual Theory: Methodologies of Textual Scholarship and Editorial Practice in the Study of Jewish Mysticism* (Magnes, 2013).

Bar Levav, Avriel. "Ritualisation of Jewish Life and Death in the Early Modern Period," *Leo Baeck Institute Year Book* 47 (2002): 69–82.

Dunkelgrün, Theodor. "The Christian Study of Judaism in Early Modern Europe," in *Cambridge History of Judaism,* vol. 7 (Cambridge University Press, 2017), 316–48.

Fram, Edward. *The Codification of Jewish Law on the Cusp of Modernity* (Cambridge University Press, 2022).

Halbertal, Moshe. *People of the Book: Canon, Meaning, and Authority* (Harvard University Press, 2009).

Halbertal, Moshe, and Jackie Feldman. *Concealment and Revelation: Esotericism in Jewish Thought and Its Philosophical Implications* (Princeton University Press, 2007).

Idel, Moshe, and Warren Zev Harvey, eds. *Abraham Abulafia's Esotericism: Secrets and Doubts* (De Gruyter, 2020).

Kahana, Maoz. "Cosmos and Nomos: Rabbi Joseph Karo and Shabtai Zvi as Portable Heavenly Temples," *El Prezente* 10 (2016): 143–53.

Kahana, Maoz. "Hasidic Halakhah: Reappraising the Interface of Spirit and Law" (with Ariel Evan Mayse), *AJS Review* 41 (2017): 375–408.

Kahana, Maoz. "Old Prophesies, Multiple Modernities: The Stormy Afterlife of a Medieval Pietist in Early Modern Ashkenaz," *Jewish History* 34 (2021): 233–58.

Katz, Jacob. *Divine Law in Human Hands: Case Studies in Halakhic Flexibility* (Magnes, 1998).

Reiner, Elchanan. "Beyond the Realm of the Haskalah: Changing Learning Patterns in Jewish Traditional Society," *Jahrbuch des Simon-Dubnow-Instituts* 6 (2007): 123–33.

Steinsaltz, Adin. *Reference Guide to the Talmud*, ed. Joshua Schreier (Koren, 2014).

Urbach, Efraim Elimelech, et al. *The Sages: Their Concepts and Beliefs* (Harvard University Press, 1995).

Werblowsky, R. J. Zwi. *Joseph Karo: Lawyer and Mystic* (Oxford University Press, 1962).

Notes

1. Moshe Halbertal, "Histories of the Halakha and the Appearance of Halakha" [Hebrew] *Dinei Israel* 29 (2013): 1–23, and *People of the Book*; Y. M. Ta-Shma, *Talmudic Commentary in Europe and North Africa: Literary History* [Hebrew] (Magnes, 2004); E. E. Urbach et al., *The Sages*.

2. A. Steinsaltz and A. Funkenstein, *Sociology of Ignorance* (Ministry of Safety, 1987); Yosef Dan, *On Holiness: Religion, Ethics, and Mysticism in Judaism and Other Religions* [Hebrew] (Magnes, 1997).

3. "How the Zohar Was Composed" [Hebrew] *Jerusalem Studies in Jewish Thought* (1989) 1–74; also Ronit Meroz, *Spiritual Biography of Rabbi Simeon bar Yochay: An Analysis of the Zohar's Textual Components* [Hebrew] (Bialik Institute, 2018).

4. Yakov Z. Mayer, "Rav Hamnuna and Rashbi Between Ashkenaz and Sepharad" [Hebrew], in *The Zoharic Narrative*, ed. Liebes et al. (Yad Ben Zvi, 2017), and "Crying at the Florence Baptistery Entrance—A Testimony of a Traveling Jew," *Renaissance Studies* 33 (2018): 441–57.

5. Such as *Sefer Yetzirah*; see Liebes, *Theory of the Creation of the Sefer Yetzirah* [Hebrew] (Schoken, 2001).

6. Liebes, "The Messiah of the Zohar: On R. Simeon bar Yohai as a Messianic Figure," in *Studies in the Zohar* (SUNY Press, 1993), 87–236.

7. Meroz, *Spiritual Biography*.

8. Daniel Abrams, *Kabbalistic Manuscripts and Textual Theory: Methodologies of Textual Scholarship and Editorial Practice in the Study of Jewish Mysticism* (Magnes, 2013).

9. I. M. Ta-Shma, *The Revealed in the Hidden: A Study of the Halakha in the Zohar* [Hebrew] (Hakibbutz Hameuchad, 1995).

10. Liebes, "The Zohar as a Book of Halakha" [Hebrew] *Tarbiz* 64 (1995): 581–605; see also I. M. Ta-Shma, *The Revealed in the Hidden: A Study of the Halakha in the Zohar*, Expanded ed. [Hebrew] (Hakibbutz Hameuchad, 2001).

11. See, for example, Oded Israeli, *Temple Portals: Studies in Aggadah and Midrash in the Zohar* [Hebrew] (Magnes, 2013); Liebes, "Zohar and Eros" [Hebrew] *Alpayim* 9 (1994): 67–119, and "God's Qualities" [Hebrew] *Tarbiz* 70 (2000): 51–74.

12. See, for instance, Urbach, *The Sages*.

13. See Liebes, "Zohar and Eros," "God's Qualities," and "The Zohar as Renaissance," *Da'at* 46 (2001): 5–11.

14. Moshe Halbertal and Jackie Feldman, *Concealment and Revelation: Esotericism in Jewish Thought and Its Philosophical Implications* (Princeton University Press, 2007).

15. See Idel, "On the History of the Prohibition to Study Kabbalah before Age Forty" [Hebrew] *AJS Review* 5 (1980): 1–20; Ephraim Kopper, "Glosses by an Anonymous Scholar on the Words of the Sage Rabbi Yosef, Son of Rabbi Yosef the Foreigner, Who Wrote and Proclaimed Loudly against Maimonides" [Hebrew] *Kobez Al Yad: Seder Chadash* 11 (1985): 213–88.

16. See the pioneering work of Yaakov ben Tzvi Emden, *Sefer Mitapachat Sfarim* (Sifriyat Mekorot, 1870), and the adaptations by Gershom Scholem, *Major Trends in Jewish Mysticism* (Schocken, 1995), 173–204. For contemporary research, see, for instance, Leore Sachs-Shmueli, "Maimonides' Rationalization of the Incest Taboo, Its Reception in Thirteenth-Century Kabbalah, and Their Affinity to Aquinas," *Harvard Theological Review* 114 (2021): 371–92.

17. Moshe ben Israel Isserles and Asher Ziv, eds., *Shu"t HaRema* (Feldheim, 1970), 7. See Tzipporah Brody, "R. Moshe Botril" [Hebrew], in *Sefer Zichron Yisrael*, ed. Yosef Dan, vol. 1 (Hebrew University, 2006), 159–206.

18. Idel and Warren Zev Harvey, eds., *Abraham Abulafia's Esotericism: Secrets and Doubts* (De Gruyter, 2020).

19. Yosef Dan, "The 'Exceptional Cherub' Sect in the Literature of the Medieval German Ḥasidim" [Hebrew] *Tarbiz* 35 (1966): 349–72; Roi Horn, *The Baal Shem Tov and the Kabbala of the Ari* (Bar-Ilan University Press, 2021).

20. Paul Fenton, "Sufis and Jews in Mamluk Egypt," in *Muslim-Jewish Relations in the Middle Islamic Period*, ed. Stephen Conerman (Bonn University Press, 2017), 41–62.

21. See Yosef Schwartz and Ariella Sturm, eds., *"To Thee Is Silence Praise": Meister Eckhart's Reading in* Guide of the Perplexed [Hebrew] (Am Oved, 2002).

22. Liebes, *Egidio da Viterbo: De Litteris Hebraicis* [Hebrew] (Carmel, 2012); Guillaume Postel, *On the Conciliation of Nature and Grace: A Latin Translation and Commentary on the Zohar*, trans. Judith Weiss [Hebrew] (Magnes, 2017).

23. See, for example, Chaim Wirszubski, *Pico della Mirandola's Encounter with Jewish Mysticism* (Harvard University Press, 1989); Allison Coudert and Ilyas Shufani, eds., *Hebraica Veritas?: Christian Hebraists and the Study of Judaism in Early Modern Europe* (University of Pennsylvania Press, 2004); Yosef Dan, "Modern Times: The Christian Kabbalah," in *Kabbalah: A Very Short Introduction* (Oxford University Press, 2006); Pasquale Terracciano, "The Origin of Pico's Kabbalah: Esoteric Wisdom and the Dignity of Man," *Journal of the History of Ideas* 79 (2018): 343–61.

24. Idel, "Reflections on Kabbalah in Spain and Christian Kabbalah," *Hispania Judaica Bulletin* 2 (1999): 3–15.

25. Eric Nelson, *The Hebrew Republic: Jewish Sources and the Transformation of European Political Thought* (Harvard University Press, 2010).

PIETY AND KNOWLEDGE 181

26. See, for example, Anthony Grafton, Joanna Weinberg, and Alastair Hamilton, *"I Have Always Loved the Holy Tongue": Isaac Casaubon, the Jews, and a Forgotten Chapter in Renaissance Scholarship* (Belknap, 2011); Theodor Dunkelgrün, "The Christian Study of Judaism in Early Modern Europe," *Cambridge History of Judaism* vol. 7 (2017): 316–48; Coudert and Shufani, *Hebraica Veritas?*; Stephen G. Burnett, *From Christian Hebraism to Jewish Studies: Johannes Buxtorf (1564–1629) and Hebrew Learning in the Seventeenth Century* (Brill, 1996), and *Christian Hebraism in the Reformation Era (1500–1660): Authors, Books, and the Transmission of Jewish Learning* (Brill, 2012); also Abraham Melamed, *Hebraic Aspects of the Renaissance: Sources and Encounters* (Brill, 2011).

27. C. Philipp E. Nothaft, *Dating the Passion: The Life of Jesus and the Emergence of Scientific Chronology (200–1600)* (Brill, 2011).

28. Yosef Hayim Yerushalmi, *Zakhor: Jewish History and Jewish Memory* (University of Washington Press, 1982); Ram Ben-Shalom, "Myth and Classical Mythology in the Historical Consciousness of Medieval Spanish Jewry" [Hebrew] *Zion* 66 (2001): 451–94; Maoz Kahana, *Bacchus and Beyond: Jewish Interpretations of Greek and Roman Mythology in the Early Modern Era* (Haifa University Press, forthcoming).

29. See further in Maoz Kahana, "A Universe of Words: Rabbi Yosef Karo's Self-Perception as a Halakhic Codifier" [Hebrew] *Shenaton Hamishpat Ha'ivri* 31 (2020): 79–128, and "Cosmos and Nomos."

30. Uri Safrai, "R. Chaim Vital, God's Goldsmith" [Hebrew] *Pe'amim* 157 (2019): 39–74.

31. Asaf Tamari, *God as Patient: The Medical Discourse of Lurianic Kabbalah* [Hebrew] (Magnes, 2023); also Roni Weinstein, *Kabbalah and Jewish Modernity* (Littman Library, 2016).

32. Liebes, "Zohar and Eros"; Melila Hellner-Eshed and Nathan Wolski, *A River Flows from Eden: The Language of Mystical Experience in the Zohar* (Stanford University Press, 2005).

33. Jacob Katz, "Post-Zoharic Relation between Halakha and Kabbala," in *Jewish Thought in the Sixteenth Century*, ed. B. D. Cooperman (Cambridge University Press, 1983), 283–307, and *Halakha and Kabbala* [Hebrew] (Magnes, 1984).

34. Avriel Bar Levav, "Ritualisation of Jewish Life and Death in the Early Modern Period," *Leo Baeck Institute Year Book* 47 (2002): 69–82.

35. See Katz, *Halakha and Kabbala*; Moshe Chalamish, *Kabbalah in Prayer in Halakha and Custom* [Hebrew] (Bar-Ilan University Press, 2000).

36. See Tzvi Luboshitz, "'The Secret of that Herb': Mystical Smoking from Italian Sabbateanism to Hasidism," *Modern Judaism* 41 (2021): 317–38; Maoz Kahana, "The Shabbes Coffeehouse: On the Emergence of the Jewish Coffeehouse in Eighteenth-Century Prague" (Hebrew) *Zion* 78 (2013): 5–50, and "Smoke the Pipe and Win the War: A Sabbatian Smoking Ritual and Seventeenth-Century Warfare" (2024); and Elliott Horowitz, " Coffee, Coffeehouses, and the Nocturnal Rituals of Early Modern Jewry," *AJS Review* 14 (1989): 17–46.

37. Joseph Avivi, "History Needs Height" [Hebrew], in *Jubilee Volume for Rav Mordechai Breuer*, ed. M. Arendt et al. (Akademon, 1992), 709–71.

38. See Luboshitz, "'The Secret.'"

39. Ron Margolin, *Inner Religion in Jewish Sources: A Phenomenology of Inner Religious Life and Its Manifestation from the Bible to Hasidic Texts* (Academic Studies, 2021); Mordechai Pachter, "*Katnut* and *Gadlut* in Lurianic Kabbalah," *Jerusalem Studies in Jewish Thought* 10

(1992): 171–210; Tzvi Mark, "*Katnut* [Smallness] and *Gadlut* [Greatness] in the Teachings of R. Nahman of Bratslav and Their Roots in the Lurianic Kabbalah" [Hebrew] *Daat* 46 (2001): 45–80.

40. See G. Scholem, *On the Kabbalah and Its Symbolism* (Schocken, 1965).

41. See Isaiah Tishby, "The Customs of Nathan of Gaza: Letters of R. Moshe Zaccuto and the Taqqanot of R. Hayyim Abulafiya in the Book Hemdat Yamin" [Hebrew] *Kiryat Sefer* 54 (1979): 585–610.

42. See G. Scholem, *Major Trends in Jewish Mysticism* (Schocken, 1995); Mark, "*Katnut.*"

43. See Elchanan Reiner, "Wealth, Social Position and the Study of Torah: The Status of the Kloiz in Eastern European Jewish Society in the Early Modern Period" [Hebrew] *Zion* 58 (1993): 287–328; Maoz Kahana, "Changing the World's Measures—Rabbi Zeev Olesker and the Revolutionary Scholars Circle in Brody Kloyz" [Hebrew] *AJS Review* 37 (2013): 29–53, and *A Heartless Chicken: Religion and Science in Early Modern Rabbinic Culture* [Hebrew] (Mossad Bialik, 2021), 428, index.

44. R. J. Zwi Werblowsky, *Joseph Karo: Lawyer and Mystic* (Oxford University Press, 1962); Liebes, "Messiah of the Zohar"; Moshe Idel, *R. Joseph Karo and His Revelations: or The Apotheosis of the Feminine in Safedian Kabbalah* (Tikvah Center Working Paper 5, 2013).

45. Compare Kocku von Stuckrad, *Locations of Knowledge in Medieval and Early Modern Europe Esoteric Discourse and Western Identities* (Brill, 2010).

46. Amnon Raz-Krakotzkin, "Law and Censure: The Printing of the Shulkhan Arukh as the Commencement of Jewish Modernity" [Hebrew], in *Tov Elem: Memory, Community and Gender in Medieval and Early Modern Jewish Societies; Essays in Honor of Robert Bonfil*, ed. E. Baumgarten et al. (Mandel Institute, 2011), 306–335; Maoz Kahana, "Cosmos and Nomos: Rabbi Joseph Karo and Shabtai Zvi as Portable Heavenly Temples," *El Prezente* 10 (2016): 143–153; Tirza Yehudit Kalman, "Written with Iron and Lead Letter in Print': The Print Revolution and the Creation of the Beit Yosef" [Hebrew] *Pe'amim* 148 (2017): 9–25.

47. Raz-Krakotzkin, "Law and Censure"; Roni Weinstein, "Jewish Modern Law and Legalism in a Global Age: The Case of Rabbi Joseph Karo," *Modern Intellectual History* 17 (2020): 561–78. For the problematic nature of such theories, see Y. Ben Naeh, Ch. Peli and M. Idel, *Rabbi Joseph Karo: History, Halakhah, Kabbalah* [Hebrew] (Zalman Shazar Center, 2021).

48. Werblowsky, *Joseph Karo*; Kahana, "Universe"; and compare Ben Naeh et al., *Rabbi Joseph Karo.*

49. Ta-Shma, "Rabbi Joseph Karo: Between Spain and Germany" [Hebrew] *Tarbiz* 59 (1989): 153–70; Tirza Kalman, "The Use of Ashkenazi Decisors in Beit Yosef Yoreh Dea 183–200 as a Case Study" [Hebrew] *Sidra* 27 (2012): 143–66; also "'I Shall Create Halakhic Ruling . . . for That Is the Objective': The Dimension of Halakhic Ruling in Joseph Karo's Beit Yosef" [Hebrew] (PhD dissertation, Ben Gurion University, 2018).

50. Kahana, "Universe." See also Malachi ben Yaakov, *Sefer Yad Malakhi* (1767).

51. Maoz Kahana, "Cosmos and Nomos: Rabbi Joseph Karo and Shabtai Zvi as Portable Heavenly Temples," *El Prezente* 10 (2016): 143–53.

52. Chaim Tchernowitz, *Toldot Haposkim* [Hebrew] (Va'ad Hayovel, 1946); Reiner, "The Roots of Urban Jewish Communities in Poland in the Early Modern Period" [Hebrew] *Gal-Ed* 20 (2006): 13–37, and Elchanan Reiner, "Beyond the Realm of the Haskalah—Changing Learning Patterns in Jewish Traditional Society," *Simon Dubnow Institute Yearbook* 6 (2007): 123–33;

Halbertal, "Histories"; Haim Barkovitz, " The Influence of Sepharadic Sages on Modern Ashkenazi Legal Decision Making" [Hebrew] *Levavi Bamizrah* 1 (2019): 31–44; Kahana, "Universe."

53. See Reiner, "The New Instead of the Old: Changes in the Curriculum of the Polish Yeshivas in the Sixteenth Century and r. Moses Isserles' Yeshiva in Krakow" [Hebrew], in *Zekhor Davar le'Avdekha: Essays and Studies in Memory of Dov Rappel*, ed. S. Glick et al. (Bar Ilan University, 2007), 183–206; I. M. Ta-Shma, *Ha-Sifrut ha-Parshanit la-Talmud be-Eropa u-vi-Zefon Afrika: Korot, Ishim, ve-Shitot* (Magnes, 1999), 2: 141–45.

54. See Noam Samet, "*Ketzot Hahoshen*: The Beginning of *Lamdanut*" [Hebrew] (PhD diss., Ben Gurion University, 2016); Jacob Mayer and Yishai Rosen-Zvi, *Talmud: The History of Lamdanut* [Hebrew] (Magnes, 2024).

55. Jonathan Eybeschutz, *Urim veTumim al Sefer Tekfo Kohen* [Hebrew] (Jerusalem, 2014), 186.

56. Samet, "Ketzot"; Michal Tikochinsky, *Teach Me the Laws: The Beginning of Legal Scholarship in the* Minhat Hinukh *and of Its Author R. Yosef Baavad* [Hebrew] (Hebrew University, 2020).

57. See Samet, "Ketzot," 109–42; H. Soloveitchik, *Rupture and Reconstruction: The Transformation of Contemporary Orthodoxy* (Littman Library, 2021), 57–97; and Norman Solomon, *The Analytic Movement: Hayyim Soloveitchik and His Circle* (Scholars, 1993); Shlomo Tikochinsky, *Modes of Study in Lithuanian 19th-Century Yeshivas* [Hebrew] (Hebrew University of Jerusalem, 2004).

58. See Ta-Shma, *The Hebrew Book: A Historical Survey* (Keter, 1975).

59. For extensive examples, see Dov Lipz, et al., *Yehudot Lita* (3 vols.; Am HaSefer Tel Aviv, 1960); Shlomo Yehuda Spitzer, *Communities of Hungary* [Hebrew] (Moreshet Yahadut Hungarya, 2009).

1.3 Modernities

8

Citizenship

Julie E. Cooper, Tel Aviv University

HISTORIANS OFTEN describe the breakdown of the feudal and corporate structures of medieval Europe as the beginning of Jewish modernity, when Jews
sought entry as individual citizens into unified sovereign states. In Western
Europe, Jews navigated the equivocal promise of inclusion in nation-states, and
Eastern European and Ottoman Jews encountered modernity within empires
that tended to cultivate, rather than suppress, diversity. In every region, however, a change in political status signaled the onset of modernization. Thus,
historians who differ regarding when and where Jewish modernity began tend
to concur that processes of political enfranchisement were decisive for the construction of modern Judaisms. In the modern period, all Jews—regardless of
geographical location—were forced to wrestle with questions such as the following: What is the significance of formal political membership in an interna-
tionally recognized state? Does accession to equal citizenship improve Jews'
economic prospects, social standing, and political power? Which modes of Jewish identity and practice are consistent with the civic loyalty expected (often
demanded) of citizens?

Given the ubiquity of such questions, it is not altogether surprising that canonical histories have long identified accession to equal citizenship (e.g., "emancipation") as the defining event of Jewish modernity. Yet, this canonical periodization invites sustained theoretical reflection. The reflexive equation of
Jewish modernity with emancipation has become so familiar that we sometimes
forget that the fixation on citizenship—and politics more generally—is not immediately obvious. Competing explanations might trace modernization to technological developments, economic dislocations, the decline of halakhic author-

ity, or changes in family structure. (Indeed, explanations of this kind have played a role in Jewish Studies scholarship.) When historians ascribe epochal significance to Jewish enfranchisement, they advance a claim—sometimes explicit, sometimes implicit—about the constitutive role of politics and the state in shaping modern Jewish existence.

In this chapter, I take the primacy that conventional periodizations accord to political developments—in particular, to the emergence of modern state structures—as the occasion for an exercise in political theory. This endeavor is inspired by the work of political theorists—many of them of Jewish extraction (Baruch Spinoza, Karl Marx, Hannah Arendt)—who treated Jewish emancipation as a test case. Following Spinoza, Marx, and Arendt, I use the study of Jewish enfranchisement (as reconstructed by twentieth-century historians) to evaluate the conditions for legal membership in modern states and the salience of political rights.

This juxtaposition of historiography and political theory is also inspired by the work of Jewish historians. Whether consciously or not, historians who identify enfranchisement as a catalyst to Jewish modernity are doing a kind of political theory. These historians are "doing political theory" in the sense that they make a distinctive "question of regime" the critical question for Jewish history and politics. Although few of the historians surveyed attempt a formal taxonomy, they all trace the dislocations, negotiations, and reinventions that characterize Jewish modernity to variations in state forms (e.g., nation-state vs. multinational empire). In this sense, historians who date Jewish modernity to emancipation pose what political theorists would call a "question of regime": Of the many political regimes under which Jews have lived, which kinds of states are most hospitable (or most hostile) to Jewish flourishing?

In what follows, I amplify historians' theoretical assumptions regarding the power of state structures to determine Jewish self-understanding. Using concepts borrowed from Spinoza and Marx, I foreground a claim about the specificity of Jewish citizenship running through emancipation historiography. In a paradoxical fashion, historiography that dates Jewish modernity to civic enfranchisement exposes the comparative insignificance of legal citizenship status. Throughout Jewish history, formal political membership has proved less consequential than the type of polity in which Jewish enfranchisement was or was not conceivable. Instead of asking whether terms of legal membership were full or equal or identical to those of non-Jews, contemporary scholars should focus on the ways that different regimes configured membership and the varying possibilities for Jewish existence they afforded.

Spinoza and Marx: Jewish Emancipation as a Case Study for Political Theory

Jewish emancipation has long served as a touchstone for political theorists studying the prospects for inclusion in modern states. Spinoza and Marx, two theorists with notoriously vexed relationships to their Jewish heritage, are the most prominent examples of this theoretical deployment. Writing at a time of epochal transformations in the global order, Spinoza defended the kind of state that could theoretically extend equal rights to Jews. In the nineteenth century, Marx criticized liberalism's limits while participating in contentious public debates on the emancipation of German Jews. Both thinkers used the Jewish case to examine the grounds for inclusion in a realm of formal equality, as well as the kinds of freedom such a regime affords. Without making any claims for direct historical influence (of Spinoza on Marx or of Spinoza and Marx on Jewish historiography), I invoke their respective engagements with the "Jewish question" for heuristic purposes to delineate the theoretical terrain that subsequent scholars of Jewish citizenship would (wittingly or unwittingly) traverse. Spinoza and Marx represent two approaches to theorizing the contours of a state that could conceivably extend full citizenship to Jews. Consequently, their work provides a handy (if stylized) schema for articulating the theoretical stakes of Jewish Studies scholarship.

Spinoza, who advances a democratic vision, makes visible the informal demands that citizenship places on Jews and Judaism. In the *Theologico-Political Treatise*—in which Spinoza uses the words "subject" and "citizen" interchangeably—the citizen is defined in contradistinction to the slave (who advances his master's interests) and the son (who remains under tutelage): "A subject . . . is someone who does what is advantageous for the collective body—and hence, also for himself—in accordance with the command of the supreme power."[1] Acting in accordance with the sovereign's command does not violate individual freedom, because living in a republic is conducive to rational self-development. In these abstract theoretical formulations, citizenship is egalitarian. Indeed, Spinoza celebrates democracy as "the most natural state" because citizens have an equal say in shaping the laws to which they are subject. Moreover, democratic states impose no religious tests for citizenship. Responding to critics of democracy, Spinoza adduces the example of Amsterdam to prove that free republics can thrive. Amsterdam has flourished economically, Spinoza contends, because citizens of all faiths are willing to transact business with any reputable merchant.

CITIZENSHIP   187

In practice, however, modern citizenship has proved highly exclusionary. These tensions between equality and exclusion color theoretical articulations of modern citizenship. Like many of sovereignty's canonical exponents, Spinoza narrows the class of people eligible for citizenship, denying women equal rights (*Theologico-Political Treatise*, 603). Because women are naturally weaker than men, Spinoza contends, they have fewer rights and must submit to male rule. Given the theoretical underpinnings of the social contract tradition—that is, voluntary consent between naturally free individuals—the question of women's enfranchisement becomes almost unavoidable. As Spinoza demonstrates, however, theorists found myriad ways to resist the egalitarian implications of contractarian premises.

Just as women's enfranchisement becomes conceivable in a theoretical framework grounded on formal equality, so does Jewish enfranchisement emerge as a theoretical possibility. As in the case of women, however, tendentious assessments of Jewish political mettle mitigate against automatic enfranchisement. In the *Theologico-Political Treatise*, Spinoza famously entertains the possibility that Jews might establish a modern state: "If the foundations of their religion did not make their hearts unmanly, I would absolutely believe that someday, given the opportunity, they would set up their state again" (124). In the grips of an emasculating religion, Jews occupy the same marginal position to citizenship as do women. Unlike women, however, (male) Jews can graduate to become fit political subjects by assimilating norms of proper masculinity. Yet overcoming "the foundations of their religion" involves not only a gender overhaul but also requires a thoroughgoing renovation of Jewish existence. In Spinoza's state, the sovereign demands exclusive political loyalty and is the lone source of law. Nonstate normative systems, such as halakhah, lack legal standing and are recast as private religious confessions. Like any other citizen, the Jew's *political* identity and allegiance are to the state—not to the Jewish people.

In Spinoza's thought, the political template that makes Jewish enfranchisement conceivable (e.g., the sovereign state) recasts earlier forms of Jewish political community as anomalous or even pathological. Spinoza wrote in a period when Jews' economic clout in Amsterdam derived from their legal status as a foreign mercantile community operating without a charter.[2] Confronted with a community that "arrogated to itself virtually all the powers of an autonomous community or Kehillah," Spinoza predicated enfranchisement on Judaism's reconstitution as a private religious confession (29). Thus, it is scarcely surprising that European Jewish enfranchisement was not "self-evident," in the words of Paul Mendes-Flohr.[3] Enfranchisement often lagged behind the

adoption of modern concepts of citizenship and was only gained after protracted political struggle—the achievements of which were partial and revers-
able. The prospect of citizenship changes everything, in Spinoza's work, because
it entails the creation of new forms of (Jewish) religiosity consonant with the
state's demand for exclusive political allegiance.

Marx, by contrast, downplays or even dismisses the significance of formal
political membership. In "On the Jewish Question" (1843), Marx seeks to re-
frame debates about the terms of Jewish inclusion that roiled the German
intelligentsia.[4] From 1815 to 1850—the period of most intense public debate—
thousands of articles were published advocating positions ranging from outright
opposition (absent conversion), conditional or incremental emancipation, to
the demand for full civic equality.[5] Against those who debate whether the Jews
are (or could become) worthy of citizenship in nominally secular states, Marx
asks whether the conferral of equal citizenship actually merits the name "emancipation." Although "*political* emancipation certainly represents a great progress," Marx concludes, "it is not, indeed, the final form of human emancipation" (35). Extending equal rights to Jews would not liberate the Jews (or society
as a whole), Marx contends, because the state can only confer an abstract, partial
form of freedom. In the kind of state that entertains the possibility of Jewish
enfranchisement, formal equality in the public sphere is eminently compatible
with egregious inequality in the various spheres now deemed private:

> The state abolishes, after its fashion, the distinctions established by *birth*,
> *social rank, education, occupation,* when it decrees that birth, social rank,
> education, occupation are *non-political* distinctions; when it proclaims, with-
> out regard to these distinctions, that every member of society is an *equal*
> partner in popular sovereignty, and treats all the elements which compose
> the real life of the nation from the standpoint of the state. But the state, none
> the less, allows private property, education, occupation, to *act* after *their own*
> fashion, namely as private property, education, occupation, and to manifest
> their *particular* nature. (33)

Indeed, the state is parasitic upon these distinctions—which it ostentatiously
"disregards" when conferring political rights, thereby confirming the universality of the political. Thus, accession to citizenship will not free Jews from antisemitic discrimination, which continues to "act after its own fashion" in civil society. (Of course, Marx was scarcely concerned with antisemitism and sought
rather to precipitate humanity's emancipation as a species-being.) According to
Marx, the fixation of emancipation proponents and opponents on formal

CITIZENSHIP 189

political membership is misplaced, diverting attention from inequality and subordination in the private sphere.

Joining the controversy surrounding Jewish emancipation, Marx formulates a more general criticism of the kinds of freedom available in a liberal state. In his analysis, Jewish emancipation "certainly represents a great progress," but when considered from an emancipatory standpoint the conferral of rights effectively changes nothing, leaving intact the oppressive "framework of the prevailing social order" (35). If Spinoza demands a comprehensive rehabilitation of Jewish masculinity, liberal states ask nothing of those petitioning for inclusion. Indeed, Marx upholds the likely persistence of Judaism (as one instance of benighted religion) post-emancipation as a testament to the provisional nature of political liberation: "The man was not liberated from religion; he received religious liberty" (45). In Marx's analysis, one should neither ascribe epochal significance to changing citizenship regimes, nor should one expect a radical transformation, emancipatory or otherwise, to follow Jewish enfranchisement. Emancipation would change nothing then, because the liberal state institutes formal equality only to give hierarchy and subordination free rein in civil society.

Of course, there are more points of intersection between Spinoza and Marx than this schematic opposition suggests. A staunch defender of freedom of thought, Spinoza would not countenance prohibitions on Jewish belief. As envisioned by Spinoza, citizenship does not require the abolition of Judaism or any other (non-seditious) belief system. In this sense, Spinoza provides support for Marx's analysis of the liberal state, which refrains from making (formal) demands of citizens. Marx, by contrast, did not hesitate to call for the abolition of what he tendentiously called "Judaism." Recycling stock tropes of European antisemitism, Marx predicates true human liberation, unattainable in the liberal state, on emancipation from "real and practical Judaism"; that is, "huckstering and money" (48). Indeed, Marx judges the promise of liberal citizenship paltry precisely because he aspires to revolutionary transformation. Here, Marx amplifies Spinoza's informal demand for the refashioning of Jewish existence. The Jewish case allows Spinoza and Marx to expose the informal power relations that shadow formal rights discourse and—for Jews, at least—prove more consequential than rights themselves.

I present their divergent conclusions in stylized fashion—enfranchisement would change everything (Spinoza) and nothing (Marx)—to provide a theoretical framework for interpreting Jewish Studies scholarship. As we will see, the historiographical moves of scholars who made emancipation the defining concept of Jewish modernity echo the claims of Spinoza and Marx. Suffused with disappointment, the field's founding texts trace an arc that moves from the Spinozist insight that enfranchisement exacted exorbitant concessions to the Marxist conclusion that these concessions did not materially improve Jewish welfare. The Spinoza/Marx mash-up yields an ambivalent picture in which the type of political regime under which Jews live proves more consequential than their formal citizenship status.

The Historiography of Emancipation: Citizenship as a Central Category for Jewish Studies

Since the founding of academic Jewish Studies in nineteenth-century Germany, the field has been dominated by historians. Political science has played a negligible role in its development, nor have political scientists exhibited much interest in Jews or Judaism. This absence is striking, given that the central theoretical insight that emerges from the historiography of Jewish emancipation is the power of state structures to refashion Jewish existence. Despite debates about the periodization and geographical scope of emancipation, many of the most influential scholars of Jewish modernity concur that this phenomenon was its founding event. When historians date modernity to Jewish enfranchisement, they ascribe decisive agency to politics and the state. According to canonical studies, the achievement (and loss) of citizenship did not merely alter the balance of civil rights and duties or the opportunities for participation in parliamentary politics. Enfranchisement, it is claimed, instigated a fundamental transformation of Judaism—turning what was formerly a nationality into a private religious confession. In any given period, the historiography of Jewish emancipation suggests that the hegemonic mode of political organization and the place of Jews therein establish the conditions of possibility for Jewish identity, practice, and communal organization.

Yet the historiography does more than advance a claim about political causality. Studies of Jewish emancipation are themselves influenced by the political ideologies and movements such as liberalism and nationalism that emerged in its wake. Following Gershom Scholem, most scholars view the founding of academic Jewish Studies as part and parcel of the struggle for emancipation. Although the historians who founded the Wissenschaft des Judentums school in Germany in 1819 professed scholarly objectivity, their political motivations are often transparent. In the preface to his 1832 history of Jewish homiletics, Leopold

Zunz yoked advanced Judaic scholarship to the imperatives of Jewish enfranchisement: "It is high time that the Jews of Europe, particularly those of Germany, be granted right and liberty rather than rights and liberties—not some paltry, humiliating privileges, but complete and uplifting civil rights."[6] Zunz enlisted Jewish Studies to fight for what Scholem called "external" and "internal" emancipation. On the external front, Zunz and his colleagues sought to prove that Jews (and Judaism) were worthy of full citizenship. Accurate and up-to-date historical research, Zunz contended, would dispel the prejudices that continue to impede civic equality. Addressing an internal Jewish audience, Zunz sought to craft a Judaism commensurate with the demands of the state and the ideals of enlightened modernity.

For many Jews, the liberal conceptions of citizenship championed by thinkers such as Moses Mendelssohn became less credible once citizenship rights were granted. The realization that enfranchisement did not always promote integration spurred new forms of political mobilization. Scholars have long depicted Zionism—especially the political Zionism of Theodor Herzl—as a response to the failures of emancipation. The persistence of antisemitic discrimination in liberal states led Herzl to conclude that Jews would never become full and equal members of European society.

Zionism was merely one strand within a larger constellation of nationalist ideologies and movements marked by fierce internal debate. (Broadly speaking, the modifier "nationalist" indicates movements and discourses that define Jews as a national collective, as opposed to a mere "religion.") When it came to emancipation, however, nationalists from competing camps professed a shared ambivalence regarding the value of political enfranchisement. Echoing Marx, nationalists disappointed by emancipation questioned the salience of formal political membership. Persistent antisemitism exposed what political scientists call citizenship's "hollow promise": Rights on paper are insufficient, even empty, given how sharply outcomes vary in societies stratified along religious, racial, and gender lines. The point of departure for political Zionists in the West and socialist Zionists in the East was the realization that Jews' political standing was determined by factors other than citizenship status, such as civil society, economic competition, and education. At the same time, most nationalist intellectuals treated emancipation as an epochal shift on the order of the events of 70 CE. The grant of citizenship, on this view, precipitated an unprecedented transformation of Jewish identity, eroding Judaism's national foundations. Taking a page from Spinoza, nationalists viewed emancipation as a greater threat to Jewish national independence than dispersion itself.

192 CHAPTER 8

This ambivalence surrounding citizenship's transformational power colors the historiography of emancipation, which assumes a more critical tenor with the rise of nationalist ideologies. Simon Dubnow—who gained renown as a historian and activist promoting diasporic Jewish autonomy—offers a classic articulation of the nationalist historiography of emancipation.[7] In Dubnow's rendition, Russian Jewry retained an unparalleled degree of inner cohesion and cultural isolation, which were buttressed by movements such as Hasidism. Living under a hostile and backward regime, Dubnow argues, Russian Jews who absorbed modernist cultural trends achieved spiritual emancipation long before they were granted political (but not civil) rights in 1905. Yet the partial grant of rights was followed by waves of increasing repression that led to mass emigration.

Although Dubnow's outlook is marked by the distinctive political trajectories of Eastern European Jews, he locates the dawn of Jewish modernity in the West. In Dubnow's periodization, Jewish modernity dates both to the French Revolution, which inaugurated the Jews' political emancipation, and the thought of Moses Mendelssohn, which instigated a spiritual emancipation. Dubnow identified as a liberal in Russian Jewish party politics, and his portrait of nineteenth-century developments exudes a modernist faith in the power of enlightenment to free Jews from benighted superstition. Moreover, as an activist who made the demand for political and civil rights a key plank of his Autonomist Party platform, Dubnow was not inclined to dismiss the significance of 1791. In his more optimistic moments, Dubnow trusts that Jews can enjoy newfound rights without sacrificing their national identity.

Dubnow's more characteristic assessment of emancipation, however, is starkly pessimistic. In "Letters on Old and New Judaism,"[8] Dubnow mounts a fierce critique of emancipation as a form of national slavery, the latest guise of Jewish subordination. Rehearsing the history of Jews in France and Germany, he laments their willingness to commit "national suicide" in exchange for political rights (110). Even after emancipation, Dubnow argues, Western Jews were not truly equal: "True emancipation means, not only liberation of the individual human being, but also of the individual nationality" (113). To Dubnow's chagrin, many Jews willingly complied with the state's demand to adopt a "foreign" (i.e., French or German) nationality as a condition for enfranchisement. With this indictment of the concessions extracted from emancipated Jews, Dubnow flirts with political determinism. In Western Europe, Dubnow contends, the grant of formal political membership had fateful consequences. In a standard-issue nation-state that demands exclusive political allegiance, Jewish nationality is liable to wither away. The evidence from Western Europe shows that the liberal state can indeed suppress (if not extinguish) the national spirit.

Dubnow inaugurated a historical school that treats citizenship as a catalyst for the transformations—many of them sorely lamented—that reshaped Judaism in modernity. This school is nationalist in orientation, in the sense that it posits nationality as the originary (and arguably the proper) form of Jewish collectivity. Today, Salo Baron's "Ghetto and Emancipation" (1928)[9] is mostly remembered for its critique of the "lachrymose theory" of Jewish history. Against Dubnow and the Wissenschaft historians, Baron argues that medieval Jews' lack of "equal rights" did not constitute a disability, beccause no one had "equal rights" in the corporate states of the Middle Ages. In practical terms, Baron claims, medieval Jews often enjoyed greater freedoms and a higher standard of living than their Christian neighbors. Yet this controversy regarding the welfare of ghetto Jews cannot conceal a more fundamental agreement between Baron and Dubnow regarding the nature of Jewish identity. Like Dubnow, Baron concludes that "emancipation has not brought the Golden Age" (63). Baron and Dubnow arrive at this critical assessment because they both take Jewish nationality as a (historical and ideological) point of departure. Echoing Dubnow, Baron asserts that "the Jew, indeed, had in effect a kind of territory and State of his own throughout the Middle Ages and early modern period" (55). Judged against this benchmark, emancipation constitutes a loss—the loss of national autonomy—rather than a liberation. Mourning this loss, Baron hopes to resuscitate autonomy as a contemporary political ideal and complement to more familiar values of liberal equality.

Baron reiterates and sharpens Dubnow's claim about the power of hegemonic political templates to determine the contours of Jewish existence. Downplaying Jewish struggles for equal rights and the fierce opposition they provoked, Baron interprets emancipation as a foregone conclusion with the rise of the modern state: "Emancipation was a necessity even more for the modern State than for Jewry," because the modern state cannot abide autonomous corporations ("Ghetto and Emancipation," 60). Baron makes an important point, which subsequent scholars have amplified, about the institutional and conceptual foundations of the modern state, which demand the abolition of corporations. More noteworthy, however, is the extent to which Baron flirts with a kind of political determinism, reserving agency for the state. Baron's deterministic streak is even more pronounced in "Nationalism and Intolerance" (1929),[10] an essay that identifies "the *national structure* of the state" as the "underlying, uniform cause" determining whether diasporic Jews have suffered or flourished (506–7). Seeking an invariant historical law to account for marked fluctuations in diasporic Jewish welfare, Baron ascribes explanatory power to state structures—specifically, the different ways in which states configure national membership. To substantiate this claim, Baron develops a threefold taxonomy: "If we now consider the treatment of Jewry under these various types of States, we shall, while leaving out all details, be able to formulate our law as follows: *The status of the Jew is most favorable in pure States of Nationalities, most unfavorable in National States, and somewhat between the two extremes in States which include part of a nationality only*" (506).

Here, the claim for political causality pushes Baron to pose a distinctively Jewish question of regime. Riffing on the classical taxonomy—monarchy, aristocracy, democracy—Baron instructs Jews to evaluate their prospects under nation-states, multinational states, and mixed regimes. For our purposes, Baron's endorsement of the multinational state is less significant than the theoretical claim from which it derives—a theory that posits state structures as the driving force in shaping diasporic history. With this taxonomy, Baron makes explicit the political-theoretical assumptions animating most of the scholarship surveyed in this chapter.

Although Dubnow's modernist optimism waned, his nationalist premises continued to frame influential histories of emancipation through the late twentieth century. Jacob Katz built his voluminous research around the ghetto/emancipation antithesis. In *Tradition and Crisis*,[11] Katz asserts that Jews constituted a unified "national body" on the cusp of modernity, which he dates to the Haskalah in the West and the rise of Hasidism in the East (8). In *Out of the Ghetto*,[12] Katz characterizes this Jewish journey as a veritable revolution, "transmuting the very nature of their entire social existence" (1). As Spinoza intimated, enfranchisement changed everything: Traditional values no longer defined communal norms, nor did they unite Jews across the globe. With Dubnow and Baron, Katz posits an organic Jewish nation whose dissolution signals the advent of modernity—with the result that French, English, and German Jews now belong to different nations. Moreover, Katz presents emancipation as a single process in which Western European patterns reproduced themselves worldwide (with the exception of the United States and the Arab world). When Katz presents Western European trajectories as paradigmatic of Jewish modernity, he makes citizenship paramount for the constitution of modern Judaism.

Yet, in *Out of the Ghetto,* Katz also voices characteristic skepticism, which recalls Marx, of the supposed benefits of formal political membership. Having cast emancipation as a veritable revolution, Katz ultimately concedes that equal rights did not bring genuine integration. As patterns of persistent antisemitism attest, political enfranchisement was rarely a catalyst for assimilation: "Jews entered European society but did not merge with it" (216). Indeed, the political processes that promised to liberate instead placed Jews in an anomalous social position, distinguished from their neighbors by family structure, occupational patterns, and transnational loyalties. Yet enfranchisement, which inspired fierce opposition, does not merely prove a "hollow promise" but also fails to alter the deeper structures of Jewish identity: "The conception of Jews as a congregation existing merely by virtue of a common confession of faith functioned only on the theoretical level" (213). Echoing Dubnow in his more optimistic moments, Katz suggests that the religionization of Judaism was merely superficial because the state lacks the power to destroy traditional norms of communal organization and global solidarity.

Even when not expressly committed to partisan ideologies, the founding historiography of emancipation operates with nationalist assumptions. The most influential historians of emancipation presume that national autonomy is the natural state of the Jews—and hence worry that autonomy becomes impossible once being Jewish no longer defines one's position within and relationship to the state. The persistent vacillation regarding whether politics is a catalyst for transformation—the vacillation between Spinoza and Marx, in our schema—reflects these anxieties about the prospects for diasporic independence in a world of nation-states. Although historians lament the state's power to erode Judaism's national foundations, they are still disappointed when the liberal state fails to protect Jews from hostile forces, whether religious, social, or economic.

Diversifying Emancipation

Baron and Katz were born in Eastern Europe. Yet they wrote, respectively, in the United States and Israel, two countries in which Jews never underwent processes of legal emancipation because (male) Jews were never excluded from citizenship. In these comparatively young countries, Jews did not make the transition from privileges to rights, from subordination to equality. In the United States, the constitutional guarantee of religious freedom positioned Jews as equal citizens from the outset—although it did not insulate Jews from social discrimination, which persisted through the 1950s. Since Israel's establishment as a Jewish nation-state, Israeli law has enshrined privileges for Jews at the expense of non-Jewish citizens, who were subject to military rule until 1966 and still face legal, civic, and social discrimination. The ghetto/emancipation binary to which Baron and Katz recur is arguably a vestige of their Eastern European inheritance, rather than a reflection of the political conditions in the countries to which they emigrated.

Alert to these divergent historical trajectories, subsequent generations undertook comprehensive mapping projects to document the varied circumstances under which Jews across the globe gained and lost political rights. *Paths of Emancipation: Jews, States, and Citizenship*,[13] an influential edited volume, illustrates the impetus for this new global approach. In the text's introduction, editors Pierre Birnbaum and Ira Katznelson object to the nationalist orientation that permeated Katz's work. Ideological biases led scholars of Katz's generation to paint a reified portrait of premodern Judaism as a static, traditional society that enjoyed a high degree of autonomy. Having posited a primordial Jewish nationality, Katz depicts emancipation as a unitary, linear process that shattered Jewish community everywhere. To challenge the notion that Jews everywhere constituted a nation pre-emancipation, Birnbaum and Katznelson highlight the diverse trajectories that Jews traveled in different regions. Yet their volume— which includes chapters on enfranchisement struggles in Holland, Germany, France, England, Italy, the United States, Turkey, and Russia—still takes the nation-state as the basic unit of analysis.

Reverting to our theoretical schema, one could say that Birnbaum, Katznelson et al. set out to mitigate the Spinoza-style slant of previous research. The Spinoza-inspired claim that accession to citizenship irrevocably transformed Jewish existence presupposes not only a primordial Jewish nationality waiting to be shattered but also a particular kind of modern state, one that cannot abide autonomous corporations. Yet the regimes that extended rights to Jews were not equally subversive of community and culture. Given these objections, one might wonder why Birnbaum and Katznelson retain the umbrella term "emancipation." Yet their use of the category is not accidental. Indeed, it reflects these scholars' continued (if contentious) location within a Spinozist orbit. As in previous scholarship, the "emancipation" rubric signals that enfranchisement in its varying forms did transform Jewish existence, as the following assertion reveals: "Everything changed—from communal and social organization to religious practice to family life to migration patterns to employment to schooling to ideology to collective action" (*Paths of Emancipation*, 15). The comparative turn notwithstanding, Birnbaum and Katznelson and their collaborators follow Baron in linking these changes to variations in state forms. Indeed, the political determinism evident in nationalist historiography arguably prepared the subsequent turn toward multiple pathways. If enfranchisement "changes everything," then scholars must enumerate and evaluate the different regimes under which Jews lived. As Birnbaum and Katznelson recognize, "the type of state" in which Jews reside "played a considerable role in the strategies adopted by the Jews themselves" (36). In other words, different kinds of states incubate different forms of Jewish identity, activism, and communal organization. Proliferating case studies beyond Western Europe actually confirm the insight, foundational for Jewish historiography since Dubnow, that regime types (e.g., corporate polity vs. centralized nation-state) shape the possibilities for Jewish self-understanding.

The ambition to document diverse trajectories within a single historical phenomenon reaches its apotheosis in David Sorkin's encyclopedic study, *Jewish Emancipation*. Taking the earlier mentioned critique of nationalist historiography as a point of departure, Sorkin aspires to present a comprehensive treatment of emancipation as a diverse global phenomenon. Although Sorkin retains emancipation as a historiographic concept, he rejects the traditional periodization as falsely implying a decisive and radical break. In contrast to narratives that begin with the French Revolution, Sorkin dates emancipation to 1550, when Jews in select European cities "began to gain extensive privileges bordering on parity with Christian burghers and merchants" (5). By pushing the periodization back to the sixteenth century, Sorkin refutes the notion that emancipation takes one form—the abolition of estates and the blanket grant of individual rights—that then repeats itself across the globe. On the contrary, Sorkin identifies two legislative models of emancipation (conditional vs. unconditional) and three geographical regions: Western, Central, and Eastern Europe. (In what reads like something of an afterthought, Sorkin identifies the Ottoman Empire as a fourth region blending equality for religious minorities with elements of corporate autonomy [the *millet* system].) In some regions (Western Europe), civil rights were attached to residency, but Jews fought for political rights. In other regions (Central and Eastern Europe), both civil and political rights had to be won. In Sorkin's work, the term "emancipation" encompasses both the abolition of estates, which supplanted privileges with individual rights, and processes that extend privileges and move Jews into estates.

Perhaps because he resists unitary, linear narratives, Sorkin exudes a pessimism about rights that recalls Marx and the "hollow promise" critique of citizenship. In *Jewish Emancipation*, Sorkin focuses single-mindedly on legal and political history, detailing "the process of gaining, exercising, retaining, and where lost, recovering rights" (1). The singular focus on rights, to the exclusion of social and economic factors, reflects a judgment about politics as the crucial arena for understanding Jewish modernity: "Emancipation is the principal event of modern Jewish history" (354). Having expanded the geographic and temporal boundaries of the phenomenon, however, Sorkin concedes that "emancipation was ambiguous and interminable" (356). A comprehensive survey reveals that egalitarian legislation was often disregarded or implemented in haphazard and partial form. Once granted, rights were just as easily revoked. To take one example: "In Italy Jews gained emancipation five times (1796–99, 1801, 1848, 1870, 1944) and lost it four times (1800, 1813–15, 1848, 1938)" (5). Here, rights are the essence of Jewish modernity, but they are fragile and evanescent. "Jews everywhere continue to live in the age of emancipation"—which presumably means that they must engage in ceaseless contestation and political advocacy (356).

Whether intentionally or not, Sorkin tells a story riddled with disappointment. *Jewish Emancipation* opens with Nahum Goldmann's appreciation for democracy as the regime that granted Jews equality. Yet Sorkin risks implying that no regime, democracy included, is safe or "good" for the Jews. (According to Sorkin, the United States and Israel—two countries in which Jews were never subject to disabilities—partake of the same ambiguous dynamics.) Depriving readers of the consoling fantasy of the emancipatory state, Sorkin offers Jews no respite from political struggle and no exit from modernity, in all its tragic complexity.

Trapped within "ambiguous and interminable" processes of enfranchisement, we can grasp the seemingly paradoxical nature of the historiography that identifies emancipation as the foundational event of Jewish modernity. Scholars who locate civil and political rights at the heart of Jewish modernity (Spinoza's schema) are generally forced to conclude that—for Jews at least—rights are fragile or even empty (Marx's schema). For modern Jews, citizenship changes everything and nothing, it would seem.

Legal Belonging in the Ottoman World

As we have seen, scholars who take exception to the ideological and geographical biases of the founding scholarship have sought to expose diverse trajectories of enfranchisement even while retaining "emancipation" as an umbrella category. Although careful not to impose a Eurocentric template on Ottoman and North African Jews, Birnbaum and Katznelson and Sorkin nevertheless concur that European and non-European Jews participated in the same historical process. Indeed, many of the themes surveyed earlier in this chapter recur in scholarship that refracts Jews' changing relationship to the state in the Ottoman world through the emancipation prism. In the lone chapter of *Paths of Emancipation* to address Jewish citizenship outside Europe, Aron Rodrigue traces the gradual migration of modern state-building practices to the Ottoman world, depriving Turkish Jews of the autonomy they enjoyed under the *millet* system.[14] Although Rodrigue characterizes the trajectory of Turkish Jews as "emancipation without liberalism" to differentiate it from European patterns, his conclusions regarding the liabilities of the nation-state echo those of Dubnow, Baron, and Katz (260). The devolution of a multinational empire into modern nation-states consigns Turkish Jews to the status of a religious minority, and this framing makes the consequent loss of communal autonomy a benchmark for Sephardic (as well as Ashkenazic) modernity.

In recent years, by contrast, historians who elevate citizenship as a key for understanding Sephardic history have dispensed with "emancipation" as a category and concept. Two related strands of Sephardi scholarship put citizenship at the heart of Jewish modernity. On the one hand, scholars such as Julia Phillips Cohen study dynamics of loyalty and belonging among Ottoman citizens. In *Becoming Ottomans: Sephardi Jews and Imperial Citizenship in the Modern Era*,[15] Cohen reconstructs the manifold projects that Ottoman Jews undertook in the wake of the Tanzimat reforms—which extended equal citizenship without religious distinctions—to position themselves as a "model millet" (1). Cultivating civic loyalty in an imperial context was not without its complications: Jews simultaneously professed brotherhood with Ottomans of all faiths and sought to distinguish themselves from less "exemplary" minorities. Scholars have also showcased the experiences of Mediterranean Jews who opted for extraterritorial citizenship (e.g., European consular protection) instead of local forms of legal belonging. Both strands challenge the precedence that studies of Jewish modernity have long accorded to European models of state formation.

"Emancipation" proves less useful as an organizing frame for historians who study extraterritoriality, because they seek to challenge the binary opposition— one either has or lacks citizenship—that animates traditional emancipation narratives. Against scholarship that emplots modern Jewish history as a movement between these two statuses, historians such as Sarah Abrevaya Stein depict "citizenship as a spectrum: a range of conditions or possibilities that Jews could access rather than a singular possession they could or could not claim."[16] Drawing on a similar archive—"the extraterritorial privileges accorded to European subjects in the Ottoman empire"—Jessica Marglin goes one step further, proposing that we replace the term "citizen" with "legal belonging, a neutral, umbrella term that encompasses a wide range of formal bonds between individuals and states."[17] With Stein, Marglin reminds us that "legal belonging" exists on a broad spectrum. A term like "citizenship" poorly suits the nineteenth-century Mediterranean then, because populations could not be neatly divided into insiders and outsiders. In any given region, one might find citizens, nationals lacking political or civil rights, and protégés under the jurisdiction of a European consulate. (The bolder claim is that the same holds true for Europe, where women and colonial subjects had different legal statuses.)

In Stein's work, citizenship status still serves as a privileged lens for deciphering modern Jewish history—but citizenship's diagnostic power derives from the myriad forms that it has historically taken. With this insistence on the "messiness" of modern citizenship, Stein hopes to foreground the agency of Sephardic Jews, who emerge as savvy citizenship entrepreneurs. Although Stein resists the kind of political determinism that characterizes Baron's work, she remains within the Spinoza schema as expanded by Birnbaum and Katznelson. Like Rodrigue, Stein frames the Sephardic twentieth century as a journey from the multiethnic Ottoman empire to a world of nation-states. In *Family Papers*,[18] Stein uses the Levy family—whose history she relates from nineteenth-century Salonica through the present—to illustrate the ways that belonging differed in imperial and postimperial contexts: "As their empire and economy frayed, the Levys, like all the city's Jews, were destined to become nationals. What kind of nationals they became was a matter of choice. They could accept the state that formed around them; they could emigrate; or they could seek the protection of a foreign power" (54). Some of Stein's protagonists were Ottomans, some Greek citizens, and others carried European papers and may have found themselves stateless at critical junctures during World War II.

In Stein's *Extraterritorial Dreams*, it is members of the third category of protégé—Ottoman Jews who gained the legal protection of European countries—who exemplify individual agency. Exploiting the "juridical fungibility" of an imperial context and the exigencies of great-power politics, many Ottoman Jews managed to acquire the European legal status that they judged most advantageous (9). As a form of extraterritorial membership, protégé status confounds models of territorial citizenship. The protégé detaches political status from residency—in many cases, protégés never set foot in the European countries whose papers they acquired—and necessitates a degree of legal pluralism. Moreover, putting the protégé on center stage divorces citizenship from political rights such as voting, shifting the focus to matters of jurisdiction, classification, and status. Although some protégés betrayed an emotional and cultural investment in "Europeanness," they harbored no illusions about civic participation in European democracies. Only in crisis moments of war or economic catastrophe did the prospect of refuge and residence in Europe become relevant. If historians of Western Europe document Jews' profound longing to become French or German in the normative sense, Stein imputes more strategic motivations to the protégés.

Stein resists strong forms of political determinism that threaten to rob Jews of political agency. Yet she echoes some of the skeptical conclusions regarding the value of formal political membership that I grouped under Marx's schema. Historians of Ottoman Jewry are determined to avoid a lachrymose narrative that takes the utter devastation visited on Salonican Jews during the Holocaust as a foregone conclusion. Echoing Sorkin, however, Stein emphasizes the tenuousness of any legal standing (absent deeper social and political commitments). In *Extraterritorial Dreams*, she focuses on Ottoman Jews "who held, sought, or lost the protection of a European power" (2). In turbulent periods of the mid-twentieth century, the loss of rights moves to the forefront of Stein's narrative. Protégés who sought refuge during the Holocaust often found themselves at the mercy of individual bureaucrats, who could revoke or cancel their protected status. At this juncture, the state seems more like a bureaucratic maze than a normative community of belonging. As the widely divergent fates of protégés reveal, rights can mean everything and nothing, given historical contingencies, bureaucratic discretion, and luck.

Once the Western European nation-state loses its default status as the paradigmatic site of analysis, familiar assumptions like the category of citizenships are subject to revision. Yet the work of scholars such as Cohen, Stein, and Marglin nevertheless echoes some of the theoretical claims encountered in previous scholarship on Jewish citizenship. Precisely because extraterritorial legal statuses challenge models of citizenship inherited from Spinoza et al., this research amplifies the Spinoza-inspired insight regarding the decisive implications of regime type. Standard emancipation narratives presuppose a type of state in which territorial belonging is (or is alleged to be) paramount. In the multinational empires of the Islamic Mediterranean, however, carrying foreign papers was often more advantageous than formal membership in one's place of residence. The distinctive membership dilemmas confronting Ottoman Jews—and the distinctive modes of transnational commerce and community they crafted—reflect the legal possibilities afforded by the regimes under which they lived. Moreover, scholarship on the Mediterranean foregrounds persistent quandaries about Jews' place in a world of nation-states. In the Ottoman world, as in Europe, the dissolution of a multinational empire and its division into homogeneous nation-states alter the political calculus for Jews. Finally, scholars of Ottoman Jewry echo the Marx-inspired caution about the hollow promise of rights on paper, whether they take the form of citizenship or consular protection. Given the checkered historical record, showcasing extraterritoriality does little to alleviate persistent doubts about the value of legal rights absent a sincere commitment to social and economic integration.

Conclusion

At first blush, it could seem like the fierce debates about region and periodization that have roiled the study of Jewish emancipation are largely of antiquarian interest. Today, Jews have equal civil and political rights nearly everywhere. At the time of this writing, antisemitic incidents and the tenor of political discourse post-October 7, 2023, have shaken Jews' sense of security in countries once considered exceptional such as the United States. Yet formal political membership is neither controversial nor subject to debate in the countries where most Jews live. *Pace* Sorkin, it would seem that emancipation has ended or, at the very least, entered a decisive new phase. As Sorkin rightly cautions, once granted, rights can be infringed and revoked. This caution assumes greater resonance at a moment when antisemitism has emerged as one of the defining political controversies of our time. Yet contemporary Jewish politics transpires within a historical frame in which civil and political equality have emerged as default, universal norms.

At this juncture, what can the study of Jewish citizenship contribute to debates about the stakes of formal political membership? Spinoza and Marx took the prospect of Jewish inclusion as the occasion for a broader meditation on the modern state. In similar fashion, contemporary critics can derive theoretical conclusions from scholarship that ascribes epochal significance to Jewish enfranchisement. Two currents run through the diverse and contentious scholarship on Jewish citizenship: a critique of the dilemmas that the nation-state poses for Jews and the corollary insistence that different types of states afford radically different possibilities for Jewish identity, practice, and self-organization. With the exception of Baron, the latter (Spinoza-style) theme is rarely articulated as a political-theoretical proposition. I tried to amplify this theme and render it legible to theorists of modern citizenship. With this move, I rehabilitate foundational insights from the nationalist school of emancipation historiography about the near-existential significance of variations in state structures. The lament for a lost corporate autonomy makes visible the far-reaching transformations attendant on the dissolution of the old and the rise of new political regimes.

Here, it is important to make distinctions between historical claims (and their accuracy) and conceptual claims (and their richness or perspicacity). As we have seen, subsequent generations challenged the historical accuracy of nationalist emancipation narratives, accusing their predecessors of operating with a reified, ideological conception of Jewish nationhood. Yet critics who corrected these historiographical lapses nevertheless vindicated the original insight about the decisive implications of political templates. From the founding histories of emancipation onward, work on Jewish citizenship has disclosed a facet of political belonging not commonly noted in scholarship on the citizenship of, say, women or racial minorities.

With a nod to Baron, I argued that the study of modern Jewish citizenship confronts us with a distinctive "question of regime." What forms of Jewish existence are constrained and enabled by different kinds of political regimes (e.g., city-state, nation-state, federation, or multinational empire)? Baron's work poses the question in these terms and demonstrates its importance. But none of the historians—Baron included—provides a fully worked-out theoretical repertoire to probe the question whose urgency their research demonstrates. Nor has Western political theory managed to fill the void. In modernity, regime thinking loses its centrality as the "question of the best regime"—a standard topos of ancient political thought—gives way to concepts such as sovereignty. Hobbes and Rousseau continue to operate with the classical triad (monarchy, aristocracy, democracy). In their works, however, the justification for absolute sovereignty takes precedence over the question of its embodiment in a given regime, which is treated as a secondary, technical matter. The most notable attempt to incorporate the insights of emancipation historiography into political theory—that of Hannah Arendt, to whom I turn in conclusion—underscores the lack of a robust idiom for debating what I have called the Jewish question of regime.

Like Spinoza and Marx before her, Arendt drew theoretical conclusions about the value of formal political membership from "so small (and, in world politics, so unimportant) a phenomenon as the Jewish question."[19] In *The Origins of Totalitarianism*, she famously derived "the existence of a right to have rights" from the crisis that befell Jews and other stateless peoples during World War II (296). Stripped of citizenship, Arendt demonstrates, Jews found that the human rights meant to protect them in such an eventuality were worthless because no country was willing to honor them. Arendt wrote *Origins* after the

Holocaust—the historical event that arguably justified the profound pessimism of emancipation historiography. Moreover, Arendt situates herself within traditions of emancipation historiography, citing Baron and Katz approvingly (xii). In *Origins*, Arendt devotes a chapter to "the equivocalities of emancipation," narrating "the simultaneous decline of the European nation-state system and growth of antisemitic movements" (11, 9). Arendt's argument about the causes of antisemitism is predicated on the Jews' tenuous position in a specific regime, the nation-state. Express commitments to equality notwithstanding, Arendt argues, nation-states needed the Jews (specifically, Jewish bankers) to remain "outside the social body and within the sphere of the state" (30). (The historical validity of Arendt's claims regarding the vicissitudes of Jewish wealth has been largely discredited.) Despite the limitations of Arendt's historical research, her approach echoes Baron and Katz in that she foregrounds the constraints that the nation-state placed on Jewish self-understanding and organization.

When Arendt derives theoretical conclusions from the Jewish case, however, she elides distinctions between nation-states and other kinds of states, praising citizenship in the abstract. The plight of refugees prompts Arendt to endorse citizenship as an essential constituent of the human: "The calamity of the rightless is not that they are deprived of life, liberty, and the pursuit of happiness"—oppressed within a given state—"but that they no longer belong to any community whatsoever" (295). Here, formal membership in a political community is a necessary condition for realizing supposedly natural human rights. Indeed, statelessness or expulsion from the polity is tantamount to expulsion from the human: "Only the loss of a polity itself expels him [man] from humanity" (297). Writing as a theorist, Arendt uncouples the abstract concept of citizenship from the concrete regimes that enfranchised Jews. The nature of the commonwealth—nation-state vs. multinational federation vs. empire—remains unspecified and proves less important than the fact of citizenship as such. Of course, Arendt reaches this conclusion because she writes at a juncture when the alternative to citizenship is statelessness—rather than a primordial Jewish autonomy. For refugees fleeing political repression and violence, membership in any polity—nation-state, federation, or multinational empire—is undoubtedly preferable to the alternative.

As a contribution to the study of emancipation, however, Arendt's unqualified endorsement of citizenship is curious. With the jump from the nation-state to formal membership in a generic polity, Arendt diverges from her historical sources. Indeed, Arendt appears to have repressed key points of Baron's non-lachrymose conception. The historiography of emancipation accords decisive importance to the *type* of polity in which Jews reside. Although most of the scholars surveyed treat enfranchisement as an epochal break, they are not especially invested in citizenship as such. (The early proponents of Wissenschaft—who struggled to secure equal standing—prove an exception.) Rather, they examine the prospects for Jewish identity and existence afforded by the *kinds* of regimes in which Jewish enfranchisement was or was not conceivable. Indeed, given the anti-lachrymose thrust of canonical narratives, it is scarcely surprising that scholars downplay the importance of legal citizenship status. If Jews who lacked equal rights enjoyed a robust national existence in the Middle Ages, one could argue, formal political membership is less salient than Arendt contends. As Baron claimed, the idioms of liberal citizenship (rights, equality) do not fully capture the conditions that reshaped Jewish politics in modernity and must be supplemented with concepts such as autonomy.

This excursus into Arendt's work illustrates the lack of a language for translating the insights of Jewish citizenship studies into the idioms of political theory. In other works, such as *On Revolution*,[20] Arendt displays a keen appreciation for thinkers like Montesquieu who grapple with concrete challenges of regime design. Yet she proves less adept when navigating the distinctive regime dilemmas posed by Jewish history. This lacuna may stem from her admirable commitment to refugees. On a deeper level, however, it reflects a paucity of theoretical resources. Although Arendt immersed herself in emancipation historiography, she had trouble grasping its central findings as political-theoretical propositions. Jewish struggles with and over citizenship focus attention on aspects of political belonging that Western political theorists—preoccupied with the choice between liberal and republican visions of citizenship—tend to overlook. Studying modern states from a Jewish vantage point should prompt contemporary theorists to develop a richer language in which to assess the profound implications—beyond economic benefits and parliamentary participation—of state structures for minority communities.

Framed in this way, the historiography of enfranchisement speaks directly to political controversies roiling the Jewish world today. At a moment when virtually all Jews enjoy equal rights (qua Jews), the type of regime nevertheless remains a live question. Caution is required, lest we succumb to a political determinism that downplays the significance of grassroots agency, mobilization, and contestation. As history demonstrates, Jewish enfranchisement was not self-evident, despite the egalitarian underpinnings of modern citizenship theory: Jews and their allies had to fight to secure equal standing. With these caveats in mind, I nevertheless argue that contemporary ideological configurations reflect the type of states in which Jews currently live. In a period when Jewish citizenship is largely taken for granted, formal membership is less consequential for the shaping of Jewish identity than the *kind* of state to which Jews belong.

Today, Jews are full citizens in Israel, North America, and Europe—yet their modes of identity and communal organization radically diverge. As codified in the 2018 Nation-State Law, the State of Israel defines itself as the nation-state of the Jewish people. The law reflects the hold that a shared national identity—which is Jewish, rather than Israeli—has over Israeli Jews. In the United States, the constitutional guarantee of religious freedom has allowed Judaism to thrive as a private religious (or ethnic) identity. For most American Jews, national autonomy no longer registers as a desideratum. (The Satmar Hasidim, who used property ownership and religious freedom protections to create an exclusively Haredi town, constitute a notable exception). New modes of Jewish identity have begun to percolate in the smaller communities of Central Europe, whose concepts are taken not from the nation-state but from the symbolic and institutional structures of the European Union. Developments in Europe hold out the prospect of a new political grammar, in which the range of available Jewish ideologies expands beyond ethnonationalism (Israel) and liberal individualism (North America) to encompass transnational federations built on communal autonomy.

In short, contemporary Jewish politics confirms the continued primacy of state structures. At a moment when questions once thought settled (e.g., the justification for liberal democracy) have been reopened, these insights are more important than ever for Jews and non-Jews alike. Studying the history of the Jews' vexed relationship to the state pushes us to talk about citizenship in ways that go beyond standard considerations of rights and equality, liberalism, and republicanism. Jewish Studies can contribute a profound appreciation for the ways in which political regimes shape our conceptual apparatus, spiritual imagination, sense of self, and possibilities for communal organization. To realize this promise, scholars must hone a critical vocabulary that can translate historiographical claims regarding the decisive implications of state forms into theoretical discourse. Making the modern Jewish "question of regime" legible to a wide audience is the urgent task for which this chapter has laid the scholarly groundwork.

Recommended Readings

Baron, Salo W. "Ghetto and Emancipation," in *The Menorah Treasury*, ed. Leo W. Schwarz (Jewish Publication Society, 1966), 50–63.

Baron, Salo W. "Nationalism and Intolerance," *Menorah Journal* 16, no. 6 (1929): 503–15.

Birnbaum, Pierre, and Ira Katznelson, eds. *Paths of Emancipation* (Princeton University Press, 1995).

Cohen, Julia Phillips. *Becoming Ottomans: Sephardi Jews and Imperial Citizenship in the Modern Era* (Oxford University Press, 2014).

Dubnow, Simon. *Nationalism and History* (Jewish Publication Society, 1958).

Katz, Jacob. *Out of the Ghetto* (Harvard University Press, 1973).

Katz, Jacob. *Tradition and Crisis* (New York University Press, 1993).

Marglin, Jessica. "Extraterritoriality and Legal Belonging in the Nineteenth-Century Mediterranean," *Law and History Review* 39, no. 2 (2021): 679–706.

Mendes-Flohr, Paul. "The Emancipation of European Jewry: Why Was It Not Self-Evident?" *Studia Rosenthaliana* 30, no. 1 (1996): 7–20.

Sorkin, David. *Jewish Emancipation* (Princeton University Press, 2019).

Stein, Sarah Abrevaya. *Extraterritorial Dreams* (University of Chicago Press, 2016)

Stein, Sarah Abrevaya. *Family Papers* (Farrar, Straus, Giroux, 2019).

Notes

1. *Theologico-Political Treatise*, in *The Collected Works of Spinoza,* Vol. 2, ed. Edwin Curley (Princeton University Press, 2016), 289.

2. David Sorkin, *Jewish Emancipation* (Princeton University Press, 2019), 29, 33.

3. See Mendes-Flohr, "The Emancipation of European Jewry: Why Was It Not Self-Evident?" *Studia Rosenthaliana* 30 (1996): 7–20.

4. See *The Marx-Engels Reader*, ed. Robert C. Tucker (W. W. Norton, 1978).

5. Sorkin, *Jewish Emancipation*, 149–50.

6. "Scholarship and Emancipation," in *The Jew in the Modern World*, ed. Paul Mendes-Flohr and Jehuda Reinharz (Oxford University Press, 2011), 254.

7. See esp. *Nationalism and History: Essays on Old and New Judaism,* ed. K. S. Pinson (Jewish Publication Society, c. 1958).

8. *Nationalism and History*, 100–115.

9. *Menorah Treasury*, ed. Leo W. Schwarz (Jewish Publication Society, 1966), 50–63.

10. *Menorah Journal* 16, no. 6: 503–15.

11. Schocken, 1957.

12. *Out of the Ghetto* (Harvard University Press, 1973).

13. Princeton University Press, 1995.

14. "From *Millet* to Minority," *Paths*, Ch. 8.

15. Oxford University Press, 2014.

16. *Extraterritorial Dreams* (University of Chicago Press, 2016), 9.

17. "Extraterritoriality and Legal Belonging in the Nineteenth-Century Mediterranean," *Law and History Review* 39 (2021): 680, 682.

18. Farrar, Straus and Giroux, 2019.

19. *The Origins of Totalitarianism* (Harcourt Brace, 1979), viii.

20. Viking, 1963.

9

Colonialism

Ethan B. Katz, University of California, Berkeley

Terminology and Typology

The story of overseas empires haunts the modern Jewish condition. The most significant developments of modern Jewish history, including the struggle for civic emancipation, the rise of modern antisemitism, the emergence of Zionism and the State of Israel, and the Shoah, were all profoundly affected by colonialism. Yet colonialism in Jewish history simultaneously hovers as an omnipresent specter and remains understudied and underconceptualized.

This chapter does not treat Jews and empire writ large—a topic that would span millennia and much of the globe. Here the ambit of colonialism corresponds to the focus of the scholarly "imperial turn": overseas settler colonies and their European metropoles in modern times. Historians have interrogated a paradox that makes Britain, France, and other liberal regimes of Europe distinctive: the simultaneous rise of a set of claims about the nation-state, popular sovereignty, the public good, and universalism at home and about violent conquest and subjugation on a large scale overseas. Even when they offered the rhetoric of universalism or the ever-delayed promise of democratic equality, settler-colonial spaces were built on racial hierarchy, dehumanization, a homogenizing nationalism, and systematic discrimination. Jews frequently had the peculiar experience of operating within the fissures and contradictions of colonial rule. Scholars of the "new colonial history" have typically seen land-based empires like the Russian, Hapsburg, Ottoman, and American ones as different. These entities shared some but not all the earlier mentioned features specific to modern overseas empires and were often more multiethnic or even multinational in their self-conception. Thus, for both historiographical and historical reasons, they are outside the scope of this chapter.

Jews across a range of imperial metropoles and peripheries were hardly monolithic in their politics or practices. Just like other ethnic and religious groups, they took up a range of positions and roles in relation to Europe's overseas empires, and this chapter in part traces that demographic reality. Yet I often center those cases (1) where Jews defined their relationship to empire in Jewish terms—whether via Jewish causes, political parties, press, pulpits, or networks—and (2) where Jews were defined as such by state or nonstate actors.

Indeed, part of our challenge remains that there is not one history of Jews and overseas colonial empires. Rather, there are at least three, which for shorthand purposes, may be called histories of emancipation, racialization, and brutalization. In the first history, Jews in the European mainland supported colonialism—sometimes unequivocally, in other cases more critically—as a vehicle for Jewish emancipation and equality. This support took two principal forms: (1) an ardent patriotism that emphasized colonial bona fides as a means to promote Jewish civic equality and (2) a Jewish "civilizing mission" to improve the material and political situation of their Jewish brothers and sisters living in overseas colonies. In the second history, colonialism had a dual impact on the racial status of Jews. From the late nineteenth century, colonialism played a pivotal role in expanding, accelerating, and actualizing the rise of race thinking, in which the emergence of modern antisemitism was fundamental. At the same time, many Jews assertively embraced racializing ideas, often to strengthen their claims of being "European" or "white." This process included a paternalistic effort to differentiate European Jews from the darker-skinned "Oriental" Jews to whom they offered aid in colonial spaces. In the third history, Jews participated actively in the colonies themselves, playing a role as soldiers or colonial settlers in the brutal work of conquest and control. These three histories are at once distinctive and interwoven. Each concerns Jews on the European mainland and those in colonized spaces. Jews in the colonies experienced the arrival of Western imperial governments, corporations, goods, and individuals as sources of potential salvation or subjugation. In time, some turned to a radical Jewish politics of resistance, joining efforts to throw off European colonial rule.

These three entangled histories have much to tell us about Jews' multivalent relationships to European powers like Britain, France, Germany, and Italy and to their colonial ventures from the Antipodes to Algeria. They also offer a useful typology for responding to a challenge that Arthur Hertzberg posed more than seven decades ago. At the beginning of *The Zionist Idea*, Hertzberg declared, "Zionism exists and it has had important consequences, but historical theory does not really know what to do with it."[1] This challenge remains substantially the case today. Although historians have increasingly situated Israel/Palestine within the wider history of empire, seldom have they done so with regard to the history of specifically Jewish engagements with colonialism. To address Zionism's implications for Jewish and world history more fully, we must cast the question of Zionism and colonialism in the latter light. In so doing, we find overlooked points of connection and rupture that illuminate both parallels and contrasts.

France and Britain: Making the World More Humane for Jews

The rise of modern colonial empires was paradoxically part and parcel of the era that Holly Case calls the "Age of Questions," when Western polities had to negotiate the rise of liberalism with the status not only of Jews but also of women, people of color, immigrants, the poor, the ill, and other groups seen as others.[2] In this context, the contradictory relationship of empire to emancipation was the central story in the Jewish encounter with colonialism. After centuries during which Jews had regularly negotiated changing terms of residence, legal status, and patronage with sovereigns, states, and empires while experiencing regular bouts of violence and expulsion, the prospect of equal citizenship appeared to many as a harbinger of greater stability in a new age. Simultaneously, the growing presence of many of the same European powers across Eurasia and Africa presented challenges and possibilities for many Jews of the mainland and the colonies. In both France and Britain, expanding imperial possessions and spheres of influence in the nineteenth century gave many Jews the occasion to buttress their liberal and patriotic credentials by supporting humanistic, liberal visions of imperial intervention. Simultaneously, many Jewish liberals defended the rights and needs of their brothers and sisters in far-off "Eastern" lands.

In the French case, as the empire grew in the nineteenth century, Jewish participation in broader French colonial missions—including their more brutal aspects—expanded too. By the 1880s, mainland French Jewish soldiers were gaining distinction as participants in imperial conquest and subjugation from the Maghreb to the Far East. They served as everything from infantry to artillery to interpreters to medical staff to generals, and they often met violent ends while on assignment. In the early 1890s, enough of these Jewish officers had perished in the colonies to elicit a special memorial prayer service at the Grand Synagogue in Paris for Jewish military officers killed overseas, with military brass and Jewish community notables in attendance. The community's patriotic fervor, like that of their Christian compatriots, burned particularly brightly for those sons who had taken up the sword of empire.[3]

Simultaneously, the decades following the Damascus Affair of 1840 witnessed the rise of a new Jewish international solidarity movement. French Jews like Adolphe Crémieux, who were prominent both in national liberal politics and the Jewish community, sought to uplift their coreligionists in North Africa, the Levant, and the Balkans whom they saw as backward, ossified, and in dire economic and political straits. In so doing, they strengthened both their own claims to civic equality and the more democratic strains in French politics that underlay such claims. The Alliance Israélite Universelle (AIU), founded in Paris in 1860, was the first international Jewish solidarity organization in the modern world. Emerging in the context of the fierce political battles in mid-century France between ultramontane Catholic conservatives and anticlerical liberals, the AIU represented in equal measure an effort to cement the alliance of French Jews with the latter group. In the process, such Jews helped forge a newly secular version of French political and cultural expansion overseas, framed around "civilization" rather than Catholicism. This all aligned with a wider, long-term effort on the part of community leaders to "regenerate" France's Jewish population: The Revolution of 1789 and the Napoleonic Sanhedrin had laid the legal foundation, but becoming fully accepted citizens demanded education, reform, and modernization.

Franco-Jewish leaders believed such efforts should extend well beyond the Hexagon (the country of France). Founded to combat discrimination against Jews across the Maghreb, the Mashriq, and the Balkans, the AIU made its greatest impact through a sprawling international network of schools that carried out a specific version of the famed *mission civilisatrice*. Filled with North African and Ottoman-born teachers trained in Paris, these schools aimed to forge a "Francophone" model of a modern, enlightened, Western-educated, laicized Jewish youth. In addition to Hebrew and Jewish history, students learned secular subjects like math and science and became proficient in French language and culture. The reach and long-term impact of the organization were formidable: At its height in 1913, there were 183 AIU schools educating nearly 44,000 students from Morocco to Greece to Palestine.[4]

Almost no territories where the AIU rose to prominence were under direct French colonial rule until the late nineteenth and early twentieth century, when Tunisia (1881) and Morocco (1912) became French protectorates. The case of French Algeria was quite different, constituting the most intensive merging of colonial and emancipationist aims and practices in the Francophone orbit.

Within a few years of its invasion in 1830, the French state treated Algeria less like an overseas outpost and more like an extension of France proper.[5] Jewish leaders in mainland France followed suit: In 1842, with the help of the War Ministry, the Central Consistory in Paris—the state-run, official representative body of the French Jewish community—sent a fact-finding mission to Algeria. The resulting report concluded that Algerian Jews, although living in poverty, could be "regenerated" and might be useful to the project of French domination.[6] In 1845 the Consistory founded branches in Algiers, Constantine, and Oran.[7]

On the ground in Algeria, the consistories were in many respects what Valerie Assan terms "instruments of French domination," cooperating closely with the colonial authorities.[8] On the part of both colonial and consistorial authorities, the rabbis became divided into "French" and *indigènes*. The *rabbins indigènes* were paid significantly smaller salaries than their "French" counterparts and barred from the highest posts.[9] At the same time, Assan contends that an important divergence of objectives distinguished "Jewish colonialism" in Algeria from French colonialism broadly: The Consistory aimed ultimately to emancipate the Jews of Algeria, a goal that they would substantially realize in 1870.[10] Crucial to this process was the gradual assimilation of Jews' legal standing to the French civil code via a series of ordinances and decrees from 1830s through the 1860s.

Throughout, Algerian Jews were never simply passive objects; they resisted, negotiated, and appropriated France's civilizing notions and efforts.[11] At a critical moment, the Central Consistory in December 1869 submitted a petition demanding equal French citizenship. With separate versions in French and Judeo-Arabic, this petition was signed by 1,228 Jewish men in the region of Algiers on behalf of an overall Jewish population of 34,000. This appeal to the imperial authorities reflected long-standing cultures of petition among Jews in both French and Islamic lands.[12] These processes unfolded in the northern portions of Algeria but culminated in the metropolitan city of Tours, where on September 4, 1870, the Government of National Defense had been formed. There, Adolphe Crémieux as justice minister emancipated the Jews of Algeria with a decree that would forever bear his name.

In years to come, French Jewish leaders often punctuated this emancipationist narrative with notes that linked the fate of Algerian Jews to the particularities of Franco-Judaism. In 1889, rabbis across France celebrated the centennial of the French Revolution with sermons declaring France "the new Jerusalem" and proclaiming the occasion "the anniversary of our deliverance . . . our modern Passover!" Chief Rabbi of Algiers Isaac Bloch marked the occasion by declaring that, even though Algerian Jews were "latecomers among the sons of France," when the French landed at Sidi-Ferruch in 1830, the "Algerian Israélites were [already] convinced that the new France, formed by the principles of '89, carried in the folds of its flag not hatred and persecution but love, justice, and liberty."[13]

Over the ensuing decades, the interrelationship between liberal notions of empire in Algeria and Jewish rights there became further cemented. During World War II, in October 1940, the pro-German Vichy regime stripped Algerian Jews of their French citizenship. Over the next three years, numerous Jewish resisters and community leaders endeavored to restore independent French sovereignty and eventually to place the Free French in power in Algeria. They viewed this as the linchpin for the reinstatement of their citizenship (eventually undertaken by Charles De Gaulle in October 1943). During the Algerian War for Independence (1954–62), Algerian and French Jewish leaders feared that Jews' security depended on French rule; they worked feverishly to ensure that, whatever the outcome, France would guarantee their citizenship.

These efforts succeeded in part because at the very same moment Algerian Muslims were being cast out of the nation. In fact, for Jews in French Algeria, emancipation and racialization were hardly separable stories from the start. Across the nineteenth century, French reformists and policy makers debated whether both Jews and Muslims in Algeria were capable of "becoming French."[14] For policy makers and colonists alike, the two groups' statuses were always entwined. It was in significant part the proximity between Jewish and Muslim culture in North Africa and the Middle East that shaped French Jewish ideas about the "Eastern question" and the need to bring "civilization" to the indigenous Jews of Muslim lands. French Jewish reformers and their allies drew repeated contrasts between stereotypes of the veiled, domesticated, unexposed Arab Muslim woman beyond the reach of civilization and the increasingly free, open, educated, and civilized Algerian Jewish girl. Muslims, they implied, were much further removed from (white) Europeanness, and Jews were much closer to it.

Yet simultaneously, racialization meant a backlash against emancipation: Antisemitism became a major political program in the three major urban centers of Algeria. Between the late nineteenth century and the 1930s, Algiers, Oran, and Constantine all elected mayors with antisemitic platforms. During the Dreyus Affair, anti-Jewish violence in Algeria was far more virulent than in the mainland. At its height, Edouard Drumont, dubbed "the Pope of Antisemitism," was one of the four proudly antisemitic deputies—of six total—elected to parliament from Algeria. For the settler classes in Algeria, Jewish emancipation represented the danger that the racial hierarchy underlying the colonial edifice could be overturned: If one group of natives could become citizens, then one day so could the rest of them. Likewise, the furious resistance provoked by the Crémieux Decree in Algeria was among the major reasons why Jews in French Tunisia and Morocco never acquired French citizenship en masse.[15]

The connections between antisemitism and colonialism proved highly polyvalent. In the late nineteenth century, French writers, including not only Drumont but also Guy de Maupassant, Maurice Barrès, and Émile Zola, created a stock character of public scandal and popular literature: the Jewish colonial conspirator, blamed for imperial overreach and its threatening backwash on the mainland. For instance, Drumont and others alleged that the French invasion of Tunisia in 1881 was the product of financial and political schemes orchestrated by Jews in France and Tunisia. By tying Jews to colonization in such a way, antisemites could link stereotypes about Jews as economically exploitive with those that classified Jews as racially other: Suddenly, Jews across the Mediterranean appeared as a single power-thirsty international entity.[16]

———

A few years after the rabbinical pronouncements marking the centennial of the French Revolution, British Jewry had its own occasion to show fealty to crown and empire: the 1897 celebration of the Diamond Jubilee of Queen Victoria. Michael Adler, minister of Hammersmith Synagogue, declared the "political and social condition of [our fellow Jews] at the present moment in the British Empire" was "better than at any previous period of the exile."[17] Israel Abrahams, speaking at the Central Synagogue, linked empire not only to Jewish but also to broader emancipation: "With off-shoots in all countries and climes, embracing under its banner men widely differing on race, in religion, and in language, England alone of all the empires of Europe has grown to understand that national life needs differentiation in a union of many forces on behalf of progress and righteousness."[18]

Just two years later, the Boer War gave British Jews the opportunity to lend more material support to imperial war and conquest. While the British were fighting an unexpectedly difficult war against the Afrikaners for control of South Africa, British Jews were largely unified and vocal in their support. Nathan Adler, chief rabbi not only of England but also the British Empire, gave a sermon in the war's early weeks where he invoked Jewish theology to insist that, no matter the aspiration to peace, "certain wars are inevitable"; waging this conflict, he maintained, was necessary to support "England's sons in distant lands."[19]

Both the community newspaper, the *Jewish Chronicle*, and *Der Yidisher Ekspres*, a newspaper for Eastern European Jewish immigrants allied with both Zionism and Orthodoxy, praised Jewish soldiers at the front. Featuring substantial reporting and photography of Jewish soldiers, the former claimed that the Jewish casualty rate was almost twice that of general losses; the latter extolled the war as "an opportunity [for Jews] to show thanks to the country which has taken them in and given them freedom."[20] In his research on Jews in the British Empire, David Feldman has persuasively contended that at the same time "there was in both newspapers an undercurrent of uneasy concern that at any moment emancipation might be brought into question."[21]

Like in France, the frequently close entanglement between the quest for full acceptance by British Jews and the work of empire was rooted in the nineteenth century. In contrast to the secular form of liberal internationalism that Jews joined in France, in the British case the cause of Jewish relief became linked with campaigns for the abolition of slavery, "civil and religious liberty," and Christian humanitarianism. These campaigns were underlaid by the "three interlocking pillars" of British imperial ideology—commerce, Christianity, and civilization—and the "special resonance" that each had for Jews.[22]

If Adolphe Crémieux was the most ubiquitous figure in the early decades of the Jewish encounter with French imperialism, in the British case that role was played by Crémieux's close ally during the Damascus Affair, Sir Moses Montefiore. For five decades, Montefiore served as president of the Board of Deputies of British Jews; throughout that time, he focused his energy on the plight of Jews overseas. When humanitarian disasters occurred, he led fundraising efforts and undertook numerous missions to aid Jewish communities in Europe, the Middle East, and North Africa. His greatest engagement was with Ottoman Palestine, which he visited seven times from 1827 to 1875, building relationships with local communities and raising considerable sums on their behalf. Montefiore also became a de facto agent of British interests, helping, for instance, cultivate an enduring attachment to the empire and its ruling family among many Jews in Palestine.

Active in abolitionist circles in the 1830s, Montefiore built relationships with non-Jewish liberals around causes like antislavery, which in turn became linked for many with Jewish relief. A number of Radicals such as the Whig rationalist Lord Brougham and the Irish Catholic MP Daniel O'Connell embraced antislavery and Jewish relief as paired causes within a larger reform effort for "civil and religious liberty."[23] Alliances of Jews, Evangelicals, Quakers, and Radicals took the lead in advocating for the protection of Jews at critical moments such as the Damascus Affair and the 1872 campaign against the persecution of Jews in Rumania. At such moments, the wider power of the empire, even in lands it did not control, became crucial. And Jews often drew surprising strength from groups across the empire: In the 1850s and 1860s, relief funds for Jews in Palestine and Morocco generated support from British subjects in places like Jamaica, Auckland, Toronto, and Hong Kong.

If Jews used the British imperial context to mobilize for their own purposes, so too did the empire draw strength from its support for Jewish causes. Embracing Jewish relief as a British concern helped the empire construct and sustain a self-conception as a shining light for freedom across the globe and so legitimize its overseas reach. Sometimes, as in the aftermath of the Anglo-Persian War of 1856–57, British demands for Jewish relief furthered their broader efforts to defend "humanity" and "civilization"; in other cases, like Morocco in the same era, Jewish efforts to increase consular protection ran counter to British interests in keeping the territory neutral. Either way, however, Jews could speak within a framework of moralistic language around "civil and religious liberty" and the higher imperial callings of Christianity and civilization; this granted their demands significant purchase with British officials.

As in the French case, promoting Jewish emancipation through the empire— whether at home or overseas—was often ultimately a matter of defending Jews as good imperial citizens. The connection was apparent in Jewish support for the campaign in South Africa at the turn of the century. This pairing of Jewish patriotism and advocacy occurred again in the war's aftermath, following a 1904 government report that lamented the physical condition of the volunteers in the war. In the face of xenophobic attacks on free immigration, defenders of Jewish immigrants used the report to contrast the alleged weakness of the British working class with the vitality and nurturing practices of Jewish mothers and fathers. Jewish immigrants from Eastern Europe, they maintained, did not drain imperial resources but instead constituted just the sort of vigorous citizens whom the empire needed.[24]

The specter of race was not always so subtle. The previous year, efforts by Israel Zangwill and others to find a colonial haven for Jews led briefly to the possibility of settling Jews in a portion of British East Africa (today Kenya, although the episode would later be known as the "Uganda offer"). At a time when British officials were worried by the slow pace of European settlement in the East African highlands, their outreach to Theodor Herzl was one among a series of attempts to recruit so-called white settlers to the area. Equally steeped in racialized assumptions, an anonymous columnist in the *Jewish Chronicle* wrote,

"It is land without a people to be offered to a people without a land. . . . The only inhabitants are a few nomadic Masai."[25] The settler community in the capital of Nairobi, however, had its own racial ideas about Jews. Settlers' alarm at word of the proposal caused their leader Lord Delamere to send a telegram to the *Times of London* that read, "Feeling here very strong against the introduction of alien Jews. Railway frontage fit for British colonization 260 miles. Foreign Office proposes give 200 miles best to undesirable aliens."[26] At a protest meeting in Nairobi soon after, one speaker expressed the fear that the natives would learn quickly that Jews were "not white men according to their own ideas," and then the natives "would be influenced by them and their own low code of morals."[27]

Across the great expanse of the British Empire, Jewish emancipation offered a framework for myriad political engagements—with racialization frequently present as well. In 1919, the wealthy Baghdadi Jew of British Calcutta, David Ezra authored a petition asking that the British authorities grant Baghdadi Jews in India exemption from the Indian Arms Act of 1878.[28] This act barred Indians from having weapons but made exceptions for some minority groups, including Europeans, Armenians, and Americans. Ezra tried to argue that Jews, because of their lifestyle (European), loyalty (British), and origins (purportedly Sephardic), should be exempted as well. Although the Home Department rejected this petition, ten years later, Ezra tried once more but changed his argument: He contended that the Baghdadi Jews in India should be recognized not as a privileged minority but simply as Europeans themselves. Ezra and some other Baghdadi Jews were concerned that their power would decline as the majority Hindu electorate that they were a part of expanded. This memorial, with 115 signatories among the prominent Baghdadi Jews living in Calcutta, insisted that "all natural born British subjects of the Jewish Community living in the European style and domiciled in Bengal" should become part of the European electorate.[29]

In Ezra's first petition, he made a distinction between foreign Jews (the Baghdadis) and natives in the Benei Israel community. In his subsequent campaign, he went much further, insisting that Jews' race was widely known to be "European" and "white." In September 1929, in a letter to a leader of the Bombay Jewish community, Ezra even wrote, "It is an accepted and established fact in the civilized world that the Jewish race is a white one," and thus "British Jews of pure descent have a right to be included by Government in their political classification of European no matter where they were born," given that the European electorate "was obviously formed to represent the White races domiciled in India."[30] Like so many pleas for the acceptance of Jewish whiteness, underneath

Ezra's claims lay his own experience of anti-Jewish exclusion in certain social settings, including in 1907 from the Bengal Club, a European gentlemen's club that ironically was on property Ezra himself owned. Ezra's real estate holdings in Calcutta were so considerable that the club's organizers had not realized he owned that land. When he ordered the property vacated, they offered him membership. He refused but allowed them to continue to operate the club there.[31]

Italy and the Kaiserreich: Stouter Jewish Citizens for Racy-er Empires

Living under nation-states established much later than England or France, Jews in Italy (unified in 1861) and in Germany (unified in 1871) were part of empires that also rose and fell more rapidly. In their imperial engagements through the framework of emancipation, they both mimicked and departed from their British and French counterparts. As Italy moved to build an empire in parts of Africa beginning in the 1890s, Italian Jews—equal citizens since just after unification—were substantially supportive.[32] Jewish leaders undertook what Shira Klein describes as "a three-way relationship" between Italian Jewry, colonial authorities, and native Jewish communities in Tripoli and Benghazi in Libya, as well as the Falashas and a few other small communities in Ethiopia and Eritrea.[33] As in the French and British cases, Jews on the mainland both Orientalized and sought to aid their colonized coreligionists.

Jewish support for Italy's quest for a "place in the sun" came early and often. Not long after Italy began to colonize Eritrea, Leopoldo Franchetti, deputy in the Italian parliament and scion of what had once been among Italy's most prominent Jewish families, became the new colony's counselor for agriculture in 1891. His appointment prompted multiple organs of the Italian Jewish press to express their happy wishes for his great success. During the Italian invasion of Libya in 1911, Jewish support was quite visible. Livorno's chief rabbi wrote a special prayer for victory that was read each Shabbat morning in Italian synagogues. The president of the Roman Jewish community expressed his hope that Italy's "civilizing mission" would triumph. Many Jews joined the invading armies and were celebrated in the Jewish press; others appeared on the donor rolls of the Italian war cause.

Yet it was as the skies began to darken on Italian emancipation that Jewish colonial fever reached its peak. In the 1930s, Mussolini undertook a second phase in the Fascist Revolution that called on Italians to cease to be "a race of slaves" and become "a race of lords"; that is, powerful imperial citizens. Seeking to fashion Italy into an African empire, he established legal hierarchies around race, and by 1938 these laws targeted Jews.[34] In this environment, Jews seemed to double down on their imperial patriotism by asserting their belonging in the new "race of lords": During what proved to be a ruthless invasion of Ethiopia in 1935–36, not only did many Jews volunteer to fight, but more notably, a number of Jews also supported the war in explicitly Jewish terms. Community leaders urged Jewish women to give their wedding rings, gold, and expensive jewelry to the "Gold for the Fatherland" campaign in support of the invasion. On the first anniversary of Italy's victory, Jewish youths in Florence paraded through the garden of the synagogue playing music and wearing fascist youth uniforms. With imperial racism and concomitant antisemitism growing, Jews seemed more eager than ever to perform imperial loyalty as a defense of their increasingly vulnerable position within the Italian nation.

During the same era, Italian Jews extended their emancipationist and racialized imperialism to the embattled Jewish populations of the colonies. Despite their relatively small numbers (barely 39,000 in the 1931 census), mainland Italian Jews confidently devoted attention to the thousands of Indigenous Jews in Tripolitania (some 21,000), Cyrenaica (nearly 3,000), Eritrea (less than 200), and Ethiopia (50,000 Falashas). They referred to these Jews repeatedly as their "brothers." Faced with a combination of harshly enforced government restrictions on their livelihoods and their religious practices, on the one hand, and frequent hostility and even violence from local populations, on the other, Jews in colonies like Libya and Eritrea regularly appealed directly to their coreligionists in the metropole for protection. Jews on the peninsula in turn took a predictably paternalistic attitude that reflected their own assumptions about racial superiority. As in French Algeria, the Italian Jewish community insisted on imposing Italian rabbis, rather than relying on Indigenous ones, and granted colonized Jewish communities little representation on Jewish governing councils. At times, such attitudes provoked significant resistance from Indigenous Jews, who could, for instance, refuse to accept an outsider rabbi or oppose efforts to reform local religious customs.

At the same time, race simultaneously undergirded the vulnerability of Jews in the colonies and the terms that they used to promote their own rights. In 1932, objecting to the way that Jews were treated in the criminal justice system, Asmara's Jewish leader Shoa Menachem Joseph lamented, "The condemnation [of Jews] is carried out in the same way as for the Indigenous people." He differentiated Jews sharply from the latter, defined as an "uncivilized race [with its] unfamiliar laws, habits and feelings." Like in French North Africa, however, avoiding association with other Indigenous groups was nearly impossible. The conquest of Abyssinia in 1935–36 set in motion Italian fears of racial contamination that led to laws of separation, first from the territory's Black population and eventually from the Jews in Libya.[35] This escalation helped set the stage for the 1938 racial laws and the violence and internment experienced by Libyan Jews during the Holocaust.

———

In an important contrast with France, Britain, and Italy, the Kaiserreich had long focused its imperial holdings and ambitions substantially in Europe, rather than overseas. Given its small African holdings, the German Empire was not home to any populations of Indigenous Jews who could appear to be in need of a "civilizing" or humanitarian mission on the part of their continental coreligionists.[36] Moreover, many German Jews were transfixed in the nineteenth century by the "allure of the Sephardic," perceiving the Jews of medieval Islamic Spain in particular as a model for German Jewish education and integration. Thus, it was not the Jews of Arab lands but rather the *Ostjuden* immigrating to Germany that were seen as in need of civilization, acculturation, and modernization. In these circumstances, international Jewish solidarity played little role in the German-Jewish engagement with empire. Simultaneously, the emergence of colonial possessions and outlooks in Germany coincided with the twinned rise of political antisemitism and race science and eugenics. Just when German Jews were achieving civic emancipation after unification, they faced the growing sentiment that they remained outsiders. Support for colonialism offered a path inward to fit changing times—away from the receding humanistic cult of *Bildung* and toward the more *volkish*, ethnoracial chauvinism emerging by the end of the nineteenth century.[37]

This effort was on full display in 1913 for the the twenty-fifth anniversary of Kaiser Wilhelm II's rise to the throne. Ludwig Geiger, son of the famous founding father of Reform Judaism, Abraham Geiger, and himself then editor of the *Allgemeine Zeitung des Judentums* (*AZdJ*), the principal organ of German Jewry, wrote a rather obsequious essay in his newspaper to mark the occasion. Praising the Kaiser as a builder of empire, Geiger somewhat implausibly ignored the sovereign's well-known bellicosity toward native populations; instead he credited him for wise restraint that cultivated successes like the Kiautschou (Jiaozhou) in China and the discovery of diamonds in German South West Africa (present-day Namibia, SWA hereafter).[38] This laudatory editorial in the *AZdJ* was representative of a wider trend in which a number of visible German Jews raced to associate themselves enthusiastically with imperial progress as a way to burnish their nationalist credentials.

The primary colonial arena in the German context was one of unusual complexity for Jews: the war of annihilation against the Herero and Nama peoples in 1904–5 in SWA. When a group of warriors from the Herero, the majority native ethnic group, responded to large-scale land seizures by German settlers with a violent insurgency, they provoked a series of conflicts that led eventually to a brutal campaign of repression. By the end of hostilities, the Germans had wiped out approximately 80,000 Herero and Nama, representing around 80 percent of the former and 50 percent of the latter populations, respectively. This brutal campaign entailed dehumanization, concentration camps, efforts to create German "living space," and the use of brutal "final solutions." These components have led several scholars to connect—in however jagged a manner—the campaigns of extermination in SWA to those against Jews by the Nazis a generation later.[39]

But in this case, Jews were among the perpetrators. Of 15,000 white inhabitants in SWA, between 300 to 400 were Jewish. Jews even had their own synagogue in Swakopmund, the largest town in SWA. The German forces that arrived in SWA to put down the Herero uprising included Jews. Altogether, this meant that in SWA, more than in most places, Jews were involved in brutalization measures such as resettlement, repression, and even genocide.[40]

At the very same time, Jews faced the interlaced rise of antisemitism and German colonial stereotypes. The Pan-German League, founded in 1891, began as a colonialist lobbying group; in time it expanded its *volkish* racial ideology to become one of the most radical and virulent antisemitic organizations in Germany.[41] (Conversely, German colonialism's fiercest critics regularly caricatured—and frequently with anti-Jewish stereotypes—the figure of Bernhard Dernburg, a man of Jewish ancestry who served from 1903 to 1911 as Germany's colonial director and then colonial secretary.[42])

The challenges of race for Jews in colonial Germany help explain the ardent pride expressed in the Jewish press regarding Jewish participation in the colonial wars in SWA. In response to a lengthy speech in the Reichstag by Deputy Friedrich Bindewald in 1907 in which he attacked the motivations and actions of Jews in the colonies, the *AZdJ* highlighted the widespread patriotism of the Jews against the Herero. Elsewhere the *AZdJ* underscored that the *Frankfurter Zeitung* had included mention of Jewish volunteers who fought in battles against the Herero and were on a German colonial expedition to China.[43] Thus, German Jews had to navigate competing considerations of patriotic loyalty, racial demarcation, and moral critique as SWA became an important site for negotiating their relationship to the Kaiserreich.

———

As this highly episodic survey suggests, from the corridors of European capitals to the fields of the bush, three stories of Jews and colonialism—of emancipation, racialization, and brutalization—that may appear distinct at first glance unfolded across more than a century in an uneven, frequently simultaneous, entangled, and paradoxical fashion. If the linkages between colonialism and emancipation both opened and motivated possibilities for greater Jewish mobility across political boundaries, some of these same connections also etched new boundaries around the increasingly ubiquitous lens of race. All at once, mainland and Indigenous Jews had a contentious relationship defined by both fraternal bonds and racially tinged paternalism; struggled against systems of structural racism and antisemitism; and echoed colonial racial stereotypes in an effort to solidify their own European bona fides. Both groups participated frequently in the most optimistic aspirations of the colonial project. Joining a far larger number of European Christians who dominated the work of colonization, some Jewish soldiers and occasionally settlers also took part in the brutal work of conquest and repression.

In time, the nexus of emancipation, racialization, and brutalization in the Jewish encounter with colonialism engendered growing critique and opposition in distinctly Jewish terms. In the German context, the Jewish writer and scientist Hermann Glenn wrote in 1917 that Judaism should be the "conscience of humanity" in the age of imperialism by helping curb the latter's worst excesses.[44] Already in 1913, when Mahatma Gandhi led his first *satyagraha* ("holding onto truth") campaign in South Africa, Jews such as the lawyer Henry Polak, the architect Hermann Kallenbach, and Gandhi's personal assistant Sonja Schlesin played indispensable roles. During the era of decolonization in the mid-twentieth century, numerous Jews combined aspects of Jewishness and leftist politics, ranging from trans-Mediterranean networks of Jewish communists to intellectuals and writers like Hannah Arendt, Albert Memmi, and René Sirat who linked Holocaust memory and anticolonial critique. In recent years, historians have begun to illuminate more fully this alternative history of Jews and colonialism.[45]

The Question of Zionism

Where do emancipation, racialization, and brutalization fit into the history of Zionism and Israel, particularly in comparison with the other instances of Jews and colonial history discussed here? In brief, all three histories were present from early on, but each has taken new forms in the Zionist context. Here I can only sketch the outlines of continuities and disjunctions, but I hope that, as the field of Jews and colonial history grows, the issue will receive much more scholarly attention.

Zionism, like the stories of Jews and colonialism, has often operated in what postcolonial theorist Homi Bhabha terms the "in-between spaces."[46] The groups and entities within these spaces reveal how colonial practices, through their obsession with fixed boundaries, often undermine the very dualities that they seek to construct. At its origins, Zionism was at once a revolt against European homogenizing, racializing policies *and* a product of European hegemonic and imperial culture.[47] By many measurements, Zionism was, at its origins, an anticolonial movement seeking collective emancipation.[48] In a manner parallel to the situation of subjects in the French and Dutch Empires, European Jews in the nineteenth century experienced citizenship as a quid pro quo arrangement wherein they had to prove their fitness for European civilization. Two other parallels were the establishment of agricultural colonies for both Jews and the Indo-European poor and the intellectual responses of Jews in the Haskalah and Reform movements, who took up many themes analogous to those of efforts for cultural renewal among subject populations in colonial Asia and Africa. In each instance, reviving ancient language and culture was crucial to a process of a subaltern people achieving greater national consciousness. Set in this historical context, pre-state Zionism suddenly sounds similar to other Indigenous movements for reform or independence that we may know better—from Haiti to West Africa to the Indian subcontinent.

Moreover, early Zionism was in many respects shaped by a different imperial framework—that of the Russian, Hapsburg, and Ottoman multinational empires. Surrounded in their birthlands by ethnonationalist movements that articulated flexible formulas for what Simon Dubnow called "independence within empire," figures such as Leo Pinsker, Ahad Ha'am, and Theodor Herzl echoed such outlooks.[49] They envisioned substatist territorial entities of Jewish culture that, if located in Palestine, would most likely exist under the sovereignty of the Ottoman Empire.[50] As Herzl met with Ottoman, Wilhelmine, and British officials, his great ambition was to secure "a charter." The watershed moment of the Balfour Declaration in 1917 did not promise Jews a state of Palestine but rather "the establishment in Palestine of a national home."

But just as other anticolonial movements relied frequently on the appropriation of the "master's tools," so too did Zionism. Jews like Herzl drew on the rise of nineteenth-century European ideas such as nationalism, romanticism, Orientalism, and the connection between ethnicity and nationhood—ideas that had often helped subjugate Jews but could be turned toward a different kind of Jewish liberation than the one that seemed to be repeatedly forestalled in the protracted emancipation process. As they unfolded across the late nineteenth and early twentieth centuries, many necessary prerequisites for Jewish colonization in Palestine—including financial support, the notion of a "civilizing mission," the connection between such a mission and western agricultural technologies, and Orientalist ideas about Arab culture, to name but a few—were only thinkable in the wider context of European overseas expansion.

In this manner, Herzl seems almost inevitably a paradoxical prophet whose aptness for the role could have been matched by few of his peers. Even though his experience of antisemitism and upbringing in Hapsburg Vienna led him to call for a new kind of collective Jewish emancipation and to rebel against the colonized condition of Jews in Europe, he also knew and supported many methods and assumptions of European overseas colonialism. By posing frequently as enthusiasts of colonialism, sometimes as soldiers of colonial repression, and occasionally even as settlers, Jews in other colonial settings were learning new ways of being European as they still sought to fulfill the "liberal offer" of equal citizenship. Zionism took these approaches that much further. If Jews were to gain the emancipation and normalization that they were denied within Europe, they would still do so, in the schema of Herzl and many of his successors, as Europeans. And if settlement in Palestine, with its long-standing and sizable Arab population, was the answer, alliance with the great powers and the methods of colonialism—including specific forms of racialization and brutalization—would be all but inevitable.

We might say that Zionism was aligned with both meanings of emancipation from the earlier history of Jews and colonialism: (1) colonialism as Jewish emancipation and (2) anticolonialism as a form of Jewish emancipation (in both instances proponents expressed ideas about universal rights that would liberate Jews). Zionism brought these two strands together. Not only did early Zionists have much in common with anticolonial movements but in its early decades the Israeli state also made fruitful alliances with movements of the Global South, some of which saw Israel as a model of anticolonial struggle and postcolonial society. Over time, however, the tension of being "colonized colonizers" proved too much to sustain.

In part, this reflected another key departure of Zionism. From French Algeria to Italian Libya, the same modes of adapting to European ideas and institutions, which often blurred lines between Jews and European settlers and made equality seem more attainable, simultaneously hardened and racialized divisions between Jews and their Indigenous neighbors. Conversely, long-standing commonalities between Jews and the majority Indigenous population around elements of shared culture threatened to separate Jews racially from their aspirations to western acceptance and civic emancipation. In Palestine these twinned processes looked different. There emancipation, in the form of Jewish self-determination in Jews' historic homeland, necessitated a two-pronged process of racialization. In the first place, Jews who migrated from around the world had to stake a claim to indigeneity. Although Palestine had always remained home to a small Jewish community, now a much larger one was transforming itself into native sons and daughters of their ancestral land. Concurrently, the same Jews had to differentiate themselves more sharply from two groups of Arabs—first, the long-standing Arab inhabitants of Palestine, and second, the Jews from Arab lands who arrived in waves in the early years of the state. The former faced growing encroachment on their land, followed by massive displacement and second-tier citizenship; the latter were relegated to the physical and social margins of the young Jewish state and instructed to abandon their Arab heritage for the Labor Zionism of the Ashkenazic founding generations.

In a kind of dialectic, the same developments helped accelerate the return of another form of racialization in the Jewish diaspora. In an era of resurgent antisemitism globally that began in the late twentieth century, some of Israel's fiercest critics essentialized the Jewish state as a uniquely malevolent, colonialist hegemon. Frequently echoing tropes like those of Jewish power, cabal, finance, or bloodthirst, such demonization conjured older antisemitic attacks on Jews as colonial conspirators.

But what was most distinctive historically was that this second phase, of necessity, entailed brutalization, the road less traveled by most Jews who had taken a hand in earlier colonial projects. In contrast to other contexts where Jews treated colonial rule as a means to equality, achieving the aspiration to collective emancipation in the form of full Jewish sovereignty required violence and dispossession on a wide scale. Not only were some 700,000 Palestinians displaced in the course of the state's creation in 1948–49 but also in the same period and the years following more than 400 Palestinian villages and towns were systematically destroyed and all but obliterated from the landscape. Even if the brutality of these early years might be seen as less a form of colonial conquest and more the product of an anticolonial civil war or of violence typical in other postcolonial settings, the colonial dimensions became more marked after Israel's military exploits in the 1967 Six-Day War. Rather than retreat immediately, the Israelis elected to occupy the West Bank, Gaza, and the Sinai and create a regime of military rule and, in time, a hierarchical settler society with two sets of dramatically differentiated legal, cultural, social, and physical realities.

By the early twenty-first century, with millions of Palestinian Arabs living without basic rights in the West Bank and the Occupation and its daily humiliations normalized for the foreseeable future, the fundamentally dehumanizing aspects of colonial rule—for both ruler and ruled—seemed inescapable facets of Israeli life. Even as Zionism remained the long-standing national liberation struggle of a subaltern people, seeking to live in freedom and security in a portion of its ancestral homeland, it also appeared more inseparable than ever from colonial conceptions, ideologies, modes, and practices.

Conclusion

If we are to remember that Zionism and Israel do not exist outside history, we must situate both their nationalist and colonialist elements within broader Jewish engagements with nation and empire in modern times. In contemporary discourse, debates around the term "colonial" have become hyperpoliticized, often generating more heat than light. For opponents of some strands of contemporary Jewish politics—Zionism, in particular—the term "colonial" has become less of an analytical category than an accusation, a cudgel with which to bludgeon the target of their ire. Often, Zionism's harshest critics, both Jewish and non-Jewish, have used the label of "colonial" to paint Israel as a uniquely evil regime without precedent or as a dramatic and misguided departure from any previous iterations of Jewish politics. By the same token, many of Israel's staunchest defenders have depicted any attempt to treat Zionism within a colonial frame as merely an effort to delegitimize Israel's very existence.

In reality, colonialism has long been central to modern politics; thus, as long as there has been Jewish politics, Jews have found themselves implicated in various ways in imperial projects. As we have seen across a wide chronological and geographical sweep, Jews have experienced colonialism as a site of emancipatory possibilities, racializing logics, and brutalizing endgames. Jews have frequently been in the roles of colonizer, colonized, or, most often, something in between. From the Global North to South, numerous Jewish individuals and groups have marshaled Jewish institutions, traditions, and platforms to support, leverage, critique, or oppose a wide range of colonial regimes, practices, and ideologies. The long history of Zionism includes each of these tendencies.

In that context, Zionism should not be regarded as an exceptional (or exceptionally malevolent) chapter in the history of Jewish politics but rather as a continuation of Jewish participation in broader international politics in modern times. It is only in this historical context that we can we begin to render normative assessments regarding the justice, or lack thereof, of the current regime and politics of the State of Israel.

Recommended Readings

Ariel, Ari. "Colonialism, Collective Violence, and the Jewish Communities of Libya and Yemen," *Tema* 12 (2012): 48–76.

Boum, Aomar, and Sarah Abrevaya Stein, eds. *The Holocaust and North Africa* (Stanford University Press, 2018).

Chasin, Stephanie M. *British Jews and Imperial Service: Nationalism, Pan-Islamism and Zionism in Mandate Palestine and Colonial India* (Bloomsbury Academic, 2024).

Eraqi Klorman, Bat-Zion. "Yemen, Aden and Ethiopia: Jewish Emigration and Italian Colonialism," *Journal of the Royal Asiatic Society* 19 (2009): 415–26.

Feldman, David. "Jews and the British Empire c. 1900," *History Workshop Journal* 63 (2007): 70–89.

Greene, Abigail. "The British Empire and the Jews: An Imperialism of Human Rights," *Past and Present* 199 (2008): 175–205.

Katz, Ethan. *The Burdens of Brotherhood: Jews and Muslims from North Africa to France* (Harvard University Press, 2015).

Katz, Ethan, Lisa Moses Leff, and Maud Mandel, eds. *Colonialism and the Jews* (Indiana University Press, 2017).

Shumsky, Dmitry. *Beyond the Nation-State: The Zionist Political Imagination from Pinsker to Ben-Gurion* (Yale University Press, 2018).

Tsur, Yaron. "Colonial and Post-Colonial Jewries," in *The Cambridge History of Judaism*, Vol. 8, ed. M. B. Hart and T. Michels (Cambridge University Press, 2017), 221–56.

Vogt, Stefan, ed. *Colonialism and the Jews in German History: From the Middle Ages to the 20th Century* (Bloomsbury Academic, 2022).

Vogt, Stefan, Derek J. Penslar, and Arieh Saposnik, eds. *Unacknowledged Kinships: Postcolonial Studies and the Historiography of Zionism* (Brandeis University Press, 2023).

Notes

1. *The Zionist Idea: A Historical Analysis and Reader* (Jewish Publication Society, 1997), 15.

2. Holly Case, *The Age of Questions* (Princeton University Press, 2018).

3. Derek Penslar, *Jews and the Military: A History* (Princeton University Press, 2013), 108–15, esp. 110–11.

4. For figures and country-specific data, see Michael Laskier, Sara Reguer, and Reeva Spector Simon, *The Jews of the Middle East and North Africa* (Columbia University Press, 2003).

5. See Todd Shepard, *The Invention of Decolonization: The Algerian War and the Remaking of France* (Cornell University Press, 2006), 20.

6. See Lisa Moses Leff, *Sacred Bonds of Solidarity: The Rise of Jewish Internationalism in 19th-Century France* (Stanford University Press, 2006), 129–31; Joshua Schreier, *Arabs of the Jewish Faith: The Civilizing Mission in Colonial Algeria* (Rutgers University Press, 2010), esp. 51–57 and 88–89.

7. Michael Shurkin, "French Liberal Governance and the Emancipation of Algeria's Jews," *French Historical Studies* 33 (2010): 274.

8. Valérie Assan, *Les consistoires israélites d'Algérie au XIXe siècle: "L'alliance de la civilization et de la religion"* (Paris: Armand Colin, 2012), 420.

9. In time, *rabbins indigènes* were incorporated into the consistorial system but only on an ad hoc basis. Despite repeated petitions from these rabbis to both the consistory and French administration, their salaries and statuses remained decentralized, dependent on the needs and resources of local communities, rather than the state. See Assan, *Les consistoires.* My thanks to Rachel Schley for her assistance in better understanding this issue.

10. Assan, *Les consistoires*, 423.

11. This is a central argument of Schreier, *Arabs*. Assan, *Les consistoires*, illustrates the significant limitations on the consistories' power.

12. See Avner Ofrath, "'We Shall Become French': Reconsidering Algerian Jews' Citizenship, c. 1860–1900," *French History* 35 (2021).

13. "Israel et la Révolution Française," 73, and Zadoc Kahn, "Allocution," in Benjamin Mossé, ed., *La Révolution française et le rabbinat français* (Avignon, 1890), 100.

14. See Schreier, *Arabs*, 143–76.

15. The cases were not identical. In Tunisia there were opportunities such as the 1923 Morinaud Law that enabled many more Jews to apply for French citizenship. By contrast, in Morocco Jews rarely could become French citizens and actually remained *dhimmis*, subjects of the Moroccan sultan with a status inferor to that of Muslims under Islamic law.

16. Dorian Bell, *Globalizing Race: Antisemitism and Empire in French and European Culture* (Northwestern University Press, 2018), chaps. 2 and 5; see also Ethan B. Katz, "An Imperial Entanglement: Antisemitism, Islamophobia, and Colonialism," *American Historical Review* 123 (2018): 1190–209.

17. Quoted in David Feldman, "Jews and the British Empire c. 1900," *History Workshop Journal* 63 (2007): 70.

18. Quoted in Feldman, "Jews," 70.

19. Quoted in Feldman, "Jews," 77.

20. Quoted in Feldman, "Jews," 77.

21. Feldman, "Jews," 77.

22. Abigail Greene, "The British Empire and the Jews: An Imperialism of Human Rights," *Past and Present* 199 (2008): 178, 187. This article is my main source for further discussion here of nineteenth-century Britain.

23. Quoted in Greene, "British Empire," 189.

24. Feldman, "Jews," 79.

25. Quoted in Feldman, "Jews," 85.

26. Quoted in Feldman, "Jews," 83.

27. Quoted in Feldman, "Jews," 83–84.

28. The discussion of the Ezras and Baghdadi Jews of India is based on Elizabeth E. Imber, "A Late Imperial Elite Jewish Politics: Baghdadi Jews in British India and the Political Horizons of Empire and Nation," *Jewish Social Studies* 23, no. 2 (Winter 2018): 48–85.

29. Imber, "Late Imperial," 54.

30. Imber, "Late Imperial," 56, 57.

31. Imber, "Late Imperial," 63.

32. Throughout the discussion of Italy and the wider context of emancipation there, I am indebted to David Sorkin, *Jewish Emancipation: A History across Five Centuries* (Princeton University Press, 2019), esp. 172–75; 303–4.

33. Shira Klein, "A Place in the Sun: Italian Jews and the Colonization of Africa," unpublished paper shared at CalJEMM workshop, October 28, 2018. There is precious little published to date on Jews and Italian colonialism. Klein's nascent work and particularly this paper have formed the basis for much of my discussion of Italy.

34. For the wider Italian context in this era, see Michele Sarfatti, *The Jews in Mussolini's Italy: From Equality to Persecution* (University of Wisconsin Press, 2006).

35. See Jens Hoppe, "The Persecution of Jews in Libya between 1938 and 1945: An Italian Affair?," in *The Holocaust in North Africa*, ed. Aomar Boum and Sarah Abrevaya Stein (Stanford University Press, 2019), 55–56.

36. Abraham Doron, "Between Concern and Difference: German Jews and the Colonial 'Other' in South West Africa," *German Studies* 40 (2022): 41–42, and "Reforming Identities: Jews' Experience of German Colonial Expansion," *Postcolonial Studies* 25 (2021): 248–69.

37. Doron, "Between Concern," 43–44. Also see George L. Mosse, *German Jews beyond Judaism* (Indiana University Press, 1985) and *The Crisis of German Ideology: Intellectual Origins of the Third Reich* (University of Wisconsin Press, 2021).

38. Doron, "Between Concern," 45.

39. On the points raised here, see esp. Benjamin Madley, "From Africa to Auschwitz: How German South West Africa Incubated Ideas and Methods Adopted and Developed by the Nazis in Eastern Europe," *European History Quarterly* 35 (2005): 429–64; Isabel V. Hull, "Military Culture and the Production of 'Final Solutions' in the Colonies," in *The Specter of Genocide*, ed. R. Gellately and B. Kiernan (Harvard University Press, 2003), 141–62. For a good overview of the highly contested debate over the relationship between colonialism and the Holocaust in Germany and elsewhere, see Thomas Kuhne, "Colonialism and the Holocaust: Continuities, Causations, and Complexities," *Journal of Genocide Research* 15 (2013): 339–62.

40. Doron, "Between Concern," 53.

41. Stefan Vogt, "From Colonialism to Antisemitism and Back: Ideological Developments in the Alldeutsche Verband under the Kaiserreich," in *Colonialism and the Jews in German History: From the Middle Ages to the 20th Century*, ed. Stefan Vogt (Bloomsbury Academic, 2022), 134–55.

42. Axel Stahler, "'Our Dernburg'—'The New Moses': The German Empire's 'Jewish' Colonial Director and the Satirical Press," in Vogt, *Colonialism and the Jews*, 156–84.

43. Doron, "Between Concern," 57–58.

44. Quoted in Doron, "Between Concern," 50.

45. On Jews in anticolonial politics, see work by Alma Rachel Heckman, Joel Beinin, Pierre-Jean Le Foll Luciani, Ethan B. Katz, and Orit Bashkin. On the relationship between Holocaust memory and anticolonial critique (including the important role of non-Jews such as Jean-Paul Sartre, Frantz Fanon, and W. E. B. Dubois), see esp. Michael Rothberg, *Multidirectional Memory: Remembering the Holocaust in the Age of Decolonization* (Stanford University Press, 2009); Bryan Cheyette, *Diasporas of the Mind: Jewish and Postcolonial Writing and the Nightmare of History* (Yale University Press, 2014); Ethan B. Katz, "Muslims as Brothers or Strangers? French Jewish Thinkers Confront the Moral Dilemmas of the French Algerian War," in *The Stranger in Early Modern and Modern Jewish Jewish Tradition*, ed. C. Bartlett and J. Schlor (Brill, 2021), 202–39.

46. Homi Bhaba, *The Location of Culture* (Routledge, 1994), 1–2, cited in Stefan Vogt, Derek J. Penslar, and Arieh Saposnik, "Introduction: Unacknowledged Kinships," in *Unacknowledged Kinships: Postcolonial Studies and the Historiography of Zionism*, ed. Vogt et al. (Brandeis University Press, 2023), 10.

47. See citation and discussion in Vogt et al., "Introduction: Unacknowledged Kinships," in *Unacknowledged Kinships*, 1–26.

48. The ensuing discussion is deeply indebted to Penslar's essay, "Is Zionism a Colonial Movement?" and the forum on this essay some years after its initial publication (including Penslar's response) in *Colonialism and the Jews*, ed. Katz et al. (Indiana University Press, 2017), Part 3. Penslar recently sharpened his comparative framework for Zionism as in part a form of settler colonialism in "Zionism as Colonialism," in his book, *Zionism: An Emotional State* (Rutgers University Press, 2023).

49. Dubnow quoted in Dmitry Shumsky, *Beyond the Nation-State: The Zionist Political Imagination from Pinsker to Ben-Gurion* (Yale University Press, 2018), 48.

50. This is the compelling argument of Shumsky, *Beyond the Nation-State*, esp. 1–23, 33–36, 43–48, 78–80, and 119–21.

10

Catastrophe

Mark Roseman, Indiana University

THE HOLOCAUST has an uneasy place in Jewish Studies. On the face of it, it is everywhere, which is hardly surprising given its impact on Jews and Judaism. Yet much of the research pertaining to the Holocaust continues to be conducted by scholars outside the field, raising questions far removed from things Jewish. Holocaust historians who find themselves within the Jewish Studies orbit often arrive with trajectories very different from their peers and worry whether their courses are "Jewish" enough to carry credit. In part this reflects an age-old tension as to whether the proper subject of Jewish Studies should be "Jews" or "Judaism." But even a Jewish historiography very much concerned with Jews has had a surprisingly ambivalent relationship to the Holocaust. As David Engel has shown so eloquently, many celebrated scholars of modern Jewish history deliberately did not engage with the subject, seeing it as somehow disconnected from the history of the Jewish people, particularly from the Jewish people as agents of history.[1] Behind these simple facts lies the question David Vital asked: Is the Holocaust "in some crucial and decisive sense not only an event in but also peculiar to Jewish history, and comprehensible ultimately only in its terms?"[2] The alternative would be to see the Holocaust as Jewish only in the sense that a meteor hitting interwar Vilna would be Jewish—as Jewish in suffering and Jewish in impact but utterly extraneous in cause and nature.

One answer, of course, is that there is a very Jewish story to be told—that of victim responses and experiences. This has in recent years become a central focus of historical research, reviving questions that were raised in the very early postwar years by survivor historians in the German DP camps, in Poland, and in France. Even here one must still ask whether the behavior was simply that of human beings under extreme duress or did it bear the marks of distinctively Jewish traditions, community structures, and outlooks. But it is a reasonable generalization to say that the more historians have shifted their attention to the world of the victims, the more comfortable their scholarship feels in the Jewish Studies context. This is all the more so because recent work has tended to emphasize Jews' collective experiences and agency, rather than simply the existential dilemmas of individuals in extremis. Yet however resourceful victims managed to be, it was not they who determined the nature of the genocide, and they affected its progression only on the margins.

If in the Jewish Studies context the Holocaust sometimes does not feel Jewish enough, a recent strident debate in Germany, with strong international involvement, has revolved around the question whether the Holocaust is being too zealously guarded by Jews (or by an unholy alliance between Germany, Israel, and US Jewry) and willfully secluded behind the label of uniqueness, thereby preventing links and parallels between colonial and other violence and the Holocaust from being explored.[3] The public exchanges in what has been dubbed the "Historikerstreit 2.0" have often been removed from the interests and findings of historical scholarship; indeed, much of it at least purported to revolve around questions of public memory and the politics and ethics thereof, even if in fact historical claims were being advanced below the surface.[4] But some interventions, particularly those from Dirk Moses's recent book, *The Problems of Genocide*,[5] have raised substantive questions about the Holocaust as history and implicitly about what it might mean now to understand the Holocaust as a Jewish phenomenon.

What has not been commented on in this debate is the strained relationship between the claim of Jewish ownership and that of uniqueness. For, if the Holocaust were indeed unique, that would make it quite unlike other events and catastrophes, including Jewish ones. Yet, as we will see, claims of uniqueness tend to go hand in hand with the idea that the Holocaust represented some distinctively and characteristically Jewish fate. This chapter thus pursues two parallel lines of inquiry. On the one hand, it asks about the relationship between claims about the Holocaust's uniqueness and its Jewishness. On the other, it draws on the wealth of recent scholarship about the Holocaust and other genocides to ask how distinctive the Holocaust really was. In so doing, it arrives at some conclusions about both the uniqueness and the Jewishness of the Holocaust.

Unique but Jewish?

The sense that the Holocaust was unprecedented emerged even while it was unfolding. Contemporary victim accounts might initially have harkened back to earlier Jewish episodes of persecution or even to biblical scourges, but the overwhelming sense was increasingly of something unparalleled, beyond belief. Not only the victims but also well-informed non-Jewish observers shared this perception of a "crime without a name" (Churchill) or of "a terrible crime against the dignity of mankind, a crime that cannot be compared with any other in the history of mankind" (second leaflet of the White Rose).[6] After the war, the liberation of the camps offered new evidence of unprecedented horror. Hannah Arendt was among the first to express in more intellectual terms the idea that a fundamental new threshold had been crossed that should never have been crossed but might happen again.[7]

To be unprecedented, a phenomenon must in some sense be discontinuous with what has gone before. Indeed, many Jews at the time could not assimilate what was happening into their understanding of the world. For Orthodox Jews, the cruelty and the threat of total annihilation called into question God's covenant and thus the meaning of Jewish history. Zionists in the United States and in Palestine found it hard to adjust to the imminent threat of total annihilation. Even after the war, many still could not absorb the fact that the Holocaust had negated their cherished assumptions about the protection that a Jewish state might offer to a troubled diaspora. The Nazis' global war against the Jews had been halted at the gates of Palestine only because of Allied military campaigns, campaigns that had not been waged to save the Jews.[8]

If what had happened bore no relationship to past experience, how was it connected with Jewish history? Some definitions of the Holocaust's uniqueness—of which Eli Wiesel is the most famous exponent—insist on its incomprehensibility as an event outside history. Being beyond comprehension and outside history would indeed constitute a metaphysically unique event, but this usage is belied both by the many efforts to list quite concretely what makes the Holocaust stand out from other atrocities and by the explicit or implicit linkage in popular imagination, in Israeli scholarship, and indeed in Wiesel's own discourse between the Holocaust and some larger sense of Jewish vulnerability and hatred for Jews.

As the Holocaust began to attract more scholarly attention in the 1960s and 1970s, postwar Israeli and Jewish scholars emphasized its unique character.

"Never since the dawn of history had the world witnessed such a campaign of extermination," argued Jacob Talmon at a major conference on the Holocaust and the "rebirth" of Israel, held at Yad Vashem in 1973. What made the Holocaust stand out was its conscious and explicit planning, its systematic execution, the absence of any emotional element, and the decision to eliminate everyone without any possibility of reprieve.[9] Although many agreed with Talmon's conclusion, their grounds for doing so varied. For Yehuda Bauer, it was the planetary comprehensiveness, the clear commitment to kill all, that made the Holocaust something more even than a genocide as defined by Raphael Lemkin and the United Nations. For other authors, it was the Nazi vision that made the Holocaust unique. "The attempt at total physical eradication may sometimes be identical," wrote Saul Friedländer, "but the motivations are quite different: in that sense, the Nazi exterminatory drive against the Jews remains unmistakably singular."[10] Dan Diner's highly influential claim that the Holocaust represented a rupture in civilization had yet another premise—that, by going to such efforts to round up and destroy valuable human capital during a total war, the Nazis revealed an irrationality that utterly overturned the precepts of enlightened society.

In many cases, claims about uniqueness were linked rather paradoxically to long-standing antisemitism and Jews' status in modern gentile society. The US historian Lucy Dawidowicz, although an ardent defender of the Holocaust's uniqueness, argued that a straight line could easily be drawn from Luther to Hitler.[11] Talmon's paper that began with uniqueness was, in fact, mostly about antisemitism and the place of Jews in modern society. On one level it is obvious that some measure of continuity must bridge the "rupture," some element of repetition join with the unique. But the paradox is that the claim of uniqueness coexisted with the explicit or implicit argument that the Holocaust's horrific face reflected explosive characteristics of Judeophobia or some version of it. The assertion of Holocaust uniqueness was thus entangled with arguments about antisemitism's uniqueness or Jews' unique place in the world. Talmon wrote of the "uniqueness" of Jewish history, and Jacob Katz of the "unique fascination" of German Jewish history.[12] In short, the claim of uniqueness, although widely shared and deeply felt, was surprisingly complex, surprisingly ambivalent, and one might add, often surprisingly untested. It represented a strange amalgam of genuine shock at something horrific and new, on the one hand, and a sense that what had been revealed was the true face of persistent Jewish hatred, on the other.

Defining the Catastrophe

For Jewish communities under attack from the Nazis, it was obvious that this was a Jewish catastrophe. Although biblical catastrophe may resonate in the Yiddish word *Churbn* more than in the Hebrew *Shoah*, the two terms have in common that they were coined by Jews to connote the fate of Jews. However, much postwar scholarship that relates to the Holocaust sought to explain a catastrophe that was defined and demarcated differently. Postwar trials were conducted under the rubric of war crimes and crimes against humanity. At Nuremberg, considerable space was given to the Jewish fate, but only as an extreme variant in a more general litany of Nazi atrocities. It was only in the Eichmann trial that "Crimes against the Jewish people" would figure as a central category (although the Israelis had earlier used it to charge Jewish collaborators with the Nazis).[13]

From the 1950s onward, German and other western historians of Germany turned to the problem of Nazi Germany with greater intensity. Their focus was on the collapse of democracy and on how the regime had managed to steer Germany into a disastrous war and a disastrous defeat. For those using Marxist theories of fascism to interpret Nazism, the Holocaust was a disastrous byproduct of the central drama—the effort by big business to retain control by exploiting the irrational prejudices of the petit bourgeoisie. Totalitarian theory accorded regime ideologies more weight and could thus acknowledge murderous antisemitism more but did not develop explanatory models with the Holocaust in mind. That meant that, even when in the 1970s and early 1980s scholars engaged in bitter debates about the origins of the "Final Solution," the principal term used in the scholarship at the time, the arguments used were not developed to respond to the enormity of the Holocaust but were rather system theories that were being deployed in this context. In 1978 the historian Leonard Krieger offered a telling review of recent scholarship on Nazi Germany. In his intelligent but deracinated discussion, the regime's murderous violence is almost invisible. If he had been writing even just ten years later, the Holocaust would have been far more present. And yet, Krieger concluded with this remark referring to the Holocaust that "everything we write about the Nazis bears explicit as well as implicit marks of the same monstrous provocation."[14] The Holocaust was both out of focus and in scholars' minds at the same time.

Beginning in the 1980s, a new generation of scholars entered the field. After 1991, research into the Holocaust became infused with new energy by the release of Nazi documents that had been held in the Soviet Union. Two new paradigms emerged that shifted the boundaries of the "catastrophe" once again. First, historians now recognized the breadth and seriousness of the Nazis' racial policy, which groomed and supported those who were seen as valuable parts of the community and disciplined, excluded, and eliminated all those groups deemed unfit. Well over three hundred thousand Germans were sterilized before the outbreak of war on ostensibly genetic grounds. More than two hundred thousand were killed after war began. Indeed, the disabled were the first group under the Nazis to be subject to a planned program of elimination. If measured relative to the prewar population, the decimation of the Roma population in Europe proved to be in the same league as that of European Jewry, although definitive statistics remain hard to come by: More than two hundred thousand Roma were murdered by the same horrific mixture of forced neglect, shootings, and gassings. From this perspective anti-Jewish measures were just part of a war against undesirables waged by the racial state.

The other paradigm was that of imperial conquest, as the scale of Nazi population and resettlement plans in the East came into view. The famous Wannsee conference was preceded seven months earlier by another meeting of similar ranks who casually envisaged the deaths of tens of millions of Soviet citizens through the ruthless commandeering of foodstuffs. The first group to die off the battlefield in the millions was Soviet POWs, two million in the first half-year of the war alone. Settlement policies conjoined with utterly ruthless warfare and merciless antipartisan campaigns saw the decimation of populations in Ukraine, Byelorussia, and other territories in Eastern Europe and envisaged the removal or elimination of up to 90 percent of respective European ethnic groups after the war.

Against this background, it is not surprising that even the Holocaust as a label became open to discussion. The creation of the US Holocaust Museum generated some hefty debates, and although the museum largely opted for the narrower definition, President Carter's opening speech cast a much wider net to include some eleven million victims of the Nazis, which caused some consternation among Israeli scholars.[15] Clearly, different definitions of the catastrophe lead to different conclusions about its relationship to Jewish history. Our task now is to ask how they might relate to one other.

The Deaths of Others

Narrative choice has its limits.

Even Hayden White, who famously wrote that "any given set of real events can be emplotted in a number of ways,"[16] has come to recognize that the

Holocaust might impose (or remind us to impose elsewhere too) certain kinds of constraints on the stories we tell.[17] The Historikerstreit of the 1980s was in part about challenging false causal equations. Auschwitz was not simply a response to the Gulag, as the historian Ernst Nolte claimed.[18] It also challenged false moral equivalencies. You could not, as the historian Andreas Hilgruber proposed with his book *Zweierlei Untergang* (The Twofold Disaster), treat the Holocaust and Germany's defeat as parallel tragedies.[19] But the scholarship of the 1990s and beyond offered no such facile or intolerable juxtapositions. So how far have the historiographies of racial policy and imperial conquest enclosed or superseded Jewish narratives of the Holocaust?

Historians have demonstrated clear institutional and policy links between measures against Jews and those of other groups. Laws were applied to Sinti and Roma in analogy to anti-Jewish legislation, even if the former were also subject to police measures of segregation and control before they were extended to Jews. Sinti and Roma were alongside Jews on the first deportation trains from the Reich, they were murdered by the same Einsatzgruppen in the occupied Soviet Union, and they were killed in the gas ovens at Auschwitz. Although policy against the disabled was largely disconnected from anti-Jewish measures in the 1930s, the use of gas for murder was tried out on them, and the personnel required for this operation would later be transferred to the Operation Reinhard extermination camps in fall 1941.

Perhaps the most important aspect of the new work was the way it demonstrated the intellectual commitment and professional energy of groups of educated elites across the gamut of racial policy. Whereas Nazi racial ideology had been treated earlier as the irrational if deadly fantasy of a mentally unbalanced coterie, the impact and extent of systematic race thinking now emerged clearly. Social questions were redefined as biological ones. Criminologists, youth, welfare bodies, and experts, pedagogues, and other professionals talked the language of biology and proposed ruthless bio-policies. There were clear overlaps and symmetries between these initiatives and the targeting of Jews as an alien element in the population. The question of what made the policy makers and perpetrators tick, and where sincere belief left off and cynical gameplaying took over is, however, complex and one to which we will return.

In recent scholarship, "imperial" policy has become understood as even more entangled with the final solution. "Imperial" is something of a misnomer, because Hitler envisaged territory progressively cleansed of foreign elements (albeit with some limited space allotted to deracinated "Slavic" slaves) and added to an expanding Germany. If Hitler's vision approximated to imperial models at all, then it was closest to settler colonialism—except that the Nazis planned the removal from the center in advance, complete with statistical tables and agricultural rationales, and this planning depended on the enthusiastic involvement of intellectual and professional elites.[20] During the 1930s and thus well before the regime had engaged in its official planning, agronomists, geographers, historians, and others had proposed far-reaching population resettlement and displacement to solve perceived agricultural inefficiency in the East. "Ostforschung" in universities and regime quangos (an acronym for quasi-autonomous nongovernmental organization) laid the groundwork for the massive resettlements and expulsion plans formulated during the war under Himmler's leadership. The intellectual exercises among the experts of "the East" included removing Jews alongside other groups, both to achieve general land clearance and reduced population density, as well as specifically targeting Jews' middle-man functions in rural economies.

After the invasion of Poland, absorption of its territories into Germany prompted the deportation of both Jewish and non-Jewish Poles. The SS staffs entrusted with settling incoming ethnic Germans were also involved in expelling the unwanted. The creation of the extermination camps in the Lublin area from 1941, spearheaded by Odilo Globocnik under Himmler's supervision, was linked to proposed German settlement projects. Later in 1942, the murder of Polish Jews would be accelerated in part because of the pressure to transfer Polish foodstuffs into the Reich to follow Polish forced labor, making it expedient to eliminate those for whom the Reich had no use. More generally, as already indicated, the language of mega-exploitation and mass removal and mass death that accompanied both mid-range settlement plans and short-run civilian management in wartime provided an ominous drumbeat against which anti-Jewish policy was formulated.

These findings have dramatically altered the contexts in which we place anti-Jewish policy. Given the measures already undertaken or planned toward the Roma and Sinti, for example, it is no longer possible to claim that anti-Jewish measures were designed to be total and anti-gypsy policies partial. Yet in other ways, scholarship has explicitly or implicitly underlined distinctions between Jews and the rest. Above all, the urgency and centrality of the war against the Jews find no parallel, which is a major reason why, by the time the war turned against Germany, so little of the imperial planning had even been initiated and why the murder of Jews continued until the war's last hours. Jews were treated variously as a race, an anti-race, or a people and increasingly singled out as part of a global conspiracy conniving with the Allies against Germany. It was the image of a global enemy, directing or in cahoots with the Allies, that the Nazis were most successful in conveying to a people at war.

Even if it unfolded in the context of broader settlement plans, the Nazi Jewish project was not a function of those plans. It began at home, extended beyond any territory the Nazis wished to claim, and continued long after all hope of expansion had gone. It is true that in significant ways the murder of Jews has been shown to have been conducted with a certain rationality—dispossessing them of assets that could be used for social projects in Hungary, or redistributing their property in knockdown sales at home, or reducing demand for food in occupied areas so that grain and (non-Jewish) forced labor could be transferred to the German home front. But it is also true that the halfway recognizable logics that motivated quite a bit of the Nazis' ruthless social engineering—permanent territorial acquisition, subduing enemy combatants, increased economic efficiency, and so forth—only marginally applied to Jews as a target. Indeed, as recent comparative work makes clear, most of the recognizable comparable logics and contexts that favor genocide elsewhere do not work in the case of the Jews, unless you do the same mental pyrotechnics as the Nazis and construe Jewry as a concerted and organized international threat.

The Holocaust, Jewish History, and Antisemitism

Acculturated German Jews blamed the mass of Eastern Jews who arrived during and after World War I for fostering antisemitism. At the same time, Orthodox German Jews blamed their acculturated counterparts for trying to disguise who they were and arousing suspicion. At various times and places Orthodox Jews blamed unobservant Jews for exciting God's wrath. Later, ultra-Orthodox Jews in Israel would blame the Zionists for having done so. After the war, Hannah Arendt accused the Jewish Councils of working assiduously to assist the Nazis. Raul Hilberg (uniquely!) went so far as to build Jewish compliance into his understanding of uniqueness: "For the first time, also, the Jewish victims, caught in the straitjacket of their history, plunged themselves physically and psychologically into catastrophe. The destruction of the Jews was thus no accident."[21] But for most observers, the Holocaust was not a function of Jewish behavior. If there was a link between Jewish history and the origins and course of the Holocaust, then it must primarily be a history of the hostility that Jews engendered.

The historiography on this issue has been extraordinarily diverse in focus, methods, and conclusions. For some, antisemitism is merely a kind of interpretive gap filler, as meaningful in explaining violence against Jews as saying antimannism is responsible for violence against men. For Enzo Traverso, it was not antisemitism that gave rise to the Holocaust but that Auschwitz had "invented" antisemitism, because it conferred "the appearance of a coherent, cumulative, and linear process on a body of discourse and practices that, before Nazism, had been perceived in the various European countries as discordant, heterogeneous and in many cases decidedly archaic."[22]

For Jews living under Nazi rule, particularly in the zones of the most atrocious violence in the East, hatred of Jews, psychological deformation, and Germanness were intrinsically linked. The contempt and ruthlessness of Germans of every stamp suggested an almost universal adherence to Nazi ideology. But for the victims, ideas shaded into a psychological deformation, even monstrosity. The implacable, unearthly inhumanity of the persecution, even before the era of the extermination camps, felt very different from the everyday antisemitism that many Eastern Europeans knew from the interwar period. During the war, the avarice and corruptibility of the miserable Lithuanians or Ukrainians who had been enlisted as auxiliaries marked them as humanly recognizable to many Jewish observers (if often also bestially violent) in a way that the Germans were not. The German hatred for Jews was thus understood as part of a package that eluded understanding and was tied into the psychological character of their tormentors. Complicating the picture was that many Jews who, through work or some other often enforced context, had prolonged contact with Germans noted a range of different types. In this way participation in the violence of the Holocaust project was a complex, inexplicable phenomenon, with the place of ideas and ideology obscure.

The perception that antisemitism was a psychological deformation persisted into the postwar era. In early postwar German reckonings, antisemitism was resolutely purged of that link to the national character that it held for the survivors. The scholarly focus was on Hitler's diseased obsession with the Jews. In Germany and elsewhere, the postwar decades saw a great deal of interest in identifying the seminal experience that had led Hitler to his obsession, a search that prompted the historian Hans Ulrich Wehler to ask whether it mattered if Hitler had had one testicle or perhaps three.[23] Postwar German jurisprudence treated antisemitism, like sadism, as a personal attribute or "base motive," and in relation to crimes committed under Nazi rule, this could make the difference between a mere accessory charge and an outright murder conviction. In the United States, the German Jewish émigré Theodor Adorno, building on studies of antisemitism conducted by the transplanted Frankfurt School, offered the "authoritarian personality" as an explanation for it, a theory that accorded well

CATASTROPHE 241

with the increasingly psychologized understandings of racial tension and prejudice in the Cold War United States.[24] In all these interpretations, antisemitism
had become a personal syndrome or a tic, largely removed from a history of
Jewish–gentile relations.

When Israeli and Jewish scholars turned to study the Holocaust, however,
they saw antisemitism instead as an inheritance that provided the motive force
for destruction. Historiographical surveys tend to group German historians
such as Klaus Hildebrand or Eberhard Jäckel together with Jewish and Israeli
scholars like Saul Friedlander or Yehuda Bauer as "intentionalists," arrayed
against the "functionalists"; however, on a subtle but fundamental level, the two
German camps were closer to one another than to the "Jewish" side. The most
important point was that for the German historians, the protagonists, except for
Hitler and perhaps a few others, were not particularly ideologically motivated
by antisemitism or anything else. For the intentionalists, Hitler's supreme power
enabled his plan to be put into practice, whereas for the functionalists, power-
hungry players duked it out under the mantle of Hitler's vague but murderous
licensing rhetoric.

Israeli and Jewish scholars, however, viewed the world differently. For one
thing, they often assumed antisemitism was influential on a broader societal
plane. "All the fears of the middle- and lower-middle class Germans," wrote
Shmuel Ettinger, "all streamed into the flood waters of anti-Semitism on which
the Nazis were borne to power."[25] For another, they saw antisemitism as a destructive force in itself. For German intentionalists like Ernst Jäckel, as indeed
for the Frankfurt School's Max Horkheimer and Adorno, antisemitism ac-
counted for the target but not for the character of the crime, whose origins lay
elsewhere: For Jäckel it lay in Hitler's "bottomless criminality and inhumanity"[26] to which was yoked the destructive energies of a totalitarian state. For a
Bauer, an Ettinger, or a Friedländer, by contrast, it was antisemitism's own distinctive character (or that of a particular brand of antisemitism) that explained
both the animus behind it and the monstrousness of the crime.

The question was how to reconcile the claim of antisemitic continuity with
the Holocaust's uniqueness. For some Israeli scholars, continuity was the dominant note. In 1944 Ben-Zion Dinur saw hatred and destruction as an intrinsic
and persistent part of Jewish and gentile history.[27] For Jacob Katz, too, although
offfering a more sophisticated account of its nineteenth-century transmogrifica-
tion, the enduring legacy of Christianity's premodern rejection of Judaism was
key.[28] Other authors zeroed in on critical turning points closer to the Holocaust.
The villain of the piece might be the Enlightenment coupled with the gentile

world's inability to throw off its Christian prejudice against the Jews. The need to find a new "post-religious" definition of Jewry's faults ended up disastrously focusing on the person and not the faith. Or it might be emancipation, which had removed the safety barrier between Jews and gentiles, rendering the Jew increasingly invisible and in turn exacerbating inherited suspicions. Some authors focused on intellectual developments that were more narrowly characteristic of the German-speaking world—in Wagner's intellectual circle, in the character of German nationalism, and so forth. Saul Friedländer's argument that the end of the nineteenth century saw among the Bayreuth circle the emergence of a "redemptive antisemitism," in which a mystical version of racial antisemitism fused with a decidedly religious vision, has been widely influential.[29]

For historians trained in the history of ideas, who conceived of history as a relay race in which one influential thinker passes the baton to the next, the nineteenth century and particularly its last quarter really did look like the critical period of intellectual ferment. But as historians came to embrace social and then cultural history, a raft of social and cultural studies of German Jewry appearing from the 1980s onward challenged lachrymose readings of late nineteenth-century German history.[30] The relatively limited circles of antisemitic thinkers, with their even more limited contemporary political impact, came to seem more like a resource on which the Nazis happened to draw than an explosive mixture just waiting for a spark. "It is not that the past (of anti-Semitism) produced the present (of the extermination)," writes Alon Confino, "not that the ancient hatred led to the Holocaust, but that the Nazis interpreted anew the past of Jewish, German, and Christian relations to fit their vision of creating a new world. . . . It is the Nazis who made sense of, and gave new meaning to, past anti-Semitism, not so much the other way around."[31]

As historians shifted to looking at politics and violence in relation to antisemitism, the transformative period came to be seen as the aftermath of World War I. It was then that new kinds of antisemitic movements and a global panic emerged, which gave the Jewish issue an explosive political quality across Europe (and indeed in North America). Moreover, the more historians of the Holocaust shifted their attention to collaboration in Eastern Europe, particularly after the publication of Jan Gross's *Neighbors* in 2001, the more the political constellation of the interwar period came to seem a central element in explaining the breadth of anti-Jewish violence.[32]

Like all panics, the global antisemitic panic after World War I was a complex phenomenon, whose unfolding dynamic left the original catalysts far behind.

The massive convulsions, violence, and population displacements of war were joined by those of the Russian and European revolutions, in which Jews played a prominent and visible role. Wartime fantasies about Jewish power morphed into a widespread fear of "Judeo-Bolshevism."[33] The global fear of Jewish influence was reinforced by the 1920 translation into English of the bogus *Protocols of the Elders of Zion*. Civil war in Russia saw unprecedented anti-Jewish violence, whereas for counterrevolutionary groups across Europe, violent antisemitism became part and parcel of their vocabulary. New or reformed postimperial states became sites of ethnic conflicts in which Jews became unwillingly embroiled, as Omer Bartov's study of Buczacz showed so eloquently.[34] The Paris Treaties' efforts to protect minorities were denounced as a Jewish imposition. It may have been only after the Versailles terms were announced that Hitler became an out-and-out antisemite. In the 1930s the global economic crisis reopened old wounds. As Nazi Germany gained in prestige, smaller European states felt encouraged to fly the antisemitic flag. Finally, the Hitler–Stalin pact bequeathed to the USSR a band of territory from the Baltics to Poland in which the communists exploited ethnic tensions, often inserting Jews in leading positions where barriers had existed before. The post–World War I myth of Judeo-Bolshevism gained new momentum.

In short, when the Germans began their concerted campaign against Jews in Poland and then in Baltic, Ukrainian, and Byelorussian territory and when they enlisted the assistance of Allies and well-disposed Eastern European powers in removing the rest of European Jews, they could draw on regional patterns of conflict and violence and transnational networks of anti-Jewish sentiment. In ethnically contested regions, the German invasion or example triggered a considerable degree of autochthonous violence—Hungarian deportations of Jews into the German firing lines, unhinged Romanian violence in Transnistria up to 1942, Bulgarian deportations to extermination camps from acquired Greek territory, Ukrainian and Polish murders of Jews in contested Galician lands, and so on.

There is no mistaking the power of a long-established trope of Jews as clandestine anti-Christian conspirators. Such tropes played a role everywhere, and Eastern Europe church leaders often enjoyed a far more central presence in fomenting antisemitism than they had in the evolution of radical antisemitism in Germany. But the explosive and violent combination after 1918 of the legacy of wartime violence, the European civil war between communists and anticommunists, and the fierce interethnic rivalries in former imperial territories created a highly specific context.

None of this new work on the European context, of course, challenges Germany's primary role in unleashing the Holocaust. A critical area of recent research relates to participation and perpetration in Germany itself. Daniel Goldhagen was widely criticized in the mid-1990s when he claimed that Germans shared a special kind of "eliminationist" antisemitism that made killing Jews seem plausible and indeed desirable.[35] There were obvious problems with the claim—not least that the evidence for this especially murderous antisemitism before the Nazis came to power was relatively thin. But the force and energy of Goldhagen's writing, and his unwillingness to conceal the kinds of routine but graphic violence inflicted by ordinary Germans on Jews, brought the question of motivated participation in the Holocaust to the fore.

Starting in the 1980s but accelerating in the 1990s, scholarship on the perpetrators gained steam, embracing ever-widening circles of upper and middle levels of leadership and increasingly also lower levels and the grassroots. It certainly echoed Goldhagen's claim of agency and active involvement at all levels but has been much less univocal on the protagonists' motivation and mindset. The early research on the racial state and a series of regional studies of occupation and the final solution in the occupied East emphasized the hard-headed rationality of the actors and the logics of settlement, development, or food supply. Another body of work, associated particularly with studies on the SD and the SS, detected cohorts or networks of "ideological warriors," who brought with them values and styles from the 1920s that dovetailed well with Nazism and helped give the SS administration such energy and purpose. Here, what was being foregrounded was not the cold rationality of the modern state but the outlook and assumptions of a cohort formed during and after World War I. Antisemitism was part of this group ethos, but above all what Ulrich Herbert, Michael Wildt, and others identified was radical ethnonationalism and a ruthless style that Werner Best dubbed "heroic realism."[36] Finally, as research moved down the ranks, scholars' approaches (with exceptions like Goldhagen) became more situational, analyzing the way "ordinary men" (Christopher Browning) adapted to the circumstances with which they were confronted, eliminating cognitive dissonance by internalizing the logic of murder or drawing on organizational logic, notably the ability of Nazi organizations and structures to socialize and shape the men who worked in them.[37]

These different interpretations reflect, in part, diversity among the protagonists, which is not surprising given that recent work has found that hundreds of thousands of men, and some women, were involved in the project of murder in one form or another. There were ideologues, sadists, loyalists, technocrats, opportunists, reluctant participants, and more. The disagreement on motives also reflects difficulties in interpreting the sources. There is no question that assumptions, rhetoric, and violence against Jews became common currency among a wide circle of perpetrators, but it is less clear how to evaluate the sincerity, authenticity, and opportunism of that rhetoric. Recent studies by Alon Confino and the late Boaz Neumann have reemphasized the seriousness and coherence of the Nazi vision but do not explore where the vision came from or how to understand the relationship of individual participants to it. Neumann explicitly eschews explanation.[38] Confino, as we know, sees preceding antisemitism as a resource from which the Nazis freely assembled their own ideology, although what prompted them to do so and what was the boundary between "Nazi" and "German" are unclear.

Partly out of a sense that the key to understanding the perpetrators may lie in the society from which they came, attention has shifted to the stance and attitudes of the population as a whole. In fact, popular antisemitism in Germany has been the subject of considerable research ever since the 1980s. Strong evidence emerged, for example, of a growing rift between Jewish and non-Jewish society in the Weimar era. For a large nationalist movement, the new marker of ultra-patriotism and loyalty to the "Volk" was the assertion that Jews did not belong to it. Jews themselves were split on whether to be more militantly self-assertive or more self-effacing in the wake of this change.

After 1933 abrupt shifts in Jewish policy were not always popular—the boycott of Jewish stores in 1933 met with a very mixed response—but research has shown that even anti-Nazi observers, who had wanted to believe that most Germans were hostile to the Nazis, had to admit that non-Jewish German society adapted and participated in the new order with remarkable alacrity. The violence of Kristallnacht evoked some consternation at the destruction and disorder but also considerable participation from ordinary citizens. Aryanization of Jewish property was driven forward by willing purchasers at knockdown prices. Once the war began, the Nazis seem to have been particularly successful in persuading Germans that it was a Jewish war and that the persecution of Jews and the opposition of the Allies were somehow connected. The long-held claim that the population was unaware of what was happening the East has been disproven; returning troops shared knowledge of the mass shootings of Jews, and rumors of extermination centers were widespread. The clear evidence for this is provided by the widely attested rumors and worries that the bombing campaigns were a reprisal for what was being done to the Jews. Even if most of the population was not actively involved in Jewish persecution, the importance of this echo chamber is increasingly evident, and the position of the bystander has grown in importance.

In many ways, older German historiography, which saw antisemitism as Hitler's personal craze, has been utterly debunked. The readiness of government, academic, military, and other elites to press forward with antisemitic agendas is as striking as the degree to which the larger population accepted the idea that the war was to some extent a Jewish war. But reflecting on the fate of Roma and Sinti is always a salutary corrective. Even when the fate of the Roma and Sinti was not on Hitler's agenda and did not figure in party speeches, mobilize popular sentiment, or command the ideological limelight, state and party agencies ramped up persecution all the way to extermination. Nazi Germany's capacity to inflict violence, its ability to mobilize and sharpen sentiment, and its concomitant tendency to radicalization were not themselves the result of some destructive logic contained within antisemitism. To help us place antisemitism's function, we need to look briefly at comparative cases of genocide.

The Holocaust and Other Genocides

Since the 1990s, the field of genocide studies has taken off, and interest in comparative research has grown considerably. We now have a clearer sense, for example, not only of the scale of settler genocides in the Antipodes and the Americas but also of the degree to which liberal intellectual circles embraced and welcomed the eradication of inferior races. The emergence of modern, ethnically based nation-states created a new set of risks, particularly after the multiethnic empires collapsed. By some counts there were almost one hundred genocides and partial genocides in the first half of the twentieth century.[39] Many genocidal campaigns in the recent past have been localized and partial, but others like the Armenian or later the Rwandan genocides were nationwide projects of elimination. It is hard to compare levels of extremity, but the "extravaganzas of cruelty"[40] that pervaded the Holocaust, absolutely extraordinary though they were, seem to have been a feature of other genocides and mass violence.

In analytical terms, scholars have found much that unites the Holocaust with other genocides and mass atrocities. In Germany, as elsewhere, it was a major societal crisis—in fact, two, separated by less than a decade: the aftermath of defeat in 1918 and then the depression after 1929—that brought a radical elite to the fore. In Nazi Germany as elsewhere, the violent ideology purveyed by this elite presented removal of another group as the key to national salvation, a message that in all cases was disseminated and repeated through various media. Whether it was the Ittihadist Special Organization in the Armenian genocide, the Rwandan youth Interahamwe, or the SS, special party-linked organizations outside the normal state apparatus spearheaded killing operations, even if in all cases killings extended well beyond those groups to include military and civilian groups. Ethnic stereotypes, security worries, and the desire for the wealth of the persecuted group intermingled with material motives particularly important in incentivizing public participation. Comparison shows the Nazis' bio-racism was not at all a precondition for wanting to eliminate other groups, but the overlaying of religious and ethnic differences was a common, though not universal, fuel for murderous antagonism. In many cases, the stresses and opportunities of war were critical for enabling murderous ethnic projects. Finally, genocide or partial genocide often involves groups that are seen as somehow linked to an external threat. This ties the Holocaust to other genocides, even though the fantastical element of construing Jews in this way is more extreme than in many other cases. Many more such themes and patterns could be named.

Yet, it is noteworthy that many of the most impressive recent attempts to offer comparative historians of modern ethnic violence have difficulty fitting the Holocaust into their models. In his field-changing survey, *The Dark Side of Democracy: Explaining Ethnic Cleansing*, Michael Mann, for example, found that many of his central arguments did not fit the Nazi case and concluded that "the Holocaust had too many peculiarities to fit easily into any general model. All general explanations of murderous ethnic cleansing have suffered from taking this case as the model."[41] Christian Gerlach's search for an alternative to the genocide concept, *Extremely Violent Societies: Mass Violence in the 20th Century World*, with its focus on the emergence of new elites and their economic motives, fails to offer a convincing model of the Holocaust.[42] Mark Levene's magisterial *Crisis of Genocide*, although it offers a remarkable survey of many of the developments in which the Holocaust was entangled, focuses its argument on the developments in the rimlands or what elsewhere have been called the "shatter zones" of empire. Although it is true that much of Nazi mass murder did indeed take place in the rimlands, exploiting or intensifying the ethnic rivalries of those areas, it is also clear that the war against the Jews had different roots, and Levene himself acknowledges that European antisemitism does not fit in his model.[43] Finally, Dirk Moses's effort to locate the Holocaust in a long-term pattern of nations

248   CHAPTER 10

seeking to achieve an illusory "permanent security" suffers not only from the underdefinition of what distinguishes permanent security from other kinds of national aims but also ignores the striking and distinctive irrationality in the Nazis' claim that Jews represented a threat.[44]

Uniqueness, Jewishness, and the Holocaust

The Holocaust stands out as a genocide pursued across a highly diverse imperial space, using the different available intermediaries and structures that the Nazis found or left in place in the different parts of their realm. That it went well beyond the territory that the Nazis were intending to settle is also striking. Remarkably, the Nazis sought to render the war against the Jews global. The Holocaust was distinctive also in the use of special industrial killing sites and in organizing long-distance transports of people to be killed there. Perhaps most distinctive is that Jews fulfilled so few of the criteria of what constitutes a threat, even if one acknowledges that paranoid fantasy is characteristic of almost every genocide. German Jews were not competing for land, were not an economic threat to the new ascendant elites in Nazi Germany, were not an organized political grouping competing for power, were not an ethnic-linguistic grouping demanding special status, and, above all, were not in league with foreign powers in any sense that threatened national security. Of course, it is significant that the Nazis said and believed that Jews *were* many of these things. But the distance between that claim and any objective measure both detaches the Holocaust from other cases and makes understanding the violence that much more difficult.

What we can also see, however, is that research within Nazi Germany and comparative research outside it have significantly narrowed what uniqueness might mean. What is clear is that much of the raw horror of the Holocaust is not unique; indeed, it has been repeated far more often than we would like to believe. Yet there may well be something about Auschwitz that continues to pose a distinctive challenge to our understanding of humanity, and we should not belittle the sensation that it does. There is also something entirely unearthly about the psychological and political journey that was necessary to turn Jews into a threat that needed to be destroyed—although we might say that also about the putative conspiracies invoked by Stalin or the Cambodian fantasy of the "New People." That too carries a distinctively troubling charge. But these analytical distinctions, and the questions they raise about antisemitism and the interwar conjuncture, cannot sustain the moral and political weight of the claim of uniqueness as it has again been voiced in recent German debates. There was nothing Jewish about being exposed to a horrific genocide, although sadly it was a Jewish fate to be so.

Where does all this leave the Holocaust's place in Jewish Studies and particularly in Jewish history? Whether "Jewish" or not, the Holocaust's impact on the Jewish world requires its inclusion in any curriculum. Work on Jewish responses to Nazi persecution, both within and outside the Nazi sphere of influence, in any case easily stakes a claim to being a "Jewish" topic. Yet, as we have seen, the growing recognition of intersections between anti-Jewish policy, on the one hand, and other parts of the Nazi racist and expansionist agenda, on the other, has intensified the degree to which Holocaust scholars have to engage with material well outside the Jewish world. If that is discomforting, it is, however, a discomfort shared with many other parts of Jewish historiography, not least given scholars' increasing recognition (evident in other parts of this volume) that the history of Jewish communities and practices intersected with, was strongly influenced by, and in turn influenced those of the non-Jewish world around them. It is also no peculiarity of the Holocaust that the study of antisemitism ends up almost always being more about non-Jewish perceptions than about Jews themselves. To fulfill its brief, Jewish Studies regularly must look beyond the boundaries of the Jewish world, and here the Holocaust is no exception.

Recommended Readings

Bartov, Omer. *Anatomy of a Genocide: The Life and Death of a Town Called Buczacz* (Simon & Shuster, 2018).

Bloxham, Donald. *The Final Solution: A Genocide* (Oxford University Press, 2009).

Cohen, Boaz. *Israeli Holocaust Research: Birth and Evolution* (Routledge, 2013).

Confino, Alan. *A World without Jews: The Nazi Imagination from Persecution to Genocide* (Yale University Press, 2014).

Dawidowicz, Lucy. *The War against the Jews, 1933–1945* (Holt, Rinehart and Winston, 1975).

Engel, David. *Historians of the Jews and the Holocaust* (Stanford University Press, 2010).

Hanebrink, Paul A. *A Specter Haunting Europe: The Myth of Judeo-Bolshevism* (Belknap, 2018).

Hilberg, Raul. *The Destruction of the European Jews* (Yale University Press, 2003; first pub. 1961).

Katz, Jacob. *From Prejudice to Destruction: Anti-Semitism, 1700–1933* (Harvard University Press, 1980).

Kershaw, Ian. *The Nazi Dictatorship: Problems and Perspectives of Interpretation* (Arnold, 2000).

Levene, Mark. *The Crisis of Genocide* (Oxford University Press, 2013).

Moses, Dirk. *The Problems of Genocide* (Cambridge University Press, 2021).
Traverso, Enzo. *The Origins of Nazi Violence* (New Press, 2003).

Notes

1. *Historians of the Jews and the Holocaust* (Stanford University Press, 2010).

2. "After the Catastrophe: Aspects of Contemporary Jewry," in *Lessons and Legacies I: The Meaning of the Holocaust in a Changing World*, ed. Peter Hayes (Northwestern University Press, 1991), 132.

3. For a useful collection of the contributions to the debate, see https://serdargunes .wordpress.com/2021/06/04/a-debate-german-catechism-Holocaust-and-post-colonialism/ ?fbclid=IwAR2ggEdPcMjKQjA-B9lF-HkjMHHj7EvNrlkkmNAi1NMadkbLOWdlUvMneZY.

4. Mark Roseman, "Memory or History," *Central European History* 56 (2023): 289–93, and see the other essays in the forum.

5. Cambridge University Press, 2021.

6. Translated from the original German leaflet at www.bpb.de/themen/nationalsozialismus -zweiter-weltkrieg/weisse-rose/61015/flugblatt-ii/.

7. "'What Remains? The Language Remains': A Conversation with Günther Gaus," in Hannah Arendt, *Essays in Understanding, 1930–1954: Formation, Exile, and Totalitarianism* (Knopf Doubleday, 2011), 14.

8. Dan Diner, "Cumulative Contingency: Historicizing Legitimacy in Israeli Discourse," in *Beyond the Conceivable: Studies on Germany, Nazism, and the Holocaust* (University of California Press, 2000), 201–17.

9. "European History: Seedbed of the Holocaust," *Midstream* 19, no. 5 (1973): 3–25.

10. "Some Aspects of the Historical Significance of the Holocaust," *Jerusalem Quarterly* 1, no. 37 (1976): 40–41; cited in Daniel Blatman, "Holocaust Scholarship: Towards a Post-uniqueness Era," *Journal of Genocide Research* 17 (2015): 23.

11. *War against the Jews, 1933–1945* (Holt, Rinehart and Winston), 23.

12. Jacob Talmon, "Uniqueness and Universality of Jewish History," *Commentary* 24 (July 1957): 1–14; Katz, "The Unique Fascination of German-Jewish History," *Modern Judaism* 9 (1989): 141–50.

13. Laura Jockusch, "Prosecuting 'Crimes against the Jewish People': The Eichmann Trial and the History of a Legal Concept," in *The Eichmann Trial Reconsidered,* ed. R. Wittmann (University of Toronto Press, 2021), 75–103.

14. "Nazism: Highway or Byway?" *Central European History* 11 (1978): 21.

15. Michael Berenbaum, "The Uniqueness and Universality of the Holocaust," *American Journal of Theology and Philosophy* 2, no. 3 (1983): 85–96.

16. Hayden White, "The Question of Narrative in Contemporary Historical Theory," *History and Theory* 23 (1984): 20.

17. Todd Presner, "Intersectional Methodologies in Holocaust Studies," in *The Holocaust in North Africa,* ed. A. Boum and S. Abrevaya Stein (Stanford University Press, 2018), 246.

18. *Der Europäische Bürgerkrieg, 1917–1945: Nationalsozialismus und Bolschewismus* (Propyläen, 1987).

CATASTROPHE 251

19. *Zweierlei Untergang: Die Zerschlagung des Deutschen Reiches und das Ende des Europäischen Judentums* (W. J. Siedler, 1986).

20. The argument here is explored in greater length in Roberta Pergher and Mark Roseman, "The Holocaust: An Imperial Genocide?" *Dapim: Studies on the Holocaust* 27 (2013): 42–49.

21. *Destruction of the European Jews*, cited in Emil L. Fackenheim, "Raul Hilberg and the Uniqueness of the Holocaust," *Holocaust and Genocide Studies* 4 (1988): 491.

22. *The Origins of Nazi Violence* (New Press, 2003), 6.

23. Cited in Ian Kershaw, *The Nazi Dictatorship: Problems and Perspectives of Interpretation* (Arnold, 2000), 72.

24. *The Authoritarian Personality* (Harper, 1950).

25. "The Origins of Modern Antisemitism," in *The Nazi Holocaust: Historical Articles on the Destruction of European Jews: Vol. 2, The Origins of the Holocaust*, ed. M. Marrus (Mecklermedia, 1989), 243.

26. My translation from Jaeckel, *Hitlers Herrschaft: Vollzug einer Weltanschauung* (DVA, 1986), 145.

27. Cited in Shmuel Ettinger, "Jew-Hatred in Its Historical Context," in *Antisemitism through the Ages*, ed. S. Almog (Pergamon, 1988), 3.

28. *From Prejudice to Destruction: Anti-Semitism, 1700–1933* (Harvard University Press, 1980), 319.

29. *Nazi Germany and the Jews: Vol. 1, The Years of Persecution, 1933–1939* (Harper Collins, 1997), 87 ff.

30. For a review of this trend, see Mark Roseman, "Between Acceptance, Exceptionalism and Continuity: German Jewry, Antisemitism and the Holocaust," *Contemporary European History* 19 (2010): 55–74.

31. *A World without Jews: The Nazi Imagination from Persecution to Genocide* (Yale University Press, 2014), 11.

32. This context is admittedly not the dominant note in *Neighbors: The Destruction of the Jewish Community in Jedwabne, Poland* (Princeton University Press, 2001). For a recent powerful emphasis on continuity from the the post–World War I period to the Holocaust, see Jeffrey Veidlinger, *In the Midst of Civilized Europe: The Pogroms of 1918–1921 and the Onset of the Holocaust* (Metropolitan, Henry Holt, 2021).

33. Paul A. Hanebrink, *A Specter Haunting Europe: The Myth of Judeo-Bolshevism* (Belknap, 2018).

34. *Anatomy of a Genocide: The Life and Death of a Town Called Buczacz* (Simon and Shuster, 2018).

35. *Hitler's Willing Executioners: Ordinary Germans and the Holocaust* (Vintage, 1997).

36. Herbert, *Best: Biographische Studien über Radikalismus, Weltanschauung und Vernunft, 1903–1989* (J. H. W. Dietz, 1996); Wildt, *Generation des Unbedingten: Das Führungskorps des Reichssicherheitshauptamtes* (Hamburger Edition, 2002).

37. Browning, *Ordinary Men: Reserve Police Battalion 101 and the Final Solution in Poland* (HarperPerennial, 1993).

38. *Die Weltanschauung des Nazismus: Raum—Körper—Sprache* (Wallstein, 2010).

39. Mark Levene, *The Crisis of Genocide,* Vol. 2. *Annihilation: The European Rimlands 1939–1953* (Oxford University Press, 2013), 425.

40. Eva Hoffman, *After Such Knowledge: Memory, History, and the Legacy of the Holocaust* (Public Affairs, 2004), 43.

41. Cambridge University Press, 2005, 503.

42. Cambridge University Press, 2010.

43. For a discussion of the peculiarities of antisemitism during and after World War I, see *Crisis of Genocide*, Vol. 2, 77–94.

44. Dirk Moses, *The Problems of Genocide* (Cambridge University Press, 2021).

11

Culture

Olga Litvak, Cornell University

ENGLISH SPEAKERS put the word "culture" to various uses; the third edition of the *Oxford English Dictionary* (*OED*, 2008) boils down a rich and complicated lexical history to seven general categories, at least two of which are relevant to disciplines included in the field of Jewish Studies. The first descends from the eighteenth-century philosophical concept of the aesthetic and relates, broadly speaking, to the invention of a new subjective faculty of judgment called "taste" and to the programmatic distinction of "beauty" from other categories of objective value (i.e., the value attached to objects). In this rubric, "art" constitutes the "social practice of culture" and refers to a "self-consciously post-traditional activity whose value is internal to the vocation of practicing it."[1] The second owes its origins to developments in twentieth-century anthropology and encompasses every kind of meaning-making activity that a group of people may employ to place their experience "in some sort of comprehensible, meaningful frame."[2] Here, "culture" refers more broadly to "the symbolic dimensions of social actions—art, religion, ideology, science, law, morality, common sense."

The remit of this chapter is confined to the first category; accordingly, my principal concern is the "aesthetic turn" in nineteenth-century Jewish experience and expression. The anthropological and ethnographic concept of culture and its transformative methodological impact on Jewish Studies, evident in the "cultural turn" of the field at the turn of the millennium and signaled by the publication of a "new history" called *Cultures of the Jews* in 2002, is the focus of chapter 21, in the third part of this volume.[3] The intersection between Jewish Studies and the dedicated study of specific artistic "cultures" (literary, musical, and visual) is likewise addressed, respectively, in chapters 16–18, to which this historical survey of the Jewish "question of culture" may serve as an introduction.[4] In this context, it should be noted that the pragmatic division of labor that allocates the study of Jewish culture or cultures to several university departments, a division reflected in the organization of this book, should not be taken to imply that the ways in which this term has been used have nothing in common. On the contrary, the spread of "culture" across the length and breadth of this volume (and of the humanities and social sciences) signals that both the conceptual affinity and the historical relationship between its several meanings (implicit and explicit)—a range of family resemblances registered by the *OED* and certainly not confined to the multiple functions of the term "culture" in Jewish Studies—deserve more sustained scholarly attention.[5]

The first cultural turn in Jewish history involved two parallel nineteenth-century developments that gave social purchase to the significance that Kant assigned to perception of the aesthetic as a discrete faculty of human judgment and to the concomitant emphasis that post-Kantian philosophy placed on the autonomy of art, a word used to designate both a modern vocation and the privileged status of a material object (a literary text, a picture, a musical composition, a piece of furniture) commanding aesthetic interest.[6] Dramatic social changes attendant on the process of political emancipation and on the rise of a global commercial economy encouraged Jewish consumption of culture, underwritten by programmatic arguments for the moral transcendence of art and the spiritual significance of sensibility and imagination.[7] At the same time, the expansion of an aesthetically literate audience stimulated the entry of Jewish artists, writers, and composers into the production of culture, which had been newly liberated from clerical censorship and aristocratic patronage. In some sense, both these emergent patterns of behavior represent aspects of Jewish *embourgeoisement*—Jewish entry into the liberal professions and Jewish identification with middle-class standards of personal deportment, moral responsibility, conjugal loyalty, and civic duty—but they are not traceable to the same set of attitudes, and their relationship may, in many cases, be described as adversarial. To put it another way: Cultural work performed by Jewish artists (especially work explicitly marked for consumption by Jews) cannot be read as an unequivocal endorsement of Jewish cultural ambitions and a reflection of Jewish *embourgeoisement*. Indeed, the primary difficulty confronting the student of modern Jewish culture in its formative period is that its creation seems to have been motivated by a contrarian desire to subvert the normative category of the aesthetic from which contemporary culture derived its value and to outrage the feelings of its modern Jewish consumers. Despite modern Jewish enthusiasm for aesthetic experience (which, by the end of the nineteenth century, had become sufficiently familiar to constitute a ready-made object of parody), modern Jewish culture manifests a distinctly self-destructive anti-aesthetic streak.[8]

The Jewish encounter with culture involved an act of translation; yet the Hebrew word *tarbut*, mobilized for the purpose by Ahad Ha'am (1856–1927), the Russian founder of "spiritual Zionism," and eventually absorbed into modern (Israeli) Hebrew as the Jewish equivalent of culture, came loaded with heavy ideological baggage and postdated the Jewish domestication of the German *Kultur* (and its Russian loanword, *kul'tura*) by almost a century.[9] The lasting appeal of *Kultur* to the readers of Ahad Ha'am (even to those who did not share his nationalist commitments) and the Zionist transvaluation of *tarbut* were inseparable from the epoch-making changes in the organization of Jewish collective life that loosened communal discipline and provided young and literate men with points of entry into new service professions that rewarded personal ambition with material comforts and social privileges. The successful pursuit and enjoyment of such goods entailed a new kind of schooling, informed by a pedagogical ideal of "acculturation"—the acquisition of culture. In Germany, this ideal went by the evocative name of *Bildung*, which means something like "self-formation."[10] The modern Russian word for "education" (*obrazovanie*), similarly rooted in the word for "image" or "form," is almost a transliteration of *Bildung*, in pointed contrast to the native Russian word for "teaching" (*uchenie*). In nineteenth-century Hebrew the word *haskalah* similarly stood for *Bildung*, distinguished both from "occupational training" (*hinukh*) and ethical "teaching" (*torah*). Like the German *Bildung* and the Russian *obrazovanie*, the pursuit of *haskalah* entailed self-cultivation and personal refinement, faculties of thought and feeling that depended on a serious and high-minded engagement with art. Under the name *haskalah*, Jewish proponents of *Bildung* first introduced the German concept of culture into the Jewish lexicon. The movement they founded (called "the Haskalah" and misleadingly translated as "the Jewish Enlightenment") in the last quarter of the eighteenth century may also be credited with inventing the idea of a distinctive "Jewish culture," the ethos of which was, in fact, countercultural.[11]

In the project of middle-class self-fashioning, undertaken with a view toward upward mobility, the pursuit of culture became identified with what Schiller called the "aesthetic education of mankind." The "formation" of character attuned to the responsibilities and demands of modern life—the subjective imperative of shaping oneself and one's conduct—depended on the objective appreciation of "form," the source of intersubjective consensus (the glue) that effectively transcended the friable political bonds of citizenship and the doctrinal divisions of confession to hold society together. In this scenario, the possession and display of culture in the home served as the signifier of successful *embourgeoisement,* an ideal of self-creation that exercised a powerful attraction for upwardly mobile individuals who were neither born into aristocratic privilege nor baptized into the ruling Christian faith.[12] An expanding *Bildungsbürgertum* in German-speaking cities thus included a growing number of affluent Jews, many of them educated at secondary schools and universities, whose social credentials were effectively underwritten by their purchasing power and by their expensive cosmopolitan tastes.[13] On the urban frontier of late imperial Russia, a diploma-ed Jewish intelligentsia likewise entered into the ranks of "educated society" (Rus. *obshchestvo*), newly opened in the wake of the Great Reforms, which permitted select categories of the czar's Jewish subjects to move beyond the Pale of Jewish Settlement and up into the empire's professional and commercial elites.[14] The process had a marked effect. In the entrepôts of middle-class Europe, Jewish men and women were to be seen buying the latest novels, visiting art exhibitions, attending the opera and the theater, gathering at home for musical and literary evenings, and paying respects to the distinctly modern genius of Pushkin, Goethe, Beethoven, Balzac, and Walter Scott. By the end of the nineteenth century, the bourgeois drawing room had become "an overinvested site of cultural meaning," an intimate theater of secular ritual.[15] If middle-class domesticity exemplified the power of culture to act as a progressive, civilizing force, then Jewish acculturation bespoke the universal promise of emancipation. But not everyone believed. Doubts arose where they might have been least expected—that is to say, precisely among the creators of literature and art meant for modern Jewish consumers.

To begin with, there is the problem of nostalgia. Despite the attractions of acculturation into middle-class life and the adoption of bourgeois patterns of consumption, modern Jewish culture exhibited, almost from its very beginnings—as Richard Cohen puts it in "Nostalgia" (1998)—"the urge to retrieve aspects of a community that could no longer be reconstituted" precisely "in those modern settings where the processes of integration into European society were the most developed."[16] In the Jewish art of mid-century Western and Central Europe, the "Jewish past"—characterized by public observances and domestic devotions—became "a source of cultural inspiration" for people whose Jewish affiliations were increasingly tenuous. In Germany, the manufacture of decorative household objects depicting "religious themes" and marketed to middle-class Jewish consumers became a "cottage industry" (169). Paris, the birthplace of self-consciously modern artistic experimentation and home to the most emancipated Jewry in Europe, produced Jewish artists who felt they had a "duty to portray a dying Jewish world" (177).

A sense of longing for "traditional Jewish society" combined with a moral imperative to place it at the center of modern Jewish culture was not confined to Jewish painters. Modern Jewish literature, written by and for middle-class Jews, was driven by the same nostalgic impulse to idealize the traditional life of the "Jewish masses."[17] Although scholarship explains this tendency by reference to feelings of "disorientation and emptiness" occasioned by the shock of displacement from Jewish communal life (156), it seems that Jewish nostalgia was cultivated consciously and deliberately and not merely as a reflexive response to loss. The "contradictory attitudes" toward the old world that studies of modern Jewish culture in Western and Central Europe trace to the "rapid disintegration of traditional Jewish observance" (185) were already in evidence in Eastern Europe, where the old world was still very much alive and where traditional Jewish observance showed no signs of disappearing.

Indeed, Dan Miron sees this "paradox" as a defining feature of *maskilic* literary activity, exemplified chiefly in the development of modern prose fiction in Yiddish, the vernacular of the "Jewish masses" in Eastern Europe.[18] The Haskalah, says Miron, objected to Yiddish as a "social and cultural barrier between the Jews and their non-Jewish environment" (221). Furthermore, Jewish writers deplored Yiddish on specifically aesthetic grounds as the antithesis of linguistic decorum: "Its speakers," Miron writes, "were constantly referred to as 'stammerers' and their speech was often compared to meaningless noises produced by animals" (219). Yiddish was the repository of Jewish resistance to *Bildung*, an obstacle to Jews behaving like "educated middle-class Europeans" (223). And yet, apparently in pursuit of this ideology, the same writers "brought about the opening of this language to undreamt-of artistic and intellectual prospects" (220). They achieved this impressive feat of culture-making by the same richly imaginative means as Jewish painters were to use a short while later in France and Germany:

> With a typically anatomical intent, [Jewish writers] set about analyzing and recording various facets of the vast panorama of traditional Jewish cultural behavior.... They did this with gusto and with a *sense of mission*, and they managed to cover such broad areas of the traditional Jewish milieu, and endow their works with such a potently suggestive sense of descriptive plenitude, that it became a commonplace that for all of its ideological bias, nineteenth-century

Yiddish literature contained a complete and faithful replica of the social, economic and cultural scene of the time (221; emphasis added).

Here, incidentally, we get an impression of the way in which the aesthetic conception of *Kultur* fed into the anthropological. But for our purposes what is important is Miron's emphasis on a "sense of mission"—the same "duty" that apparently drove French Jewish painters to concentrate their attention on the cultural reproduction of traditional Jewish piety. According to Miron, this "sense" had less to do with a lingering sentimental attachment to the old ways than with feelings that were decidedly more rebarbative and self-aware. When a Jewish writer describes a venerable custom giving way to Jews acting like middle-class paragons, "we are not sure that this modernization meets entirely with his approval" (235). In reading the comments of Jewish writers on "the actual changes which the cultural behavior of Eastern European Jewry was undergoing ... changes which they themselves propagated and celebrated," one "realizes that this celebration almost always leaves a bitter aftertaste" (233). What passes under the name of nostalgia apparently served the articulation of a sense that the prospect of Jewish *embourgeoisement* was not altogether a happy one. For purveyors of modern Jewish culture, it was Yiddish-speaking "poor Jews" who, paradoxically, embodied Jewish "plenitude." In them, wrote Leopold Kompert (1822–86), an exemplary emancipated Jew (university-educated, civic-minded, urban, and German-speaking) and the author of *Geschichten aus dem Ghetto* (Leipzig, 1848), "lies our kernel, our power, our Judaism. The beautiful, delicate and inspiring that we possess is found in these crippled and afflicted creatures."[19]

Kompert's startling assertion that beauty, delicacy, inspiration—aesthetic values associated with *Bildung*—inhere in deformity and affliction, which are apparently characteristic of poor traditional Jews, brings us to the crux of the matter that Miron first brought to scholarly attention: The *maskilic* embrace of Yiddish, the language of "meaningless noises," points to the lively resistance to form as constituting modern Jewish culture. This is the basic tendency of which nostalgia is merely a symptom and which Kompert's sublimation of Jewish disability and dispossession (abjection) brings so dramatically to the fore. Miron's paradox is not, in fact, confined to *maskilic* Yiddish literature but may be said to inflect the modern Jewish imagination working in various literary, visual, and musical registers and in a number of languages, including Hebrew, the language-elect of Jewish collective emancipation, and English, the language that more than any other testifies to the spectacular triumph of Jewish *embourgeoisement* across the Atlantic.[20] In style, as well as in substance, modern Jewish culture looks less like a tribute to the Jewish achievement of *Bildung* and more like a parody of Jewish aspirations toward middle-class status, middle-class comforts, middle-class subjectivity—toward which, it must be said, the authors of that culture themselves aspired and which, in many cases, their own conspicuous success (like that of Leopold Kompert) signified. On the other side of middle-class nostalgia for the old lies the *maskilic* critique of the new.

It is a singular and historically significant fact that *maskilic* literature, ideologically committed to *Bildung*, nevertheless failed to produce a single modern educated Jewish hero who is not, in one way or another, punished or compromised (reduced, deformed) by his author. Here are three famous examples of what happens to a modern Jewish protagonist who is supposed to represent the path toward "modernization" creditably negotiated by thousands of his historical contemporaries. The eponymous hero of *The Autobiography of Solomon Maimon* (1792–94), the first German Jewish "novel of self-formation" (*Bildungsroman*), is subjected by his author—who resists any kind of simple identification with his character—to the most hilarious mockery.[21] Maimon appears in Berlin not so much to learn from others as to outsmart them; his life is a parody of social climbing, and his real "enlightenment" is treated as the product of Jewish learning, rather than of any kind of higher education; he fails to finish his course at university and dismisses his studies there as beneath his Jewish genius. At the same time, his attempts at "cultivation" boil down to visiting brothels, and his native Eastern European coarseness highlights the hypocrisy and insipidity of "culture." In *The Autobiography*, the attempt at *Bildung* results in dissipation, both literal and figurative. Its protagonist's encounter with modern culture leads to radical skepticism and, finally, narrative disintegration into allegory, which exposes his quest for self-improvement and a modern philosophy of life as frivolous and intellectually trivial.

The most popular Hebrew novel of the nineteenth century, Abraham Mapu's *Love of Zion* (1851), presents itself as a defense of the middle-class ideal of companionate marriage and appears to perform the romantic integration of personal desire and the social good.[22] The hero and heroine exemplify the virtues of self-cultivation. However, the pair is named Amnon and Tamar, sending the reader back to the original pair of that name. The biblical Amnon and Tamar feature in a story about rape, incest, and the disintegration of the royal house of David; the resolution in the biblical story is more apocalyptic than progressive. In fact, an apocalyptic fear of social collapse shadows Mapu's seemingly happy marriage plot. The final union between the lovers can stand, it seems, only with the return of paternal authority at the end. Amnon cannot defend his own romantic choice. The conclusion thus arrests this paragon of bourgeois autonomy in a regressive state of permanent childhood.

Joseph Perl's *Revealer of Secrets* (1819), the first example of a Jewish social novel and the first Jewish novel to be written in Hebrew, appears to elevate its cultivated protagonist, the richly endowed Mordechai Gold, above the uncouth, vulgar, and corrupt Hasidim who scheme against him in a convoluted plot.[23] The problem here is that even though the latter are defeated, the ending is hardly a triumph for middle-class propriety. Although the author clearly identifies with Gold and works very hard to expose his Hasidic antagonists as lecherous and deceitful, they seem to enjoy a kind of vitality and zest for life that Perl denies to his hero. At the conclusion of the novel, Gold remains isolated, childless, and possibly impotent. Moreover, the book ends on a nihilistic note of disintegration: One of the villains explodes in an apoplectic fit, the fate of his body—broken into pieces—mirroring nicely the radical diffraction of meaning that the meandering epistolarity of Perl's novel introduces into Jewish literature.

All three examples exhibit the irresistible pull of disfiguration that characterizes the *maskilic* attempt to bring about the aesthetic education of the Jews and to put the ideal of *Bildung* into practice. But no one communicated the contradictions besetting the *maskilic* engagement with culture more explicitly or more directly than Sh. J. Abramovich (1836–1917), a writer who worked in both Yiddish and Hebrew and who might well be single-handedly responsible for communicating these contradictions to his twentieth-century successors. His younger contemporary, S. N. Rabinovich (1859–1916), more popularly known by his alter ego Sholem Aleichem,[24] famously appropriated Abramovich as the "grandfather" of his own literary vocation; in fact, it was largely through Rabinovich's mediation that Abramovich's approach to the problem of form exercised its influence on twentieth-century Jewish literature.

The early work of Abramovich includes impressive instances of deformation of various kinds: moral (Takif, the confessional antihero of *The Little Man*), intellectual (Yisroelik, the madman of *The Nag*), and physical (the eponymous protagonist of *Fishke the Lame*). Moreover, Abramovich's entire oeuvre is shot through with repeated evocations of the distorted, the unfinished, the partial, the fragmented, and the broken.[25] Very few of his books have anything like a proper ending; most also seem to begin in the middle. Abramovich actively embraced this aspect of his self-consciously "uncultivated" art not merely on the level of practice but as his personal aesthetic creed. Sounding very much like Kompert, Abramovich—who reduced his own literary persona to the voice of a Jewish book peddler diminutively named "Mendele" (little Mendel)—affiliated

CULTURE 261

the modern Jewish imagination with the "poor Jew."[26] "I was destined," he wrote in the author's introduction to a new edition of *Fishke the Lame* (1888),

> to lower myself to the lowest rung of Jewish life, the very cellars. My heritage consists of rags and rot. I am constantly preoccupied with beggars, with the poor and the miserable, with the useless small-timers, clowns and other such creatures, squalid and vile. I dream only of scroungers. The Jewish beggar's pack, that enormous, everlasting Jewish burden, hovers ceaselessly before my eyes. Everywhere I turn, it flickers before me. Every story I try to tell, the beggar's pack comes immediately to mind.[27]

Abramovich's "beggar's pack" represents the antithesis of "culture" not so much because a beggar's basic needs do not rise to such a demand but because the "pack"—the Yiddish word here is *torbe,* far closer to the word "bundle" than to the word "pack," which carries a vague suggestion of compactness and order—is a collection of random bits and pieces, trifles, scraps, and fragments: things, in other words, that have been discarded. In their present devolved condition, they have no meaning, no shape, and no integrity.

What is most interesting about Abramovich's manifesto, however, is not its content but the way in which his exposition parodies the idea of culture as finished form. Instead of form, what Abramovich gives us here (and what he makes great use of in his fiction) is a list, the opposite of the ideal of internal coherence by which "culture" distinguishes itself from "nature"—the same striving by means of which the formal and deliberate qualities of "art" distinguish themselves from the disorganized condition of "life."[28] Of course, in his actual life, Abramovich represented art's highest achievement, a deliberate formality that his own imagination apparently resisted. While dreaming of Jewish "scroungers," Abramovich slept not on the floor of any cellar but in the comfortable bed of a deeply cultured modern *bourgeois* and woke to breakfast with his cultivated, well-read wife and his equally cultured and well-educated—Russian-speaking—children. Although his literary work gravitated toward the "crippled and the afflicted," Abramovich made his home in the city of Odessa among professionally educated, Russian-speaking, middle-class Jews who venerated his talent and ensured his financial security by supporting his appointment to the directorship of the largest local Jewish charity school. In this capacity, Abramovich oversaw the *Bildung* of poor Jewish children and supported their entry into a more respectable station of life. The contradictions between imaginative and social aspirations embodied in the person of Abramovich and in his work continued to trouble future purveyors of Jewish culture.

Jewish engagement with "culture" went hand in hand with Jewish *embourgeoisement*. But Jewish culture itself neither reflected nor reproduced the ideal of aesthetic wholeness associated with this process. From its beginnings, it was driven by a contrarian tendency to exploit the appeal to the imagination involved in the creation of art in the name of subverting the *embourgeoisement* not so much of Jews as of Judaism: its containment within the formal confessional parameters of a faith (Ger. *Glaube*).[29] Even though the Haskalah championed the improvement of Jewish taste, the education of Jewish sensibility, and the expansion of the Jewish curriculum to include music, art, and literature, its own wares were resolutely anti-bourgeois and profoundly suspicious of the teleology of cultural progress. By the end of the long nineteenth century, Jewish writers—followed in short order by Jewish musicians and Jewish artists—had produced an impressive body of work that was meant to be consumed by the cultivated classes, comprising middle-class Jewish men and women who could afford to attend concerts and exhibitions, collect artworks, and buy new books. But this same body of work actively antagonized its own consumers, collectively and individually; mocked their social aspirations; dismissed their Jewish commitments as superficial, self-serving, and ill-informed; and pulled back from the aesthetic educational program of Jewish modernity to embrace the archaic, the abject, and the unsightly. Scandalously, modern Jewish culture often insisted on biting the middle-class hand that fed it. In the twentieth century, the counterintuitive *maskilic* achievement that launched a Jewish anti-aesthetic of deformation on the world proved both generative and profound. Although its cultural ideology focused on *obrazovanie*, the most characteristic feature of twentieth-century Jewish cultural practice, shaped by the poetics of the Haskalah, was *bezobrazie*.

Bezobrazie is a potent word that means both "deformation" (reduction to formlessness) and "scandal" and, of course, suggests the undoing of whatever it is that the ideal of "education" or, more precisely, "formation" (*Bildung* or in Russian, *obrazovanie*) was supposed to do. *Unbildung* would be the closest German equivalent, but it lacks the suggestion of deliberate moral outrage.[30] In fact, *bezobrazie* is frequently translated as *Schande* both in German and in Yiddish; this hits the right moral note but just misses the reference to the aesthetic, implicit in *Bildung/obrazovanie*, the master concept that underwrote its commitment to culture/*kul'tura*/*Kultur*. By the beginning of the twentieth century, the Jewish artist had emerged as a first-class *bezobraznik*, a troublemaker, a disturber of middle-class peace, an imp, and a perpetrator of mischief, whose vocation it was to place the tastes of Jewish "educated society" (Ger. *gebildetes Pub-*

likum, Rus. *obshchestvo*) on the defensive, to disturb its hard-won sense of social and personal decorum, to induce radical discomfort and shame, and to unravel the carefully knit fabric of its aesthetically pleasing home life. A *bezobraznik* is an iconoclast, a breaker of images, a prophet of wrath.

To be sure, the collective biography of Jewish art in the modern period cannot be reduced to this type. It is enough, in this context, to mention the counterexample of N. M. Shaikevitsh (1849–1905), known by his acronym as Shomer. Shomer published more than 200 novels in Yiddish, more than 50 Yiddish plays (the plots of which drew largely on his prose) and 15 novels in Hebrew. Most of his output (a word that is exactly descriptive of his productivity) consists of middle-class fables of socioeconomic ascent; Shomer has the distinction of being the only Jewish author in the nineteenth century to achieve these same feats of *embourgeoisement* entirely by means of the income he earned from writing fiction that dispensed the nostrum of upward mobility.[31] His popularity was a perpetual thorn in the side of his more sophisticated contemporaries.[32] Although Jewish literary criticism relegates Shomer's work to the netherworld of *shund* (rubbish), no historian would deny his role in the "acculturation" of the Jewish reading public. The same might be said of Leon Uris (1924–2003), the author of the phenomenally successful American Jewish novel *Exodus* (1958), which served the same function for Jewish immigrants from the Soviet Union, and of Sheldon Harnick (b. 1929) and Jerry Bock (1928–2010), creators of the musical *Fiddler on the Roof* (1964), which continues to carry on the same kind of cultural work even now.[33]

And yet, the fact remains that the anti-aesthetic of *bezobrazie* is a constitutive feature of the modern Jewish imagination. Twentieth-century examples of the Jewish artist—visual, musical, and literary—as *bezobraznik* come readily and forcefully to mind. Modern art includes such eminent troublemakers and disturbers of middle-class peace as Marc Chagall (1887–1985), a painter who made visual deformation of Jewish reality a specialty; El Lissitzky (1890–1941); Mark Rothko (1903–70); and Barnett Newman (1905–70): They were original creators (not merely exponents) of artistic styles deliberately resistant to the appeal of form. In the work of Chagall and Lissitzky (which is, otherwise, very different), it is possible to discern a shared connection between the nineteenth-century pull of Jewish "nostalgia" and the way in which twentieth-century Jewish artists made use of abstraction; this is a connection that deserves more study. In music, no figure deserves the title of *bezobraznik* more than Arnold Schönberg (1874–1951). Indeed, the singular phenomenon of Schönberg emerges with particular salience against the background of the dramatic success of the middle-class

Jewish domestication of classical music; it also exemplifies the ambiguities of "culture" as a Jewish concept, an exemplary "complex word" that signifies both the desire for a certain kind of thing *and* the contrarian desire to blast the certainty and smash the thing itself to pieces.[34] For it was classical music, more than any other form of artistic expression, that seems to have galvanized the middle-class Jewish romance with "culture," defined by a longing for well-ordered forms. For this reason, the disruptive figure of Schönberg looms much larger in this story than his relative marginality on the spectrum of modern Jewish cultural expression might, at first, suggest.[35]

Schönberg did many things, including writing an opera about Moses—but one of his uncredited achievements may have been his murderous, if unintended, thrust against the cultural ambitions of every nineteenth-century Jewish mother who paid for a lifetime of violin or piano lessons. After Schönberg, it was much harder to predict just what the results of such cultural investment would be. And this is just the point: Although Jewish consumption of culture was the logical outcome of its institutionalization by *maskilim*, its production was, from the beginning, driven by an iconoclastic impulse to deface the romantic cult of beauty, to disfigure Goethe's "beautiful soul," and to reduce well-integrated modern forms—the novel, for instance, or, in Schönberg's case, its musical equivalent, the symphony—to a state of anarchic, atonal shapelessness; that is, to make pictures, books, and music that had the express purpose to cause scandal and to get on people's nerves. Viewed from this perspective, the totality of modern Jewish culture looks like a highly paradoxical Schönbergian *Skandalkonzert* (the name given to a notorious concert of experimental music that Schönberg conducted in Vienna in the spring of 1913, two months before the equally scandalous Paris premiere of Stravinsky's *Rite of Spring*)—a riotous unity that remains very difficult to accord with the idea of culture as "sweetness and light," exemplified chiefly by formal "harmony."[36] Modern Jewish culture is fully complicit in the revolutionary, not to say anarchist, effort to overturn such pieties; long before Schönberg, there was Heinrich Heine (1797–1856), who subjected the Romantic cult of "poesy" to devastating irony. But the only possible rival for Schönberg's place as modern culture's paradigmatic Jewish troublemaker is the supreme *bezobraznik* of twentieth-century Jewish literature, the American novelist Philip Roth (1933–2018).

Now, it is undoubtedly true that modern Jewish writing produced a disproportionate share of *bezobrazniki*. Sholem Aleichem (Abramovich's self-anointed "grandson")—whom some of his early readers called a "Jewish Cossack"—was one. Although his reception in the United States (largely in English translation)

CULTURE   265

has turned him into an icon of Jewish sentiment, his best-known works—the monologues that comprise *Tevye the Dairyman* and the *Railroad Stories*—stage an assault on middle-class Jewish preoccupations with money and status.[37] Adopting a deliberately loose "conversational" style, Sholem Aleichem perfected the art of unreliable narrative: Most of his speakers (including Tevye) are self-deluding narcissists. Sholem Aleichem also has the distinction of introducing the figure of the artist as *bezobraznik* into the repertoire of Jewish literature, first in the title character of *Stempenyu* (1888) and then in the "wandering stars" of his late novel about a Jewish theatrical company (1909–11). Then, there is Shai (S. Y.) Agnon (1887–1970), whose work may be read as a study in the poetics of disfiguration. His first full-length novel, a digressive mock epic called *The Bridal Canopy* (1931), is a parody of the middle-class marriage novel, and his master-piece *Only Yesterday* (1945) is a sustained improvisation on the theme of mad-ness. Agnon's short stories are also generically indeterminate and hard to fit into any modern theory of narrative; likewise, his characters represent striking and often discordant combinations of obsessive pathology and traditional piety. Agnon bears comparison to two of his Jewish contemporaries, Franz Kafka (1883–1924) and Isaac Babel (1894–1940), who were similarly attuned to the liter-ary possibilities of deformation. Kafka's *Dearest Father* (a letter that the author actually addressed to his father, a paragon of middle-class success, unpublished until 1953) reads like a manifesto of *bezobrazie*.[38] In verse, it is enough to men-tion H. N. Bialik (1873–1934), whose work dwells with a compulsive fascination on images of physical decomposition and apocalyptic chaos.[39] In this respect, Bialik had a loyal disciple in the refractory poetic persona of Uri Zvi Greenberg (1896–1981), who abandoned every poetic measure for extended vatic dis-courses, many of them uncomfortable performances of individual and collective agony. Greenberg's work effaces the boundaries of poetic speech in the same way that Agnon's work defies the distinction between different kinds of literary prose, it seems, to question every other kind of normative distinction that organizes the inner world of the modern Jewish reader.

It is, of course, possible to argue that the increasing appeal to *bezobrazie* reflected in twentieth-century Jewish culture is a function of Jewish historical experience in the twentieth century, but Roth's body of work challenges the neatness of this interpretation. For one thing, engagement with the subject of the Shoah inspired Roth's most conventionally structured and politically affir-mative book: a counterfactual middle-class Jewish fable called *The Plot against America* (2004). At the same time, Roth's treatment of the same subject matter elsewhere in his oeuvre shows a distinctly provocative proclivity toward *bezobrazie*: Like his nineteenth-century predecessors, Roth refuses to elevate culture above what we might call the ground floor (Abramovich's "very cellars") of human behavior. No work signifies this tendency more clearly than *Portnoy's Complaint* (1969), which subjects the liberal conscience of its *gebildete* (an obsessively cultured and educated) Jewish protagonist, ironically named Alexander—the conqueror of the world and the original purveyor of classical culture to eastern barbarians—to the most outrageous authorial ridicule. Roth's modern Jewish antihero—a narcissist who leaves his girlfriend stranded in Greece, the birthplace of European civility, to seek a psychoanalytic cure for impotence—is the latest exemplar in a line of modern Jewish protagonists intentionally disfigured by their authors: Alex Portnoy is a direct descendant of Solomon Maimon. Roth exposes Alex's middle-class cultural pretensions as a self-serving affectation and lowers his dream of erotic independence to the level of a relentless masturbatory instinct. *Portnoy's Complaint* continues to scandalize middle-class Jewish readers.[40] So do Roth's later works, *Sabbath's Theater* (1995) and *American Pastoral* (1997), notable for the way in which they bring aesthetic discipline into question and for the way they capture Roth's *maskilic* discomfort with Jewish *embourgeoisement*, already evident in *Goodbye, Columbus* (1959) and in the extraordinary short story, "Defender of the Faith" published in the same early collection.

Looking back from a vantage point informed by the difference between *Portnoy's Complaint* and *The Plot against America,* we struggle to position modern Jewish art within a modern Jewish "canon": an exemplary list of essential works defined by some intransitive metaphysical quality and reducible to an expression of ethnic belonging, emotional attachment, or political conviction. None of these suffice to account for the specific structural and dramatic tensions that inflect the art of Philip Roth. On the contrary, the irrepressible tension between culture and anarchy that we have been tracking through this chapter all the way to Roth is in its own way a powerful argument for ideology implicit in the invention of "Jewish art." Instead of pursuing the obscure object of modern *Jewish* culture, we might turn our attention to the eminently historical subject of modern Jewish *culture*: the involvement of Jews in the production and consumption of modern painting, music, and literature as part of a second-order investigation of the aesthetic.

Recommended Readings

Avishai, Bernard. *Promiscuous: Portnoy's Complaint and Our Doomed Pursuit of Happiness* (Yale University Press, 2004).
Biale, David. *Jewish Culture between Canon and Heresy* (Stanford University Press, 2023).

Cohen, Richard. *Jewish Icons: Art and Society in Modern Europe* (University of California Press, 1985).

Ledehendler, Eli. *Jewish Immigrants and American Capitalism, 1880–1920: From Caste to Class* (Cambridge University Press, 2008).

Miron, Dan. "Folklore and Antifolklore in the Yiddish Fiction of the Haskala," in *Studies in Jewish Folklore,* ed. Frank Talmage (Association for Jewish Studies, 1980), 219–49.

Mosse, George. "A Cultural Emancipation," in *German Jews beyond Judaism* (Hebrew Union College Press, 1985), 1–20.

Nester, Adi. *Unsettling Difference: Music, Drama, the Bible, and the Critique of German Jewish Identity* (Cornell University Press, 2025).

Peleg, Yaron. *Directed by God: Jewishness in Contemporary Israeli Film and Television* (University of Texas Press, 2016).

Schweid, Eliezer. *The Idea of Modern Jewish Culture* (Academic Studies Press, 2008).

Seidman, Naomi. *The Marriage Plot, or How Jews Fell in Love with Love and with Literature* (Stanford University Press, 2016).

Shavit, Zohar, and Yaakov Shavit, "Jewish Culture: What Is It?," in *Cambridge History of Judaism*, Vol. 8, ed. Hart and Michaels (Cambridge University Press, 2017), 677–98.

Wisse, Ruth R. *The Modern Jewish Canon: A Journey through Language and Culture* (University of Chicago Press, 2000).

Notes

1. Michael Levenson, *Modernism* (Yale University Press, 2011), 8.

2. See Clifford Geertz, "Thick Description: Toward an Interpretive Theory of Culture," in *The Interpretation of Cultures: Selected Essays* (Basic Books, 1973), 3–30.

3. David Biale, ed., *Cultures of the Jews: A New History* (Schocken, 2002).

4. The quotation is from the title of Geoffrey H. Hartman's *The Fateful Question of Culture* (Columbia University Press, 1997). This book is a spirited defense of the nineteenth-century Romantic concept of "culture" as critique from the relentlessly affirmative "culturalism" of the late twentieth century. His "question" about the relationship between culture and the imperatives of social and political order is eminently pertinent to the question posed by this chapter: What is the relationship between modern Jewish culture and modern Jewish life?

5. On the relationship between the uses of culture in this chapter and its deployment in the context of anthropology, see Louis Dumont, *German Ideology from France to Germany and Back* (University of Chicago Press, 1994).

6. For the intellectual background, see Paul Guyer, *A History of Modern Aesthetics*, Vol. 1 (Cambridge University Press, 2014). On the importance of the Kantian category of the aesthetic for the "cultural life" of the nineteenth century, see the studies in *The Impact of Idealism: The Legacy of Post-Kantian German Thought*, Vol. 3, ed. C. Jamme and R. Cooper (Cambridge University Press, 2013). For a critical reflection from the perspective of the twentieth century, see Wolf Lepenies's essay, *The Seduction of Culture in German History* (Princeton University Press, 2006).

7. On the connection between *embourgeoisement* and the moral elevation of culture, see Terry Eagleton, *The Ideology of the Aesthetic* (Blackwell, 1990).

8. For examples of parody of the nineteenth-century Jewish enthusiasm for "culture," see Thomas Mann, "The Blood of the Volsungs [1905]," in *The German-Jewish Dialogue: An Anthology of Literary Texts, 1749–1993*, ed. R. Robertson (Oxford University Press, 1999), 152–78; and Oscar Wilde, *The Picture of Dorian Gray* [1891] (Penguin, 2010), 72–73. In Wilde's novel the world-weary aesthete, Sir Henry Wotton, speaks with ironic admiration of a Jewish theatrical manager with "an extraordinary passion for Shakespeare," who had the "great distinction" of ruining himself "over poetry." In Mann's story, the object of Jewish "passion" for art is the music of Wagner.

9. See Zohar Shavit and Yaakov Shavit, "Jewish Culture: What Is It?" in *Cambridge History of Judaism*, Vol. 8, ed. M. Hart and T. Michels (Cambridge University Press, 2017), 677–98, esp. 679–81. The word *tarbut* (from the root R-B-H) refers to "development" or "growth." In both biblical and rabbinic usage, it is associated with taking up alien and transgressive behavior; see Num 32:14 and BT Hagigah 15a, BT Berakhot 7a, and Sanhedrin 106b. The expression *yatza letarbut ra'ah* means something like "departed for evil ways" or "came to wickedness."

10. See W. H. Bruford, *The German Tradition of Self-Cultivation: "Bildung" from Humboldt to Thomas Mann* (Cambridge University Press, 1975).

11. On the translation problem and its interpretive consequences, see Olga Litvak, *Haskalah: The Romantic Movement in Judaism* (Rutgers University Press, 2012).

12. On the appeal of *Bildung* to German Jews, see George Mosse, "A Cultural Emancipation," in *German Jews beyond Judaism* (Hebrew Union College Press, 1985), 1–20.

13. The pioneering study of this process is Marion Kaplan, *The Making of the Jewish Middle Class: Women, Family and Identity in Imperial Germany* (Oxford University Press, 1991). See also Till van Rahden, *Jews and Other Germans: Civil Society, Religious Diversity, and Urban Politics in Breslau, 1860–1925* (University of Wisconsin Press, 2008).

14. See Steven J. Zipperstein, *The Jews of Odessa: A Cultural History, 1794–1881* (Stanford University Press, 1986); Benjamin Nathans, *Beyond the Pale: The Jewish Encounter with Late Imperial Russia* (University of California Press, 2002); and Natan M. Meir, *Kiev, Jewish Metropolis: A History, 1859–1914* (Indiana University Press, 2010).

15. Levenson, *Modernism*, 181.

16. "Nostalgia and 'The Return to the Ghetto,'" in Cohen, *Jewish Icons: Art and Society in Modern Europe* (University of California Press, 1998), 157.

17. See Cohen, "Nostalgia," 178–84; Jonathan M. Hess, *Middlebrow Literature and the Making of German-Jewish Identity* (Stanford University Press, 2010), esp. chap. 2; and Maurice Samuels, *Inventing the Israelite: Jewish Fiction in Nineteenth-Century France* (Stanford University Press, 2010), esp. chaps. 4 and 5.

18. Miron, "Folklore and lore in the Yiddish Fiction of the Haskala," in *Studies in Jewish Folklore*, ed. Frank Talmage (Association for Jewish Studies, 1980), 219–49.

19. Cited in Cohen, "Nostalgia," 181.

20. On American Jewish *embourgeoisement*, see Eli Lederhendler, *Jewish Immigrants and American Capitalism, 1880–1920: From Caste to Class* (Cambridge University Press, 2008).

21. *The Autobiography of Solomon Maimon*, ed. Y. Y. Melamed and A. P. Socher (Princeton University Press, 2018).

22. Abraham Mapu, *Love of Zion and Other Writings* (Toby, 2006). For analysis of the plot, see Litvak, *Haskalah*, 136–46.

CULTURE 269

23. Joseph Perl, *Revealer of Secrets* (Routledge, 1996).

24. "Sholem-aleichem" is a Yiddish greeting, which means "How-do-you-do?" and was so used by S. N. Rabinovich in reference to his literary persona.

25. See Amir Banbaji, *Mendele and the National Narrative* (Ben Gurion University, 2009).

26. On the relationship between Abramovich and "Mendele," see Dan Miron, *A Traveler Disguised: The Rise of Modern Yiddish Fiction in the Nineteenth Century* (Schocken, 1973).

27. *The Three Great Classic Writers of Modern Yiddish Literature*, ed. Zuckerman et al. (3 vols.; Joseph Simon/Pangloss, 1991), 1:172–73; transl. altered; for the Yiddish original, see Abramovich, "Fishke der krumer," in *Ale verk fun Mendele Moykher-sforim* (17 vols.; Mendele, 1911–13), 11:6–7.

28. For an example of Abramovich's literary use of the list as a signifier of chaos, see Litvak, *Haskalah*, 168.

29. On this process, see Leora Batnitzky, *How Judaism Became a Religion: An Introduction to Modern Jewish Thought* (Princeton University Press, 2011).

30. Educated Jewish readers of German referred to knowledge of Yiddish not merely as undesirable, useless, and faulty but also as *Unbildung*: active ill/literacy; see Jeffrey Shandler, *Yiddish: Biography of a Language* (Oxford University Press, 2020) 110.

31. See Sophie Grace-Pollack, "Reishito shel shomer be-yidish," *Ḥulyot* 2 (1994): 69–87.

32. See Justin Cammy, "Judging *The Judgment of Shomer*: Jewish Literature versus Jewish Reading," in *Arguing the Modern Jewish Canon: Essays on Literature and Culture in Honor of Ruth R. Wisse*, ed. Cammy et al. (Harvard University Press, 2008), 85–127.

33. See Alisa Solomon, *Wonder of Wonders: A Cultural History of Fiddler on the Roof* (Metropolitan Books, 2013).

34. On "complex words," see William Empson, *The Structure of Complex Words* (Chatto and Windus, 1951).

35. But see Adi Nester, "The End of Abstraction and the Beginning of the People: On Law and Representation in Arnold Schoenberg's *Moses und Aron*," *German Quarterly* 93 (2020): 19–36.

36. Matthew Arnold was the primary English-speaking exponent of the nineteenth-century ideal of "culture" as the perfected form: the "harmonious expansion of *all* the powers which make the beauty and worth of human nature." See Arnold, *Culture and Anarchy and Other Writings*, ed. Collini (Cambridge University Press, 1992), 62.

37. See Sholem Aleichem, *Tevye the Dairyman and the Railroad Stories* (Schocken, 1987).

38. See Kafka, *Dearest Father* (Alma Classics, 2008).

39. See Hamutal Bar-Yosef, *Decadent Trends in Modern Hebrew Literature* [Hebrew] (Ben Gurion University, 1997). Bar-Yosef positions Bialik's poetics within the context of European "decadence," an affinity that seems highly attenuated and for which she has little historical evidence. It seems more productive to think about Bialik's poetics of mortality, decomposition, and "decline" (which Bar-Yosef also locates in the work of J. H. Brenner and M. J. Berdyczewski) in connection with the Jewish genealogy of *bezobrazie*.

40. On the critical and popular response to *Portnoy's Complaint,* see Bernard Avishai, *Promiscuous: Portnoy's Complaint and Our Doomed Pursuit of Happiness* (Yale University Press, 2004).

PART 2

Ideas and Expression

12

God and the Sacred

Sarit Kattan Gribetz, Yale University

THIS CHAPTER highlights religious dimensions of ancient Judaism from the biblical through the Second Temple and rabbinic periods, identifying key concepts and practices that developed in the course of antiquity and in the context of many different communities across considerable temporal and geographic distance. It takes a thematic approach to the sources. Over the long span of time and in the diverse texts and contexts that this chapter addresses, different ideas, practices, institutions, and norms existed at any given time and also changed over time. Yet, despite this heterogeneity, it can be productive to think across chronological periods, geographical locations, and textual and material corpora to illuminate overarching trends and shared themes that arise between and among them, including ritual practices, formations of communities, transmission of traditions, constructions of space and time, cosmologies, and theologies. It was during this period that many of the main cornerstones of Jewish practice solidified and ideas about commandedness, dedication, and vigilance regarding their adherence took root.[1]

There are several conceptual challenges and opportunities associated with investigating the religious dimensions of ancient Judaism. For example, the category of "religion" is a modern concept that is not easily applied to antiquity nor to Judaism. Yet, scholarship in the field of religious studies has demonstrated that thinking carefully about the constellation of concepts we now call "religion" can be helpful in thinking about the ancient world. This is the case even if those living in that ancient world did not necessarily use the same language—nor even the same conceptual categories—that we do, because it shifts our attention to new and important dimensions of our sources that might otherwise be overlooked or marginalized. (Investigating the language and concepts used in and by our ancient sources is also important, of course.) Moreover, although the field of religious studies relies on philological, historical, and cultural analysis and is interested in how texts are composed and transmitted, it also gravitates to the stories those sources tell, the rituals they prescribe, the laws and norms they promote, the categories they develop, the identities they cultivate, the communities they form, and the legacies they instantiate.[2]

The field of religious studies also provides frameworks for exploring concepts such as sacredness, divinity, and theology and their place within social and cultural matrices—both how ancient authors and their communities conceived of God and the heavenly realm and how such conceptions permeated other dimensions of social organization, cultural production, and ritual practice. In other words, central categories and questions from the modern discipline of religious studies help us reconfigure the ways in which we study ancient Judaism and its textual and material remains. Doing so also affects how we understand the formation of religion as an idea, because Judaism itself was formed as part of the process by which the category of religion emerged, both within the broader Greco-Roman world and in complicated conversation with the development of Christianity and other traditions within that same context.[3]

The discipline of religious studies has also been interested, particularly in the past few decades, in non-elite members of society and the ways in which our sources might provide access, however indirect, to their contributions and contexts. In addition to examining long-studied canonical texts, the field of religious studies has relatedly encouraged the analysis of extra-canonical texts and non-literary sources—including documentary evidence, liturgical poetry, material culture, architecture, and art—because they provide new angles to examine ancient communities and practices. Scholars have also provided tools for situating these diverse types of sources in the spatial and experiential contexts in which they might have been used or read; these tools help us understand the role the sources played not only in the development of ritual, legal, theological, or doctrinal discourse but also in the messy daily lives of individuals, who navigated between the quotidian and existential in myriad ways. Such approaches represent capacious views of religion as a subject of study and stem from an understanding that religion encompasses many aspects of life and society.

Thus, all evidence from antiquity—from oil lamps to ritual baths to sundials; to amulets and incantation bowls, documentary papyri, mystical literature, homilies, epigraphy and burial inscriptions, graffiti, coins, frescoes, and mosaics; to the many texts that were composed, recited, and transmitted—contribute

GOD AND THE SACRED 275

important dimensions to our understanding of the forms of Judaism that were created over this long period and of the different communities and practices that emerged in that time.

This chapter proceeds in two parts. The first half focuses on conceptions of and interactions among space, time, and ritual. It identifies the role that space in general and that certain places and institutions in particular played in ancient Judaism, including the Temple (along with its sacrifices and purity practices), synagogues, and urban and rural landscapes. It also examines the practices and rituals associated with time—the annual calendar, the Sabbath, festivals, prayer, the life cycle, and daily rituals—as they developed from biblical sources through Second Temple and rabbinic texts. The second half of this chapter turns to conceptions of God and the heavenly realm, addressing more directly the question of divinity in ancient Judaism, including how ritual devotion and ir/reverence participated in the formation of ancient Judaism and laid important foundations for the Judaism(s) that followed in the medieval and modern periods. Conceptions of space, time, ritual, sacredness, divinity, community, and identity are all integrally related to one another and provide helpful ways of approaching the formation of ancient Jewish communities, texts, rituals, and histories.

Space, Time, and Ritual

Several institutions, practices, and ideas played central roles in Jewish antiquity: the Temple and sacrifice; the calendar and festivals, including the Sabbath; purity and prayer practices; lifecycle events and rituals; Torah study; and synagogue communities.

In biblical sources, the Tabernacle and Temple play central roles in conceptions of nation, community, and worship. The Tabernacle, conceived in written sources as the tent of meeting and prophecy, as well as priestly sacrificial practices, was located at the center of the Israelite encampment in the wilderness and at the front of the entourage when the nation moved from location to location. The Temple, a more permanent and grandiose structure in Jerusalem, envisioned by David and built by Solomon (and, after its destruction, rebuilt in the Persian period and remodeled and expanded by Herod the Great in the first century CE), is also presented as Israel's cultic center. In addition to tithes and sacrificial offerings that were brought for various reasons, liturgical and musical practices developed in the Temple. Economic institutions in Jerusalem and travel routes throughout the greater region facilitated pilgrimage, especially during the three pilgrimage holidays. (Biblical sources also spend considerable energy warning readers to stay away from cultic places outside Jerusalem and from idolatrous gods.)

Ancient sources cultivate multiple conceptions of the sacredness associated with the Temple. Some imagined that God's presence inhabited the Tabernacle and Temple, which were thus fashioned as God's home (e.g., Exod 25:8); others describe the space as the meeting place between heaven and earth where, for example, the bottom of God's heavenly robe reached the interiors of the Temple (e.g., Isa 6:1). Yet others argue that although God resides in the heavens, the Temple serves as God's earthly address, to which prayers ought to be directed, even though God does not dwell—and indeed cannot be contained—in any particular place (e.g., 1 Kgs 8:27). Biblical and Second Temple sources developed additional ideas about the Temple's sacredness and about alternative (often heavenly) temples, which were posited as solutions to the Temple's destruction and as critiques of the earthly Temple (e.g., the biblical books of Ezekiel and Ezra, the Temple Scroll among the Dead Sea Scrolls). Alternative temples and spaces of worship existed as well, including at Elephantine, Mount Gerizim, Leontopolis, and Qumran (on the emergence of synagogues, see the later discussion).

A large proportion of rabbinic sources are similarly focused on the Temple, including its sacrifices and other rituals; even though they were composed after its destruction, they refer to it in the present tense, maintaining it as an imagined realm still relevant long after its physical destruction.[4] Other rabbinic passages bemoan the Temple's destruction.[5] Biblical narratives associated with creation, the patriarchs, and other important historical moments came to be associated with the space of the Temple, such that by Late Antiquity, the location of the Temple was also considered the origin of the world's creation and the binding of Isaac—and, in early Islamic sources, where Muhammad's night journey and ascent to heaven occurred. Rabbinic texts develop theories of sacred space that encompass the area of the Temple along with the broader region. One passage in the Mishnah, for instance, lists the ten degrees of holiness, in which the first is the Land of Israel, the second are cities enclosed by a wall, and the third is Jerusalem. The list narrows its focus on the Temple precinct, such that the final holiest place is the Holy of Holies.[6]

Ancient sources discuss rituals and practices associated with the Temple, including an elaborate system of sacrifices and offerings that were no longer practiced after the Temple's destruction and a system of purity and impurity that remained relevant well beyond the Temple even when it stood and that continued to be practiced in various forms throughout Late Antiquity and beyond after its destruction.[7] Leviticus 1–5 outlines the five types of offerings—*olah, minhah,*

GOD AND THE SACRED   277

shelamim, hattat, and *asham*—that are often translated as burnt offering, grain offering, offering of well-being, purification offering, and offering of restitution (although there is much scholarship on the identity and purpose of each of these offerings). Leviticus 11–15 and Numbers 19 present rules and regulations associated with different forms of impurity, which can stem from dead creatures (animal carcasses, human corpses, dead insects, etc.); impure substances (semen, ashes of the red heifer); people with scale disease and genital discharges (including menstruation) after childbirth; and certain objects (garments and houses) afflicted with mildew or mold.[8] These rules were adapted by different communities and made more or less stringent in each.[9] Whether and when these became widespread practices is difficult to determine, as is the case with so much that is based on ancient sources that are primarily prescriptive; however, material evidence suggests that, at some point, concerns about impurity led to the construction of ritual baths (*mikvaot*) throughout the city of Jerusalem and in other cities and towns where Jews lived.[10] These sacrificial and purity practices were just as important for their structuring of time (e.g., daily, weekly, and festival offerings; schedules for the duration of various forms of impurity and the purification rituals that followed) as they were for conceptions of space.

Other practices mentioned in biblical sources—for example, circumcision and prohibitions against consuming non-kosher animals—also remained important in the Second Temple and rabbinic periods.[11] Although biblical sources provide basic guidelines for these practices and Second Temple sources reference many of them, rabbinic texts provide the most comprehensive set of discussions and guidelines about practices of daily life. Over the course of Jewish antiquity, customs, practices, and norms developed regarding lifecycle events and family life, including conversion, betrothal, engagement, marriage, and divorce; caregiving, including childrearing, education, and eldercare; and death, burial, and morning. Daily prayers, other recitations (such as the Shema), and embodied practices such as donning phylacteries also became increasingly standardized.[12]

Biblical passages outline festivals and the dates on which they ought to be celebrated. Leviticus 23 begins with the Sabbath on the seventh day of each week and then proceeds to list Passover and the Festival of Unleavened Bread, the Festival of Weeks (Shavuot), the Festival of Trumpets (Rosh Hashanah), the Day of Atonement (Yom Kippur), and the Festival of Tabernacles (Sukkot), all of which are also discussed elsewhere in the Hebrew Bible. Many of these festivals are associated in biblical sources with the agricultural cycle, and some with important events found in biblical sources. The division of time into seven days, an innovation of ancient Israel, and its signature day of rest, the Sabbath, are presented in biblical sources as a remembrance of both God's creation of the world and the subsequent decision to rest, as well as Israel's redemption from enslavement in Egypt. The weekly Sabbath was associated with the seven-year Sabbatical cycles related to agricultural practices and the Jubilee year (the fiftieth year following seven cycles of seven years), which addressed land ownership, debt, and social order. Second Temple sources suggest that, by the end of that period, the Sabbath was not only a day on which certain activities were prohibited but also one that was marked with festive meals and other rituals. The book of Jubilees, composed in the second century CE, orders world history in cycles of seven years, offering a privileged place to the weekly Sabbath and the Sabbatical years in its cosmology. Rabbinic sources discuss Sabbath practices and customs extensively.

Beyond mentioning the dates of festivals, biblical sources do not provide much material regarding the construction of a calendar. The origins and precise functioning of ancient Israelite and Jewish calendars are thus somewhat mysterious. References to the calendar—or rather, to competing calendars—burst onto the scene when calendrical practices became matters of controversy, especially in the later Second Temple period. Different communities advocated for different types of calendars. Those associated with the Dead Sea Scrolls firmly believed that a solar calendar fulfilled scriptural instructions, whereas others, probably those associated with the Jerusalem Temple, preferred a luni-solar calendar, anchored in lunar months but adjusted for the solar seasons through a system of intercalary months. Whether the use of different calendars caused extreme social and ideological upheaval or simply represented accepted calendrical pluralism is difficult to untangle, given that extant sources on this subject stem from primarily one, highly polemical community. But the stakes were certainly high, because calendars not only served social, political, and economic functions but also represented the synchronization of earthly and heavenly time, such that using the proper calendar and declaring accurate festival dates were deemed essential for worshiping God correctly.

By the period of the composition of our earliest rabbinic sources, whatever calendrical controversy had unfolded generations earlier seems to have died down. Only faint traces of earlier disputes remain in rabbinic sources; for example, a story in Mishnah Rosh Hashanah in which two rabbis disagree about the proper procedure for accepting conflicting testimony about the phases of the moon and thus when a new month should begin.[13] The rabbinic solution seems to have been to accept the rabbinic calendar that was declared based on the original accepted testimony—whether it was astronomically accurate or not—as the calendar sanctioned by God, even if that testimony is later discovered to be astronomically impossible. The rabbinic calendar (at first observed, later fixed, even later calculated) continued to develop through the rabbinic period and beyond, so that as late as the ninth and tenth centuries rabbinic communities found themselves debating decisions about calendrical calculations, intercalation, and festival times.[14] Calendrical discrepancies sometimes became major communal disruptions and at other times were viewed as acceptable parts of a temporally pluralistic society.

One dimension of time worth noting is the seasonality of the year. The annual festivals do not only punctuate the year with special days, each with their own sets of rituals, practices, and liturgies. They also create different seasons in which specific themes, histories, narratives, and polemics become more dominant. For example, by Late Antiquity, the fall cycle of festivals featured Rosh Hashanah, the New Year, which was associated with the shofar, renewal, and judgment; Yom Kippur, the day of atonement; and Sukkot and Shemini Atzeret, associated not only with the fall harvest and the sojourn of the Israelites in tabernacles in the wilderness but also a time of joy, related especially to the Temple and its dedication. Hanukkah marked the winter, first with its narrative of military victory over the Greeks and, eventually, the miracle of oil in the Temple. The spring began with Purim, a holiday celebrating the survival and triumph of diaspora communities threatened with genocide; it was followed by Passover, the festival during which the exodus from Egypt was enacted through sacrifice, study or storytelling, and the consumption of unleavened bread. After Passover, forty-nine days of the Omer were counted, culminating in the festival of Shavuot, which came to mark revelation at Sinai and the giving of the Torah, in addition to the early summer harvest. The summer months turned primarily to mourning, when the siege of Jerusalem and then destruction of the Temple(s) and other devastating events in Jewish history were marked through fast days.

This overview flattens the complicated historical processes through which each of these festivals and its rituals developed from biblical through Second Temple and rabbinic sources.[15] But it also highlights how, by the end of the rabbinic period, we can identify not only a calendar and a set of festivals but also defined annual and seasonal cycles in which historical narratives, agricultural rhythms, and communal practices defined the contours of Jewish communities and how they experienced and marked time. In addition, there were days on which fasting was either mandated—for example, as a strategy to beseech God for rain in periods of drought—or prohibited, such as on days of particular joy.[16]

Alongside mandated times of celebration or mourning stood other sets of times—those of empires and competing communities—that Jews were urged to resist from adopting (but that many probably marked as well). The Jewish calendar thus marked periods not only of heightened practice and communal participation but also of vigilance to separate and establish difference for fear of adopting too many practices associated with forbidden others.

In addition to the Temple and its associated institutions, more local places of gathering and worship emerged, some of which were frequented daily and played an especially important role during Sabbaths and festivals. Synagogues, the earliest of which are contemporaneous with the later Second Temple period, served as communal places of meeting, study, charity, and eventually worship, including readings of Torah and Prophets (in both Hebrew and often in Aramaic translation, called *targum*), daily and Sabbath prayer services, homilies, and liturgical poetry. They also housed Torah scrolls and sacred writings. By the end of the rabbinic period, dozens of synagogues existed throughout the region of the Galilee and elsewhere as part of the fabric of urban and village life.[17] Synagogues, in some places located in the center of town and in others on the periphery, were built in local architectural and artistic styles, many of which featured mosaics and frescos (more on these later). Their hall for worship included a *bima* (altar), seating, a *ner tamid* (eternal light), and a shrine for Torah scrolls. Many synagogues were large complexes with courtyards, foyers and atriums, water installations, and other infrastructure as well. Some included dedicatory inscriptions and, less frequently, quoted biblical or rabbinic passages. Many synagogues faced Jerusalem, gesturing toward the sacredness associated with that city and its temple, even centuries after its destruction.

The relationship between synagogues and other communal institutions when the Temple was still standing differed from that with rabbinic study houses in later periods. Although rabbinic authorities, for example, might have wielded more sway in contexts of rabbinic Torah study, their power seems to have been somewhat diminished in synagogue contexts, in which many rabbinic liturgical practices were adopted but some rabbinic prohibitions—for example, against figural art—were largely ignored, and where other (competing?) communal figures, such as the *paytan* (liturgical poet), stood at the center and women could occupy leadership positions rarely afforded them in rabbinic contexts.[18] Personal piety through prayer, study, and other means existed alongside synagogue worship.[19]

Rabbinic study houses, too, emerged in the first and second centuries, first less formally and eventually as powerful institutions and academies (*batei mi-*

drash and *yeshivot*) in Palestine and Babylonia.[20] Because Torah study was regarded as a sacred endeavor, these spaces of learning, legal theorization, exegesis, and debate constituted an important part of the ancient Jewish sacred landscape. The Babylonian Talmud, for instance, describes rabbinic husbands leaving their wives for extended periods of time to dedicate themselves to Torah study as an expression of love of God and scripture, even at the expense of family life.[21] (For more on rabbinic texts and culture, see chapter 3, "The Rabbis.")

In addition to the Tabernacle, Temple, ritual baths, synagogues, and study houses, other spaces played significant roles in ancient Jewish life. The home became a place for domestic piety through the requirement to hang *mezuzot* on doorframes (and later, in Babylonia, the practice of burying incantation bowls beneath a home to protect it from harm); childrearing and pedagogical practices conceived as essential to children's religious formation; Sabbath preparations and meals, which extended from Friday evening through Saturday evening; and kosher laws that required constant diligence in slaughtering and cooking habits.[22] Courtyards and alleyways, especially through the ritual of the *eruv*, transformed the seams of homes and neighborhoods into communities,[23] and city limits circumscribed travel on the Sabbath and required prayers of protection to traverse at other times.[24] Likewise, agricultural fields were not only sowed and harvested but were also presented in biblical and rabbinic sources as places associated with care for the poor, through practices such as *leket* (not picking up produce that fell in the harvesting process), *shiheha* (not returning to harvest produce that was forgotten in the field), and *peah* (leaving a corner of one's field for the poor to harvest).[25] Farmers were also beckoned to be careful in their farming practices so as not to crossbreed species, a practice forbidden in biblical law and further elaborated on in rabbinic sources—similar prohibitions were applied to mixtures of animal species and fibers used for weaving—so that vigilance extended to these other contexts as well. Cemeteries, catacombs, and tombs, often located outside cities and villages, likewise required special rituals of burial, mourning, and purity and became places of devotion and sometimes pilgrimage; monumental tombs marked the topography, including alongside main roads from which travelers could easily see such large structures.[26]

Certain spaces (like times) were presented as potentially dangerous; for example, temples and places of "foreign" (idolatrous) worship, places of entertainment such as theaters and stadiums, roads between cities, markets before festivals, bathhouses, and latrines, which, in some periods and contexts, were imagined to be a prime location for demons. The world thus consisted not only of spaces, times, and rituals incumbent on Jews but also spaces, times, and rituals from which Jews were encouraged to abstain or remain vigilant to maintain their identities, communities, and ways of life.

God and the Heavenly Realm

Ancient Jewish sources, in their wide-ranging constructions of spaces, times, and rituals—as well as in their development of Jewish communal life writ large—do not convey a single approach to God and the heavenly realm. Biblical writings, Second Temple texts, rabbinic literature, liturgy, art, and apotropaic sources provide a diverse array of perspectives and beliefs that each, in its own way, relates to divinity and sacredness in how it approaches the world. Mapping some of these notions highlights the diversity and depth of ancient Jewish communities and their engagement with the world, one another, and God.

The texts preserved among the Dead Sea Scrolls, discovered in a series of caves adjacent to the ancient settlement of Qumran, provide examples of some of the ways in which members of a single community in the Judean desert imagined their relationship to one another, other communities, and the divine sphere. According to their writings, members of this community were dissatisfied with the leadership of the Temple cult in Jerusalem and its approach to issues such as purity and sacrifice. Fearing the divine consequences of improper practice and promoting their steadfast commitment to serve God correctly, they relocated to the desert, creating a community and way of life that they believed aligned with scripture and divine expectations. This group established its own communal rules, including standards for entry, full membership, and expulsion; plans for the apocalyptic war they expected, in which God would destroy their enemies whom they labeled the "children of darkness" (in contrast to themselves, the "children of light); strict halakhic guidelines for the observation of ritual purity, the Sabbath, and other central practices; a solar calendar, which they believed embodied God's instructions for organizing time and observing festivals; sacred historiography that mapped the Sabbatical cycles onto biblical history, synchronizing divine and human time; and liturgical texts that were recited daily, weekly, or annually and that often described angelic worship as mirroring the community's own worship practices.

One such example is the collection of the "Songs of the Sabbath Sacrifice," which describe the heavenly Temple, the angelic priesthood, and angelic praise of God as angels surrounded God's throne.[27] This liturgical collection combines the sacredness of space, namely the heavenly Temple, with the sacredness of time, exemplified by the organization of the thirteen songs recited on each of

GOD AND THE SACRED 283

the Sabbaths in the first quarter of the year. Through these songs, along with other liturgical practices, this human community sought to emulate the angels in every aspect of their daily lives.

The Dead Sea Scrolls are not a unified canon of texts that reflect the coherent set of beliefs and practices of a specific community; instead, they promote various ideas that sometimes contradict one another or present competing values. Still, the collection provides scholars with a corpus of texts, some of which were written by and for this community and others of which were composed earlier but adopted by the community, that integrate conceptions of God and other divine beings, sacred space and time, rituals, and liturgies—and that seem to have been put into practice in some way by a single community at Qumran.

Two first-century authors likewise provide examples of the different ways in which God and divine intervention were conceived during this period. The Jewish philosopher Philo of Alexandria, who lived in the decades before and after the turn of the millennium, composed dozens of treatises on biblical and philosophical topics, some of which address the topic of God explicitly and others that incorporate conceptions of the divine more implicitly. In most of his writings, Philo navigates between philosophical commitments (including Platonic and Stoic interlocutors) and interpretations of biblical texts, which he considered to embody God's revelation.[28]

For example, in *On the Origins of the World*, Philo draws on Platonic philosophical ideas to explain the opening chapters of Genesis. In his presentation, God first creates the world of Ideas, from which the material world is thereby created. Philo maintains God's atemporality and the creation of the entire world in a single instant by interpreting the steps of Genesis in logical rather than chronological order.[29] This view of creation is a good example of the way in which Philo's conception of God bridges philosophical and scriptural commitments. He presents this analysis of the world's creation—and the idea of God and God's engagement with the created world—as an introduction to the law. In another work, *Special Laws*, he presents many rituals and laws for a broad, predominantly non-Jewish audience, making the case for the value of such practices. In his section on festivals, for example, Philo systematically describes the theological, philosophical, and practical rationale undergirding each festival, weaving in basic principles about God and the created world in these explanations.[30]

The historian Josephus Flavius, who was born to a priestly family in Judea in the mid-first century CE and who later relocated to Rome as a client of the Flavian emperors after the destruction of Jerusalem, published several works, including an account of the Jewish revolt against Rome and a twenty-part history of the Jews from biblical origins through his own day. His writings reveal how he imagined God to operate in the everyday lives of individuals and in the political and religious structures of which they were a part, although in ways that differ substantially from the theological and philosophical orientation of Philo's writings.[31] His account of the Temple's destruction, for example, places the blame on rogue Roman soldiers and Jewish internal strife, but in a deeper sense he suggests that it was God's divine will to destroy the Temple. God operated in every small step that led to ultimate defeat, and thus the destruction was not evidence of God's lack of control but rather of God's infinite power. This is but one example of the ways in which Josephus suffuses his historical works with theology. Josephus also outlines the theological and ritual distinctions between the Jewish groups of his day, including the Pharisees, Sadducees, and Essenes. His descriptions of these schools provide scholars with a valuable source for understanding what beliefs about issues, such as the body, soul, and resurrection of the dead, and rituals, such as those related to purity, unified and divided various communities in the late Second Temple period (such discussions also animate the writings of Paul, the gospels, and the book of Revelation). According to Josephus, the distinctions between such groups were not only a social phenomenon but also were rooted in disagreements about tradition, practice, and belief.

Rabbinic sources vary in their approaches to God. Early rabbinic texts do not engage many of the theological questions that preoccupied Christians in the same period, although they do explore the relationship between revelation and interpretation, as well as the question of divine inspiration in law and scripture and the power of prayer.[32] The Babylonian Talmud and other later rabbinic works, however, do develop conceptions of God that differ in meaningful ways from earlier sources.

A passage in the Babylonian Talmud (b. Berakhot 6a–b), for example, meditates on God's presence in the world. The text posits that God can be found in many contexts: in the space of the synagogue, among any group of ten people who have gathered to pray, among three people who sit in judgment, or in the company of two people who busy themselves with Torah study. The text notes that the divine presence even exists when a single person sits and studies Torah. This narrative suggests that each of these activities—praying, judging, and studying—represents a sacred activity that draws God near (it is worth noting that the examples evoked in this passage are limited to ritual and social practices associated with adult Jewish men: the obligation of communal prayer, proffering judgment, studying Torah, and donning phylacteries are couched as gendered

GOD AND THE SACRED   285

requirements in the Babylonian Talmud). But what about God? Does God also engage in rituals and activities that foster human–divine relationships, or is cultivating this relationship solely the responsibility of the people of Israel? The continuation of this passage explains that God maintains a relationship with Israel by wearing phylacteries that contain a series of biblical verses that glorify Israel as God's people. God's phylacteries and the embodied and textualized daily practice associated with them thus bind God to Israel, just as Israel's phylacteries declare love of and devotion to God.

Other rabbinic sources likewise describe God engaging in other acts of devotion, including kneading, wrapping, binding, braiding, and tying, such as when God forms the first human out of earth or when God adorns Eve, braiding her hair for her first encounter with Adam.[33] Rabbinic sources portray God consulting the angels about whether to create human beings; when the angels caution God against doing so, God defies the angels' wishes and forms the first human. Leviticus Rabbah explains that God serves as a perpetual matchmaker, pairing couples (an extension of God's work of creation, when animals and eventually the first humans are fashioned in pairs) and thereby maintaining cosmic order. In another feat of creation, attested in many rabbinic compositions including the Mishnah, God crafts a series of mystical creations, including the rainbow from the Noah story, Moses's staff, and the manna in the wilderness, during twilight between the sixth day of creation and the first Sabbath, a time that is as fleeting as it is mysterious and is associated especially with the divine. Through these creations, God has prepared in advance the idiosyncratic objects and phenomena that would later play important roles in Jewish history. Lamentations Rabbah and the Babylonian Talmud depict God mourning the destruction of the Temple in Jerusalem, crying throughout the night and teaching the angels how to mourn, including shaving their heads and wearing sackcloth. Such embellishments of biblical narratives vividly imagine the practical dimensions of God's acts of creation and in the created world. They emphasize that God's daily routine—from the very start of the world's creation until the present—entails caring for the world's creations, maintaining order, acting as matchmaker, engaging with the Torah, and partaking in rituals—all of which imbue the world and its inhabitants with different forms of divine presence.[34]

Rabbinic sources do not idealize God, however; they are at times irreverent. In one of the most widely taught rabbinic narratives today (b. Bava Metzia 59a–59b, referred to in shorthand as the "Oven of Akhnai"[35]), a rabbinic dispute about a matter of ritual purity is resolved not through divine sanction but through majority rabbinic opinion. A dramatic scene describes a rabbi invoking heaven to demonstrate that his opinion on a matter of law is correct. He performs a series of supernatural feats (a tree uproots itself and moves, a stream flows uphill, the walls of the study house begin to sway, and even a heavenly voice affirms the rabbi's position)—only to be reprimanded by his colleagues in the study house when they insist that the Torah and its laws are "not in heaven" but rather exist in the human domain for rabbis to legislate. When the prophet Elijah asks God for his opinion, God laughs in approval, declaring, "My sons have defeated me, my sons have defeated me!" This story echoes sentiments present in early rabbinic discussions about declaring new moons, discussed earlier. The idea that rabbinic deliberation, discussion, and debate determine the proper parameters for practice and that this process is sanctioned by God, even when God might disagree with the individual decisions made by the rabbis, is a uniquely rabbinic approach to the divine.

Rabbinic texts also sometimes offer bitter critiques of God, especially when reflecting on human suffering. Although this phenomenon is anchored in biblical traditions—most notably, Abraham's defense of Sodom and the book of Job—such "theologies of protest," as Dov Weiss terms them, flourished in Late Antique rabbinic sources, such that the Judaism that emerges in this period is "a religion that tolerates, even celebrates, arguing with God."[36] These protests are often voiced by biblical characters and embedded in rabbinic calls to avoid criticizing God, and yet, as Weiss argues, they convey "a profound ambivalence or even sympathy for the irreverent expression."[37]

Pictorial depictions from Roman Galilee and the broader region are another source for how Jews in this period imagined God and the divine realm. A series of synagogue floor mosaics from Sepphoris, Hamat Tiberias, Bet Alpha, Huqoq, and elsewhere depict scenes including the binding of Isaac, the Temple and its utensils, and the zodiac, which usually included the four seasons, the twelve months of the year, and the sun—portrayed in the guise of the Greco-Roman sun deity—along with the moon and stars at the center.[38] The synagogue at Dura Europos includes frescos of biblical events and features the hand of God a number of times, depicting God's intervention in human affairs. Such images brought representations of God, narratives about God acting in history, and worship of God through the Temple cult into the heart of the community and its sacred spaces. Complementing passages from rabbinic sources discussed earlier, which insist that the divine presence finds itself in synagogues, these mosaics literally produce portraits of God and a record of God's intervention in history within the space of the synagogue. God was also invoked in the context of death, burial, and mourning. Graffiti at Beit Shearim, for example, warns intruders to stay out of the graves or face the wrath of God.[39]

In addition to descriptions and depictions of God, ritual, literary, exegetical, legal, liturgical, apotropaic, mystical, and magical sources from the Second Temple and rabbinic periods extensively develop ideas about the heavenly or transmundane realm and the intermediary figures, including angels and demons, that populated the earthly and heavenly realm. Mika Ahuvia writes, "An array of sources from antiquity attests that people took for granted that the invisible realm was crowded with mediating beings: angels could be found at home, on the streets, in the synagogues as well as in the multilayered heavens."[40] Such figures inhabited the world and thus needed to be contended with—whether they were summoned for assistance or warded off for protection. They also populated texts, through which they served literary and conceptual roles.[41] Annette Yoshiko Reed explains that transmundane beings not only "embodied the conviction that truth could travel from the highest heavens down into the quotidian domains of human life" and played "a part in theology, theodicy, and the theorization of the structure and workings of the cosmos" but also that "writings about transmundane powers emerge as a Jewish knowledge-practice" that marshaled spirits "in the service of organizing and theorizing knowledge."[42] Angels were invoked in liturgical poetry as well.[43]

Many Jews in Palestine wore amulets, and those in Babylonia commissioned incantation bowls to attract divine or angelic healing or intercession, as well as to protect themselves from demons and other dangers, both when they were out and about and when they remained at home.[44] Still others commissioned magical texts and treatises, with instructions for warding off unwanted situations.[45] The world was full of hardships, painful illness, unfortunate heartbreak, devastating infertility, unsettling financial insecurity, pesky in-laws, frightening sexual assault, and unrelenting demons, and Jews turned to such material and ritual practices to keep themselves and their family members safe. Some circles gravitated toward mystical forms of piety, developing a corpus of Hekhalot literature that describes mystical union with the divine and picks up on themes in earlier Jewish sources, including Second Temple traditions. These magical and mystical practices, previously assumed to stand apart from the rabbinic sphere, are now understood to be far more integrally related and often overlapping.[46]

Discussions about the nature of God and correct ways of worshiping God also stood at the center of some religious controversies. In addition to the Second Temple tensions mentioned earlier, select rabbinic sources participated in broader theological debates about the unity and diversity of God, especially as Christians developed binitarian and trinitarian theologies and rabbis reimagined earlier Jewish conceptions of the divine, including traditions about Wisdom, Torah, or the angel Metatron existing alongside God at creation. Rabbinic passages grapple with the Hebrew Bible's various names for God, including those in the plural such as *elohim*, prompting some readers of the biblical text to wonder about the possibility of multiple deities.

This tension between absolute monotheism and the embrace of lower yet still heavenly divinities could suggest the simultaneous repulsion and attraction that some rabbinic figures might have felt to alternative conceptions of God held by the communities among which they lived.[47] Often, at the heart of such disagreements were interpretations of biblical passages and theological perspectives attached to opposing readings that were narrated as encounters between heretics (termed "*minim*") and the rabbinic sages they confronted with exegetical challenges.[48] Echoes of such theological disagreements also appear in the daily liturgy as it developed in the rabbinic period, which came to include a disavowal of heretics in the Amidah prayer; competing theological conceptions, especially about who will participate in the messianic redemption, likewise molded Jewish prayer rituals.[49] It has been suggested that rabbinic sources reacted to theological discourse among Christians by redirecting their attention to other realms of inquiry, insinuating that theology as a discipline of study should not occupy rabbinic energy.[50] According to this view, rabbinic figures thus separated themselves from their Christian counterparts not only—or even primarily—through distinct notions about God's identity but instead through advocating for a different realm of inquiry, eschewing the theological for alternative intellectual modes and methods of inquiry.

Recommended Readings

Alexander, Elizabeth Shanks, and Beth A. Berkowitz, eds. *Religious Studies and Rabbinics* (Routledge, 2017).

Balberg, Mira. "Ritual Studies and the Study of Rabbinic Literature," *Currents in Biblical Research* 16 (2017): 71–98.

Bohak, Gideon. *Ancient Jewish Magic: A History* (Cambridge University Press, 2011).

Fonrobert, Charlotte Elisheva. *Menstrual Purity: Rabbinic and Christian Reconstructions of Biblical Gender* (Stanford University Press, 2000).

Hachlili, Rachel. *Jewish Funerary Customs, Practices, and Rites in the Second Temple Period* (Brill, 2005).

Kattan Gribetz, Sarit. *Time and Difference in Rabbinic Judaism* (Princeton: Princeton University Press, 2020).

Levine, Lee. *The Ancient Synagogue: The First Thousand Years* (Yale University Press, 2005).

Noam, Vered. "Megillat Taanit: The Scroll of Fasting," in *The Literature of the Sages,* Vol. 3, ed. Safrai et al. (Brill, 2006).

Schäfer, Peter. *Two Gods in Heaven: Jewish Concepts of God in Antiquity* (Princeton University Press, 2020).

Stern, Karen. *Writing on the Wall: Graffiti and the Forgotten Jews of Antiquity* (Princeton University Press, 2018).

Tabory, Jacob. "Jewish Festivals in Late Antiquity," in *Cambridge History of Judaism,* Vol. 4, ed. S. T. Katz (Cambridge University Press, 2006), 556–72.

Weiss, Dov. *Pious Irreverence: Confronting God in Rabbinic Judaism* (University of Pennsylvania Press, 2017).

Notes

1. Tzvi Novick, *What Is Good, and What God Demands: Normative Structures in Tannaitic Literature* (Brill, 2010); Mira Balberg, *Fractured Tablets: Forgetfulness and Fallibility in Late Ancient Rabbinic Culture* (University of California Press, 2023).

2. On the integration of religious studies and ritual studies in the study of rabbinics and ancient Judaism, see, e.g., Elizabeth Shanks Alexander and Beth A. Berkowitz, eds., *Religious Studies and Rabbinics* (Routledge, 2017); Mira Balberg, "Ritual Studies and the Study of Rabbinic Literature"; and Naftali Cohn, *Ritual: An Ancient Jewish Perspective* (forthcoming).

3. For various approaches to this complex topic, see Daniel Boyarin, *Border Lines: The Partition of Judaeo-Christianity* (University of Pennsylvania Press, 2006); Leora Batnitzky, *How Judaism Became a Religion* (Princeton University Press, 2011); Jörg Rüpke, *Religion: Antiquity and Its Legacy* (Oxford University Press, 2013); and Brent Nongbri, *Before Religion: A History of a Modern Concept* (Yale University Press, 2015).

4. Mira Balberg, *Blood for Thought: The Reinvention of Sacrifice in Early Rabbinic Literature* (University of California Press, 2017).

5. Galit Hasan-Rokem, *Web of Life: Folklore and Midrash in Rabbinic Literature* (Stanford University Press, 2000).

6. Sarit Kattan Gribetz, "Holiness in the Mishnah," in *What Is the Mishnah? The State of the Question,* ed. Cohen (Harvard University Press, 2022).

7. Naphtali Meshel, *The "Grammar" of Sacrifice: A Generativist Study of the Ancient Israelite Sacrificial System in the Priestly Writings with a "Grammar" of Σ* (Oxford University Press, 2014); Jonathan Klawans, *Impurity and Sin in Ancient Judaism* (Oxford University Press, 2000); Mira Balberg, *Purity, Body, and Self in Early Rabbinic Literature* (University of California Press, 2014); Charlotte E. Fonrobert, *Menstrual Purity: Rabbinic and Christian Reconstructions of Biblical Gender;* (Stanford University Press, 2000); Shai Secunda, *The Talmud's Red Fence: Menstrual Impurity and Difference in Babylonian Judaism and Its Sasanian Context* (Oxford University Press, 2020).

8. Balberg, *Purity.*

9. On impurity in the Dead Sea Scrolls, see, e.g., Martha Himmelfarb, "Impurity and Sin in 4QD, 1QS, and 4Q512," *Dead Sea Discoveries* 8 (2001): 9–37.

10. Yonatan Adler, *The Origins of Judaism: An Archaeological-Historical Reappraisal* (Yale University Press, 2022).

11. On circumcision, see Shaye J. D. Cohen, *Why Aren't Jewish Women Circumcised? Gender and Covenant in Judaism* (University of California Press, 2005); on kashrut, see Jordan Rosenblum, *The Jewish Dietary Laws in the Ancient World* (Cambridge University Press, 2016).

12. Ruth Langer, *Jewish Liturgy: A Guide to Research* (Rowman & Littlefield, 2015).

13. Steven D. Fraade, "Theory, Practice, and Polemic in Ancient Jewish Calendars," in *Legal Fictions: Studies of Law and Narrative in the Discursive Worlds of Ancient Jewish Sectarians and Sages* (Brill, 2011).

14. Sacha Stern, *Calendar and Community: A History of the Jewish Calendar, 2nd Century BCE to 10th Century CE* (Clarendon, 2001), and *The Jewish Calendar Controversy of 921/2 CE* (Brill, 2019).

15. See, e.g., Jeffrey L. Rubenstein, *The History of Sukkot in the Second Temple and Rabbinic Periods* (Brown Judaic Studies, 1995); and Vered Noam, "The Miracle of the Cruse of Oil: The Metamorphosis of a Legend," *Hebrew Union College Annual* 73 (2002): 191–226. For an introduction to the calendar and festivals, see Jacob Tabory, "Jewish Festivals in Late Antiquity," in *Cambridge History of Judaism*, Vol. 4, ed. S. T. Katz (Cambridge University Press, 2006).

16. Vered Noam, "Megillat Taanit: The Scroll of Fasting," in *The Literature of the Sages*, Vol. 3, ed. Safrai et al. (Brill, 2006); Julia Watts Belser, *Power, Ethics, and Ecology: Rabbinic Responses to Drought and Disaster* (Cambridge University Press, 2015).

17. Lee Levine, *The Ancient Synagogue: The First Thousand Years* (Yale University Press, 2005); Steven Fine, *Sacred Realm: The Emergence of the Synagogue in the Ancient World* (Oxford University Press, 1996).

18. Bernadette Brooten, *Women Leaders in the Ancient Synagogue* (Brown Judaic Studies, 1982).

19. For one example, see A. J. Berkovitz, *A Life of Psalms in Jewish Late Antiquity* (University of Pennsylvania Press, 2023).

20. Jeffrey L. Rubenstein, "Social and Institutional Settings of Rabbinic Literature," in *Cambridge Companion to the Talmud and Rabbinic Literature*, ed. Charlotte Fonrobert and M. Jaffee (Cambridge University Press, 2007).

21. Daniel Boyarin, *Carnal Israel: Reading Sex in Talmudic Culture* (University of California Press, 1995).

22. Sarit Kattan Gribetz, "Sacred Spaces," in *Companion to Jews and Judaism in the Late Antique World, 3rd Century BCE—7th Century CE*, ed. G. Kessler and N. Koltun-Fromm (Wiley Blackwell, 2020).

23. Charlotte E. Fonrobert, "The Political Symbolism of the Eruv," *Jewish Social Studies* 1 (2005): 9–35.

24. Gil Klein, "Sabbath as City: Rabbinic Urbanism and Imperial Territoriality in Roman Palestine," in *Placing Ancient Texts: The Ritual and Rhetorical Use of Space*, ed. M. Ahuvia and A. Kocar (Mohr Siebeck, 2018), 53–86; Sarit Kattan Gribetz, "'Lead Me Forth in Peace': The Wayfarer's Prayer and Rabbinic Rituals of Travel in the Roman World," in *Journeys in the Roman East: Imagined and Real*, ed. M. Niehoff (Mohr Siebeck, 2017), 297–327.

25. John Mandsager, "Agriculture and Industry," in *Companion to Late Ancient Jews and Judaism*, ed. N. Koltun-Fromm and G. Kessler (Wiley & Sons, 2020), 495–510. On charity in

ancient Judaism more generally, see Gregg E. Gardner, *The Origins of Organized Charity in Rabbinic Judaism* (Cambridge University Press, 2015).

26. Rachel Hachlili, *Jewish Funerary Customs, Practices, and Rites in the Second Temple Period* (Brill, 2005).

27. Carol Newsom, *Songs of the Sabbath Sacrifice: A Critical Edition* (Scholars, 1985).

28. Maren Niehoff, *Philo of Alexandria: An Intellectual Biography* (Yale University Press, 2018).

29. Roberto Radice, "Philo's Theology and Theory of Creation," in *Cambridge Companion to Philo*, ed. A. Kamesar (Cambridge University Press, 2009).

30. Sarit Kattan Gribetz, "The Festival of Every Day: Philo and Seneca on Quotidian Time," *Harvard Theological Review* 111 (2018): 357–81.

31. Jonathan Klawans, *Josephus and the Theologies of Ancient Judaism* (Oxford University Press, 2012).

32. Steven D. Fraade, *From Tradition to Commentary: Torah and Its Interpretation in the Midrash Sifre to Deuteronomy* (SUNY Press, 1991); Azzan Yadin-Israel, *Scripture as Logos: Rabbi Ishmael and the Origins of Midrash* (University of Pennsylvania Press, 2004), and *Scripture and Tradition: Rabbi Akiva and the Triumph of Midrash* (University of Philadelphia Press, 2015); and Christine Hayes, *What's Divine about Divine Law? Early Perspectives* (Princeton University Press, 2015). On Second Temple sources, see Hindy Najman, *Seconding Sinai: The Development of Mosaic Discourse in Second Temple Judaism* (Brill, 2003), and Judith H. Newman, *Before the Bible: The Liturgical Body and the Formation of Scriptures in Early Judaism* (Oxford University Press, 2018).

33. On the long history of imagining God as embodied, see Benjamin D. Sommer, *The Bodies of God and the World of Ancient Israel* (Cambridge University Press, 2011).

34. Sarit Kattan Gribetz, *Time and Difference in Rabbinic Judaism* (Princeton University Press, 2020).

35. See Jeffrey L. Rubenstein, *Talmudic Stories: Narrative Art, Composition, and Culture* (Johns Hopkins University Press, 1999).

36. Weiss, *Pious Irreverence: Confronting God in Rabbinic Judaism* (University of Pennsylvania Press, 2017), 2.

37. Weiss, *Pious Irreverence*, 51.

38. On these synagogue mosaics, see Rina Talgam, *Mosaics of Faith: Floors of Pagans, Jews, Samaritans, Christians, and Muslims in the Holy Land* (Penn State University Press, 2014).

39. Karen Stern, *Writing on the Wall: Graffiti and the Forgotten Jews of Antiquity* (Princeton University Press, 2018).

40. Mika Ahuvia, *On My Right Michael, On My Left Gabriel: Angels in Ancient Jewish Culture* (University of California Press, 2021), 2.

41. Annette Y. Reed, *Demons, Angels, and Writing in Ancient Judaism* (Cambridge University Press, 2020); Ahuvia, *On My Right*; Sara Ronis, *Demons in the Details: Demonic Discourse and Rabbinic Culture in Late Antique Babylonia* (University of California Press, 2023).

42. Reed, *Demons*, 11.

43. Tzvi Novick, "Israel, the Nations, and the Angels in a Qillirian *Silluq* for Rosh Ha-Shanah," *Oqimta* 9 (2023): 37–66.

44. Gideon Bohak, *Ancient Jewish Magic: A History* (Cambridge University Press, 2011); Ortal-Paz Saar, *Jewish Love Magic: From Late Antiquity to the Middle Ages* (Brill, 2017); Yuval Harari, *Jewish Magic before the Rise of Kabbalah* (Wayne State University Press, 2017); Michael Schwartz, *The Mechanics of Providence: The Workings of Ancient Jewish Magic and Mysticism* (Mohr Siebeck, 2018); Rivka Elitzur-Leiman, *"As a Charm upon Your Heart": Jewish Aramaic Amulets in Early Byzantine Palestine* (forthcoming).

45. Michael A. Morgan, *Sepher Ha-Razim: The Book of Mysteries* (Society of Biblical Literature, 1983).

46. See Ra'anan Boustan, *From Martyr to Mystic: Rabbinic Martyrology and the Making of Merkavah Mysticism* (Mohr Siebeck, 2005); Moulie Vidas, *Tradition and the Formation of the Talmud* (Princeton University Press, 2014); Avigail Manekin-Bamberger, "Jewish Legal Formulae in the Aramaic Incantation Bowls," *Aramaic Studies* 13 (2015): 69–81. Simcha Gross and Avigail Manekin-Bamberger, "Babylonian Jewish Society: The Evidence of the Incantation Bowls," *Jewish Quarterly Review* 112 (2022): 1–30.

47. Peter Schäfer, *The Jewish Jesus: How Judaism and Christianity Shaped Each Other* (Princeton University Press, 2012), and *Two Gods in Heaven: Jewish Concepts of God in Antiquity* (Princeton University Press, 2020).

48. Michal Bar-Asher Siegal, *Jewish-Christian Dialogues on Scripture in Late Antiquity: Heresy Narratives of the Babylonian Talmud* (Cambridge University Press, 2019).

49. Ruth Langer, *Cursing the Christians? A History of the Birkat HaMinim* (Oxford University Press, 2012).

50. Emanuel Fiano, *Three Powers in Heaven: The Emergence of Theology and the Parting of the Ways* (Yale University Press, 2023).

13

Philosophy

Yonatan Y. Brafman, Tufts University

WHAT IS JUDAISM, and who is a Jew? Some preliminary answers to these questions are necessary for Jewish Studies to have an object of study. Both recent introductory texts and theoretical reflections on Jewish Studies have offered a variety of answers. As I show in this chapter, these responses suffer from confusion about the concepts of "religion" (What is Judaism?) and "identity" (Who is a Jew?). This confusion stems from academic Jewish Studies' differentiation of itself from traditional Jewish learning and from the ever-changing social, cultural, and political circumstances of modern Jews. From a philosophical perspective, it also stems from views about normativity and its role in academic inquiry. By normativity, I mean claims that go beyond empirical description, like whether an object is red or whether an event occurred, and that express judgments about what ought to be believed or done; specifically, ethical, political, or theological claims. Because these cannot be settled by an appeal to common experience and they express judgments about belief and practice, many people think that normativity has no place in the academy. In North American academia more broadly, religion and identity are often assumed to be outside the realm of normative evaluation, although for different reasons. Religion is most often considered within a confessional model of faith, a legacy of specifically Protestant assumptions. Claims about religion are considered "beyond reason," whereas those about identity are considered self-validating.

In this chapter, I argue that both assumptions are mistaken because they ignore the way that all claims, even those about religion and identity, operate in a "space of reasons." Because reasons can be given for and against religious and identity claims, both can be evaluated. Recent trends in philosophy, especially

293

the philosophy of religion, concerning normativity contain the solution to these problems in Jewish Studies. When suitably reconfigured, Jewish Studies has the capacity to expand the philosophy of religion beyond its Christian preoccupations, incorporating the moral, legal, and political interests of Judaism and forging connections with the corresponding branches of philosophy.

The State of the Field

Scholars of religion often use concepts like belief or ritual in their historical, philological, or anthropological investigations without critically examining them. As Kevin Schilbrack has argued, philosophers of religion should attend to these concepts, clarify their assumptions, and, if necessary, propose revisions.[1] Within this framework, I examine recent introductory texts and methodological reflections on Jewish Studies, reading them closely and critically to assess their philosophical presuppositions, particularly their conceptions of religion and identity and their views of normativity.

Introductions to Jewish Studies

As evidenced by its title, Michael Fishbane's *Judaism: Revelation and Traditions* purports to take "Judaism" as its object of analysis, which he defines as "the religious expression of the Jewish people based upon a Torah believed given them by God and on the teachings of this Torah as elaborated by trained sages for the sake of sanctifying human behavior and guiding nearness to God."[2] Two elements stand out in this definition: Judaism is anchored in the Jewish people, and Judaism is the Jewish people's religious expression. Of course, this first element immediately raises the question, Who is the Jewish people? If "the Jewish people" is read collectively, it seems to fall prey to what Jacob Neusner called the "peoplehood-and-history theory of Jewish historiography . . . [which] presupposes that a single, clearly defined entity, 'the Jewish people,' has produced a unitary and linear history."[3] This idea of the Jewish people has been highly influential in scholarship in support of Jewish nationalism, because it reifies the Jewish people into an organic whole. Alternatively, "Jewish people" could refer to individual Jews. But who determines who is considered a Jew? Fishbane notes that membership in the Jewish people has historically been determined by descent or conversion. He also observes that exclusively matrilineal descent is not present in the Hebrew Bible nor is it universal among contemporary Jewish movements.

Turning to the second element of the definition, we may ask, What is a "religious expression," and is it a distinct area of culture or consciousness? Fishbane certainly details how the Torah includes ethical, civil, and political regulations that do not fit easily into currently widespread notions of religion. However, he does not allow their inclusion to modify his original definition of Judaism. Is it the belief that the Torah is revealed by God and oriented toward sanctification and closeness to God that makes it religious? But this seems too restrictive, because it excludes views about the Torah and its purposes that do not refer to the supernatural from being part of Judaism. Moreover, as theorists of religion have argued, the conception of religion as a discrete area of culture that is focused on private faith and salvation is a Protestant notion that has been exported and applied to other traditions and communities, including "Judaism."[4]

These questions about identity and religion raise a larger issue concerning normativity in Jewish Studies: Is it possible to identify its object—whether Jews or Judaism—without making normative claims? That is, on what basis can we rule out or rule in individuals, communities, texts, ideas, or rituals as Jewish? And how do scholarly judgments about what is Jewish, which are necessary to delineate an area of study, differ, if at all, from intracommunal claims about who or what is Jewish? Fishbane presents a capacious definition of Judaism, but it is normative insofar as it asserts certain features—the Jewish people, religious expression, not to mention belief in the revelation of the Torah, interpretation by sages, sanctification, and nearness to God—as definitive of Judaism.

Other introductions to Jewish Studies are sensitive to these concerns and so thematize questions about Jewish identity and mobilize theories of religion. Yet they also become enmeshed in difficulties as they try to avoid making normative claims. Michael Satlow's *Creating Judaism: History, Tradition, Practice* defines the academic study of Judaism as non-essentialist and non-normative.[5] An essentialist definition states necessary and sufficient conditions for inclusion within a category. Such a definition of Judaism would posit certain beliefs or practices that are required for some text, figure, or movement to count as part of Judaism. Likewise, an essentialist definition of Jewishness would stipulate certain features that an individual or community must possess to count as Jewish. Obvious examples would be consistency with theological doctrines like Moses Maimonides' Thirteen Principles of Faith for Judaism or matrilineal descent for Jewishness. Satlow maintains that these criteria would be too limiting—they would rule out too much of Judaism or Jewishness—and would be normative. That is, instead of engaging in the tasks of description, understanding, and explanation, they would make judgments about what is truly and authentically Jewish. Such judgments are fine for Jewish communities but not for scholars of them.

Satlow instead draws on the philosopher Ludwig Wittgenstein's notion of family resemblance and its application by the theorist of religion J. Z. Smith to develop what he calls a "polythetic chart" of Judaism. Wittgenstein suggests that just as the resemblance among biologically related family members cannot be described using all-or-nothing criteria but rather through sharing a set of physical features that are overlapping (e.g., some family members have the same eye color but not the same hair color, whereas others have the same hair color but not the same eye color), so too inclusion within a conceptual category should not be reduced to essential criteria but should be conceived as sharing in overlapping characteristics.[6] Judaism, on this view, is a "family of traditions" that can be plotted on three maps: Israel, textual tradition, and religious practice. These are not topics on which every form of Judaism or Jewish community will agree. They are instead a field of debate or, as Satlow calls it, citing the theorist of religion Talal Asad, a "conversation" (12). Every Jewish community will develop a stance on who is Israel, will relate to textual traditions, and will enact religious practices and so participate in the conversation that is Judaism.

Satlow's maps are more open to the diversity of Jewish traditions and communities than Fishbane's definition, yet normativity creeps into his approach as well. Although he presents these three maps—Israel, textual tradition, and ritual practice—as equal, the category of Israel is basic. The canonical texts and religious practices are those of "Jewish communities." (8–9). Moreover, in introducing the map of Israel, Satlow writes, "By Israel I refer to self-identity, the act of identifying as a member of am Yisrael and the particular self-understanding of what that identification means. All groups that self-identify as Jews 'count,' and, however much other Jewish communities contest their identity, their own self-characterization puts them on the map.... Being part of Israel begins with the claim to be, not with some outsider judging whether that claim is correct" (8).

However, claiming to be Israel is not identical to claiming to be part of the Jewish people. Christians, for one, claim to be Israel while denying being part of the Jewish people. Conversely, I can report that most undergraduates in American universities are surprised to find out that "Israel" originally referred to a people, not a nation-state. This is a reversal, because as Cynthia Baker has argued, those who currently refer to themselves as Jews historically did refer to themselves as Israel.[7] In any case, Satlow's immediate identification of Israel with Jewish people takes for granted a sociological referent—people who currently claim to be Jews—and then links it to a more enduring theological category, Israel, even as it extends it on the margins.

This extension has limits, however, and they become apparent in Satlow's brief mention of Black Hebrews and his slightly longer discussion of Messianic Jews: Both are noted as boundary cases. Satlow appeals to "ideological, historical, and social factors" to explain the "widespread Jewish rejection of Messianic Judaism as 'Judaism.'"[8] These factors are helpful in explaining why other Jewish communities reject Messianic Judaism as Judaism, but they do not explain why a scholar committed to a non-essentialist and non-normative approach to Judaism should.

Satlow's requirement of reciprocal recognition—acceptance by both parties—for participating in the Jewish conversation is too strong, because it would not even apply to the institutions of the contemporary United States. By recognizing patrilineal descent, Reform Judaism accepts as "Israel" individuals whom both Orthodox and Conservative Judaism do not. And although some Conservative Jews might see themselves as in dialogue with Orthodox halakhic decisors by responding to their rulings, Orthodox decisors would deny that they are part of the same conversation. The scholar might insist that, despite these denials, Orthodox and Conservative halakhists are participating in the same conversation about ritual practice because they refer to similar texts—the Talmud and its interpreters—and even read them according to similar methods; however, this would privilege the judgment of the scholar about what counts as the "same" conversation and "similar" methods. There is no abstract standard for such determinations, which can only be made within a social practice and shared understanding about how things ought to be done.[9] Normativity reemerges even within scholarship.

From a philosophical perspective, this is not a problem. As Wittgenstein who introduced the family resemblance model suggested, all concept application is normative, even when the standards cannot be fully articulated.[10] All definitions—whether essentialist or polythetic—are normative, because they make judgments according to standards about whether something falls under a category. The only question is what sorts of normative claims are permitted within a discipline and why.

Once we realize that the issue is not a normative versus a non-normative approach to the study of Judaism but rather what type of normativity is accepted, we can better analyze the relation between religion and identity in Jewish Studies. In this context, Aaron J. Hahn Tapper's *Judaisms: A Twenty-First-Century Guide to Jews and Jewish Identities* is instructive.[11] Whereas Satlow assumes the centrality of Jewish identity even as he notes the importance of textual tradition and ritual practice, Hahn Tapper, as his title indicates, directly centers identity and specifically modern Jewish identity. Judaism, on his view, "is the sum total of the ways that Jews have communicated, and continue to communicate, their Jewishness, which includes the collective canon of Jewish ideas and rituals" (3). Judaism consists of ideas and rituals that are expressions of Jews' Jewishness.

Jewishness is described as a form of identity, and identity, in turn, is understood to be a basic human need (2). Modern identities, Hahn Tapper notes, are complex and porous, drawing on many sources. Yet, citing the philosopher Charles Taylor, he still maintains they are based on individuals' expression of their authentic selves. He thus shows how prevalent ways of defining Jewishness—as religion, culture, ethnicity, nationality, or race—fail to account for Jews' various expressions of Jewishness. Of course, this is circular reasoning because to call into question ways of defining Jewishness is already to assume that these individuals, communities, and expressions are Jewish. That is, unless one already assumes that individuals' authentic self-assertions are decisive for identity.

Hahn Tapper considers Jewish individual and communal narratives based on this understanding of identity. Narratives are stories and collective memories that shape self-understanding of who we are, where we came from, and where we are going. They may not be factual, in the sense of being based on events that happened or propositions that obtain. Instead, they are based on what he calls "truths": "A community's 'truth' often describes the reasons behind that group's practices and beliefs. It does not need to be factual, though it certainly can be. 'Truths' are central to identities, whether individual or collective, because we orient toward the truth as if it is factual" (14).

Hahn Tapper is uninterested in evaluating whether, in his terms, these truths are factual. However, there are two related problems with this stance. First, as he notes, the Jewish individuals and communities he is presenting take their "truths" to be factual or simply true in the ordinary sense of the term. They do not understand them as merely their narratives based on subjectively held beliefs. Second, his readers—beginners in Jewish Studies—are likely interested in the truth of certain claims in a commonsense factual sense; for example, whether the Mossad conducted bombings in Iraq to scare the Jewish population to leave, as some Iraqi Jews apparently think, or whether the State of Israel abducted Yemenite babies for adoption or medical experimentation, as some Yemenite Jews seemingly believe (123, 127–28). Hahn Tapper certainly takes his readers' interest in the factual truth for granted when he begins his discussion with what he calls the "common Jewish narrative"—Abrahamic origin, exodus from Egypt, revelation at Sinai, exile from the Holy Land, and persecution—only then to question it against the findings of historical research and to complicate it by showing who and what it includes and excludes. The commitment to accepting the "truths" of Jewish individuals and communities is not consistently kept.

Nor is the acceptance of all self-assertions of Jewish identity. Hahn Tapper explicitly considers whether there are boundaries to Jewish identity, noting three characteristics that set a group at the margins of Jewishness: "(1) claiming to be the *true* descendants of the biblical Israelites (i.e., authenticity); (2) rejection of rabbinic authority; and (3) denial that they are Jewish although others say they are" (219). Only the last characteristic is not problematic within his model. The others are more questionable. He admits that, like Karaites and Messianic Jews who are placed at the margins, Reform Jews reject rabbinic authority, yet he insists that their "Jewishness is widely accepted." To explain this, he maintains that, unlike those other groups, Reform Jews "are simply too large a group to marginalize" (224). But, as with Satlow, whether other Jews recognize an individual or group as Jewish and why is a non sequitur within Hahn Tapper's model. Otherwise, one would have to choose which Jews' recognition matters and according to what criteria do they give or withhold it. In fact, this is what eventually happens in the cases of the Samaritans and the African Hebrew Israelites. They too are placed at the margins because they both claim "exclusive Jewish authenticity." This marginalization is certainly puzzling if self-assertion is primarily what matters for identity. However, what seems to matter here is that other Jews—the "mainstream Jewish community"—have not accepted them as Jews, likely because of the exclusionary nature of their identity claim (222). But, again, such reciprocal recognition and a commitment to pluralistically accepting others who claim to be Jews do not follow from Hahn Tapper's model of identity or application of it to Jewishness. Instead, it seems to assume a certain conception of a big-tent Jewish community that is then tweaked.

In sum, these recent introductions to Jewish Studies struggle to achieve their respective goals of taking a non-normative perspective on Judaism (Satlow) and centering claims of Jewish identity (Hahn Tapper). In both cases, normative claims reappear—for Satlow about what counts as the same conversation and thus as Judaism, and for Hahn Tapper about what makes for a valid identity claim and so for Jewishness. Both assume a referent for the Jewish community, which is then stretched slightly, enough to include various forms of Second Temple Judaism, the array of contemporary Jewish movements, and Jews of diverse ethnic backgrounds but not so much as to include Black Hebrews, Samaritans, Messianic Jews, and African Hebrew Israelites. This inconsistency is the result of having started out down a dead end. Instead of trying to do without normative claims, which is impossible, such claims should be thematized, and then arguments should be offered about why some are acceptable while others are not within Jewish Studies.

Theoretical Reflections on Jewish Studies

These inconsistencies are also apparent in two books in the Rutgers series, "Key Words in Jewish Studies," which "seeks to introduce students and scholars alike to vigorous developments in the field by exploring its terms." The books on Jewish Studies and on Jews, by Andrew Bush and Cynthia Baker, respectively, when read together show that the field struggles with the categories of religion and identity because of misperceptions about normativity.

Bush's *Jewish Studies: A Theoretical Introduction*, the lead-off book within the series, makes crucial assertions about religion and identity as it describes the relation between traditional Jewish learning and academic Jewish Studies.[12] In his view, they are not just separate intellectual undertakings but also compete for a role in Jewish self-formation. Jewish learning is the study of specific Jewish "contents"—the Hebrew Bible and rabbinic literature, for example—by Jews for the purpose of fulfilling covenantal obligations. The transition from Jewish learning to Jewish Studies "reenacted the intellectual history of Western universities" because it involved the removal of religious authority (4). Jewish learning is thereby secularized—in the original meaning of the term—as it becomes Jewish Studies. But it also involves a shift in the presumed subject and object of study. Bush writes, "Studying Jews . . . has meant taking Jews and what they do as an object of study, for the purpose of producing, testing, and disseminating knowledge about Jews, regardless of who happens to be doing the studying" (1). Because it is not seen as the fulfillment of a religious obligation nor is supervised by religious authority since it has no religious goal, Jewish Studies may be conducted by Jews and non-Jews alike. Moreover, instead of the primary objects being Jewish texts, ideas, or norms, its object is Jews themselves. Texts, ideas, or norms are important insofar as they are the cultural products of Jews.

This again raises the question of Jewish identity that, Bush maintains, is a key term in Jewish Studies. It connects Jewish Studies to other areas of the university curriculum and to contemporary theories of identity, because the field recognizes "identity as a conglomerate of disparate elements, simultaneously present, but differential[ly] active" (63). An individual or their cultural product may be simultaneously Jewish and non-Jewish because Jewishness has no essence or intrinsic features. Jewish Studies, he suggests, may be "reconceive[d] based on "theories of alterity, heterogeneity, and provinciality" (92). Indeed, whereas Jewish learning stresses the unity and continuity of tradition, Jewish Studies, in Bush's telling, indicates rupture and simultaneously makes modernity—with its valorization of change, newness, and hybridity—a cultural resource for Jews. It not only shows Jews as a people with a history but also reconstructs Jewish memory—another key word according to Bush—by recovering Jews at the border zones where "all parties are both imitating and imitated, in a complex balance of mimesis and alterity" (89). Hybrid Jews are the object of Jewish Studies; recovering the hybridity of Jewishness for modern Jews is also its purpose.

Cynthia M. Baker's *Jew*, perhaps subverting its intentions, gives reason for skepticism of Jews as an object of study for Jewish Studies.[13] It also makes clear the normative purposes that guide such efforts. As indicated, Baker points out that historically Jews did not refer to themselves as such. She writes, "The most persistent meanings and force of the term *Jew(s)* derive . . . from an antique Christian worldview in which *the Jews* foundationally function as a kind of originary and constitutional alterity, or otherness" (4). Before the rise of Jewish Studies, "creation of knowledge about *Jew(s)* was . . . a non-Jewish enterprise" with the implicit aim of "constructing and sustaining non-Jewish identities" through the casting of "the Jew" as other (50). It is only in the present era that "Jewish" becomes a self-identification that allows Jews to control its meaning. Jewish Studies thus becomes part of "modern subject- or self-formation" by "producing an ever-expanding pool of cultural resources for constructing identities" (66). In fact, Baker maintains, "Studying Jews can be characterized as a kind of 'secular' practice of Jewishness" because it functions as a "workshop for constructing, deconstructing, examining and critiquing ideas about *Jew* as self" (67, 77). It is a "space for Jewish identified scholars to come build for themselves a native discourse about Jews" (77).

There are, however, problems with this theoretical account of Jewish Studies. It is hard to see how Jewish Studies can serve as a such a "native" discourse, given that, as Bush indicates, Jewish Studies began by differentiating itself from traditional Jewish learning. It understands itself precisely as a break from the "native." Moreover, Jewish Studies' preoccupation with identity—with that of Jews of the past, with the construction of modern Jewish identities, and with contemporary theories of subjectivity—is arbitrary from a scholarly perspective that rejects normativity. Rather than stemming from the object of study, it arises from the conditions of scholars of Jewish Studies, participants in the academy, and the wider culture. It then guides what should be studied and which contributions are considered worthwhile in the field. It thus serves as a norm of scholarship in Jewish Studies, even while other forms of normativity, especially those construed as religious, are ruled out of bounds.

Normativity in Scholarship, Identity, and Religion

As the foregoing shows, Jewish Studies does, in fact, make normative claims about Judaism, Jewish communities, modern Jewish identity, and identity itself. It excludes only certain normative claims—those that are construed as religious—while allowing in others, such as pluralistic yet bounded claims about the Jewish community, claims about the hybridity of Jewish identity, and theoretical accounts of identity. This is not surprising in view of philosophical accounts of normativity and its role in interpretation and concept applications. Indeed, theoretical reflection on Jewish Studies gains from an engagement with philosophy, especially the philosophy of religion. The philosophy of religion also stands to benefit from engagement with a suitably configured Jewish Studies.

The philosophy of religion has undergone a reassessment in the past years. Along with Schilbrack's *Philosophy and the Study of Religion: A Manifesto*, Thomas A. Lewis's *Why Philosophy Matters for the Study of Religion & Vice Versa* takes stock of the field and sets out a new vision for it.[14] Although, as their titles indicate, these works are mainly concerned with the study of religion, their arguments also have implications for Jewish Studies. Moreover, both propose that the philosophy of religion must broaden its interests beyond epistemological questions concerning the rationality of belief in God that it inherited from Christian theology by attending to other religions and their interests. These include ritual, ethics, and politics, which are issues that are well developed in Jewish texts.

The Pervasiveness of Normativity

Common to Schilbrack and Lewis is a rejection of the facile differentiation of academic religious studies from theology based on the latter's normativity. This differentiation also prevents the incorporation of the philosophy of religion into the academic study of religion, because the former, like theology, explicitly makes normative claims. These, however, are not about God and what God demands humans believe and do; rather, they are about the reasons that are offered in support of such claims about what to believe and do in theology, as well as in other areas like religious ethics. The philosophy of religion evaluates those reasons to determine whether they are justified, the beliefs they support true, and the actions they back moral. Some scholars of religion, however, dismiss such evaluation as out of place in the study of religion. Religious studies, in their view, must be restricted to description and explanation. This, of course, is reminiscent of the distinction between traditional Jewish learning and academic Jewish Studies in the recent introductory works and theoretical reflections. Jewish learning stands to Jewish Studies as theology stands to religious studies. The rejection of Jewish learning and theology as normative is constitutive for Jewish Studies and religious studies, respectively.

But the distinction between legitimate and illegitimate disciplines that is centered on normativity is untenable. Schilbrack identifies two arguments in support of this distinction. The first claims that only those disciplines like the sciences and social sciences that appeal to the evidence of experience belong in the academy. However, he argues that all academic work is based on assumptions about what counts as "valuable, reasonable, and real."[15] This is borne out in the current state of Jewish Studies. The second claims that the task of scholars is "to explain the ways in which religions are, like other human institutions, ideologically driven modes of social formation" (194). He counters this by showing how it relies on a particular anthropology in which humans are simply nodes in nexuses of power and by proposing another in which "humans are purposive agents who can and sometimes do weigh reasons" (194).

Lewis likewise insists that "normativity is pervasive."[16] He identifies two assumptions that underwrite religious studies' opposition to theology and suspicion of the philosophy of religion: The first is the presumption that only theologians make normative claims, whereas the second is that normative claims concerning religion are simply matters of faith and so cannot be evaluated. He shows that both assumptions are false. Normative claims expressly feature in philosophy and political science, and yet these disciplines' place in the academy is secure. Normative judgments are also subtly present in a scholars' assessments of the materials, individuals, or communities they study; for example, when they evaluate an institution as oppressive, when they identify an activity as expressing a basic human need, or when they displace religious self-understanding with an explanatory account of "what's really going on here" (47–50). There is nothing intrinsically problematic about normative judgments. They only become questionable when they are shielded from question or asserted based on appeals to authority. The assumption, moreover, that the normative claims of religions cannot be evaluated because they are held on faith is, Lewis writes, a "theological presupposition that continues to haunt discussions of religion" (45). The only positions that should be ruled out are those that refuse to subject their normative judgments to critical scrutiny; this applies to theologians, philosophers, historians, anthropologists, and other scholars alike.

This intervention into the relationship between the philosophy of religion and the study of religion has implications for Jewish Studies. It breaks down the artificial division between it and Jewish learning based on the issue of normativity. Normativity, again, is pervasive, and so its reappearance in introductory texts and theoretical reflections on the field is understandable. What matters is the type of normative claims that are made and the willingness to defend them.

The Normativity of the Study of Jews and Judaism

Schilbrack offers a typology of approaches in religious studies that may be applied usefully to Jewish Studies. He distinguishes among description, explanation, and evaluation. Some scholars are interested in describing religious phenomena in terms of the self-understanding of their practitioners, whereas others explain them by external factors like politics, economics, or the environment, of which their practitioners might be unaware. Still others, philosophers of religions, engage in the evaluation of the reasons offered by religious practitioners for their beliefs and norms. Each of these approaches involves normative judgments.[17] The legal theorist Ronald Dworkin's late writings about interpretation help spell out these judgments as they apply to the interpretation of texts, events, and concepts, including those of Jews and Judaism.[18]

Dworkin's interpretive theory of law has been influential in the Jewish Studies subfield of rabbinic literature.[19] He argues that judicial decision making cannot be reduced either to the simple application of rules or the instrumental pursuit of goals. It is instead an interpretive act in which the judge both describes and justifies the law. Judges do this by attributing moral and political principles to the law and then showing how they are expressed in previous cases and how they support their current rulings.[20] But Dworkin also generalizes this model of interpretation, applying it to any constructive intellectual undertaking, including legal theory, as well as to historical research and philosophical analysis. Each of these areas of inquiry are normative insofar as they require standards for what is a proper theory, account, or argument. These standards, in turn, are established by views of what is the purpose of the area of inquiry.

Dworkin usefully distinguishes between collaborative, explanatory, and conceptual interpretation. Collaborative interpretation often takes place in areas like law, theology, and literature. Explanatory interpretation typically takes place in history and the social sciences. Conceptual interpretation occurs in philosophy. Importantly, these are not distinguished by the presence or absence of norms, the standards and purpose that guide inquiry. They are instead distinguished by *whose* standards and purpose guide it and the *relation* between the interpreter and the object of interpretation.[21]

In collaborative interpretation, the interpreters—whether a jurist, theologian, or ordinary reader—are oriented by a purpose that they take themselves to share with the author of the text. They attempt to advance that purpose through their interpretation. Such collaborative interpretation characterizes Jewish learning. Despite their distances in place and time, as well as in social and intellectual backgrounds, participants in Jewish learning see themselves as sharing a purpose with the authors of the texts they study. They may well disagree among themselves about what that purpose is. Kabbalists, for example, might read the Hebrew Bible to uncover the inner life of God, whereas halakhists might read it to implement the commandments. Yet they each attribute a purpose to the text and interpret the text to advance it.

Explanatory interpretation, in contrast, does not purport to share a purpose with the author of the text, because the interpreters—whether historians or social scientists—are oriented by a purpose that they take themselves to share with their present audience: other scholars and the wider public. Political events or economic activity, for example, may only be tangential concerns of the Hebrew Bible. Yet a political historian or an economic researcher might see them as the key to understanding human phenomena and so the purpose of their discipline. They will thus interpret the text in view of that purpose, even without attributing it to the text itself. Jewish Studies, as described in its recent introductory works and theoretical reflections, engages in explanatory interpretation. It is oriented by purposes that it—perhaps rightly—takes itself to share with a contemporaneous scholarly and lay audience. These purposes center around questions of identity in general and Jewish identity in particular. It sees its task to complicate notions of Jewish identity, to provide cultural resources to those who are already living self-consciously hybrid Jewish identities, and to participate in the theorization of identity.

Traditional Jewish learning and academic Jewish Studies differ over what standards and goals orient their interpretations and over whom they take themselves to share these purposes. But both types of claims—religious and

306 CHAPTER 13

identitarian—can be evaluated, as can the concepts that underwrite them. In fact, better concepts of identity and religion are available than those that currently operate in Jewish Studies.

Identity and Religion Revisited

Dworkin, again, is instructive, because he offers a third model of interpretation. Despite their differences, collaborative and explanatory interpretation both distinguish between an author and interpreter. The interpreter interprets a text produced by an author. In contrast, in conceptual interpretation, we interpret our own concepts and practices. Some concepts apply to natural kinds—things like water or plants. Individuals share these concepts when they agree about when they apply and the consequences of their application. Criterial concepts, likewise, have antecedent conditions for their application, even though they may sometimes be vague; they include such things as being a triangle or being bald.

Interpretive concepts, in contrast, do not have antecedent conditions; their meaning depends "on the best justification of the role it plays for us" in our practices.[22] They include not only such moral concepts as "goodness" or "justice," but also ones like "identity" and "religion." These concepts are contested; there are no previously set criteria for their application. Dworkin writes, "People who use [such] concepts do not agree precisely about it means, they are taking a stand about what it *should* mean."[23] We try to give an account of our usage of the term "justice," for example, that also shows it to be something we ought to pursue. The same holds for "identity" and "religion." They are concepts that are developed through interpretation involving both description and justification. Because definitions must account for their usage and show why they are things we should care about, they thus have the capacity to illuminate how these concepts currently function and to revise our understanding of them. As I have shown, introductions to Jewish Studies struggle with the concept of identity, on the one hand, making self-assertion as being a Jew crucial, while on the other, putting limitations on Jewishness. Theoretical reflections complicate matters by celebrating alterity, heterogeneity, parochiality, and hybridity, but do not offer fleshed-out accounts of identity.

Because of its significance in contemporary discourse, identity is an important topic in recent philosophy. Kwame Anthony Appiah's *The Ethics of Identity* develops a helpful account of identity that sets it in a rich social context and has normative implications.[24] It illuminates Jewish identity.

Collective identities pick out "kinds of persons," which are brought into being by the creation of the label for them (*Ethics of Identity*, 65). They have a threefold structure. First, there must be a social conception of the label. People within society must know about the label and apply it either to themselves or to others in roughly similar ways. Second, among those people to whom the label is applied, at least some must identify with it. It must be a source of value for them, leading them to think, act, and even feel certain ways in their own lives and in their relationships with others (21–26).[25] Lastly, people behave toward others based on that label; they treat them as someone who is that kind of person (67–69). According to this account, being Jewish requires the existence of the category and some consensus concerning who is a Jew and what it is to be Jewish. Some individuals and communities must identify with being Jewish. And individuals and communities must be treated as Jews by others, whether Jews or non-Jews.

Being Jewish is thus a social status that requires the cooperation of many different individuals. Jewish identity cannot be understood simply as an individual's identification as a Jew, because there must be a vague shared understanding among Jews and non-Jews about what makes someone a Jew, and others must treat the individual as a Jew. This explains why reciprocal recognition—acknowledgment by other Jews—suddenly appears in Satlow's and Hahn Tapper's discussion of groups at the margins of Jewishness.

Being Jewish is also a normative status. A rough consensus about what makes someone a Jew means an agreement about who ought to be labeled a Jew. The application of this label also has ethical and political implications, because individuals and communities so labeled are treated—for better and for worse—as Jews. Lastly, identification as a Jew must make a practical or even political and ethical difference in one's life. It must be one's reason for thinking, doing, and feeling certain things. There also must be some alignment between the reasons that people give for their Jewishness and the social conception of Jewishness. These reasons cannot be completely idiosyncratic, although they can be contested in certain respects. And, of course, the social conception can shift over time as new normative judgments are incorporated into and old ones are discarded from the social conception of Jewishness.

Indeed, claims about Jewish identity, like all identity claims, are subject to rational evaluation against the background of other, currently unquestioned, elements of the identity. This happens all the time. Consider, for example, debates among Jewish Democrats and Republicans, who each cite their Jewishness as a reason for their political positions. These debates might involve weighing priorities that both acknowledge flow from their Jewish identity—social welfare for the needy versus support for the State of Israel. But they might turn to an evaluation of those priorities themselves: Do Jewish values really demand universal healthcare or a modern nation-state? And these questions can be answered by appealing to a wide range of sources—history, memory, texts, values, and norms—that are considered Jewish even as their Jewishness can be called into question at some later point in the debate.

This is true even of the sources considered "religious." Within the history of Judaism, it is a commonplace that the meaning of texts—whether the Hebrew Bible, the Talmud, or later codes and commentaries—is not transparent and so is subject to debate. Such debate proceeds by supporting one's reading by showing how it makes sense of more features of the text than its competitors and how it is consistent with other Jewish texts. Others propose an alternative that shows that the initial reading missed something in the original text or that distinguishes it from other texts. Thus, reasons are offered for understanding a religious text in a certain way and for deriving values and norms from it.[26] Moreover, inspection of both practical and theoretical halakhic writings shows that is difficult to locate uniquely "religious claims." Instead, one finds a panoply of types of reasons, including ethical, prudential, aesthetic, political, and theological considerations. In fact, halakhic discussion often concerns what types of reasons are being offered.[27] Seldom does one find arguments like "because it is the command of God" or "because the Torah says so," and even when one does find them, they do not function as "conversation stoppers." One can still ask philosophical and theological questions like "Why does God command it?" or "Why does the Torah say so?" or interpretive and practical questions like "Is that really how to understand God or the Torah?" or "Is that really how to apply the reading in action?" Because of the casuistic and dialectical character of halakhah, it is difficult to construe it as involving rationally unevaluable religious claims.[28]

The model for identity as self-assertion, which has been so influential in Jewish Studies, is religion, when religious claims are understood as confessionals of faith. Both are considered unevaluable, even as they are distinguished in Jewish Studies' differentiation of itself from Jewish learning. Jewish learning is associated with arational religion, whereas Jewish Studies concerns self-validating identity. Yet, ironically, this conception of religion and, in turn, identity is belied by traditional Jewish learning itself! Religious claims as confessionals of faith seldom feature within it. Both religious and identity claims are evaluable, and their evaluation should be considered appropriate topics in Jewish Studies.

Conclusion

In introductions to Jewish Studies, claims about "common Jewish narratives" or even about inclusion within "Israel" are already being evaluated in the field. These normative judgments should be made explicit and open to contestation. Recognizing the pervasiveness of normativity would also mean that subfields currently at the margins of Jewish Studies because of their connection to normativity would be moved to the center. These include the study of halakhah and of Jewish philosophy. Although both subfields are represented in Jewish Studies, the appropriate methods for examining them are restricted. To distinguish its academic study from the learning of rabbis and decisors, halakhah is usually studied philologically, historically, and doctrinally as opposed to focusing on understanding its reasoning and developing its concepts. So too, Jewish philosophy is commonly conducted as intellectual history because of anxiety about making constructive theological claims in the university. But if all subfields of Jewish Studies make normative claims, then what really matters for academic respectability is whether these claims are allowed to be challenged or not. And this applies to every subfield and topic, from halakhah and philosophy to history and ethnography.

An engagement between Jewish Studies and the philosophy of religion thus allows Jewish Studies to resolve some of its major difficulties. Once Jewish Studies has been suitably reconfigured through this engagement, it has much to contribute to the philosophy of religion. The way that Jewishness transcends cultural, political, and intellectual classifications and the development of Judaism as a private faith in modernity have already served to call into question the category of "religion." The realization that faith claims seldom feature in Jewish debates about texts, beliefs, and norms supports the philosophy of religion's position that religious discourse involves reason-giving and so can be rationally evaluated. Moreover, this realization provides new topics and connections for the philosophy of religion beyond epistemological questions concerning the rationality of religious belief. Halakhah's preoccupation with norms and agency, for example, has natural connections with moral and legal philosophy. And contemporary liberal Jews' concern with social justice has obvious links with political theory and community organizing. The philosophy of religion enables Jewish Studies to evaluate these phenomena by overcoming its differentiation from Jewish learning, while Jewish Studies allows the philosophy of religion to transcend the preoccupations of Christian theology.

Recommended Readings

Appiah, Kwame Anthony. *The Ethics of Identity* (Princeton University Press, 2005).

Asad, Talal. *Genealogies of Religion: Discipline and Reasons of Power in Christianity and Islam* (Johns Hopkins University Press, 1993).

Baker, Cynthia. *Jew* (Rutgers University Press, 2017).

Batnitzky, Leora. *How Judaism Became a Religion: An Introduction to Modern Jewish Thought* (Princeton University Press, 2011).

Dworkin, Ronald. *Justice for Hedgehogs* (Belknap, 2013).

Farneth, Molly. *The Politics of Ritual* (Princeton University Press, 2023).

Lewis, Thomas A. *Why Philosophy Matters for the Study of Religion & Vice Versa* (Oxford University Press, 2015).

Magid, Shaul. *American Post-Judaism: Identity and Renewal in a Postethnic Society* (Indiana University Press, 2013).

Saiman, Chaim N. *Halakhah: The Rabbinic Idea of Law* (Princeton University Press, 2018).

Schilbrack, Kevin. *Philosophy and the Study of Religion: A Manifesto* (Wiley-Blackwell, 2014).

Notes

1. *Philosophy and the Study of Religion: A Manifesto* (Wiley-Blackwell, 2014).

2. *Judaism: Revelation and Traditions* (HarperOne, 1987), 18.

3. As cited in Noam Pianko, *Jewish Peoplehood: An American Innovation* (Rutgers University Press, 2015), 107.

4. See, for example, Talal Asad, *Genealogies of Religion: Discipline and Reasons of Power in Christianity and Islam* (Johns Hopkins University Press, 1993); and, developed in the context of modern Judaism, Leora Batnitzky, *How Judaism Became a Religion: An Introduction to Modern Jewish Thought* (Princeton University Press, 2011).

5. Columbia University Press, 2006, 5–12.

6. Wittgenstein, *Philosophical Investigations* (Wiley-Blackwell, 2009), para. 66ff.

7. *Jew* (Rutgers University Press, 2017), 3, 49–50.

8. Satlow, *Creating Judaism*, 54.

9. Wittgenstein, *Philosophical Investigations*, para. 185.

10. For the classic statement of this not-uncontroversial reading, see Saul Kripke, *Wittgenstein on Rules and Private Language* (Harvard University Press, 1982).

11. University of California Press, 2016.

12. Rutgers University Press, 2011.

13. Rutgers University Press, 2017.

14. Oxford University Press, 2015.

15. *Why Philosophy*, 192.

16. *Why Philosophy*, 8.

17. *Why Philosophy*, 177–89.

18. For an earlier iteration of this argument, see Yonatan Y. Brafman, "Philosophy, Interpreter of Halakha," *Studies in Judaism, Humanities, and the Social Sciences* 1, no. 2 (2018): 69–82.

PHILOSOPHY 311

19. See all the articles in *Dine Israel*, vol. 25.

20. See Ronald Dworkin, *Law's Empire* (Hart, 1998).

21. *Justice for Hedgehogs* (Belknap 2013), 134–39.

22. *Justice,* 158.

23. *Religion without God* (Harvard University Press, 2013), 7.

24. Kwame Anthony Appiah, *The Ethics of Identity* (Princeton University Press, 2005).

25. Appiah, *Ethics of Identity*, 21–26.

26. On this, see, for example, Menachem Fisch, *Rational Rabbis: Science and Talmudic Culture* (Indiana University Press, 1997).

27. Yonatan Y. Brafman, *Critique of Halakhic Reason: Divine Commandments and Social Normativity* (Oxford University Press, 2024).

28. Abraham (Avi) Sagi, *Avi Sagi: Existentialism, Pluralism, and Identity*, ed. H. Tirosh-Samuelson and A. W. Hughes (Brill, 2015), 59–102.

14

Lived Religion

Rachel B. Gross, San Francisco State University

ON A HOT and humid July day in 2012, visitors to the Hester Street Fair on New York's Lower East Side sampled the wares of Gefilteria, a purveyor of artisanal "Old World Jewish foods" remade for the sensibilities and palates of twenty-first-century hipsters. Writer Rose Surnow described the scene:

> People ordering from Gefilteria . . . were practically having a religious experience. A woman named Hillary McGrath took one bite of the gefilte crostini and seemingly went into a trance. I've never seen fish affect someone like that. 'This was the first time in fifty years that I had that same exact sensory feeling as I had eating my grandparents' gefilte. It really brought me back to my childhood,' she said by way of explanation.[1]

What happens if we take this moment seriously as a religious experience? Gefilte fish is a ball or loaf of finely chopped fish, usually whitefish, pike, or carp, cooked in a broth, and usually served chilled. It became a popular dish among Central and Eastern European Ashkenazi Jews, and it was adapted—and turned into a shelf-stable product—by twentieth-century American Jews. Gefilteria's gefilte fish reimagined the dish as a tricolor sliced loaf of sustainably sourced whitefish, pike, and salmon.[2] As Surnow's description demonstrates, for some Jewish diners, the experience of tasting artisanal gefilte fish on a hot summer day was an emotional experience. It created a sense—however ephemeral—of community in the present, helped consumers narrate their lives, connected them to remembered ancestors, and encouraged them to recall larger stories about Jewish migration. These are all components that we can understand as features of religious practice.

As this moment demonstrates, if we open ourselves to thinking broadly about what counts as "religion," the religious experiences of U.S. Jews can include a wide and sometimes surprising array of practices, objects, spaces, and participants. The academic approach of lived religion focuses our attention on the ways in which people enact their religious identities, including through seemingly ordinary actions such as eating, cooking, shopping, reading, or entertaining, as well as through more traditional religious activities or experiences recognized as spiritual. Most people do not recognize many of the practices of lived religion as religious actions similar to celebrating a holiday or reciting prayers; they are instead seen as the mundane practices that provide the structure of our lives or the leisure activities that we engage in throughout the week.

But the study of lived religion helps us break down an artificial distinction between "religious" and "secular" activities. It helps us understand not only how people who do not see themselves as religious make meaning in their lives but also how people who do see themselves as religious make meaning both within and beyond practices and places that are traditionally understood as religious. The study of lived religion of contemporary U.S. Jews helps us understand how Jews of all genders, ages, and religious affiliations—or lack thereof—enact their Judaism in their everyday lives. This approach helps us go beyond what community leaders say Jews should be doing and instead ask questions about what they are doing.

Although the study of lived religion is primarily an academic exercise, such scholarship can also be of use to non-academic Jews seeking language to help articulate how they find Jewish and religious meaning through a wide range of experiences. Unlike some social-scientific scholarship designed to guide Jewish communal practices and the large-scale philanthropy that supports it,[3] studies of lived religion generally aim to articulate what it is that Jews are already doing. Sometimes, studies of lived religion may celebrate or critique those practices, but their primary aim is always description and analysis of what Jews are already doing.

Religious studies scholarship on the lived religion of U.S. Jews has several origins. The most immediate is the development since the 1990s of the approach of lived religion within the subfield of U.S. religious history. Going further back, we can also find the roots of the study of Jews' quotidian practices in the work of early twentieth-century ethnographers of Jewish culture in Eastern Europe, which was later continued by the start of anthropologists' ethnographic study of U.S. Jews in the 1970s. Taken together, these academic developments have led to an exciting field of study that helps us understand how American Jews perform their Jewish identities and create Jewish meaning in their lives through everyday activities and how laypeople understand ritual practices.

Lived Religion in the United States

The study of lived religion in the United States emerged in the mid-1990s as religious studies scholars and those in related fields reflected on who and what had been the subject of scholarship on the history of "religion." Religious studies scholarship had focused on the study of ideas and texts, largely by elite religious leaders. The term "lived religion" originated at a 1994 conference at Harvard Divinity School (HDS) organized by American religious historian David D. Hall. The conference attendees were mostly historians, but they also included sociologists and religious studies scholars; most participants were scholars of American Protestantism, although there were notable exceptions. The conference and a related course at HDS were funded by the Religion Division of the Lilly Endowment, which had a stated interest in promoting the study of "daily life," especially among Protestant laypeople. Conference papers were published in the volume *Lived Religion in America: Toward a History of Practice*.[4] Although the field has diversified in the last twenty years—including, as we see, engaging in significant scholarship on Jews—the roots of the study of U.S. lived religion are firmly in the study of Christianity and, especially, Protestantism.

From its outset, the lived religion approach was intended not only to expand the range of data but also to highlight religious actors who had been previously overlooked by both religious leaders and academic scholarship. Nancy Ammerman, a sociologist who contributed to the 1997 *Lived Religion* volume, writes, "Studying lived religion began as something of a rebellion. Where, we asked, were the religious lives of women, children, poor people, and people of color?"[5] Adapting the phrase "lived religion" from its use in French sociology of religion (*la religion vécue*), these scholars began to ask questions about "the everyday thinking and doing of lay men and women." They built on and adapted the study of "popular religion," which emphasized what laypeople did apart from clergy. In contrast, scholars of lived religion resist an overly rigid division between religious leaders and everyday practitioners, understanding that leaders and laypeople engage in many of the same sanctioned and unsanctioned patterns of behavior. Moreover, in many religious traditions, it is often less than clear who should count as a "religious leader," so studies of "high and low" religion are less useful or relevant to analysis.[6]

From its beginnings, scholarship on lived religion has encouraged questions about "meaning"[7] and has led to a broad understanding of what counts as religion. In many ways, the abstract concept of religion is a modern Protestant creation. Although uses of the word date back to Roman and early Christian settings, the origins of how we understand the term today lie in Protestants' efforts to differentiate their religion from Catholicism and from European colonizers' efforts to distinguish their Christianity from non-Christian religions around the world. Both these efforts tended to see "good," "true," or "high" forms of religion as those that emphasized personal faith and belief, rather than those that emphasized communal practices and rituals.[8]

Nonetheless, the concept of religion is often fluid and changes in different contexts. In the United States, defining religion both socially and legally has been essential to issues of religious freedom. Discussions of religious freedom have been used to strengthen white Protestants' claims to racial and religious supremacy, and historical and recent court cases have addressed the intersection between everyday activities and religion. Racial and religious minorities, including Jews, have deliberately defined certain practices and beliefs as religious to improve their status and situation in the United States.[9]

For many scholars of lived religion, the word "religion" functions as an umbrella term that helps facilitate conversations about how individuals, families, communities, or even nations create and sustain meaning. As Jonathan Z. Smith writes, "'Religion' is not a native term; it is a term created by scholars for their intellectual purposes and therefore theirs to define." Just as linguists define "language" and anthropologists define "culture," religious studies scholars define "religion" as the scope of their academic inquiry (194). In his studies of U.S. Catholics, Robert A. Orsi has defined religion as "the totality of their ultimate values, their most deeply held ethical convictions, their efforts to order their reality. . . . More simply stated, *religion* here means 'what matters.'"[10] In his later scholarship, Orsi identifies religion as "a network of relationships between heaven and earth involving humans of all ages and many sacred figures together." These networks include relationships with "saints, ancestors, demons, gods, ghosts, and other special beings," as well as sacred relationships among the living.[11] Another influential scholar, Thomas Tweed, defines religions as "confluences of organic-cultural flows that intensify joy and confront suffering by drawing on human and suprahuman forces to make homes and cross boundaries."[12] In her studies of religion and consumer culture, Kathryn Lofton emphasizes communities' shared interests and passions: "Whatever else religion might be, it is a way of describing structures by which we are bound or connected to one another."[13] These definitions have been continually adapted and reformulated by other scholars to fit specific case studies. The focus of scholars of Christianity on the transcendental, for instance, does not always apply to studies of U.S. Jewish practices. Regardless of which precise definition scholars use, the study of lived religion helps scholars raise questions about how Americans create meaning in their lives and answer existential questions through a wide range of practices.

Significantly, the study of lived religion developed more or less in tandem with the study of "material religion"—the study of material culture or the physical stuff of religious practice and identity—and many scholars use both approaches. Like lived religion, material religion developed as an approach to better understand people's tangible experiences of religion, in addition to understanding religion through texts or dogma. As the editors of the journal *Material Religion* explained in their first issue, "Religion is not regarded as something one does with speech or reason alone, but with the body and the spaces it inhabits. . . . Religion is what people do with material things and places, and how these structure and color experience and one's sense of oneself and others."[14] Colleen McDannell's *Material Christianity* explores a particularly important early innovation in this approach.[15] McDannell documents how theologians and other religious leaders had often denigrated or dismissed religious images and material practices as inauthentic or unimportant religious practices. In contrast, she takes seriously souvenirs and relics, Lourdes water, and "Praise the Lord" T-shirts as ways that everyday people have practiced and expressed religion.

Commerce, in particular, is often dismissed as a profane activity. But what we spend our money on often illuminates our values more than our words do. Scholars of lived religion help us see religion in ordinary activities generally considered "secular." These scholars identify religion and religious practices in baseball, Coca-Cola, Tupperware, celebrity worship, weight-loss culture, and the American office, to name just a few subjects. Broadening the category of religion in this way helps us take seriously the structures, commitments, and activities that shape everyday life. Anything can become a religious object, depending on how it is used and understood. Expanding the conventional definitions of religion to include everyday practices and materials identifies the social value placed on them and the communities developed around them. Eating a pastrami sandwich or fangirling Kim Kardashian—as Lofton analyzes—can be a religious activity, not just because it is personally meaningful but also because it is part of a shared cultural framework ascribing specific kinds of meaning to those activities.[16]

Jewish Ethnography

Ethnographies of contemporary Jews also have antecedents in the work of European Jewish collectors and ethnographers of the early twentieth century. In 1891 Jewish historian Simon Dubnow lamented the lack of historical writing on Jewish experience in Eastern Europe and called on the public to collect and preserve historical materials.[17] Inspired by Dubnow and by the Russian intellectual and revolutionary movement of "going to the people"—learning from and about the simple folk of the Russian peasantry—Eastern European Jews took up the task of collecting and recording their cultures. Between 1912 and 1913, the writer and political activist Shloyme Zanvil Rapoport, known by his pseudonym S. An-sky, led the Jewish Ethnographic Expedition into the Russian Pale of Settlement, the territory between the Black and Baltic Seas to which most of Russia's Jews had been legally restricted since the 1790s. In the beginning of the twentieth century, around five million Jews lived in the Pale, making it the largest Jewish population in the world. Many lived in predominantly Jewish market towns or shtetls. "Members of different Hasidic sects, *misnagdim* [non-Hasidic Orthodox Jews], Communists, Jewish Socialists, and Zionists of various orientations all inhabited the same communities; indeed, they could even be found in the same families."[18] The Jewish Ethnographic Expedition documented the remarkable diversity of Jewish practices and beliefs in this region.

As Jeffrey Veidlinger writes, Russian populists who went "to the people" were divided in their intentions for doing so.[19] "Was it to learn from them? Or was it to teach them? And what exactly were they to be teaching or learning?" (3) Russian Jewish ethnographers were similarly divided between those who observed, critiqued, and celebrated traditional Russian Jewish cultures. An-sky hoped that the ethnographic project would inspire a renaissance of new Jewish cultural creations that built on and reimagined Eastern European Jewish traditions. In contrast to the nineteenth-century German Wissenschaft des Judentums (Science of Judaism) movement—generally seen as an antecedent to contemporary academic Jewish Studies—which "imagined history as a science divorced from contemporary politics and external influences," Russian Jewish ethnographers saw their work as a "a political gesture, intertwined with the defenses of the legal rights of Jews in the empire" (5). Although An-sky's dreams of a Jewish cultural renaissance were dashed by the Russian Revolution, the question about the purpose of Jewish ethnography lingers in studies of Jewish lived religion.[20] Who is this work for? Is it intended to describe, celebrate, or critique Jewish practices?

The work of these early twentieth-century ethnographers became significant as historical documents. But they also established a scholarly tradition of Jewish ethnography, one that has continued in the work of anthropologists, sociologists, linguists, ethnomusicologists, historians, literary scholars, visual artists, playwrights, and musicians, among others.[21] A significant change in the study of U.S. Jews came from the work of anthropologist Barbara Myerhoff. Myerhoff had been a highly regarded anthropologist of Indigenous Mexicans and had studied rituals of the Huichol people. But, as Myerhoff later recalled, in a period of increasing ethnic and racial pride and emphasis on communities' self-empowerment, the anthropologist took seriously comments from communities of color who told her to "study your own." Myerhoff's groundbreaking research on elderly Jews who met at a senior center in Venice, California, resulted in an award-winning short documentary with filmmaker Lynn Littman (1977) and a celebrated book, both called *Number Our Days* (1979).[22] Neither U.S. Jews, the elderly, nor American urban populations had previously received much attention from anthropologists, whose field had developed from studying "exotic," non-western, and often colonized peoples. Among other influences, Myerhoff's work opened up possibilities of scholarship on contemporary U.S. Jews.[23] At the same time, the field of religious studies was professionalizing and developing in the 1960s and 1970s, and religious studies scholars, among others, would turn to ethnography and other approaches to the study of quotidian practices.

U.S. Jewish Lived Religion

Building on these legacies, Jewish Studies scholars researching U.S. lived religion have focused attention on the ways that U.S. Jews enact their Judaism and Jewish identity outside rabbinic law and practice. Turning aside from communal questions about what is "good for the Jews," they instead ask what U.S. Jews are really doing and how we can interpret their actions. These scholars pay attention to activities both within and beyond the major recognizable institutions of Jewish identity in the United States, such as synagogues, Jewish Community Centers, Jewish Federations (umbrella philanthropic organizations), and Zionist organizations. They study both the Jewish "nones"—a sociological term for the religiously unaffiliated—and Jews affiliated with Jewish organizations of all kinds. Lived religion approaches have been particularly useful for drawing attention to the religious work of American Jewish women and complicating the ideas of who counts as a religious or communal leader in U.S. Jewish contexts.

Like other scholars of lived religion, these scholars often wrestle with definitions of religion. This is particularly challenging in the study of Jews and Judaism. The political emancipation of Jews, which allowed Jews to become citizens of modern western nation-states over the course of the eighteenth through early twentieth centuries, required Jews to define Judaism as a voluntary religious association. Before emancipation, European Jewish communities had largely governed themselves. As newly minted citizens in modern nation-states, Jews gave up their communal autonomy and used the language of religion to articulate themselves as a group. In the United States, Jews continued to characterize religion as an individual matter of belief and choice, rather than one mandated by ethnicity and community. In the mid-twentieth century, a period of American church growth in general, U.S. Jewish leaders worked to frame their shared endeavors as religion to demonstrate Jews' Americanness.[24] But by the 1970s and 1980s, as a white ethnic revival developed, U.S. Jews of European ancestry emphasized Jewishness as an "ethnicity" to articulate Jewish difference, even as they benefited from their increased recognition as white.[25] These political histories have led to distinctions between "Jewish religion" and "Jewish culture" that do not adequately capture the range of ways that American Jews make meaning: Studies of lived religion trouble the seemingly easy application of these categories.[26]

The study of American lived religion began with historical scholarship, and although this chapter focuses on research on contemporary Jews, it is important to note that Jewish Studies scholars continue to apply lived religion approaches to U.S. Jewish history in many significant works. For example, Shari Rabin examines the changing ritual and communal practices of nineteenth-century Jews on the move in the American West.[27] Laura Yares demonstrates the significance of nineteenth-century Jewish Sunday schools, an institution created by women, for the development of uniquely U.S. Jewish religious thought and practice.[28] Turning to the twentieth century, Sarah Imhoff explores the religious life and thought of American-born Zionist writer Jessie Sampter, who was physically disabled due to post-polio syndrome and whom we might understand as queer.[29] Much of the scholarship on contemporary Jews below builds on historical research or blends historical and contemporary methods (to avoid repetition?).

In the next several subsections, I examine developments in the scholarship on U.S. Jewish lived religion that draws on approaches of material culture studies, ritual studies, food studies, and media studies. I then address work that helps us expand the boundaries of who is included in these studies and areas in which there is a need for further research. It is also worth noting that the boundaries of any scholarly approach are never entirely clear-cut. Most but not entirely all the scholarship I address is by religious studies scholars who study U.S. Jews and explicitly refer to the approach of lived religion; a select few works are by scholars in related disciplines who use similar approaches. In any case, I do not intend this to be a comprehensive list of scholarship to date; instead, it is a representative survey of the field.

Material Religion

Like other scholars of lived religion, Jewish Studies scholars using the approach regularly turn toward material religion to understand how American Jews perform their Judaism. Vanessa Ochs's study of the Jewish home exemplifies this work.[30] As Ochs writes, "In Judaism and, I imagine, most other faith traditions, the spiritual is material. Without things, in all their thingness, there is no Passover, only an idea of Passover; and a faint and fuzzy idea it would be, like honor, loyalty, and remorse—like, perhaps, God, and more surely, monotheism. Things denote one's belonging, one's participation, possibly one's convictions" (493). Ochs interviewed a Jewish informant and takes the reader on a tour of objects in her home, including both objects that are overtly Jewish and seemingly ordinary objects that signify Jewishness to Ochs's informant. This work opens a new way to think about how American Jews express their Judaism in their everyday lives.

Other scholars of lived religion and material culture continue to draw our attention to objects that we might otherwise overlook but that serve as insightful windows into Jewish practice. Their work also requires us to expand which practices we pay attention to as "religious." For example, in *Painted Pomegranates and Needlepoint Rabbis*, Jodi Eichler-Levine examines the religious dimensions of the Jewish crafting movement, emphasizing how crafting can create religious communities and serve as an act of spiritual resilience.[31] As do many studies of material religion, Eichler-Levine uses material culture as a means of accessing religious actors' affect and emotions.

The intersection of lived religion and material culture can also draw our attention to spaces that we might overlook as sites of Jewish practice. Drawing on her ethnographic research, Laura Yares examines a Jewish museum gift shop as a site where object lessons are conveyed by Jewish community leaders and at which Jews of many types express their own Jewish identity and religious practices through consumer engagement or lack of engagement.[32] My own book, *Beyond the Synagogue*, identifies Jewish genealogical societies, historic synagogues used as museums, children's books and dolls, and artisanal delis as objects and sites of Jewish religious practice that provide standardized models of nostalgia for Eastern European Jewish heritage.

Ritual Studies

Jewish Studies scholars of lived religion have particularly been drawn to studying rituals. These are often traditionally "religious" moments, which another scholar might study in terms of how rabbis and other traditional religious authorities describe how these performances *should* be enacted. But scholars of lived religion are interested in how Jews actually perform these rituals, what they mean to practitioners, and how practitioners continue to develop and change them. For example, Dianne Ashton's *Hanukkah in America* places furious debates about American Jews' "December dilemma" in historical context, presenting a history of American Jews through their engagement with the holiday.[33] Ashton makes the case that "Hanukkah festivals . . . set in motion a dynamic relationship between clergy and laity" (75) in which lay women, in particular, shaped Hanukkah practices in family homes. She also attends to the changing public nature of the holiday, from nineteenth-century pageants to Chabad's development of public menorah lightings since the 1970s.

In another study of how Jews actually practice and understand a traditional holiday, folklorist Gabrielle Anna Berlinger examines the sukkah, a temporary ritual hut constructed for the week-long holiday of Sukkot, as a powerful ritual expression of contemporary Jews' identities and politics through case studies in Bloomington, Indiana, Brooklyn, and Tel Aviv.[34] Berlinger employs the approach of "vernacular religion,"[35] which is closely related to "lived religion" in its focus on "religion as it is lived: as human beings encounter, understand, interpret and practice it," but was developed from folklore studies and anthropology, rather than religious studies (51). Using the temporary ritual structure of the sukkah, which has both rigid traditional requirements and room for creative expression, Berlinger examines "how people integrate and make meaning from the disparate elements of their past, present and future through daily expressions of their creative agency" (12).

Notably, Vanessa L. Ochs's *Inventing Jewish Ritual* identifies the ways that American Jews have changed traditional ritual practices and created new ones to suit life in the late twentieth and early twenty-first centuries, from wedding booklets that explain Jewish wedding practices to the display of Holocaust Torahs.[36] Although one might erroneously assume that such a study focuses only on religiously liberal Jews, Ochs makes the case that Jews of all religious affiliations engage in ritual change; most notably, she includes a case study of Chabad Lubavitch women's tambourines, used in anticipation of the Lubavitcher Rebbe, Menachem Mendel Schneerson, "rising up" as the messiah around the time of his death in 1994 (167).

Food Studies

Closely related to studies of material culture and ritual is the study of that most intimate of materials, food. In the early 2000s, scholars of religion began to apply their studies of lived religion and material religion to studies of food, and there is a burgeoning field of Jewish food studies, both within and beyond religious studies. As an area of humanistic study, food studies has developed gradually since the 1990s and is now a vibrant field of inquiry. Scholars of North American lived religion began to turn to food studies in the early 2000s, notably with an American Academy of Religion seminar that resulted in an 2014 edited volume, *Religion, Food, and Eating in North America*.[37] As Martha Finch writes in the introduction to that volume, "Because it is necessary for basic human survival, food is at the heart of religious life: not only does it provide physical nourishment and sustenance, but those who eat also invest what is (and is not) eaten with deep and compelling values" (xi). Food has long been recognized as a distinctive part of Jewish religion and culture, so it is perhaps not surprising that U.S. Jewish food studies is an expandng field. Two notes of caution are needed regarding Jewish food studies: Jews' attention to food should not be confused with Jews having a more special relationship to food than any other people; all human cultures create meaning through food practices, though it is sometimes less overtly articulated or recognized, especially in mainstream religious cultures. See, for instance, Daniel Sack's *Whitebread Protestants*.[38] Moreover, Jewish food culture is often confused with Ashkenazi food culture, which dominates U.S. Jewish food practices but does not delineate it.

Jonathan Brumberg-Kraus provides an excellent exploration of the many ways that food practices can function as religious practices for contemporary U.S. Jews, beyond traditional ritual and holiday practices: "Jewish food traditions are 'sacred' not just because they're old, or not just because the holy rabbis and sacred texts tell us so, but also because for those who practice them, they continue to evoke powerful feelings and meanings" (x).[39] Brumberg-Kraus describes creative ways that Jews find meaning in food practices as "culinary midrash," building on the Jewish tradition of creative engagement with religious texts. Importantly, he addresses the ways that rejecting kashrut, traditional Jewish dietary laws, can also be an engagement with Jewish food practices in itself, even if it is a nontraditional one.

In studies of food, as in other subjects, scholars of lived religion point us to new or unexpected sites of religious practice. Adrienne Krone's work helps us understand Jewish farms as sites of religious practice.[40] Her studies of contemporary Jewish farms around the country analyze Jewish farm staffers' and program participants' expression of Jewish ethics and their restatement of Judaism as an earth-based religion. My own work examines artisanal delis as sites of religious practice, where, like Krone's farmers, restaurateurs articulate sustainability as a Jewish value and reimagine Ashkenazi cuisine for the twenty-first century.[41]

Some important recent work attends to how Orthodox Jewish food practices, like all other people's food practices, are not just a simple matter of "following rules" but also are a constant reimagination of religious practices in new contexts. Jody Myers examines how Orthodox Jews sustain and demarcate their communities through food practices, focusing on the primarily Orthodox Jewish neighborhood of Pico Robertson in west Los Angeles.[42] Anthropologists Rachel Z. Feldman and Ayala Fader's research on the trade in raw milk between Amish farmers and Orthodox Jews in Lancaster County, Pennsylvania, examines food as a site of collaboration between two insular communities, both of which aim to push back against mainstream U.S. norms and regulations.[43] Like other works of food studies, these studies are particularly adept at pointing us to the negotiation of the borders and boundaries of religious practice. Where Feldman and Fader direct us to the integral work of non-Jewish producers in the creation of "Jewish food," Myers highlights how food practices can both shore up and undercut notions of "communal unity."

Media Studies

Other scholars have turned toward media studies, including studies of literature and television. Although there is some overlap with the burgeoning field of popular culture studies within the field of Jewish Studies, lived religion scholars are primarily interested in reception history and everyday practice. For example, Jodi Eichler-Levine's *Suffer the Little Children* draws attention to children's literature as a serious site of religious engagement in a study of U.S. Jewish and African American children's literature.[44] Eichler-Levine's interest in the books lies in how they represent and shape communal conversations about suffering and trauma and their intersection with ideas of childhood. Likewise, communication studies scholar Jeremy Stolow's *Orthodox by Design* focuses on the practices of Orthodox Jews, specifically the design and use of prayer books and other products by ArtScroll, the world's largest Orthodox Jewish publishing house.[45] Like many other scholars of lived religion, Stolow is attentive to media—in this case, largely print media—production and reception alongside issues of practice. *Orthodox by Design* also follows the lived religion principles of attention to both recognized religious authorities and the practices of laypeople.

Turning to other forms of media, Yiddish Studies scholar Jeffrey Shandler's *Jews, God, and Videotape* explores a range of intersections between American Jewish ritual practices and media throughout the twentieth and early twenty-first centuries, from sound recordings of cantors to photographic and video documentation of Jews' lifecycle events.[46] More recently, Laura Yares and Sharon Avni examine the Saturday Night Seder, a widely publicized online broadcast in April 2020, as a digital media event, a broad space of Jewish dialogue, and a site of ritual change and expression during the particular historical circumstances of the early period of the COVID pandemic.[47] Authors of lived religion and media take the approach, in Stolow's words, that "'religion' can only be manifested through some process of mediation. . . . By the same token, every medium necessarily participates in the realm of the transcendent."[48]

Expanding Boundaries and Further Directions

As scholarship on contemporary communities, studies of Jewish lived religion intersect with heated ongoing debates about how to understand and how to fund Jewish communities. In particular, lived religion scholars have weighed in on the so-called American Jewish continuity crisis. Since the mid-twentieth century, U.S. Jewish communal leaders have worried loudly that American Jews' religiosity is declining. These communal leaders define Jewish religiosity narrowly, in terms of practices that can be measured in sociological studies, such as attending synagogue, keeping kosher, or sending children to Jewish religious schools. In the decades since then, these fears have been seemingly confirmed in widely accepted social-scientific studies that seem to demonstrate an American Jewish "continuity crisis" or a "marriage crisis," the latter emphasizing communal fears about marriages between Jews and non-Jews. Dismay over intermarriage and its effects on Jewish religious continuity has been articulated in sociological language from the pulpit, by Jewish organizations, and in large-scale philanthropy. Proponents of the continuity crisis rely on divisions between activities seen as "good for the Jews"—largely those identified as religious Jewish practices, which these leaders want to encourage—and those activities seen as "bad for the Jews"—generally, cultural Jewish practices seen as encouraging secularism, assimilation, and intermarriage, which they want to discourage. These studies have guided the determination of which American Jews count, literally and metaphorically, and they have influenced the funding and aims of local and national Jewish communal organizations. In recent years, some Jewish Studies scholars have begun to push back against these narratives and to demonstrate the ways in which they have been constructed—especially, the ways these constructed narratives harm Jewish women—although this continues to be a matter of fervent debate.[49]

To this end, lived religion has expanded to whom we pay attention when we talk about U.S. Jewish religion. As part of the pushback against the so-called continuity crisis, some scholars of lived religion have refuted the idea that interfaith romantic relationships and, especially, Jewish-Christian interfaith co-parenting are "bad for the Jews." Works like Jennifer A. Thompson's *Jewish on Their Own Terms*[50] and Samira Mehta's *Beyond Chrismukkah*[51] refocus the conversation on the lived experiences of interfaith families and how they understand their religious practices. Like other works discussed in this chapter, Mehta blends analysis of media reception with ethnography and interviews to develop a more complete picture of lived experiences. Importantly, this scholarship on interfaith families helps us see that Jewish families and communities include non-Jews, as well as Jews.

In another direction, sociologist Emily Sigalow's *American JewBu* sheds light on an often discussed but previously underanalyzed group, U.S. Jews who have turned to Buddhism.[52] Building on her extensively researched history of the movement of U.S. Jewish Buddhists, Sigalow pushes back against popular perceptions of contemporary Jewish Buddhists as a frivolous anomaly by taking their religious practices and organizations seriously. Likewise, Jody Myers's study of practitioners affiliated with the Kabbalah Centre in Los Angeles significantly pushes the boundaries of "who counts" in Jewish Studies.[53] As Myers explains, the Kabbalah Centre is best understood as a new religious movement. It draws on Jewish and Christian mystical traditions, and its adherents include people of Jewish and non-Jewish backgrounds. Although mainstream American Jews largely reject the Kabbalah Centre as "Jewish," Myers makes an important case that understanding the practices of its practitioners helps us understand the history of U.S. Judaism and its ever-uncertain boundaries.

Other new work points us toward the embodied ways that religion is performed, drawing our attention to the ways that gender, power, and authority reset in bodily expression and perception. The research being done on the embodied nature of gender, sexuality, and religion is particularly exciting. In addition to Imhoff's work on the queer and embodied nature of Jessie Sampter's Zionism, mentioned earlier, Cara Rock-Singer's work on the Kohenet Priesthood Institute brings into focus gendered aspects of ritual and religious authenticity.[54] S. J. Crasnow's ethnographic research has included studies of how trans Jews reinterpret and expand religious rituals to affirm trans identity.[55] Both Rock-Singer and Crasnow's work draws attention to the importance of embodied experiences, presentations, and identities in U.S. Jewish ritual activity.

Increasingly, scholars are attentive to the intersection of race and religion. Cultural anthropologist Henry Goldschmidt's powerful ethnography of Black and Chabad Lubavitch residents of the Crown Heights neighborhood in Brooklyn argues that the violence in that neighborhood in August 1991 was the product of a "collision of social realities" in which Black and Lubavitch groups fundamentally understood race and religion differently.[56] Still, there is a considerable need for more research that explicitly analyzes the ways many U.S. Jews continue to think about themselves in terms of race and ethnicity, even if they are sometimes uncomfortable with that language. Sarah Imhoff and Hillary Kaell have made an important foray into this research by comparing the conversations of mainstream Jews and Messianic Jews about DNA, race, and Jewish identity.[57] More recently, scholars are becoming attentive to the gaps in literature on non-Ashkenazi and non-white Jews, including Sephardi and Mizrachi Jews and Jews of color. Samira Mehta examines different understandings of the term "religion" held by white American Jews and non-Christian or Jewish Asian Americans and its impact on marriages between such individuals.[58] A complementary study is *JewAsian: Race, Religion, and Identity for America's Newest Jews*, a qualitative study of the intersections of race, religion, and ethnicity in households that are Jewish American and Asian American by married sociologists Helen Kiyong Kim and Noah Samuel Levitt.[59] The "Jews of Color: Histories and Futures" project, led by Mehta at the University of Colorado Boulder, will encourage future studies of the diversity of U.S. Jewish communities.

In the last few years, public attention has increasingly been drawn to Jews' varied approaches and understandings of antisemitism and Zionism. Although there is a substantial historical literature on these topics, as well as an increasing number of community and national sociological and anthropological studies, there is room for religious studies scholars attentive to lived religion to carefully analyze case studies of how Jews enact and understand their Judaism in light of feelings of security and insecurity in the United States and in relation to the State of Israel. There are also an increasing number of excellent studies of U.S. Jews' engagement with sound and music, primarily by ethnomusicologists, and their uses of language, especially by linguists; to date, however, religious studies scholars have been less attentive to these creative forms of expression.

The study of lived religion has opened new avenues of study about what practicing Judaism and embodying Jewish identity look like in the United States. Conversations centered around religion's meaning and, as Orsi writes, "what matters" can offer scholars and non-academic Jews new ways to understand Jews' everyday lives and ritual activities. Although the term "lived religion" may fall out of fashion in the coming years, this approach has given scholars fresh ways to study the objects, food, and media that Jews create, consume, and engage with in their everyday lives and to explore new ways to attend to their marked moments of ritual.

Recommended Readings

Brumberg-Kraus, Jonathan D. *Gastronomic Judaism as Culinary Midrash* (Lexington, 2018).

Crasnow, S. J. "On Transition: Normative Judaism and Trans Innovation," *Journal of Contemporary Religion* 32 (2017): 403–15.

"Editorial Statement," *Material Religion: The Journal of Objects, Art, and Belief* 1 (2005): 4–9.

Eichler-Levine, Jodi. *Painted Pomegranates and Needlepoint Rabbis: How Jews Craft Resilience and Create Community* (University of North Carolina Press, 2020).

Gross, Rachel B. *Beyond the Synagogue: Jewish Nostalgia as Religious Practice* (New York University Press, 2021).

Krone, Adrienne. "Ecological Ethics in the Jewish Community Farming Movement," in *Feasting and Fasting: The History and Ethics of Jewish Food*, ed. Aaron S. Gross et al. (New York University Press, 2020), 273–86.

Krone, Adrienne. "'A Shmita Manifesto': A Radical Sabbatical Approach to Jewish Food Reform in the United States," *Scripta Instituti Donneriani Aboensis* 26 (2015): 303–25.

Mehta, Samira K. *Beyond Chrismukkah: The Christian-Jewish Interfaith Family in the United States* (University of North Carolina Press, 2018).

Myers, Jody. *God's Table: How Foodways Create and Sustain Orthodox Jewish Communities* (Wayne State University Press, 2023).

Ochs, Vanessa L. *Inventing Jewish Ritual* (Jewish Publication Society, 2007).

Rock-Singer, Cara. "Milk Sisters: Forging Sisterhood at Kohenet's Hebrew Priestess Institute," *Nashim: A Journal of Jewish Women's Studies & Gender Issues* 37 (Fall 2020): 87–114.

Thompson, Jennifer A. *Jewish on Their Own Terms: How Intermarried Couples Are Changing American Judaism* (Rutgers University Press, 2014).

Yares, Laura. "The Material Inventories of Millennial Jewish Affective Learning and Consumer Culture at the National Museum of American Jewish History Gift Shop," *Material Religion* 18, no. 2 (2022): 161–81.

Notes

1. Rose Surnow, "Gefilte Fish, Bringing Sexy Back," *Haaretz*, August 1, 2012.

2. See Rachel B. Gross, *Beyond the Synagogue: Jewish Nostalgia as Religious Practice*.

3. See Lila Corwin Berman, Kate Rosenblatt, and Ronit Y. Stahl, "Continuity Crisis: The History and Sexual Politics of an American Jewish Communal Project," *American Jewish History* 104 (2020): 167–94.

4. Edited by David D. Hall (Princeton University Press, 1997).

5. Nancy Tatom Ammerman, *Studying Lived Religion: Contexts and Practices* (New York University Press, 2021), 6.

6. Hall, *Lived Religion,* vii–xiii.

7. Hall, *Lived Religion,* ix.

8. Jonathan Z. Smith, *Relating Religion: Essays in the Study of Religion* (University of Chicago Press, 2004).

9. Tisa Wenger, *Religious Freedom: The Contested History of an American Ideal* (University of North Carolina Press, 2017), 17–18.

10. Robert Orsi, *The Madonna of 115th Street: Faith and Community in Italian Harlem, 1880–1950* (Yale University Press, 1985), xliii.

11. Robert Orsi, *Between Heaven and Earth: The Religious Worlds People Make and the Scholars Who Study Them* (Princeton University Press, 2005), 2.

12. Thomas Tweed, *Crossing and Dwelling: A Theory of Religion* (Harvard University Press, 2006), 54.

13. Leigh Eric Schmidt, *Consuming Religion* (University of Chicago Press, 2017), 5.

14. S. Brent Plate, David Morgan, and Crispin Paine, "Editorial Statement," *Material Religion* 1 (2005): 5.

15. Yale University Press, 1995.

16. *Consuming Religion.*

17. Cecile Esther Kuznitz, *Yivo and the Making of Modern Jewish Culture* (Cambridge University Press, 2014), 18.

18. Nathaniel Deutsch, *The Jewish Dark Continent: Life and Death in the Russian Pale of Settlement* (Harvard University Press, 2011), 1.

19. *Going to the People: Jews and the Ethnographic Impulse* (Indiana University Press, 2016), 1–24.

20. Deutsch, *Jewish Dark Continent,* 12.

21. Jeffrey Veidlinger, *Going to the People* (Indiana University Press, 2016), 2.

22. E. P. Dutton.

23. Riv-Ellen Prell, "Barbara Myerhoff," in *Shalvi/Hyman Encyclopedia of Jewish Women,* 2009, online at jwa.org.

24. Laura Levitt, "Impossible Assimilations, American Liberalism, and Jewish Difference: Revisiting Jewish Secularism," *American Quarterly* 59 (2007): 807–32; Leora Batnitzky, *How*

Judaism Became a Religion: An Introduction to Modern Jewish Thought (Princeton University Press, 2011).

25. Matthew Frye Jacobson, *Roots Too: White Ethnic Revival in Post-Civil Rights America* (Harvard University Press, 2006).

26. Gross, *Beyond the Synagogue*.

27. *Jews on the Frontier: Religion and Mobility in Nineteenth-Century America* (New York University Press, 2019).

28. *Jewish Sunday Schools: Teaching Religion in Nineteenth-Century America* New York University Press, 2023).

29. *The Lives of Jessie Sampter: Queer, Disabled, Zionist* (Duke University Press, 2022).

30. "What Makes a Jewish Home Jewish?" *CrossCurrents* 49 (1999/2000): 491–503.

31. University of North Carolina Press, 2020.

32. "The Material Inventories of Millennial Jewish Affective Learning."

33. New York University Press, 2018.

34. *Framing Sukkot: Tradition and Transformation in Jewish Vernacular Architecture* (Indiana University Press, 2017).

35. Leonard Norman Primiano, "Vernacular Religion and the Search for Method in Religious Folklife," *Western Folklore* 54 (1995): 37–56.

36. Jewish Publication Society, 2007.

37. Benjamin E. Zeller, et al. *Religion, Food, and Eating in North America* (Columbia University Press, 2014).

38. Palgrave, 2001.

39. *Gastronomic Judaism as Culinary Midrash*.

40. Adrienne Krone, "'A Shmita Manifesto': A Radical Sabbatical Approach to Jewish Food Reform in the United States," and "Ecological Ethics in the Jewish Community Farming Movement."

41. *Beyond the Synagogue*.

42. *God's Table: How Foodways Create and Sustain Orthodox Jewish Communities*.

43. Feldman, Rachel and Ayala Fader, "Illiberal Jewish-Christian Encounters: Political Temporalities in Amish Country Tourism." *Journal of the American Academy of Religion* 92 (2024): 62–87.

44. New York University Press, 2013.

45. University of California Press, 2010.

46. *Jews, God, and Videotape: Religion and Media in America* (New York University Press, 2009).

47. "'Saturday Night Seder' and the Affordances of Jewish Cultural Arts during COVID-19," *Contemporary Jewry* 41 (2020): 3–22.

48. Jeremy Stolow, *Orthodox by Design* (University of California Press, 2010), 125.

49. Berman et al., "Continuity Crisis."

50. *Jewish on Their Own Terms: How Intermarried Couples Are Changing American Judaism*.

51. *Beyond Chrismukkah: The Christian-Jewish Interfaith Family in the United States*.

52. *American JewBu: Jews, Buddhists, and Religious Change* (Princeton University Press, 2019).

53. *Kabbalah and the Spiritual Quest: The Kabbalah Centre in America* (Praeger, 2007).

54. "Milk Sisters," = and "On the Altar of *Shekhina*: The Kohenet Hebrew Priestess Institute and the Gendered Politics of Jewish Revival," in *Jewish Revival Inside Out: Remaking Jewishness in a Transnational Age*, ed. D. Moterescu and R. Werczberger (Wayne State University Press), 245–68.

55. "On Transition: Normative Judaism and Trans Innovation," *Journal of Contemporary Religion* 32 (2017): 403–15.

56. *Race and Religion among the Chosen Peoples of Crown Heights* (Rutgers University Press, 2006).

57. "Lineage Matters: DNA, Race, and Gene Talk in Judaism and Messianic Judaism," *Religion and American Culture* 27 (2017): 95–127.

58. "Asian American Jews, Race, and Religious Identity," *Journal of the American Academy of Religion* 89 (2021): 972–1005.

59. *JewAsian: Race, Religion, and Identity for America's Newest Jews* (University of Nebraska Press, 2016).

15

Language

Sarah Bunin Benor, Hebrew Union College—Jewish Institute of Religion

LANGUAGE IS CENTRAL to social life. Through our words, pronunciations, and grammar, we communicate not only conversational content but also social information. We align ourselves with some people and distinguish ourselves from others, expressing multiple allegiances sometimes even within the same sentence. Members of diasporic, ethnic, and religious groups tap into multiple repertoires of linguistic features that indicate both their unique traits and their commonalities with those outside their group. These features might include elements of ancestral languages and dialects that reflect historical migration patterns or words for cultural practices and orientations important to the group.

Jews—a diverse religious, diasporic, and multiethnic group—participate in these trends. Through language, they have indicated their multiple allegiances: as residents of and (to varying extents) integrated into the surrounding society and as constituting a distinct communal entity and subgroups, inspired by ancient texts and ancestral migration patterns. In most locations throughout the Jewish diaspora, Jews have spoken a variant of the language of their non-Jewish neighbors, distinguished to varying extents. In a few communities, they have maintained a language that originated elsewhere, incorporating influences from the languages of their new non-Jewish neighbors. And in modern Israel, they embraced a re-vernacularized version of their ancient language, Hebrew. In all these contexts, Jews have regularly modulated their language, using more or fewer textual and other Jewish features depending on audience, topic, and genre.

This chapter offers an introduction to the history of Jewish languages, their distinctive features, and their contemporary use. It weaves in findings and trends from scholarship on how Jews use language and theoretical understandings of what constitutes a "Jewish language." By analyzing the cultural domain of language, Jewish Studies scholars gain insight into the inner lives of Jews, their relations with non-Jews, and the commonalities and diversity of Jews around the world.

Naming Jewish Languages

Although some scholars consider language varieties to be "Jewish languages" only if they are written in Hebrew letters or are mutually unintelligible to their non-Jewish neighbors, others find these criteria limiting (see more on this later). Recent research has argued that contemporary Jews are continuing the diasporic linguistic practices of previous eras by speaking Jewish varieties of their local languages, even if these language varieties are not written in Hebrew letters and are intelligible to local non-Jews. Whether some Jewish communities are seen as speaking separate languages or just dialects of the local language, Jewish Studies scholars can learn a great deal by including all Jewish communities— past and present—in the comparative study of Jewish languages. Therefore, this chapter takes an expansive approach, including in the category "Jewish language" any language variety spoken or written by Jews that differs to some extent from the surrounding non-Jewish language variety. It offers examples not only from long-standing Jewish languages like Judeo-Arabic and Bukharian (Judeo-Tajik) but also from new Jewish languages like Jewish Russian and Jewish Swedish. New Jewish languages are generally called "Jewish X," rather than the more archaic term "Judeo-X."

Each Jewish language has been referred to in multiple ways by various people and at various times. A common appellation has been variants of the word "Jew," "Jewish," or "Judaism," such as *Yiddish*, *Juhuri* (Judeo-Tat, spoken in Azerbaijan and Dagestan), *Al-Yahudiyya* (Judeo-Arabic), *Judezmo* (Ladino/Judeo-Spanish), and *Hulaula* (Jewish Neo-Aramaic, from *Y'hudautha*). Words meaning "our language" have also been common, such as *Lishana Deni* and *Lishanet Noshan* for Jewish Neo-Aramaic and *Zuhun Imu* for Juhuri. Rabbinic literature in Hebrew often referred to Jewish languages as *La'az*, meaning "foreign language"—for example, the many Old French translations of Hebrew words in Rashi's commentaries—to contrast them with Hebrew. Several languages were also referred to with a variant of the name of their non-Jewish correlate, such as *Taytsh* (German) for Yiddish and *Spanyol* (Spanish) for Ladino. We also find hyphenated versions, equivalent to Judeo-X or Jewish X, such as *Yiddish-Taytsh* (Jewish German) and modern academic appellations for most languages in English, Hebrew, and other languages of scholarship. Taken together, these language names suggest that insiders and outsiders have viewed Jewish languages either as distinctly Jewish, related to their non-Jewish correlate, or a combination of the two.

History

The history of Jewish languages is marked by empire change, expulsions, and migrations. Originally speaking Hebrew, the Jews gradually learned Aramaic when the Babylonian and Persian Empires controlled Palestine. They learned it because of their forced migration to Babylon and economic and cultural pressure to speak the more prestigious language in the Holy Land. But Jews' Aramaic was heavily influenced by Hebrew, to such an extent that the language of some biblical and rabbinic texts can be classified as Judeo-Aramaic. This influence came in part from the earliest bilingual Hebrew-Aramaic speakers but continued over the centuries because Jews maintained Hebrew for liturgical purposes— the recitation and study of biblical texts and prayers. The influence of Aramaic can also be seen in the writing system: The Aramaic alphabet replaced Paleo-Hebrew symbols and continues to be used as the alphabet we know today as Hebrew.

Subsequent empire changes and migrations led to Jews speaking Judeo-Greek, Judeo-Persian, and Judeo-Arabic and, later, Judeo-Italian, Judeo-Georgian, and several other "Judeo-" languages throughout the Middle East, North Africa, Europe, and Western Asia. Like Judeo-Aramaic, these Jewish variants were similar to the surrounding languages but were influenced to varying extents by Hebrew (and Aramaic) and usually were written in Hebrew letters. They sometimes differed in other ways by using distinctive pronunciations or grammatical features. These linguistic differences were caused by both internal and external factors. Internal factors included Jews studying biblical and rabbinic texts; reciting blessings, prayers, and songs in Jewish ritual contexts; and wanting to maintain some degree of separation from the surrounding society. External factors included restrictions on Jewish participation in specific professions or institutions, especially educational systems. Wherever Jews lived, their speech and writing reflected that the Jewish community was both a part of and apart from the local society.

The two most famous diaspora Jewish languages, Yiddish and Ladino, are exceptions in this history, because they are *post-coterritorial*, meaning they were maintained away from their lands of origin. Jews who spoke Western Yiddish, also known as Judeo-German, moved eastward from areas where their neighbors also spoke varieties of German to areas where their neighbors spoke Slavic and other languages, including Czech, Polish, Belarusian, and Hungarian. Rather than adopt those languages for day-to-day in-group communication, they maintained their Germanic language and incorporated influences—words, pronunciations, and grammatical features—from the new local languages. Similarly, Jews who were expelled from Spain in the late fifteenth century moved to other regions, including Morocco, Turkey, and Greece: Rather than adopting Arabic, Turkish, Greek, and other new local languages, they maintained their Judeo-Spanish for centuries. Even so, they had some knowledge of those languages, and gradually, some words—especially from the dominant Ottoman Turkish and Moroccan Arabic—became part of Judeo-Spanish, also known as Ladino, Judezmo, Spanyol, and, in North Africa, Haketia.

In addition to Yiddish and Ladino, several Jewish languages have differed so much from the local non-Jewish correlate that Jews and non-Jews could not understand each other's (in-group) language. In some cases, this was because Jews gradually changed their language, and in other cases it was because Jews maintained their language when their non-Jewish neighbors shifted to a different language. For example, in the Kurdish region of Iran, Iraq, and Turkey, Jews and Christians in the same town sometimes spoke varieties of Neo-Aramaic that were mutually unintelligible. Similarly, Juhuri is different enough from Muslim Tat that Muslims and Jews cannot understand each other. Recent scholarship conceptualizes Jewish communities as located along a continuum of linguistic distinctness: Some spoke very similarly to their non-Jewish neighbors, and others spoke very differently. For example, in Damascus, Judeo-Arabic and Muslim Arabic were generally mutually intelligible, but in Baghdad, they were often not.

Distinctive Features

Jews' language has differed from that of their non-Jewish neighbors because of several factors. Their reverence for and maintenance of sacred texts—the Bible and rabbinic literature—in their original languages led to Hebrew and Aramaic influences, especially words and the writing system. Jews' historical migrations led to influences from languages spoken in previous locations along their journey. They often had contact with various groups of non-Jews, leading to influences from their languages. In addition, they often maintained contact with Jews in other regions of their current language territory, or they migrated within that territory and were influenced by other regional dialects of their current language. And although their integration into the surrounding society was reflected in their use of local languages, their insularity led to both archaic linguistic features—when local non-Jews changed an aspect of their language and Jews did not—and innovative linguistic features when Jews changed an aspect of their language and non-Jews did not.

Hebrew and Aramaic Influences

The most common and salient distinctive feature of Jewish languages is the presence of words from Hebrew and Aramaic. Throughout history, most Jewish communities maintained a situation of diglossia—the stable communal use of two languages for different purposes; They spoke various vernaculars while studying and praying in Hebrew and Aramaic. Therefore, it is not surprising that these languages would influence the spoken languages. Hebrew and Aramaic words are especially common when referring to concepts not found in the local non-Jewish language, such as Jewish rituals, holidays, and halakhic (Jewish legal) constructs. Sometimes different languages refer to the same concept with different Hebrew or non-Hebrew words. For example, the holiday of Tu Bishvat, the new year of the trees, is called *mooedeh ilanoot* (holiday of the trees) in Judeo-Persian, *khamishoser* (fifteen) in Yiddish, *mzade 'ilane* (gift of the trees) in Hulaula, and various forms of *Tu Bishvat* (fifteenth of the Jewish month of Shevat) in some other languages, such as *tubizvat* in Judeo-Italian and *tubisbat* in Judeo-Arabic and Haketia. Some languages use words not from Hebrew or Aramaic, such as *fǝth ǝl-ʿúd* (blossoming of the dry tree) in Tunisian Judeo-Arabic, *shbídi pherobá* (seven species) in Judeo-Georgian, *meva xūri* (fruit eating) in Bukharian, and *las frutas* (the fruits) in Ladino.

Hebrew and Aramaic words are not limited to concepts distinctive to Jewish communities: They are also used for referents that do have non-Jewish correlates. Especially common are euphemisms for taboo concepts like body parts and death, such as *rimonim* (pomegranates, breasts) and *beth axaim* (house of life, cemetery) in Judeo-Greek. Another common use of Hebrew/Aramaic words is for secretive language referring to non-Jews and their holidays and religious figures. The word *arel*, meaning uncircumcised, is used in many Jewish languages to refer to "non-Jew" in general or "Christian" in particular. Muhammad is known as *mashugga* in several varieties of Judeo-Arabic and *misiga* in Judeo-Borujerdi (a non-Persian language spoken in Iran)—variants of the Hebrew word for "crazy," which is how Muhammad is characterized in some medieval Hebrew texts. Hebrew and Aramaic words are even used for interjections and adverbs that have equivalents in the local non-Jewish language. Examples include *bekitser* (briefly, in sum) and *teykef-umeyad* (immediately) in Western Yiddish; *afillu* (even so) and *vadday* (of course) in Haketia; and *avade* (of course) and *mamash* (to a high degree) in Jewish English.

When Hebrew words are used within other languages, they are integrated to varying degrees into the grammatical system of the target language. Nouns generally use Hebrew plurals, such as *sefarim* for *sefer* (book, Torah, or any book of the Jewish religious canon) in many languages, but sometimes they use the plural system of the local language, such as *mazamir* for *mizmor* (song) in Judeo-Arabic. Verbs can be integrated directly, such as Judeo-Italian *gannavi* (she steals) from Hebrew g*anav* (steal), or they can be integrated using a helping verb, such as Juhuri *monuho birɛ* (to die), which combines Hebrew *menuḥa* (rest) with Tat *birɛ* (to be). Many Jewish languages have instances of both systems.

In addition, the pronunciation of Hebrew words is influenced by the local language and by various historical Hebrew pronunciation traditions, so that even though Jews around the world use many common words, they pronounce them differently. Several historical Hebrew sounds, including those represented by *ʿayin* (ע), *waw* (ו), *teth* (ט), and *thaw* (ת), differ significantly, as do gemination (consonant doubling), stress, and vowels. For example, the Hebrew word *moʿed* (holiday) is pronounced *moʿēd* in Judeo-Arabic, *moqédi* in Judeo-Georgian, *mongéd* or *monyédde* in Judeo-Italian, *mwed* in Ladino, and *móyed* in Yiddish. The Hebrew word *tallit* (prayer shawl) is *ṭallít* or *tallét* in Judeo-Arabic and Jewish Neo-Aramaic, *taléd* or *taléde* in Judeo-Italian, *talé* in Ladino, and *tális* in Yiddish. Some Jewish languages include sounds not used by local non-Jews, especially in Hebrew-origin words, such as *ḥet* and *ʿayin* in Bukharian and Jewish Neo-Aramaic and [x] (spelled "ch" or "kh") in Jewish English (from Yiddish and Hebrew *chet* and *chaf*).

In some cases, Jews use a Hebrew word in combination with a non-Hebrew word that has the same meaning. Examples include *helluf-ḥazir* (pig, lit. pig-pig) in Judeo-Arabic from Sefrou, Morocco; *mayim akhroynim vaser* (hand-washing after meal, lit. last water water) in Yiddish; and *boni mangasim tovim* (good deeds, lit. good good deeds) in Judeo-Italian. Doubled phrases like these are sometimes used for emphasis or to indicate that the Hebrew word has changed in meaning or use. They might also demonstrate some speakers' low awareness that they are using Hebrew and non-Hebrew words with the same meaning.

From the twentieth century onward, Hebrew has also influenced Jewish languages through an additional source: Modern Israeli Hebrew. We see this in the many languages spoken by immigrants to Israel, including Jewish versions of Amharic and Russian. However, we also see it in new Jewish languages spoken in the diaspora, like Jewish English and Jewish Latin American Spanish. For example, Jewish Swedish includes Modern Hebrew words like *hadracha* (leadership), *dati* (religious), and *göra mangal* (to make a barbecue). Modern Hebrew also provides pronunciation norms for contemporary Jewish languages, such as pronouncing *het* as [x], which is higher in the throat than the historical [ḥ], and deleting the *shva-na* between two initial consonants, as in *psukim* (verses) and *brit* (covenant) in Jewish English, rather than *pesukim* and *berit* (both Yiddish influences on Modern Hebrew).

The Hebrew/Aramaic texts of the Jewish tradition also influence spoken languages through translation, because many Jewish languages include direct translations of Hebrew phrases. In Egyptian Judeo-Arabic, translations of Hebrew texts mark the definite direct object with *ilā* to translate the Hebrew direct object marker *et*; for example, *kullǝna ʿarfīn ʾila š-šariʿa* (all of us are learned in the Torah), a translation of *kulanu yodʿim et ha-Torah* from the Passover Haggadah; other varieties of Arabic would not include the underlined word. In some cases, direct translations can also be found in spoken Jewish languages, such as the Jewish English phrases "may her memory be for a blessing" and "the world to come," translations of Hebrew *zichronah livrachah* and *ʿolam ha-ba* that sound odd in non-Jewish English.

Textual Influence in Writing

Hebrew/Aramaic texts have historically provided a writing system for many Jewish languages. Most Jewish languages that arose in the Middle Ages were and continue to be written in Hebrew/Aramaic characters. Here is an example from a Judeo-Italian prayerbook from the early sixteenth century:

דּוֹמֵידַית פּוֹרְטֶיצִי אֶלוֹ פּוֹפּוֹלוֹ סוּאוֹ דָּרַה דּוֹמֵידַית בִּינִידִיצִירָה לוֹ פּוֹפּוֹלוֹ סוּאוֹ אִין פָּאצִי
Domedet fortezze allo popolo suo darà Domedet benedicerà lo popolo suo en pace

This is a translation of the Hebrew verse from Psalms 29:11: "May the Lord grant strength to His people; may the Lord bless His people with peace." Vowels are represented not only by the diacritic markings (*nikkud*) but also by the Hebrew characters *waw, yod, alef,* and *hey*. Eastern Yiddish uses a similar system, but *ayin* represents the [e] sound, and various combinations of consonants are used for sounds that do not exist in Hebrew, such as *zayin-shin* for [zh] (like *je* in French). Eastern Yiddish also uses other distinctive combinations of characters, such as a double *vov* representing [v]. Here is an example from twentieth-century Yiddish poet Celia Dropkin, with the *ayin*, double *vov*, and *zayin-shin* bolded:

עאיך בין **א** צירקוס דאַמ

Ikh bin a tsirkus dame

I am a circus lady

אַלן **זש** ישן קין **וו** און טאַנץ צ

Un tants tsvishn kinzhaln

And dance between daggers

Jewish writing systems tend to change over time. For example, in different eras, Judeo-Arabic writing reflected to various degrees the Arabic writing system, the Hebrew writing system, or the actual pronunciation. In some cases, diacritics were added to Hebrew letters, based on similar diacritics in Arabic, such as צ̇ for ض [ḍ], ק̇ for ق [q], and פ̇ for ف [f]. Some long-standing Jewish languages, such as Judeo-Georgian and Jewish Malayalam, were historically written in the local alphabets, not Hebrew letters. Languages that Jews acquired during modern times, such as Jewish English, Jewish Hungarian, and Jewish Russian, are generally written in their local alphabets because of more universal education and literacy.

Other Contact Languages

In addition to Hebrew and Aramaic, some Jewish languages exhibit influences from other historical Jewish languages, reflecting more recent migration patterns. In Ladino, the word for "to read Torah" is *meldar*, an influence from an ancient language spoken by the ancestors of Ladino speakers: (Judeo-)Greek *meletaō* or (Judeo-)Latin *meletare*. The Ladino word for "Sunday" is *alhad*, from *al-ḥadd*, which is from the (Judeo-)Arabic spoken in the Iberian Peninsula before Spanish was the dominant language, enabling Jews to avoid calling Sunday *domingo* (Lord). For similar reasons of intentional distinction, the Yiddish word *bentsh* (bless) comes from a Romance language spoken by the ancestors of some

Yiddish speakers—likely (Judeo-)Italian *benedice*—because Jews wanted to avoid the German word *segenen*, which means not only "bless" but also "make the sign" (of the cross). Contemporary languages that are closer to the generation of mass migration exhibit much more influence from ancestral Jewish languages. For example, Jewish English has many words and grammatical influences from Yiddish, and Jewish French has many words from North African Judeo-Arabic.

Ancestral languages also influence the Hebrew/Aramaic component of Jewish languages, including which words are used, how they are pronounced, and how they are integrated into the grammatical structure of the new language. This is particularly evident in contemporary languages. Jewish English includes many Hebrew words that are influenced by Yiddish, the language spoken by a large percentage of Jewish immigrants to English-speaking countries. Examples include *shaleshudes* (third meal of Shabbat, from *shalosh seudot*, three meals), *taleysim* (prayer shawls), and *pasken* (render a halakhic decision). These Hebrew-origin words are influenced in their pronunciation, morphology, and meanings by their parallel forms in Yiddish. One Yiddish and Jewish English word, *sheygets* (non-Jewish male, from Hebrew *sheqeṣ*—abomination), reflects historical influence from Judeo-French: The consonant in the middle of the Hebrew word *sheqeṣ* changed from [k] to [g] in line with similar changes in medieval French. The word was maintained by German-speaking Jews and was passed down through Eastern Yiddish to Jewish English.

Other languages spoken nearby also provide influences. Yiddish and Ladino (post-coterritorial languages) include words and grammatical features from the new coterritoral languages: Polish, Belarusian, Hungarian, and others in the case of Yiddish; and Turkish, Greek, Serbo-Croatian, and others in the case of Ottoman Ladino. Many Jewish languages were spoken in multilingual regions, and their lexicons particularly reflect that contact. Juhuri, for example, includes words from Turkic languages like Azeri and Kumyk, as well as Persian, Arabic, and, more recently, Russian. Jewish Neo-Aramaic includes structural influences from Kurdish and Azeri Turkish in word order and pronunciation. In one area of the Kurdish region, the word "they" is *diyey* among Christians but *dohun* among Jews, and what Christians pronounce as [th] and [dh] (as in "think" and "this") becomes [l] among Jews—both influences on Aramaic from other regional languages, reflecting the differential exposure to these languages among Christians and Jews. This sound change is why the language is called *Hulaula*, stemming from *Y'hudautha*, meaning Jewish.

International languages of prestige also influence Jewish languages. In the nineteenth and twentieth centuries, the Alliance Israélite Universelle and other organizations established schools throughout the Middle East and Mediterranean regions, including Morocco, Tunisia, Turkey, and Iran; the language of instruction was either French or Italian. These new situations of language contact resulted in lexical influences from French and Italian on local Jewish languages like Ladino, Judeo-Arabic, Judeo-Median (non-Persian languages spoken in Iran), and Judeo-Persian.

Migrated Regionalisms

Another feature common in many Jewish languages is migrated regionalisms: dialectal features from one region used in a different region, where the same language is spoken in both regions. Migrated regionalisms reflect two trends: historical migrations of Jews from one region to another within a given language territory, and past and present contact between Jewish communities. Examples include a plural article from southern Italy used in Judeo-Italian in central and northern Italy, a verb form from Morocco and a plural form from Baghdad found in Judeo-Arabic in Cairo, and New York pronunciations like "orange" as "ahrange" used in Jewish English in other parts of the United States. Another instance of this phenomenon is Jewish varieties of Neo-Aramaic in towns around Kurdistan that resemble each other more than the language of nearby non-Jews. Table 1 gives some vocabulary in three Jewish communities and one Christian community, all within a small radius. Most are similar or identical in the Jewish dialects but quite different in the Christian dialect. This similarity likely reflects contact and migration between the Jewish towns.

TABLE 1. Christian and Jewish Neo-Aramaic in four towns in Kurdistan

	Christian-Barwar	Jewish-Betanure	Jewish-Amedia	Jewish-Nerwa
now	*diya, hadiya*	*ʾatta*	*ʾatta*	*ʾatta*
tomorrow	*təmməl*	*bənhe*	*qadöme*	*qadome*
big	*goṛa*	*ʾəṛwa*	*ʾuṛwa*	*ʾuṛwa*
to stand	*klaya*	*ḥmala*	*ḥmala*	*ḥmala*

Archaic Features

Another way that Jews distinguish their language is by preserving archaic features that local non-Jews have stopped using. An example is Jewish Malayalam (and its Muslim correlate), which retains the dative case marker -*ikkə*, even though it disappeared in Christian and Hindu Malayalam in the fifteenth century. Cairo Judeo-Arabic uses the verbal pattern *fuʿul*, whereas the standard Egyptian dialect replaced it with *fiʿil*. In Yefren, Libya, the historical Arabic [q] sound (like a [k] but lower in the throat) is retained in most words, but local Muslims have changed that sound to [g]. Archaisms are especially common in post-coterritorial languages. Some dialects of Ladino, for example, retain the Latin-origin [f] at the beginning of words, as in *fazer* (to do/make), but Spanish around the world changed that sound to [h] and then deleted it, as in *hacer*. Although archaic features are common, it is inaccurate to say that Jews tend to preserve older forms of the language. It is clear from the multilingual influences discussed earlier that Jews' language is not an exact replica of an earlier non-Jewish language. In addition, Jews distinguish their languages in other ways, thereby creating not only archaisms but also innovations.

Innovative Features

Jews' language can differ from that of their non-Jewish neighbors (or the non-Jewish neighbors of their ancestors in the case of post-coterritorial languages) in various ways in addition to the features already discussed. These differences can be quite minor, or they can be as significant as a completely different system of pronunciation and grammar. Judeo-Georgian has few structural differences from Georgian, but some words and intonation (pitch patterns) are used in distinctive ways. For instance, the Georgian word *jamaati* means "a mass gathering," but in Judeo-Georgian it also refers to "a *minyan* (prayer quorum)." And in Kutaisi, a city in western Georgia, Jews and non-Jews can often guess who is Jewish based on their intonation in asking questions. Yiddish has many structural differences from German, such as in word order, case, and pronunciation: These innovations are not attributable to language contact or archaism. An example of independent innovation in Ladino is the switching of the sounds [rd] to [dr]; for example, *vedre* compared to Spanish *verde* (green).

Another area of innovation is avoiding elements of the surrounding language that seem un-Jewish (too Christian, Muslim, etc.) and instead using distinctive

342 CHAPTER 15

Jewish words: This phenomenon is referred to as *l'havdil* (distinguishing) language. In many cases the words selected are from Hebrew, Aramaic, or other Jewish languages, such as the Ladino *alhad* and Yiddish *bentsh*, discussed earlier. Sometimes, however, *l'havdil* words come from the base language. Two examples are found in Jewish Amharic, which lacks the other distinctive features discussed earlier because Jews in Ethiopia did not recite or study Hebrew and Aramaic texts or maintain contact with other Jewish communities. Orthodox Christian Amharic speakers mention Mary when congratulating a woman who has recently given birth: *ankwan Maryam marāččaš* (it is good that Mary has pardoned you). Jews avoid this Christian reference, instead opting for *ankwan agzi'abher bäsälam gälag-gäläš* (it is good that God has relieved you peacefully). Similarly, Ethiopian Jews call a particular grasshopper *ya-muse faras* (Moses's horse), whereas Christians call it *ya-maryam faras* (Mary's horse). Moses also appears in entomological terminology in Yiddish in another instance of *l'havdil* language: A term for ladybug is *moyshe rabeynes kíele* (Moses Our Teacher's little cow), a Judaized version of similar terms for ladybug in other influencer languages, such as Russian (God's cow) and German (Mary's beetle).

Variation

Jewish languages can have more or fewer distinctive linguistic features depending on several sociopolitical factors. A major factor is to what extent Jews in a particular community are integrated socially, economically, and educationally with their non-Jewish neighbors or are restricted to certain professions, residential areas, and schools. This can affect whether Jews maintain a language, as in postcoterritorial languages like Ladino and Yiddish, or learn the new local language soon after migration. It can also influence whether Jews use archaic and innovative features. Influences from other languages and regional variants spoken by Jews can correlate with how much time has elapsed since Jews' migration from a different language territory and with how much contact they maintain with other Jewish communities. In addition, the extent to which Jews study and recite sacred texts plays a role in Hebrew/Aramaic influences and writing systems.

Linguistic distinctness can also change over time. Research suggests that when Jews migrate to a new country or language area, they tend to acquire that language to a large degree and then, over time, the community's language often becomes more and more distinct from the local non-Jewish language. We see this trend playing out in Jewish English today. Younger Jews are more likely than older Jews to use some influences from Yiddish, such as the word *by* meaning

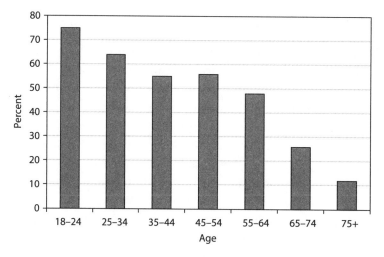

FIGURE 1. Percentage of Orthodox Jews who report saying "staying by us" (meaning "at our house"), by age

"at," rather than just "near." This trend is especially common in Orthodox communities (Figure 1).

Age is not the only variable that correlates with inter-speaker variation—language diversity between individuals—within a particular Jewish community. Jews who have more contact with their non-Jewish neighbors tend to speak more similarly to them. Those who spend more time studying sacred Jewish texts tend to use more Hebrew and Aramaic words. Gender and socioeconomic status can lead to language diversity, because boys and those with more means are often given more intensive Jewish education. Therefore, scholars studying historical periods should not assume that all community members spoke the same way that elite men wrote in the texts that have survived. In addition, Jews from various ancestral origins might maintain elements of their ancestral languages that do not spread to the rest of the community, such as Jews with Ladino-speaking ancestry using *bragas* (underwear) and *lonso* (bear, stupid person) in Jewish English.

Finally, we see intra-speaker variation: Individual Jews vary linguistically, depending on their setting, topic, and, especially, audience. When speaking to another Jew about a Jewish-specific topic in a Jewish communal context, they will likely use more distinctive Jewish features. They might not be aware of or able to modulate all features that distinguish them from non-Jews, but they likely code-switch to some extent.

Non-Jews' Use of Jewish Language

Although the linguistic features described earlier generally distinguish Jews from their non-Jewish neighbors, these features have sometimes spread beyond the Jewish community. This has been especially common in professions dominated by Jews, such as goldsmiths in Egypt, furriers in Italy, and horse and cattle dealers in Switzerland and Germany. Jews in these professions began using Hebrew and Aramaic words with each other as a means of speaking secretively in a way that their customers would not understand, and then their language developed into a broader professional jargon that came to be used also by their Christian and Muslim colleagues. In Alexandria, Egypt, Jewish goldsmiths used Hebrew words like *ganneb* (thief, from *ganav*) and *enaymak* (look out, from *enayim*—eyes), and these words became part of the broader goldsmiths' jargon, including among Muslim and Christian practitioners.

Beyond the professional domain, Jewish-origin words have sometimes become part of the broader language. Judeo-Greek words of Hebrew origin, such as *emeth* (truth), and *pasal* (fool, originally "unacceptable") became part of colloquial Greek, especially in Ioannina where the Judeo-Greek-speaking Jewish community was centered. In the Netherlands today, the Dutch population uses Hebrew-origin words that entered Dutch through Western Yiddish. They refer to prison as *bayis* (from Hebrew *bayit*—house) and Amsterdam as *mokum* (from Hebrew *makom alef*—place A—because Amsterdam starts with A or *alef*). This trend can also be seen in the United States today, where Yiddish-origin words like *klutz* and *chutzpah* have spread beyond Jewish English to the broader population.

In addition to select words diffusing beyond Jewish communities, there is also historical evidence of select non-Jews becoming proficient speakers of Jewish languages. Some Muslims in Iran could speak Jewish varieties of Iranian languages, and, in parts of Eastern Europe, some Christian nannies who worked for Jewish families picked up Yiddish and even taught Hebrew prayers to Jewish children. Studying instances like these sheds light on the diversity of relations between Jews and non-Jews and the porous boundaries at times between communities.

Jewish Language Shift, Endangerment, and Post-Vernacularity

Throughout the centuries, some Jewish languages, such as Judeo-French and Judeo-Catalan, became obsolete as Jews emigrated or shifted to more prestigious languages. The nineteenth and twentieth centuries saw major shifts in Jews' language use caused by their emancipation and the Enlightenment, as well as by governments that implemented nationalist policies requiring official languages for education. Jews in Italy, Greece, and Iran, for example, learned standard Italian, Greek, and Persian, gradually reducing the distinctive features of their long-standing Jewish language varieties. Another major factor in language shift during this period was massive waves of immigration, sparked by persecution and economic factors. When Jews moved from Central and Eastern Europe, North Africa, the Middle East, and Asia to the Americas, Israel, Western Europe, and elsewhere, they felt economic and social pressure to learn the new local languages—English, French, Spanish, and so on. As in previous centuries, Jews spoke these languages with Hebrew words and other distinctive features, but in most cases, they did not write them with Hebrew letters because of more widespread literacy. In Israel, language policies required immigrants to learn Modern Hebrew, and diaspora languages were stigmatized and disincentivized. The Holocaust also led to language changes, when millions of speakers of Yiddish, Ladino, Judeo-Italian, Judeo-Greek, and Krymchak (Crimean Judeo-Turkic) were murdered.

Today, most long-standing Jewish languages are endangered, spoken primarily by the elderly, and not transmitted from parent to child. The major exception is Yiddish, which is vibrant in Hasidic communities around the world. In addition, young people in one town, Qırmızı Qəsəbə, Azerbaijan, still speak Juhuri, but they all also speak other languages. The endangerment of most long-standing Jewish languages has led to some "post-vernacular engagement": people engaging with and celebrating a language even when they have limited speaking ability. Jews in Rome attend theatrical performances in Judeo-Italian, and Jews in several countries sing and listen to songs in Ladino, for instance. Israeli Jews of various ages participate in nostalgic, metalinguistic activities surrounding their ancestral Judeo-Arabic, Jewish Neo-Aramaic, and Jewish Malayalam, including singalongs, lectures and conversations about the languages, and language classes. Post-vernacular Yiddish can be found in Ashkenazi communities around the world, such as in song, comedy, material culture, and language learning; many non-Jews also participate in post-vernacular Yiddish activities, especially in Europe.

Hebrew throughout History

So far, this chapter has discussed how Hebrew has influenced diaspora Jewish languages, but when and how have Jews used Hebrew itself? Hebrew was the primary spoken language of the Israelites, and ancient Jewish texts are written in various forms of Hebrew, including Biblical and Mishnaic. Since the (gradual) shift to Aramaic in antiquity, most Jewish communities maintained a situation of diglossia, speaking various vernaculars while studying and praying in Hebrew and Aramaic. Elite Jews, mostly men, also wrote in Hebrew and Aramaic, including in letters to Jews across linguistic boundaries, business and communal records, and legal documents such as *ketubot* for marriage and *gitin* for divorce. Throughout the Middle Ages and early modern period, Hebrew writing was influenced by local languages and by admiration for various earlier forms of Hebrew.

One of the most significant changes in Jewish linguistic history was the "revival" of Hebrew in the late nineteenth and early twentieth centuries, which led to the decline of most long-standing Jewish languages. The Hebrew revival is more accurately characterized as "re-vernacularization": Jews in Palestine began to learn the language not just for prayer, study, and writing but also as an everyday language of communication, and subsequently transmitted it to their children. The re-vernacularization drew on European nationalist language ideologies, Enlightenment Hebrew literary productivity, and a history of Jews from diverse linguistic communities using basic spoken and written Hebrew as a lingua franca. The process was facilitated by large waves of Jewish immigration from multiple locations to Palestine, corpus planners like Eliezer Ben-Yehuda, and schools and other organizations dedicated to promoting Hebrew.

Although ideological revivalists disincentivized the use of Yiddish, Ladino, Judeo-Arabic, and other languages spoken by Jews, these languages, especially Yiddish, ultimately influenced Modern Hebrew in many ways. For example, the word *chanukia* (Chanukah menorah) comes from Ladino, and *ko'ev li ha-beten* ("my stomach hurts," lit. "hurts [masc.] me the stomach [fem.]") imitates Yiddish *es tut mir vey der boykh* (lit. "it hurts me the stomach"). In part because of influences from non-Hebrew languages, contemporary Israelis often misunderstand elements of biblical and rabbinic literature. For example, in Biblical Hebrew, the word צְלִיל (as in Judges 7:13) would be pronounced *tsəliyl* and means "bread," but in Modern Hebrew it is pronounced *tslil* and means "sound." The differences are so significant that some linguists call the language "Israeli Hebrew" rather than "Modern Hebrew." Even so, most Israelis consider their language a continuation of the Hebrew language spoken by their ancient ancestors and used in sacred contexts by their more recent forebears. Because of the engineered nature of re-vernacularization, Modern Hebrew and Biblical/Rabbinic Hebrew are more similar to each other than the ancient and modern varieties of languages that were used continuously throughout the centuries, like Ancient and Modern Greek. In Jewish communities around the world, learning and engaging with Modern Hebrew has become an important means of enacting Jewish identities and diasporic ties to contemporary Israel.

New Research Directions

Contemporary research on Jewish languages has taken new approaches to determining what is and is not a Jewish language. Many scholars and commentators have debated whether to consider certain linguistic entities spoken by Jews to be stand-alone languages or merely dialects of a non-Jewish language. How does one distinguish between the two? Some use intelligibility as a criterion. If two language varieties are mutually intelligible, they are dialects of the same language; if they are not, they are separate languages. But this method is complicated by the fact that speakers of language A may say they understand language B, but speakers of language B may say they cannot understand language A. Political autonomy and writing systems also play a role in distinguishing between languages and dialects. The oft-cited quip, "A language is a dialect with an army and a navy," points to the role of power in these designations. But if political autonomy alone were the distinguishing criterion, no Jewish language varieties except Hebrew (ancient and modern) would be considered a language. The fact that many historical Jewish languages were written in Hebrew letters leads some to consider them separate languages, but this does not help in classifying languages that were not written, nor does it take into account that some languages differed from their non-Jewish correlates only by the writing system and a few other minor features.

Because of these complications, some recent scholars have declared the language–dialect question unanswerable and instead focus on speakers' and outsiders' discourses about how to classify the language varieties. A more productive question—and one that has become more common in contemporary scholarship—is to what extent various Jewish language varieties have differed from their non-Jewish versions and how those differences have correlated with historical factors. The same question can be asked on a more microlevel about subgroups of Jews, individual Jews, and individual conversations or even utterances by individuals.

Another trend in research on Jewish languages is a focus on language ideologies: speakers' and outsiders' views about how language is used and should be used and how different people speak differently. Language ideologies are central in research on how contemporary Jewish educational institutions approach language, especially Yiddish in Hasidic communities and Hebrew in diaspora Jewish schools and summer camps. Historical research has found that Jewish speech was often subject to negative commentary and even ridicule, because non-Jews who spoke similar languages perceived Jews' language varieties as corrupted. These critiques stem not only from the language differences described earlier but also reflect Jews' low status, because the language of marginalized groups is generally stigmatized. A sixteenth-century observer criticized Yiddish as "mutilated" German, focusing on differences in pronunciation (such as Yiddish *un* vs. German *und*, meaning "and") and the integration of Hebrew words. Later, even assimilated German Jews who spoke German fluently were accused of *mauscheln* or *jüdeln*, derogatory terms for "speaking like a Jew." Non-Jewish writers sometimes portrayed Jewish language in negative, often comedic, ways in plays and other literature. For instance, from the seventeeth to the twentieth centuries, every year at Carnival in Carpentras, France, a Catholic priest would dress up as a rabbi and recite a mock Jewish sermon that included many distinctive linguistic features of Judeo-Provençal. Jews sometimes internalized and perpetuated these negative ideologies and encouraged their coreligionists to learn the standard or more widespread versions of their languages.

However, in modern times, many Jewish communities have embraced their distinctive language. Influenced by other European language movements of the nineteenth century, Jewish activists worked not only to re-vernacularize Hebrew but also to standardize and raise the status of Yiddish and to create and spread a new universal language, Esperanto. Finally, descendants of speakers of many Jewish languages have adopted nostalgic stances toward these languages, engaging with them in post-vernacular ways and raising their status from stigmatized "jargons" to communal symbols of unity and ethnic pride.

Conclusion

Within Jewish Studies, the subfield of Jewish linguistic studies can be illuminating not only to linguists but also to historians, sociologists, literary scholars, and others. By analyzing how Jewish communities in various eras and locations have spoken and written, we can gain a better understanding of everyday Jewish life, relations between Jews and non-Jews, historical migration patterns, and Jews' continuing engagement with sacred texts. The genesis and maintenance of distinctive linguistic features could be due to internal factors, such as Jews wanting some degree of separation from non-Jews and maintaining their own educational systems, or it could be caused by external factors, such as residential and professional restrictions that limit Jews' access to the surrounding language. Analyzing these distinctive features and comparing them across communities can shed light on these internal and external historical forces and give us a better understanding of the relative integration and separation of Jews in their surrounding societies.

In addition, linguistic research can spotlight communities that have been largely neglected within Jewish Studies more broadly. For example, recent research on Judeo-Hamedani, Judeo-Kashani, and other Jewish Median languages has brought new attention to the diversity of Iranian Jews, a group that has been featured very little in Jewish Studies research and teaching. In addition, comparative analysis that brings together Jews from India, Italy, Georgia, and Azerbaijan offers an alternative to the hegemony of Ashkenazi communities within Jewish studies. By focusing on language, we can gain a better understanding of the commonalities and the diversity of the Jewish people past and present.

Recommended Readings

Benor, Sarah Bunin. "Towards a New Understanding of Jewish Language in the 21st Century," *Religion Compass* 2/6 (2008): 1062–80.

Benor, Sarah Bunin, ed. n.d. "Jewish Languages," online at jewishlanguages.org.

Edzard, Lutz, and Ofra Tirosh-Becker, eds. *Jewish Languages: Text Specimens, Grammatical, Lexical, and Cultural Sketches* (Harrassowitz, 2021).

Fishman, Joshua A., ed. *Readings in the Sociology of Jewish Languages* (Brill, 1985).

Hary, Benjamin, and Sarah Bunin Benor, eds. *Languages in Jewish Communities, Past and Present* (De Gruyter Mouton, 2018).

Kahn, Lily, and Aaron Rubin, eds. *Handbook of Jewish Languages* (Brill, 2015).

Rubin, Aaron, and Lily Kahn. *Jewish Languages from A to Z* (Routledge, 2021).

Shandler, Jeffrey. *Adventures in Yiddishland* (University of California Press, 2005).

Spolsky, Bernard. *The Languages of the Jews: A Sociolinguistic History* (Cambridge University Press, 2014).

Weinreich, Max. *History of the Yiddish Language*, ed. Paul Glasser, trans. Shlomo Noble and Joshua A. Fishman (2 vols.; Yale University Press, 2008).

Wexler, Paul. "Jewish Interlinguistics: Facts and Conceptual Framework," *Language* 57 (1981): 99–149.

Zuckermann, Ghil'ad. *Revivalistics: From the Genesis of Israeli to Language Reclamation in Australia and Beyond* (Oxford University Press, 2020).

16

Literature

Shachar Pinsker, University of Michigan

TODAY, JEWISH LITERARY studies is a lively and flourishing academic field or, more precisely, several loosely connected subfields. Side by side with the study of modern *belletristic* prose fiction, poetry, and plays written in the variety of languages in which Jews have expressed themselves, scholars study the literary aspects of classical Jewish texts: the Hebrew Bible, rabbinic texts, *piyutim* (liturgical poetry), Kabbalistic and Hasidic texts. For a long time, the two basic questions at the center of Jewish literary studies have been what makes a Jewish text "literary," and what makes a literary text "Jewish"? These questions have preoccupied and animated the minds of many, even though it is difficult, perhaps impossible, to give them a definitive answer. In the volume *What Is Jewish Literature?* editor Hana Wirth-Nesher wrote, "While the last two decades have witnessed a steady increase in Jewish Studies programs and Jewish literature courses, there is no consensus nor is it likely that there will ever be one about defining the subject under study."[1] This observation is as true today as it was in 1994, but the lack of consensus and accepted definitions is one reason for the vitality and creativity of Jewish literary studies.

Questions about what makes a Jewish text "literary" and what makes a literary text "Jewish" go back to the early nineteenth century to the Jewish scholars of the Wissenschaft des Judentums movement, the forerunners of contemporary Jewish Studies. These scholars were trained in German universities and studied what they understood to be Jewish literature in the context of the academic and intellectual climate of their time and place. The foundational text of Wissenschaft, Leopold Zunz's "Etwas über die rabbinische Litteratur" (Something on Rabbinical Literature, 1818) is an essay-cum-manifesto usually considered as

LITERATURE 351

ushering in the field of modern Jewish historiography. In fact, for Zunz and others who followed in his footsteps, Jewish scholarship begins with a critical study of Jewish literature comprising not only postbiblical Jewish texts such as the Talmud and collections of Midrashim but also texts such as treatises on astronomy and fragments of zoology written in Hebrew and Aramaic.

This understanding of literature might surprise us today, but we must remember that the broader sense of literature as "a totality of written or printed works" was common at the time in all European languages; only later did it give way to more exclusive definitions based on criteria of imaginative, creative, or artistic value. It is also important to remember the Latin origin of the word and institution of *literature* and that the Hebrew word *sifrut* to designate it was only coined around 1860 as a translation. In a 1995 lecture, Jacques Derrida, the French thinker who was born in Alegria to a Jewish Sephardic family, said, "Literature is a Latin word. . . . In all European languages, even languages in which Latin is not dominant like English or German, *literature* remains a Latin word." Derrida asks readers to "take account of the latinity" in the "institution of literature" and to pay attention to its "Christendom," as linked to the "Roman Church . . . Roman law, the Roman concept of the State, indeed of Europe." Given this entanglement, Derrida posits the question: "Does there exist, in the strict and literal meaning of the word, something like literature, like an institution of literature and a right to literature in non-Latin-Roman-Christian culture?"[2]

In a sense, this was the question that preoccupied Wissenschaft scholars. Although they were deeply influenced by the Enlightenment, they were compelled by the rising nationalism of the nineteenth century to imagine and describe Jewish literature vis-à-vis European literature. It was a new and revolutionary endeavor, but also an apologetic one. Christian scholars always studied the Hebrew Bible as the "Old Testament," and even those who celebrated it as a sublime literature by and large dismissed and neglected what was written by Jews after the Bible.[3] Against this, some Wissenschaft scholars attempted to show that Jews *do* have literature and that Jews' continuous literary history reflects, following the Romantic doctrine of Johann Gottfried von Herder, a *Volksgeist*—a national spirit or essence. At the same time, when Johann Wolfgang von Goethe articulated a new concept of *Weltliteratur* (world literature), writing, "National literature is now rather an unmeaning term; the epoch of world literature is at hand, and everyone must strive to hasten its approach," Wissenschaft scholars wanted to demonstrate that Jewish writing could and should be included in it.

In an essay written in 1845, Zunz acknowledged "the peculiar character" of Jewish literature. He argued that "by participating in the intellectual currents of the past and contemporary world, sharing its fights and sufferings, [Jewish literature] becomes . . . a complementary element of general literature, albeit with its own organism that, understood by general laws, helps to understand the universal."[4] Zunz emphasized the role of Jews as cultural brokers and mediators, who were well suited to the civilizational model Goethe called forth that was based on intellectual exchanges.[5] This was something that Moritz Steinschneider, a bibliographer and historian of culture who was a student of Zunz, picked up on in his essay "*Jüdische Literatur*" (Jewish Literature).[6]

Steinschneider struggled to define Jewish literature along lines of nationality because he knew that Jews did not conform to the German nineteenth-century idea of a nation based on a common origin (*Abstammung*), a common native country (*Vaterland*), and a common language (*Sprache*). Yet, he contended that one must study and understand Jewish literature on its own because, throughout its history, Jewish literature followed trends prevalent in the countries and peoples in which it was written; at the same time, it also has created specific literary genres or forms that cannot be compared to anything outside it. Steinschneider, the first to conceptualize a continuous Jewish literary history, divided it into four periods, from the canonization of the Bible until the eighteenth century. The four periods are more or less parallel to the familiar division into ancient, medieval, early modern, and modern times, but their division is also based on a Hegelian paradigm. Steinschneider thought that Jewish literature reached its high point in the Middle Ages as a synthetic outcome of early medieval Jewry's encounter with its main antithesis: Arabic science and philosophy.[7]

The fruits of the Wissenschaft approach became evident only later in 1886, after the folding of the Wissenschaft project. That was when Gustav Karpeles published his large book in two volumes, *Geschichte der judischen Literatur* (History of Jewish Literature), which was the first comprehensive study of the subject. For Karpeles, Jewish literature was "the aggregate of writings produced by Jews from the earliest days of their history up to the present time, regardless of form, of language, and . . . of subject-matter." All works produced by Jews, he wrote, "constitute only one class," because all "are infused with the spirit of Judaism and subordinate themselves to its demands."[8] The concept of Jewish literature that Karpeles constantly highlighted was the interconnection between Jewish and general literature that in his mind (and this was common to most Wissenschaft scholars) was inherent in the juxtaposition and interaction of halakhah (as particular) and aggadah (as universal). Karpeles included in his history not just ancient and medieval literature written in Hebrew and Aramaic but also the writing of Benedict Spinoza and of Moses Mendelssohn; the poetry and prose of nineteenth-century German Jewish writers such as Heinrich Heine; and the historical novels of Berthold Auerbach, Ludwig Philippson, and Marcus Lehmann.

Despite this seemingly inclusive approach, Wissenschaft scholars and their intellectual heirs were not interested in the contemporary belletristic literature that emerged in the late eighteenth and throughout the nineteenth century in Hebrew, Yiddish, Ladino, Arabic, and languages other than German when Jews embraced new genres of literature in unprecedented ways as the Haskalah movement spread. They also ignored and dismissed mystical and Hasidic texts that were written in the same period: Those texts did not conform to their notion of literature. It is only toward the end of the nineteenth century that the global scale and the significance of new forms of Jewish writing became evident. This was accompanied by a growing debate regarding this literature. The debate was first conducted among critics and writers and later by academically trained scholars. Among the questions asked were the following: What was "new" about the modern Jewish literature? In what ways was this literature a break or a continuation of older trends such as the "Golden Age" of Jewish poetry in medieval Spain (written in Hebrew and Arabic), the Hebrew poetry of the Italian Renaissance, or the Yiddish romances of early modern Europe? What were the relationships between literature written in Jewish languages such as Hebrew and Yiddish (as well as Ladino and Judeo-Arabic) and literature written by Jews in German, Russian, French, English, and other non-Jewish languages that Jews have spoken and read?

By the early twentieth century, scholars such as Wilhelm Bacher, S. Levy, and Meyer Waxman continued the legacy of Wissenschaft scholarship in their explorations of a growing corpus of Jewish literature.[9] The most impressive achievement of Wissenschaft-inflected Jewish literary scholarship in the twentieth century was that of Israel Zinberg, who was a chemical engineer and critic who wrote in Russian and Yiddish and was influenced both by Wissenschaft and by Marxist thought. Zinberg published, in Yiddish, his magnum opus, *History of Jewish Literature: The Struggle of Mysticism and Tradition against Philosophical Rationalism*, between 1929 and 1937 in the Soviet Union. In this book, Zinberg presented a continuum that began with Jewish writing in medieval Spain and ended in the late nineteenth century. In contrast to earlier Wissenschaft scholars, Zinberg's understanding of Jewish literature was all-encompassing, including not only poetry, prose, and philosophy but also mystical and Hasidic texts in Hebrew, Yiddish, Ladino, and non-Jewish languages such as Arabic, Italian, German, French, Russian, and Polish. Zinberg conceptualized Jewish literature, using the topos of the "people of the book" that originated in the Qur'an, as a diasporic literature. Of the Jews, he wrote, "Those homeless wanderers, all this could be clearly reflected only in their literary creativity. And indeed, being closely connected with their life of exile, this creativity had to be originally interwoven with their intimate world of sorrows and hopes."[10]

Although Zinberg paid attention to Yiddish—mostly old Yiddish literature written before the nineteenth century—in his history, the academic study of modern Jewish literature in Hebrew and Yiddish was inaugurated by Nahum Slouschz and Meir Pines, scholars who wrote doctoral dissertations at the French Sorbonne.[11] These studies were written in the prevalent positivist context that presumed the existence of direct causal ties between literary texts and the biography of the writers as revealed in their diaries, letters, and other relevant archival materials; the influences of other literary texts; and the historical and political background against which texts were written. The positivist methodologies were increasingly used in the service of the new national Jewish political movements, Zionism and Jewish diaspora nationalism, that emerged at the turn of the century. The Zionist understanding of Hebrew literature can be seen best in the work of Joseph Klausner, who studied at Heidelberg University and was active as a critic, editor, and historian in Odessa before World War I. By 1925 Klausner was appointed as the first professor of modern Hebrew literature in the newly established Hebrew University. In his six-volume literary history, Klausner focused on modern Hebrew literature, which he understood as *the* national Jewish literature. It did not begin with literature of the Haskalah in Germany but with the poetic works of Rabbi Moshe Haim Luzzatto in early eighteenth-century Italy, and its end point was the literary Hebrew flowering in Eastern Europe at the end of the nineteenth century. Klausner arranged a literary map of neoclassical, romantic, and naturalist periods, a periodization that was somewhat artificially modeled on the standard histories of French and Russian literatures.[12]

Klausner's literary scholarship embodied a Zionist-Hebraist approach that was countered by a parallel Yiddishist-national approach seen in the work of scholars such as Zalman Reyzen and Max Weinrich at the YIVO Institute, which was established in 1925 in the East European city of Vilna; the Hebrew University in Jerusalem opened that same year. There was considerable resistance to these competing national Jewish literary studies that focused either on Hebrew or Yiddish literature. One of the main questions that occupied scholars and critics in

Europe, North America, and Palestine was the question of the unity of Jewish literature against the multilingualism and fragmentation of Jewish life and letters that did not map well onto a neat construction of national literature. Ba'al Makhshoves (the penname of Isidor Elyashev) wrote *Tsvey shprakhn—eyneyntsike literatur* (Two Languages—One Literature) in 1918, which emphasized the unity of Jewish literature in the two languages of Ashkenazi Jews: Yiddish and Hebrew: "We have two languages and a dozen echoes from other foreign languages, but . . . we have only one literature."[13] In the late 1930s, Shmuel Charney (Niger) in the United States extended this assumption to the Jewish literary past, offering the hypothesis that postbiblical Jewish literature was always bilingual, matching Hebrew, the holy tongue (*loshn koydesh*), with a non-Hebraic language—Aramaic, Greek, Arabic, and then the Jewish languages Yiddish and Ladino—and using each for different literary purposes.[14] In Mandatory Palestine, Dov Sadan developed his own inclusive notion of a unified *Sifrut Yisrael,* "literature of the Jewish people." In Sadan's definition, Jewish literature is written in Hebrew and Yiddish and by Jewish writers writing in non-Jewish languages for a Jewish audience. Sadan also charted an ideological triad of secular nationalism, Hasidism, and anti-Hasidic rabbinical orthodoxy. According to Sadan, modern Jewish writing in the modern period was evolving in different and seemingly irreconcilable directions—he was acutely aware of the radical fragmentation of modern Jewish life in general—but he believed it to be a temporary situation and predicted that the future, in which Jewish culture would thrive in Israel, would bring about a grand synthesis of all the various splinters.[15]

Because Jewish literary studies in the first half of the twentieth century were conducted against the background of a fiercely competitive ideological environment, literary scholars were called on to explain not only what literature was like but also what it should be. For such scholarly figures as Yosef Klausner, Max Weinreich, Shmuel Charney (Niger) and Dov Sadan, Baruch Kurzweil, and Shimon Halkin, a cultural prognosis was as important as a critical and historical analysis. They were all born in Eastern and Central Europe and were active in the 1940s and 1950s within the context of the Yishuv and birth of the young State of Israel (Halkin was for many years a Hebraist in the United States). They had witnessed the traumas of the Holocaust and the dissolution of Jewish life in Europe, as well as the rise of new Jewish life in Israel and the United States. In the writings of these scholars, a half-century of important conceptual research peaked but also reached its end.

The rise of comparative literature in the United States as a discipline during the 1950s and 1960s coincided with the growth and institutionalization of Jewish

Studies in the United States (the Association for Jewish Studies was created in 1969) and the establishment of Comparative Literature departments at Hebrew University and Tel Aviv University. René Wellek, who founded the department of Comparative Literature at Yale University in 1947, identified "literariness" as the central issue of the study of literature, based on the literary theory developed in Russian Formalism and in Prague and French Structuralism. Using the model of linguistics to approach literature as a system, Wellek declared the proper subject of comparative literature to be the study of literariness across national boundaries and the analysis of a work as a stratified structure of signs and meanings with its own aesthetic value and "substantial identity" throughout various readings.[16] It is in this intellectual atmosphere that Binyamin Hrushovski (Benjamin Harshav) founded what became known as the Tel Aviv School of Poetics, with a department of literary theory and journals in Hebrew and English that made Tel Aviv a world center of literary studies.

These scholars studied Hebrew and Yiddish literature not by itself but as part of a general theoretical approach to poetic forms. The establishment of the Tel Aviv School was couched in terms of militant opposition to a norm of ideological criticism that was presumably dominant in Israel at the time, but this claim should be taken with a grain of salt. After all, Hrushovski, who was born in Vilna and survived the Holocaust in the Soviet Union, wrote Yiddish and Hebrew poetry, translated Yiddish poetry into Hebrew, and was a significant member of what became known as the "statehood generation" of Hebrew literature; other members were Natan Zach and Yehuda Amichai, as well as a member of the Yiddish group "Yung Yisroel." Hrushovksi's scholarly work had begun with studies in prosody—the patterns of rhythm and sound—in the history of Yiddish and Hebrew poetry and only then moved toward more abstract levels of theoretical statement.

Within the context of the Tel Aviv School, Itamar Even-Zohar developed an influential "polysystem theory" to explain the total systematic situation of a literature—its resources, mode of existence, and the interrelations among its systems—which controls how the system functions. He declared that "only a nationalistic approach, or a racist anti-Semitic one, or ignorance . . . would adopt the term 'Jewish literature' on the basis of origin of writers," thus seemingly rejecting the concept of Jewish literature that was advanced by people like Zinberg or Sadan.[17] At the same time, his polysystem was built, at least in part, on a set of phenomena in nineteenth-century Jewish literature: the transfer of cultural materials between language traditions, the fluctuating prestige of different genres within a literature, and the phenomenon of literary multilingualism—the interplay within the same population between Russian, Hebrew and Yiddish. As Alan Mintz has claimed, certain peculiarities of Jewish literature—three millennia of poetic activity, the acknowledged excellence of biblical narrative, the multilingual situation of modern Jewish literatures—presented temptingly unique specimens for structural analysis.[18]

Hrushovski and Even-Zohar inspired new research into Jewish literature in areas such as Yiddish popular literature in the nineteenth and twentieth centuries, the development of the Hebrew crime story in the 1930s, Hebrew children's literature, the shifting norms of Hebrew fiction from the Palmach generation to the generation of the 1960s, studies on allusion and intertextuality, and the theory and function of literary translation.[19] It is also important to mention studies by Menakhem Perry and Meir Sternberg that paid attention to what became known as "Bible as literature." Perry and Sternberg's analysis of the biblical story introduced a literary perspective of narrative gaps and a process of filling gaps that were novel at the time.[20]

Meanwhile, in the United States, the other major center of postwar Jewry, there was much new Jewish literary activity and much critical writing about American Jewish writers, but scholarship was lagging. "There were few, if any, courses offered in American universities on Jewish literature," wrote Arnold Band three years after receiving his PhD in comparative literature from Harvard University in 1959. But this was about to change significantly in the following years. The main force bringing studies of modern Jewish literature to American students and readers was Robert Alter, who like Band, had studied comparative literature at Harvard but had devoted much of his attention since the early 1960s to modern Jewish writing in Hebrew (Alter and Band were the first to introduce the brilliance of the Hebrew writer S. Y. Agnon, who won the Nobel Prize in 1966, to American audiences), English, Yiddish, German, French, and Russian. Alter examined these texts against a backdrop of biblical and rabbinic literature, emphasizing the ongoing tension between language and history, with "language" as the abode of symbolism, holiness, and the artistic imagination and "history" as the vehicle of crisis, destruction, and loss of faith.

Although at this time there seemed to be a deep divide between literary scholarship in Israel and the United States, in fact there was much interconnection. For example, Dan Miron, who was a student of Dov Sadan and Shimon Halkin in Jerusalem and had made a name for himself as an emerging critic and scholar of Hebrew literature, studied Yiddish with Uriel Weinrich at Columbia University and wrote his PhD dissertation on the Yiddish writing of the nineteenth-century bilingual writer S. Y. Abramovitch (Mendele Mocher

Sforim).[21] Miron has since written major studies on the emergence of the novel in Hebrew and Yiddish fiction and a reevaluation of Hebrew poets H. N. Bialik and Natan Alterman. He continued to split his attention between Hebrew and Yiddish literature and published both in Hebrew and in English while teaching and training students at the Hebrew University and at Columbia University. Hrushovski-Harshav, the main force behind the Tel Aviv School, moved in 1986 to teach at Yale University; in the same year he edited and translated, together with his wife Barbara Harshav, *American Yiddish Poetry: A Bilingual Anthology*, a pioneering collection and study that opened the eyes of many to the riches of Yiddish modernism and its importance in American Jewish writing.[22] The connections between scholarship in Israel and United States were also evident in the rise of the literary approach to the Bible, marked by Alter's pioneering *The Art of Biblical Narrative*,[23] a highly influential book that put "the Bible as literature" on the scholarly map. Alter was indebted to studies on biblical narrative published by Perry, Sternberg, and others from the Tel Aviv School.

By the 1970s and 1980s, Jewish literary scholarship had reached maturity and was being expanded by scholars in the United States, Israel, and to some extent in Europe, especially when the Cold War ended with the collapse of the Soviet Union. This was also the time when American Jewish writing came of age. In 1977, Irving Howe edited a well-received anthology titled *Jewish-American Stories*, in which he created an arc of tradition that extended from short stories by East European writers Sholem Aleichem, Isaac Babel, and Isaac Bashevis Singer (who wrote in Yiddish or Russian) and Henry Roth (who wrote in English) to American-born writers such as Philip Roth, Delmore Schwartz, Cynthia Ozick, Saul Bellow, and Grace Paley. In his introduction, Howe described the stories he collected, somewhat whimsically, as "regional literature" in the sense that it possessed a distinct thumbprint, what Howe called its "inescapable subject": a "literary consciousness resulting from an encounter between an immigrant group and the host culture of America."[24] Many saw the publication of Howe's anthology as ushering in a distinct body of what we have come to know as American Jewish literature, which most readers, critics, and scholars accepted.[25]

Among other developments in this period, we can mark the moment in 1981, when two young scholars of Hebrew and Yiddish literature, Alan Mintz and David Roskies, established *Prooftexts: A Journal of Jewish Literary History*. It was inaugurated with the declaration that it "encompasses the study of medieval and modern Hebrew and Yiddish literature, literary approaches to classical Jewish sources, and Jewish literatures in European languages." Within a few years, *Prooftexts* had established itself as the most important journal in the field. It brought renewed attention not only to literary approaches to the Bible but also to Hasidic and early rabbinic texts and, as indicated by the title *Prooftexts*, a chief concern for the text, textuality, and intertextuality.

This coincided with a brief but intense period of interest among literary critics and theorists in midrash, especially the apparent similarities between it and the commentaries and criticism of the poststructuralist thought of Derrida, Jacques Lacan, Roland Barthes, and others. Perhaps the most impressive product of this moment was Geoffrey Hartman and Sanford Budick's anthology *Midrash and Literature*, which put together the work of prominent scholars of rabbinic literature alongside theorists (like Derrida) and scholars of comparative literature to explore methodological aspects of midrash in rabbinic practice, the interrelationship between midrash and kabbalistic texts, and the presence of midrash in texts of modern Jewish writers such as Franz Kafka, S. Y. Agnon, and Paul Celan.[26] How can we explain this sudden interest? As David Stern wrote, "Midrash has long been known to Western scholars, but mainly as either an exegetical curiosity or a source to be mined for facts about the Jewish background of early Christianity. The perspective of contemporary literary theory has placed midrash in a decidedly new light." Stern explained that midrash had come to epitomize "a discourse that avoids the dichotomized opposition of literature versus commentary and instead resides in the dense shuttle space between text and interpreter."[27]

The encounter between biblical and rabbinic texts and literary approaches was an exciting and energizing moment, and there is still good scholarship being conducted in these areas.[28] There is also renewed interest in the Hasidic literature of the eighteenth and nineteenth centuries and its interaction with the literature of the Haskalah. Scholars use literary analysis to study the hagiographic work on the life of *tzadikim* in Hasidic stories such as the tales of R. Nahman of Braslav, which some earlier scholars saw as marginal and other as integral to the Jewish literary complex.[29] However, contemporary Jewish literary studies is mostly preoccupied with what Lital Levy and Allison Schachter have recently dubbed as "the secularizing belletristic Jewish cultures that emerged as early as the 18th century and reached their apex in the mid–20th century."[30]

It is on this modern domain that most scholars in the field focus, even if there is little agreement on what "belletristic Jewish literature" is or was. As Anita Norich claimed, throughout the twentieth century scholars of Jewish literature devoted much attention to "questions of identity, nomenclature, boundaries, and intersections, seeking a definitive identity for the texts they study or simply a working definition of their subject," only to discover that "the question of what constitutes Jewish literature is as intractable as any other question about identity."[31]

In the early 2000s, scholars like Ruth Wisse tried to delineate modern Jewish literature as an autonomous, pseudonational entity with its own "canon," and Michael Kramer tried to define modern Jewish literature once and for all as literature written by Jews, which he understood in racial terms.[32] However, most contemporary scholars seem to reject these notions and tend to align with Dan Miron's suggestion in his 2010 book *From Continuity to Contiguity*[33] that it is futile to search for a single unified Jewish literature based on the identity of the writers or for a clearly defined modern Jewish canon. Instead, they accept the reality of what Miron calls the "modern Jewish literary complex" (405) as "a multifarious entity consisting of different connected, semi-connected and unconnected particles" (275) that is "vast, disorderly, and somewhat diffuse" (276). According to Miron, the challenge of anyone facing such a bewildering subject is to resist the temptation to find false harmony and unity and at the same time to avoid abandoning altogether the very category of "Jewish literature." Miron makes it clear that the modern Jewish literary complex lacks the basic markers of what is commonly understood as a "national literature": a shared geography and a shared language. Viewed from today's vantage point, as much as Zionist ideology stipulated that a unity of common geography, language, and people would be achieved, the current circumstances of Jewish life and literature prove this ideology wrong. Moreover, even Israeli literature cannot be seen as a "normal" national literature because it has been created in a host of languages—not only Hebrew but also Yiddish, Arabic, Russian, and others—and by both Jews and non-Jews. Instead of bemoaning this situation as "abnormal" and in need of repair, Miron accepts and even celebrates Jewish literature as an irregular assemblage contingently cobbled together, claiming that the Jewish literary complex must be open-ended and be ever ready to apply itself to whatever literary corpus is experienced as "Jewish"—particularly when such a corpus seems totally alien in language, form, and content to anything previously identified as Jewish.

Miron proposes "contiguity" as the principle that must inform a new Jewish literary theory. Thinking about relationships between different phenomena in terms of contiguity may be an alternative to essentialist definitions that instead focus on the experiential element: "A Jewish writer (who can, as a matter of course, be also an American or a French or a German writer) is a writer whose work evinces an interest in or is in whatever way and to whatever extent conditioned by a sense of *Judesein*, being Jewish, or is being read by readers who experience it as if it showed interest and were conditioned by the writer's being Jewish" (405). Accordingly, Miron suggests that Jewish literary studies should focus on contiguities: proximities, unregulated contacts, and moments of close adjacency. As an example of contiguity in the Jewish literary complex, Miron reads side by side two modern Jewish writers, Franz Kafka and Sholem Aleichem, who wrote in different languages (German and Yiddish) and places and had very different experiences of "being a Jew in the world"; yet both reacted in their writings to a "similar Jewish situation of persecution and weakness" (360).

I dwell at some length on Miron's book because it captures well many of the current preoccupations and themes in Jewish literary studies. For example, in Hana Wirth-Nesher's 2006 book, *Call It English,* she writes about a problem in the subfield of American Jewish writing: "When read in the framework of American literature," this body of literature "has often been regarded as one among other European ethnic literatures of the United States, and when read in the framework of Jewish literature, it has often been detached from the American literary and cultural forces that have also shaped it." However, for Wirth-Nesher, these approaches cannot account for the "unique contribution of Jewish American writing to the evolution of a transnational, multicultural American literary history."[34] Thus, she focuses her analysis on transnationalism—multilingualism, translation, hybridity, diasporas, and homelands—some of the key issues that preoccupy modern Jewish literary studies today and not only in the subfield of American Jewish literature.

Another good example of recent scholarship is Naomi Seidman's 2016 book, *The Marriage Plot,* in which she studies the effects of European literary and sexual conventions on Jewish sexual structures and analyzes the literary character of Jewish sexual modernity. Using insights from Ian Watt's *The Rise of the Novel,* in which he showed how novels came into prominence in eighteenth-century Europe with the rise of the middle class and of literacy, Seidman shows that parallel processes took place in Jewish society in Europe during the nineteenth century and lingered until the late twentieth century. She discusses Jewish texts that range across languages (German, Yiddish, Hebrew, English), locations (Central and Eastern Europe, Palestine, America) and genres from memoirs and autobiographies to poems, short stories, novels, and storytelling in films.[35] Thus Seidman also engages with the same issues of contiguity, translation, multilingualism, and transnationalism that Miron, Wirth-Nesher, and Chana Kronfeld identified as central to the study of Jewish literature in recent decades.[36] However, her study breaks new ground in two major preoccupations of contemporary Jewish literary studies: (1) gender and sexuality and (2) the question of "high" and "low" or canonical and popular literature.

Considerations of the importance of gender and sexuality have revolutionized and invigorated Jewish literary studies since the publication of the pioneering 1992 book *Gender and Text in Modern Hebrew and Yiddish Literature*.[37] Although Jewish literary studies since its inception tended to focus on "great texts" written by "great men," in recent decades many studies influenced by feminist approaches have recovered writings by Jewish women who were marginalized and often misconstrued; a host of new translations have drawn attention to this writing and to its previous absence from conversations about Jewish literary history.[38] Other studies productively used gender and sexuality as a tool of analysis in Jewish literature written and read by both men and women. They focused, for example, on the distinctive features of Hebrew and Yiddish literature, in which the Hebrew tradition is associated with a masculine educational system and Yiddish language and literature with a denigrated femininity; on gender and nation-building in Zionist and Israeli literature; and on the reading habits and expectations of Jewish readers as governed by gender.

Questions of reading and readership—Who reads? What are they reading and why?—are related to rethinking the rigid dichotomy between "high" culture and "low" or mass culture that had been accepted in Jewish literary studies. Popular literature, however we define it, has been a fixture of Jewish cultural life long before the onset of modernity. Both in the Ashkenazi and the Sephardi worlds, popular forms provided reading material "for women" that was enjoyed by men as well, if only as a guilty pleasure acknowledged to occupy a "lower" cultural plane than the sacred texts men were expected to study. Since the mid-eighteenth century, new definitions of belletristic literature relegated popular forms of writing and reading to the margins, but readers continued to enjoy and consume a variety of texts in new forms of distribution such as mass journalism. New attention to these forms has recovered neglected writers and texts from the nineteenth and twentieth centuries in Israel, the Americas, and Europe. Marat Grinberg has productively explored what Jews in the Soviet Union in the second half of the twentieth century read and what was on their bookshelves. This inquiry yielded surprising insights on Soviet Jews' reading culture and their lives in the aftermath of the Holocaust. We discovered that, although the public Jewish presence was routinely delegitimized, reading uniquely provided many Soviet Jews with an entry to communal memory and identity.[39]

Alongside studies of the history of the Jewish "bookshelf" and the materiality of the Jewish book,[40] there is currently a renewed interest in Jewish cultural products ranging from newspaper feuilletons; to popular literature (known sometimes as *shund*, a pejorative Yiddish term that refers to serialized pulp novels and popular theater) of romance, detective fiction, and "middlebrow" Jewish novels; and to more contemporary popular forms such as graphic novels and films.[41]

These new studies consider in a comparative manner literature and cultural products created in both Ashkenazi and Sephardi or Mizrahi culture. From its inception in the Wissenschaft des Judentum movement, Jewish literary studies explored medieval Jewish literature in the Iberian Peninsula written in Hebrew, Aramaic, or Arabic but largely ignored modern Sephardi and Mizrahi Jewish writing in the Middle East, Europe, and South America. The most prestigious language of the modern Sephardic and Mizrahi diaspora, particularly in the belletristic realm, was French, and much Jewish writing was produced in that language both in France and in the larger diaspora.[42] There was also a good deal of translation from French to Ladino, Judeo-Arabic, and literary Arabic not only of "high" but also of popular literature, as well as both "religious" and "secular" original texts written in these languages,[43]

One of the most exciting developments is Jewish literary studies is a budding comparative study of "high" and "low" culture in Hebrew, Yiddish, Ladino, Judeo-Arabic, and European languages such as French, German, English, Spanish, Russian, and Polish. This new arena of comparative multilingual study, conducted by scholars in the United States, Europe, and Israel, is emerging alongside a renewed interest in the concept of world literature within a global literary market of the twenty-first century.[44] Contemporary scholars in Jewish literary studies are returning to some of the very basic questions that preoccupied Zunz and his followers in the early years of the nineteenth century. However, as Benjamin Schrier argued, in the twenty-first century, scholars can no longer assume the Jewishness of any text as "a stable, coherent, and signifying phenomenon underwritten by the legibility of population . . . but rather the dynamic, contested product of the struggle."[45] Scholars today tackle the peculiarity of Jewish literature as a body of texts that highlight tensions between universalism and particularity and between religion, secularism, and modernization, They approach these ever-present questions with different assumptions and methodologies and the completely different corpus of Jewish writing that has been created since then, as well as a new critical attention to the categories of Jewishness and of literature.

Recommended Readings

Alter, Robert. *The Art of Biblical Narrative* (Basic Books, 1981).

DeKoven Ezrahi, Sidra. *Booking Passage: Exile and Homecoming in the Modern Jewish Imagination* (University of California Press, 2003).

Hartman, Geoffrey, and Sanford Budick, eds. *Midrash and Literature* (Yale University Press, 1986).

Jelen, Sheila E., et al., eds. *Modern Jewish Literatures: Intersections and Boundaries* (University of Pennsylvania Press, 2011).

Krammer, Michael. "Race, Literary History, and the Jewish Question," *Prooftexts* 21, no. 3 (2001): 287–321.

Kronfeld, Chana. *On the Margins of Modernism: Decentering Literary Dynamics* (University of California Press, 1996).

Levy, Lital, and Allison Schachter. "Jewish Literature/World Literature: Between the Local and the Transnational," *PMLA* 130, no. 1 (2015): 92–109.

Miron, Dan. *From Continuity to Contiguity: Toward a New Jewish Literary Thinking* (Stanford University Press, 2010).

Norich, Anita. "Under Whose Sign? Hebraism and Yiddishism as Paradigms of Modern Jewish Literary History," *PMLA* 125, no. 3 (2010): 774–84.

Roskies, David G. "Modern Jewish Literature," in *The Modern Jewish Experience: A Reader's Guide,* ed. Jack Wertheimer (New York University Press, 1993), 213–27.

Sokoloff, Naomi B., Anne Lapidus Lerner, and Anita Norich, eds. *Gender and Text in Modern Hebrew and Yiddish Literature* (Jewish Theological Seminary of America, 1992).

Stavans, Ilan. *Jewish Literature: A Very Short Introduction* (Oxford University Press, 2021).

Stern, David. *Midrash and Theory: Ancient Jewish Exegesis and Contemporary Literary Studies* (Northwestern University Press, 1996).

Wirth-Nesher, Hana, ed. *What Is Jewish Literature?* (Jewish Publication Society, 1994).

Notes

1. Wirth-Nesher, "Defining the Indefinable: What Is Jewish Literature?," in *What is Jewish Literature?* ed. H. Wirth-Nesher (Jewish Publication Society, 1994), 3.

2. Derrida, *Demeure: Fiction and Testimony* (Stanford University Press, 2000). Compare with Cynthia Ozick's essay "Literature as Idol: Harold Bloom," in *Art & Ardor* (E. P. Dutton, 1983).

3. The exception was a group of Christian Hebraists who studied postbiblical Jewish literature in the early modern period. On this topic, see Allison P. Coudert and Jeffrey S. Shoulson, eds., *Hebraica Veritas? Christian Hebraists and the Study of Judaism in Early Modern Europe* (University of Pennsylvania Press, 2004).

4. Leopold Zunz, "Die jüdische Literatur" (1845), in *Gessamelte Schriften*, Vol. 1 (Gerschel, 1875), 42. Quoted and translated by Andreas B. Kilcher, "'Jewish Literature' and 'World Literature': *Wissenschaft des Judentums* and Its Concept of Literature," in *Modern Judaism and Historical Consciousness: Identities, Encounters, Perspectives*, ed. A. Gotzmann and C. Wiese (Brill, 2007), 299–325.

5. Clémence Boulouque, "Between Assonance and Assimilation: Literature as a Hyphen in the Wissenschaft des Judentums," in *Frontiers of Jewish Scholarship: Expanding Origins, Transcending Borders*, ed. A. O. Albert et al. (University of Pennsylvania Press, 2022), 103–20.

6. In *Allgemeine Encyclopädie der Wissenschaften und Künste*, ed. J. S. Ersch and J. G. Gruber, Vol. 27 (1850).

7. Steinschneider, *Jewish Literature from the Eighth to the Eighteenth Century* (Longman, Brown, Green, 1857). For an analysis of Steinschneider's understanding of Jewish literature and the internalized orientalism that lies in it, see Irene E. Zwiep, "From Dialektik to Comparative Literature: Steinschneider's Orientalism," and Reimund Leicht, "Moritz Steinschneider's Concept of the History of Jewish Literature," *Studies on Steinschneider* (Brill, 2012), 137–74.

8. Karpeles, *Jewish Literature and Other Essays* (Jewish Publication Society, 1895), 10–11.

9. Bacher, Wolf, and Levy, "What is 'Jewish' Literature?" *Jewish Quarterly Review* 16 (1903): 300–329.

10. Zinberg, *History of Jewish Literature*, Vol. 1 (Press of Western Case University, 1972), xxiii–xxvi.

11. Schloutz, *La Renaissance de la littérature hébraïque: 1743–1885* (Paris, 1902); Pines, *Histoire de la Littérature Judeo-Allemande* (Paris, 1911).

12. Klausner, *History of New Jewish Literature* [Hebrew] (6 vols.; Jerusalem, 1930–50).

13. Ba'al Makhshoves, "Tsvey shprakhn—eyneyntsike literatur," *Petrograder Tageblatt* (Petrograd, 1918), repr. *Geklibene verk* (Cyco-Bicher Farlag, 1953). Wirth-Nesher's English translation, "Ba'al Makhshoves' 'One Literature in Two Languages,'" appears in *What Is Jewish Literature?*, 69–77.

14. Shmuel Niger, *Di tsveyshprakhikeyt fun undzer literatur* (Louis Lamed Foundation for the Advancement of Hebrew and Yiddish Literature, 1941); transl. *Bilingualism in the History of Jewish Literature* (University Press of America, 1990).

15. Sadan, *About Our Literature* [Hebrew] (Ha-maḥlakah Le-'inyane Ha-mo'ar Vehe-ḥaluts, 1950).

16. Wellek, *Concepts of Criticism* (Yale University Press, 1963).

17. Even-Zohar, *Papers in Historical Poetics* (Porter Institute, 1978), 80–81.

18. See Mintz, "On the Tel Aviv School of Poetics," *Prooftexts* 4 (1984): 215–35.

19. See David G. Roskies, "Jewish Literary Scholarship after the Six-Day War," in *The State of Jewish Studies*, ed. S. J. D. Cohen and E. L. Greenstein (Wayne State University Press, 1990), 165–84.

20. Perry and Sternberg, "The King through Ironic Eyes: Biblical Narrative and the Literary Reading Process," *Poetics Today* 7 (1986): 275–322; orig. Hebrew publication in 1968.

21. Miron, *A Traveler Disguised: The Rise of Modern Yiddish Fiction in the Nineteenth Century* (Schocken, 1973).

22. Harshav and Harshav, *American Yiddish Poetry: A Bilingual Anthology* (University of California Press, 1986). Mainstream American audiences were first introduced to the range of Yiddish stories and poem in English translation with Howe and Goldberg, *A Treasure of Yiddish Stories* (Viking, 1954), and *A Treasury of Yiddish Poetry* (Holt Rinehart and Winston, 1969).

23. Basic, 1981.

24. Howe, *Jewish-American Stories* (Penguin Books, 1977), 3.

25. For a recent critical discussion of the subfield of Jewish American literature with important implications for the field as a whole, see Benjamin Schreier, *The Rise and Fall of Jewish American Literature: Ethnic Studies and the Challenge of Identity* (University of Pennsylvania Press, 2020).

26. Hartman and Budick, *Midrash and Literature* (Yale University Press, 1986).

27. David Stern, "Midrash and Indeterminacy," *Critical Inquiry* 15 (1988): 132–61.

28. See, for example, Jacqueline Vayntrub, *Beyond Orality: Biblical Poetry on Its Own Terms* (Routledge, 2019), which revises earlier studies by James Kugel and Robert Alter.

29. Yonatan Meir, *Literary Hasidism: The Life and Works of Michael Levi Rodkinson* (Syracuse University Press, 2016); Yitzhak Lewis, *A Permanent Beginning: R. Nachman of Braslov and Jewish Literary Modernity* (SUNY Press, 2020); Tsippi Kauffman, "Thoughts on the Seam between Hasidic Literature and Haskalah Literature: The Works of Joseph Perl," *Prooftexts* 38 (2021): 347–68; Hannan Hever, *Hasidism, Haskalah, Zionism: Chapters in Literary Politics* (University of Pennsylvania Press, 2023).

30. Levy and Schachter, "Jewish Literature/World Literature: Between the Local and the Transnational," *PMLA* 130, no. 1 (2015): 92–109.

31. Norich, "Under Whose Sign? Hebraism and Yiddishism as Paradigms of Modern Jewish Literary History," *PMLA* 125, no. 3 (2010): 774–84.

32. Wisse, *The Modern Jewish Canon: A Journey through Language and Culture* (Free Press, 2001); Michael Krammer, "Race, Literary History, and the 'Jewish' Question," *Prooftexts* 21 (2001): 287–321.

33. Miron, *From Continuity to Contiguity: Toward a New Jewish Literary Thinking* (Stanford University Press, 2010).

34. Wirth-Nesher, *Call It English: The Languages of Jewish American Literature* (Princeton University Press, 2006), xii.

35. In one chapter, Seidman moves from autobiographies of Salomon Maimon and M. A. Günzburg, in the early nineteenth century to Avraham Mapu's novel *Love of Zion* (1853), Y. L. Gordon's narrative poem "The Tip of the Yud" (1878), S. Y. Abramovitsh's novella "The Travels of Benjamin the Third" (1878), Erica Jong's novel *Fear of Flying* (1973), and Woody Allen's film *Love and Death* (1975). See Seidman, *The Marriage Plot: Or, How Jews Fell in Love with Love* (Stanford University Press, 2016).

36. Kronfeld's pioneering study, *On the Margins of Modernism: Decentering Literary Dynamics* (University of California Press, 1996), has inspired much of the current critical attention to translation, multilingualism, and transnationalism in the context of Jewish literary history.

37. Naomi B. Sokoloff, Anne Lapidus Lerner, and Anita Norich, *Gender and Text in Modern Hebrew and Yiddish Literature* (Jewish Theological Seminary of America, 1992).

38. Shirley Kaufman et al., *Hebrew Feminist Poems from Antiquity to the Present: A Bilingual Anthology* (Feminist Press, 1999); Dvora Baron, *The First Day and Other Stories* (University of California Press, 2001); Wendy I. Zierler, *And Rachel Stole the Idols: The Emergence of Modern Hebrew Women's Writing* (Wayne State University Press, 2004); Carole B. Balin, *To Reveal Our Hearts: Jewish Women Writers in Tsarist Russia* (Hebrew Union College Press,

LITERATURE 367

2000); Sheila E. Jelen and Shachar M. Pinsker, *Hebrew Gender and Modernity: Critical Responses to Dvora Baron's Fiction* (University Press of Maryland, 2007); Kathryn Hellerstein, *A Question of Tradition: Women Poets in Yiddish, 1586–1987* (Stanford University Press, 2014).

39. Grinberg, *The Soviet Jewish Bookshelf: Jewish Culture and Identity between the Lines* (Brandeis University Press, 2022).

40. Barbara E. Mann, *The Object of Jewish Literature: A Material History* (Yale University Press, 2022).

41. S. Baskind and R. Omer-Sherman, eds., *The Jewish Graphic Novel: Critical Approaches* (Rutgers University Press, 2008); Jonathan M. Hess, *Middlebrow Literature and the Making of German-Jewish Identity* (Stanford University Press, 2010).

42. Maurice Samuels, *Inventing the Israelites: Jewish Fiction in Nineteenth Century France* (Stanford University Press, 2010).

43. Marjorie Agosín, *Memory, Oblivion, and Jewish Culture in Latin America* (University of Texas Press, 2005); Matthias B. Lehmann, *Ladino Rabbinic Literature and Ottoman Sephardic Culture* (Indiana University Press, 2005); Olga Borovaya, *Modern Ladino Culture: Press, Belles Lettres, and Theater in the Late Ottoman Empire* (Indiana University Press, 2011); Monique Balbuena, *Homeless Tongues: Poetry and the Languages of the Sephardic Diaspora* (Stanford University Press, 2016).

44. Lital Levy and Allison Schachter, "A Non-Universal Global: On Jewish Writing and World Literature," *Prooftexts* 36 (2017): 1–26; Shachar M. Pinsker, *A Rich Brew: How Cafés Created Modern Jewish Culture* (NYU Press, 2018), 1–26.; Susanne Zepp et al., *Disseminating Jewish Literatures: Knowledge, Research, Curricula* (De Gruyter, 2020); Saul Noam Zarrit, *Jewish American Writing and World Literature: Maybe to Millions Maybe to Nobody* (Oxford University Press, 2020).

45. Schrier, *Rise and Fall of American Jewish Literature*, 169. See also Adam Zachary Newton, *Jewish Studies as Counterlife: A Report to the Academy* (Fordham University Press, 2019).

17

Music

Edwin Seroussi, Hebrew University of Jerusalem

JEWISH STUDIES have been slow to embrace the sonic dimension of Jewishness as a fundamental constituent of the field and as a potential venue for revisiting its paradigms. Addressing the uniqueness of nonverbal sound, of which music is its most prominent instance, as a gateway to the complexities of the "Jewish" while also suggesting paths for future research comprises the core of this chapter.[1] It begins with general remarks that are critical to the understanding of how music operates and why it offers alternative venues to untangle the "Jewish," understood as either culture, religion, civilization, ethnicity, or nationality. It then moves into an exploration of the concept of "Jewish music" at three different but intersecting discursive levels: as the practice of music by Jews in the past and present, as a field of scholarly inquiry since the late nineteenth century, and as a label in the contemporary market of musical products.

"Jewish music" as a concept did not exist until the mid-nineteenth century. On the wings of a thriving Wissenschaft des Judentums, a learned and reflexive interest in the subject (usually in the category of synagogue music) developed mostly among practitioners undergoing a process of professionalization; that is, cantors of predominantly modernizing German-speaking Jewish communities. This statement does not mean that in earlier times Jews did not maintain musical repertoires conceptualized by them (or by their neighbors) as integral to their culture, whether they were distinctive from or in conversation with repertoires of non-Jews. They certainly did, but they just did not refer to it as "Jewish music."[2]

Escaping the "Jewish music" trap—the preoccupation with defining unique clusters of musical parameters (such as scales, modes, and melody types) as

368

specifically Jewish—should lead to research questions differing from those that had guided most studies of music in Jewish Studies. One may consider, for example, the historical, social, economic, and technological processes that have generated music listened to or conceived as Jewish either by large audiences or by small communities. What are the authorities or power relations within the music market that compose, produce, reproduce, label, archive, sell, and promote certain music as Jewish? Which historical processes are embedded in the diffusion of music that circulates today as Jewish? How are sonic qualities of Jewish music that many deem prestigious, such as "authentic," "ancient," or "traditional," constructed and deployed in different discursive fields like marketing strategies, pedagogic texts, and academia? These and other questions comprise the kernel of this chapter, whose goal is not to provide conclusive answers but rather to inspire alternative lines of inquiry.

On Music

A few words about music as a unique human phenomenon are required to justify its centrality in Jewish Studies. Music emerges from the human domestication of an intangible natural resource, sound, eliciting physiological and mental responses that recent research on musical cognition addresses as both "biological"—our innate ability to synchronize clapping or tapping with a steady pulse—and "cultural," generating emotions such as joy, sorrow, or pleasure that are learned within specific social and temporal contexts.[3] Put differently, the same sonic formation may elicit different responses from or have diverse meanings to different individuals and collectives, and these meanings shift over time for the individual or whole communities.

Music also has materiality and is fundamental to human interactions: It is an integral constituent of the social fabric. During the course of history, music was reified, acquiring monetary value and creating a market that generates revenues for its creators, practitioners, and mediators. The economy of music led to the valorization of musical expertise, the need for institutions that trained practitioners, social esteem of musicians in demand, centers of power controlling such prestige, regulations such as copyrights, and many intermediaries invested in musical commodities from instrument makers to music publishers and artists' agents.

In short, music is a humanly conceived sonic icon, index, and symbol that generates tangible and intangible value, as well as networks of social relations. Humans have recruited music for a variety of intimate and collective goals, such as prompting emotions and passions; coordinating human behavior and labor; enhancing and structuring rituals; delineating identities; constructing and deconstructing communities and nations; advancing political agendas, even torturing; and more prosaically serving as the background for everyday life as the nonverbal soundtrack of existence. Lastly, the borderlines of music itself are open-ended; that is, what counts as "music" in a particular cultural or historical context may count as "noise" in another. As Frigyesi has shown in her study of *minyanim* (synagogue service quorums) of aged World War II survivors in communist Budapest and Prague, an occasional visitor to some of their rituals would have been perplexed by their rather "unmusical" yet compelling ritualistic sound.[4]

Is Jewish Music Possible?

Taking into consideration these general remarks about the import of music as a human activity, one can appreciate its enormous, still uncharted potential for studying Jewishness. Facing the plethora of contemporary music practices labeled "Jewish" in performances, recordings, archives, composition competitions, scores, catalogs, and websites—to name a few contexts and technologies of music production, storage, and consumption—one can conclude that "Jewish music" is, as Gershon Scholem wrote to Theodor Adorno, "something downright inconceivable."[5] Or vice versa, one could argue that potentially any "non-Jewish" music can become conceptualized as Jewish under specific historical circumstances, as can be seen (or rather heard) in the wholesale embracing of *maqam*-based music by Jews throughout the Islamic world.[6] Moreover, Jewish music can be nurtured by non-Jews in non-Jewish contexts, as occurred with the explosion of Eastern European Jewish instrumental music ("klezmer") among non-Jewish musicians and audiences since the 1970s.[7]

Despite these theoretical predicaments and their implied critique of the concept of Jewish music, one can say that there has never been so much music circulating in markets as "Jewish" and talking (academic talk included) about Jewish music as today. Moreover, despite the subjectivity involved in establishing signification in any music, a wide audience, at least in the West, can typify today certain musics as "Jewish" when they hear them. Whether these judgments regarding the Jewishness of a certain music, informed by stereotypes hammered in by the mass media or by the authority of scholars or "influencers," are historically accurate is irrelevant. Research concerns should focus on how and why this vast discursive field, linguistic and musical, about "Jewish music" came into being.

Jewish music as a concept emerged with the rise of the modern concept of nationhood among European Jews during the long nineteenth century. Following the evolving idea of "national music" in European musical Romanticism,[8] late nineteenth-century practitioners engaged in Jewish music research reasoned that if a Jewish nation in its modern sense exists despite millennia of dispersion and if each nation possesses distinctive musical traits, then some "universal" core of Jewish music must be embedded in contemporary Jewish practices.[9] Soon however, this idea ran into a cul de sac. Imperial colonial expansion led to the encounter of European Jews with the very different sounds of their North African and Middle Eastern brethren, posing major questions regarding the viability of a "Jewish music" legacy shared by all Jews. The search for an ancestral common musical denominator (or its refutation) informed early theoretical postulates in Jewish music research and, in fact, set its agenda.

The emergence of the "science of music" (*Musikwissenschaft*, musicology) as an academic discipline coincided in time and place with the increasing interest in Jewish music. This new field of inquiry developed in the same habitat as modern Jewish nationalism did—in urban centers such as Vienna, Paris, and Berlin—and its pioneers were assimilated Jews or Jews who converted to Christianity.[10] Despite this Jewish DNA of early musicology, the organic integration of music studies within Jewish Studies developed gradually, as both disciplines initially seemed to run along parallel courses. This phenomenon can be partly attributed to the hermetic character of music as a language, especially in early musicology that emphasized as its object of inquiry music scores that few could read and an analytical terminology that few commanded. Synagogue cantors slowly recruited the tools of the new science of music, such as the systematic collection of data (archival and ethnographic), philological techniques, and comparative methodologies in their endeavor to unearth the assumed primordial Jewish music.[11] In addition to the anxiety caused by scores and music theory jargon, Jewish Studies scholars were also wary of the main venue of Jewish music transmission: orality. Orality relied on memory, and early Jewish Wissenschaft disparaged memory as an undependable repository of reliable documentation in favor of written sources.[12]

Enter recording technologies (after about 1900) that could facilitate the preservation and retrieval of Jewish oral traditions. These technologies were slow to turn into accessible tools for research, although early commercial recordings comprised a quasi-ethnographical documentation. Commercial recordings were also frowned on by some influential Jewish practitioners-scholars such as the great cantor, composer, and music writer Pinchas (Pinkhes) Minkowsky of

Odessa (1859–1924): He vehemently opposed recordings on religious grounds (depleting the embodied experience of live prayer) and economic ones (the immoral import of market capitalism).[13] Only after World War II did major music ethnographic undertakings became possible with the development of cheaper, portable, and efficient recording technologies.

Before the advent of recordings, scholars of Jewish music and Jewish music practitioners (a dichotomy hard to demarcate in the past) had to rely on transcriptions of oral traditions using Western notation. However, this graphic means could not encode the totality of the performances by living sources. Moreover, each time the same piece was played, it sounded slightly different, forcing subjective judgments by transcribers as to what is essential to a piece of music and what is circumstantial. Despite these limitations, modern European Jews adopted Western musical notation *tout court* beginning in the early nineteenth century; this is attested by the substantial archives and libraries of Jewish music still available despite so much destruction due to natural causes, negligence, or wars.[14]

Technologies that fix music to preserve it for further generations, whether in written, mechanical or digital form, run against the very nature of music as an art whose essence is time and whose experience is immediate and corporeal. Domesticating music by caging it with graphic descriptions on paper and materials like wax cylinders, shellac records, or hard drives therefore calls for scholarly reflection because music research depends on the competences and agendas of those who create, duplicate, and distribute these products.

Tracing "Jewish Music"

Considering the complexity of Jewish music as a concept and the problematics of its conservation, a productive strategy to avoid the pitfalls of defining it is to address the practices that delineate its perimeters of inclusion and exclusion. Such practices comprise actions, such as writing about, composing, printing, broadcasting, selling, and consuming music tagged as "Jewish." Just consider the decisions of record store owners (old-fashioned brick and mortar ones or online platforms) about what to include in the shelf labeled "Jewish music" and to what extent previous decisions by producers and marketing strategies affect the stores' display. Moving into even earlier stages in this chain of decision making that shapes Jewish music, think about each musician's choice regarding what to record as "Jewish" and what record label to approach to advance their music as "Jewish." One could ask from which resources does a musician draw the music she deems "Jewish." A family tradition? Scores on a library shelf? Earlier recordings?

The access that scholars of Jewish music had to data constrained their writings so that individual contingency (who can read the data), accessibility to resources (who can reach the data), and power relations (who controls the data) determined their contents. In turn, scholarly works informed and inspired musical creativity, performances, recordings, and festivals, as well as reception and criticism. These interactions generated a process by which acts of "inscribing" and performing Jewish music nurtured each other in constituting the field of Jewish music studies.[15]

In these acts of writing and performing, of creating, receiving, and criticizing, the preoccupations and agendas of influential agents and power brokers—musicologists, educators, performers, producers, publishers, critics, and investors—play a crucial role in establishing the ever-shifting boundaries of Jewish music as both a discursive field and a performative one. Put differently, the writing and performing strategies deployed by these agents are marked by their access to resources, aesthetic ideals, tastes, and remunerative considerations as much as by personal and communal concepts of Jewishness and Jewish heritage. Whether actors identified themselves as Jews or not, these strategies are relevant to research projects, as is the entanglement of Jews with their non-Jewish surroundings.

How do all these considerations contribute to a more integrative approach to music within Jewish Studies? How can music expand the horizons of Jewish Studies beyond written texts or visual artifacts? In the next section, there are short illustrations that exemplify issues of music research that may inspire new research within Jewish Studies. These snippets stress agency rather than musical products—actions such as collecting, archiving, teaching, performing, and consuming music—and they emphasize collectivities constituted around musical practices.

The Challenge of a Silent Jewish Musical Past: The Written Archive

The uncovering of the past and its multiple interpretations based on surviving written sources has been a methodological paradigm in Jewish Studies. However, what is known about music in the Jewish past are only traces of musical memories that have survived into the present. These traces constitute an archive, a repository of textual fragments dispersed (in fact "hidden") within larger texts (such as responsa), rare music scores (since the late eighteenth century), and sounds (since 1900) that both inform present-day writings and facilitate renewed performances. Such remnants of written and oral testimonies about past musical practices endured through a process of selection that is obscured by the passing of time, natural disintegration, censorship, and plain forgetting.[16] Reconstructing the Jewish musical past based on such precarious data demands a careful cross-examination of disparate and fragmentary sources.

Music per se was rarely an object of extensive discussion on the Jewish bookshelf, and yet attitudes related to it—contexts of performance, qualifications of performers, the origin of melodies—can be gleaned from the Bible up to recent halakhic pronouncements. Other literary genres (travelogues, *musar* literature, poetry) offer access to the musical experiences of (mostly adult male) Jews and their approaches to music in the past. Halakhic texts are concerned with practical issues, such as the permissibility and limits of music in rituals, the qualifications of performers (*hazzanim*, cantors), gender issues (*kol be-isha*, the talmudic ban on hearing the voice of a woman), the contested use of musical instruments (*klei zemer*), new technologies (whether the recording of liturgical music is allowed), and relations to the music of the Other (the permissibility of adopting foreign melodies to prayers). Mystical texts address the influence of music on the body and the soul of the individual and community, considering music as a technique to induce prophesy and to communicate with the Divine, cleave to it or even sway its inner workings.[17]

An example of a medieval source rich in information about music is *Sefer Hasidim* (Book of the Pious). Originating in the Rhineland, this compilation is widely considered to be a major resource for studying medieval German Jewry. From it we learn about divergent practices in the performance of prayers, particularly the core prayer of services, the Amidah or "Eighteen." The authors ponder the desired rhythm of this prayer's performance, reproaching those who rush it and recommending slowing it down with *niggun*: "When you are eager to praise [God, or a King] with pleasant voice and a song of praise, if it was customary to rush without *niggun* and that was the way you were used to [pray], accordingly you should not do it in a rush but at ease with your melodious voice and with a loud voice as it is written, to raise the voice with joy (Ezra 3:12, 'for joy [they] shouted aloud')."[18] Such an argument discloses the tensions and the shifting models in the aesthetics of Ashkenazi liturgical performance almost a millennium ago. This text is an early record of the modern term *niggun*—voicing aloud the prayer melodiously and with clear articulation has a certain theurgical potential, meaning that God listens more willingly to prayers performed in this manner. *Niggun* opens the gates of heaven, an idea that will permeate deliberations about the role and power of music in prayer into the modern era. The shifting from an aesthetic based on the art of the Eastern European cantor (*hazones* in Yiddish) to the experience of communal singing (*niggunim*) in contemporary America is but one example.[19]

Religious poetry (*piyyutim*)—texts performed musically—offers another example of data about musical practices.[20] Manuscripts and printed collections of *piyyutim* include quotations of the names or first lines of songs (in Hebrew or vernacular languages) to whose tune a poem is sung ("sing to the melody of . . ."). Such quotations provide a glance into song repertories practiced by Jews in the past that otherwise would remain concealed.[21] In North Africa and the Middle East, such collections of poetry include instructions regarding musical modes (a concept similar to scales) and rhythmic patterns, further enriching our knowledge about musical practices of Jews and their affinity to those of their non-Jewish neighbors.

A notable example of such collections of *piyyutim* can be found in the oeuvre of R. Israel Najara (ca. 1550–ca. 1628), a remarkable Ottoman Sephardic poet active in Safed, Damascus, and Gaza; his musical poetry had a decisive impact on the devotional practices of Jews throughout the Middle East and North Africa. Najara set the vast majority of his religious poetry to the melodies of the Turkish, Arabic, Spanish, Greek, and even Persian songs he heard in the vast territories of the multidenominational Ottoman Empire at its height. Moreover, Najara mastered the Ottoman *makam* system and arranged his poems according to these musical modes, launching a musical practice that would reverberate continuously until the present.[22]

More ethnographical by nature are travelogues that offer a rich if yet unexplored source of information about past musical practices. Two examples are *Nach Jerusalem!* (2 vols., 1858) and *Aus Egypten* (1860), detailed orientalist accounts of the travels of the Viennese literate Ludwig August Frankl in the Middle East, in which he describes musical performances he witnessed in the Jewish communities he visited in the Middle East. Memoirs of Jewish musical practitioners, such as the autobiography of cantor, composer, teacher, ethnographer. and scholar Abraham Moshe Bernstein (1866–1932),[23] are yet another literary genre providing vivid insights into the social fabric of music making in Jewish societies. Lastly, the modern Jewish press offers a trove of data about venues of performances, obituaries of performers, the selection and installation of musical personnel and instruments, the commission of new music, the sale of musical scores, and the publication of commercial recordings.[24]

Iconography, the visual representation of musical scenes and artifacts, is another source from which one may glean data (even if imagined) about past musical activities. Medieval illuminated manuscripts and, later, plates in printed books provide such information. A depiction of King David holding a harp in the *Leipnik Haggadah* (Amsterdam, 1738, Biblioteca Rosenthaliana, Ms. HS. ROS 382, fol. 20b) shows him performing from a music score opened on a piece titled "Hodu le-Pesah." This is an early testimony of a cantor's music manual, a tool adopted by Western Ashkenazi *hazzanim* whose earliest surviving specimens are from the late eighteenth century. This image allows the acquisition of notated musical literacy by cantors to be assigned to an earlier period than was previously thought. Modern visual ephemera, such as postcards, offer interesting data about musical practices and practitioners at a time when the new technology of photography started to emerge. Moreover, some postcards even included musical scores, such as those issued by the Jewish National Fund containing Palestinian Hebrew songs.[25]

Yet, none of this array of visual images of musical scenes and of texts—from short statements to longer writings discussing musical issues or providing information about musical performances—provide a tangible clue about the actual sound of Jewish music in the past. Only scores can generate such knowledge. Paradoxically, the earliest specimens of "Jewish music" in musical notation were published by non-Jews. These rare documents are a rather fragmentary product of the initiative of Hebraists, early modern encyclopedists, and Orientalists beginning in the sixteenth century. Interest in contemporary Jewish performance practices as archaeological remnants of templar music, as clues to the beginnings of church music, or even as a source for the renewal of Christianity's lost musical glory motivated these early notations of specimens of Jewish music. Specimens of this type include Johannes Reuchlin's musical transcription of the *te'amim* (biblical cantillation signs) in his *De accentibus et orthographia linguae hebraicae* (Hanau, 1518) and a few Sephardic and Ashkenazi tunes from the Venetian ghetto transcribed by Benedetto Marcello (1686–1739) and incorporated into his psalm settings, the *Estro poetico-armonico* (Venice, 1724–27).[26]

Early modern European music histories published since the mid-eighteenth century usually opened with a chapter on "Hebrew Music" paired with ancient Greek music, both considered as the foundation of western (read: Christian) musical civilization. These chapters were based on interpretations of the music data provided by Scripture. However, some of these books also incorporated proto-ethnographic materials drawn from contemporary Jewish practices. The section dedicated to the "Music of the Hebrews" in the multivolume history of music by the Belgian music historian François-Joseph Fétis (1784–1871) is a notable example.[27] Positioning "the Hebrews" under the category of "Semites" (versus the "Aryans") within a racialized taxonomy of musical cultures, Fétis summarizes the antiquarian literature on Israelite music that emphasized the glory of rituals in biblical times and mourns the disappearance of this ancient Hebrew musical lore. A proof of this loss is the diversity of the Jewish musical present, where the psalms "are chanted in absolutely different manner in the Orient, in Germany, in Spain and in England." Fétis shows this diversity with musical notations from contemporary Jewish practices available to him. In another passage, he claims to the contrary that "the traditional chants, and the modes of accented recitation and mixed chanting, are therefore the only sections of the musical liturgy in use at the synagogues of Europe that may be considered as deriving from the ancient music of the Temple of Jerusalem" (476). By addressing in one text musical data from biblical times and modern sources, Fétis unintentionally advanced a paradigm based on an innate contradiction: claiming continuity in chant transmission from Temple times to the present while admitting musical variety in contemporary synagogue practices.[28] Fétis's text, however, needs contextualization. He quotes profusely from the musical scores in Samuel Naumbourg's *Zemirot Yiśra'el, Chants religieux des Israëlites* (Paris, 1847). Naumbourg, the German-born cantor of Paris, expressed in his own writings ideas similar to those found in Fétis's writing (and embedded them in the subtitle to his work "From the Earliest Times to Our Days"). Therefore, ideas about the antiquity and modernity of synagogue music circulated in Europe from Jews to non-Jews, and vice versa.

Studying such unexplored texts on Jewish music shows how Jewish Studies can benefit from expanding its vistas into the musical realm. The Naumbourg–Fétis texts (and scores) show how entrenched modern epistemes of continuity and rupture, memory and forgottenness, authenticity and imitation that are found in discourses about music (racialized, apologetic, or both) can be productive beyond the confines of musicology. This concealed dialogue between an immigrant German cantor-composer active in a major musical metropolis of his time (Paris), who probably inherited concepts about his own lore from his predecessors in Munich, and one of the most influential Christian music historians offers a distilled illustration of the potential music has for Jewish Studies.

Writing liturgical Jewish music in western notation was, as mentioned, a turning point not only in practical terms—freezing for posterity the fleeting sounds of Jewish music—but also in the promotion of wider and extramural discourses about Jewish music. These writings increased exponentially throughout the long nineteenth century, from discrete samples up until the 1830s to a flood of production toward the beginning of the twentieth century. By then, most cantors, synagogue music composers, or choirmasters were able to write and publish versions of the liturgy for themselves, their choirs, or, in the case of liberal congregations, for instruments (usually the organ).[29] These scores comprise a wide span of selections, from attempts to transcribe as accurately as possible oral traditions transmitted from a distant past to new music bearing no traces of previous Jewish practices but embracing musical techniques and aesthetic ideals of the surrounding non-Jewish society.[30] For example, the strong impact of opera, the musical genre that dominated the European urban soundscape throughout the nineteenth century, is notable. Scores also teach us about relations between local versus regional musical traditions, the individual skills of their producers, and the financial resources of the congregations (maintaining large choirs versus small ones) that sustained such publications.

Since the early twentieth century, colonialism, general and Jewish (e.g., the network of schools of the Paris-based Alliance Israélite Universelle or the Berlin-based Hifsverein), and Zionism brought western musical notation beyond Europe, expanding the Jewish music archive with samples from North Africa and the Middle East. Music notation was used in the Grand Synagogue of Wahran (Algeria) during the colonial period, questioning pervasive dichotomies in Jewish Studies along the Reform versus Orthodox divide that were sonically challenged by the religious hybridity of colonial Algerian Jewry.[31] Abraham Z. Idelsohn's publications, based on his fieldwork in late Ottoman Palestine, combined early comparative musicological savvy, technologies of sound recording sponsored by an imperial agency (the Vienna Phonogrammarchiv of the Austro-Hungarian Imperial Academy of Sciences), and the typographical resources and marketing capabilities of German powerhouses of music publishing. Yet, the use of musical notation by Jews outside Europe remained exceptional, with oral tradition remaining the venue of transmission. Only after postcolonial relocation, mainly in Israel, were the musical traditions of Jews from the Middle East and North Africa registered in musical notation.[32]

Toward the end of the nineteenth century, as part of their engagement with the emerging discipline of folklore, Jews and non-Jews started to collect, transcribe, and publish Jewish folk songs in Jewish languages, mostly Yiddish and Ladino. Concern with preserving and studying the voice of "the people"—the rural non-elitist population or women—was symptomatic of the emergence of modern Jewish nationalism. At the same time, these enterprises exposed another modern anxiety: the preoccupation with forgetting the authentic voices of the nation under the steamroller of modernization.

Modern Jewish intellectuals, from Abraham Danon (1857–1925) in the Ottoman Empire working under French scholarly models to his contemporaries Peysekh Marek (1862–1920) and Shaul Ginsburg (1866–1940) who were active in the Russian Empire under the aegis of Russian folkloristics, engaged in the collection and publication of folk songs. They conceptualized these repertoires as the most genuine musical and poetical expressions of the Jewish nation beyond the realm of religious practices. Moreover, these sources were also perceived as potential raw materials for cultural regeneration.[33]

Although these initiatives of folk song collection derived from the elites, there was a democratizing aspect to the archiving practices of Jewish folk songs, which systematically heard and recorded the musical voices of women and the underprivileged. At the same time, such collections opened the doors to other spaces of Jewish musical activity beyond the synagogue and into the intimate privacy of the home or open public spaces, such as the café, the cabaret, musical theater, and eventually the recording studio.

Folk and liturgical music documentation generated another layer in the evergrowing Jewish music archive: that of the popular Jewish song. The industrial printed format of the modern popular song, sheet music, contributed to the massive dissemination of folk songs, liturgical snippets, and new songs in Jewish languages (mostly Yiddish and Hebrew) in arrangements for voice and keyboard.[34] By the late twentieth century, these popular songs became conceptualized, at times for marketing purposes, as "folk," their origins blurred by time. Studying this new popular music by Jews or addressing Jewish subjects can therefore be a productive field of research leading to a tighter integration of Jewishness with race, religion, nation, and ethnic and cultural studies, as well as raising questions about how Jews shaped modern popular music beyond the Jewish community.[35]

Another significant format that transformed Jewish songs into a new product is the multilayered songster. Produced mostly on behalf of Jewish educational institutions, youth movements, and modernizing synagogues, the Jewish songster incorporated the most diverse array of musical layers, such as simple liturgical melodies for congregational singing, Jewish folk songs, new settings of modern Jewish poetry, and non-Jewish songs adopted by and performed in Jewish contexts.[36]

The eclectic plurality of songsters in terms of genre, language, and origin of the songs they included collapsed time and place of origin, exposing again the inherent modernity of Jewish music. It also disclosed the skills, resources, and agendas of those involved in the production and distribution of the songsters. Some songsters were in fact musical *siddurim*, providing a succession of congregational melodies for different services, whereas others catered to summer camps or Zionist clubs in which communal singing became a vital ritual.[37] These song repertoires created communities and transmitted sets of values and ideals through the agency of music.

The vast repository of manuscripts and printed publications of liturgical, folkloric, popular, and all the musical genres in between, as well as the texts surrounding them (editorial notes, analyses, commentaries) discussed in this section, which comprise "the archive" of Jewish music, is still far from being explored. This archive encapsulates the sonic experience of Jews in the past, offering alternative venues for understanding issues such as the multifaceted reciprocal relations of Jews to the Other, the consolidation and reconfiguration of Jewish community identities around sonic assets, gender relations, and how Jews cope with intracommunal social processes and with external factors such as voluntary and forced displacements, ghettoization, acculturation, assimilation, modernization, cosmopolitanizing, and globalization.

A Revolution: The Jewish Sound Archive

Beyond the bookcases of the "Jewish music archive" loom the recorded music shelves, the "Jewish sound archive." In a world saturated by recorded sound accessible at any time and in any place, it is hard to envision how the invention of mechanical sound reproduction dramatically transformed the ways of experiencing music. Experiencing music detached from the bodies that produced it entails a shift of epistemological proportions. The ability to freeze and reproduce countless times what was once a unique and fleeting musical performance changed beyond recognition the production and consumption of music. Eventually, sound recordings also allowed for unimaginable possibilities of sound manipulation, from editing multiple takes to sampling.

Jews plunged into the new technologies of sound reproduction with determination and enthusiasm. They have been recorded throughout a vast geographical area since 1900 and were at the vanguard of the recording industry on a global scale. Recordings allow us to listen to a relatively distant Jewish sonic past. But what is the nature of this recorded past? Who decided whom and what to record? How did technological limitations coerce music that existed in the unlimited timespans and spaces of oral performances? Who heard these recordings, and how did the act of listening change the ways music was performed orally after the exposure to recordings? These are just some of the methodological questions posed by recordings, commercial or ethnographic, of Jewish music.

Access to the older recordings—wax cylinders and different formats of 78 rpm records that dominated the industry until about World War II—is still limited. Such access demands digitization and the building up of metadata to accompany the recordings. This old sonic repository is unique because it reflects actual practices of the pre-recording era largely untouched by editorial considerations because of the thin borderline then separating ethnographic from commercial recordings.

With the advent of cheaper and more portable recording hardware, the Jewish sound archive grew exponentially in two directions. The long-play record, cassette, CD, and digital file nourished the Jewish strand of the global music industry. This industry catered to diverse audiences, some of whom were very intimate with the Jewish community while others looked into an amorphous public. At the same time, new recording capabilities facilitated ethnographic fieldwork, which grew dramatically after World War II and created its own shelves within the sound archive. Eventually the mere accumulation in the archive of diverse media, commercial and ethnographic, flattened the differences between them, and the archive became a repository of sound serving both research and renewed creativity.

Recent studies have shown the productive potential that this sonic repository has to enlighten historical, social, and interdenominational issues in Jewish Studies in very diverse geographical areas in the twentieth century.[38] Moreover, the role of Jews in the development of the recorded music industry opens another venue for questioning the relations between Jews, the music market, and social mobility.[39] Considering the umbilical cord connecting commercial recordings to popular music since the launching of the recording era, it becomes clear that not only "the Jewish sound archive" but also the entire music industry are extremely productive areas for grappling with the relations among Jewishness, ethnicity, race, and social mobility.

Institutionalizing Jewish Music

Producing the "Jewish music and sound archives" and making their resources available required institutional backing, but so did many other aspects of Jewish music cultures. Institutionalization covers different aspects of music making, such as the training of professional music personnel, the printing of music, its recording, and curating and researching.

Studying the institutionalization of synagogue cantors' training, for example, illuminates aspects of modernization in European and American Jewry. Until the mid-nineteenth century, cantors' schooling was based on apprenticeship within the synagogue (as children's choristers accompanying renowned *hazzanim*) or within the family, as a trade transmitted from generation to generation similarly to other music trades such as instrumentalists, the *klezmorim*. Institutions for the training of cantors emerged from rationalizing governmental regulations that demanded a uniform training and accreditation of cantors, such as the Lehrerseminar in Germany. Jewish associations, such as rabbinical and teachers' seminars, cantors' guilds, and klezmer ensembles, began in the late nineteenth century to institute formal and informal training programs.[40] Formalized transmission of cantorial and other musical specializations spread during the twentieth century beyond Europe. Training of Ashkenazi cantors in the United States diversified as cantorial schools became affiliated with Jewish denominations (Conservative, Orthodox, Reform, Renewal) that each promoted its own liturgical music agenda.[41] Outside the United States, training frameworks developed only after the 1980s in supra-denominational institutions such as the Abraham Geiger Kolleg in unified Germany. This project reflects the renaissance of the Jewish community in that country and its liturgical soundscapes while contributing at the same time to the final demise of the "original" German Jewish traditions in favor of repertoires that cater to an entirely new community of immigrants.[42]

In the Middle East and North Africa, in contrast, liturgical music apprenticeship continued to exist within traditional chains of transmission until late in the colonial period when European models of training clergy made some inroads. Such an example was the school Em Habanim in Casablanca that had in the 1940s a loosely organized cantorial program. After the relocation of Jews from Arab countries in Israel, a loosely defined "School of Sephardic Cantors" was established in the 1980s in Israel by Renanot–Institute of Jewish Music. Among other training grounds dedicated to music transmission in systematic contexts, one can mention the proliferation of "camps," short-term retreats dedicated to klezmer and Yiddish songs, that started in New York in 1985 and later spread to Canada and Germany.[43]

To meet the training needs of these schools, written music materials, scores and scholarly writings from as early as the mid-nineteenth century in Europe, and instructional recordings were produced, all of which enriched the Jewish music archive. Companies specializing in the printing of Jewish music also emerged, as well as record labels, radio stations, and radio programs dedicated to the subject. These institutions comprised a network with each node feeding the other. In the United States, for example, Tara Publications provided scores for an array of Jewish contexts of musical performance. As a supermarket of scores of musical genres from different traditions, Tara was an agent in the dissemination of repertoires that until their publication were confined to members of one community.

The past four decades or so have witnessed dramatic growth in the institutionalization of Jewish music research, with the establishment of research institutes, music chairs at universities, composition competitions, online courses, academic journals, blogs, and conferences. Jewish music special interest groups were established at eminent musicological societies, where until recently this was a nonsubject. In their turn, Jewish Studies academic associations, reflecting a growing recognition of music as an integral component of their mandate, also established specialized groups. The question remains as to whether such compartmentalization of music interest groups within musicological or Jewish Studies academic structures contributes to their integration into such professional societies or sets them apart.

Musical Communities

Jewish music is categorized horizontally along a mix of fuzzy categories that combine ethnohistorical communities (Sephardic, Ashkenazi), areas (Eastern European, North African), nation-states (Moroccan, German, Italian), religious orientation (Orthodox, Reform), music genre (cantillation, *nussach*, *niggun*), performers (cantorial, klezmer, choral), languages (Yiddish, Ladino, Arabic), contexts of performance (liturgical, weddings), and any combination of these groupings. Although these categories offer legitimate strategies for addressing the field from a distinct angle, rethinking Jewish music around the notion of communities opens, as Shelemay suggests "opportunities . . . to explore musical transmission and performance not just as expressions or symbols of a given social grouping, but as an integral part of processes that can at different moments help generate, shape, and sustain new collectivities."[44] Musical communities are then aggregates of individuals sharing a "musical capital" and actively engaged in maintaining, transmitting, preserving, and renewing it beyond the categories mentioned earlier. The perimeters of musical communities are difficult to delineate, and yet Jewish music has been and still consolidates collectivities at the most diverse social levels.

Despite methodological and theoretical challenges, sorting out the otherwise indomitable corpus of music associated with Jewish spaces and bodies according to musical communities can be a most productive strategy for those archiving, cataloging, and researching Jewish music. Reconsidering how Jewish musical collectivities emerge in relation to the earlier mentioned categories that still dominate classifications, from sound archives to online playlists, can also enrich Jewish Studies.

As a people ultimately forged by dispersion, Jews traditionally group, musically speaking, around repertoires transmitted within a lineage, factual or imagined, of family and close community ties anchored in territorial units from small villages to nation-states and to imperial or transnational levels. Liturgical music communities exemplify such groupings, combining a shared sense of ancestry and allegiance to a distinctive lineage of rabbinical authority and version of the prayer book, all reinforced by a routine of cyclical performances. Democratic participation in the performance of prayer creates strong community bonds, more than any other type of music. No wonder then that for many practitioners and outside observers, Jewish music means synagogue music.

What binds the sense of belonging to a Jewish community of prayer? Analyzing contemporary performances or the perceptions of performers regarding their repertoire reveals lineages of transmission (collective memory) and discontinuities (collective forgetting) that forge communities through liturgical music. Decisions about what to maintain and what to change in liturgical music reveal awareness both of belonging to unbroken lineages and the strategies of survival under shifting social conditions.

Do communities that keep the label "Spanish-Portuguese" comprise a coherent synagogue music community that traces its pedigree back to their founding fathers, the *conversos* who returned to Jewish practice since the mid-sixteenth century? Or is each such synagogue a discrete musical community because of the diverse historical circumstances in Amsterdam, London, Bayonne, Gibraltar, Livorno, or New York? What was the nature of that "original" music practice of Spanish-Portuguese Jews, if there ever was one? How did Jews who were detached from the practice of Judaism for several generations constitute a liturgical music repertoire? How did Jewish immigrants who relocated in the twentieth century, joining "Spanish-Portuguese" synagogues in the cities mentioned earlier, negotiate their musical lore vis-à-vis local practice?

When attending services in each Spanish-Portuguese synagogue one can literally "hear" their social history; for example, in the similarities of certain High Holiday and Ninth of Av melodies with those of "Eastern Sephardic" synagogues (remnants of Ottoman Sephardic cantors hired to serve "Western Sephardic" synagogues early in their history); of the input of German Jews who preferred to join the "aristocratic" Spanish-Portuguese synagogue of New York rather than Eastern European ones; of Moroccan, Iraqi, and Persian Jews who joined the Amsterdam and London synagogues after World War II; or of opera composers active in Livorno's synagogue in the nineteenth century.

Yet these synagogues shared in the past a common pool of cantors, and some of them auto-documented their musical lore in musical notation. Thus, despite noticeable sonic differences between "Spanish-Portuguese" liturgical music communities, one can listen today to shared threads of musical memory, as well as modern revivals based on archival sources. More recently, the internet has facilitated the renewal of exchanges of "authentic" Spanish-Portuguese liturgical music between different centers (http://www.sandpcentral.org).

Liturgical music studies then have a potential for refining questions such as how Jewish communities evolved around musical capitals in a specific locality or how these capitals were transferred across great distances by individual performers on the move. Mobility (by free will or by force) generated musical contacts, exchanges, hybridization, and erasures that can still be heard. By the modern period, the variety of Jewish liturgical music communities was staggering, and yet members of each community could still conceive of themselves also as members of larger aggregates, of "imagined musical communities." Jewish Studies scholars can therefore benefit from listening to the diverse constellations of contemporary Jewish musical communities, rather than imposing on them rigid binaries such as Eastern/Western or Sephardic/Ashkenazi ones.

A similar approach can be applied to Jewish musical communities built around Jewish folk songs that parallel but do not always coincide with liturgical music communities. Here the proficiency in, interest on, and longing for songs in Jewish vernacular languages are the underlying motivation. Many of those participating in such folk-song–oriented music communities perceive belonging to them as an alternative to synagogue affiliation. One can articulate a Jewish sense of belonging by participating in a Yiddish song circle meeting regularly, rather than attending synagogue services.

Liturgical and folk song communities are not necessarily two binary opposites but rather ends of a continuum as prayers can become folk songs, and vice versa. An example of such a crossover music community is one centered on the singing of *piyyutim*, not as liturgical songs but rather as a cultural asset whose performance creates bonds between individuals belonging to diverse ethnohistorical backgrounds outside the synagogue. This phenomenon that started in Israel at the turn of the twenty-first century also exemplifies the agency of modern corporate Jewish philanthropy (the Avi Chai Foundation in this case) in creating contemporary musical communities that challenge conventional binaries, not only the liquid religious/secular divide but also the ethnohistorical one. The same principle can be applied to Hasidic *niggunim* that were detached from their communities of origin to become Jewish folksongs via Zionist filters performed in new musical communities, such as youth movements or summer camps.[45] In this case too, binaries of Jewish Studies collapse, including the one regarding oral versus written cultures, because *niggunim* turned into modern Hebrew songs are transmitted both orally and in songsters.

The realignment of Jews according to citizenship in nation-states (including Israel) created unprecedented musical strategies of being (or remaining) sonically Jewish. Modern nation-based Jewish musical collectivities produced "national liturgies" and "national Jewish archives." "National liturgies" consist of attempts to create a soundscape that symbolically encompasses the musical lore of members of diverse Jewish ethnohistorical communities sharing citizenship within a modern nation-state.

These "national" Jewish liturgies were top-down musical projects that met with partial success. France's Third Republic and Victorian England, where centralizing Jewish institutions—the Consistoire Central Israélite de France, Board of Deputies of British Jews, and United Synagogue of Great Britain—consolidated diverse ethnohistorical communities, produced musical liturgies that combined Ashkenazi and Sephardic elements in an effort to consolidate a sense of cohesiveness at the level of ritual within a subaltern Jewish collective embedded in a nation-state.[46] In the United States, a "nussach America" (American liturgy) emerged from grassroots practices related to the centralization of the training of cantors by Conservative, Orthodox, and Reform denominations.[47]

A similar phenomenon occurred in the early years of Israel within the national religious movement that attempted to create a "nussach achid" (integrated liturgy) incorporating Sephardic-Mizrahi melodies within an Ashkenazi liturgical framework. Changes in the political configuration on which this musical initiative relied were a major factor in its demise. Today the national religious movement is musically redefined by a new repertoire dominated by tunes authored by Shlomo Carlebach and his acolytes. Paradoxically, this new aesthetics links Israeli synagogues to a global trend that weakens the "national moment" in Jewish liturgical music.

Other institutions, differing in their profile, organization, and sources of funding, developed in nation-states where Jewish communities or individual agents promoted local Jewish music with the support of state agencies and private philanthropy; for example, the European Center for Jewish Music in Hanover (Germany), the Jewish Music Institute in London, the European Institute of Jewish Music in Paris, and Yuval Italia in Milan (now the Center for Contemporary Jewish Documentation). Each institution is engaged in activities of preservation and the diffusion of music mostly deriving from the Jewish traditions that developed within each nation-state.

Lastly, one must note the unique status of "Jewish music" within the state of Israel where Jews comprise a majority. This unprecedented development challenges the study of music in Jewish Studies as it does in other scholarly disciplines. One could argue that all the musical facilities of the State of Israel—its archives, libraries, printing press, record companies, as well as all institutions of learning and venues of performance—are a legitimate subject of "Jewish music" inquiry. Without entering the intractable and ideologically loaded relationship between the spheres of Jewishness and Israeliness in academia, music—because it is an open system of signification—is precisely the field that can illuminate such relations from new perspectives. By musically deconstructing Israeli Jewish society, one can see the productiveness of abandoning schemes that contrast futile musical categories based on territory and nationalism. Music labeled Jewish, Israeli, or both flows from and into Israel as just another node in the Jewish musical map in a continuous exchange that blurs the sense of place and time in the conception, performance, reception, and preservation of musical repertoires.

New Age Jewish musical communities, a kind of antithesis to the communities described earlier, have proliferated since the 1960s in the ambiguous spaces that bridge metamorphosed traditional liturgies and antinominalist spirituality. These circles, often created around the idea of Jewish renewal, offer their membership diverse types of communal experiences mediated by bundles of musical items sorted out from the Jewish past (i.e., from the archive), borrowed from other religious faiths, and new creations.[48] This musical porosity reflects the great fluidity of contemporary Jewishness, tilted by nationalism (territorial or diasporic), ethnicity, competing denominations, decentralized spiritual authority, and, as ever in Jewish history, the specter (or blessing) of assimilation.

Finally, Jewish musical communities can be centered on gender. Gender-based musical communities emerged from segregation (and from the agency that such segregation eventually generated), such as Orthodox women singing, or by choice, as in the case of feminist Jewish music initiatives that of late have created their own repertoires. In addition, LGBTQ Jewish communities enroll music making and consumption as one component of their social strategies.[49]

Focusing on musical communities can be a productive strategy for examining how music can enrich Jewish Studies. Such a strategy explores how repertoires are constructed, canonized, and renewed by the dynamics of memorialization, forgetting, and innovation. An ever-shifting array of agents with diverse degrees of power within the community—cantors, composers, educators, synagogue officials, and music publishers—and allegiance to place (locals, immigrants, invited performers) constitute these repertoires. Cohesiveness is not a necessary staple of musical communities, because they constantly evolve over time and place; they split and reconstitute themselves, allowing individuals to navigate among different musical options or even participate in several communities at the same time. Such omnivorous Jewish music clients offer another example of how difficult it is to impose categories on the variety of ways of being musically Jewish or of experiencing Judaism through music without affiliating to any specific Jewish institution or even identifying as Jewish. Being formally Jewish (in any variant of Jewishness) is certainly not a sine qua non of being a creator or consumer of Jewish music.

Concentrating on communities does not necessarily imply ethnographic presentism. The history of the Jews can be also examined via musical lenses, illuminating how religious movements or ethnic constellations were negotiated through and defined by music. The contribution of music studies to elucidating the origins and development of Hasidism in mid-eighteenth-century Eastern Europe can be substantial and surprising (even subversive). Certainly, the more recent emergence of the disputed concept of "Mizrahi Jews" in Israel since the 1970s can be illustrated through music studies in a clearer manner than by any other field of scholarly inquiry.[50]

Music in Jewish Studies Today and Beyond

Despite its potential to enrich every scholarly discipline addressing Jews and Jewishness beyond musicology, music has remained on the peripheries of Jewish Studies. Listening, actively or figuratively, to music associated with Jews and

Jewishness and considering music as a unique resource for the study of the Jewish experience past and present do not require musicological training. Certainly, musicologists are equipped to illuminate, through musical analysis, layers of signification in repertoires performed by Jews or conceptualized as Jewish. However, studying music from alternative perspectives—historical, cultural, sociological, anthropological, aesthetical, economical, or technological—can be no less productive. It can facilitate music's full integration into Jewish Studies beyond the insights that musicology offers. Many enlightening studies quoted in this chapter were penned by non-musicologists. They can serve as an inspiration for future endeavors.

There are methodological challenges, however, to a potential "musical turn" in Jewish Studies. The internet has revolutionized the access to repositories of music in all formats while at the same time generating contexts of performance and new and unexpected musical communities. With this widespread availability of endless quantities of soundbites and music images (videos, as well as scanned scores) has come the need to select the chaff from the wheat. One can, of course, trust the authority of databases of established institutions, such as universities and major public libraries. However, some major repositories remain in private hands, and some are not cataloged. A casual family recording uploaded to YouTube may be the only available source for a certain musical item, event, or context. Improving online searching tools, perhaps with the contribution of AI, and the processing of data mining into visual representations can sharpen research questions about Jews and music that can be integrated by Jewish Studies scholars beyond musicology.

How can music contribute to "big questions" in Jewish Studies, such as differences in the Jewish experience under Christianity and Islam, a vexing question treated by scholars from diverse disciplines?[51] How did the ethical and aesthetic attitudes of these two major religious systems and political powers toward music affect Jewish musical cultures, or vice versa? To what extent was Jewish agency in music constructed as a resistance to or co-optation of non-Jewish musical norms and institutions? Those interested in colonial studies can examine the impact of European Christian imperial expansion into the lands of Islam and its aggressive policies of cultural and economic domination on both Jews and Muslims through the lenses of music. The importation of new musical instruments, notation, educational systems, and, later, recording technologies, radio, and cinema affected not only musical creativity but also led to the reification of music as an object of consumption and altered its venues of transmission—shaking the delicate social ecology that connected Jews and Muslims through music before European colonialism. Investments of Jewish capital in musical enterprises in the Islamic realm and the tensions this investment caused comprise another venue for the examination of modern Judeo-Islamic encounters. After almost all Jews, and among them a large contingent of prominent musicians, were uprooted (willingly or by force) from the lands of Islam, their music became a field for a wider exploration of issues, such as the construction of memory, nostalgia, belonging, and cultural appropriation. These are some issues related to a "big question" in Jewish Studies that can be illuminated anew through music.

Recommended Readings

Bohlman, Philip V. *The World Centre for Jewish Music in Palestine, 1936–1940: Jewish Musical Life on the Eve of World War II* (Clarendon Press, 1992).

Cohen, Judah M. *Jewish Religious Music in Nineteenth-Century America: Restoring the Synagogue Soundtrack* (Indiana University Press, 2019).

Guesnet, François, Benjamin Matis, and Antony Polonsky, eds. *Jews and Music-Making in the Polish Lands: Polin 32* (2020).

HaCohen, Ruth. *The Music Libel against the Jews: Vocal Fictions of Noise and Harmony* (Yale University Press, 2011).

Hammarlund, Anders. *A Prayer for Modernity Politics and Culture in the World of Abraham Baer (1834–1894)* (Svenskt visarkiv/Statens musikverk, 2013).

Harrán, Don. *Salamone Rossi: Jewish Musician in Late Renaissance Mantua* (Oxford University Press, 1999).

Loeffler, James. *The Most Musical Nation: Jews and Culture in the Late Russian Empire* (Yale University Press, 2010).

Móricz, Klára. *Jewish Identities: Nationalism, Racism, and Utopianism in Twentieth-Century Music* (University of California Press, 2008).

Schwartz, Dov. *"The Soul Seeks Its Melodies": Music in Jewish Thought* (Academic Studies, 2022).

Shelemay, Kay Kaufman. *Music, Ritual, and Falasha History* (Michigan State University Press, 1989).

Shelleg, Assaf. *Jewish Contiguities and the Soundtrack of Israeli History* (Oxford University Press, 2014).

Seroussi, Edwin. *Sonic Ruins of Modernity: The Sephardic Song Today* (Routledge, 2023).

Slobin, Mark. *Fiddler on the Move: Exploring the Klezmer World* (Oxford University Press, 2000).

Summit, Jeffrey A. *Singing God's Words: The Performance of Biblical Chant in Contemporary Judaism* (Oxford University Press, 2016).

Wood, Abigail. *And Now We're All Brothers: Singing in Yiddish in Contemporary North America* (Ashgate, 2013).

Notes

1. For the nonverbal sonic dimension of Judaism, see Edwin Seroussi, "Music: The 'Jew' of Jewish Studies," *Jewish Studies—Yearbook of the World Union of Jewish Studies* 46 (2009): 3–84; Judit Frigyesi, "The 'Ugliness' of Jewish Prayer—Voice Quality as an Expression of Identity," *Musicology* 7 (2007): 99–118, and "The Sound Issue" of *AJS Perspectives* (2015). For core issues and biographical updates, see Edwin Seroussi, "Jüdische Musik," in Die *Musik in Geschichte und Gegenwart Online*, www.mgg-online.com/articles/mgg15539/2.0/mgg15539. This chapter refers only to selected works to show how diverse issues have been addressed. Online resources, most especially in the main reference tool for music studies, *RILM: Abstracts of Music Literature* now under EBSCOhost (www.ebsco.com), provide extensive resources. A search for "Jewish music" in this platform produced 10,009 results in January 2024.

2. Philip V. Bohlman, *Jewish Music and Modernity* (Oxford University Press, 2008), xx.

3. The idea of music as a domestication of a natural resource was suggested by Attali as the primordial stage, a ritualistic one, in the evolution of the economy of sound; Jacques Attali, *Noise: The Political Economy of Music* (University of Minnesota Press, 1985).

4. Judit Niran Frigyesi, *Writing on Water* (Central European University Press, 2018).

5. Gershom Scholem, *A Life in Letters, 1914–1982*, ed. Anthony David (Harvard University Press, 2002), 404.

6. *Maqam* (Arabic), *makam* (Turkish), *mugham* (Azeri), *maqom* (Uzbek), and other cognates refer to the scales, modes, and melodic formulas underlying most music in the lands of Islam. See Mark Kligman, *Maqām and Liturgy: Ritual, Music, and Aesthetics of Syrian Jews in Brooklyn* (Wayne State University Press, 2009).

7. Magdalena Waligórska, *Klezmer's Afterlife: An Ethnography of the Jewish Music Revival in Poland and Germany* (Oxford University Press, 2013). For the evolution of the term "klezmer music," see Walter Z. Feldman, *Klezmer: Music, History, and Memory* (Oxford University Press, 2016), xiv–xviii.

8. The literature on this subject is vast. For a succinct overview, see Philip V. Bohlman, "Music before the Nation, Music after Nationalism," *Musicology Australia* 31 (2009): 79–100, esp. 83–92.

9. "National" appeared as early as the late 1830s in Salomon Sulzer's introduction to the first volume of his *Schir Zion* (Vienna, ca. 1839). He defines the oldest stratum of Ashkenazi (southern German) liturgical music as *National-melodie*. However, Sulzer's sense of Jewish "national" music at this early stage of his life was premature and Eurocentric.

10. Esther Schmidt, "Nationalism and the Creation of Jewish Music: The Politicization of Music and Language in the German-Jewish Press prior to the Second World War," *Musica Judaica* 15 (2000): 1–31.

11. The most ambitious enterprise is the introductory essays to Abraham Z. Idelsohn, *Hebräisch-orientalischer Melodienschatz* (10 vols.; Benjamin Herz, 1914–32). Idelsohn's ideas and methodology were rooted in postulates circulating among musicologists in central Europe, some of whom were not Jewish, at the turn of the twentieth century. See Yonatan Turgeman, "Neima Kedosha: The Problem of the Scholar-Composer in Modern Jewish Musicology" [Hebrew] (PhD. diss., Hebrew University of Jerusalem, 2023).

392   CHAPTER 17

12. See Yaakov Elman and Israel Gershoni, *Transmitting Jewish Traditions: Orality Textuality and Cultural Diffusion* (Yale University Press, 2000), 1–26.

13. James Loeffler, "The Lust Machine: Recording and Selling the Jewish Nation in the Late Russian Empire," *Polin: Studies in Polish Jewry* 32 (2020): 257–77. Minkowsky's position was not shared by his colleagues, many of whom were quick to embrace the new technology.

14. Important repositories of Jewish music are the Department of Music of the National Library of Israel that incorporates the Jacob Michael collection amid private estates of composers and musicologists; the Klau Library of the Hebrew Union College in Cincinnati housing the Eduard Birnbaum Collection of Jewish Music; the Library of the Jewish Theological Seminary of America with estates of cantors, composers, and music scholars; the University of Pennsylvania that now incorporates the Eric Mandell Collection formerly at Gratz College; the Vernadsky National Library of Ukraine that holds the collections of Russian scholars since imperial times, most particularly Moshe Beregovski; and the Center for Jewish History in New York City. Institutions dedicated to Jewish music, such as the l'Institut Européen des Musiques Juives in Paris and the Europäische Zentrum für Jüdische Musik at the Hochschule für Musik, Theater und Medien Hannover, have holdings of primary sources.

15. These issues have been discussed in programmatic articles. See Israel Adler, "Problems in the Study of Jewish Music," in *Proceedings of the World Congress on Jewish Music, Jerusalem, 1978*, ed. Judith Cohen (Institute for the Translation of Hebrew Literature, 1982), 15–27; Philip B. Bohlman, "Music," in *Oxford Handbook of Jewish Studies*, ed. Martin Goodman et al. (Oxford University Press, 2002), 852–69; Kay Kaufman Shelemay, "Mythologies and Realities in the Study of Jewish Music," *World of Music* 37 (1995): 24–38; Mark Slobin, "Ten Paradoxes and Four Dilemmas of Studying Jewish Music," *World of Music* 37 (1995): 18–23; Judah M. Cohen, "Whither Jewish Music? Jewish Studies, Music Scholarship, and the Tilt between Seminary and University," *Association of Jewish Studies Review* 32 (2008): 29–48; Heidy Zimmermann, "Was heißt 'jüdische Musik'? Grundzüge eines Diskurses im 20. Jahrhundert," in *Jüdische Musik? Fremdbilder, Eigenbilder*, ed. John Eckhard and Heidy Zimmermann (Böhlau, 2004), 11–32, and review of this last cite in Daniel Jütte, "Jüdische Musik und Geschichte jüdischer Musiker," *Aschkenas* 15 (2005): 243–55. Also Joshua S. Walden, ed., *Cambridge Companion to Jewish Music* (Cambridge University Press, 2015); Tina Frühauf, ed., *Oxford Handbook of Jewish Music Studies* (Oxford University Press, 2023).

16. For the earliest surviving music scores in manuscript, see Israel Adler, *Hebrew Notated Manuscript Sources up to circa 1840: A Descriptive and Thematic Catalogue with a Checklist of Printed Sources* (2 vols.; Henle, 1989).

17. Israel Adler, *Hebrew Writings concerning Music in Manuscripts and Printed Books from Geonic Times up to 1800* (Henle, 1975); Jonathan L. Friedmann, *Music in Jewish Thought: Selected Writings, 1890–1920* (McFarland, 2009).

18. First edition of *Sefer Hassidim* (Bologna, 1538), para. 158 (fol. 23a-b).

19. Ari Kelman and Jeremiah Lockwood, "From Aesthetics to Experience: How Changing Conceptions of Prayer Changed the Sound of Jewish Worship," *Religion and American Culture* 30 (2020): 26–62.

20. Ezra Fleischer, "On the Musical Agenda of the 'Sephardi Revolution' in the Forms of the Medieval Hebrew Song" [Hebrew], *Yuval 7: Studies in Honor of Israel Adler*, ed. Eliyahu Schleifer and Edwin Seroussi (2001) Hebrew sect., 5–22.

21. Edwin Seroussi with Rivka Havassy, *Incipitario sefardí: El cancionero judeo-español en fuentes hebreas (siglos XV–XIX)* (Spanish National Research Council, 2009). For this phenomenon in early Yiddish song collections, see Diana Matut, *Dichtung und Musik im Frühneuzeitlichen Aschkenas* (Brill, 2010).

22. Israel Najara, *She'erit Yisrael by Zemirot Yisrael*, ed. Tova Beeri and Edwin Seroussi (2 vols.; Ben-Zvi Institute and Rosen Foundation, 2023).

23. Edward Blank YIVO Vilna Online Collections (https://archives.cjh.org/repositories/7/resources/3614).

24. For the contribution of the Jewish press, rare manuscript scores, and ephemera to the study of music in a modern community in flux, see Francesco Spagnolo, "The Musical Traditions of the Jews of Piedmont (Italy)" (PhD diss., Hebrew University of Jerusalem, 2007).

25. See Hans Nathan and P. V. Bohlman, *Israeli Folk Music Songs of the Early Pioneers* (A-R Editions, 1994); Natan Shahar, *Israeli Songs of Keren Kayemet* (Keren Kayemet le-Yisra'el Archive, 1994).

26. For Reuchlin, see Hanoch Avenary, *The Ashkenazi Tradition of Biblical Chant between 1500 and 1900: Documentation and Musical Analysis* (Tel Aviv University, Ministry of Education and Culture, 1978). For Marcello, see Edwin Seroussi, "In Search of Jewish Musical Antiquity in the 18th-Century Venetian Ghetto: Reconsidering the Hebrew Melodies in Benedetto Marcello's Estro Poetico-Armonico," *Jewish Quarterly Review* 93 (2002): 149–200.

27. François-Joseph Fétis, *Histoire Générale de la Musique Depuis les Temps Plus Anciens Jusqu'à Nos Jours*, Vol. 1 (Didot, 1869), 369–476.

28. The Anglophone world contributed similar texts, such as William C. Stafford, *A History of Music* (1830) (Boethius Press, 1985); David Aharon De Sola and Emanuel Aguilar. *The Ancient Melodies of the Liturgy of the Spanish and Portuguese Jews* (Wertheimer, 1857); Carl Engel, *The Music of the Most Ancient Nations, Particularly of the Assyrians, Egyptians, and Hebrews* (Murray, 1864).

29. Edwin Seroussi, "The Jewish Liturgical Music Printing Revolution: A Preliminary Assessment," *Studies in Contemporary Jewry* 31 (2020): 100–36, and in *Textual Transmission in Contemporary Jewish Cultures*, ed. A. Bar Levav and U. Rebhun, 99–136.

30. Philip V. Bohlman, "The Age of Jewish Music Collecting," in *Music, Libraries, and the Academy: Essays in Honor of Lenore Coral*, ed. James P. Cassaro (A-R Editions. 2007), 81–103.

31. The use of the organ in Wahran was challenged by the Chief Rabbi of Mandatory Palestine, Abraham Isaac Kook, disclosing the tensions that musical strategies generated across modern Jewish mentalities. See Gabriel Abensour, "A Letter from Algerian Rabbi David Askénazi to Rabbi Kook Advocating for the Use of the Organ in Synagogue Services," *Zutot* 20 (2023): 1–18.

32. See Isaac Levy, ed., *Antología de la liturgia judeo-española* (10 vols.; Ministry of Education and Culture, Jerusalem, 1959–80).

33. Abraham Danon, "Recueil de romances judéo-espagnols chantées en Turquie," *Revue des Etudes Juives* 32 (1896): 102–23, 263–75; 33 (1897): 122–39, 255–68. The collection of Yiddish folk songs by Ginsburg and Marek, *Evreiskiia narodnyia piesni v Rossii* (1901), was reprinted with commentaries by Dov Noy (Bar Ilan University Press, 1991). Both collections contain only lyrics. Non-Jewish Spanish scholars Ramon Menéndez Pidal and Manuel Manrique de

Lara, who were engaged in searching for the roots of their own legacy that they assumed was preserved by Sephardic Jews in "the Orient," continued Danon's work. See Diana Díaz González, "La labor de folclorista de Manuel Manrique de Lara en el contexto de su vida y obra," *Cuadernos de música iberoamericana* 23 (2012): 45–66. The Russian Empire was also the scene of attempts to document Jewish folksongs. A celebrated enterprise benefiting from the modern technology of sound recording was the An-Sky expedition. Among the earliest products of this initiative was Susman (Zinoviy) Kiselgof's *Lider-zamelbukh far der yidishe shul un familie* (Berlin, 1912) and Zinovy Kiselgof, Leonid Guralnik, and Evgeny Khazdan, eds., *Jewish Folk Melodies* (Jewish Community Center of St. Petersburg, 2001). On Kiselgof, see Lyudmila Sholokhova, "Zinoviy Kiselhof as a Founder of Jewish Musical Folklore Studies in the Russian Empire at the Beginning of the 20th Century," in *Klesmer, Klassik, jiddisches Lied: Jüdische Musikkultur in Osteuropa*, ed. Karl-Erich Grözinger (Harrassowitz, 2004), 63–72. The accumulated materials of ethnographic expeditions by Soviet Jewish musicologist and folklorist Moshe Beregovski appeared mostly posthumously. See *Jewish Musical Folklore*, Kiev: Vernadsky National Library, 2013–23 (www.audio.ipri.kiev.ua). On Beregovski, see Michael Lukin, "Method and Myth: M. Beregovski's Contribution to the Study of the Traditional Yiddish Folksong," in *Musik Traditionen* 4, ed. Ulrich Morgenstern and Thomas Nußbaumer (Böhlau, 2019): 107–42. The YIVO institute in Vilnius provided further impetus to the publication of folksongs and niggunim. See Abraham Moshe Bernstein, *Muzikalisher pinkes: Nigunim zamlung fun yidishn folks-oytser, mit tekst un erklerungen* (Jewish Historical Ethnographical Society of the Name of Sh An-ski in Wilno, 1927).

34. Mark Slobin, *Tenement Songs: The Popular Music of the Jewish Immigrants* (University of Illinois Press, 1982). Ladino folksongs appeared in other formats. See Alberto Hemsi, *Coplas sefardíes (Chansons Judéo-espagnoles) for Voice and Piano, Alexandria (Egypt): Édition orientale de musique and Paris: The Author, 1932–1973*. Hemsi based these arrangements on his ethnography; see his *Cancionero sefardí*, ed. Edwin Seroussi et al. (Hebrew University of Jerusalem, 1995).

35. Because of the centrality of race issues in U.S. society, most research in this area relates to American Jews. See Charles Hersch, "'Every Time I Try to Play Black, It Comes out Sounding Jewish': Jewish Jazz Musicians and Racial Identity," *American Jewish History* 97 (2013): 259–82 (and the copious bibliography in n. 4); Jonathan Karp, "Blacks, Jews, and the Business of Race Music, 1945–1955," in *Chosen Capital: The Jewish Encounter with American Capitalism*, ed. Rebecca Kobrin (Rutgers University Press, 2012): 141–67; Jeffrey Paul Melnick, *A Right to Sing the Blues: African Americans, Jews, and American Popular Song* (Harvard University Press, 1999); Jon Stratton, *Jews, Race, and Popular Music* (Routledge, 2017); Ari Katorza, *Stairway to Paradise: Jews, Blacks, and the American Music Revolution* (De Gruyter, 2021).

36. An early specimen is Abraham Zvi Idelsohn's *Sefer Hashirim* (Berlin, 1912), subsequently expanded and reprinted in several editions. For a contextual analysis of one songster, see Edwin Seroussi, "Songs That Young Gershom Scholem May Have Heard: Jacob Beimel's *Jüdische Melodieen, Jung Juda* and Jewish Musical Predicaments in Early Twentieth-Century Berlin," *Jewish Quarterly Review* 110 (2020): 64–101.

37. The three volumes of *Zamru Lo: Congregational Melodies, Prayers, Zemirot, Hymns*, compiled and edited by Moshe Nathanson (Cantor's Assembly of America, 1955, 1960, 1974), is one such aggregate. Nathanson was a pioneer agent in the transatlantic transmission of

Hebrew songs from Palestine to America, as well as in blurring the religious/secular divide. See Moshe Nathanson, *Manginoth Shirenu: Hebrew Melodies, Old and New, Religious and Secular* (Hebrew Publication Co., 1939). For imported "Palestinian" Hebrew songs, see Eli Sperling, *Singing the Land: Hebrew Music and Early Zionism in America* (University of Michigan Press, 2024). Similar musical repertoires circulated between Eretz Israel and Europe during the interwar period; see Joseph Jacobsen and Erwin Jospe, *Hawa Naschira! = Auf! Lasst Uns Singen!* (A. J. Benjamin, 1935), reprinted with a *Lexikon,* ed. Dagmar Deuring et al. (Dölling und Galitz Verlag, 2001).

38. See Michael Aylward, "Early Recordings of Jewish Music in Poland," *Polin: Studies in Polish Jewry* 16 (2020): 60–63; Christopher Silver, *Recording History: Jews Muslims and Music across Twentieth-Century North Africa* (Stanford University Press, 2022); Veronika Seidlová, "The Social Life of Jewish Music Records from 1948 Czechoslovakia by Hazzan Josef Weiss," *Lidé města (Urban People)* 24 (2022): 225–62.

39. Jonathan Karp, "The Roots of Jewish Concentration in the American Popular Music Business, 1890–1945," in *Doing Business in America: A Jewish History,* ed. Steven J. Ross et al. (Purdue University Press, 2018), 123–44.

40. For the training of cantors in mid-nineteenth-century Germany, see Geoffrey Goldberg, *Between Tradition and Modernity: The High Holy Day Melodies of Minhag Ashkenaz according to Ḥazzan Maier Levi of Esslingen* (Jewish Music Research Centre, 2019), 43–60. The training of *klezmorim* in Eastern Europe is discussed in Feldman, *Klezmer.*

41. Judah M. Cohen, *The Making of a Reform Jewish Cantor: Musical Authority, Cultural Investment* (Indiana University Press, 2009).

42. Sarah M. Ross, *The Moralization of Jewish Heritage in Germany: Sustaining Jewish Life in the Twenty-First Century* (Lexington Books, 2024).

43. For the transmission of Yiddish song, see Mark Slobin, "A Hundred Years of Yiddish Song Mobility," *Arts* 10, no. 3 (2021): 65; for klezmer camps, see Henry Sapoznik, "KlezKamp and the Rise of Yiddish Cultural Literacy," in *American Klezmer: Its Roots and Offshoots,* ed. Mark Slobin (University of California Press, 2002), 174–86.

44. Kay Kaufman Shelemay, "Musical Communities: Rethinking the Collective in Music," *Journal of the American Musicological Society* 64 (2011): 349–90.

45. On Hassidic *niggunim* as Zionist songs, see Yaakov Mazor, "From Hassidic Niggun to Israeli song" [Hebrew] *Katedra* 115 (2004): 95–128.

46. For England, see Charles Heller, "Masters of the London Blue Book—Marking 350 Years since the Resettlement of Jews in England," *Journal of Synagogue Music* 31 (2006): 67–76. For France, see Gérard Ganvert, "La musique synagogale à Paris à l'époque du premier temple consistorial (1822–1874)" (PhD diss., Sorbonne, 1984).

47. Boaz Tarsi, "Observations on Practices of 'Nusach' in America," *Asian Music* 33 (2002): 175–219.

48. Jeffrey A. Summit, *The Lord's Song in a Strange Land: Music and Identity in Contemporary Jewish Worship* (Oxford University Press, 2000).

49. Ellen Koskoff, *Music in Lubavitcher Life* (University of Illinois Press, 2000), 120–40; Gordon Dale, "Music and the Negotiation of Orthodox Jewish Gender Roles in Partnership Minyanim," *Contemporary Jewry* 35 (2015): 35–53; Judah Cohen, "Musical Alternatives: Debbie Friedman in Houston, 1978–1984," *Journal of Jewish Education* 88 (2022): 75–94.

50. Amy Horowitz, *Mediterranean Israeli Music and the Politics of the Aesthetic* (Wayne State University Press, 2010); Motti Regev, *When the Guitar Scratches a Song of Longing: Electric Guitars and Mizrahiyut in Israeli Pop-Rock* [Hebrew] (Lamda, 2023).

51. Mark R. Cohen, *Under Crescent and Cross* (Princeton University Press, 2008) and "Islam and the Jews: Myth, Counter-Myth, History," in *Jews among Muslims: Communities in the Precolonial Middle East*, ed. S. A. Deshen and W. P. Zenner (New York University Press, 1996), 50–63.

18

Visual Culture

Maya Balakirsky Katz, Bar Ilan University

THANKS TO THE GROWING number of scholars engaged in nontextual or extra-textual "objects," we can no longer consider the history of art an esoteric or beleaguered academic specialization in Jewish Studies. The early distaste of Jewish scholars for art evolved from the chauvinistic disciplinary attitudes of the first art historians toward the definition and function of art. With the deep-seated marginalization of minority arts in the founding years of art history, the first scholars of Jewish art had to argue first principles. They sought to prove that Jews made art throughout their history and enjoyed a creative spirit based on the basic definitions of humanity and the history of civilizations. In short order, these intrepid scholars in early art history and adjacent departments convinced the most innovative Jewish Studies scholars that "Jews" and "art" are a mutually constructive relationship. As the rebel pioneers of the Jewish visual field began to unlock the languages of art, they simultaneously began to question the tenets of the discipline in which they were trained in the history of fine arts in German and Viennese universities.

Only after Jewish Studies embraced some of the methodologies of art history did the academic study of Jewish art begin to develop in earnest. No longer needing to legitimize the existence of Jewish creativity, art historians turned to identify a new set of first principles focused on subjective aspects of Jewish art throughout the ages. Their exploration was supported and deepened by the work of scriptural scholars. In Jewish Studies journals and academic forums, Talmud scholars slowly convinced text scholars that Scripture did not forbid art, with scholars emerging from Hasidism convincingly arguing that it even demanded art. Scholars who identified the blossoming of modern Jewish art in the context of the Jewish national project of emancipation and Zionism in previous decades have been joined more recently by scholars exploring the renewed interest in the production of "authentic" Jewish art in the context of premodern, modern, and postmodern messianic movements.

It is perhaps ironic that after a century of academic study, the field currently concludes that Jews have not made much fine art in the first definitions of "*Kunst*" and that the vast majority of all their other "stuff" was distorted, destroyed, and publicly burned. This situation helps explain the outsized effort that the field of Jewish art has exerted on behalf of archival, preservation, cataloging, and institutionalization efforts. Art historians have found careers in the academy and the exponential growth of Jewish museums, libraries, and community centers worldwide.

This growth in the Jewish institutional world has influenced some of the most significant developments in Jewish Studies. With history and Scripture being the two most stable subfields in Jewish studies, scholars of Jewish art reshaped the field by insistently overturning the conclusions that research had arrived at without examining the evidence that "objects" provided. At the same time, the debate forced art historians to seriously consider "objects" in relationship to "words," which was difficult for those trained in classic art history departments. These developments have brought the field closer to the original aims of Jewish Studies by taking us closer to Jewish experiences, what the first scholars of Wissenschaft des Judentums called "historical Judaism."

Disciplinary Formation and Its Longitudinal Repercussions

Efforts to reconcile the political and theoretical investments of art history and Jewish Studies, both of which have since independently exceeded the specificity of their ethnic and geopolitical origins, have been critical in defining the stakes of the historical project of the Jewish people. Even a brief outline of the parallel developments of these disciplines reveals the essential irreconcilability of the philosophical foundations of the two fields. First theorized by Johann Joachim Winckelmann and his heirs, art history developed into a highly conservative meta-theory of art used to map "western civilization" from its roots in classical culture through a line of succession that ended in German culture. One can easily see the fault lines in a theory seeking to prove that Hellenism played the primary role in the moral development of western civilization. Still, German Jews, who were not about to argue that Judaism played the primary role in developing German morality, came up against an entirely different problem.

Because the field privileged the study of "masterpieces," Jews were left out of the "Family of Man."

We must qualify the term "masterpieces" because of the damage this term has suffered in recent years. Masterpieces are those works that were seen to have influenced the development of representation primarily through considerations of subject matter and style. German Jews were not looking down their noses at masterpieces; they craved to understand every flourish of the brushstroke that made those pieces into masters. The problem was not with the masterpieces. During the nineteenth-century struggle for emancipation, Jewish scholars versed in German *lettres* began to notice that the style-oriented schemes of art history excluded Jews who could neither boast of a national style nor generally operate outside avant-garde artistic currents. Under the art-historical proposition that national character reveals itself through art, Jews were effectively written out of the rise of the modern nation-state.[1] German-language art history used an innovative reading of the Second Commandment's prohibition against the making of idols as a prooftext of Jewish iconoclasm, which became a critical mainstay throughout the nineteenth and twentieth centuries.[2] Richard Wagner, Jacob Burckhardt, Arthur Gobineau, and Max Weber applied the medieval conception of Jewish "blindness," which initially had a theological connotation referencing the Jewish obstinacy in rejecting Christ as the universal savior, to refer to a literal inability of Jews to create and spiritually apprehend art.

The field of Jewish Studies sought to theorize the conspicuous absence of Jews from the plastic arts from a more generative perspective and to find a place in the national schemata of art history for a people differentiated by creed, race, history, cultural orientation, and, most significantly, structural position. Identifying uniquely Jewish works of art in the established criteria of what constituted the "arts" made the effort frankly embarrassing. Christianity erected monumental architecture, public sculptures, and grand narrative paintings in the spirit of the oft-quoted Latin maxim *"Ars longa, vita brevis"* (Art is enduring, life is brief"), and Islam, Buddhism, and Hinduism created some of the world's most significant monuments in their transformation of the Arabic and Asian worlds. In contrast, Jewish art and architecture reflected the reality of a minority culture that claimed few monumental works in the West or the East. Wissenschaft scholars faced an imagined tabernacle of biblical narrative, a destroyed Second Temple of Jerusalem, relatively modest architectural proportions, and derivative styles in their ceremonial and liturgical arts. Scholars searching for a uniquely Jewish architecture had the *sukkah*, the temporary ritual hut erected outdoors for the autumn holiday of Sukkot, and the "eruv," a barely visible ritual string that ritually transforms an outdoor space into a shared courtyard, thereby allowing Jews to carry objects outdoors on the Sabbath. Given the Jewish lacuna of art masterpieces, Jewish Studies scholars embraced the prevailing myth of the "artless Jew" in German art history, famously expressed by historian Heinrich Graetz as "paganism sees its god, Judaism hears Him."[3]

Scholars in yet another emerging field forged in the German language—psychoanalysis—began to reinterpret the Second Commandment, the totemic prooftext for the myth of the artless Jew, as a theory of the uniquely Jewish contribution to the history of art. In *Totem and Taboo* (1912–13), Sigmund Freud proffered the much-maligned Second Commandment in German art history as originating "not from any objection to the plastic arts, but from a desire to deprive magic (which was abominated by the Hebrew religion) of one of its tools."[4] In reinterpreting the meaning of the Second Commandment as a scriptural resistance to the embodied spiritualism of paganism (and implicitly of Christianity), Freud separated the attitude of the Second Commandment from religion and prescribed the autonomy of the symbolic object from the action. Taking the sentiment to a logical extreme, art historian Leo Steinberg would later justify the Jewish Museum's exhibition of non-Jewish artists of the New York School with the argument that modern art is essentially Jewish because of its renunciation of representation.[5]

Freud's Berlin-based colleague Karl Abraham elaborated on the Second Commandment's formative influence on art history. Comparing the prohibition against the creation of an image of the "only (paternal) God" to the First Commandment's instruction to apprehend and recognize only one God, Abraham argued that Judaism internalizes conflict to "see and don't see" in relation to the One Father, in contrast to an externalization of conflict into a divided Godhead.[6] Abraham attributed the internal conflict in "see and don't see" to the creative sublimations of the Oedipal situation, in contrast to the continual and unresolvable struggles with doubt between the Father and the Mother of obsessional neurotics and, by suggestion, of Christian artists.[7] The psychoanalytic turning of the dialogic tables from the artlessness of the "Father Religion" of Judaism to the obsessive artistic preoccupations of the "Son Religion" of Christianity allowed scholars to shamelessly probe the projection of internalized conflict onto the external object, the inherent ambivalence at the center of creative work, the sexual and aggressive drives underpinning the making of art, and the negotiation of competing desires and affective states in its consumption. In short, it is difficult to overstate the influence of the psychoanalytic shift from an object- to subject-oriented approach to art across the humanities and, in the present context, the critical role this shift played in studies on the relationship between Jews and the history of art.

Several factors dramatically lifted the depressed state of scholarship on Jewish art and visual culture. The nineteenth-century emergence of Jewish artists in the fine arts demonstrated that Jewish emancipation significantly influenced Jewish aesthetic sensibilities and creative production hitherto thought inaccessible to Jews. Archaeological finds in the early twentieth century significantly extended the timeline of Jewish creativity back in time from Late Antiquity (third to seventh centuries CE). Archaeological excavations unearthed such a rich trove of Jewish representational culture in Israelite palaces at Megiddo dating from as early as the eighth and ninth centuries BCE, at Jewish catacombs in Rome, and in synagogue mosaics across Palestine, Syria, and Greece that the evidence eventually toppled the entrenched view that biblical prohibitions against idolatry reflected a Jewish history devoid of art. Archival scholars also rediscovered medieval Jewish manuscript illumination and Jewish printing and book culture.

The institutionalization of Jewish art began earnestly with the birth of the first Jewish museums in Europe during the long *fin de siècle*. In 1947 the Jewish Museum of New York opened at its new location on Fifth Avenue on "Museum Row": Its inaugural exhibition on the Ten Commandments in Jewish art was a display of the uninterrupted Jewish history of art from the 1923–33 archaeological excavations of the floor-to-ceiling mosaics at the Dura Europos synagogue in Syria to contemporary Jewish art. Ernst Cohn-Wiener's *Jewish Art: Its History from the Beginning to the Present Day*, initially published in German, heralded the scholarly reassessment of the existence of Jewish artistic history by including both the ancient and modern eras of Jewish art in its overview.[8] A growing number of German Jewish scholars followed in the wake of Cohn-Wiener with surveys of Jewish art in the 1940s, such as Franz Landsberger's *A History of Jewish Art* and Karl Schhwarz's *Jewish Artists of the 19th and 20th Centuries*.[9] The peak of the retrospective scholarly revision of the existence of a Jewish artistic tradition was reached by the non-Jewish scholar Ernst Goodenough in his thirteen-volume *Jewish Symbols in the Greco-Roman Period*.[10]

Historians of Jewish art have needed help integrating some of the most formative Jewish-born and German-educated art historians of the twentieth century, such as Aby Warburg, Erwin Panofsky, and Ernst Gombrich. Their explicit dismissal of Jewish art as "derivative," "primitive," and "oriental" left scholars confused and pushed them to search for new definitions of Jewish art.[11] The critique of these scholars has been essential to historiographic analyses of discourses on Jewish art. Still, their achievements in laying the groundwork for the methodological and theoretical infrastructure for the study of religion and art cannot be dismissed if we are to understand the *academic* relationship between Jews and the arts.[12] Given the increasing recognition of contemporary Jewish artists and the exponential growth of an archaeological archive, it is fair to question why the most preeminent Jewish-born art historians continued to trade in empirically debunked propositions in their ecstatic embrace of the externalized spiritualism of Christian art. Yet, suppose we return to their innovations. In that case, we can see their embrace of religious aesthetics as a reclamation of an area previously denied to Jews in the ghetto and as their correction of the interpretive "mistakes" their predecessors made about Christian art, the objective of the scientific critique on the humanities.

In turning to the *means* for the knowledge of the past, we find that many of the first German Jewish art historians widened the field of art history in ways that bypassed and transformed diachronic accounts of the march of national schools. Aby Warburg's *Bilderatlas* project—a compendium of photographic and print copies of artworks that idiosyncratically structured western civilization by maintaining symbolic forms, character types, and gestural language across time and place—sought to undo what he termed the *grenzpolizeiliche Befangenheit* (border-police–style closed-mindedness) of disciplinary practice. Another German Jewish historian of Renaissance and Christian art, Erwin Panofsky, developed Warburg's iconological approach to studying art into a methodological theory that essentially displaced subject matter and style considerations to the lowest strata of understanding, devoid of any "cultural" knowledge. In his 1936 essay "Race, Nationality, and Art," artist and art historian Meyer Schapiro, another Jewish art historian specializing in medieval Christian art, offered a clue to Jewish art-historical passions for Christian art when he asserted that Jewish art was essentially antinomian, conditioned by a spiritual experience quite apart from dominant Christian cultures.[13] In applying novel approaches to the hegemonic cult of images in the European canon, these Jewish art historians revealed aspects of ugliness that lay beneath the formation of a beauty canon.

Ernst Gombrich, another Jewish-born and German-educated art historian, spoke openly about some of these issues when he recognized that the history of art preceded and even produced the Jewish question. In 1960, ten years after he published the single most popular art-historical blockbuster, *The Story of Art,* in which he evaluated ancient Jewish art as "primitive," Gombrich reconsidered his position. Writing to psychoanalyst Adrian Stokes in 1960 that he "discovered how much art history had been misused" for the propagation of race theory and Marxist economic theory, Gombrich stated that these "pseudo-historical religions" rested on the basic "scientific" assumptions of art history that amounted to "a denial of the unity of mankind."[14] Gombrich took a second stab at Dura Europos in his *Art and Illusion* (1960, 113), arguing that the Old Testament ban on "graven images" not only separates the cult from the object but *creates* the conditions for tolerating the visual object. Invoking both talmudic and art-historical sources, Gombrich suggested that Jewish artists may appear more representationally "primitive" than their pagan and Christian neighbors but actually they were more *perceptually* advanced. Inclined to distinguish between media and to attain a level of comfort with "secular" and even "profane" media, Jewish culture showed remarkable tolerance toward what was foreign to them. For Gombrich, this promise of consciousness, of trespassing boundaries between life and death, inside and outside, has informed the history of art as we know it.[15] Informed by his collaborative work with art historian and psychoanalyst Ernst Kris, Gombrich theorized that what we refer to as the artistic style of "primitivism" was not the work of "primitive peoples"; instead, those who could tolerate the "regression" that the distortion of reality requires were those who had achieved stable boundaries between subject and object.[16]

Beginning as early as World War II, scholars, either implicitly or explicitly, traced dehumanizing church imagery vilifying Jews to the genocidal campaigns of the Holocaust. In concrete iconographical studies of the Jewish subject in Christian art, Joseph Reider's essay "Jews in Medieval Art" (1942) and Bernhard Blumenkranz's *The Medieval Jew in the Mirror of Christian Art* (1966) turned Crusade-era Christian art into a mirror in which Jews could see themselves reflected in the eyes of the Other.[17] In the 1990s, Heinz Schreckenberg and Ruth Mellinkoff published veritable encyclopedias of the signs of Jewish Otherness in volumes illustrated by more than a thousand images.[18] More recently, scholars Sara Lipton and Dana E. Katz have reminded us that the image of the Jew in Christian art reveals more about Christian self-representation and the parts of their state of mind they wanted to disown; furthermore, in the spirit of the dictum that "life follows art," these artistic representations came to shape perceptions, social policy, and popular attitudes toward Jews.[19] At the same time, every historian of Jewish art will have to wade through this challenging material, making it possible to consider Jewish artistic production against the backdrop of the mainstream aesthetic tropes they encountered of themselves.

The Institutionalization of Jewish Art

Although disciplinary formation speaks to the inter-ethnic national discourse, the rise of intra-Jewish art practices, Judaica collecting, the birth of the Jewish museum, and the Zionist embrace of a universalist Jewish art left an enduring imprint on intra-Jewish approaches to the study of art. Wissenschaft scholars framed the consumption of world art as a *Jewish* cultural enterprise with religious imperatives. This trend began with the bilingual Hebrew and German edition of the "Philippson Bible" (1858), in which the printer illustrated Ludwig Philippson's lengthy commentaries on the latest scientific discoveries of the objects and utensils described in the text with more than five hundred images, many of which were wood engravings from the British Museum. The "Philippson Bible" treated world art as mediating the passage from word to image and image to word. The influence of this approach could be seen in Freud's collection of antiquities, which reproduced in one-to-one correlation the objects illustrated in the Philippson Bible, and Daniel Sperber's eight-volume *Minhage Yisrae'el* (1989–2007) that traces the development of Jewish lifecycle traditions from the evidence of more than two millennia of objects and images.[20]

The first collectors of overtly Jewish art and artifacts embraced a mission of Jewish historical preservation of a culture threatened with extinction, whether caused by the repeated catastrophes of the Jewish diaspora or the pull of modernity. The consumption, collection, and theorization of Judaica and art that illuminate Judaism eventually led to the birth of the new institution of the Jewish museum, in which Jews performed themselves both as biblical subjects and as contemporary citizens. The first of these Jewish museums were established in Vienna at the end of the nineteenth century with collections of objects that participated in the construction of Jewish historical experiences; these were primarily ceremonial objects, liturgical art, archaeological finds, plans and pictures of Holy Land environs, and documentary records of ancient Egyptian or Assyrian monuments related to Jewish history and the holy Scriptures.

The institutional founders of Jewish museums across Central and Eastern Europe and the United States wrestled with questions about their nature, mission, and role and what sort of works should be exhibited. Because the ensuing discourse continues to inform the self-image of contemporary Jewish museums, scholars have shown a sustained interest in the wave of ethnographic projects in the first decades of the twentieth century that collected material still in use for the museological project. In one such expedition in 1912–14, S. An-sky and his team of semi-professional collectors (*zamlers*), including a photographer, a musicologist, artists, and students of the so-called Higher Courses on Oriental Studies, amassed a treasure trove of phonographic recordings, photographs, and artifacts belonging to the religious elite from Hasidic households and simple Jews. The results remain the basis for new observations and evaluations of how people interacted with their "things" in Jewish communities across Eastern Europe and Central Asia and the ethnographic museological projects they inspired.

Although Jewish museums and Judaica collections demonstrated the existence of a wealthy Jewish visual culture, they judiciously sidestepped the debates about Jews in art history, which revolved primarily around the fine arts. In the Russian Empire, where Jews had not yet achieved emancipation and attitudes toward art developed in an ideational environment far removed from the foundational Austro-German texts in art history, populist intellectuals called Jewish artists to join the avant-garde struggle to overthrow European notions of the fine arts. The efforts to promote a distinctly modern "Eastern Semitic" architectural, sculptural, and painting style by Russian art critic Vladimir Stasov and Jewish Orientalist Baron David Ginzburg in the 1890s and Solomon Vermel's and Abram Efros's retrospective description of Jewish elements in art in the early 1900s as prone to abstraction, primitivism, the folk, the Orient, and melancholy legitimized the development of Jewish Orientalism as an authentic expression of Jewish national art.

A new layer was added to intra-Jewish debates on the politicization of art at the Fifth Zionist Congress (1901) when delegates from Germany applied the European art model to imagine the Jewish nation and representatives from Russia stormed out in protest. Before the question of the role of "culture" in the Zionist agenda was resolved, Martin Buber took the stage on the first day of the Congress. He announced an exhibit of forty-eight works by eleven Jewish painters working in diverse national contexts.[21] Russian delegates were not offended that Jews engaged in what might be considered Jewish art. Still, Buber's promotion of a *universalist* "Jewish art" flew in the face of what they felt constituted a shared Jewish identity. For religious delegates, the notion of a collective aesthetic identity between Jewish artists of French, Dutch, Russian, and German backgrounds suggested the replacement of religion as the basic common denominator among world Jews with some undefinable yet essentializing "culture."

Since its founding in 1906, the Bezalel Art Institute in Jerusalem has attracted scholars for its engagement with the Jewish art question as a prehistory to Israeli art. On the one hand, the relationship between the new institution and its place in Jerusalem made a strong claim on the Jewishness of the enterprise. On the other hand, the application by Boris Schatz, founder of the Bezalel school, of this unique relationship to his representation of and practices in Bezalel provoked controversy among religious Jews; it peaked in reaction to the sort of rhetoric exemplified by Schatz's utopian work, *Yerushalayim ha-Benuya* (Jerusalem Rebuilt, 1924), that appealed to the redemptive process of artistic creation and claimed that the museum would become part of the messianic Jerusalem.[22] Likewise, Schatz's application of European academic styles to familiar Jewish and Zionist symbols universalized Jewish particularism in ways that unsettled the exponents of an Eastern framework for considering Jewish art. Zionists like Max Nordau and Ahad Ha'am rejected the East as a template for Jewish culture for a Jewish Palestine, which they envisioned, as Nordau put it, as "a wall against Asian barbarity."[23] As Bezalel exported the European conceit of a national school of art that it had imported into Palestine across Eastern Europe and as disparate Jewish artists exhibited their work in group shows under the banner of Jewish art, the claim of a "Jewish" painting, the threshold of the European academy, provoked heated critical debates that still remain relevant.

Expanding Disciplines

In all the ways that new fields and institutions helped assuage the historical rifts between art history and the arts of the Jews, the two disciplines first found mutual epistemological ground only in the late twentieth century when the disciplinary critique from within art history transformed art history departments in U.S. universities. As the discipline of art history expanded its disciplinary boundaries in response to critical reevaluations of the categories of genius and masterpieces, taste and canon formation, and the role of collecting and patronage in the processes of art professionalization, Jewish Studies scholars were able to participate in the field from the center, rather than in the periphery of art-historical concerns. The art-historical accommodation of a nonhierarchical "visual culture," as it came to be called in the 1990s, was initially launched on behalf of Christian studies by scholars David Morgan, Sally M. Promey, S. Brent Plate, and Colleen McDannell, among others; it has played a critical role in advancing new theoretical and methodological approaches in Jewish Studies.[24]

Contemporary scholars no longer need to justify why Jews may have been at pains to materialize their identities in monumental ways, but focus instead on identifying and understanding the alternative artistic practices that Jews developed to participate in the cultural life of their nations and within their communities. Scholars approach noncanonical, even mundane, material from essential art-historical concerns of representation, asking how Jewish painters, printers, metalsmiths, filmmakers, and so on, materialized themselves, their worlds, their relationship to God, and their intermediaries in media-specific ways. They seek to understand how the objects that Jews did produce during their unbroken histories in both the Christian and Arabic worlds shed light on the ways that localized tradition can be transported into new contexts through a priori flexible and reproducible structures and symbols. Thus, rather than attempting to tie Rembrandt to his subjects in the Jewish quarter of Amsterdam, today's scholars are much more likely to ask how Menasseh ben Israel's articulation of a special Jewish relationship to mass media in seventeenth-century Amsterdam affected Sephardic identity. They are also more likely to situate the archaeological excavation of ancient Jewish life beyond its practical historical value to consider its effects on contemporary artistic revival. Thus, the Dura Europos tradition became a source for Warner Brothers set designer Hugo Ballin's 1929 murals for a Los Angeles sanctuary that depicted the history of the Jewish people through the transformative power of cinema and offered Reform Judaism a new visual theology that exceeded its German origins.

As art historians brought the analytical systems developed in feminist theory, ethnic studies, and postcolonialism to their discipline, scholars of Jewish art enjoyed new relevance. Without discarding the notion that a work of art can and does function as a primary source and "art history" as a historiographical model that actively organizes historical data points into national and scholarly discourse, Jewish art scholars can return to the visual field of analysis as the primary object of study. As art history integrated the issues surrounding spectral politics theorized by Jacques Derrida and Roland Barthes, Holocaust scholars James E. Young, Monica Bohm-Duchen, and Barbie Zelizer were among the first to develop new analytic tools for assessing the role of the artistic "apparatus" in resisting cultural hegemony, aiding memory work, and confronting the past. Stuart Hall's thesis that identity is constructed "within, not outside representation" has opened the floodgates for Jewish Studies' analyses of the history of representation, the foremost concern of art history, in shaping Jewish identity.[25] Scholars interested in Jewish engagements in popular culture pay special attention to the features in a genre or medium that reproduce and thus resist dominant modes of representation. We have seen eye-opening expositions on the technology of spatial miniaturization in world's fairs, the mimetic nature of live-action film, representational juxtapositions in graphic novels, aural and visual remains in modernist theater, the theorization of the autonomy of objects in stop-motion animation, and the referent of photography: These have all served to reveal how Jews performed themselves and shaped their worlds. In step with older methodologies in the study of "masterpieces," scholars of Jewish visual culture aim to identify what particular works revealed those features to other artists so that they became *conventions*; in what ways other artists revealed the artificiality of these conventions after they were no longer recognizable as such; and how artists exploit the genre- and medium-specific tools of representation to shift the perceptual ground beneath us.

By and large, today's scholars do not attempt to define what is really "Jewish" about the arts that Jews produce but go directly to elucidating *Jewland*, a mythical place one can see. The citizens of Jewland are its artists, performers, set designers, producers, theoreticians, consumers, censors, and media communities. Scholars explore the visual language of Jewland, a world perpetually trying to create symbols for itself, whether painted, dreamed, installed, projected, borrowed, or reclaimed. They strive to elucidate Jewland approaches to the visual and the material, whether employed in the principle of "worship through materiality" (*avodah be-gashmiyut*), to reach the Divine (*devekut*), to heal (*tikkun*) the soul, or to fix the world (*tikkun olam*)—in the hopes of heralding the messianic age through the performance of "unifications" (*yihudim*) or to elevate the profane through "intention" (*kavvanah*) and attain blessing through the exchange of financial support (*pidyon ha-nefesh*). Scholars seek to understand the imports and exports into Jewland, whether from the paganistic past or to the universalizing screen of popular culture. Examples abound, such as Galit Hasan-Rokem's explorations of immigrant transformations of Jewland through the new medium of postcards; Glenn Dynner and Batsheva Ida Goldman's reincarnations of new spiritual leadership in Jewland through ink, silk, and metalwork; Laura Arnold Leibman's study of the entry of a Black enslaved woman into Jewland through portraiture and family heirlooms; and Jodi Eichler Levine's study of the stitching together of women's Jewland communities in North America through embroidery and quilting.

Scholars have accessed new, orthogonal areas of Jewish experience by turning to this rich interdisciplinary terrain. At the same time, the academic legitimation of the existence of Jewish art and its institutionalization in the academy also forced Jewish art studies to confront the same critiques that art history faced in general. The still unresolved areas of this broadening of art history have come from the postcolonialist review in the context of Israeli statehood, the use of nontextual material in the study of religion, and attitudes toward analyzing a single work of art in the field of Jewish Studies.

In the first area, Edward Said's *Orientalism*[26] identified Orientalism as a mode of western imperialism and, through its influential reception history, problematized the relationship between Jews and the Orient. The Orientalizing of Jews was primarily studied from the perspective of Jews as Orientalists, indiscriminantly applying what Said theorized of Christian identity formation in the West to Jews emerging in North Africa and Russia—countries that did not often fall into the category of the "West" and that saw themselves as sitting at the crossroads between East and West for most of their histories. Israeli scholars, primarily based at the Hebrew University, looked at Jews as the subject, even in self-representation, of Orientalism, striving to show that they had a stake in eastern and western identities in ways that often resisted the colonialist project. In a contemporary political climate in which Jewish intellectuals are revisiting the Zionist project in the context of the Israeli–Palestinian conflict, these issues have assumed an intra-Jewish discursive nature.[27]

The second central area of contention has emerged in the study of religion. Perhaps because classical art history, from Winckelmann to Schatz, conceived art in relationship to nation and peoplehood—a fraught secular proposition—religious communities have generally eschewed the concept of western art in inverse proportion to the widespread embrace of visual media. At the same time, one need not be a historian to perceive a gaping chasm between Orthodox religious life (as practiced in the synagogues, schools, and yeshivot) and the art world (as practiced in museums, galleries, and universities) and, even more so, "popular culture" (as practiced online, in professional sports, cinemas, and television). However, I refer specifically to the premises undergirding the category of a universalist "Jewish art." If religious delegates stormed out of the Fifth Zionist Congress in 1901 for its inclusion of art as a category of Jewish identity, the premise that art is constructive of religion, devotional practices, and the interpretation of the written word conflicts with contemporary religious attitudes that approach the textual tradition as a blueprint for action. Religious communities do not debate the notion that one's viewing practices play a profound if perhaps unconscious role in the formation of beliefs, emotional and intellectual development, and adjacent cognitive heuristics, assumptions, and tenets of faith.[28] Rather, they guard their visions against the profane and sacralize their own media for the dissemination of religious culture and promotion of a religious "worldview."

It is worth keeping in mind these intra-Jewish culture wars on the street when thinking about the ways that the work of art is framed in the study of religion in the academy. It is not unusual, for example, to see the third-century

Dura Europos synagogue with its wall-to-ceiling biblical cycles, nudes, and anthropomorphized images of God make claims on the contemporaneous rabbinical texts that railed against representation. These studies have not only shed important light on the limits of textual analysis and rabbinical authority but also tend to rescue the ancient powers of the religious image from contemporary religious attitudes. We have not yet adequately understood how the transition to writing culture transformed the visual expression of theology, influenced religious engagements in civic-public-secular visuality, and changed attitudes toward Jewish visibility in the Roman border city of Dura Europos.[29] The specific scopic telos of religious experience still awaits the complexity that scholars have applied to gender, ethnic, and national categories of Jewish art. A focus on the visual and material landscapes of religion provides additional bridges to understanding the mutual accommodations that religion and modernism have reached, while studies of a nonhierarchical spectrum of religious expression have been critical to developing an understanding of lived religion in ways that preempted theological concepts. As they continue to interrogate contemporary methods of historical reconstruction, scholars are searching for new analytic tools to access the future of ancient Jewish image-makers and to revisit veteran discourses, such as magic, in the process.

If scholars use "things" to study people, I call the methodological modes for conceptualizing religious material culture and the sensory apparatus "thinging." Thinging refers to the theology of the material world, including the internalization and performance of visual theology. To some degree, these are parallel processes, but the study of "thinging" specifically concerns the materialization of the Divine creator, his creative functions, and his creations.

In addition to the challenges that accompanied the academic legitimization of the existence of Jewish art in the discipline of art history, a third constellation of issues facing art historians come from Jewish Studies. The most persistent issue still revolves around legitimation. In something of an ironic twist, the work of art has not achieved its autonomy as being worthy of understanding in its own right in Jewish Studies, partly because the field has not yet reached a consensus on what approach to take to the work of art. Although it is generally understood that an analysis that clears up long misunderstood puzzles in Isaac Babel's *Red Cavalry* does not need to exemplify a broader Jewish attitude, art historians are still burdened with explaining the significance of their objects of study not for their aesthetic influence but for their Jewish value. Scholars who finally broke the visual code in the use of symbolism in a single enigmatic work of Marc Chagall or Camille Pissarro are asked to delineate what makes such symbolism "Jewish." Scholars of art are often accused of atomization and are driven to diminish a singularly transcendent and influential work through attempts to demonstrate its historical prevalence through a collection of similar objects for empirical evidence.

These challenges will undoubtedly continue to inform future research. In asking how the individual, personal, specific, and singular provide historical insight, we also reproduce the founding questions of art history and Jewish Studies and their antithetical histories. In seeking to identify the relationship between the extraordinary, the ordinary, and the most mundane object to the macro-culture, economy, and society in which it was imbued with meaning, we continue the work of the confusing "and" in the interdisciplinary study of "Jews and art."

Recommended Readings

Baskind, Samantha, and Larry Silver. *Jewish Art: A Modern History* (Reaktion, 2011).

Bilski, Emily D., and Emily Braun. *Jewish Women and Their Salons: The Power of Conversation* (Yale University Press, 2005).

Cohen, Richard. *Jewish Icons: Art and Society in Modern Europe* (University of California Press, 1998).

Fine, Steven. *Art and Judaism in the Greco-Roman World: Toward a New Jewish Archaeology* (Cambridge University Press, 2010).

Goldman-Ida, Batsheva. *Hasidic Art and the Kabbalah* (Brill, 2018).

Grossman, Grace Cohen. *Jewish Museums of the World* (Hugh Lauter Levin Associates, 2003).

Kirshenblatt-Gimblett, Barbara, and Jonathan Karp, eds. *The Art of Being Jewish in Modern Times* (University of Pennsylvania Press, 2008).

Mahan, Jeffrey. *Media, Religion and Culture: An Introduction* (Routledge, 2014).

Manor, Dalia. *Art in Zion: The Genesis of Modern National Art in Jewish Palestine* (Routledge, 2005).

Olin, Margaret. *The Nation without Art: Examining Modern Discourses on Jewish Art* (University of Nebraska Press, 2001).

Schrijver, Emile. "The Eye of the Beholder: Artistic Sense and Craftsmanship in Eighteenth-Century Jewish Books," *Images* 7, no. 1 (2013): 35–55.

Soussloff, Catherine, ed. *Jewish Identity in Modern Art History* (University of California Press, 1999).

Stern, Sacha. "Figurative Art and Halakha in the Mishnaic-Talmudic Period," *Zion* 61 (1997): 397–419.

Stout, Daniel A. *Media and Religion: Foundations of an Emerging Field* (Routledge, 2012).

Tumarkin Goodman, Susan, ed., *The Emergence of Jewish Artists in Nineteenth-Century Europe* (Jewish Museum, 2001).

Notes

1. Margaret Olin, *The Nation without Art: Examining Modern Discourses on Jewish Art.* Also see Kalman Bland, *The Artless Jew: Medieval and Modern Affirmations and Denials of the Visual* (Princeton University Press, 2000).

2. On rabbinical responsa on the question of Jewish attitudes toward images, see Vivian Mann, *Jewish Texts on the Visual Arts* (Cambridge University Press, 2000); Joseph Gutmann, "Is There a Jewish Art?," in *The Visual Dimension: Aspects of Jewish Art*, ed. Clare Moore (Westview, 1993), 1–23.

3. Heinrich Graetz, *The Structure of Jewish History* (Jewish Theological Seminary of America, 1975), 68.

4. Freud, *Totem and Taboo*, in *Standard Edition of the Complete Psychological Works of Sigmund Freud* ed. J. Strachey (24 vols.; Hogarth, 1953–74) [SE] 13: 80 [vii–162].

5. *The New York School: Second Generation; Paintings by Twenty-Three Artists Exhibited from March 10 to April 28, 1957* (Jewish Museum of the Jewish Theological Seminary, 1957).

6. Abraham, "Über Einschränkungen," 76–77, in *Selected Papers on Psycho-Analysis* (Karnac, 1997), 222–23.

7. Abraham, "Über Einschränkungen," 68, in *Selected Papers,* 214.

8. Ernst Cohn-Wiener, *Jewish Art: Its History from the Beginning to the Present Day* (Wasservogel, 1929).

9. Franz Landsberger, *A History of Jewish Art* (Union of American Hebrew Congregations, 1946), and Karl Schwarz, *Jewish Artists of the 19th and 20th Centuries* (Philosophical Library, 1949).

10. Ernst Goodenough, *Jewish Symbols in the Greco-Roman Period* (13 vols.; Pantheon, 1953–68).

11. See Emily Bilski, "The Jew as Asiatic Interloper," in *Berlin Metropolis: Jew and the New Culture, 1890–1918* (University of California Press, 1999), 17–21. For a review of early Jewish art histories and the treatment of Jewish art as "derivative," see Eva Frojmovic, "Buber in Basel, Schlosser in Sarajevo, Wischnitzer in Weimar: The Politics of Writing about Medieval Jewish Art," in *Imagining the Self, Imagining the Other: Visual Representation and Jewish-Christian Dynamics in the Middle Ages and Early Modern Period*, ed. E. Frojmovic (Brill, 2002), 1–32.

12. See Matthew Rampley, "Aby Warburg: *Kulturwissenschaft,* Judaism and the Politics of Identity," *Oxford Art Journal* 33 (2010): 317–35.

13. Meyer Schapiro, "Race, Nationality, and Art," *Art Front* 1 (March 1936): 10–12.

14. Gombrich-Stokes correspondence, June 15, 1960, quoted in Rachel Dedman, "The Importance of Being Ernst: A Reassessment of E. H. Gombrich's Relationship with Psychoanalysis," *Journal of Art Historiography* 7 (2012): 22.

15. Gombrich, *Art and Illusion* (Princeton University Press, 2000), 94.

16. See Ernst Kris, *Psychoanalytic Explorations in Art* (International Universities, 1952; orig. Vienna, 1934]).

17. Joseph Reider, "Jews in Medieval Art," in *Essays on Antisemitism,* ed. K. S. Pinson (Conference on Jewish Relations, 1942), 45–56; Bernhard Blumenkranz, *Le Juif medieval au miroir de l'art chrétien* (Études augustiennes, 1966).

18. Heinz Schreckenberg, *The Jews in Christian Art: An Illustrated History* (SCM, 1996); Ruth Mellinkoff, *Outcasts: Signs of Otherness in Northern European Art of the Late Middle Ages* (University of California Press, 1993).

19. Sara Lipton, *Images of Intolerance: The Representation of Jews and Judaism in the Bible moralisée* (University of California Press, 1999); Dana E. Katz, "Painting and the Politics of Persecution: Representing the Jew in Fifteenth-Century Mantua," *Art History* 23 (2000): 475–95.

20. Ana-Maria Rizzuto, "Freud's Disrupted Idealizations, Religious Unbelief, and His Collection of Antiquities," in *Psychohistory in Psychology of Religion: Interdisciplinary Studies*, ed. J. A. Belzen (Rodopi, 2001), 91–112; Daniel Sperber, *Customs of Israel* [Hebrew] (8 vols.; Mossad Harav Kook, 1989–2007).

21. Max Nordau, *On Art and Artists* (Fisher Unwin, 1907; orig. German, 1905).

22. See Schatz's utopian work, *Jerusalem Rebuilt* [Hebrew] (Bezalel Academy, 1924), chap. 1.

23. Alina Orlov, "First There Was the Word: Early Russian Texts on Modern Jewish Art," *Oxford Art Journal* 31 (2008): 401.

24. For a review essay on the current scholarship on religion and media, see David Morgan, "Religion and Media: A Critical Review of Recent Developments," *Critical Research on Religion* 1 (2013), 3:347–56; *Sacred Gaze* (University of California Press, 2005), and *Visual Piety: A History and Theory of Popular Religious Images* (University of California Press, 1998). Also see S. Brent Plate, *Religion, Art, and Visual Culture: A Cross-Cultural Reader* (Palgrave, 2002); Sally M. Promey, "The 'Return' of Religion in the Scholarship of American Art," *Art Bulletin* 85 (2003): 581–603; and Colleen McDannell, *Material Christianity: Religion and Popular Culture in America* (Yale University Press, 1995).

25. Stuart Hall, "Cultural Identity and Diaspora," in *Identity: Community, Culture, Difference*, ed. J. Rutherford (Lawrence and Whishart, 1990), 222.

26. Edward Said, *Orientalism* (Vintage, 1978).

27. J. Lockard and Jan Elsner, "Jewish Art: Before and after the Jewish State (1948)," in *Empires of Faith in Late Antiquity: Histories of Art and Religion from India to Ireland,* ed. Jan Elsner (Cambridge University Press, 2020), 293–319.

28. Michal Shaul, *Holocaust Memory in Ultraorthodox Society in Israel* (Indiana University Press, 2020).

29. Karen B. Stern, *Writing on the Wall: Graffiti and the Forgotten Jews of Antiquity* (Princeton University Press, 2018).

19

Yiddish

Anna Shternshis, University of Toronto

ONE OF THE BIGGEST paradoxes of Yiddish studies is how a language so central to Ashkenazi culture and history for the past thousand years can remain on the margins of the scholarship of Jewish Studies. The terms "Yiddish" and "margins" seem to go together, both when Jewish Studies as a field is in question, and in what matters Yiddish studies addresses—the lives and works of everyday life, women, and literature. In today's climate these issues are now central to what scholars are interested in. Perhaps this explains why the field of Yiddish was one of the most vibrantly represented at meetings of the 2023 American Association for Jewish Studies and why Yiddish scholarship books receive prizes in non-Yiddish categories. For example, in 2022 Rachel Rojanski's *Yiddish in Israel* won the prestigious Jordan Schnitzer Book prize in the category of Modern Jewish History and Culture: Europe and Israel.[1] A finalist for that category was another book on Yiddish studies, *A Citizen of Yiddishland: Dovid Sfard and the Jewish Communist Milieu in Poland*, by Joanna Nalewajko-Kulikov.[2] Both books study fields that have expanded into new horizons because of Yiddish. Rojanski challenged the myth that Yiddish culture has been suppressed in Israel by looking beyond ideological slogans and examining actual developments: Yiddish magazines, publications, and centers that existed in the country despite its supposed ban on Yiddish. Similarly, Nalewajko-Kulikov revises the history of postwar Poland by looking into the life and writing of Yiddish writer Dovid Sfard, a central figure in the Communist Party of Poland after World War II; instead of considering his work as being that of a "puppet" or as "brainwashed," this analysis examines postwar European Yiddish culture as it developed across borders and discusses what happens to our perspective on Cold War Eastern Europe when Yiddish is put front and center.

A quick glance at what is happening in the field of Yiddish today reveals that field-changing insights appear when scholars analyze the literature and culture of Jewish women, the reception of Jewish literary texts, everyday life, and contemporary Jewish culture. Prioritizing Yiddish gives voice to lesser-known authors, Hasidic Jews, and ritual practices. In some areas, addressing Yiddish can revise the entire scholarship. Take, for example, Russian Jewish studies. Although the majority of Russian Jews spoke or understood Yiddish in the early twentieth century, the story of Soviet Yiddish culture is still obscure. Without Yiddish one cannot truly appreciate the experimental works of art, literature, theater, and music that developed in the Soviet Union in the 1920s, including the paintings of El Lissitzky, Alexander Tyshler, and Marc Chagall. Similarly, how can we fully understand the history of the Soviet punitive system if we do not study the experiences of Jewish prisoners in the Soviet gulag, such as poet Moisei Teif, teacher Shifra Lipshitz, or musicologist Moisei Beregovsky? The list of questions is long, and although the answer to all these questions is "no," the Yiddish story is still on the margins.

The puzzle of Yiddish is double-sided. To continue with the example of Russia, neither specialists in Soviet Jewish history nor specialists in Yiddish studies are knowledgeable about Soviet Yiddish culture. For Soviet Jewish historians, it is marginal because of the language; for Yiddish specialists, it is marginal because it concerns Soviet Jews. And Soviet Jewish studies are marginal because of the Cold War. Yet how Yiddish studies became separated from the studies of modern Jewish history is a bigger puzzle. Of course, this question does not concern solely Russian Jewish studies but also applies to American Jewish studies. In some places, such as in Poland, this is no longer the case, but for the most part we still face the same questions: Why is Yiddish still on the margins, and what happens when it is not? This chapter discusses some of the central issues of the field.

Question 1 of the Past: Is Yiddish a Real Language?

Yiddish is a Germanic language, with its origins dating to the 1100s, and its first written sentence, "Thank you to those who brought a prayer book to this house of learning," to 1272. Born in the German Rhine Valley, it traveled with Jews to the Polish-Lithuanian Kingdom and the Russian, Austro-Hungarian, and Ottoman Empires. Until 1939 it served as a vernacular and written language of the majority of Ashkenazi Jews. Although Germanic in origin, it was largely used by Jews in Slavic lands. One of the greater mysteries in Jewish history is why

Jews never developed a Jewish language based on a Slavic one, such as Polish, Ukrainian, or Russian. Instead, Yiddish incorporated no more than 10 percent of Slavic words into its vocabulary, along with about 20 percent of Hebrew-origin words.

Today, when linguists take delight in analyzing language origins, they call such languages "hybrid." Yiddish, however, was not so lucky; for centuries it was referred to as "bastardized jargon" or a "women's tongue" or "marketplace vernacular," but more often as an embarrassment. It was Jewish culture's skeleton in the closet, something that betrayed that not all Jews spoke impeccable German, won Nobel Prizes, or led world industries. Some lived in small towns, were poor, and enjoyed low-taste theater performances and ballads—in Yiddish. It was not until Max Weinreich, a linguist who miraculously escaped Europe soon after Hitler came to power, wrote his four-volume study called *History of the Yiddish Language*, published in Yiddish posthumously in 1973, that Yiddish was referred to as a "serious" language.[3]

Maybe this embarrassment led to the next paradox in modern Jewish history: Given that the history of Yiddish and the history of Ashkenazi Jews are the same from about 1100 until about 1939, it is astonishing that Yiddish studies, broadly defined—ranging from culture to history to linguistics—continues to remain on the margins of Jewish Studies. Even in fields such as Holocaust studies, where one would think studying Yiddish-language sources would be of central interest, these materials remain largely unread—even important ones such as the miraculously preserved archive by historian Emmanuel Ringelblum documenting lives and deaths of Jews in the Warsaw Ghetto (although it was finally published, in Poland, so there are no more excuses![4]). Similarly, most works of Yiddish literature, especially those written by women, are just beginning to surface. First spoiler alert: Women's literature is one of the more promising areas of Yiddish studies today.

The marginality of Yiddish as an academic field has its roots in the period when Jewish Studies, Wissenschaft des Judentums, began to develop in nineteenth-century Germany. German Jewish intellectuals who formed the movement, including founder Eduard Gans, a student of German philosopher Georg Hegel, wished to study Jewish literature, culture, and history as that of a people, rather than a religion. They believed that this approach would enable the development of Jewish Studies as a respectable field, worthy of inclusion into university curricula. Proponents of Jewish Enlightenment, these founders of the movement thought of Jewish Studies from the point of view of its contributions to European civilization: for example, the Hebrew Bible. But in contrast to traditional Jewish studies, which did not dispute the divine origins of the text, the proponents of the new movement called for free interpretation of the text without worrying about religious or any other practical consequences. Similarly, studies of Talmud, Midrash, and works of Jewish philosophers, such as Maimonides, promised to put Jewish Studies into the European academy.

None of the texts that these scholars considered important were written in Yiddish, which was barely spoken then by German Jews. Yiddish, in fact, was the language of everything that intellectuals believed was "wrong" with Jewish civilization: low-taste sentimental ballads, chivalric romances like the sixteenth-century *Bovo-buch*, and the eighteenth- and nineteenth-century Hasidim with their "primitive" tales and hagiographies of rebbes who spoke to God directly and performed miracles. Yiddish seemed to create bawdy narratives, whereas Hebrew provided the necessary depth that allowed one to study it in another serious language, German. Even though it was Germanic in origin, Yiddish did not seem worthy of study; instead, it was a secret that one needed to hide.

Question 2 of the Past: Is Yiddish Literature a Real Literature?

Writing in Yiddish was always presented as a choice that needed to be justified— even by writers of works that the world later came to know as classics of Yiddish literature. Sholem Rabinowitch (1859–1916) wrote in Yiddish under the pen name Sholem Aleichem (translated as both "Hello" and "Peace upon you"). He adopted a pen name because he was terrified that his stock market buddies would learn that he wrote in Yiddish. No one remembers those stockbrokers today, and no one knows the name Rabinowitch, but Sholem Aleichem is still the most famous Yiddish author. Themes of his novel *Tevye the Dairyman*, featuring a father unable to catch up with his five daughters who bring aspects of modernity into his rapidly changing world, still captivate eager audiences. The American adaptation in the musical *Fiddler on the Roof* has remained an international hit since it appeared on Broadway in 1964, and amateur productions of it are still popular in Eastern and Western Europe, Asia, the Americas, Australia, and Africa. Sholem Aleichem's predecessor, Sholem Abramovich (1836–1917), also wrote under a pen name—Mendele Mocher Sforim (Mendele, the Book Peddler), which disguised both his identity and his social and economic standing. Abramovich worked as a school principal, and he felt that he was too sophisticated, educated, wealthy, and urban to speak to his uneducated, small-town poor readers on their level, so Mendele served as both his translator and narrator.

Sholem Aleichem, Mendele Mocher Sforim, and later Y. L. Peretz (1852–1915) enjoyed popularity among millions of readers. Their audience was transnational, living in the Russian Empire including Poland, Germany, the United States, Canada, France, and Australia. Famously, Sholem Aleichem's funeral in New York attracted more than 100,000 mourners. Yet, literary studies of these authors, let alone thousands of others who created important works in Yiddish, were rare until recently.

The first Yiddish literary critic also wrote under a pen name, just like the authors whom he analyzed. Isidor [Yisroel] Eliashev (1873–1924) was known as Bal Makhshoves (Man of Thoughts). He studied the works of Abramovich and other Yiddish writers and wrote five volumes of literary criticism, not for aesthetic reasons or to deepen an understanding of these texts, but because he believed that the Yiddish language represents the Jewish collective soul. He hoped other Jewish intellectuals would be inspired by their people's wisdom and embrace Yiddish as their antidote to assimilation. In the early twentieth century, when Bal Makhshoves was writing, assimilation and conversion seemed like the most pressing issues faced by Jews in Europe and the Americas, and Yiddish seemed like a possibly effective solution.

In the early Soviet Union, Yiddish was treated as the language of Jewish workers and thus the only acceptable part of the Jewish heritage suitable for communist ideology. Yiddish studies functioned in the newly created institutions of Jewish Studies. Critics such as Max Eric, Meir Veiner, Israel Zinberg, and Yeheskel Dobrushin wrote some of the most insightful analyses of Yiddish literary works. However, because they wrote in Yiddish, and, more importantly, they were working in communist institutions, their scholarship was later dismissed as "ideologically driven."

In the United States, Yiddish literary criticism was neither supported by the state apparatus nor influenced by its ideology. The result was the development of a new school of interpretation. Even though many critics on both sides of the Atlantic knew each other or even came from the same families, their views on Yiddish literature differed significantly. The most famous example is two brothers who were both literary critics, Daniel and Shmuel Charney. Both tried to emigrate to United States; Shmuel succeeded, but Daniel was turned away on Ellis Island because of his health. Both became crucial figures in Yiddish literary world. Daniel was instrumental in creating the Marxist school of interpretation of Yiddish literature, whereas Shmuel, who took the pen name Niger, got a job at the Yiddish *Forverts* and served as a major gatekeeper for Yiddish voices worldwide.

Before World War II, the question was how to use Yiddish properly; after the war, the issue became how not to forget that it existed. About five million Yiddish speakers were murdered during the Holocaust, and Jews in North America switched to using English, Jews in Israel switched to Hebrew, and Jews in the Soviet Union spoke Russian. Yiddish became a symbol of a destroyed civilization. Scholarship focused on creating encyclopedic resources: Zalman Reyzen's *Leksikon fun der Yidisher literatur* (Dictionary of Yiddish Literature) listed hundreds of Yiddish writers and their works; Zalmen Zilbercweig's *Leksikon fun dem yidishn teater* (Dictionary of Yiddish Theater)[5] and Chaim Beider's *Leksikon fun Yidishe shrayber in Ratn* (Biographical Dictionary of Soviet Yiddish Literature)[6] systematized, alphabetized, and asserted that Yiddish culture exist(ed) and it was vast. The discussion of what to do with Yiddish ended: These encyclopedias and dictionaries proved that Yiddish is a real language, with a history, philology, literature, and linguistics, and that Yiddish literature is real, with its classics, its centers, its schools, and trajectories. The trouble was that most of its European speakers were killed during the Holocaust, and those who were spared, except for some Hasidic groups, saw no need to speak it. Yiddish was quickly becoming a symbol, a memorial, and a monument to a civilization that was never taken seriously.

In 1947 Uriel Weinreich, Max Weinreich's son, published *College Yiddish,* the first textbook designed for college learning. It had excellent grammar sections prepared with a degree of German meticulousness, simple texts, and vocabulary that screamed, "Yiddish is a proper language, not the one of the marketplace." Generations of Yiddish students who used this textbook learned to speak a language that was grammatically correct, with proper vocabulary, but it was one that no native speaker of Yiddish actually spoke: It lacked an idiomatic structure, informalities, profanities, and yes, the flavor of the marketplace and intimacy—the very elements that drove students to embrace Yiddish and to study the world that no longer existed. For Weinreich and his students, Yiddish teaching was prescriptive, not descriptive. His goal was for students to speak a Yiddish that never existed except in the imagination of the scientific workers of YIVO, the Institute for Jewish Research that was founded in Berlin and Vilna in 1925 and moved to New York in 1940. Fast forward seventy-five years after the first edition of *College Yiddish*, and the current struggle of Yiddish-language programs and of learners is to restore the idiomatic authenticity of the language Weinreich tried to standardize.

Ironically, in the fight to restore authenticity, scholars have turned to the past much more often than to the present. Instead of studying the vernacular of Hasidic Jews, who still speak Yiddish daily in parts of the United States, Israel, and Canada, scholars have turned to the tapes of recorded Yiddish speech—from the 1960s, 1970s, or even 1990s—to explore dialects, pronunciation, and the colloquial expressions that Weinreich worked to eliminate in *College Yiddish*. Why not study the Hasidim? Here is another irony: Their language did not seem to be an authentic, pure form of Yiddish because it borrowed heavily from English and Hebrew, and it abandoned proper grammar, often ignoring rules that standard Yiddish prescribed.

Spoiler #2: Today, the study of Hasidic Yiddish is the most promising, fast-developing, and exciting area of the field, ranging from linguistics to anthropology to studies of everyday life. Maybe this turn of interest signifies the change that many of us are hoping for: Yiddish studies are changing from prescriptive to descriptive, and scholars may be abandoning their mission to educate and instead may finally embrace learning from the people.

Being a symbol or a means to achieve a political or cultural goal is both the blessing and the curse of Yiddish studies. It was a blessing because there was always something to study, but it was also a curse, because scientific Yiddish was not sufficient in its own right: Without a purpose, it became mere jargon again. Yiddish scholarship, or Yiddish studies, developed in the context of having to prove something. In the early twentieth century, political thinker Ber Borokhov essentially established the field by stating that Yiddish language is a vernacular that reveals the "real" Jewish people: workers, craftsmen, beggars, women, and members of the Jewish working class. For Borokhov, the goal was to find the heart of Jewish nationhood, and Yiddish seemed like a good foundation, if analyzed properly, to achieve that aim.[7] His political approach initiated the field of Yiddish studies, which focused on linguistics, philology, and literary analysis. Borokhov died in 1917 at the age of thirty-six, but his work on Yiddish studies still remains relevant—not only in the field of Yiddish linguistics but also in its major assumption: Studying Yiddish has always been seen as a political, if not radical, choice, and there had to be an explanation for why one needed to bother.

After the Holocaust, the focus of Yiddish studies shifted. Yiddish no longer seemed like the most important Jewish vernacular, and studies in the field gradually focused on history, rather than the present or the future. The center of Yiddish studies moved to the United States and Israel, where the impulse to "normalize" the quickly disappearing Yiddish language and literature, to bring it into conversation with the field of comparative literary analysis, animated Yiddish literary studies of the 1970s to 1990s. In the 1970s Columbia professor Dan Miron published the first English-language book-length analysis on Sholem Abramovich, *A Traveler Disguised*.[8] Just as Abramovich was Yiddish literature's first classic author, Miron's study of his works has become a foundational text in Yiddish literary studies and is now a classic. Later Miron wrote a book on Sholem Aleichem and produced other works that embarked on serious literary analysis of the works whose authors worked so hard to conceal themselves.[9] The third major author of Yiddish literature, Y. L. Peretz, received his first serious monograph in 1991, when Harvard professor Ruth Wisse placed him as a founder of modern Jewish culture in her book solely devoted to his work.[10] Later, Wisse's brother, Jewish Theological Seminary professor David Roskies, began a conversation about Yiddish authors belonging to a canon of Yiddish storytellers. He started his groundbreaking work with the stories of Nachman of Bratzlav, the late eighteenth- to early nineteenth-century Hasidic leader, whom he referred to as the founder of modern Yiddish literature, and ended with Isaac Bashevis Singer, the only Yiddish writer who has won the Nobel Prize for literature.[11] Although these studies did not embrace the entire corpus of Yiddish literature—none, for example, discuss any female authors—they certainly turned Yiddish literature into a field of study in North America, which has gradually developed to incorporate more authors, more movements, more lenses. Miron, Roskies, and Wisse trained new generations of Yiddish scholars worldwide. It is because of their work that we can now talk about the future of the field.

Today's Questions

In his 2015 article "Yiddish Studies from a New Perspective,"[12] Mikhail Krutikov argued that the future of the field of contemporary Yiddish studies lies in gender studies, political theory, and Holocaust studies. He also proposed that we look beyond the English-speaking world for the most innovative scholarship and turn our attention to Germany and Poland, where Yiddish studies functions in the context of ideas of tolerance and multiculturalism. In other words, all the features for which Yiddish was ostracized and looked down on in the past—such as being the "language of everyday life," "the language of women and uneducated men," "the marketplace tongue," and more—are now precisely what scholarship in Jewish Studies and humanities at large value most. Yiddish gives access to the histories, literatures, and cultures of people who, although they represented most Jews, previously remained on the margins of scholarship. In the past few decades, scholars of European Jewish Studies, especially history, have been divided into those who work with Yiddish sources and those who apologize that they do not.

Russian/Soviet Jewish Experience

When it comes to Jewish history, some of the major advances in Russian and Soviet Jewish history have come from people who work with Yiddish sources. Zvi Gitelman and Mordechai Altshuler paved the way in the 1970s with their books on Jewish sections of the Communist Party[13]; their extensive use of Yiddish sources enabled them to argue how many Soviet policies toward Jews derived from the Yiddish-language Bundist ideology. Gennady Estraikh pioneered the exploration of Soviet Yiddish linguistics in the early Soviet Union,[14] and Jeffrey Veidlinger wrote a book-long monograph on the Moscow State Yiddish Theater (where he argued that this theater is a window into early Soviet Jewish culture—a revolutionary argument, compared to his predecessors, who spoke of the Jewishness of Trotsky, Lenin's treatment of the Jewish question, or even examined Isaac Babel).[15] Kenneth Moss wrote a 400-page book about the Jewish renaissance, mostly in Yiddish, and the Russian Revolution.[16]

David Shneer, arguably the most innovative and daring scholar of our generation, used Yiddish to tell new imaginative stories of Jewish idealism: the Jewish press of the 1920s, the post-Soviet Jewish diaspora, queer studies, and the global antifascist movement.[17] Elissa Bemporad wrote a new history of Jews in Minsk of the 1920s and was able to argue, using Yiddish and Russian-language newspapers, that many Minsk Jews maintained their traditions to a much larger extent than previously believed.[18]

My own work, on Soviet Jewish popular culture of the 1920s and 1930s, has almost entirely focused on Yiddish sources; they enabled me to trace the emergence of a new Soviet Jewish identity expressed in Yiddish-language plays, songs, brochures, and other genres of popular culture: Soviet Yiddish culture was filled with a communist spirit yet was grounded in many Jewish traditions. The field of early Soviet Jewish studies, in short, has been transformed by Yiddish, and there is so much more to explore: the history of the Kiev-based Kultur Lige and the lives of individual cultural actors—poets, philosophers, writers, directors, actors, educators, painters, scientists, musicians, and folklorists, especially women. Yiddish opens doors to exciting, meaningful scholarship by Mikhail Krutikov, Amelia Glaser, Sasha Senderovich and many others.[19]

Old Yiddish

In the area of early modern studies, which is especially popular in Europe (in Germany, France, and the Netherlands) and Israel, there is an explosion of interest in old Yiddish literature that was previously overlooked. Anthologies by Gerold Frakes and book-length monographs by Jean Baumgarten, Chava Turniansky, Claudia Rosensweig, and Shlomo Berger have revived interest in the *Bovo Buch*, an early modern Yiddish chivalry novel; *Shmuel Buch*, a popular retelling of stories of Solomon; Hasidic tales; and stories of the supernatural. These texts bridge Jewish studies and the history of reading, leisure, and early modern everyday life. The memoir by Glückel of Hameln, written in the seventeenth century by an extraordinary businesswoman who wanted to use writing to cure herself of melancholy, has always attracted scholarly attention, but few read it in Yiddish.[20] Glückel's talent as a writer, as well as the events that she describes—the aftermath of war, the expulsion of the Jewish community from Hamburg, the Black Plague, and more—make the text central in both early modern Jewish history and Yiddish studies. Because this is a rare text written by a woman, there is even more interest in it today, when scholars are looking for women's own voices, rather than those who speak on their behalf.

Women/Gender Studies

What women read, what they thought, and how they lived their lives were of primary interest to scholars of early modern history. There is much exciting work to be done in Yiddish women and gender studies: For instance, there is only one monograph on *Tsene Rene*, one of the most popular and influential books of East European Jewry, popularly known as the "women's Bible"; there is no monograph on *Thines*, Yiddish renditions of Psalms; there are no books on the early stories of the supernatural in Yiddish folklore—the golem (zombies), dybbuk, *shedim,* and other mystical creatures; and much, much more. If done right—that is, in conversation with digital humanities, contemporary global approaches, and book history—these studies can represent exciting developments in the field. Working with original Yiddish sources (rather than translations) should put any serious scholar on the map.

One of the largest gaps in the field and so one of the most promising directions is the analysis of literature written by hundreds of women authors: The insights generated by this scholarship will change and challenge the way we understand Yiddish literature. Naomi Seidman's pioneering work, which challenged the presumption of the position of Yiddish literature in the Jewish cultural sphere as "female" as opposed to Hebrew "male," opened the conversation about the actual women writing in Yiddish, notably their invisibility in the canon.[21] Seidman in her later works and other American and Canadian scholars, including Kathryn Hellerstein, Anita Norich, Sheva Zucker, Faith Jones, Alison Schachter, and Frieda Forman, have paved the way in bringing women's voices into the story of Yiddish narratives. Their brilliant translations and analyses have introduced Celia Dropkin, Kadia Molodowsky, Ester Kreitman, Anna Margolin, Shira Gorshman, and many other women Yiddish poets and prose writers to a larger audience. Some of the most exciting scholarship in the field of Yiddish studies is with "newly discovered" women's writing, including stories by Fradl Shtok (translated and annotated by Allison Schachter and Jordan Finkin),[22] Rivka Levin's children's literature (anthologized and analyzed by Miriam Udel),[23] and Shira Gorshman's unusual stories as analyzed by Faith Jones.[24]

The newest scholarship on Yiddish women writers relies on these works and asks new questions. For example, Zohar Weiman Kelman, in her book *Queer Expectations: A Genealogy of Jewish Women's Poetry*, argues that Jewish women writers turned to poetry to write new histories, developing "queer expectancy" as a conceptual tool for understanding how literary texts can both invoke and resist what came before.[25] Similarly, Allison Schachter, in her *Women Writing Jewish Modernity, 1919–1939*, makes a case that women wrote prose in Yiddish and Hebrew that challenged the patriarchal norms of Jewish textual authority and reconceptualized Jewish cultural belonging.[26] Weiman Kelman and Schachter focus on American authors. Yiddish specialists in Poland are among the cutting-edge scholars who produce work analyzing Yiddish women writing in the context of contemporary culture in Poland: Karolina Szymaniak, Joanna Lisek, and Bella Szwarcman-Czarnota. We are still seriously behind when it comes to literature produced by Soviet Yiddish women (and many men too) and Yiddish literature created in South America and Mexico, and Canada. The fact that there are still no monographs on most Yiddish women writers, including Chava Rosenfarb, one of the most talented Yiddish writers, who wrote a breathtaking novel set in Lodz ghetto,[27] means that there is still much work to do.

Pushing Boundaries of Imagination

When one brings together Yiddish and almost any other aspect of European history and culture, new dimensions and new directions pop up. Take, for example, Holocaust studies. David Roskies paved the way for Yiddish Holocaust literature in North America when he published *Against the Apocalypse.*[28] Many more untranslated Yiddish-language diaries, letters, journals, notes, poems, short stories, songs, interviews, and even photo epitaphs are still largely unintegrated into Holocaust studies. Once these materials are translated into a more popular language, such as German, Hebrew, Polish, Russian, or English, their significance increases. Two conclusions arise from this observation: One is that translation is the future, and another is the importance of integrating documents into new studies before they are translated. Here are a few examples. The Yiddish-language archive by Emmanuel Ringelblum collected in the Warsaw Ghetto is almost fully digitized but yet is barely used; the archive of the Kiev Cabinet for Studies of Jewish culture is barely studied (it has materials on Yiddish music from the 1920s and 1930s, including songs from Bela Tserkov recorded in 1938, just a few years before the Nazi invasion); and the same goes for the Yiddish-language holdings of the Ontario Jewish Archive and all Yiddish-language interviews of the Shoah Foundation.

Why bother with these documents? Because when one does, one rewrites history. For example, Justin Cammy has translated and annotated a memoir by Avrom Sutzkever—a well-known Yiddish poet, a war veteran, a partisan, and survivor of the Vilna ghetto.[29] It is an important contribution not only to Yiddish studies but, significantly, also to the history of the Nuremberg Trials, the Cold War, and the Holocaust in the Soviet Union. A few years prior to that, Mikhail Krutikov published a new intellectual biography of Yiddish literary critic Meir Wiener and by doing so highlighted how closely integrated Yiddish was into European society of the 1920s, from Germany to France to Poland to Russia.[30] This book illustrates how much we lack knowledge of how prewar society dealt with issues of minorities, race, religion, and secularism or how closely Yiddish intellectuals interacted with their Jewish and non-Jewish contemporaries. For example, Wiener personally knew Lenin and Rabbi Kook, corresponded with Martin Buber and Hugo von Hofmannsthal, and argued with Gershom Scholem and Georg Lukacs. His intellectual biography brings Yiddish to the forefront of the intellectual discourse of interwar Europe.

Perhaps one of my favorite examples of how Yiddish studies can expand our understanding of prewar European culture is the story of Judah Leman's Yiddish brochure on Einstein's theory of relativity. In 1921 Albert Einstein supervised the preparation and publication of a concise summary of his renowned theory of relativity. He taught physics to Russian refugees in Berlin, and his student Leman helped translate for them (into Yiddish); he eventually wrote this book to introduce Eastern European Jews to Einstein's theory. Jordan Chad, who found the book and translated it into English, argued, in his beautiful introduction, that Leman managed to produce the most accessible summary of the theory in any language.[31] The project contributes both to the history of science and the history of Jews in Europe, and it would be impossible without Yiddish.

To work on projects like this, one needs to have expertise in the Yiddish language, including an ability to read handwritten manuscripts, in-depth knowledge of at least one but preferably two languages, and some interdisciplinary training. But the result—new, exciting findings that push and challenge the boundaries of human knowledge—can truly be rewarding.

Digital Humanities

A few words about digitization. During the COVID-19 pandemic, when trips to libraries and archives were impossible, many graduate students and more senior researchers kept saying, "Thank God we live in the age of digitization and virtual archives." Indeed, with so many things digitized—and Yiddish studies is at the forefront of this—it seemed that one does not need to leave the house to do groundbreaking cutting-edge research. The Yiddish Book Center holds 11,000 fully digitized titles of Yiddish books, and these titles and the content are fully searchable. The National Library of Israel holds many fully digitized Yiddish dailies, including *Haynt*, published in Poland between 1908 and 1939; *Der Moment* (1910–39); and the Yiddish *Forverts* (New York, 1897–1979), along with 272 Yiddish periodicals from many countries. YIVO holds dozens of fully digitized Yiddish archives from Poland and Lithuania online. The list of Yiddish digital resources grows daily, although it is still hard to find materials from the Soviet Union. With fully searchable texts, the possibilities for imaginative research are boundless: How did Yiddish press cover the Beilis Trial of 1913 or Hitler's rise to power? How did readers learn about the newest trends in fashion? How many times was the story of the Rabbi of Kotsk covered in the Yiddish press in Poland? What exactly is transnational about Yiddish theater? How did Yiddish culture address race? The presence and accessibility of Yiddish digital resources will push the boundaries of our imagination and enable new exciting research.

Yiddish Music, Dance, Summer Programs, and Communities

Universities provide avenues for the serious study of Yiddish, but even more important are Yiddish summer programs, where students and interested members of the public spend an intensive few weeks learning the Yiddish language, culture, and music in an immersive environment. This is where people interested in Yiddish professionally or as a hobby meet and spend days and nights conversing with each other in Yiddish (sometimes because this is the only language they have in common, sometimes because they are committed to improving their competency), and they form friendships and networks associated with Yiddish. Yiddish summer communities of YIVO in New York, the Medem Center in Paris, Tel Aviv University, Wroclaw in Poland, Vilnius in Lithuania, Oxford in England, and Amherst, Massachusetts, in the United States are centers of otherwise dispersed Yiddishland, where people who need Yiddish for academic research or who feel marginalized by mainstream Jewish communities for being queer or secular or not being significantly attached to Israel or being interested "just in music" can find their place. Studies of new programs like these are beginning to appear, as are studies of queer Jewish identities associated with Yiddish, interviews with summer school students and faculty, and articles based on the future of Yiddish and Yiddish studies. This area of study is very self-aware, self-reflexive, and well documented because almost every participant of such summer programs believes they have a unique path to Yiddish, and their stories find receptive listeners.

Nearly every Yiddish program has a significant evening component that is usually centered on music: They are collective performances of singing, jamming, and dancing. Many participants began studying Yiddish because they were intrigued by Yiddish music, which they sometimes heard from family members or at concerts. Almost every Yiddish musician is a scholar too, researching the origins of the songs, the people who sang and collected them, and their audiences. Excellent histories of Klezmer music by Zeev Feldman, Joel Rubin, Henry Sapoznik, and others have been published, as well as a book by Sonia Gollance on the history of Yiddish dance.[32] Although it seems that the number of studies of the so-called Klezmer renaissance or revival is decreasing, there is still room for creating new scholarship-inspired musical performances.

In the past few years, we have seen a shift from monographs into blends of archival and artistic products. Examples include David Shneer's and Jewlia Eisenberg's production of Yiddish songs by Lin Jaldati; Naomi Seidman's multimedia production of Bais Yakov culture; and my own work with artist Psoy Korolenko on reconstructing Yiddish music created in Ukraine during World War II in the form of a performance and a lecture-concert. Multimedia productions are gaining popularity in the Yiddish world. The Digital Yiddish Theater Project, YIVO's Ruth Rubin archive online, collections of Yiddish-language interviews by the Yiddish Book Center, the Yale-based Fortunoff Video Archive's Songs from

Testimonies, and videos of the Aheim project—all these are promising and exciting avenues of research and potential research productions. One gap in these offerings is the availability of Yiddish films—more than one hundred have been made, but almost none are available in open access or via streaming. Once Yiddish films become more accessible, there will be more books, monographs, articles, and documentaries about Yiddish cinema, and it will become another promising research area. Works by J. Hoberman, Zehavit Stern, and Rebecca Margolis have paved the way, but there is so much more to do.

Hasidic Yiddish

Most speakers of contemporary Yiddish wear Hasidic or other ultrareligious garb. Educational systems, prayer houses, community organizations, and popular Hasidic culture, including music (not Klezmer!), are thriving. As Dovid Katz points out, the future of Yiddish lies most likely with the half-million Hasidim who speak Yiddish to their many children and who, a generation or two from now, will most likely have very different legacies from the thousand-year-old Yiddish culture that we study today.

Yet Hasidic Jews of the twenty-first century are the least-studied Jewish group, partially because they are extremely insular and distrusting of largely secular Yiddish studies scholars, and few scholars seem interested in approaching this community. Studying Hasidic Yiddish requires a degree of rebellion from the tradition of Yiddish scholarship. One needs, for example, to let go of an attachment to standard Yiddish and to be open to a descriptive, rather than prescriptive, approach to studying Yiddish linguistics. One also should stop lamenting the lack of interest among Hasidim in contemporary "authentic" Klezmer music, as carefully restored from ethnographic collections of the early twentieth century, and embrace the fact that Hasidim like either *nigunim* or, for celebrations, music that largely relies on computer sound effects. Hasidic literature is not rooted in Ayzik Meyer Dik or even Rav Nachman's stories—but it is entertaining and read by thousands of native speakers of Yiddish, even though people who study Yiddish to gain insight into culture are completely unaware of it. The future, I think, is with scholars like linguist Chaya Nove, who studies Satmar Yiddish linguistics, and Kriszta Eszter Szendroi, who is completing a dictionary of Hasidic Yiddish. Other areas of Hasidic Yiddish culture, such as music, literature, theater, and film, are still waiting to be studied. Similarly, sociologists, anthropologists, and historians who study the community are waiting for Yiddish specialists to enter the field—which I suggest is the real future of academic studies of Yiddish.

Epilogue

Aaron Lansky, founder of the Yiddish Book Center, has famously stated, more than once, that Yiddish has outwitted history. He means that Yiddish has survived, even though its death has been predicted in almost every generation for the past few hundred years. Yiddish studies seems to keep reinventing itself. In addition to studies of literature and the language itself, Yiddish opens insights into the past of Jewish people that are impossible to gain from other languages. Knowledge of Yiddish helps scholars in other disciplines too. Diaspora studies, for example, can rely on Yiddish studies for exploring questions of home, belonging, margins, negotiating spaces, and, of course, always living as a minority. Genocide studies scholars can turn to Yiddish to learn how languages find words for unimaginable violence. Similarly, for scholars of refugee studies, Yiddish testimonies offer insights into the direct voices of people forced to flee in the past. Finally, for the stories of the present, Yiddish opens some doors into the least researched and insular Hasidic communities.

Recommended Readings

Baumgarten, Jean. *Introduction to Old Yiddish Literature* (Oxford University Press, 2005).

Estraikh, G. *Soviet Yiddish: Language Planning and Linguistic Development* (Clarendon, 1999).

Fishman, David E. *The Rise of Modern Yiddish Culture* (University of Pittsburgh Press, 2005).

Glaser, Amelia. *Songs in Dark Times: Yiddish Poetry of Struggle from Scottsboro to Palestine* (Harvard University Press, 2020).

Krutikov, Mikhail. *Yiddish Fiction and the Crisis of Modernity, 1905–1914* (Stanford University Press, 2001).

Miron, Daniel. *The Image of the Shtetl and Other Studies of Modern Jewish Literary Imagination* (Syracuse University Press, 2000).

Miron, Daniel. *A Traveler Disguised: A Study in the Rise of Modern Yiddish Fiction in the Nineteenth Century* (Schocken Books, 1973).

Norich, Anita. *Writing in Tongues: Translating Yiddish in the Twentieth Century* (University of Washington Press, 2013).

Nove, Chaya R. "The Erasure of Hasidic Yiddish from Twentieth Century Yiddish Linguistics," *Journal of Jewish Languages* 6 (2018): 111–43.

Roskies, David G. *A Bridge of Longing: The Lost Art of Yiddish Storytelling* (Harvard University Press, 1995).

Seidman, Naomi. *A Marriage Made in Heaven: The Sexual Politics of Hebrew and Yiddish* (University of California Press, 1997).

Seidman, Naomi. *Translating the Jewish Freud: Psychoanalysis in Hebrew and Yiddish* (Stanford University Press, 2024).

Shneer, David. *Yiddish and the Creation of Soviet Jewish Culture, 1918–1930* (Cambridge University Press, 2004).

Shternshis, Anna. *Soviet and Kosher: Jewish Popular Culture in the Soviet Union, 1923–1939* (Indiana University Press, 2006).

Yudkoff, Sunny S. *Tubercular Capital: Illness and the Conditions of Modern Jewish Writing* (Stanford University Press, 2019).

Notes

1. Rachel Rojanski, *Yiddish in Israel* (Indiana University Press, 2020).

2. Joanna Nalewajko-Kuliko, *A Citizen of Yiddishland: Dovid Sfard and the Jewish Communist Milieu in Poland* (Peter Lang, 2020).

3. *Geshikhte fun der yidisher shprakh* (Yidisher Visnshaftlekher Institut, 1973).

4. *Notes from the Warsaw Ghetto* [English] (i-books, 2006).

5. Elisheva, 1931ff.

6. Alveltlekhn Yidishn Kultur-Kongres, 2011.

7. See Borochov and Mitchell Cohen, *Class Struggle and the Jewish Nation* (Routledge, 2020).

8. Daniel Miron, *A Traveler Disguised: A Study in the Rise of Modern Yiddish Fiction in the Nineteenth Century* (Schocken, 1973).

9. Daniel Miron, *The Image of the Shtetl and Other Studies of Modern Jewish Literary Imagination* (Syracuse University Press, 2000).

10. Ruth Wisse, *I. L. Peretz and the Making of Modern Jewish Culture* (University of Washington Press, 1991).

11. David Roskies, *A Bridge of Longing: The Lost Art of Yiddish Storytelling* (Harvard University Press, 1995).

12. Mikhail Krutikov, "Yiddish Studies from a New Perspective," *In Geveb* (online, 2015).

13. Zvi Gitelman, *Jewish Nationality and Soviet Politics: The Jewish Sections of the CPSU, 1917–1930* (Princeton University Press, 1972), and Mordechai Altshuler, *The Yevsekstiya in the Soviet Union (1918–1930): Between Nationalism and Communism* [Hebrew] (Hebrew University, 1980).

14. Gennady Estraikh, *Soviet Yiddish: Language Planning and Linguistic Development* (Clarendon, 1999).

15. Jeffrey Veidlinger, *The Moscow State Yiddish Theater: Jewish Culture on the Soviet Stage* (Indiana University Press, 2000).

16. Kenneth Moss, *Jewish Renaissance in the Russian Revolution* (Harvard University Press, 2009).

17. David Shneer, *Yiddish and the Creation of Soviet Jewish Culture, 1918–1930* (Cambridge University Press, 2004).

18. Elissa Bemporad, *Becoming Soviet Jews: The Bolshevik Experiment in Minsk* (Indiana University Press, 2013).

19. For instance, Krutikov, *Der Nister's Soviet Years: Yiddish Writer as Witness to the People* (Indiana Univesity Press, 2019); Glaser, "Taking Yiddish to Court," *East European Jewish Affairs* 50 (2020): 289–91; and Senderovich, *How the Soviet Jew Was Made* (Harvard University Press, 2022).

20. *The Memoirs of Glückel of Hameln* (Schocken Books, 1977).

21. Naomi Seidman, *A Marriage Made in Heaven: The Sexual Politics of Hebrew and Yiddish* (University of California Press, 1997).

22. Fradl Shtok, *From the Jewish Provinces: Selected Stories* (Northwestern University Press, 2022).

23. Miriam Udel, *Honey on the Page: A Treasury of Yiddish Children's Literature* (New York University Press, 2020).

24. Faith Jones, "Between Mountains." *Bridges* 14 (2009): 129–32.

25. Zohar Weiman Kelman, *Queer Expectations: A Genealogy of Jewish Women's Poetry* (SUNY Press, 2018).

26. Allison Schachter, *Women Writing Jewish Modernity, 1919–1939* (Northwestern University Press, 2022).

27. Chava Rosenfarb, *The Tree of Life: A Trilogy of Life in the Lodz Ghetto* (3 vols.; University of Wisconsin Press, 2004–2006).

28. David Roskies, *Against the Apocalypse: Responses to Catastrophe in Modern Jewish Culture* (Harvard University Press, 1984).

29. Justin Cammy, *From the Vilna Ghetto to Nuremberg: Memoir and Testimony* (McGill-Queen's University Press, 2021).

30. Mikhail Krutikov, *From Kabbalah to Class Struggle: Expressionism, Marxism, and Yiddish Literature in the Life and Work of Meir Wiener* (Stanford University Press, 2011).

31. Judah Leman, *Einstein's Theory of Relativity: The Einstein-Approved Summary for Non-Scientists* (independently published, 2017).

32. Sonia Gollance, *It Could Lead to Dancing: Mixed-Sex Dancing and Jewish Modernity* (Stanford University Press, 2021).

PART 3

Interactions and Identity

20

Sociology

Ilana M. Horwitz, Tulane University

SOCIOLOGY IS THE STUDY of human society and its social structures and dynamics. Studying Jews through the lens of sociology means looking at how Jews influence the societies in which they live and how they are influenced by those societies. The "sociological imagination," a term coined by C. Wright Mills, enables us to see connections between Jews' personal experiences and the larger forces of history. How Jews choose to educate their children, the way they form families, how they practice religious rituals, how they organize their communities, how they choose ethnic and racial categories, how they adapt their language to fit into different groups: All of these are *social facts* that are products of human interaction with persuasive or coercive power that exist externally to any individual.

Sociological research often begins with a puzzle: What causes what to happen? Sociologists conduct research to systematically analyze social conditions and possible solutions. They do this through sociological research methods, such as surveys, interviews, participant observations, content analysis, and experiments. Sociologists then make comparisons across cases to find patterns and create hypotheses about how societies work now or how they worked in the past. Based on their research findings, sociologists then develop theories, models, and perspectives to further understand how and why the social patterns exist.

I begin this chapter by briefly describing the origins of American Jewish sociology. I then explain how sociology is done by outlining different research methods, with examples of recent studies using those methods. Finally, I explore the emerging trends and challenges in the field. Readers should note the geographical scope of this chapter and its timespan. First, except for a few studies about Israelis, I focus almost exclusively on research based on data from the United States.[1] Second, after discussing the roots of American Jewish sociology, I focus on research published between 2014 and 2022. Samuel Heilman, Rela Geffen Monson, and Shaul Kelner provide deeper histories of American Jewish sociology and synthesize articles published before 2014.[2]

How It Began? Roots of American Jewish Sociology

Marshall Sklare—the "dean" of the sociology of American Jewry who is credited with making the sociological study of American Jewry an accepted area of specialization within American sociology—carried out some of the earliest and most significant sociological studies of American Jews in the 1950s and 1960s.[3] One of the central puzzles and social patterns that Sklare sought to explore in postwar America was the remarkably high rates of Jewish identification amidst plummeting rates of traditional Jewish religious practice (e.g., dietary laws and weekly service attendance). What does it mean to be a "good" Jew without religious observance? To explore this, he embarked on two community studies, the most well-known being his studies of "Lakeville," a suburban community where Jews made up about 25 percent of the population.[4] Lakeville was also an interesting case because of its diverse Jewish population: Lakeville's Jews were both of German and East European origin and included second-, third- and fourth-generation Jews, and even members of the first generation. The multigenerational nature of Lakeville allowed for an empirical test of the third-generation hypothesis, which posits that second-generation migrants are eager to assimilate the cultural norms of their host country, whereas third-generation migrants are more likely to revert to those of their grandparents' generation, thereby asserting their difference from mainstream culture. The Lakeville study, which measured levels of home observance and synagogue attendance by generation, showed that third-generation migrants have a slight upturn in home observance and synagogue attendance.

Over the past several decades, studies of American Jews have become more sophisticated, using new methods and expanding their inquiries beyond questions of assimilation, acculturation, suburbanization, and economic mobility. In the next section, I outline commonly used sociological methods and how they have been used to study Jews and Jewish institutions between 2014 to 2022, both within the sociology of American Jewry and in sociology more broadly.

How Is It Done? Sociological Methods

Survey Research

Much of the survey-based research of American Jews uses large-scale national population studies, such as the Jewish Federation's National Jewish Population Survey (NJPS) surveys of 1990–91 and 2000–1 and the Pew Research Center's studies of Jewish Americans of 2013 and 2021. Several large Jewish communities have also commissioned their own community studies, including the 2011 New York Jewish Community Study, the 2017 Bay Area Community Study, and the 2019 Greater Philadelphia Study.[5] These national and community studies address questions, such as the following: What is the size and location of the Jewish population? Who comprises Jewish households? How do different people connect to and engage in Jewish life? And how is the community growing, changing, and evolving? Periodic measurement of the size and behaviors of the Jewish population helps Jewish federations, foundations, and nonprofits set funding and planning priorities and determine the cost, quality, and availability of Jewish education, social services, and cultural activities. These surveys also identified important trends, such as rising rates of intermarriage (1990 NJPS), rising rates of Orthodox Jews (2011 NY community study), the rise of Jewish "nones" (2013 Pew), and the increasing racial and ethnic diversity of American Jews (2021 Pew). However, methodological design decisions made by researchers, such as the choice of a sampling frame, mode of data collection, nonresponse follow-up protocols, and the definition of eligibility, can have significant impacts on population estimates.[6]

Scholars also use surveys originating outside the population and community studies. For example, Adina Bankier-Karp and Michelle Shain were curious how COVID-19 affected the mental health of Orthodox Jews and how religious resources cushion the effects of isolation and the deprivation of religious gatherings over time.[7] They used data from the COVID-19 Community Portrait Study, a longitudinal study surveying members of eleven Orthodox Jewish synagogues in four communities at three time points during COVID-19. They found two competing effects on participants' religious resources. Although group resources decreased as a result of the pandemic, psychosocial resources were strengthened. A Closeness-to-God Index predicted lower levels of depression and anxiety, less perceived stress, and less loneliness. Participation in congregational prayer also predicted lower stress and less loneliness, but the magnitude of the effect was smaller. The findings provide empirical support for theoretical frameworks emphasizing the positive effects of religion on mental health and suggest that psychosocial resources enable religious coping during particularly challenging times.

Another way to use survey data is to combine datasets. For example, Ira Sheskin and Harriet Hartman used data from Decade 2000, which combines data from twenty-two Jewish community studies.[8] This dataset includes 19,800 twenty-minute interviews and is a random sample of 547,000 Jewish households. It allowed the researchers to test the theory that an individual's Jewish identity, especially in terms of its behavioral manifestations, is influenced by interactions with other Jews in the community. They found that considerable variation exists in Jewish identity measures and depends on the type of denominational profile that exists in the individual's community. That is, Orthodox Jews, for example, behave differently in a community with a significant Orthodox population than in a community with a small Orthodox population.

Surveys can also yield useful open-ended data. For example, Helana Darwin constructed a survey with open-ended questions to understand the meanings of Jewish women's kippot.[9] She selected survey methods instead of interview methods because she wanted to involve as many voices and perspectives as possible. Her analysis of 576 Jewish women who wear kippot reveal that this religious practice is fraught with social sanctions based on the women's simultaneous gender deviance and religious deviance.

Depth Interviews

Depth interviews involve conversations between the researcher and research subject. They are designed to capture in-depth responses of a select group of people to better understand their lived experience. For example, Ari Kelman and colleagues wanted to interrogate the prevalent conception of Jewish identity as an individualized endeavor of meaning-making.[10] In a departure from common studies of identity, which ask people to report on their Jewish identities, Kelman and his team conducted life-story interviews with fifty-eight postboomers. The interviews revealed fundamentally relational expressions of Jewish identity: Respondents constructed narratives of their Jewish identities that were inseparably linked to both Jews and non-Jews from their past and present. The researchers proposed that Jewish identity can be understood primarily as a relational phenomenon that is constructed through social ties, rather than as a product of individual meaning-making. Other recent studies that rely on interviews include study of Jewish American Buddhists—Jewish Americans who are embracing a dual religious identity, practicing Buddhism while also staying connected to their Jewish roots[11]—and Zalman Schneur Newfield's study of people who exit the ultra-Orthodox Jewish sects of Satmar and Lubavitch.[12]

Participant Observation

Participant observation, often referred to as ethnography, aims to uncover the meanings people give to their actions by observing those actions in practice. For example, Mijal Bitton conducted ethnographic fieldwork to understand how a community of Syrian Sephardic Jews construct their collective.[13] The puzzle Bitton wanted to solve was about ethnic assimilation: How is it that fourth- and fifth-generation individuals in the Syrian Sephardic community still have a potent ethnic identity that shapes their daily lives and structures elements such as marriage, occupation, and residential choices? The Syrian Sephardic community is also a unique social group because they have attained high levels of social cohesion and communal maintenance, like that of Jewish Ashkenazi Haredi communities in the United States, but without adopting a similar scripturalist and ideological approach toward Jewish law. To study these paradoxes, Bitton investigated the nature of social boundaries in this community as a participant observer. She observed central communal institutions, attended communal events, and conducted interviews.

Other recent examples of participant observation and ethnographic work include my study of how families make decisions about Hebrew school,[14] and Ayala Fader's study of married ultra-Orthodox Jews who lead "double lives" by secretly exploring the outside world through the internet.[15] Fader participated in online forums and Facebook groups where Jewish doubters congregated to discuss their beliefs and experiences; attended events such as Shabbat services, Passover Seders, and secular Jewish gatherings; and conducted in-depth interviews with Jewish individuals who self-identify as doubters, heretics, or atheists.

Content Analysis

Content analysis is a systematic analysis of content, such as a written work, speech, or film. For example, Emily Sigalow and Nicole Fox examined three decades of award-winning Jewish children's literature as a medium to explore how religiosity is constructed differently for men and women.[16] They demonstrate how these books produce and perpetuate gendered religious stereotypes that associate men with agency and women with communion. They also show how these books construct images of a "domestic Judaism" for women and a "public Judaism" for men and how women have been symbolically annihilated from these books' titles and central character roles. Sigalow and Fox argue that the gender stereotypes evident in these books matter to society because they produce and enforce gender inequalities in religiousness.

Content analysis is often combined with other methods. For example, in her study of regulatory and organizational nonconformity using the case of Hasidic educational institutions, Matty Lichtenstein combined content analysis with interviewing.[17] First, she analyzed legal, administrative, and policy materials, such as New York state and city educational laws, policy documents, and legal case texts. Second, she conducted a multilingual (English, Hebrew, Yiddish) textual analysis of the landscape of Hasidic education, reviewing hundreds of education-related materials, including educational texts, lobbying documents, and newspaper, magazine, and website media sources. She also interviewed professional lobbyists, informal advocates, educational and social services agency employees, educational administrators, and state officials involved in regulatory or legislative matters pertaining to Hasidic schools. Lichtenstein shows that in response to dominant state-promoted norms of secular education, religious educational advocates have gradually developed a multilevel toolkit of flexible legitimizing tactics—compliance markers, category conflation, and discursive resonance—that position them as deserving of state support.

Another recent example that combines content analysis with other methods is Sara Bunin Benor, Jonathan Krasner, and Sharon Avni's study of Jewish summer camp[18]: It uses a mixed-methods approach that combines in-depth interviews with camp directors; surveys with campers and staff members; an analysis of camp websites, social media, and other promotional materials; and an analysis of historical sources, such as newsletters and other publications from Jewish summer camps; oral histories and personal narratives from former campers, counselors, and directors of Jewish summer camps; and documents and books on the history of Jewish summer camps in the United States.

Content analysis is often used in historical sociology, which integrates sociological and historical approaches to comprehend the past, the evolution of societies over time, and its influence on the present. The discipline highlights the significance of using complementary comparative analysis to investigate both the past and present in tandem to grasp how specific historical occurrences align with broader societal advancements and ongoing predicaments. Historical sociologists tend to use data from written reports, newspaper articles, journals, diaries, artwork, and other artifacts that date to the period being studied. For example, Robert Braun used the case of resistance during the Holocaust to examine a broader argument about the clandestine collective action dilemma, which faces the dual challenge of secrecy and mobilization.[19] He traced successful and failed rescue attempts of Jews by combining a collection of postwar testimonies gathered for an honorary pension program with postwar trial transcripts of pro-Nazi collaborators and literature on nonrescuers. His statistical analyses of postwar testimonies and arrest records demonstrate that Catholic rescue groups were more successful in Protestant regions, and vice versa, because a minority position facilitated mobilization while reducing exposure. Braun argues that it is the distinctive local position of groups that enables the production of underground movements.

In another study Braun used local variation in antisemitism in Weimar Germany before the Holocaust to show how national border crossings act as focal points for xenophobia.[20] He used data on antisemitic themes in children's stories by looking at the genre of folk tales known as *Kinderschreck* (children's fright) to capture local variation in popular antisemitism. Kinderschreck is an oral tradition of storytelling widespread in Central Europe during the nineteenth and twentieth centuries. It was deployed by parents to discipline children through the inducement of fear. The setup of Kinderschreck stories has two components: a spatial location and a bogeyman. Parents would tell their children to stay away from a certain place (e.g., a river, cornfields) or bogeymen would come and get them. In some villages, the bogeyman was the "Forest Jew," "Blood Jew," or "Wandering Jew." Braun also retrieved all antisemitic incidents reported in local Centralverein reports between 1919 and 1932, the last year before the Nazi takeover. The Centralverein is the archives of the largest secular Jewish organization in twentieth-century Germany, which set up a decentralized research center consisting of more than 650 local chapters and 70,000 members tasked with documenting antisemitic incidents across the country. Information on antisemitism was gathered through careful reading of local newspapers and magazines, as well as the collection of complaints by fellow Jews.

Experiments

Experimental methods are research techniques that involve the manipulation of one or more independent variables to observe their effect on a dependent variable. These methods are designed to establish cause-and-effect relationships between variables by controlling for alternative explanations. Experimental methods allow for greater control over variables, increased precision and replicability, and the ability to test theories and establish causal relationships. There, however, are very few examples of this kind of research in American Jewish sociology. One such study is by Moshe Semyonov and colleagues who conducted a "factorial survey experiment" to compare the impact of immigrants' traits on anti-immigrant sentiment among majority and minority populations in Israel.[21] The study used a fractionalized sample of 252 vignettes that described potential immigrants by six characteristics—gender, continent of birth, education, religion, level of religiosity, and reason for migration—organized into 42 decks of 6 vignettes each. The vignettes were presented to two national representative samples of the Jewish (majority) and of the Arab (minority) populations in Israel, who were then asked to express attitudes toward admission and the allocation of rights to hypothetical immigrants. According to the analysis, Arabs expressed more supportive attitudes toward immigrants than Jews did. The most influential characteristic that shaped attitudes toward immigrants was their religious origin, with Jews expressing a preference for Jewish immigrants and objecting to non-Jewish immigrants, especially Muslims, whereas Arabs favored non-Jewish immigrants, especially Muslims. The findings suggest that preferences regarding ethnic and cultural homogeneity play a more significant role in shaping attitudes toward immigrants than the threat of economic competition.

Another example is a field experiment by Michael Wallace, Bradley Wright, and Allen Hyde, who examined whether employers discriminate in hiring against various religious groups.[22] Researchers sent fictitious resumes to advertised job openings across the American South. The resumes were randomly altered to indicate affiliation with one of seven religious groups or a control group. The study found that job applicants who expressed a religious identity were 26 percent less likely to receive a response from employers. Discriminatory treatment was highest toward Muslims, pagans, and atheists, whereas a fictitious religious group and Catholics experienced moderate levels of discrimination. Evangelical Christians encountered relatively little discrimination, and Jews appeared not to face any discernible discrimination. Additionally, the study found some evidence that Jews might receive preferential treatment over other religious groups in employer responses. The results align with models of religious discrimination rooted in secularization theory and cultural distaste theory.

Where Is American Jewish Sociology Going?

Emerging Trends

Based on recent research, we can see several important trends emerging in American Jewish sociology. First, conversations about Jews and Jewish institutions have moved from a niche audience comprising mostly other social scientists of Jews and Jewish communal organizations to broader sociological audiences. Second, there is an increasing focus on the heterogeneity of the Jewish community, with more attention being given to the role of racial, ethnic, gender, and socioeconomic diversity. Third, there are increasingly sophisticated analytic methods and larger datasets that allow sociologists to figure out how and why social patterns exist. Finally, there is increased attention to the role of applied and public sociology, which has made sociological research about Jews and Jewish institutions more relevant and useful to non-academic audiences.

Broadening Discourse

For most of the twentieth century and the early part of the twenty-first century, scholarly conversations about Jews took place in specialty journals devoted to the social-scientific study of Jews, such as *Contemporary Jewry*. However, sociological interest in Jews has recently increased among the broader group of sociologists of religion, with several studies of Jews being published in journals like *Journal for the Social Scientific Study of Religion* (JSSR), *Sociology of Religion* (SOR), and *Review of Religious Research* (RRE). Perhaps the most notable shift over the past five or so years is the publication of articles about Jews or Jewish institutions in leading general sociology journals, such as the *American Sociological Review* (ASR) and *American Journal of Sociology* (AJS), indicating that the case of Jews can be used to illuminate and test broader sociological phenomenon. For example, Lichtenstein's AJS article used the case of Hasidic educational institutions, which do not comply with state-level curricular requirements yet receive state funding and regulatory accommodation, to examine how nonconforming collective actors, whose alternative values and practices fundamentally conflict with core norms of their field, present themselves as legitimately deserving of regulatory support and accommodation.[23] Braun's AJS and ASR articles used the cases of antisemitism and the Holocaust to consider broader questions about civil society and intergroup relationships in times of social upheaval.[24] Horwitz and colleagues' ASR article used the case of girls raised by Jewish parents to examine how and why higher education is stratified by gender and religious subculture.[25]

Jews and Jewish institutions have also captured the attention of sociological theorists outside Jewish Studies. For example, Iddo Tavory's book, *Summoned: Identification and Religious Life in a Jewish Neighborhood*, won the American Sociological Association's Theoretical Agenda-Setting award in 2016.[26] An ethnography of a Jewish neighborhood in Los Angeles, *Summoned* illustrates how Orthodox Jews are called into being as they are called on by organizations, prayer quorums, the nods of strangers, whiffs of unkosher food floating through the street, or antisemitic remarks. Two articles using the case of Jews were also published in *Theory and Society,* a leading sociological theory journal. Taylor Paige Winfield used the case of Emile Durkheim, who was raised in a traditional Jewish environment with a rabbinic-thought model, to consider how scholars' intellectual development is shaped by their upbringing.[27] And Michal Kravel-Tovi used the case of American Jewry to consider the relationship between population statistics and narratives of scale and to show how scale-making can be a useful lens through which to comprehend the persuasive power and emotional impact of numeric constructs such as smallness.[28]

Jews have also become an interesting case for scholars of race and ethnicity. For example, sociological research on ethnoraciality typically suggests that individuals who physically resemble the majority group are more likely to identify with that group, in accordance with social identity theory. However, Adam Horowitz presents a counterargument to this assumption based on his interviews of White, Black, Asian, Latino/a, and multiracial Jewish converts.[29] He finds that converts who are phenotypically similar to the Jewish prototype are more likely to pass as Jewish by birth, which leads to sustained anxiety about their outsider status. In contrast, converts who are visibly different from the Jewish prototype do not see passing as an option and therefore do not experience the same level of anxiety, allowing them to immediately work toward a sense of belonging. Thus, those who least resemble Jewish phenotypic stereotypes are able to attain a sense of belonging within Jewishness more easily. This case challenges the literature's expectations and suggests that obvious phenotypic dissimilarity can have a beneficial effect on identificational processes by releasing the pressure to fit a group prototype.

Attention to Diversity

Racial and Ethnic Diversity

Sociological studies of Jews have historically focused almost exclusively on Ashkenazi Jews, but increasing racial and ethnic diversity in the United States and among Jewish Americans has led scholars to conduct more research centering the narratives of non-White or non-Ashkenazi Jews and often considering how they have been marginalized, minoritized, or underrepresented in canonical narratives of American Jews. Examples include Laura Limonic's study of Latin American Jewish immigrants and Bitton's study of Syrian Sephardic Jews.[30] In 2023 *Contemporary Jewry* and *the Journal of Jewish Education* devoted special issues to Jewish diversity.

The increased attention to the racial diversity of Jews has led the scholars Aaron Hahn Tapper, Ari Kelman and Aliya Saperstein to examine how American Jews fit into existing social-scientific and historical categories.[31] At times, American Jews are categorized as an ethnic group and at other times as a religious one, which has led to confusion among Jewish communal leaders who seek to understand and protect their communities. This intersection of sociological methods and Jewish communal concerns highlighted a need to account for the racial and ethnic diversity of American Jews, and to address this, Hahn Tapper, Kelman, and Saperstein analyzed 175 survey instruments from American Jewish population studies and community portraits conducted since 1970. They discovered that the focus on questions of religious practice and the concomitant avoidance of questions regarding race and ethnicity resulted in a "religio-racial formation" of American Jews as White. They argue that this approach has marginalized or excluded non-White Jews while maintaining Jewish communal access to Whiteness without explicitly claiming it.

Gender Diversity

There has been increased attention to the intersection of gender and Jewish life, with articles using the case of Jews being published in top specialty journals such as *Gender and Society*. For example, Darwin used the case of Jewish women who wear kippot to examine how gender and religious scripts are inextricably intertwined.[32] Michal Frenkel and Varda Wasserman used the case of Haredi Jewish women in the Israeli high-tech industry to explore how gender–religiosity intersectionality affects ultraconservative women's participation in the labor market and their ability to negotiate with employers for corporate work–family practices that address their idiosyncratic requirements.[33]

Other recent studies examining the intersection of gender and religion include those of Yosef Sokol and colleagues, who examined how gender, cultural affiliation, and shifting cultural affiliation affect the age at first marriage within Yeshiva Orthodoxy and Modern Orthodoxy,[34] and Landon Schnabel, Conrad Hackett, and David McClendon, who used Pew data to demonstrate that Israel diverges from the typical pattern of women appearing more religious than men.[35] They suggest that gender gaps arise, at least in part, because religions are gendered institutions with gendered norms, expectations, and incentives that vary from religion to religion.

In the coming years, we should expect to see increased scholarly attention given to the role of gender and sexuality in Judaism, as organizations like Keshet provide more attention to LGBTQ Jews and camps like Tawonga create all-gender cabins. One forthcoming book on this topic is Orit Avishai's *Queer Judaism: LGBT Activism and the Remaking of Jewish Orthodoxy in Israel*, which draws on interviews to examine how Orthodox Jewish LGBT persons in Israel became more accepted in their communities.[36] Avishai's book documents a vibrant, proud LGBTQ Orthodox community in Israel that began in anonymous chatrooms and backrooms in the early 2000s but is now out in the open.

One area of inquiry currently in its nascent stages, but that will likely become increasingly popular, is the role of gender fluidity and what it means for people to navigate a religion with gendered elements when they identify as gender nonconforming. For example, Darwin draws on interviews with 44 religious and formerly religious nonbinary people, some of whom were Jewish, to illustrate the regulatory impact of binary gender ideology on religious practitioners.[37]

Socioeconomic Diversity

Socioeconomic diversity in the American Jewish community has received much less scholarly attention from sociologists than gender, racial, and ethnic diversity, primarily because scholars assume that American Jews are not an especially socioeconomically diverse group. Indeed, American Jews have been among the most socioeconomically advantaged religious and ethnic groups in the United States in the late twentieth and early twenty-first centuries. On common measures of education, income, and economic security, American Jews are faring much better than the rest of the U.S. population. For example, Jews are about twice as likely to have a bachelor's degree and almost three times as likely to have a postgraduate degree. In terms of income, Jews are about six times as likely to report household incomes over $200,000, and Jews are almost twice as likely to say they are financially comfortable. About one-quarter of Jews struggle to pay bills, which is only half as much as U.S. adults.

However, there are important differences in socioeconomic status across different demographic measures, including religious affiliation, age, gender, region, race/ethnicity, and immigration status. In terms of religious denomination, Haredi Jews are half as likely to have a bachelor's degree and two to three times as likely as Jews of other denominations to be struggling financially. In terms of age, Jews over 65 are less educated and earn less but live more comfortably, whereas Jews 30–49 are the most financially insecure age bracket. In terms of gender, women's educational attainment is rising while men's educational attainment is falling among younger cohorts. In terms of region, Jews in the South are the least educated. In terms of race/ethnicity, Jews of color are less educated and less affluent than White Jews; Sephardic/Mizrahi Jews are less educated but not much poorer than Ashkenazi Jews. In terms of immigration status, immigrants are just as educated but less economically secure than native-born Jews.[38]

Given that there is more socioeconomic diversity in the Jewish community than scholars previously thought and given the sizable population of economically precarious Jews, some scholars have started to research this issue. For example, Sascha Lascar and I (2021) interviewed thirty-six low-income Jewish parents in the Philadelphia region, finding how social ties helped people navigate the economic setbacks of COVID-19.[39] In another study, Laurence Kotler-Berkowitz and Ira Sheskin examined the relationship between social class and social cohesion among American Jews by pooling data from twenty-seven local Jewish community studies into one data file with 24,733 cases.[40] They found modest positive relationships between social class and social cohesion: As social class status increases, so too do felt connections to the local Jewish community. In the coming years, we should expect to see more attention to the topic of socioeconomic diversity.

More Sophisticated Data and Analytical Methods

Longitudinal Data

Almost all of the data on American Jews are cross-sectional, meaning that information is collected at a single point in time from a group of individuals or units that represent a population or a sample.

Longitudinal data, in contrast, refers to data that are collected over time from the same individuals or units. This type of data allows researchers to study changes or trends in a particular phenomenon or characteristic over time; in other words, the main difference between cross-sectional and longitudinal data is the time dimension. Longitudinal data are more useful for studying changes over time and for identifying the causal relationships between variables, whereas cross-sectional data are more useful for describing the characteristics of a population or sample at a particular point in time. However, although longitudinal data have many benefits in terms of explaining social patterns, obtaining it is expensive and time-consuming.

In the past few years, there have been an increasing number of studies using longitudinal data. For example, rather than relying on retrospective surveys of people in adulthood, I followed 3,238 adolescents for thirteen years by linking the National Study of Youth and Religion (NSYR) to the National Student Clearinghouse. The NSYR is a four-wave multimethod longitudinal study of adolescents first recruited in 2002 with a nationally representative sample of 3,290 adolescents and a unique Jewish oversample of 80 additional adolescents. My colleagues and I then analyzed 107 longitudinal interviews with 33 girls from the NSYR, who were interviewed repeatedly between adolescence and emerging adulthood. By following girls from adolescence to adulthood, we could examine how girls' educational, professional, and familial aspirations panned out.[41]

Another longitudinal study is Sivan Zakai's study of how American Jewish children come to think and feel about Israel, tracking their evolving conceptions from kindergarten to fifth grade.[42] Zakai collected data in several ways, including in-depth interviews with children between the ages of seven and thirteen to gather their thoughts, feelings, and beliefs about Israel; observations of children in various educational settings, analysis of various cultural and educational materials such as textbooks, curricula, and educational videos; and surveys with children about their attitudes toward Israel. Zakai argues that, over the course of their elementary school education, children develop and express deep interest in complex issues such as the intricacies of identity and belonging, conflicting ways of framing the past, and the demands of civic responsibility.

Big Data

Big data is a powerful new resource for social-science research that may advance our understanding of human behavior and social phenomenon in a way never before possible. There are multiple types of big data that offer new opportunities in specific areas of social investigation. One type is administrative data, which are derived from the operation of administrative systems (e.g., data collected by government agencies for the purposes of registration, transaction and record-keeping). Examples of administrative data include educational records, tax filings, or even synagogue attendance records. Administrative data cover the entire population of beneficiaries, reducing the likelihood of data-quality issues, such as caused by social desirability bias and poor recall, and making it more accurate than self-reported survey data. These datasets often attempt to reach the entire population of relevant participants, thereby reducing selection bias. The advantages of using administrative data include cost and time savings, the possibility of obtaining accurate data, and a large sample size at low cost. Administrative data infrastructure has the potential to improve social-science research, enabling researchers to evaluate policies and interventions and to address novel questions. Analyzing administrative data also has the potential to bridge basic and applied research and provides opportunities to understand the social world better in contexts where stakeholders are ready to act based on research results.

Very few studies about Jews or Jewish institutions, however, have used administrative data. One example is a study by Ronit Pinchas-Mizrachi, Beth Zalcman, and Efraim Shapiro, who examined the difference in mortality rates between Haredi and non-Haredi Jews in Israel by using data gathered from the Israel Population Registry, Education Registry, Ministry of Health, and the Israel Central Bureau of Statistics.[43] The dataset included information on 1,230,636 Jewish Israeli citizens collected between 1996 and 2016. The researchers found that the mortality rate was significantly lower among the Haredi population compared to the non-Haredi population, even after adjusting for sex, age, marital status, number of children, education, and socioeconomic status.

Another example of administrative data is "Bar Mitzvah to the Bar," a study of educational outcomes among girls with a Jewish upbringing.[44] My colleagues and I linked the National Study of Youth and Religion (NSYR) to the National Student Clearinghouse to obtain detailed records on college attendance and graduation of all participants who were in wave 1 of the NSYR. This data linkage allowed us to overcome a common limitation of longitudinal research: Respondents who dropped out of the study after Wave 1 or who graduated from a postsecondary institution after the study ended (in 2013) lacked complete educational outcome data. Because of the NSC match, we could identify all the higher education institutions an individual ever attended or from which they graduated, even for respondents who dropped out after the first NSYR wave or completed college after the last wave of data collection in 2013.

Artificial Intelligence

Text mining (also referred to as text analytics) is an artificial intelligence (AI) technology that uses natural-language processing (NLP) to transform the free (unstructured) text in documents and databases into normalized, structured data suitable for analysis or for driving machine-learning algorithms. There are no examples from American Jewish sociology, but Ildikó Barna and Árpád Knap explore antisemitism in contemporary Hungary by analyzing articles related to Jews from the far-right site, Kuruc.info.[45] Their corpus contained 2,289 articles from the period between February 28, 2016, and March 20, 2019. To identify latent topics in the text, they employed one of the methods of NLP—topic modeling using a machine-learning method—and extracted fifteen topics. They found that racial antisemitism, which was unmeasurable by survey research, is overtly present in the discourse of Kuruc.info. Moreover, they identified topics that were connected to other types of antisemitism.

Broadening of Applied and Public Sociology

"Applied sociology" and "sociological practice" refer to interventions using sociological knowledge in an applied setting. Jewish communal agencies, long concerned with assimilation and the future of American Jewry, have historically looked to social science to inform their programs and have funded applied social research on the Jewish population, most of which is published as research reports that do not undergo the peer review process.[46] In his 2014 review of American Jewish sociology, Kelner noted that "the question, 'Whither the Jews?' still looms large in contemporary public policy-focused research." In 2023, almost a decade later, this question remains important, but we also see communal organizations moving beyond it to better understand different populations and how to serve them. Recent examples include the study of Jewish college students commissioned by the Jim Joseph Foundation, the study of Jews of color commissioned by the Jews of Color Initiative, and a study of the New York Jewish community, the Covid-19 Pandemic Impact Study commissioned by UJA.[47]

Public sociology is a subfield of the wider sociological discipline that emphasizes expanding the disciplinary boundaries of sociology and engaging with non-academic audiences. It is perhaps best understood as a style of sociology, rather than a particular method, theory, or set of political values. The goal of public sociology is to make social research accessible to journalists, policy makers, and general readers. *The Conversation*, an outlet that aims to unlock the knowledge of researchers and academics to provide the public with insight into society's biggest problems, has published dozens of articles about Jews by anthropologists, political scientists, and historians; they have covered topics such as why some strictly observant Jewish communities disobeyed public health guidelines during COVID, how antisemitic speech is driven partly by algorithms, how social distancing unravels the bonds that keep society together, what hate symbols were present during the U.S. Capitol riot, how antisemitic conspiracy theories contributed to the hostage-taking at a Texas synagogue, how marriage trends and political views are undermining the notion of a unified American Jewish identity, how Jewish–Christian families navigate the "December Dilemma" of putting up a Christmas tree, how Jews of color and non-Ashkenazi Jews are bringing attention to new Hanukkah traditions, how the political climate on college campuses differs from what the public sees in headlines and via social media, and how digital technology offers new ways to teach lessons from the Holocaust.

Recommended Readings

Bitton, Mijal. "Liberal Grammar and the Construction of American Jewish Identity," *American Sociologist* 53 (2022): 625–43.

Darwin, Helana. "Redoing Gender, Redoing Religion," *Gender and Society* 32 (2018): 348–70.

Frenkel, Michal, and Varda Wasserman. "With God on Their Side: Gender–Religiosity Intersectionality and Women's Workforce Integration," *Gender and Society* 34 (2020): 818–43.

Horwitz, Ilana, and Ariela Keysar, eds. *Methodology* (special issue), *Contemporary Jewry* 39 (2019).

Horwitz, Ilana, et al., "From Bat Mitzvah to the Bar: Religious Habitus, Self-Concept, and Women's Educational Outcomes," *American Sociological Review* 87 (2022) n.p.

Kelner, Shaul. *American Jewish Sociology* in *Oxford Bibliographies in Jewish Studies*, ed. David Biale (Oxford University Press, 2014).

Kelner, Shaul. *Tours That Bind: Diaspora, Pilgrimage and Israeli Birthright Tourism* (New York University Press, 2010).

Lichtenstein, Matty. "Legitimizing Tactics: Hasidic Schools, Noncompliance, and the Politics of Deservingness," *American Journal of Sociology* 127 (2022): 1860–916.

Newfield, Zalman Schneur. *Degrees of Separation: Identity Formation While Leaving Ultra-Orthodox Judaism* (Temple University Press, 2020).

Tavory, Iddo. *Summoned: Identification and Religious Life in a Jewish Neighborhood* (University of Chicago Press, 2016).

Wertheimer, J., *The New American Judaism: How Jews Practice Their Religion Today* (Princeton University Press, 2018).

Winfield, Taylor Paige. "Rereading Durkheim in Light of Jewish Law: How a Traditional Rabbinic Thought-Model Shapes His Scholarship," *Theory and Society* 49 (2020): 563–95.

Notes

1. The *Jewish Journal of Sociology*, which highlighted many of the international developments in the sociology of Jewry, closed in 2015. These studies are now located at the European Jewish Research Archive (EJRA), which is a project of the Institute for Jewish Policy Research (JPR).

2. Samuel C. Heilman, "The Sociology of American Jewry: The Last Ten Years," *Annual Review of Sociology* 8 (1982): 135–60; Rela Geffen Monson, "The Sociology of the American Jewish Community," *Modern Judaism* 11 (1991): 147–56; Shaul Kelner, "American Jewish Sociology" (2014), http://www.oxfordbibliographies.com.

3. Chaim I. Waxman, "Psalms of a Sober Man: The Sociology of Marshall Sklare," *Contemporary Jewry* 4 (1977): 3–11.

4. Mashall Sklare and Joseph Greenblum, *Jewish Identity on the Suburban Frontier: A Study of Group Survival in the Open Society* (Basic, 1967).

5. These can be accessed through www.jewishdatabank.org/databank.

6. See David A. Marker et al., "Jewish Community Studies in the Twenty-First Century," *Contemporary Jewry* 41 (2021): 349–68.

7. Adina Leah Bankier-Karp and Michelle Shain, "COVID-19's Effects upon the Religious Group Resources, Psychosocial Resources, and Mental Health of Orthodox Jews," *Journal for the Scientific Study of Religion* 61 (2022): 197–216.

8. Ira M. Sheskin and Harriet Hartman, "Denominational Variations across American Jewish Communities," *Journal for the Scientific Study of Religion* 54 (2015): 205–21.

9. Helana Darwin, "Jewish Women's KIPPOT: Meanings and Motives," *Contemporary Jewry* 37 (2016): 81–97.

10. Kelman et al., "The Social Self: Toward the Study of Jewish Lives in the Twenty-First Century," *Contemporary Jewry* 37 (2016): 53–79.

11. Emily Sigalow, *American JewBu: Jews, Buddhists, and Religious Change* (Princeton University Press, 2019).

12. Zalman Schneur Newfield, *Degrees of Separation: Identity Formation While Leaving Ultra-Orthodox Judaism* (Temple University Press, 2020).

13. Mijal Bitton, "Liberal Grammar and the Construction of American Jewish Identity," *American Sociologist* 53 (2022): 625–43.

14. Ilana Horwitz, "Foregrounding the Family: An Ethnography of How Families Make Decisions about Hebrew School," *Contemporary Jewry* 39 (2019): 155–72.

15. Ayala Fader, *Hidden Heretics: Jewish Doubt in the Digital Age* (Princeton University Press, 2020).

16. Emily Sigalow and Nicole S. Fox, "Perpetuating Stereotypes: A Study of Gender, Family, and Religious Life in Jewish Children's Books," *Journal for the Scientific Study of Religion* 53 (2014): 416–31.

17. Matty Lichtenstein, "Legitimizing Tactics: Hasidic Schools, Noncompliance, and the Politics of Deservingness," *American Journal of Sociology* 127 (2022): 1860–916.

18. Sarah Bunin Benor, Jonathan Krasner, and Sharon Avni, *Hebrew Infusion: Language and Community at American Jewish Summer Camps* (Rutgers University Press, 2020).

19. Robert Braun, "Minorities and the Clandestine Collective Action Dilemma: The Secret Protection of Jews during the Holocaust," *American Journal of Sociology* 124 (2018): 263–308.

20. "Bloodlines: National Border Crossings and Antisemitism in Weimar Germany," *American Sociological Review* 87 (2022): 202–36.

21. Moshe Semyonov et al., "The Impact of Immigrants' Characteristics on Anti-Immigrant Sentiment among the Jewish Majority and the Arab Minority in Israel," *Journal of Ethnic and Migration Studies* 49 (2023): 4266–87.

22. Michael Wallace, Bradley R. E. Wright, and Allen Hyde, "Religious Affiliation and Hiring Discrimination in the American South: A Field Experiment," *Social Currents* 1 (2014): 189–207.

23. "Legitimizing Tactics."

24. "Minorities" and "Bloodlines."

25. Ilana Horwitz et al., "From Bat Mitzvah to the Bar: Religious Habitus, Self-Concept, and Women's Educational Outcomes," *American Sociological Review* 87 (2022).

26. Iddo Tavory (University of Chicago Press, 2016).

27. Taylor Paige Winfield, "Rereading Durkheim in Light of Jewish Law: How a Traditional Rabbinic Thought-Model Shapes His Scholarship," *Theory and Society* 49 (2020): 563–95.

28. Michal Kravel-Tovi, "Ambivalences of Smallness: Population Statistics and Narratives of Scale among American Jewry," *Theory and Society* 52 (2022): 293–331.

29. Adam L. Horowitz, "Obviousness: The Unexpected Benefit of Phenotypic Dissimilarity," *Ethnic and Racial Studies* 40 (2017): 1900–1918.

30. Laura Limonic, *Kugel and Frijoles: Latino Jews in the United States* (Wayne State University Press, 2019); Bitton, "Liberal Grammar."

31. Aaron Hahn Tapper, Ari Y. Kelman, and Aliya Saperstein, "Counting on Whiteness: Religion, Race, Ethnicity, and the Politics of Jewish Demography," *Journal for the Scientific Study of Religion* 62 (2022): 28–48.

32. "Redoing Gender, Redoing Religion," *Gender and Society* 32 (2018): 348–70.

33. Michal Frenkel and Varda Wasserman, "With God on Their Side: Gender–Religiosity Intersectionality and Women's Workforce Integration," *Gender and Society* 34 (2020): 818–43.

34. Yosef Sokol et al., "Examining Average Age at First Marriage within Orthodox Judaism: A Large Community-Based Study," *Journal for the Scientific Study of Religion* 61 (2022): 710–25.

35. Landon Schnabel, Conrad Hackett, and David McClendon, "Where Men Appear More Religious than Women: Turning a Gender Lens on Religion in Israel," *Journal for the Scientific Study of Religion* 57 (2018): 80–94.

36. Orit Avishai, *Queer Judaism: LGBT Activism and the Remaking of Jewish Orthodoxy in Israel* (New York University Press, 2023).

37. "Navigating the Religious Gender Binary," *Sociology of Religion* 81 (2020): 185–205.

38. Based on my analysis of Pew 2020 data.

39. Ilana M. Horwitz and Sasha Lascar, "Ties in Tough Times: How Social Capital Helps Lower-Income Jewish Parents Weather the Economic Hardship of COVID-19," *Contemporary Jewry* 41 (2021): 161–83.

40. Laurence Kotler-Berkowitz and Ira M. Sheskin, "Social Class and Social Cohesion among American Jews," *Review of Religious Research* 64 (2022): 497–520.

41. Horwitz et al., "From Bat Mitzvah to the Bar."

42. Sivan Zakai, *My Second-Favorite Country* (New York University Press, 2022).

43. Ronit Pinchas-Mizrachi, Beth G. Zalcman, and Ephraim Shapiro, "Differences in Mortality Rates between Haredi and Non-Haredi Jews in Israel in the Context of Social Characteristics," *Journal for the Scientific Study of Religion* 60 (2021): 274–90.

44. Horwitz et al., "From Bat Mitzvah to the Bar."

45. Ildikó Barna and Árpád Knap, "Antisemitism in Contemporary Hungary: Exploring Topics of Antisemitism in the Far-Right Media Using Natural Language Processing," *Theo-Web. Zeitschrift Für Religionspädagogik* 18 (2019): 75–92.

46. Jonathan Krasner, "On the Origins and Persistence of the Jewish Identity Industry in Jewish Education," *Journal of Jewish Education* 82 (2016): 132–58.

47. Eitan Hersh, "Jewish College Students in America: A Report to the Jim Joseph Foundation" (2022) at jimjosephfoundation.org; Tobin Belzer et al., "Beyond the Count: Perspectives and Lived Experiences of Jews of Color" (2021) at jewsofcolorinitiative.org.

21

Anthropology

Michal Kravel-Tovi, Tel Aviv University

IF *THE PRINCETON COMPANION TO JEWISH STUDIES* had been published twenty or thirty years ago, the main narrative of this chapter would have revolved, I suspect, around the fraught relationship between anthropology and Jewish Studies. I imagine that this chapter would have discussed the double marginality of this subfield in both its home fields: why, in its formative years, anthropology tended to disregard Jews as research subjects and why Jewish Studies, as developed in North American and European universities, did not invite anthropology to its bustling interdisciplinary table.

Several conceptual and review essays from the last two or three decades have explored precisely this marginality. These include Jonathan Boyarin's "Jewish Ethnography and the Question of the Book,"[1] Virginia Dominguez's "Questioning Jews,"[2] and Jonathan Webber's "Modern Jewish Identities: The Ethnographic Complexities."[3] Interrogating and historicizing these relations, these accounts engaged productively with the unique otherness of Jews and the incompatibility of this precise uniqueness with the kinds of otherness that generally preoccupy anthropologists. They provided insights into some of the most profound—albeit unspoken—biases informing both anthropology and Jewish Studies, pointing toward a more reflexive and mutually productive *Jewish anthropology*. (In using this term, I build on Jonathan Boyarin's work, mostly *Palestine and Jewish History: Criticism at the Borders of Ethnography*[4] and "Jewish Ethnography and the Question of the Book," even though the way he construes this term is more prescriptive and ideological in nature).

The rubric of Jewish ethnography is expansive and loosely defined. My usage of the term is intentionally descriptive and inclusive, denoting a systematic up-close ethnographic exploration of mundane Jewish cultural life through both scientific and artistic means. The great majority of Jewish ethnography today takes the form of the anthropological study of Jewish life. It is pursued within the scholarly discipline of anthropology—the science of humanity, which focuses on the organizing cultural dimensions of the human experience—primarily by relying on ethnographic immersions in the lives of those under study. This immersion is a way of establishing rapport with research subjects through prolonged fieldwork using participant observation, open-ended and narrative interviews, and the study of their textual representations, material culture, and activities in digital spheres.

But even the seemingly straightforward linkage between Jewish ethnography and the anthropological study of Jews is more elusive than one might think. To the extent that anthropology unfolded across the nineteenth and twentieth centuries in convergence with overlapping disciplines (such as race science and folklore)—and at a time when these disciplines themselves were in the making—it is no wonder that the boundaries of Jewish ethnography are not self-evident. In addition, works in Jewish ethnography can be traced not only along the multiple histories of anthropology as an academic field but also in nonscientific ethnographic representations of Jews (such as in museum exhibitions) and in related disciplines such as sociology, cultural studies, and education that all adopt, to some extent, ethnographic methods and questions.

Although the previously accepted narrative of a thin dialogue between anthropology and Jewish Studies captures certain, even decisive, periods in the development of Jewish ethnography, it is nonetheless an imprecise narrative; its relevance to the current moment is on the wane. This chapter is written from the current vantage point of a generally stable and relatively productive moment of Jewish ethnography. The intersection of anthropology and Jewish Studies needs no further justifications or apologies. To be sure, the subfield neither takes center stage within anthropology nor has precedence in Jewish Studies over classic disciplines like history or philosophy. And yet, anthropologists have become welcomed and active interlocutors in Jewish Studies conversations, and works on Jews and Jewish life are increasingly finding space in prime anthropology outlets. In part, this new situation can be attributed to academic changes, both intra- and interdisciplinary. These include a heightened attention within anthropology to the workings of history and a greater epistemological openness within Jewish Studies to nontextual methodologies and objects of research, such as rituals and material culture, for example, and to probing the contemporary.

Just as importantly, Jewish ethnography is flourishing, relatively speaking, simply because so much is going on and grabbing the attention of anthropologists. Jewish life, broadly defined, is teeming and bubbling in old, new, and renewed ways. Above all, current Jewish life is underscored by a vibrancy, intensity, and inventiveness worthy of note. The current burgeoning of Jewish ethnography is largely a response to a range of multivalent realities, in which individuals and groups engage with Jews, Jewishness, and Judaism from many angles and with different intentions in mind. In and through these processes, they also modify, challenge, invigorate, and invent the forms and contents of Jewish life. By documenting these unfolding dynamics on the ground, anthropologists themselves participate in shaping Jewish life. As they chronicle the realities they study, they inescapably help make space for them and attract public attention to them—affirming, reifying, and transmitting them.

Whether this Jewish creativity reverberates within or transgresses the conventional boundaries of Jewish life, anthropologists meticulously document what it can teach us about Jews, Jewishness, and Judaism: how people claim Jewish belonging, seek Jewish recognition, experiment with Jewish religiosity, express piety in a particular Jewish fashion, pursue social justice from Jewish sensibilities, produce and consume Jewish objects and spaces, engage with the Jewish past, work hard to secure a Jewish future, and devise cultural interactions with other Jews and non-Jews alike. The list is long and could be longer, attesting to the ever-expanding and inventive articulations of Jewish life.

I offer the term "Jewishland" to capture the anthropological engagement with these inventive dynamics and to refer to the bustling social and political landscape in which Jewish relatedness (i.e., identity, belonging, and affinity) and Jewishly related forms of culture and meaning find expression and recognition, usually through practice, discourse, political claims, and social relations. The term is also a nod to the focal themes at the heart of my cartographic account of the field, constituted as they are by encounters, experiments, and new frontiers. The greater part of this chapter is dedicated to describing the directions that the anthropological study of Jews and Jewish life has taken over the last three decades or so. Most of the works that shape my take on the current field were written by scholars trained in and identifying with the field of anthropology—but I am also influenced by works at the sometimes blurred boundaries between anthropology, sociology, folklore, cultural, and performance studies.

But before unraveling these threads of research, a brief outline of previous trajectories is in order.[5]

Past Trajectories

The ethnographic exploration of Jews took root in Eastern and Central Europe during the late eighteenth century and developed from the turn of the twentieth century until the interwar period. In opposition to the early scholars of Jewish Studies who were keen on decoding Jewish history, which was usually written from the standpoint of the elite, advocates for the anthropological study of Jews aspired to consider the present realities of the common Jew. This initial interest was folklorist in nature, directed at systematically documenting Yiddishkeit culture and its materialization in artifacts, melodies, proverbs, fables, lullabies, superstitions, and anecdotes. Documentation was seen as a means of salvaging, if not invigorating, a diasporic culture that seemed doomed to collapse. The An-Sky ethnographic expeditions to the Pale of Settlement, aimed at recording oral and musical relics and gathering material culture, were emblematic of this cultural mission. As Andreas Kilcher and Gabriella Safran suggestively demonstrate in their edited volume *Writing Jewish Culture: Paradoxes in Ethnography*, these early ethnographic explorations blended scientific logic and artistic prose, realism and fiction.[6] Altogether, they formed an impressive corpus of academic publications, literature, and museum exhibitions.

Even though some of the founding fathers of academic anthropology in both Europe and the United States hailed from Jewish backgrounds, they did not generally train their anthropological gaze on Jews. For Franz Boas, the German Jewish immigrant who established American anthropology at the turn of the twentieth century, evading Jews in research was a deliberate attempt to minimize Jewish difference. His was part of an ideological agenda to prove the assimilability of the Jews in the promising new world.

But this premise could not be maintained for long. In the wake of the destruction of European Jewry, to disregard Jews ethnographically came to mean an additional act of erasure, which was no longer a morally defensible option. In what could be seen as a post-Holocaust ethnographic tribute of salvage, the widely read retrospective *Life Is with People: The Culture of the Shtetl* by Mark Zborowski and Elizabeth Herzog reconstructed recollection of *shtetl* life, redeeming once again the memory of East European Jewish culture.[7] As Barbara Kirshenblatt-Gimblett shows in her account, "Imagining Europe: The Popular Arts of American Jewish Ethnography," in the succeeding decades various popular artistic and literary ethnographic representations animated this memory, allowing vast publics of post–World War II Americans and American Jews to indulge in nostalgia and to imagine a pre-Holocaust Europe.[8]

In the 1970s Barbara Myerhoff's *Number Our Days*, a compelling monograph that was later adapted into a documentary, provided a nuanced vista of the life of elderly Jews from Europe in the United States, granting American Jews further engagement with tropes of loss and nostalgia.[9] *Number Our Days* carved a niche for the anthropological interrogation of American Jews. Inspired by this groundbreaking work, several other monographs and volumes from the 1970s and 1980s told the stories of specific American Jewish settings (i.e., local communities, neighborhoods, and congregations of various denominations), significantly expanding this niche. These publications include Samuel Heilman's *The People of the Book*,[10] Jack Kugelmass's *The Miracle of Intervale Avenue: The Story of a Jewish Congregation in the South Bronx*,[11] and Riv-Ellen Prell's *Prayer and Community*.[12] In due course, these books themselves became landmarks for the next generation of anthropologists of American Jewry.

As expected, Israel has been another key locus of Jewish ethnography. Jewish ethnography in Israel as an academic endeavor germinated in the twentieth century, first in the 1930s and 1940s under the disciplinary canopy of folklore and then under anthropology during the 1970s. Israel's national revival and its diverse immigrant populations made it an ideal "natural laboratory" for examining Jewish heterogeneity and the making of a collective national culture. As Orit Abuhav shows in her *In the Company of Others: The Development of Anthropology in Israel*, anthropologists—in their capacity as "experts of *others*"—seemed perfect for the task of documenting the manifold and seemingly "exotic" Israeli Jewish realities unfolding in immigrants' villages, kibbutzim, and development towns.[13]

Over the last two or three decades, these loci of Jewish ethnography have changed dramatically. Currently, the anthropological study of Jewish life happens in numerous localities, some more obvious than others. Post-Holocaust East European geographies once mourned as Jewish graveyards and settings in the Global South never imagined as part of the global Jewish landscape are now joining the more obvious settings of New York City and Israel. These new frontiers stretch but also contest the established boundaries of both Jewish life and Jewish ethnography.

Anthropologists follow Jewishly related engagements wherever they take place. Moreover, they increasingly do so while tracing the flow of ideas, initiatives, and objects across Jewish locations. This research orientation has been reinforced by methodological developments within anthropology; in particular, anthropology has distanced itself from its once axiomatic scheme of a bounded field-site endeavor and has equipped itself with the means to study interscaled and multisited dynamics. This tendency within anthropology opened the way for the study of Jewish life in its increasingly globally dispersed iterations.

In what follows, I map the current anthropological study of Jewish life, proposing several thematic clusters.[14] Neither neatly divided nor exhaustive, these clusters nevertheless provide perspectives on where the anthropology of Jewish life is currently at and where it is heading.

Contemporary Contours

Jewish Relatedness

Anthropologists show that the landscape that Jewishly related publics inhabit has undergone substantial diversification over the last several decades, its boundaries becoming increasingly blurred and porous. Seeking to make sense of these shifts, anthropologists bring to this endeavor both the liberal bent of cultural anthropology and the discipline's analytic interest in identity-making, boundary-making, and meaning-making. Ultimately, they chart an evidently inclusive framework, one that encompasses experimental, contested, and hybridized formations of Judaism and Jewishness.

If one takes the perspective of Jewish religious law and tradition, the individuals and groups inhabiting Jewishland are not necessarily Jewish. Jewish relatedness is neither performed nor claimed by people who identify as Jews. Assorted iterations of Jewishness proliferate not only beyond the borders imposed by religious law, but also, more generally, in widening margins of Jewish life. Intent on documenting these iterations, anthropologists demonstrate the inherent instability and flexibility of the Jew/ish signifier. Religion, ethnicity, nationality, race, and kinship can all converge or diverge in different ways to produce diverse Jewishly related attachments.

Anthropologists study the interpretative and practical mechanisms through which groups and individuals stake claims of all sorts to Jewish relatedness. Among many, I refer to Bruce Haynes's *The Soul of Judaism: Jews of African Descent in America*[15]; *Thin Description: Ethnography and the African Hebrew Israelites of Jerusalem* by John L. Jackson Jr.[16]; Janet L. Jacobs's *Hidden Heritage: The Legacy of the Crypto-Jews*[17]; Naomi Leite's *Unorthodox Kin: Portuguese Marranos and the Global Search for Belonging*[18]; Don Seeman's *One People, One Blood: Ethiopian- Israelis and the Return to Judaism*[19]; Rachel Feldman's *Messianic Zionism in the Digital Age: Jews, Noahides, and the Third Temple Imaginary*[20]; and my own book, *When the State Winks: The Performance of Jewish*

Conversion in Israel.[21] Patrilineal Jews; Jewishly involved spouses of recognized Jews; non-Jewish immigrants to Israel from the former Soviet Union; Messianic Jews; Beta Israel and Feres Mura Ethiopian Jews; Karaite Jews; Samaritans; Judaizing groups, including the self-identified descendants of Marrano Jews, the Lemba of South Africa and Zimbabwe, the Abayudaya of Uganda, and a myriad of other Indigenous groups asserting claims to the Jewish origins of the Lost Tribes; and Black Hebrews and Israelites within African and Caribbean American communities—these and other groups constitute a kaleidoscope of Jewishly related identities, whose refractions seem to offer endless answers to the question of "Who is a Jew?" In fact, some of these groups prefer describing themselves as Israelites or Hebrews, rather than as Jewish, rendering the latter signifier irrelevant to their self-understanding.

Anthropologists trace the moral and economic exchanges among all the groups just listed and mainstream Jewish organizations and associations. Those Jewishly related groups on the margins often long to belong but become unavoidably entangled in the hierarchical politics of recognition vis-à-vis established communities. They look up to key rabbinic authorities and depend on resources flowing from the center of Jewish life—the United States, Europe, and Israel—but they also insist on pursuing their idiosyncratic identity work and understandings of Jewish commitments, regardless of the potentially subversive quality these understandings take in mainstream Jewish terms. Jews at the center of Jewish life are just as invested in these encounters, taking them as an opportunity to act on their Jewish agendas. For example, some American Jews arrive at this encounter as tourists or Jewish professionals, with the intention of projecting their inclusive, highly democratized, and multiracial vision of Jewish life on those who experiment with Jewish relatedness; some pious Religious Zionist Israelis arrive at this encounter holding a missionary and messianic script about the ingathering of the exiles. Driven by a sense of politico-religious calling and by an enchantment with the histories and myths of the Jewish people, they seek to bring the various publics into dialogue and alliance with mainstream Jewry.

Ultimately, these encounters between the center and the margins of Jewishland establish reciprocal—if uneven—moral, spiritual, and economic exchanges. These encounters have much to say about the centrifugal and centripetal forces shaping contemporary Jewish life. Anthropological works provide us with crisp, minute details of these encounters as experienced by differently positioned actors. Just as importantly, they point at the macro-level configurations of power and ideology—Zionism, postcolonialism, globalization, and capitalism—that enabled or even catalyzed these encounters in the first place.

Vernacularized Engagements with Jewishness

Anthropologists pay attention to the fact that scientific data travel far and wide in Jewishland, mediating various contemporary engagements with Jewish identity, origin, and conduct. Specifically, studies show that in numerous spheres, genetics, biomedical knowledge, and sociodemographic statistics help determine the ways in which the essence and boundaries of Jewish life are negotiated. Influenced by developments in science and technology studies, anthropologists of Jewish life demonstrate how scientific discourses about Jews are propagated and naturalized, as well as how the cultural authority of science lends credibility to various identity endeavors that, in turn, draw on significant interpretive leverage vis-à-vis the original discourses. By following the circulation of scientific truths among and across Jewishly related publics, anthropologists illuminate the decisive role played by social-scientific knowledge in the constant production and reproduction of the Jewish collective and selves. In other words, by following the mundane uses and understandings of scientific concepts, anthropologists can reveal how the vernacularization of scientific knowledge helps make Jewish claims and subjectivities.

The manifestations of such a vernacularization abound. Social scientists and geneticists receive public platforms to present their findings; Jewish media outlets cover the publication of new sociodemographic surveys; Jewish institutions draw on these surveys to frame and promote their communal services; rabbis come to master or at least speak the language of particular fields of expertise when catering to their audiences; and individuals adopt and then adapt scientific discourses in their own search for identity, belonging, and meaning. A wide range of mainstream Jews, self-claimed Jewishly related individuals, Jewish professionals, Judaizing groups, and communal organizations mobilize scientific reasoning in their Jewish activities. Altogether, these actors help popularize scientific discourses pertaining to Jewish life.

Medical information and Jewish genetics are today probably the most salient domains of these vernacularized engagements with Jewishness. Here, they serve as an illuminating instance of these broader processes. The field of Jewish genetics has gained currency in the last several decades. This flourishing is rooted, first, in accelerated developments within genetics itself and the especial appeal of Jewish populations as epistemic objects. But it is also connected to the varied publics eager to ingest this sort of knowledge for their various needs—from making more informed medical decisions to basing identity narratives in essentialist, biologist-driven "evidence." Susan Kahn shows, in her *Reproducing*

Jews: A Cultural Account of Assisted Conception in Israel, that genetic data are used to inform individuals' choices and communal arrangements concerning marriage and family planning among Orthodox Jews[22]; Ben Kasstan's *Making Bodies Kosher: The Politics of Reproduction among Haredi Jews of England* shows how Haredi Jews respond to biomedical interventions, given their own local theorization of the Jewish body.[23] Sarah Imhoff and Hillary Kaell's article, "Lineage Matters: DNA, Race and Gene Talk in Judaism and Messianic Judaism," shows how genetic lingo (i.e., DNA, genes) is conducive to constructing flexible but significant notions of Jewish lineage among Messianic Jews.[24] Noah Tamarkin's *Genetic Afterlives: Black Jewish Indigeneity in South Africa* finds that the research subjects of genetic studies—specifically his interlocutors, the Lemba of southern Africa—further the production of genetic knowledge by theorizing from their own standpoint the data created by their bodies.[25] In *The Genealogical Science: The Search for Jewish Origins and the Politics of Epistemology,* Nadia Abu El-Haj demonstrates how Jewish genetics have spread across the unfettered, democratized, and interactive venues of the digital world, where ancestry-testing companies offer Americans the seductive promise of discovering one's roots.[26] In this highly commercialized setting, consumers of DNA testing in the United States and elsewhere have become conversant in simplified genetic discourses, indulging in turning genetic probabilities into new genealogical possibilities of connectedness.

The Production of "Jewish Culture"

The concept of culture is the hallmark of anthropology. As such, it presents anthropologists with the most powerful (if abstract and debated) analytic focus as a distinct discipline. For anthropologists of Jewish life, the concept of culture provided the mandate to enter Jewish Studies in the first place and to contribute to nuanced understandings of practices, social structures, and meanings. Theoretical debates about its conceptual histories aside, "culture" afforded anthropologists a voice in a conversation dominated by the study of Jewish text and the opportunity to show (rather than tell) the benefits of exploring cultural productions—Jewish rituals, artifacts, happenings, exhibitions, and popular culture. Alongside ethnographic explorations of reading and living with Jewish texts, anthropologists draw on expansive notions of culture to point at the material, embodied, and ritualized (both formalized and improvised) dimensions within Jewish life.

The first thing we gain by looking at "Jewish culture" is the understanding that the making of Jewish culture entails the making of Jewish subjects. To engage with "Jewish culture" is to be invested in a world in which the content and know-how of Judaism matter. To produce, display, absorb, and shape Jewish stuff is to produce and reproduce the bearers of Jewish habitus and sensibilities. It also means the production and reproduction of individuals as Jews in places where they interact with others and understand themselves as Jews: where they let Jewish themes, doctrines, practices, jokes, fictions, songs, and objects animate their life and provide structure and meaning, enjoyment and comfort.

Several anthropological studies have called attention to the role of Jewish culture in pursuing the biological and demographic goals of Jewish continuity. Relatedly, others have unpacked the extended role of Jewish communal institutions in cultivating—through cultural engagements—Jewish subjects. When Jewish families may be lacking cultural intimacy with Jewish stuff, institutions compensate for it by extending their responsibility. Joshua Friedman and Moshe Kornfeld's article "Identity Projects: Philanthropy, Neoliberalism and Jewish Cultural Production" is an important contribution in this direction.[27] To the extent that the reproduction of "Jewish culture" is entangled with the biological reproduction of Jews, studying the first provides a vista into one of the most anxiety-filled collective Jewish endeavors in a post-Holocaust world.

The second thing we gain is an important perspective on the inventive dynamism of Jewish life. As Vanessa Ochs teaches us in her *Inventing Jewish Ritual*, we need to break the false dichotomy between tradition and innovation, between perpetuation and alteration.[28] The study of a "Jewish culture" in the making leads us thus to study both the top-down and bottom-up forces that imagine and create anew the substance, form, and order entailed in "doing Jewish." It helps us perceive how individuals and institutions draw on existing cultural repertoires, without necessarily taking them as an objectified, finalized, ready-made given. They knead, stretch, and plasticize "Jewish culture." The artistic, performative, consumerist realities unfolding around "Jewish culture" run the gamut from tentative to acclimatized. Unpacking the work invested in materializing them pushes us to unnaturalize, demysticize, and historicize the materials that Jewish life is made of.

Finally, the third benefit is the appreciation of another element in the flow of the "Jewish" signifier and the blurring of the Jewish/non-Jewish fault line. Constantly on the move, this signifier travels not only among those who claim Jewish identity and recognition but also among those who identify as non-Jews but who for various reasons are drawn into zones of Jewish cultural production. Jewish books, music festivals, Jewishly associated souvenirs for tourists, T-shirts with slogans in Yiddish, "Israeli" sandals—all these items and others pass through the hands of manifold social actors. Erica Lehrer's discussion in *Jewish Poland Revisited: Heritage Tourism in Unquiet Places* of the non-Jewish Poles who play a part in maintaining Poland's Jewish heritage industry[29] and Magdalena Waligorska's description in *Klezmer's Afterlife: An Ethnography of the Jewish Music Revival in Poland and Germany* of German residents enjoying themselves in a local klezmer festival show that non-Jews are more than bystanders in these scenes.[30] In her *Jewish on their Own Terms: How Intermarried Couples Are Changing American Judaism,* Jennifer Thompson shows how non-Jewish women married to Jewish men in the United States raise their children as Jewish through cultural engagements.[31] Playful or deadly serious, institutionalized or grassroots in nature, rooted in nationalized or transnational settings, the worlds of cultural production that these non-Jewish actors help imagine and fashion are "Jewish," yet they make room for or are even dependent on the presence of non-Jews.

Jewish Travels in Time and Space

Over the last few decades, anthropology has increasingly engaged with questions of temporality; that is, how people organize, perceive, and feel about time. This attention to temporality is driven, in part, by the centrality of time as an organizing principle in human cultural life; it is also a backlash against earlier moments in the history of the discipline when anthropology focused on the ethnographic present in ways that flattened studies to a synchronic exploration of realities ostensibly frozen in time.

The anthropological study of Jews follows this broader interest in temporality, seeking to illuminate the temporal coordinates orienting Jewish life. Anthropologists ask how Jews locate themselves in time, working on time through popular perceptions and historiographies of the past, memory work, schemes of decline and continuity, as well as through predictions and forecasts of the future. In sum, anthropologists show that Jews travel in time.

Just as interestingly, studies show that Jews take temporal journeys by taking spatial voyages. Their movement across time and space is inseparable. To give some ethnographic substance to this claim, as I show in my work, Lubavitcher Hasidic Jews work on their seemingly failing messianic present by re-presenting the past and the (deceased/disappeared) Rebbe and by cultivating urgent expectations toward the imminent onset of a messianic future. They do so by traveling to the Hasidic court in Crown Heights, Brooklyn, where they encounter the Rebbe in the here and now.[32] As Jackie Feldman shows in his work, Israeli Jewish high schoolers learn how to relive and witness the horrors of the Holocaust by traveling en masse to Poland to walk the cursed land of Auschwitz-Birkenau.[33] Jack Kugelmass shows that American Jews engage with cardinal moments in American Jewish (hi)story by consuming, nostalgically, the Lower East Side as a once-Jewish space filled with the Eastern European Jewish authenticity of new immigrants.[34] And, to give a final example, Naomi Leite demonstrates that British Jews go further back in time, revisiting the historical drama of the expulsion of Jews from the Iberian Peninsula via tourism in Jewish Portugal, providing an opportunity to reconnect with the "lost and found" offspring of the Marranos.[35] In all these examples, space compresses a sense of time, activating temporal codes that, in turn, enable certain social relations, cultural meanings, and collective identities.

Sometimes, the Jewish voyages in time and space analyzed by anthropologists are their own. Drawing on autoethnography—a method of self-reflection used to illuminate wider social and cultural formations—they grapple with their biographical ruptures to analyze broader questions about journeys, displacement, and the return of Jews. Examples of this include Ruth Behar's *An Island Called Home: Returning to Jewish Cuba*[36] and André Levy's *Return to Casablanca: Jews, Muslims and an Israeli Anthropologist.*[37]

Jewish Pieties and Religiosities

Religious piety, as with religion more generally, is construed in anthropological studies as an expanded concept, shaped by its intersection with politics, nationality, morality, ethnicity, urbanity, class, race, and gender, among other concepts. Sharing this understanding, anthropologists working in Jewish contexts show how Jewish spiritual modes of prayer, devotional religious literacy, asceticism, and meticulous orthopraxis are strictly political, politicized, and gendered. Jewish piety and religiosity are inseparable from nationalistic politics, spatialized sacred geographies, and gendered moral scripts. How settlers in Hebron are devoted to inhabiting Greater Israel and interact in specific ways with their Palestinian neighbors; how religious Zionist publics in Israel take on themselves the sacred "national mission" of adapting Jewish conversion to newcomers from the Former Soviet Union; and how ultra-Orthodox women justify the moral grounding of their family planning strategies are but three of the many examples of the multifaceted forms in which Jewish piety is studied anthropologically.

The greater share of anthropological works on Jewish piety and religiosity focuses on Orthodox and ultra-Orthodox (Haredi) Jews. This focus bears witness to the perceived "otherness" of secluded pious Jews and the fascination that this otherness poses for the (mostly secular, liberal, and feminist-oriented) Jewish anthropologists who study them. Studying Orthodox piety constitutes, thus, an exercise in tolerance and cultural relativism—and a critical engagement with the limits of liberalism. Anthropological interest in Orthodox lives is nothing new, particularly in Israel. Pioneering works by Tamar El-Or on the literacy of Hasidic women, Nissim Leon on soft-ultra Orthodoxy among Sephardi Jews, and Nurit Stadler's work on yeshiva life all attest to this long-time attention. In this specific political moment, given the demographic rise of Orthodox Jews primarily in Israel and the United States, the communal reactions to COVID, and the alignments of Orthodox Jews with non-Jewish and right-wing conservative forces, this scrutiny is on the rise.

Within the enhanced interest in Orthodox and often politicized forms of piety, greater attention is being given to marginalized Orthodox subjects, such as women, returnees to the religious fold (*baalei tshuvah*), those leaving the Jewish fold (*hozrim bitshuvah* or "off the *derech*"), and the LGBTQ+ community, each with their own positioned version of Jewish piety. The works of Ayala Fader, Orit Avishai, and Michal Raucher lead this thread of scholarship.

In addition, there is a rich body of literature engaging with highly heterogeneous revivalist forms of non-Orthodox Jewish religiosity and spirituality; for example among Reform Jews and New Agers. Rachel Werczberger and Daniel Monsterscu's *Jewish Revival(s): Inside Out* unpacks New Age agendas, the thirst for a sense of authenticity, and religious creativity, pointing at the ceaseless resourcefulness of religiosity in a postsecular age.[38]

Piety and religiosity are not understood as an isolated dyadic experience between an individual and his or her God but rather as a collective disposition highly mediated by semiotic, material, and social forces. From this perspective, piety and religiosity are studied as a work in progress, a product of relentless labor to do better and become a better Jew by sustaining distinctions vis-a-vis other Jews and non-Jews and refining both self and community. Piety is thus construed as an achievement of sorts, sometimes a fragile one. Unsurprisingly, those who fail in the attempt to become pious Jews capture more and more of the anthropological imagination. This is evidenced, for example, in studies of ex-Orthodox Jews who left the fold (OTD, "off the *derech*") and in Ayala Fader's ground-breaking study of the *Hidden Heretics: Jewish Doubt in the Digital Age* who live both in and outside the Orthodox community.[39]

The Jewish Question

Anthropology has historically oscillated between studying "The human culture" in its entirety and studying diverse human cultures across local contexts, and between studying "humankind" with its broad common denominator and studying the human experience in its endless cultural instantiations. Building on this foundational fluctuation within anthropology, we can point at a resonating—albeit highly specific—tension between universalism and particularism in the anthropological study of Jews. The subfield is likewise moving back and forth between two poles: studying "The Jew" and studying Jews.

The figure of "The Jew" emerges, perhaps unintendedly, as a somewhat essentialized construct with persistent features: most notably, difference, otherness, displacement, cosmopolitanism and, often, embeddedness in a minority situation. Ethnographic representations seem to reify these images simply by recurrently paying attention to these shared dimensions in the contemporary Jewish experience, across contexts and locations. At the same time, anthropologists go to great lengths to introduce historical and political nuance to their portrayals of these features and to situate the anxious engagements of Jews and Jewish communities with their difference within distinct national settings and shifting political moments.

The Jewish Question—the highly burdened construct denoting the unique position of Jews as marginal and unfitting others in nineteenth-century Europe—has made inroads into anthropological discussions. It can be read as an overarching metaphor for inquiry into the figure of "The Jew" and his or her recurring, as if endless, otherness. At the same time, it serves as a point of departure for discussions about the diverse and locally situated circumstances of awkward belonging for Jews—of particular "Jewish questions," as it were.

The current political moment, pregnant with heightened xenophobic, racialized, and antisemitic sentiments and incidents, including toward Jews, begs for empirical probe. Anthropologists contribute greatly to this accumulating endeavor. The current moment proves that the Jewish Question is not a thing of the past, confined to the original European context in which this trope originated: Instead, it is an open-ended question. New and unfolding realities in the United States and Europe compel Jews to clarify to themselves and to their compatriots their loyalties, given their diasporic, minority situation. Even in (or partially because of) the unprecedentedly secure post-Holocaust realities of Jews wielding considerable economic and political power, anthropologists show that the difference is still a source of deliberation and sometimes agony for Jews across contexts.

A few examples will suffice. In *Sweet Burdens: Welfare and Communality among Russian Jews in Germany*, Sveta Roberman interrogates the resurrection of Jewish life in contemporary Germany, where the long-established politics of remorse and restitution for Holocaust victims led, in the 1990s, to the institution of a generous immigration policy for Russian Jews fleeing the collapsing Soviet Union.[40] The convoluted relations that these newcomers have fostered with the German state, with the organized Jewish community, and with their own Jewishness are all tainted by notorious historical imageries of "the Jew" and his place in society. In his *Symptoms of Modernity: Jews and Queers in Late Twentieth-Century Vienna*, Matti Bunzl pursues a comparative historical ethnography of Jews and queers, taking these two groups as the principal twin markers of outsiderness within the homogenizing identity project of the modern nation-state.[41] Bringing antisemitism and homophobia into a shared conversation, Bunzl tackles how these groups contested their imposed exclusion from Austria's public sphere and how they rose to prominence within its urban life. The increasing integration of Austrian Jews and queers, argues Bunzl, signifies the transition from Europe's modernity toward postmodernity, in which Muslims and Islamophobia embody the current iteration of the Jewish problem. Relatedly, Kimberly Arkin pleads for the analytic recuperation of the Jewish Question in contemporary France, where Jews are struggling with how exactly to belong to France; see her *Rhinestones, Religion, and the Republic: Fashioning Jewishness in France*.[42] Although political observers and scholars alike are focusing on the predicaments of Muslim Frenchness, Jewish communal organizations, as depicted by Arkin, are engrossed in fighting antisemitism and producing Jewish Frenchness. To give one last example, Marcy Brink-Danan demonstrates in her *Jewish Life in 21st-Century Turkey: The Other Side of Tolerance* that, despite being regarded as Turkey's model minority and an icon of Turkish tolerance, Jews live with ongoing security anxieties fed by antisemitic occurrences.[43] Playing simultaneously the role of patriotic citizens and cosmopolitan subjects, Jews occupy a tense space in which their sameness and difference are constantly negotiated. Altogether, these and other anthropological accounts help us understand the mundane socialities that the Jewish Question adopts as an open-ended question.

By Way of Conclusion

A recurring trope in the anthropological study of Jews asserts that "Jews are good to think with." A paraphrase of French anthropologist Claude Lévi-Strauss's popular maxim, "good to think with," the idea is that Jews provide useful, even paradigmatic, case studies through which to ponder broader prob-lematizations, including issues of race, lived religion, modernity, postsecularity, identity, and memory. To some degree, this rhetorical formula is used to justify and centralize the anthropological study of Jews, crediting it with potential theo-retical weight and value.

Without either reinforcing or questioning the assumption that Jews are indeed "good to think with," I want to pay attention to an implicit method-ological bias embedded in the anthropological literature on Jews—and, hence, in what can be learned from it. Anthropologists study Jews and others who are Jewishly affiliated in domains and moments when Jewishness or Judaism matters to them: when they do Jewish things, think through Jewish lenses, speak Jewish languages, agonize over Jewishly related predicaments, and form Jewishly associated collectives of all sorts. But Jews, people with a Jewish back-ground, and people identified as Jews are obviously located in countless set-tings unmarked by an engagement with Jewishness. They work on Wall Street, or at the Haifa port, or in Cape Town tourist industries; they volunteer with humanitarian movements, shop online, throw out or recycle their garbage, and live their life in manners unspecified or unrelated to Judaism, Jewishness, or a Jewish communal life. The bias toward Jewishly related cultural dynamics produces rich accounts of ritual, religious, literary, institutional, and political dimensions of Jewish life, but it also leaves us with too thin a knowledge of the unmarked, undetectable textures of Jewishness. A dispersionist approach, to borrow the vision of historian David Hollinger—who offered to take "fuller account of the lives in any and all domains of persons with an ancestry in the Jewish diaspora, regardless of their degree of involvement with communal Jewry and no matter what their extent of declared or ascribed Jewishness"[44]— can potentially illuminate the mechanisms and domains where Jewishness matters in imbedded ways.

In *Jew*,[45] her contribution to the series Key Words in Jewish Studies, religious studies scholar Cynthia Baker writes that, for Jewish Studies scholars, "studying Jews often informs and expresses who and what they understand themselves to be; Jewish studies frequently serves as a locus of self-exploration" (66). Anthro-pologists are no different. Most of the anthropologists working in Jewishly re-lated fields identify in one way or another as Jews. Thus, the Jewish qualifier in *Jewish ethnography* refers not only to the subject matters but also to the identity of researchers. Their ethnographic investigations become a venue for reflexivity on the Jewish components in their life and self. This was the case, for example, with Barbara Myerhoff, the American Jewish anthropologist mentioned earlier in this chapter. At a time when ethnic revivals invited Americans to explore their other-than American identities, fieldwork among Jews allowed her to reconnect with her suppressed Jewish identification and to become the Jew she never thought she would ever want to be. This was also the case with anthropologist Ruth Behar, whose return to her homeland was not simply a return to Cuba but also to Jewish Cuba.

Because ethnographers constitute the research tool of their study, their encounter with themselves as Jews is always a telling ethnographic encounter among Jews. The set of exchanges, relative positionings, and mutual gazes during fieldwork are all taken as potentially revealing materials deserving scrutiny and attention. The kinds of Jews they discover they are or being seen as and the internal boundaries—but also affinities—between them and their research subjects point insightfully to fundamental aspects of the research field itself. More than just bringing Jewish competence and familiarity to their research, Jewish ethnographers bring themselves as mirrors, conduits, and interlocutors into a Jewish intersubjective space.

Beneficial as these dynamics often turn out to be, I hope that more anthropologists, unrelated personally to the Jewish world or hailing from its margins, will find their place within the collective endeavor of Jewish ethnography. Such a move can further push and complicate the anthropological study of Jewish encounters, experiments, and frontiers, bringing new perspectives to the inventive Judaisms whose unfolding we are currently witnessing.

Recommended Readings

Arkin, Kimberly. *Rhinestones, Religion, and the Republic: Fashioning Jewishness in France* (Stanford University Press, 2013).

Fader, Ayala. *Mitzvah Girls: Bringing Up the Next Generation of Hasidic Jews in Brooklyn* (Princeton University Press, 2009).

Goldschmidt, Henry. *Race and Religion among the Chosen People of Crown Heights* (Rutgers University Press, 2006).

Kasstan, Ben. *Making Bodies Kosher: The Politics of Reproduction among Haredi Jews in England* (Berghahn, 2019).

Kelner, Shaul. *Tours That Bind: Diaspora, Pilgrimage and Israeli Birthright* (New York University Press, 2010).

Lehrer, Erica. *Jewish Poland Revisited: Heritage Tourism in Unquiet Places* (Indiana University Press, 2013).

Ochs, Vanessa. *Inventing Jewish Ritual* (Jewish Publication Society, 2007).

Prell Riv, Ellen. *Fighting to Become Americans: Assimilation and the Trouble between Jewish Women and Jewish Men* (Beacon, 2000).

Seeman, Don. *One People, One Blood: Ethiopian Israelis and the Return to Judaism* (Rutgers University Press, 2010).

Tamarkin, Noah. *Genetic Afterlives: Black Jewish Indigeneity in South Africa* (Duke University Press, 2020).

Notes

1. *Anthropological Quarterly* 64 (1991): 14–29.

2. *American Ethnologist* 20 (1993): 618–24.

3. *Journal of Jewish Studies* 43 (1992): 246–67.

4. University of Minnesota Press, 1996.

5. My focus is on the social and cultural anthropology of Jewish life. To read more about the work of physical anthropologists in Jewish studies, see, for example, M. Hart, "Measuring and Picturing Jews: Racial Anthropology and Iconography," in his *Social Science and the Politics of Modern Jewish Identity* (Stanford University Press, 2000) and F. Gelya, "Jews, Multiculturalism and Boasian Anthropology," *American Anthropologist* 99 (1997): 731–45.

6. Indiana University Press, 2016.

7. Schocken, 1952.

8. In *Divergent Jewish Cultures: Israel and America*, ed. D. Dash Moore and S. Ilan Troen (Yale University Press, 2001).

9. Simon & Schuster, 1978.

10. University of Chicago Press, 1983

11. Columbia University Press, 1986.

12. Wayne State University Press, 1989.

13. Wayne State University Press, 2015.

14. For earlier reviews—and alternative thematic mapping—of an anthropology of Jews and Jewish life, see Marcy Brink-Danan, "Anthropological Perspectives on Judaism: A Comparative Review," *Religion Compass* 2/4 (2008): 674–88, and "Anthropology of the Jews" (2012) at oxfordbibliographies.com.

15. New York University Press, 2018.

16. Harvard University Press, 2013.

17. University of California Press, 2002.

18. University of California Press, 2017.

19. Rutgers University Press, 2010.

20. Rutgers University Press, 2024.

21. Columbia University Press, 2017.

22. Duke University Press, 2000.

23. Berghahn, 2019.

24. *Religion and American Culture* 27 (2018): 95–127.

25. Duke University Press, 2020.

26. University of Chicago Press, 2012.

27. *American Jewish History* 102 (2018): 537–61.

28. Jewish Publication Society, 2007.

29. Indiana University Press, 2013.

30. Oxford University press, 2013.

31. Rutgers University Press, 2013.

32. Michal Kravel-Tovi and Yoram Bilu, "The Work of the Present: Constructing Messianic Temporality in the Wake of Failed Prophecy among Chabad Hasidim," *American Ethnologist* 35.1 (2008): 64–80.

33. *Above the Death Pits, Beneath the Flag: Youth Voyages to Poland and the Performance of Israeli National Identity* (Berghahn Books, 2022).

34. "Green Bagels: An Essay on Food, Nostalgia, and the Carnivalesque," *YiVO Annual of Jewish Social Science* 19 (1990): 57–80.

35. Leite, *Unorthodox Kin.*

36. Rutgers University Press, 2007.

37. University of Chicago Press, 2015.

38. Wayne State University Press, 2022.

39. Princeton University Press, 2020.

40. SUNY Press, 2015.

41. University of California Press, 2004.

42. Stanford University Press, 2013.

43. Indiana University Press, 2012.

44. Hollinger, *After Cloven Tongues of Fire: Protestant Liberalism in Modern American History* (Princeton University Press, 2013), 141.

45. Rutgers University Press, 2017.

22

Law

Suzanne Last Stone, Cardozo School of Law, Yeshiva University

WHAT HAVE we learned and what are we learning about Jewish law and legal thought? Against all odds, the academic study of Jewish law and legal thought is burgeoning, and more significantly, theories of law have become important resources for scholars working across a variety of disciplines, including history, philosophy, literature, and anthropology, within the Jewish Studies academy in the United States and in Israel. For example, the study of early Jewish narrative, both in the Bible and the later aggadah, now often focuses on how this literature functions as law, transmitting norms through the telling of stories of social interaction. Jurisprudential theories play an increasing role in unpacking rabbinic writings from the Talmud through the responsa literature and a vital role in charting the transformations inaugurated by the rise of the modern state in the internal understanding of what precisely is the rabbinic tradition. Perhaps the greatest surprise is that jurisprudential theories are foundational in Jewish Studies scholarship that focuses on gender and feminist critique.

This new interest in law is not confined to scholars dealing with the rabbinic tradition and conversant with halakhah. Newly available archival material has allowed Jewish historians to chart the startling degree of jurisdictional and normative pluralism in the medieval and early modern periods. Jewish and non-Jewish litigants used one another's courts, and Jewish legal codes were cited and applied by imperial courts just as Jewish courts cited and made use of non-Jewish laws. Thus, Jewish historians are now taking part in a wider conversation about global legal pluralism in which the Jewish historical experience is but one example. In short, since the 1980s, we can speak of a genuine "legal turn" in the Jewish Studies academy.

The recent flourishing of academic writing about Jews and their legal tradition is "against all odds" because, unlike the established disciplines of Jewish literature, Jewish history, and Jewish religious studies, Jewish law and legal thought is not a developed discipline in the Jewish Studies academy. The centuries-long enterprise, the Talmud, the primary Jewish text that comes down to us from the ancient world, was long studied in the academy, of course, but primarily through literary, philological, historical, and cultural lenses: It took the place of law in academic writings to describe rules on topics as diverse as what constitutes theft and how to offer sacrifices in the Temple, found in the Hebrew Bible and the Mishnah and then interpreted and analytically elaborated in the Talmud: wisdom, instruction, ethics, ritual, custom, and practice. To a large extent, the academy participated in the Jewish Enlightenment response to the long-standing Christian critique of Judaism as rigidly law-centered, obsessed with external rules rather than inwardness, ethics, and spirituality. The negative view of law as a central feature of Judaism played a large role in the redefinition of Judaism as a religion, with religion defined largely in Christian terms.

What then prompted a new, positive evaluation of law and of its place in the study of Judaism? The legal turn in Jewish studies scholarship began as a very American story. New theories of law that were articulated in the American legal academy for a largely non-Jewish American legal audience played a pivotal part. These new philosophies of Anglo-American law spread to the Jewish Studies academy across the globe, in Israel and Europe no less than in the United States; it became institutionalized in several programs dedicated to fostering an interdisciplinary conversation between Jewish Studies and legal theory. The next two sections tell the story of how these new legal ideas penetrated the Jewish Studies academy, and the final section provides an overview of the new scholarship produced to date as a result of the legal turn. This chapter concludes with some comments about the implications of adopting a conceptual category termed "law."

The Challenge of Positivism

To understand how Anglo-American theories and philosophies of law became an important resource in Jewish Studies, why the turn to law and legal thought was so late in arriving, and why it still has its methodological resisters, we first need to engage a persistent jurisprudential puzzle: What is law? And is the term "law" (or, for that matter, the term "religion") a category unto itself—a conceptual absolute that is universally applicable to any culture, against which we can measure, for example, rabbinic writings—or is law itself a cultural construct? In the context of today's modern state, the positivist paradigm dominates our understanding of the legal system. Law is recognized in terms of its sources, and these sources are human and political (the state and its officials). Although John Austin and Jeremy Bentham in the nineteenth century understood this primarily in terms of power (commands of the sovereign and the imposition of sanctions), H. L. A. Hart introduced the necessity of legitimacy, understood as sources of law tacitly agreed on as a matter of social fact by the officials of the legal system.[1] Hart is offering a conceptual absolute: He sets forth criteria that must be met for a cultural undertaking to qualify as law. As such, he is concerned with marking off a domain of law that is distinct and autonomous from moral obligations or values, on the one hand, and from politics, on the other. Another important part of the positivist picture of law is that it also divorces rules from the reasons for—and arguments over—the rules. The law consists only of the rules of the system and not the arguments for or against those norms.

Given this positivist picture, the discipline of law seemed of marginal utility in the Jewish Studies academy. First, nonstate norms of behavior, no matter how internally obligating they might seem, are rarely law from the vantage point of positivism. Indeed, the close association of law with the state is a large part of the story of how other normative orders within the state's borders, including Judaism, reinvented themselves as a "religion" and used the vocabulary of rites and rituals or ethics to describe their practices and precepts, a pattern continued in the academic study of Judaism. The rabbinic tradition, moreover, did not seem to fit positivist definitions of law that emphasized sovereignty and enforcement powers. The halakhah discusses sanctions, and in the premodern period, Jews lived in semi-autonomous communities and held considerable enforcement powers. But both in theory and in practice, enforcement was not a central feature of rabbinic writing and culture long before the rise of the modern state. Finally, the most characteristic feature of the talmudic tradition—the preference for extended and multigenerational arguments over the articulation of any single rule of practice—seemed to fit the idea of philosophy far more than the idea of law.

Internal developments within Jewish legal history also contributed to marginalizing the halakhic enterprise as a central topic for understanding Judaism. Paradoxically, the increasing internal adoption of a positivist model of law by Jewish legal practitioners themselves led to marking off halakhah as a specialist, professional activity of interest only to Orthodox adherents and comparative lawyers. In both the Hebrew Bible and the Babylonian Talmud, norms and narratives are freely intertwined, and both are products and reflections of an entire culture. In the post-talmudic period, however, a division was introduced between halakhah and aggadah, splitting law from culture. Halakhah referred to the legal sections of the Hebrew Bible and the professional legal discourse of the talmudic rabbis; the rest fell under the category of aggadah. In separating law from not-law, the post-talmudic geonim deployed criteria markedly similar to positivist understandings of law: Halakhah consists of clear-cut rules, said the geonim, and the aggadah is too fluid and subjective to form a basis for legal ruling. The geonic intervention culminated in the movement to codify rules of Jewish law in the medieval period.

As a result, halakhah also became increasingly separated from other cultural activities such as philosophy and kabbalah. Philosophy and kabbalah were seen initially as inseparable accompaniments to the law. They offered rationales for the law or described the theosophic meaning of the rules. Increasingly, these explanatory systems eclipsed the law as sources of the meaning of Judaism. This splitting apart was enabled by the rise of new religious attitudes that went hand in hand with halakhah as technique. New religious attitudes ascribed mystery to the rules or emphasized limited human understanding of their cosmic significance. Thus, just as modern positivism divorces rules from their reasons, so halakhah increasingly was seen as a body of rules divorced from reasons. Finally, with the establishment of the State of Israel, the study of Jewish law in the legal academy took wing. Yet, the Mishpat Ivri (Hebrew law) movement, as this new discipline was dubbed, had more than academic study as its purpose. It also had the pragmatic purpose of advancing the adoption of Jewish law in the State of Israel, and it took the positivist picture of Jewish law along with it because that picture was congenial to the program.

In short, both internal and external pressures combined to create a positivist picture of halakhah that emphasized sources and rules and its technical, professional, formal, and analytic study. As a result, the academic study of halakhah occurred primarily in the silo of law schools or among a small set of historians of halakhah who largely adopted the positivist picture of law as a conceptual absolute that was true for secular law and for halakhah. For example, the two preeminent historians of halakhah, Jacob Katz and his student Haym Soloveitchik, developed a methodology for charting change in halakhah (the angle of deflection) that was dependent on a positivist picture of law in which the sources of law yield logical, deductive conclusions. Departures from those conclusions

The Return of the Common Law Mind

We can trace the beginning of the legal turn in the American and Israeli Jewish Studies academies to the scholarship of two American law professors, Ronald Dworkin and Robert Cover, who were writing for an American—and not specifically Jewish—legal audience and who, in different ways, sought to disrupt the positivist picture that had gained such ascendancy since the rise of the modern state.

In a classic essay titled "The Model of Rules I" in his *Taking Rights Seriously,*[2] American legal philosopher Dworkin took on the emphasis on sources of law and rules so fundamental to positivism, in general, and to Hart's *Concept of Law,*[3] in particular. Dworkin sought to show that principles and not only rules are embedded in the legal system. In American law, these principles are generally drawn from the centuries-old tradition of equity of the Anglo-American common law or are principles of political morality embedded, per Dworkin, in the foundational text of American law, the United States Constitution. Although rules have an all-or-nothing quality and may be approached through logical, deductive methods, principles are vaguer and do not yield determinate answers. Yet, principles have a gravitational force; they have great weight. The model of rules disrupted the positivist picture on many levels. First, it unsettled the positivist idea that law, morality, and politics are separate and distinct domains, Second, it refocused attention on the judge, who interprets principles together with rules, rather than on a legislature or code. In an important later work, *Law's Empire*, Dworkin reframed law as fundamentally an interpretive activity.[4] Although this is a vast oversimplification, the basic idea is that each judge inherits the work of his or her predecessors and extends the storyline, reinterpreting and revising it in ways consonant with the past so that it retains coherence and integrity. In parsing law as an interpretive concept, Dworkin moves the focus of law from a text to a social practice, from settled fact or a matter of past official decisions (positivism) to ongoing revision. This exercise in interpretation is impossible unless law is a social practice that involves its participants in arguing over the purpose or point of the practice. These purposes are not outside the legal tradition: They are embedded in the accumulated past of the tradition and retrieved from within.

Dworkin's theory of law departed from positivism in one more important respect. It had its roots in a particular jurisprudence: the Anglo-American common law tradition. Rather than present law as a conceptual absolute, Dworkin set forth to describe the concept of law in the culturally contingent Anglo-American legal system. Indeed, Dworkin remains the best modern articulator of the theory of law and style of legal reasoning that characterize the classical common law tradition.

It is worth briefly highlighting the common law style of legal thought because so many aspects of law that modern positivism emphasized and that made the conceptual category of law seem irrelevant for academic studies of the formative sources of rabbinic Judaism (the Hebrew Bible and the Talmud) are not features of the common law tradition. Instead, classical common law could be described as an ongoing, institutionalized argument about norms.

Classical common law consists entirely of cases, which are extended narratives of social interaction. Unwritten rules are extracted from a story of social interaction and even applied to the very case from which it has been extracted. Often, a rule extracted from one narrative is reformulated in light of comparison to other stories, whether real—actually decided cases—or imagined; that is, hypotheticals. Contrary to popular imagination, which treats prior decided cases as binding precedents on the order of a codified rule or statute, classical common law viewed prior cases (and even parliamentary legislation) as no more nor less authoritative than hypotheticals: All these narratives are a means to explore the ambit of a rule. Rules are "taken up" and not laid down. Rules are constantly in the process of formulation, acceptance, rejection, or revision in light of the particulars and concreteness that the narratives provide, as well as the principles discerned from the narratives, as they accrue over time.

The common law tradition flourished before the rise of the modern state, and although it persisted long after the state came into being, it does not lend itself well to a single hierarchical structure. Common law power structures are diffuse and decentralized, and the common law was highly sensitive to local practices and customs. Unity was achieved through collaborative discourse. Various institutions of the common law supported that process, most especially the system of discipleship and the various Inns to which jurists belonged and to which they retreated for long periods of time, engaging in scholastic legal discussion. Although many of these institutions no longer exist, the common law tradition has continued to persist, especially in the United States. Common law thinking continues to dominate private law and finds expression in the current split within the U.S. Supreme Court over how to read the Constitution: as a code or statute or as a body of principles.

From the vantage point of the positivists, the common law tradition was a problem to be solved. The common law is "a philosophy" or "disputable Art," not law, Hobbes wrote.[5] The common law is "a thing merely imaginary," Bentham added, for "whatever the alleged rules of common law are, they cannot be rules of law."[6] As the legal philosopher Gerald Postema points out, if one believes, with Hobbes, that "it is not Wisdom, but Authority that makes a Law," or with Bentham that law provides normative guidance but in a distinctive way—by issuing authoritative directives to citizens it seeks to govern—then common law is not law; for "common law denies that command, sanction, authorized institutions, or even clarity is theoretically central to law."[7] Instead, common law directs attention to the normative guidance that law seeks to provide, not through authoritative command but through the institutionalizing of collaborative argument and deliberation over norms.

The Babylonian Talmud, with its multigenerational argument over norms, naturally invites comparison to the common law style of legal thought. The grounds for conceptual comparison lie in a variety of structural similarities that go beyond their shared argumentative and discursive approach to legal practice, however. They include a strong judiciary/jurist class and a weak or nonexistent legislature, social institutions that have all the features of a gerontocracy (students sit at the feet of their masters absorbing the technique of innovation within tradition), the emphasis on embedding law in a community, the preference for local solutions over global consistency, and the role of narratives in legal reasoning. This tradition of legal thought, as filtered through Dworkin's writings, became a major resource for a variety of new and interesting approaches to rabbinic legal and literary material in the Jewish Studies academy.

Even more influential in ushering in the legal turn in academic Jewish Studies was a remarkable essay by the late Yale law professor Robert Cover, "The Supreme Court, 1982 Term—Foreword: Nomos and Narrative."[8] This essay was a response to a U.S. Supreme Court decision made the year before. In criticizing the decision, Cover set forth his understanding of "what is law" in powerful and poetic language. On its face, that understanding was informed by the Anglo-American common law tradition, by the growing body of American constitutional law scholarship attempting to theorize the legitimacy of the Supreme Court via the idea of a community of discourse (a body of scholarship that included Dworkin), and by contemporary anthropological writings about humans as makers of meaning. But it also was informed by Cover's understanding of the

Jewish legal tradition, a topic he addressed in other short pieces. Although the Jewish legal tradition was mentioned only in passing in "Nomos and Narrative," most academics within the field of Jewish Studies experienced an immediate shock of recognition on first encountering the article.

The article is so rich that it is impossible to do it justice in a single paragraph; here, I merely highlight a few themes around which Jewish Studies scholarship has since coalesced. Cover presented two models of law that he termed the "imperial" and the "paideic." The imperial model is the familiar modern, positivist view of state law in which law is primarily about maintaining order and emphasizes abstract rules, hierarchy, and enforcement. Law in the paideic model, by contrast, is richly particularist, meaningful, and expressive. It is both the product and ongoing guardian of a specific community's history and ideals. Law in this model is invariably set within a larger series of narratives that tell the history, aims, and longings of the community. Cover, like Dworkin before him, conceives of law in the paideic key as interpretive. It is an ongoing argument about how best to understand the law given its larger goal: to provide a path for realizing the community's ideals. Cover's definition of law thus completely separates the idea of law from the state. Much of "Nomos and Narrative" is devoted to detailing the consequences of recognizing that we live in a world of radical pluralism and of competing legal orders, even within the boundaries of a single territorial state. These legal orders are constantly clashing, engaging one another, and interacting. Moreover, because no legal order is exclusively imperial nor paideic, social order and meaning vie with one another even within a single legal order, creating legal orders that are internally pluralistic. Both the paideic model and imperial model are part of the American legal heritage, and the essay, at its core, was a plea for the Supreme Court to reemphasize the former.

The paideic legal model that Cover outlined can and has been read as an idealized account of the halakhah. (Indeed, in a recent book devoted to "the idea of halakhah"—its concept of law—Chaim Saiman begins each chapter with a quotation from "Nomos and Narrative."[9]) The article did far more, however, than present a fresh and evocative answer to the jurisprudential puzzle, "What is law?" The essay's rich interdisciplinary approach became an impetus for new interdisciplinary projects in the fields of Jewish Studies. As more fully described later, Jewish historians turned to Cover and other accounts of legal pluralism to investigate how Jews and Jewish law interacted in different periods and places with other legal systems; students of rabbinic culture were energized to investigate how law and literature are integrally connected; and Jewish feminist studies began to focus on how community and law are intertwined.

New Directions in Scholarship after the Legal Turn

The rise of philosophies of law that grew out of the Anglo-American common law heritage quickly penetrated the academic study of rabbinic legal thought. Dworkin's work provided scholars with a new vocabulary, enabling academics to describe with more clarity the role of morality in rabbinic legal exegesis, the role of principles and values in Jewish law, and the essentially interpretive aspect of rabbinic legal thought. In *Commentary Revolutions*, which cites Dworkin throughout, the Israeli academic scholar Moshe Halbertal examined tannaitic sources, showing how moral considerations influenced the choice between competing interpretations.[10] Christine Hayes investigated the early rabbinic concept of divine law and also deployed Dworkin to locate a talmudic distinction between the right law and the best law.[11] The early rabbis were aware of this distinction, Hayes shows. Deductive analysis of rules may point in one direction, but the law to be applied often moved in the opposite direction because rules are modified according to principles, such as pursuing paths of peace. The attention to the distinction between rules and principles also gave rise to a new body of scholarship examining a distinctive characteristic of modern halakhah: the transformation of ethical principles into legal rules. Whole areas, such as restrictions on speech or modest dress, whose genesis lay in ethical aspirations or custom, are increasingly turned into legal codes.[12] Scholars also began to ask, following Dworkin, where the rabbis drew their principles from, often locating their source in the prophetic writings and, most especially, in the aggadah. Thus, the Israeli scholar Yair Lorberbaum, who acknowledges the contribution that Dworkin's theories made to re-describing the relationship of halakhah and aggadah, traces the way the tannaitic rabbis fashioned a variety of legal rules around the concept of creation in the image of God, as that concept was reflected in aggadic material.[13] This scholarship retrieves the aggadah as a source of law and reunites the talmudic legacy that the post-talmudic geonim had split apart.

More recent scholarship has continued to focus on how aggadah does legal work. Moshe Simon-Shoshan has proposed that the rabbis conveyed law in two ways: through both rules and examples. Tales of the doings of rabbis and other exemplary figures are merely a different form of conveying norms of conduct.[14] Indeed, many aggadot and much biblical narrative material could be analogized to common law cases. As with the common law case, they are narratives of social interaction, with a judgment explicitly or implicitly attached that passes approval or disapproval on the reported conduct; therefore, rules may be inferred from the narrative accounts.[15] Both biblical narratives and aggadot have become increasingly important sources of law in the contemporary period. Questions about norms of war, affairs of state, and the status of Jewish secular institutions arose on the heels of the establishment of the State of Israel. Given prior exilic conditions, the halakhah was largely silent on these topics. Jurists within the Religious Zionist camp, in particular, turned to the Bible and aggadah to fill the gap.[16]

Less technically, the relationship of halakhah to aggadah and the role of storytelling in shaping the worldview of a legal community play a seminal role in new feminist scholarship. Both Tamar Ross, writing from within the Israeli academy, and Rachel Adler, writing from within the American academy, interrogate how to incorporate feminism within Judaism. Both view a commitment to halakhah as an essential marker of being Jewish, and both structure their arguments about how halakhah can change to incorporate feminism around a reading of Cover's "Nomos and Narrative." For each, law is not "a body of rules so much as an expression of the norms and values held by the community."[17]

Given its emphasis on decoupling the idea of law from the state, "Nomos and Narrative" also can be situated within a body of legal scholarship that investigates legal pluralism: the multiple legal orders that make claims on persons and how those orders interact with one another. This literature has become a central resource for Jewish historians of the medieval and early modern periods. Jewish historians are now tracing the extensive jurisdictional and normative pluralism that characterized these periods. Jews (and even non-Jews) litigated in Jewish lay courts, in rabbinic courts, and in the imperial courts. Just as non-Jewish law made its way into the rabbinic courts, Jewish law was cited and applied in the imperial courts. In the later stages of the Holy Roman Empire, for example, Jewish law was recognized as one of the many common laws that comprised the imperial legal system. The Jewish historical experience provides especially fertile ground for investigating legal pluralism; these historians join a growing group of general historians and legal theorists interested in understanding how law once operated and, indeed, with globalization, now increasingly operates across territories.

The study of legal pluralism is not confined to the medieval and early modern period. It is also a major theme of a growing body of academic literature addressing how various thinkers, especially within the Religious Zionist movement, understood the role of Jewish law in the modern State of Israel. For example, thinkers have been sharply divided over the halakhic legitimacy of the

Israeli state courts. Some held that the state courts were analogous to the Jewish community courts presided over by laypeople of the medieval and early modern period, and others argued that the legitimacy of the courts rested on its consideration of Jewish law as a source of law, even if the judges were secular Jews or even non-Jews. In short, contemporary thinkers borrowed from the earlier pluralistic models that Jewish historians are now unearthing and extended them in new ways.

Although I have emphasized new research that has been spurred by Anglo-American legal theories intended to upset the primacy of modern positivism, the most salient characteristic of the legal turn in the Jewish Studies academy is a new sensitivity to the different pictures of law that are possible, both in a positivist and in a nonpositivist register. This expanded theoretical repertoire allows academics to ask what specific concept of law is at play in different times and places and among individual rabbinic thinkers.

The Legal Turn Reexamined

The legal turn in Jewish Studies has also prompted a more self-reflective level of scholarship that reexamines a question posed at the beginning of this chapter: Is the term "law"—or for that matter, the term "religion"—a category unto itself, against which one can measure Jewish writings? In *Jewish Legal Theories: Writings on State, Religion, and Morality*, Leora Batnitzky and Yonatan Brafman offer a rich selection of readings that "attempt, explicitly, or implicitly, to characterize what Jewish law is."[18] The readings are all culled from the modern period. The theoretical question that animates the authors' collection of sources and that is addressed in its introduction is whether modern Jewish theories of law are distinctive, even if they claim complete continuity with the premodern Jewish legal past. The authors argue that modern Jewish legal theories emerge only in the framework of the rise of the sovereign nation-state, which gave rise to a "distinctly modern question: Is it possible or desirable analytically and practically to separate the spheres of law, politics, and religion from one another?" (xx) Modern Jewish writings attempting to characterize what Jewish law is all contend, in different ways, with this question, the authors argue, in contrast to the more holistic approach of premodern writings.

Yet precisely because this analytic question is so central to modernity, the debate still persists in the Jewish Studies academy about whether the category "law" is an accurate way to describe rabbinic writings and, more to the point, whether the turn to legal theory and legal philosophy as theoretical tools in academic projects is genuinely productive. The fear is that the legal turn will deflect attention from the study of texts and from the cultural innovations and imaginative energies embedded in these texts. Put starkly, the debate pits the study of a social practice aimed at delineating collective obligations and rights against the individual search for meaning and illumination found in discrete texts. Given that academic Jewish Studies, since at least Gershom Scholem, has seen itself as part of a larger modern emancipatory project to release new Jewish energies, we can expect this debate to continue.

Recommended Readings

Adler, Rachel. *Engendering Judaism: An Inclusive Theology and Ethics* (Jewish Publication Society, 1988).

Batnitzky, Leora, and Yonatan Brafman. *Jewish Legal Theories: Writings on State, Religion, and Morality* (Brandeis University Press, 2018).

Cover, Robert M. "Obligation: A Jewish Jurisprudence of the Social Order," *Journal of Law and Religion* 5 (1987): 65–74.

Cover, Robert M. "The Supreme Court, 1982 Term—Foreword: Nomos and Narrative," *Harvard Law Review* 97 (1983): 4–68.

Halbertal, Moshe. *People of the Book: Canon, Meaning, and Authority* (Harvard University Press, 1997).

Hayes, Christine. *What's Divine about Divine Law? Early Perspectives* (Princeton University Press, 2015).

Kaye, Alexander. *The Invention of Jewish Theocracy: The Struggle for Legal Authority in Modern Israel* (Oxford University Press, 2020).

Marglin, Jessica M. *Across Legal Lines: Jews and Muslims in Modern Morocco* (Yale University Press, 2016).

Saiman, Chaim. *Halakhah: The Rabbinic Idea of Law* (Princeton University Press, 2018).

Stone, Suzanne Last. "In Pursuit of the Countertext: The Turn to the Jewish Legal Model in Contemporary American Legal Theory," *Harvard Law Review* 106 (1993): 813–94.

Notes

1. H.L.A. Hart, *Concept of Law* (Oxford University Press, 1981).

2. Harvard University Press, 1977, 14–45.

3. Oxford University Press, 1961.

4. Harvard University Press, 1986.

5. Thomas Hobbes, *Dialogue between a Philosopher and a Student of the Common Laws of England* (University of Chicago Press, 1971), cited in Gerald J. Postema, "Philosophy of the Common Law," in *Oxford Handbook of Jurisprudence and Legal Philosophy*, ed. J. Coleman and S. Shapiro (Oxford University Press, 2002), 616.

6. Jeremy Bentham, *Of Laws in General*, ed. H.L.A. Hart (Athlone Press, 1970), cited in Postema, 616.

7. "Philosophy of the Common Law," in *Oxford Handbook of Jurisprudence and Legal Philosophy*, ed. J. Coleman and S. Shapiro (Oxford University Press, 2002), 617.

8. Cover, "The Supreme Court, 1982 Term."

9. Saiman, *Halakhah: The Rabbinic Idea of Law* (Princeton University Press, 2018).

10. Halbertal, *Commentary Revolutions in the Making: Values as Interpretive Considerations in Midrashei Halakhah* (Hebrew; Hebrew University, 1984).

11. Hayes, *What's Divine about Divine Law?*

12. See Benjamin Brown, "From Principles to Rules and from Musar to Halakhah: The Hafetz Hayim's Rulings on Libel and Gossip," *Dine Israel* 25 (2008): 171–256.

13. Lorberbaum, *In God's Image: Myth, Theology, and Law in Classical Judaism* (Cambridge University Press, 2015).

14. Simon-Shoshan, *Stories of the Law: Narrative Discourse and the Construction of Authority in the Mishnah* (Oxford University Press, 2015).

15. See Suzanne Last Stone, "On the Interplay of Rules, 'Cases,' and Concepts in Rabbinic Legal Literature: Another Look at the Aggadot on Honi the Circle-Drawer," *Dine Israel* 24 (2007): 125–55.

16. See Arye Edrei, "Law, Interpretation, and Ideology: The Renewal of the Jewish Laws of War in the State of Israel," *Cardozo Law Review* 28 (2006): 187.

17. Claire Sufrin, "Telling Stories: The Legal Turn in Jewish Feminist Thought," in *Gender and Jewish History*, ed. M. Kaplan and D. Dash Moore (Indiana University Press, 2011), 2.

18. Brandeis University Press, 2018, xiii.

23

Race

Bruce Haynes, University of California, Davis

THE IDEA that Jews might be a distinct race has been entertained since the earliest day of evolutionary biology.[1] Yet most Ashkenazi or Sephardic Jews and their descendants have lived their lives as white people in the United States within a context of varying levels of antisemitism. Since the late 1990s, however, the Jewish experience has been shaped by the changing nature of race in the United States.

Consequently, Jewish Studies has responded by exploring how the American system of race has shaped Jewish identity. Paying attention to critiques of society—including the emergence of critical race theory, critical whiteness, and gender studies within the academy—the critical turn recognizes the tension between European Jewish assimilation and their incorporation in the United States as white citizens in juxtaposition to African Americans' second-class status as racially disenfranchised and segregated citizens.[2] This chapter explores the unfolding political and racial contexts through which Jews, along with other immigrant groups, were integrated into the white American mainstream; the critical interrogation of whiteness and race in scholarship over the past decades; the impact of this scholarship on Jewish Studies, which has taken a decisive turn in its analysis of the Jewish experience in the United States; and the growing visibility of individuals in the United States who self-identify as non-white and Jewish—a development that challenges the prevailing narrative on the presumed whiteness of Jews.

488   CHAPTER 23

Transcending the Color Line

From a social-scientific perspective, W. E. B. Du Bois was the first to challenge the Social Darwinism of his day and argue that culture, racial discrimination, and white prejudices were at the core of differences between Black and white Americans. Whether one considers his classic essay "The Souls of White Folk," published in *The Independent* on August 18, 1910, or his analysis of the white worker in his landmark 1935 study *Black Reconstruction in America, 1860–1880*,[3] Du Bois was the first to critically think about whiteness. Scholars have since followed his lead, challenging not only the presumed immutability of racial categories but also expanding on Du Bois's ideas of "double consciousness." New terms like "hybridity" and, more recently, "intersectional identity" have been put forth to capture the multiple dimensions of our complex social identities. Today, a critical mass of scholarship in Jewish Studies identifies the intersectional, transnational, and pluralistic nature of Jewish identity.[4]

For much of the twentieth century, American Jewish identity was strongly shaped by the metaphor of "the melting pot," in which divergent groups shed their distinctive traits and identities to create a new culture. The idea, first popularized by the British Jewish playwright and novelist Israel Zangwill in his landmark 1908 play by the same name, offered an alternative to the Americanization movement, which called for the "national integration" of new immigrants through civic education programs. Yet both strategies posed a threat to a distinct Jewish culture. "Cultural pluralism"—a term coined by the German Jewish immigrant Horace M. Kallen in the early 1900s—offered Jews a middle ground between racial exclusion and total group annihilation.[5]

During the late nineteenth century, when Eastern European Jewish immigrants began arriving en masse, they were viewed by many Yankees and southerners as a potentially foreign element. (So too were other non-Protestant immigrant groups from Europe, including the Irish and Italians.) Social scientists debated which groups could blend easily into a culturally Protestant national culture, and with the rise of Social Darwinism and eugenics, the idea of race—viewed as a set of completely inheritable traits—emerged as the dominant organizing principal of political organization. Jews, a group that had long been thought of as racially and culturally distinct from Christian Europeans, evoked particular concern. Would Jews be recognized as citizens or pushed across the color line?

The idea that Jews could change from one form to another had held sway in medieval folklore and in the Lamarckian science that emerged in the eighteenth century. Writing a half-century before Darwin, the French zoologist Jean Baptiste Lamarck believed that history, climate, and geography could transform a group's religion, language, and social practices into inheritable, biological traits like temperament or color. Lamarckians distinguished between historical races—groups with heterogeneous origins that consolidated over time into a common bloodline—and natural racial groups, which corresponded to large geographic regions and were signified primarily by color. Africans were seen as a natural race, unchanged by time or environment, whereas Jews were understood to be an historical race and, like Native Americans, were mutable over time. Key to the emerging logic of racial distinctions in the United States was understanding the asymmetrical relationship between groups that were considered to be mutable like Jews and other groups, like Africans, that were not. In the heat of ethnological, sociological, and anthropological debates over whether Jews were in fact a "preindustrial" race, Jewish racial scientists embraced racist Lamarckian notions of historic races that condemned Africans to an inferior permanent state, while choosing to reject notions that Jews were an unhealthy race or nation.[6]

In the midst of a solidifying Jim Crow color line at the turn of the twentieth century, cultural pluralism provided a way for Jews to conceal their cultural distinctiveness while reconciling anxieties and questions about their whiteness; by reimagining America "as a nation of hyphenated identities," Jewish intellectuals helped construct a bridge between Jewish otherness and whiteness.[7] This one-dimensional storyline—replicated in magazines, books, and documentaries—not only ignored the presence of Jews from non-European backgrounds but also obliterated the history of Jews of African descent, as well as mixed-ancestry Jews; it also contributed to obscuring how race shaped Jewish assimilation and selfhood in America. Rather than being a pluralistic association of national, cultural, and racial diversity, most Sephardim and Ashkenazim Jews were quite willingly homogenized as white folk.

After 1910 most American Jews began adopting a hyphenated "ethnic" identity, which allowed them to be legitimately American and "white." But for Jews who remained in Europe and the Arab world, rising racial nationalism and antisemitism made assimilation and claims to whiteness unattainable. The mid-twentieth-century international environment produced Germany's infamous Nuremberg Laws, which were modeled on the racial logics of U.S. anti-miscegenation statutes. Like Africans in America, Jews were racialized as "other" in Germany and across Europe. The quantification of Jewishness under the Nuremberg Laws was an attempt to transform cultural antisemitism into biological racism, much like the racial logic deployed in the United States' one-drop rule for classifying Black Americans.

The framework of cultural pluralism also shared the stage with the "race relations cycle," an alternative model of national incorporation put forth by Chicago School sociologists Robert Ezra Park and Ernest W. Burgess. In their 1921 textbook, *Introduction to the Science of Sociology*, they asserted that competition between primordial groups progressed in a multistage trajectory from conflict toward social incorporation and amalgamation.[8] In their treatise, they defined "assimilation" as a process that melds people and groups into "a common cultural life" (735). Although they adopted the language of ethnicity, they also emphasized cultural adaptation as the key to social incorporation and economic mobility. The term "ethnicity" was used not only to describe groups as culturally distinct but also to signify which groups would be accepted—socially and politically—as white. Groups as varied as Armenians, Italian, Sicilians, Greek Orthodox, Russian Orthodox, Jews, and Poles were considered white and assimilable, whereas those arriving from China, sub-Saharan Africa, Japan, and Mexico (except those entering under the treaty of Treaty of Guadalupe Hidalgo, who were classified as white citizens for political expediency) were denied citizenship and classified as racially "other" and, by definition, of lower social rank. The "race relation cycle" would become known as the "assimilation model," and despite remnants of Social Darwinian influences, would become widely influential for decades to come. Jews were understood to be white people who "assimilated" culturally into America, rather than former racial outsiders who navigated into whiteness.

Despite being a reformer, Robert E. Park was also influenced by segregation, the Social Darwinism of Herbert Spencer, and the conservative philosophy of Booker T Washington. He embraced assumptions about primordial and evolutionary younger and older races. He believed that racial hierarchies were the result of competition and natural selection and reasoned that education could only go so far in making Blacks equal to whites. The "race relations cycle" overshadowed the important scholarship of the Atlanta School of Sociology, under the tutelage of W. E. B. Du Bois—one of the earliest scholars to apply a critical interpretation of U.S. racial dynamics and the first to wrestle with the relationship between capitalism and racial slavery.

The processes that shaped the formation of Black/white racial distinctions in the United States enabled Ashkenazi Jews to benefit from Jim Crow segregation and white privilege. (Although other non-Protestant immigrants like the Irish and Italians underwent a similar process, the uniqueness of American-style antisemitism made Jewish whiteness conditional.) Jewish ethnics were understood as having weak ancestral ties but strong cultural connections that were malleable and subject to both individual and group change but even held the potential for cultural growth; in other words, they could become white. In contrast, Indigenous people in the Americas and those from the Global South were homogenized and racialized into monolithic, stigmatized categories that did not allow for their individual or group transformation; race signified a permanent biological difference that was believed to be both essential and immutable.[9]

By the end of World War II, most Jews in the United States had been accepted as white. Meanwhile, white American sociologists built a distinctive vocabulary for understanding the Jewish experience that made whiteness invisible and sidestepped asking how ideas about race shaped Jewish life.[10] As historian Matthew Frye Jacobson and others have argued, mythical ideas about the unity of the Caucasian race helped "reconsolidate" probationary groups from Europe, like Jews, into white folk.[11]

Intermarriage between American Protestants and the newer Jews and Catholics increased. By the 1950s many began adopting the term "the triple melting pot"[12] to refer to declining national and religious boundaries between various European immigrants. By the time *Look Magazine* ran its 1964 cover story, "The Vanishing American Jew," Jewishness and whiteness had become synonymous in the public imagination. By the 1970s the focus on "intermarriage" had shifted from relationships between different European immigrant groups—that is, "white" ethnics—to interracial relationships.

Jewish political and social incorporation was followed by Jewish economic mobility, and American Jews were deemed a "model minority." By 1945, with the help of Chicago sociologist Louis Wirth, the term "minority" entered widespread use, lumping together groups with vastly difference experiences in ways that distorted the unequal power relations that helped determine their experiences. By the early 1960s scholars like Milton Gordon, Daniel Patrick Moynihan, and Nathan Glazer had embraced the language of ethnicity. Glazer and Moynihan's controversial landmark book, *Beyond the Melting Pot: The Negroes, Puerto Ricans, Jews, Italians, and Irish of New York City,* claimed that "ethnicity" provided a real experiential basis for political mobilization and social action in New York City politics.[13] Their optimistic view from the early 1960s predicted a decline in the importance of race and ethnic identity and an increase in the importance of class distinctions as different racial and ethnic groups melted into the proverbial American melting pot. New York was the case for their analysis, which did not anticipate the rise of the Black Arts, Black Power, and civil rights movements or the resurgence of ethnic identity among succeeding generations of Jewish Americans.

Into the 1970s Milton Gordon and other proponents of the assimilation model emphasized that it meant conformity to an English-speaking Protestant core culture. The focus on acculturation as a key to becoming American tended to ignore the central way that hierarchies of racial ascription systematically privileged those with light-complexioned skin tones and conferred systemic advantages to Europeans, including Jews. Although many Ashkenazi Jews had been active in the civil rights struggles, a group of Jewish intellectuals, including Norman Podhoretz and Irving Kristol, turned toward neoconservativism, rejecting the liberalism implicit in the struggle for black civil rights. They had come of age in the prewar urban slums of New York and touted their own rise to the middle class as evidence of the triumph of American meritocracy and the success of the melting pot. More than any other generation before them, these conservative-leaning Jews embraced with enthusiasm their identities as white people. In some ways, their visibility also signified to many the politics of modern-day American Jews. Meanwhile, the 1967 Arab–Israeli War (the Six-Day War), which transformed the landscape of the Sinai Peninsula, the West Bank, the Gaza Strip, and the Golan Heights, drew American Jews away from civil rights toward political concerns with the State of Israel.

Despite the resurgence of ethnic identity, Jewish cultural assimilation and rapid economic mobility had transformed American Jews into the public representative epitome of the urban, industrial, capitalist order.[14] Yet, as they tried to become less Jewish and assimilate to Anglo-cultural norms, intermarriage with non-Jews challenged their very existence as an identifiable group. Before 1970, just 17 percent of Ashkenazi Jews had married non-Jews, according to research by the Pew Research Foundation. Within a decade, Ashkenazi outmarriage rates surpassed 40 percent, and new anxieties were raised about Jewish identity and social status as many Jews economically benefited from being treated as white in America.

In the wake of the civil rights and Black Power movements, the 1970s witnessed a landmark shift in the ways that scholars understood the centrality of race and racism in producing and reproducing inequality. Ideas previously advanced by W. E. B. Du Bois, Frantz Fanon, Karl Marx, and Max Weber regained favor as a generation of scholars began engaging in more critical explorations of the structural and ideological underpinnings of race, racism, and racial inequality.

The implication for Jewish Studies was a reassessment of how race, highlighted by the Black/white binary, framed the context of the political, economic, and social incorporation of Ashkenazi, Sephardic, and many Mizrahi Jews in the United States. Research that earlier had focused on culture, ethnicity, and assimilation pivoted to investigations on "the social construction of race," racial inequality, and racial identity. The Chicago School model, which treated race and ethnicity as primordial differences based in group cultures and rendered whiteness invisible and un-interrogated, was displaced by critical explanations of the durability of racial hierarchies in society.

Whiteness Studies and Its Impact on Jewish Studies

Sociologists France Winddance Twine and Charles Gallagher claim that whiteness studies scholarship has undergone three distinct waves.[15] W. E. B. Du Bois, founder of the Atlanta School of Sociology, laid its intellectual foundations in the first wave. Black feminist legal scholars, like Kimberle Crenshaw, ushered in the second phase of whiteness studies through critical race theory within jurisprudence. The third wave centers on "whiteness as a form of power" that is "defined, deployed, performed, policed and reinvented" (5) and might best be described as whiteness studies. In contemporary Jewish Studies, scholarship has drawn insights from all three phases of critical whiteness scholarship by problematizing Jewish whiteness and the hegemony of Ashkenazi culture in representing all Jews.

The Jewish experience was explored in new ways with the publication of the five-volume series *The Jewish People in America*,[16] but it was historian David Biale's groundbreaking book, *Cultures of Jews: A New History*, that challenged the simplistic narratives of a single European origin for Jewish culture that had long prevailed. Meanwhile, a new generation of scholars was taking a more critical view of race, whiteness, and Jewish assimilation. Although they represented a diverse range of disciplines and theoretical approaches, this scholarship was often lumped together under the label "whiteness studies." Scholars in anthropology, sociology, cultural studies, literary theory, American Jewish history, law, philosophy, ethnic studies, and education all contributed to the understanding of how race categories, race identities, and racial inequalities are created and reproduced. The new conception of race understood it to be "historically situated, context specific, and subject to processes of both resistance and reproduction."[17]

In 1986 the landmark study *Racial Formation in the United States*, by sociologists Michael Omi and Howard Winant, took its place among a growing body of critical scholarship that understood race to be a socially constructed and historically specific set of ideas and processes emerging out of colonialism, slavery, and capitalism that used physical appearance to signify human value and national belonging.[18] During the 1990s such scholars as David Roediger,[19] Ruth Frankenberg,[20] Cheryl Harris,[21] Theodore W. Allen,[22] Karen (Brodkin) Sacks,[23] George Lipsitz,[24] Noel Ignatiev,[25] and Mathew Frye Jacobson[26] helped move "whiteness" to the foreground of the critical investigation of European immigrants in America and advanced the idea that the economic privileges afforded to different ethnic groups were commensurate with their level of acceptance as white folk. In short, class mobility and the juxtaposition of Jews to Black people were both causes and effects in the postwar process of Jewish acceptance within the white American mainstream.[27]

Although an academic consensus has emerged across the fields of biology, genetics, physical anthropology, and sociology that race is not a scientifically useful concept, public discourse routinely refers to race as if it were a self-evident biological fact. Much of the literature on whiteness is centered on the "social construction" of race in America, yet a growing interdisciplinary cadre of researchers have broadened their lens, examining the social, political, and intellectual history underlying the emergence of a global racial classification system. In *The Rise and Fall of the Caucasian Race: A Political History of Racial Identity*, for example, political scientist Bruce Baum outlines the racial discourses that emerged during the Age of Reason and shows how notions of racial "whiteness" and "blackness" have served as "political" or "racial projects" for the domination and exclusion of groups deemed non-white.[28]

Some observers have misunderstood the critical turn toward race among scholars, mislabeling it as critical race theory (CRT). It is in fact an orientation in legal scholarship that evolved among Black legal scholars during the 1970s and 1980s and that reached maturity in the 1990s with the broad impact of the scholarship of Derrick Bell, Richard Delgado, Kimberle Crenshaw, and Cheryl Harris. CRT is not a "theory" with a replicable, theoretical framework and may better be described as an intellectual project that critically examines the role of racial narratives within the law.[29] Over time, the framework has been adopted by other academic fields, in particular education, where the focus is on the stories and counternarratives of historically underrepresented racial groups.

Empirically, whiteness studies and race scholarship in general have tended to highlight different levels of analysis. Macro-level scholarship often investigates the historical and political creation of racial categories, whereas micro-level studies examine the people who come to occupy these categories and their social attitudes and identities. Meso-level approaches, in contrast, explore the effects of institutional and social contexts on boundary making.[30] Although whiteness scholars come from a variety of disciplines and theoretical approaches, they are unified by a critical interrogation of the social and political construction of whiteness and white identities.

The emergence of whiteness studies and the understanding of race as a primary axis of socially constructed inequality reflects a substantive intellectual shift. Over time, the new orientation in Jewish Studies, especially the critical interrogations to understanding the role of race and whiteness within Jewish life in the United States, has been impactful. This paradigm shift has fostered debate about the appropriateness of the concept of "race" in understanding the Jewish experience in the United States and around the globe. Scholars no longer see the development of racial thinking as merely a product of nineteenth-century scientific racial thought. Scholarship from medieval studies, Middle Eastern studies, women studies, Jewish Studies, history, English, comparative literature, and sociology has argued that the modern idea of "race" (what some have called "proto-race") first emerged in the late Middle Ages and the early modern era before the terminology of "race" was introduced. Both racism and antisemitism are rooted in the simultaneous formation of homogeneous Christian nations based on the racial exclusion of Jews and Moors, the colonial conquests of Indigenous peoples, and transatlantic slavery. By the fifteenth century, Jews and Muslims, along with Africans, Native Americans, Mongols, Slavs, and the Romani, were racialized as "other" and not white in the modern western imagination.[31] In fact, the first-ever compulsory mass expulsion of Jews in England, in 1290, marked a key moment in the birth of racial thinking in Europe, a period when whiteness was emerging as a normative marker of both a primordial European Christian identity and citizenship.[32]

The Growing Visibility of Non-White Jews in the Twenty-First Century

A major development reshaping scholarship on Jews and Jewish Americans has been the growing interest in and visibility of non-white Jews, sometimes called "Jews of Color." During the 1990s several factors highlighted the cultural and racial diversity of American Jewry. Changes in immigration laws brought to Israel Mizrahi Jews from northern Africa and the Beta Israel from Ethiopia, a people rumored to have existed for centuries but who were "discovered" by westerners in the late nineteenth century. The 1990s also witnessed an unprecedented growth in cross-cultural and cross-racial adoptions, spurred by the Howard M. Metzbaum Multiethnic Placement Act of 1994, which prevented federally funded agencies from delaying or denying adoptions based on a parents' or child's race. In addition, interracial marriages had been steadily increasing since the 1967 U.S. Supreme Court *Loving v. Virginia* ruling that held miscegenation laws to be unconstitutional and led to an increased number of children with mixed-race heritages, including those with one Jewish parent. The number of patrilineal-descent African-heritage and Caribbean-born Jews who wished to be recognized as Jews was also on the rise. So too were the numbers of African Americans who chose to covert to Judaism. In 1988 the black scholar and former civil rights activist Julius Lester chronicled his Orthodox conversion to Judaism in *Lovesong: Becoming a Jew*.[33] The book may have been prophetic in the way it traced his Jewish roots to American slavery and won the National Jewish Book Award. In 2023 the writer, independent scholar, culinary historian, and creator of Afroculinaria, the first blog devoted to the history of African American food culture, Michael W. Twitty, was awarded the Everett Family Foundation Jewish Book of the Year Award for his book *Koshersoul: The Faith and Food Journey of an African American Jew.*

Until recently, most scholars in communal studies or who studied Jewish identity seemed comfortable with the idea that American Jews were from Central or Eastern Europe and had, through the magic of "ethnic pluralism" become transformed from racial outsiders into white Americans. During the 1980s, when theories about multiculturalism held sway, the notion that American Jews might still be wrestling with whiteness and white identity was largely abandoned. Popular scholarship emphasized the postwar transformation of Jewish identity while largely avoiding discussion of Jewish ambivalence toward both assimilation and the concept of a "Jewish race." Today, although many Jews seem to reject the notion that Jews constitute a race, the growing interest in "Jewish genetics" since the 1990s has revived the notion among some Jews that Jewishness is biologically based while at the same time creating the fear of racial stigmatization among others.[34] Recent scholarship has shown that these kinds of scientific claims about Jewish cultural identity or religious identity are gross misunderstandings of the genetic research.[35] Genetics can only be traced to place, not to specific ethnic groups. For example, according to the National Human Genome Research Institute, although the disorder Tay-Sachs disease is highly prevalent (1/27) among Ashkenazi Jews and has been used as a marker of presumed Jewishness, there is also a high rate of incidence of the disease in the Cajun community of Louisiana. Despite the limitations of genetic testing, more than 26 million people had taken at-home DNA tests by the beginning of 2019, and by 2022, the Ashkenazi chief rabbi of Israel began requesting DNA testing to certify the Jewishness of the partners in certain marriages.[36]

Changes in the social and racial demography of the American Jewish population are leading to more nuanced studies of Jewish identity. Surveys had long focused on questions of religious practice and ignored specific questions about race and ethnicity, a practice that both resulted from and contributed to the presumption that American Jews are White.[37] Tapper and colleagues' analysis of the surveys used in 175 American Jewish population studies and community portraits since 1970 shows that the majority failed to look at questions of racial and ethnic diversity. The first comprehensive study of the American Jewish population to factor in race was the 1990 National Jewish Population Survey. It sampled 2,441 households, of which at least one member self-identified as Jewish, and found that 2.4 percent of the sample, or an estimated 125,000 individuals, also identified as black. By the turn of the millennium, no respectable survey of Jewish Americans could avoid a racial identity question. But scholarly estimates varied as to the total number of Jews in America and of "Jews of Color" (JOC), a term that activists and social demographers were increasingly adopting. Because counting Jews is not a straightforward question but rather a reflection of the variety of ways that Jewish community membership has been defined, counting non-white Jews is an even more complicated question. Are Hispanic Jews considered to be Jews of Color? How do we decide to count them? What about Sephardic and Mizrahi Jews? Do people of Iranian, Syrian, Indian, or other nonwestern backgrounds choose to identify as non-white Jews? Should these Jews be identified as non-white even if they do not identify as JOC? Which categories should we use? These are challenging questions.

Bruce Phillips outlines some of the methodological challenges demographers face in deciding who is and who is not counted as a member of the Jewish community.[38] First, numerous survey sampling designs rely on lists, distinctive Jewish names, or geography. Second, questions about race have been excluded until only recently. Third, there is no single definition of the category "Jews of Color." Fourth, an unequal distribution of Jews of Color (interreligious and interracial marriages are highest in the western states) could lead to lower estimates. And finally, not all non-white Jews may choose to self-identify as non-white, making population estimates more problematic.[39]

Survey research has tended to produce varying estimates based on sample selection. The 2013 Pew Research Center Survey—heralded by many as the "gold standard" in Jewish population surveys—reported that 6 percent of roughly

498   CHAPTER 23

5.3 million Jewish adults in the United States identified as non-white. (A year earlier, Brandeis University conducted its own national survey and found that a significantly higher number of Jewish adults—12 percent—were non-white.) The latest survey, conducted by the Pew Research Center in 2020, identified 8 percent of self-identified Jews who also identified as non-white.

Phillips cautions about these surveys' potentially low estimates and agrees with Tapper and colleagues' conclusion that younger cohorts of Jews are more likely to self-identify as non-white. In addition, more inclusive definitions of Jews lead to larger estimates of Jews of Color. In a special issue of the journal *Contemporary Jewry*, Stephen M. Cohen argues that those Jewish population studies that have moved away from using random digit dialing often paint a "deficient and distorted" picture by overlooking important population groups.[40] Ira M. Sheskin and Arnold Dashefsky, co-editors of the *American Jewish Yearbook*, use national population surveys to claim that the true estimate of Jews of Color is closer to 6 percent,[41] in contrast to the 11 to 15 percent estimate given by Kelman's research team.[42]

By the 1990s Jews of African descent were beginning to organize. One of the first public events to highlight African American Jews was sponsored by the California African American Museum in Los Angeles in December 1993. Titled "Where Worlds Collide: The Souls of African American Jews," it brought together a small but international cadre of Jews of African descent, both born Jews and Jews by choice, to talk about their personal stories. Two years later, some of the participants in that event would come together and found the Alliance of Black Jews, one of the first voluntary social advocacy groups organized by and for Jews of African descent. Former members include Black Jewish intellectuals Robin Washington, editor-at-large of *The Forward*, and Gabrielle Foreman, literary historian and digital humanist.

In the mid-1990s the late Dr. Gary Tobin and his wife Diane Tobin began a research and community-building project, Be'chol Lashon (Hebrew, "In Every Language"). Its stated mission is to "strengthen Jewish identity by raising awareness about the ethnic, racial and cultural diversity of Jewish people and experience around the globe."[43] For more than a decade, the Tobins hosted a series of "think tanks" at San Francisco's famed Fairmont Hotel, bringing together leaders of Jewish communities from around the world—from Africa, Asia, Latin America, Australia, Europe, Israel, and the United States—as well as lesbian Jews and Hebrew Israelites from outside the Jewish mainstream. The Tobins embraced a handful of Hebrew Israelite rabbis like Rabbi Capers C. Funnye Jr., Chief Rabbi of the International Israelite Board of Rabbis and the spiritual leader of Beth Shalom B'nai Zaken Ethiopian Hebrew Congregation in Chicago. These think tanks provided a lively forum for conversation, creative thinking, and developing new approaches to communal growth and allowed for the exchange of information and network building.

But Be'chol Lashon was not the first organization to seek dialogue with African American or non-white Jews. During the 1960s Hatzaad Harishon (Hebrew, "The First Step") was created to generate dialogue with and give assistance to Hebrew Israelites. The New York-based group, founded by Rabbi Irving J. Block, the Conservative Jewish founder of Beit Achim (Brotherhood Synagogue), and Yaakov Gladstone, had many initial successes despite its short lifespan. Beginning in 1966, it began producing a mimeographed newspaper that reached a national readership before being discontinued in 1972. Rabbi Block and the group sent Hebrew Israelites to day schools on scholarships and enrolled others in Jewish education courses and lectures. Some Hebrews Israelites spent summers in Israel, and a few formally converted to Judaism. Despite its disruption of the dominant narrative of Jews as white folk, few paid serious attention to the group until rhetoric scholar Janice W. Fernheimer wrote about them in her *Stepping into Zion: Hatzaad Harishon, Black Jews, and the Remaking of Jewish Identity*[44] and more recently in the *Forward*.[45]

In 2001, when the feminist journal *Bridges; A Journal for Jewish Feminists and Our Friends*, published a special issue, "Writing and Art by and for Jewish Women of Color," few, save for perhaps the editors and writers themselves, envisioned the demographic changes we see today. The growth of the internet during the 1990s was a driving force enabling non-white Jews to connect with one another and explore their Jewishness as Indigenous Jews, Latinx Jews, Asian-American Jews, Black Jews, Mizrahi, Sephardic, and as Jews of Color.[46] Meanwhile, a new cadre of Afro-Jewish scholars emerged who challenged normative understandings of Jewish identity.[47] Among them were the feminist philosopher Naomi Zack, who wrote intimately about mixed-race identity in the United States;[48] Laurence M. Thomas, author of *Vessels of Evil: American Slavery and the Holocaust*[49]; Lewis R. Gordon, author of *Fanon and the Crisis of European Man* and *Bad Faith and Anti-Black Racism*[50]; and Katya Gibel Mevorach (formerly Katya Gibel Azoulay), who wrote *Black, Jewish and Interracial: It's Not the Color of Her Skin but the Race of Your Kin, and Other Myths of Identity*.[51] These works predated the landmark *Cultures of the Jews: A New History*, edited by David Biale,[52] which decisively breaks with the Eurocentric-Ashkenazi narrative that dominates Jewish historiography and argues for a Jewish "cultural pluralism." This volume consists of essays from twenty-three international scholars across multiple disciplines. Their contributions not only represent the globalization of Jewish studies but also attest to the ways in which "Jewish culture has always evolved on a global stage" (1149).

Other researchers detailed the changes that were taking place on the ground. The lesbian feminist scholar/activist Melanie Kaye/Kantrowitz brought voice to Jews of African, Asian, Indian, and Iberian descent in her groundbreaking book, *The Colors of Jews*. In 2012 the feminist theorist Marla Brettschneider published her groundbreaking study of how race, class, and gender shape multiple dimensions of queer Jewish families titled *The Family Flamboyant: Race Politics, Queer Families, Jewish Lives*.[53] In January 2016, American Jewish historian Michael Scott Alexander and I coedited a special issue of *American Jewish History* titled "The Color Issue: An Introduction," which explored questions of color, color, and race. Later that same year, Helen Kiyong Kim and Noah Samuel Leavitt published *JewAsian: Race, Religion, and Identity for America's Newest Jews*,[54] which challenged traditional understandings of Jewish identity, intermarriage, and race.

By 2004 the noted Fanon scholar and University of Connecticut Afro-Jewish philosopher, Lewis R. Gordon, founded the Center for Afro-Jewish Studies at Temple University, signifying the growing institutional recognition of the expanding dialogue between ideas about Jewishness and Africa. Meanwhile, Hillel International created a new role—diversity talent manager—which aimed to recruit non-white, non-Ashkenazi Jews into a professional fellowship and provide new opportunities within the Hillel movement. And in 2015 the Union for Reform Judaism appointed April Baskin as "Vice President of Audacious Hospitality" to address issues of diversity in the community. Baskin, a mixed-ancestry Jew rooted in both the Jewish and African American communities and active in the Black Lives Matter movement, was one of the first activists to use the term "Jewish women of color" in public conversations. More recent initiatives include the Jews of Color Caucus, created in 2020 by the left-leaning Jews for Racial and Economic Justice, and the Jews of Color Initiative, which aims to advance racial equity in the American Jewish community and place Jews of Color at the center of Jewish leadership. Yet, although the term, "Jews of Color" has been used as an identity category by some activists, not all persons who might be classified as non-white choose to identify with that term.

As non-white Jews have become an increasingly visible part of Jewish communities and spaces, countervailing forces have raised new questions about the meaning of whiteness and white identity for Jews of European descent in America. Does rising anti-Semitic violence in the United States mean that Jews are no longer considered white by some Americans? Does the critique that Israel is a European colonial-settler society mean that Jews can only be understood as white? The historic preoccupation with the hyphenated Jewish identity, plagued by out-marriage and assimilation, was replaced with an interrogation of Jewish whiteness that drew a false dichotomy between Jews and other racialized (darker-skinned) non-white groups. Although demographers and Jewish communal leaders alike had focused on the threat of losing Jews to assimilation and out-marriage for nearly a century, discussions began shifting to the ways in which Jewish Americans view their own relationship to race.[55]

The question of whether Jews are insiders or outsiders—as Americans or as white people—has remained salient for more than a century. Just as whiteness studies scholars had reached consensus that Jews who came from Europe had gained white privilege, scholars reminded us that European Jews were not always considered white in America, nor had they always taken on identities as white people.[56]

At the center of the question of Jewish whiteness lies the question of the race of Jews. In *The Price of Whiteness*, Goldstein applies the theories of "whiteness" studies to deconstruct how America's racial color line became the standard against which Jews came to define themselves (239). His book meticulously details the shifting contexts of the late nineteenth and early twentieth centuries in which Ashkenazi Jews negotiated their competing impulses toward inclusion as white Americans and distinctiveness as Jews.

Despite the increasing visibility of non-white Jews in America, the conflation of Jewishness and whiteness persists. In a climate of "identity politics" that frames racism as the concern only of people of color while rendering Jews as white folk, competition over claims of victimhood between Jews and other minority groups has increased.[57] The presumed whiteness of American Jews has made Jewish challenges to racial antisemitism appear out of sync with their status as white people, potentially feeding more antisemitism.[58] Ever since the 9/11 terrorist attacks at the World Trade Center were blamed on Jews by conspiracy theorists, America and the globe have witnessed an increase in overt antisemitic verbal attacks and hate crimes, a trend that has intensified in the wake of the 2016 presidential election, the Covid pandemic, and violence in the Middle East. As a consequence, Jews of Color may now find themselves in contexts where they face both racism and antisemitism.

As critical whiteness studies have gained prominence in academia, Jews have become "excluded from the multicultural space of other minority groups and by the same token, following a totalized binary logic, become part of the dominant and oppressive majority."[59] We must keep in mind that to be critically conscious of the power of white skin does not mean being against white people. Some have suggested that thinking of Jews as intersectional may be a way around the Black/white binary that dominates discussions of Jewish identity in America. Meanwhile, the growing racial and cultural diversity of Jewish Americans continues unabated.

Recommended Readings

Biale, David. *Cultures of Jews: A New History* (Schocken, 2002).

Cohen, Stephen M. "Deficient, if Not Distorted: Jewish Community Studies That Totally Rely upon Known Jewish Households," *Contemporary Jewry* 36 (2016): 343–60.

Efraim Sicher, ed. *Race, Color, Identity: Rethinking Discourses about "Jews" in the Twenty-First Century* (Berghahn, 2013).

Goldstein, Eric. *The Price of Whiteness: Jews, Race, and American Identity* (Princeton University Press, 2006).

Haynes, Bruce D. *The Soul of Judaism: Jews of African Descent in America* (New York University Press, 2018).

Phillips, Bruce. "Complicating Jewish Whiteness: Jews of Color in the American West," in *Jewish Identities in the American West: Relational Perspectives*, ed. Ellen Eisenberg (Brandeis University Press, 2022).

Ratner, Sidney. "Horace M. Kallen and Cultural Pluralism," *Modern Judaism* 4 (1984): 185–200.

Schraub, David. "White Jews: An Intersectional Approach," *Jewish Studies Review* 43 (2019): 379–407.

Notes

1. See Bruce Haynes, *The Soul of Judaism: Jews of African Descent in America* (New York University Press, 2018).

2. Lewis R. Gordon, *Fanon and the Crisis of European Man* (Routledge, 1995).

3. Reprinted Free Press, 1992.

4. See Gordon, *Fanon*; Jessica Greenebaum, "Placing Jewish Women into the Intersectionality of Race, Class and Gender," *Race, Gender and Class* 6/4 (1999): 41–60; Haynes, *Soul of Judaism*; David Schraub, "White Jews: An Intersectional Approach," *Jewish Studies Review* 43 (2019): 379–407.

5. See Haynes, *Soul of Judaism*, 40.

6. Eric Goldstein, *The Price of Whiteness: Jews, Race, and American Identity* (Princeton University Press, 2006).

7. Haynes, *Soul of Judaism*, 40.

8. University of Chicago Press.

9. Victoria C. Hattam, *In the Shadow of Race: Jews, Latinos, and Immigrant Politics in the United States* (University of Chicago Press, 2007); Haynes, *Soul of Judaism*, 41.

RACE 503

10. Lila Corwin Berman, "Sociology, Jews, and Intermarriage in Twentieth-Century America," *Jewish Social Studies* 14/2 (2008): 32–60.

11. Jacobson, *Whiteness of a Different Color: European Immigrants and the Alchemy of Race* (Harvard University Press, 1998), 8.

12. See Will Herberg, *Protestant, Catholic, Jew* (Doubleday-Anchor, 1955).

13. MIT Press, 1970.

14. Goldstein, *Price of Whiteness*, 2.

15. "The Future of Whiteness: A Map of the 'Third Wave,'" *Ethnic and Racial Studies* 31 (2008): 4–24.

16. Johns Hopkins University Press, 1992.

17. Aliya Saperstein, Andrew M. Penner, and Ryan Light, "Racial Formation in Perspective: Connecting Individuals, Institutions, and Power Relations," *Annual Review of Sociology* 39 (2013): 360.

18. Routledge.

19. *The Wages of Whiteness: Race and the Making of the American Working Class* (Verso, 1991).

20. *White Women, Race Matters: The Social Construction of Whiteness* (University of Minnesota Press, 1993), and "Introduction: Local Whitenesses, Localizing Whiteness," in *Displacing Whiteness: Essays in Social and Cultural Criticism*, ed. Frankenberg (Duke University Press, 1997): 1–34.

21. "Whiteness as Property," *Harvard Law Review*, 106–8 (1993): 1707–91.

22. *The Invention of the White Race* (Verso, 1994).

23. "How Did Jews Become White Folks?," in *Race, Steven Gregory, and Roger Sanjek* (Rutgers University Press, 1994) and *How Jews Became White Folks and What That Says about Race in America* (Rutgers University Press, 1998).

24. *The Possessive Investment in Whiteness: How White People Profit from Identity Politics* (Temple University Press, 1998).

25. Noel Ignatiev, *How the Irish Became White* (Routledge, 1995).

26. *Whiteness of a Different Color.*

27. Brodkin Sacks, "How Did Jews."

28. New York University Press, 2008.

29. James R. Hackney, "Derrick Bell's Re-Sounding: W. E. B. Du Bois, Modernism, and Critical Race Scholarship," *Law and Social Inquiry* 23, no. 1 (1998): 141–64.

30. Saperstein et al., "Racial Formation."

31. Geraldine Heng, *The Invention of Race in the European Middle Ages* (Cambridge University Press, 2018).

32. Heng, *Invention.*

33. Holt.

34. Goldstein, *Price of Whiteness*, 228

35. David Goldstein, *Jacob's Legacy: A Genetic View of Jewish History* (Yale University Press, 2008); Haynes, *Soul of Judaism.*

36. Judy Malz, "Israeli Rabbinate Accused of Using DNA Testing to Prove Jewishness," *Haaretz* (2019).

37. Aaron J. Hahn Tapper, Ari Y. Kelman, and Aliya Saperstein, "Counting on Whiteness: Religion, Race, Ethnicity, and the Politics of Jewish Demography," *Journal for the Scientific Study of Religion* 62 (2023): 28–48.

38. Bruce Phillips, "Complicating Jewish Whiteness: Jews of Color in the American West," in *Jewish Identities in the American West: Relational Perspectives*, ed. Ellen Eisenberg (Brandeis University Press, 2022).

39. Phillips, "Complicating."

40. Cohen, "Deficient, if Not Distorted: Jewish Community Studies That Totally Rely upon Known Jewish Households," *Contemporary Jewry* 36, no. 3 (2016): 343–60.

41. "How Many Jews of Color Are There? Recognizing Jewish Diversity: Science and Controversy," *Contemporary Jewry* 44 (2024): 509–29.

42. Tapper et al., "Counting."

43. Haynes, *Soul of Judaism*, 14.

44. University of Alabama Press, 2014.

45. "'Hatzaad Harishon' Broke Barriers—Until Race, Identity Questions Proved Too Much," *Forward* (2022).

46. See Haynes, *Soul of Judaism;* Melanie Kaye/Kantrowitz, *The Colors of Jews: Racial Politics and Radical Diasporism* (Indiana University Press, 2007); and Michael Scott Alexander and Bruce D. Haynes, "The Color Issue: An Introduction," *American Jewish History* 100 (January 2016). Meanwhile, a new cadre of Afro-Jewish scholarship emerged that challenged normative understandings of Jewish identity.

47. Haynes, *Soul of Judaism;* Kaye/Kantrowitz, *Colors;* Alexander and Haynes, "Color."

48. "On Being and Not Being Black and Jewish," in *The Multiracial Experience*, ed. M. Root (Sage, 1996), 140–52.

49. Temple University Press, 1993.

50. Fanon (Routledge, 1995); *Bad Faith* (Humanities, 1995).

51. Duke University Press, 1997.

52. Schocken, 2002.

53. SUNY Press, 2012.

54. University of Nebraska Press, 2016.

55. Efraim Sicher, ed. *Race, Color, Identity: Rethinking Discourses about "Jews" in the Twenty-First Century* (Berghahn, 2013).

56. Goldstein, *Price of Whiteness;* Phillips, "Complicating," 328.

57. Glynis Cousin and Robert Fine, "A Common Cause: Reconnecting the Study of Racism and Antisemitism," *European Societies* 14, no. 2 (2012): 166–85.

58. Balázs Berkovits, "Israel as a White Colonial-Settler State in Activist Social Science," in *Contending with Antisemitism in a Rapidly Changing Political Climate*, ed. A. H. Rosenfeld (Indiana University Press, 2021).

59. Berkovits, "Israel," 77.

24

Gender

Laura Levitt, Temple University

ADDRESSING THE RADICAL transformative role of gender, sexuality, and women's studies in defining and learning about Jews, Judaism, and Jewishness since the 1970s, this chapter interrogates the seeming triumphalism of this very claim. As earlier chapters in this volume make clear, Judaism has always been gendered. When wasn't Judaism gendered? Can we even mark a beginning at all? There have always been Jews of different genders, and most pointedly the gender binary of male and female continues to shape Jewish languages, texts, and practices. Feminist attention to gender has challenged us to ask new questions about which legacies and stories matter and how we engage with those subjects, texts, and other materials. It has also had profound implications for how we engage with many sources that previous generations of scholars had not considered—material objects, the stuff of everyday life, the ephemera of Jewish women's lives. Gender has also significantly transformed our understanding of who gets to perform Jewish Studies scholarship, what kinds of training and critical engagement inform those who do scholarship on gender, and a myriad other topics across the subfields of Jewish Studies.

Adrienne Rich wrote long ago about her own wild patience, a patience that had taken her just so far, or is it only so far?[1] I have rewritten this sentence many times trying to decide on one of these constructions only to realize that both are at play. In many ways this chapter speaks to this gendered ambivalence. It attempts to capture the tremendous strides that have been made thus far in Jewish Studies as scholars address questions about gender, sexuality, women, and increasingly the full spectrum of embodied performances of gender beyond any simple binary of male and female. Yet, this chapter also marks the space of

505

possibility and recompense for all that remains entrenched in less capacious understandings of all these topics. It asks us to consider how much work remains to be done to make gender fully a part of Jewish Studies. The chapter focuses on three critical concerns in its three sections: "Since When?" addresses the temporal dimensions of this work; "The Logic of the Supplement" considers the dynamics that inform these feminist interventions of inclusion and transformation; and "Dispersion" shows how gender has infused Jewish Studies even as its impact may be dissipating; in other words, where the field stands now in relation to these topics.

Since When?

I posed many of these questions in the heady feminist theoretical days of poststructural and critical identity politics in the 1990s in the collection *Judaism since Gender*, which considered the many internal challenges posed by feminist scholarship within Jewish Studies, both its promises and its disappointments.[2] We insisted on making vividly clear what those of us in Jewish Studies bring to gender studies. This discussion builds on that work in three parts: "Always Already Gendered," "Since the 1970s," and "Since the 1990s."

Always Already Gendered

At least since the beginning of formal Jewish scholarship with the Wissenschaft des Judentums movement in nineteenth-century Germany, the discourse of Jewish Studies has been a masculinist one focused on the experiences, thoughts, writings, and practices of mostly Jewish men, often substituting these claims for an overall account of Jewish history, culture, and religious practice. Jewish Studies has read this European masculinist discourse as universal. Scholars like Daniel Boyarin and Sarah Imhoff among others, have turned their gaze to questions about Jewish masculinity.[3] No longer universalized in these feminist works, masculinity is something particular and worth studying in and of itself.

Scholarship on gender, sexuality, and feminist theory has brought into view the fact of gender's abiding but often invisible, undertheorized, or unacknowledged implications for how we understand not only Judaism, Jews, and Jewishness but also all kinds of communities and cultures around the world. Gender enables us to see how masculinist discourses and perspectives shaped the scholarly reading of ancient texts. Notable among scholars of the ancient world, biblical scholar Carol Meyer had us rethink ancient Judaism through the quotidian remains of everyday life, which enabled us to see ancient women. Or, by addressing early rabbinic texts in relation to grave goods and especially the remains of ancient spindle whirls and looms, Miriam Peskowitz helped us reimagine gender and labor in what she referred to as "Roman Period Judaism."[4] The basic point that gender studies scholars bring to Jewish Studies and to all the disciplines of the humanities and social sciences is that women and other gendered people were always part of the Jewish experience. For example, recent scholarship in rabbinics by Max Strassfeld shows that a range of genders are considered in complicated, often hypothetical case studies, if not always as embodied presences.[5]

Scholars of gender in Jewish Studies work alongside scholars of religion, history, anthropology, and textual studies to reconsider how and what we know, and what we thought we already knew about the (Jewish) pasts and about a full range of Jewish texts, objects, and practices. This work challenges us to rethink academic priorities, to ask different scholarly questions, and to consider the grand narratives we tell, change, or otherwise disregard.

Since the 1970s

Even though the world has always been gendered, scholars and activists only began to recognize this beginning in the 1970s. This period marks the beginning of Jewish women's activism in the broader second-wave U.S. feminist movement and in Jewish communal life, which has shaped how we think about all these matters ever since. In the 1970s Jewish feminists asked critical questions about where were women in Jewish texts, Jewish practices, and the historical records of Jewish life across the globe. They began in earnest to demand an equal role in Jewish communal life and in synagogue worship. And although a few Jewish women had served as rabbis and communal leaders before the 1970s,[6] the ordination of the first women rabbis and the first lesbian rabbis in the United States in the Reform and Reconstructionist movements happened during this decade.[7] This period also saw books and articles on Jewish women and the development of Jewish feminist journals like *Lilith Magazine,* an abiding Jewish feminist resource ever since.[8] Feminist Jews created new liturgies and rituals. Much of this early work was additive as it brought women into our understanding of sacred texts, histories, literatures, and practices. This work radically changed the norms of scholarship, bringing feminist scholars into the various subfields of Jewish Studies.[9]

Jewish feminists turned to liberationist models of inclusion—models that built on the universalized promise of classic liberalism—to challenge the status of women in Jewish life, including the academy. They considered the status of Jewish women from an assumption of human equality. For instance, Judith Plaskow's groundbreaking Jewish feminist theology, *Standing again at Sinai*, demanded the inclusion of women in all areas of Jewish life.[10] Jewish feminists also questioned how liberalism could transcend its own historical specificity as the product of a European, middle-class, male, and often Christian discourse, a critique that became more salient in the 1990s. Still, liberal promises that brought some property-owning Jewish men into western nation-states as citizens undergirded second-wave Jewish feminists' claims to equal rights and the inclusion of women in Jewish scholarship and communal life.[11]

These efforts were especially challenging in global feminist contexts; for example, the 1975 United Nations resolution that declared Zionism to be a form of racism came out of the world conference of the International Women's Year held in Mexico City.[12] Criticisms of Israel raised questions for some about antisemitism in the women's movement even as it challenged Jewish political commitments on the Left.[13] Many Jewish feminists were concerned not only about Israel but also about the ways that their Jewishness was not recognized in feminist communities. Challenges around the relationship between antisemitism and racism and issues of class led many radical Jewish feminists to oppose antisemitism alongside other forms of injustice and inequity. These efforts were a part of what became critical feminist identity politics and brought Jewish women into alliances with Black feminists and other women of color who together pushed against the limits of liberal inclusion. These radical feminists resisted demands for a politics of sameness and instead insisted on embracing difference. Spearheaded by lesbian activists, poets, and writers,[14] they came together through an acknowledgment of their differences. Their efforts were crucial to what would become intersectional, postcolonial, and other forms of critical feminist politics and theorizing, efforts that began to shape Jewish studies by the 1990s.[15]

These challenges also figured in how, by the 1990s, some in Jewish Studies had come to align themselves with canonical versions of the liberal arts, often against the more radical interventions of Black, ethnic, and gender studies.[16] Although there were and still are a wide range of Jewish Studies scholars on all sides of these issues, these remain difficult questions for Jewish feminist scholars in Jewish Studies whose efforts were further strengthened as Jewish Studies scholars began to be trained in women's studies in the 1980s and 1990s. By the

1990s Jewish feminist scholars, along with other feminist theorists, began to revisit the terms of liberal inclusion for Jews and for women in both Jewish Studies and in women's studies.[17]

Since the 1990s

Since the 1990s, Jewish feminist scholars have helped us appreciate the blind spots and structural invisibilities that mark Jewish life. These scholars have opened our eyes to other absences, including those around gender performance, sexuality, race, disability, class, displacement, and colonization.

With these concerns in mind, feminist scholars have been reshaping the study of Jewish thought and philosophy.[18] Ongoing interest in the works of Jewish women writers and of Jewish women in popular culture continues to fuel Jewish literary scholarship, and Jewish feminist ethnographers working in religious studies, anthropology, and folklore are using gender as a lens to reimagine Jewish culture and ritual.[19] And yet, even as new works continue to chip away at masculinist, heteronormative, and cisgender assumptions, these discourses continue to permeate many of the subfields of Jewish Studies. At the same time, important Jewish feminist works are often ignored in gender studies.

Since the 1990s, many scholars of gender in Jewish Studies have engaged in intersectional, transnational feminist and queer theorizing.[20] In alliance with scholars of race, ethnicity, language, class, and disability, they continue to make explicit the political stakes of all our scholarly work.[21] These efforts include reckoning with the political origins of Jewish Studies, particularly the ways that the Wissenschaft was concerned with making Judaism "a proper object of study" and, as such, a way to validate the culture, religion, and history of Jews.[22] Beginning in the 1990s, Jewish feminist and queer scholars asked powerful epistemic questions that challenged the vision of liberal inclusion espoused by many second-wave Jewish feminists. They have made clear that it was never possible to simply add women or other "others" to already existing scholarship.[23] These additions continue to demand new paradigms and new critical lenses.

The Logic of the Supplement: Addition and Transformation

In a now classic essay "Women's History," Joan Scott argues that the work of feminist scholars is "not simply a matter of adding something that had been previously missing. Instead, there is a troubling ambiguity inherent in the project of women's history, for it is at once an innocuous supplement to and a radical replacement for established history" (241).[24]

Scott offers a genealogical account of the creation and growth of this subfield of historical research and explains the complex relationship between those who study women's history and the broader field of history. She also describes how her own role as a historian of women has changed over time. Challenging what she understood as the still prevailing operative assumptions of those doing women's history, Scott begins by explaining how professionalism often masks the gender politics of history (and other fields of scholarship) as *not* always being political. The false dichotomy of history versus ideology prevents the field of history from changing and constrains the work of feminist scholars. These are, of course, abiding issues for Jewish Studies that, from its beginning, has sought to prove that Judaism was a worthy subject of study and that Jews, because they have a viable and significant history and culture, were a people worthy of both a place in the academy and citizenship. What is most significant about Scott's argument is her pointed challenge to the additive nature of feminist work—the idea that historians of women could simply add their new insights to history without having to rethink the grand narrative/s that mark French, American, Jewish, or, for that matter, world history.

Scott turns to Virginia Woolf and Jacques Derrida to explain this dilemma, which she describes in terms of "the logic of the supplement." In *A Room of One's Own*,[25] Virginia Woolf muses about the inadequacies of existing history, a history that needs rewriting because it "often seems a little queer as it is, unreal, lopsided"; that is, lacking, insufficient, incomplete. Apparently drawing back from rewriting history, Scott tentatively offers what appears to be another solution: "Why ... not add a supplement to history, calling it, of course, by some inconspicuous name so that women might figure there without impropriety?" (241).

Scott then goes on to explain the significance of this seemingly "inconspicuous" intervention. Calling attention to Woolf's sarcasm and her careful efforts to maintain a form of propriety, Scott argues that this supplement is "a complicated project" and "ambitious beyond my daring": Even as she tries to circumscribe its difficulties, the supplement evokes contradictory implications. Women are both added to history, and they occasion its rewriting; they provide something extra, and they are necessary for completion; they are superfluous and indispensable (241).

The work of addition demands a reconsideration of the frame as a whole. And so, Scott links Woolf's supplement to Derrida's efforts to "deconstruct Western metaphysics" (241). The supplement, according to Derrida, is "undecidable" because it is both an addition and a substitute or a replacement. It is something added, extra, superfluous, above, and beyond what is already fully present; it is also a replacement for what is absent, missing, and lacking and thus is required for completion or wholeness. "The supplement is neither a plus nor a minus, neither an outside nor the complement of an inside, neither accident nor essence." It is (in Barbara Johnson's words) "superfluous and necessary, dangerous and redemptive" (241).

For Scott, "the logic of the supplement" captures the ambiguity at the heart of women's history and why it must be rethought. It is not a simple addition but instead demands an epistemological transformation of the field as a whole. History must change, as indeed Jewish Studies must change.

In Scott's account, this insight creates a kind of trajectory from the additive to the epistemological. This transformation comes with a demand for theory that confronts how the addition of women to history needs to be addressed not as a minor change but rather as a transformational shift in how we do history or, in this case, Jewish Studies. In Scott's essay, the move from the additive to the epistemic is linear; one comes, it seems, to replace the other. But as I return to this generative text in the context of this chapter, I am struck by the ways this linear trajectory obscures more than it illuminates. It seems to say once others are added we can simply move on to epistemic concerns. And yet, over these many years, it seems more apt to argue that what has taken place in all kinds of fields, but in this case Jewish studies, is an ongoing interplay between additive and transformative modes of engagement. The work of inclusion, the additive, is always already bound to the epistemic. We never stopped the work of adding. That labor remains incomplete even as we continue to recalibrate our epistemic assumptions.

These dynamics best capture what gender studies continues to bring to Jewish Studies. Recent works by Laura Leibman and Samira Mehta demonstrate how this works. Leibman's *Once We Were Slaves*[26] and her award-winning *The Art of the Jewish Family*[27] are illustrative. In these works, Leibman adds profoundly to our understanding of the lives of early American Jewish women. But to tell these stories, this work also requires a radical rethinking of the archive and how we engage with material culture and the stuff of everyday life. Leibman also makes clear that scholars need to address simultaneously questions of race and class, as well as gender, as she illustrates these imbrications. Leibman allows us to appreciate not only the once invisible lives of these women but also how their racial and class identifications shift and change depending on where these women and men lived. Here the additive is profoundly bound up with epistemic and ontological concerns. Although Mehta focuses on heterosexual couples and families in *Beyond Chrismukkah*, her work on intermarriage from the mid-twentieth century to the present, she makes clear the specificity of her subjects' positions. In so doing, she does not naturalize them. Heterosexuality is not the only or the universal position, and sexuality and gender are not Mehta's only concern. This work demonstrates how the intersection of race, ethnicity, and language also shapes the dynamics of intermarriage in ways invisibilized by dominant discourses that did not in the past attend to these forms of difference.[28]

Informed by gender, ethnography, and new archives, these works demonstrate how by adding to our understanding of Jewish history and practice, we are already engaged in epistemic work. The work of Jewish scholarship changes, as do the disciplinary frames, the kinds of questions scholars ask, and the places we do this work. Recent scholarship in the field reaffirms this dynamic as it deepens our knowledge of so many aspects of Jewish lives, past and present. Examples include Elisheva Baumgarten's work on mothers and children in medieval Ashkenaz[29]; Eve Krakowski's work on girls in medieval Egypt[30]; Ayala Fader's work on contemporary Jewish Hasidic femininity[31]; and and Dalia Ofer and Lenore Weitzman's powerful work on women and the Holocaust.[32] Other contemporary Jewish feminist scholars have considered questions of Jewish women's political activism including Melissa Klapper's work on Jewish women's activism in America,[33] Joyce Antler's recent history of radical Jewish feminism, and Lihi Ben Shitrit's work on Israeli women's activism—efforts that cross the political spectrum.[34]

Dispersion

Merriam-Webster Dictionary provides several definitions for the word "disperse." When used as a transitive verb, it means "to cause to break up," as what happens when the police disperse a crowd. But it also means "to cause to become spread widely." Here, the power of what is spread is not broken up but is made more vivid.[35] When used as an intransitive verb, to disperse includes the notion of rupture: "to break up in a random fashion" where order is lost. The word can also mean to dissipate or to vanish. I conclude this chapter by respecting the promise of dissemination while considering some of the dangers built into this term, particularly the notion that what is dispersed can also evaporate or simply vanish.[36] I begin with these definitions to call attention to the ambivalence, perhaps a form of wild patience, that marks the current state of gender in Jewish Studies.

The work of gender, sexuality, and women's studies within Jewish Studies is now occurring most powerfully and productively inside its many subfields—history, literature (comparative literature, Hebrew, Yiddish, English, Arabic, Ladino, Russian, Polish, and so many other languages), religious studies, textual studies (biblical, rabbinic, and medieval), Holocaust studies, and Middle Eastern Jewish studies (Mizrahi and Sephardic histories and cultures)—and in Jewish ethnographic work, linguistic analysis, and sociology and demographic studies. In between and among these various subfields sophisticated scholarly work informed by questions of gender and sexuality is happening but not in isolation. These questions now interact and intersect with language, practice, race and ethnicity, class, and questions about national forms of identification (Israel studies). And in each of these specific venues of Jewish studies, scholars are grappling with both epistemic issues and critical efforts at inclusion: adding new voices, texts, objects, and practices to the kinds of work that constitute these subfields. This scholarship is informed both by efforts within Jewish Studies and, perhaps more importantly, the transformations around gender and sexuality that inform the broader disciplines of history, literature, anthropology, sociology, religious studies, and linguistics, to name just a few.

Perhaps what unites at least some of this work in its current dispersion is attention to queer theory, trans theory, material culture, everyday life, and issues of voice. How do we do scholarship with these issues in mind? How are we experimenting with form, using the first person, engaging ethnographically, and paying attention to material, sonic, and visual culture; ritual; and performativity as we do our work now? How do we position ourselves as participants and observers? What is the role of the writer/scholar in their scholarship? These efforts continue to saturate Jewish Studies, even though there is no central site defining this gendered work. Dispersion captures this ambivalence characterized by greater coverage and less concentration all at the same time.

What began as just adding women has complicated what we thought we already knew. It has demanded a rethinking of the grand narratives we posit, the kinds of scholarship we value as a field, and who does this kind of work. These issues are far from settled. Unlike Thomas Kuhn's notion of a paradigm shift, these challenges are still very much in play, instead following Joan Scott's later vision of feminist theory and practice as an ongoing critique.[37]

Recommended Readings

Adler, Rachel. *Engendering Judaism: An Inclusive Theology and Ethics* (Beacon, 1999).

Beck, Evelyn, ed. *Nice Jewish Girls: A Lesbian Anthology* (Beacon, 1997).

Benjamin, Mara. *The Obligated Self: Maternal Subjectivity and Jewish Thought* (Indiana University Press, 2018).

Benjamin, Mara. "Tracing the Contours of a Half Century of Jewish Feminist Theology," *Journal of Feminist Studies in Religion* 36 (2020): 11–31.

Biale, Rachel. *Women and Jewish Law: The Essential Texts, Their History, and Their Relevance for Today* (Schocken, 1984; 1995).

Hyman, Paula. *Gender and Assimilation in Jewish History: The Roles and Representation of Women* (University of Washington Press, 1995).

Ilan, Tal. *A Feminist Commentary on the Babylonia Talmud: Introduction and Studies* (Mohr Seibeck, 2007).

Kessler, Gwynn, "Judaism, Feminism, and Gender," in *Judaism 3: Culture and Modernity (RM Die Religionen der Menschheit)*, ed. Michael Tilly and Burton L. Visotzky (Kohlhammer, 2020), 169–97.

Plaskow, Judith. *Standing again at Sinai: Judaism from a Feminist Perspective* (Harper San Francisco, 1990).

Schachter, Allison. *Women Writing Jewish Modernity 1919–1939* (Northwestern University Press, 2021).

Shalvi/Hyman Encyclopedia of Jewish Women (Jewish Women's Archive online, https://jwa .org/encyclopedia).

Notes

1. *A Wild Patience Has Taken Me This Far: Poems 1978–1981* (Norton, 1981).

2. Miriam Peskowitz and Laura Levitt, eds. (Routledge, 1997).

3. Boyarin, *Unheroic Conduct: The Rise of Heterosexuality and the Invention of the Jewish Man* (University of California Press, 1997), and Imhoff, *Masculinity and the Making of American Judaism* (University of Indiana Press, 2017).

4. Meyers, *Rediscovering Eve: Israelite Women in Context* (Oxford University Press, 2012), and Peskowitz, *Spinning Fantasies: Rabbis, Gender, and History* (University of California Press, 1997).

5. See Strassfeld, *Trans Talmud: Androgynes and Eunuchs in Rabbinic Literature* (University of California Press, 2022), and Sarra Lev, "The Rabbinic Androginos and the 'Sometimes Jew': Investigating One Model of Jewishness," *Journal of Jewish Identities* 11 (2018): 75–85.

6. Early modern women leaders and rabbis include Regina Jonas and Lily Montagu. For more on these women, see the Jewish Women's Archive and its *Shalvi/Hyman Encyclopedia of Jewish Women*, online at jwa.org.

7. On the ordination of Sally Priesand in 1972, see the Jewish Women's Archive, *Encyclopedia*, online at jwa.org. This first cohort included importantly the first lesbian rabbis. See Rebecca Alpert, Sue Levi Elwell, and Shirley Idelson, eds., *Lesbian Rabbis: The First Genera-*

tion (Rutgers University Press, 2001). This activism led not only to the ordination of women but also of queer, trans, and nonbinary people as rabbis, cantors, and educators in most liberal Jewish communities, including Modern Orthodoxy.

8. On new liturgies and rituals, see Ritual Well, online at ritualwell.org, and *Lilith,* online at lilith.org. For more on these kinds of publications and practices, see Laura Levitt and Miriam Peskowitz, "Jewish Feminism, Oxford Bibliographies, Jewish Studies, 2015," Oxford Bibliographies, online; and Gwynn Kessler, "Judaism, Feminism, and Gender," in *Judaism 3: Culture and Modernity (RM Die Religionen der Menschheit),* ed. Tilly and Visotzky (Kohlhammer, 2020), esp. 169–73.

9. Earlier generations of Jewish women did engage in Jewish scholarship, including the writing of Jewish histories. Nevertheless, these scholars did not necessarily address issues of gender in their work. For a discussion of some of this early work, see the introduction to *Judaism since Gender,* 1–14, esp. 5 and nn. 7, 12–13. See also Paula Hyman, *Gender and Assimilation in Jewish History* (University of Washington Press, 1995).

10. Harper San Francisco, 1990.

11. Susannah Heschel, ed., *On Being a Jewish Feminist.* Many of these works were crossover books that introduced the broader Jewish community to Jewish feminism and its promises of a more inclusive Judaism. These works include Rachel Biale, *Women and Jewish Law: The Essential Texts, Their History, and Their Relevance for Today* (Schocken, 1984); Blu Greenberg, *Women and Judaism: A View from Tradition* (Jewish Publication Society, 1981); and Susan Weidman Schneider, *Jewish and Female: Choices and Changes in Our Lives* (Simon & Schuster, 1984).

12. On the UN resolution that was passed in 1975 and revoked in 1991, see United Nations; The Question of Palestine, Unispal Database, General Assembly Resolution 3379, online at un .org. These issues around Israel and Zionism remain contentious in feminist politics. I note these early developments to help contextualize contemporary debates.

13. On some of these challenges, see Letty Cottin Pogrebin's critical essay, "Anti-Semitism in the Women's Movement," *Ms. Magazine,* June 1982, 45–46 and 48. Pogrebin writes at some length about attending the International Women's Conference in her book, *Deborah, Golda, and Me: Being Female and Jewish in America* (Crown, 1991). Issues around Israel, especially after the 1982 Israeli invasion of Lebanon, became a focal point for contributors to the lesbian feminist anthology *Nice Jewish Girls;* later prefaces and revisions to the volume document and discuss these issues; see Evelyn Beck, ed., *Nice Jewish Girls: A Lesbian Anthology* (Persephone, 1982 and multiple reprints).

14. These efforts can be seen in feminist publishing collectives such as Sinister Wisdom that first published in the early 1980s the anthology *Tribe of Dinah* and the important volume *Yours in Struggle;* see Irena Klepfisz and Melanie Kaye/Kantrowitz, eds., *Tribe of Dinah* (Sinister Wisdom, 1986), and Elly Bulkin, Minnie Bruce Pratt, and Barbara Smith, *Yours in Struggle: Three Feminist Perspectives on Anti-Semitism and Racism* (Firebrand, 1984). These are bound to work by Black feminists and women of color, including important works such the Combahee River Collective Statement, United States, 2015, Web Archive (first pub. 1977), and Audre Lorde, *Sister Outsider: Essays and Speeches* (Crossing, 1984).

15. This work is often figured in terms of "intersectionality," a term coined by legal scholar Kimberle Crenshaw in "Mapping the Margins: Intersectionality, Identity Politics, and Violence

against Women of Color," *Stanford Law Review* 43, no. 6 (1991): 1241–99. With roots in critical feminist identity politics, Jewish feminists have been deploying these kinds of intersectional insights in their work for some time; see n.14 and for a recent rereading, see Laura Levitt, "The I in My Text: Revisiting Critical Feminist Identity Politics, Refusing the Allures of Purity," *Shofar* 37, no. 2 (2019): 91–106. For more on Jewish women of color and Jews of color, see Loolwa Khazzoom, ed., *The Flying Camel* (Seal, 2003); the archive of *Bridges: A Jewish Feminist Journal,* online; and Melanie Kaye/Kantrowitz, *The Color of Jews: Racial Politics and Radical Diasporism* (Indiana University Press, 2007).

16. See David Biale, Michael Galchinsky, and Susannah Heschel, eds., *Insider/Outsider: American Jews and Multiculturalism* (University of California Press, 1998).

17. Laura Levitt, *Jews and Feminism: The Ambivalent Search for Home* (Routledge, 1997). See also *Judaism since Gender.*

18. See Susan E. Shapiro, "A Matter of Discipline: Reading for Gender in Jewish Philosophy," in *Judaism since Gender*, 158–73; Mara Benjamin, *The Obligated Self: Maternal Subjectivity and Jewish Thought* (Indiana University Press, 2018); and Andrea Dara Cooper, *Gendering Modern Jewish Thought* (Indiana University Press, 2021).

19. For literary works, see Lori Harrison-Kahn, ed., *Superwoman and Other Writings by Miriam Michelson* (Wayne State University Press, 2019); Helene Flanzbaum, ed., "Jews, Women, and Popular Culture," a special issue of *Studies in American Jewish Literature* 41, no. 2 (2022); Allison Schachter, *Women Writing Jewish Modernity 1919–1939*; and Fradl Shtok, *From the Provinces: Selected Stories* (Northwestern University Press, 2021). For ethnographic and anthropological work, see Riv Ellen Prell, *Fighting to Become Americans: Jews, Gender, and the Anxiety of Assimilation* (Beacon, 1999); Vanessa Ochs, *Inventing Jewish Ritual* (Jewish Publication Society, 2007); and Jodi Eichler-Levine, *Painted Pomegranates and Needlepoint Rabbis: How Jews Craft Resilience and Create Community (Where Religion Lives)* (University of North Carolina Press, 2020).

20. See, for example, Daniel Boyarin, Danial Itzkovitz, and Ann Pellegrini, eds., *Queer Theory and the Jewish Question* (Columbia University Press, 2003), and Lital Levy and Allison Schachter, "Jewish Literature/World Literature: Between the Local and the Transnational," *PMLA* 130, no. 1(2015): 92–109.

21. See Julia Watts Belser, *Rabbinic Tales of Destruction: Gender, Sex, and Disability in the Ruins of Jerusalem* (Oxford University Press), published in 2018, when the Association for Jewish Studies (AJS) Taskforce on Diversity and Inclusion run by feminist scholar Karla Goldman began raising powerful structural questions about racial, ethnicity, cultural, and religious differences in the AJS.

22. On this point, see the introduction to *Judaism since Gender*, 2–5, and Robert Baird, "Boys of the *Wissenschaft*," 86–94.

23. See Miriam Peskowitz, "Engendering Jewish History," in *Judaism since Gender*, 17–39.

24. In *American Feminist Thought at Century's End: A Reader*, ed. L. Kauffman (Blackwell, 1993), 234–57.

25. Hogarth, 1929.

26. Oxford University Press, 2021.

27. Bard Graduate Center, 2020.

28. See Samira Mehta, *Beyond Chrismukkah: The Christian-Jewish Interfaith Family in the United States* (University of North Carolina Press, 2018) and "Asian American Jews, Race and Religious Identity," *Journal of the American Academy of Religion* 20, no. 20 (2021): 1–28.

29. *Mothers and Children: Family Life in Medieval Europe* (Princeton University Press, 2004).

30. *Coming of Age in Medieval Egypt: Women's Adolescence, Jewish Law, and Ordinary Culture* (Princeton University Press, 2018).

31. *Mitzvah Girls: Bringing Up the Next Generation of Hasidic Jews in Brooklyn* (Princeton University Press, 2009).

32. *Women in the Holocaust* (Yale University Press, 1999).

33. *Ballots, Babies, and Banners of Peace: American Jewish Women's Activism, 1890–1940* (NYU Press, 2013).

34. *Righteous Transgressions: Women's Activism on the Israeli and Palestinian Religious Right* (Princeton University Press, 2015).

35. The dictionary offers the example of troops coming to cover more territory, even as a third definition suggests that the term can mean "to cause to evaporate or vanish." The second set of definitions suggest that the term means "to spread or distribute from a fixed or constant source," an archaic usage meaning to "disseminate" or "disperse." (Merriam-Webster.com, 2022).

36. Strangely, the first definition I found under the term "dispersion" was "capitalized, Judaism," which took me to the first definition of the term "diaspora" and "the settling of scattered colonies of Jews outside ancient Palestine after the Babylonian exile."

37. See Kuhn, *The Structure of Scientific Revolutions* (University of Chicago Press, 1996); Scott, *Women's Studies on the Edge* (Duke University Press, 2008).

25

Mizrahi Culture

Lital Levy, Princeton University

IMAGINE A STACK of five books on your desk: a biography of a nineteenth-century Italian rabbi of North African descent[1]; a book about Israeli slapstick films featuring Mizrahi Jews[2]; a history of Jews in twentieth-century Iran[3]; a foray into the musical traditions of Syrian Jews in New York, Mexico, and Israel[4]; and a study of nineteenth-century Ladino literature and theater.[5] What do these very different books have in common? Together, do they constitute a field or even a subfield? This small but representative selection of scholarship illustrates the difficulty of defining the field of Sephardi/Mizrahi studies. A multidisciplinary field, it is premised on a contested and somewhat arbitrary religious-ethnic category of identity called "Sephardi/ Mizrahi." The name "Sephardi/ Mizrahi" itself subsumes a vast array of historic Jewish communities, covering an area stretching from Morocco to India and including culturally diverse populations who spoke different languages and did not necessarily think of themselves as Sephardic. Nevertheless, underlying the framing of Sephardi/Mizrahi studies is a common impulse: a shared sense of the urgent need to uncover the historical experiences of Jews beyond the Western and Eastern European contexts that had long dominated the narrative of Jewish history.

Research into the lives and recent histories of Sephardi and Mizrahi Jewry dates to the nineteenth century when, sensing the winds of change, Jewish rabbis and intellectuals in the Ottoman Empire and North Africa took it upon themselves to collect materials pertaining to their communities' history and customs and to disseminate the information. They published works of auto-ethnography and historical studies in their own newspapers and journals and shared them with Jewish publications based in Europe and Palestine. Pioneering studies of North African Jewry were also carried out during the colonial era by Ashkenazi and French scholars. Decades later, after the massive upheavals of the mid-twentieth century and the dislocation of most of those communities, a new recovery effort was spearheaded by Sephardi and Mizrahi Jews in Israel, who sought both a richer self-understanding of their historical origins and equitable representation in Israeli institutions and public life.

With the expansion of the field from the 1980s to the present, international scholars have come to understand that although Ashkenazi Jews made up the vast majority of the global Jewish population in the modern era, their experiences do not tell us the whole story of the recent Jewish past. The long-standing exclusion of non-Ashkenazi subjects from the general purview of modern Jewish Studies necessitated the creation of a separate scholarly space. In this sense, Sephardi/Mizrahi studies is similar to other fields that arose in response to conditions of exclusion, such as women's studies, ethnic studies, or queer studies. Although not all scholarly work on Sephardi and Mizrahi topics is driven by this mission, the idea of a field of Sephardi/Mizrahi studies emerged both from the recognition that Jewish Studies and Jewish history were too synonymous with Ashkenazi Jewish experience and from the desire for differentiation and a corrective narrative. The temporal purview of Sephardi/Mizrahi studies mainly concerns the modern era for two reasons: first, because the demographic and cultural dynamics of the Jewish world changed dramatically after the seventeeth century (in the premodern world, Jewish demographics were flipped in favor of the Islamic world); and second, because this subfield of Jewish Studies formed in response to the inequities of the broader academic discipline of Jewish Studies from the nineteenth century onward, especially the misleading characterization and incomplete understanding of the modern experience of non-Ashkenazi Jewries.

The last decades of the twentieth century and the first decades of the twenty-first century have seen a boom in research on Sephardi and Mizrahi Jewries, expressed both in the variety of topics and quantity of publications. Given the current flourishing of research, some scholars in the field are calling for new paradigms and framings that emphasize the relevance of their Jewish subject matter to regional, imperial, civilizational, or national histories (Middle Eastern and North African, Islamic, Ottoman, etc.)—and, for that matter, global histories—as opposed to sequestering it into the more isolated rubrics of Jewish history or Jewish Studies. Such a shift calls into question the continuing relevance of Sephardi/Mizrahi studies as the primary designation for studies based on non-Ashkenazi Jews.

Setting such growing pains aside, it is safe to say that from the Jewish Studies perspective, Sephardi/Mizrahi studies is a quickly growing interdisciplinary subfield. In broadest terms, it covers all aspects of the experiences of the Jewish communities of Asia, North Africa, South Asia, Central Asia, southeastern Europe, and their descendants (with the exceptions of Ethiopian Jewry and the Romaniotes, native Greek Jews who spoke a Greek dialect; for reasons beyond the scope of this chapter, Ethiopian and Romaniote Jews are currently considered distinct Jewish communities). As such, Sephardi/Mizrahi history overlaps largely (although not exclusively) with the history of Jews in the Islamic world. Among the leading questions driving contemporary Sephardi/Mizrahi studies are the following: How did non-Ashkenazi Jewries experience the transition to modernity and nationalism in the nineteenth and twentieth centuries? What were their social, economic, intellectual, cultural, and religious lives like during the two centuries prior to the disruptions of the mid-twentieth century, including their internal communal organization, contacts with other global Jewish communities, and relationships to surrounding non-Jewish societies? How did they see and understand themselves as Jews, as well as in other capacities—as residents of mixed societies, urban dwellers, imperial or national citizens, members of certain social classes, or members of professions? What contributions did they make to the major events and trends of their time and place on the local and global levels? What happened to them in the process of their emigration from their lands of origin to Israel, Europe, and the Americas? In Israel, to which most of these communities emigrated, how did Mizrahi identity and culture form, and what are the distinct experiences and histories of Sephardi and Mizrahi communities within Israeli society?

As an introduction to Sephardi/Mizrahi studies, this chapter explains this subfield's origins and trajectory, surveys recent advancements in the scholarship, and concludes with the current state of the field and future directions. This overview of Sephardi/Mizrahi studies is meant to provide a representative view of the field, but at the same time, it is important to note that "Sephardi/ Mizrahi studies" is not the sole or exclusive designation or scholarly home for most of the work in question. A given publication about Sephardi or Mizrahi Jews may speak directly to an array of scholarly fields, crossing over between Middle Eastern studies and Jewish Studies, as well as various specializations within history, sociology, cultural studies, ethnic studies, postcolonial studies, literary studies, and so forth. Over time, the intended audience for scholarship on Sephardi and Mizrahi Jews has also broadened. Literary scholars writing on Mizrahi fiction and film may be thinking of readers interested in other minority or postcolonial literatures, whereas a historian of various topics in eighteenth- and nineteenth-century Sephardic communities may be imagining historians of the Ottoman Empire as their readership. Indeed, one might argue that the ultimate success of Sephardi/ Mizrahi studies will be achieved when the label has outlived its usefulness and a separate scholarly category for the study of these communities is no longer needed.

Who Are Sephardi and Mizrahi Jews?

Sephardi/Mizrahi studies evolved in lockstep with the terms "Sephardi" and "Mizrahi" as they acquired new meaning, especially after the 1970s. "Sepharad" and "Ashkenaz" are biblical names that also took on new meanings. Sephardi became a historical and religious category denoting Jews with ancestral origins in the Iberian Peninsula (Spain); it was paired and contrasted with Ashkenazi, referring to the Jewish communities that originated in northern France and western Germany in the Middle Ages and that eventually spread throughout Eastern Europe. Sephardi and Ashkenazi Jews developed distinctive rituals and spoke different languages: Sephardi Jews spoke Ladino (Judeo-Spanish), a language derived from medieval Castilian (Spanish), or Haketia, a Judeo-Spanish variant with Arabic influences, whereas Ashkenazi Jews spoke Yiddish, a Germanic-based language with Slavic elements. By the early twentieth century, Ladino-speaking Sephardic Jews—descendants of Jews exiled from Spain and Portugal in the fifteenth century—could be found in southeastern Europe, Anatolia, the Levant, North Africa, and the Americas. However, much of the Jewish population in the Islamic world—corresponding to the Middle East, Anatolia, North Africa, Central Asia, and some sites in South Asia—did not trace their ancestry to Spain: In fact, many predated the arrival of Sephardim to these places, in some cases by millennia. There was—and still is—no single term or category encompassing Jewish populations from places as distant and different as Yemen, Iran, Iraq, Morocco, Turkey, Azerbaijan, and India. Indeed, these diverse populations lived in settings ranging from rural mountain villages to cosmopolitan cities, and their ways of life and local cultures thus varied widely. Although many communities lived in Arabic-speaking areas and spoke Jewish variations of local Arabic dialects, those dialects differed dramatically from one region to another; moreover, Jews in Iran spoke varieties of Persian, many Jews in northern Iraq spoke Kurdish/neo-Aramaic, and Jews in Central Asia spoke other languages such as Judeo-Tajik (Bukharian).

In the early twentieth century, Ashkenazi Jews comprised roughly 90 percent of the global Jewish population of about 11 million. Before the mass emigrations of the mid-twentieth century, the combined population of Asian and African Jews totaled about one million.[6] Around this time, Zionist functionaries and leaders in Palestine—themselves European Jews—began formulating racial and ethnic categories in the context of discussions about the global Jewish community. Because there was no single descriptor for the geographically diffuse and culturally diverse populations of Jews from the Middle East and North Africa (henceforth "MENA Jews"), they were often grouped together with the Ladino-speaking Jewish communities of southeast Europe under the umbrella of Sephardim. At other times, they were referred to as *Edot ha-mizrah*, the "Eastern" or "Oriental" *edot* ("tribes" or "ethnic communities"), a formulation that is now seen as outdated. As has been well documented, the Zionist establishment held generally disparaging views of the "Eastern" Jews, stereotyping them as backward, primitive, and premodern, yet they also saw them as links to the "authentic" Jewish past; Yemeni Jews, in particular, were seen by Ashkenazi Zionists as living relics of the biblical era.

After the establishment of the State of Israel in 1948, Jewish immigrants from Asia and Africa arrived en masse in the new state. The impetus for their emigration varied; although some communities were fleeing local anti-Jewish sentiment, repressive government policies, or anticolonial nationalisms in their home communities, others were drawn by long-standing religious attachments or persuaded to immigrate by emissaries of the Jewish Agency. The timing of the emigration of different communities also varied by place of origin; for example, many Yemeni and Iraqi Jews arrived within the first few years of statehood, Egyptian Jews came in the 1950s and 1960s, and North African Jews left their home countries with the end of colonial rule and arrived by the late 1960s. The nascent Israeli state was ill equipped to absorb such large numbers of immigrants, most of whom arrived impoverished, having been compelled to leave their property and assets behind. The state assigned the newcomers to unsanitary, makeshift tent cities ("transit camps," *ma'abarot*) and isolated, peripheral desert or border towns where they were beset by poor living conditions, discriminatory social policies, patronizing attitudes, and limited economic opportunity. These factors exacerbated what became known as the "ethnic problem" in Israel, whereby an entrenched social hierarchy that privileged Ashkenazi Jews and imposed a homogeneous national identity based on Ashkenazi and secular Zionist cultural norms triggered widespread resentment among Sephardi and Mizrahi Jews.

In the 1970s, activists in Israel adopted the term "Mizrahim" (Easterners) as a unifying identity to replace the patronizing *Edot ha-mizrah* and offer an alternative to the muddled use of "Sephardi." The term "Mizrahi" thus first emerged as a political label, although over the course of the past half-century, it became largely depoliticized and is now used widely to connote the large collective of Asian and African Jews (excluding Ethiopian Jewry, whose status is still seen as separate and unique). The conjoined phrase "Sephardi and Mizrahi" recognizes the more restricted definition of Sephardi referring to actual descendants of Spanish Jews as distinct from other MENA Jewry. Henceforth I use these two terms in referring to the communities in question, as well as the term MENA Jews. That said, scholars continue to debate what is the preferred terminology for African and Asian Jewish communities. Since the 1990s, some scholars have adopted the term "Arab-Jew" or "Arab Jew" (with or without the hyphen) to refer to traditionally Arabic-speaking Jewish subjects; this term has engendered its own debates and controversies, as I discuss later. At the time of writing, use of the term "MENA Jews" in English-language scholarship is on the rise.

The Decline Narrative

This background on nomenclature is relevant to the question of the formation of Sephardi/ Mizrahi studies for several reasons, including the connection of scholarship to activism, especially in understudied minority communities. Going back to the nineteenth century, the German Jewish scholars then active in the Wissenschaft des Judentums movement (seen as the origins of modern Jewish Studies) valorized medieval Sephardi Jews as paragons of the ideals of cultural assimilation and social prominence whom German Jews then hoped to emulate. But even as they turned to the distant Sephardi past for inspiration, they overlooked or ignored the activities and achievements of the actual, living Sephardi Jews who were their contemporaries. Their willful ignorance concerning their Sephardi contemporaries may be related to the assumptions behind the "decline narrative." For much of the twentieth century, experts in Jewish history subscribed to the idea that after the sixteenth century, the Sephardi and Mediterranean Jewish communities, once dominant in Jewish world history, went into decline and stopped influencing the rest of the Jewish world. For this reason, serious scholarship was directed toward the medieval and early modern history of the Jews of the Eastern Mediterranean, much of which was derived from the archive of the Cairo Geniza. By and large, despite some scholarly interest in the colonial history of Maghrebi Jews, scholars posited that the Asian and

African Jewish communities of the modern period were culturally stagnant. According to this viewpoint, Sephardi and Mizrahi communities had limited engagement with modern thought and culture, and any such engagement was a reaction to European intervention in the region, rather than a reflection of Jewish involvement in trends that originated within their surrounding local societies. Strong adherence to this narrative inhibited the development of original research that might present alternative perspectives on the plurality and heterogeneity of Jewish modernity; thus, scholars of "Jewish modernity" overlooked the modern experience of non-European Jews.

Material factors also played a role in perpetuating the decline narrative. In the nineteenth century, Ottoman Jews fled wars in southeastern Europe; for political and economic reasons, many migrated to the Americas and elsewhere in the early twentieth century. Thessaloniki, a major center of Jewish life, was destroyed by fire in 1917. In the mid-twentieth century, because of the abrupt departures of Mizrahi Jews from their native lands, many of the primary sources documenting their recent histories—community records, cultural artifacts, and texts—were lost or destroyed. Finally, the production of scholarship is linked to institutional support. It was not until the change of political winds in Israel in the late 1970s and the political rise of Sephardim and Mizrahim that historians in Israel began seriously turning to the open questions of the recent Sephardi and Mizrahi pasts. The seismic shift of 1977, when the Likud Party (with a heavily Mizrahi voter base) defeated the Labor Party in Israel's general elections for the first time since 1948, signaled a wider sociopolitical revolt against Ashkenazi domination of the Israeli public sphere; this gradually opened new possibilities for Sephardi/Mizrahi representation in culture and scholarship. The 1979 founding of the Hebrew-language journal *Pe'amim*, dedicated to the history of the Jews of the Islamic world, marked a milestone in the field's growth; other Hebrew-language journals soon followed. Still, well into the early 2000s, as Mizrahi intellectuals and activists repeatedly pointed out, official Israeli textbooks on the history of the Jewish people included negligible representation of non-Ashkenazi Jews, despite the availability of knowledge from earlier work by numerous Israeli scholars, as well as by U.S.-based scholars such as Bernard Lewis, Benjamin Braude, and Avigdor Levy, and by French Jewish scholars such as Benjamin Stora, Lucette Valensi, and Joëlle Bahloul.

Among the first wave of historians in Israel publishing on topics in nineteenth- and early twentieth-century history of MENA Jewry were self-trained scholars, often retirees who had been born and educated in the countries in question and thus held firsthand knowledge of the intellectual, cultural, and political trends of their communities of origin. Much of the Israeli scholarship at this stage dealt with the question of Sephardi and Mizrahi contributions to Zionism. In general, the most prominent focus has been Jewish–Muslim relations, a topic that is deeply and inevitably mired in contemporary politics. As a result of the political interest in this question, the scholarship tended to cleave to one of two opposing narrative templates: either that of Muslim–Jewish "symbiosis" (a term proposed by the historian Shlomo Dov Goitein) and coexistence (in Spanish, *convivencia*), as exemplified by the "Golden Age" of Islamic Spain, or its antithesis, the narrative of Muslim intolerance of Jews, as exemplified by select episodes in early Islamic history and by more recent episodes in nineteenth- and twentieth-century history such as the 1934 anti-Jewish riots in Algeria and the 1941 Farhud in Iraq, during which Jews in Baghdad were attacked and killed by mobs. It has been difficult, indeed, for scholarship involving the question of Jews and Muslims to avoid reifying one or the other of these opposing narratives, a point that has been expounded by scholars such as Mark Cohen. In today's highly politicized discourse on the Middle East and Islamic world, the temptation is strong to instrumentalize partial, selective views of history to make political claims about the present.[7]

As Michel Abitbol wrote in 2007, earlier scholarship from Europe and North America tended to characterize Jewish–Muslim relations positively in terms of symbiosis or coexistence and to attribute anti-Jewish episodes in the Maghreb to the tensions wrought by colonialism, nationalism, and Zionism. In contrast, Israeli scholars emphasized that MENA Jews in the modern period "ceased to regard themselves as an integral part of the history of the lands in which they lived for centuries" and distanced themselves from the fate of their broader communities, eschewing participation in local political movements.[8] Both approaches were overly simplistic and did not capture the complexities and contradictions of the modern experience of MENA Jews. Earlier, in 1996, Daniel Schroeter and Joseph Chetrit had advanced a different but equally incisive critique: In writing about Middle Eastern Jewish modernity, scholars leaned too heavily on ideas about "emancipation" (the process of Jews gaining political rights in Europe) and modernization that had been developed in the context of European Jewish history. In transposing these ideas onto Sephardi and Mizrahi Jewish communities, Schroeter and Chetrit argued, scholars implicitly reinforced the dichotomy between tradition and modernity that equates modernization with westernization.[9] Jews in the MENA region followed a different path to modernity for several reasons, including the powerful forces of European colonialism in the MENA region and local demographic, religious, and social dynamics. For example, in the Ottoman Empire, Jews were part of a multiconfessional society in which they were not the sole religious minority as they had been in Christian Europe. Outside Europe, Jews generally did not experience European-style antisemitism (with a few notable exceptions such as the "Damascus Affair" and adoption of the "blood libel" by Orthodox Christians in the Levant). Therefore, it was reasoned, scholarly approaches to Middle Eastern Jewish modernity should not lean on European Jewish paradigms. Similarly, in 2003, Ella Shohat critiqued the universal notion of a single "Jewish history" that denied the specificity of different Jewish experiences and rejected Arab and Muslim contexts for Jewish culture and history; she called for this notion's replacement with an approach that would show how Jewish life in different parts of the world was intimately related to different local non-Jewish contexts.[10]

The arguments of Abitbol, Schoeter, Chetrit, and Shohat are borne out by more recent scholarship that has indeed moved beyond the older ideational paradigms. For example, in a 2020 study, Dina Danon shows that in Ottoman Izmir, attitudes about social class, rather than perceptions of Jewish difference from non-Jews, were the dominant factors framing the local Sephardi community's transition into modernity.[11] This finding illustrates the inherent limitations of historical paradigms from European Jewry as explanatory models for Sephardi experiences of modernity; in Europe, Jewish difference was a paramount factor in the relationship of Jews to their broader urban, national, or imperial contexts. The MENA region followed a different path to modernity. In the Ottoman Empire, in particular, given the presence of Christian communities, Jews were part of a multiethnic society in which they were not the sole religious minority as they had been in Christian Europe.

Post-1990s Expansion and Scholarship by Area

Scholarly research on modern Sephardi and Mizrahi Jews expanded considerably in the 1980s and accelerated in the 1990s as more researchers entered the scene. With these new researchers came expansion of the field's conceptual horizons. In particular, the 1990s gave rise to groundbreaking work on Jews in North Africa and Turkey, led by scholars based in Israel, North America, and France.[12] Important contributions from the United States and France have included two volumes on Ottoman Jews; one by Stanford Shaw and the other by Avigdor Levy;[13] Norman Stillman's source text, *The Jews of Arab Lands in Modern Times*[14]; Aron Rodrigue's two books on the Alliance Israélite Universelle, an influential French Jewish educational network in the Sephardi world[15]; Joëlle

Bahloul's anthropology of an Algerian Jewish household, *La maison de mémoire: Ethnologie d'une demeure judéo-arabe en Algérie, 1937–1961*[16]; and Ammiel Alcalay's *After Jews and Arab: Remaking Levantine Culture*, a pathbreaking work that opened new vistas into the modern, transnational literary history of Mizrahi and Sephardi Jews.[17] Contributing new sources and frameworks, such works broadened the possibilities for the study of Sephardi and Mizrahi modernity as distinct from the European Jewish narrative. These works and several others by scholars in Israel, the United States, and France presented a more complex view of Mizrahi and Sephardi lives in the nineteenth and early twentieth centuries, complicating earlier assumptions about the decline of those communities and their supposed non-involvement in local culture and politics. They also expanded the discussion beyond the question of Sephardi/Mizrahi involvement in Zionism by turning to the complexities of the encounter of Sephardi and Mizrahi Jews with European colonialism and with European Jewish intervention in Middle Eastern Jewish life; for example, via the Alliance Israélite Universelle, the Anglo Jewish Association, and the Cremieux Decree issued in Algeria, as well as Mizrahi and Sephardi engagement with their local Muslim and Christian neighbors.

In the 2000s and 2010s, with the entry of a second generation of trained researchers, the field underwent a new, energetic phase of development. In the past two decades, Sephardi/ Mizrahi studies has expanded prodigiously, as measured by the number of published books, the range of languages involved, and the diversity of primary and archival sources (the multilingual Jewish press, other press sources, government records, court records, business records, memoirs and diaries, letters, dictionaries, literary works, ethnographies, cultural sources including music and film, and more). This burst of scholarship focused largely on the period between the mid-nineteenth and mid-twentieth centuries, seeking to fill in gaps of knowledge about the intellectual, political, social, economic, and cultural lives of modern Sephardi and Mizrahi communities before their disruptions after 1948; a smaller number of studies followed the communities into the later twentieth century or revisited the history of Mizrahi immigrants to Israel in the 1950s and 1960s. As the field grew dramatically in North America and in Europe, the post-2000 wave of scholarship also transformed the questions and perspectives driving the scholarship. Whereas much earlier scholarship focused on Sephardi "contributions" to Zionism, varieties of anti-Semitism in the Muslim world, or the "modernization" of Sephardi and Mizrahi Jewry via colonial projects or European Jewish intervention, the newer scholarship considered more diverse facets of the modern experience of Sephardi and

Mizrahi communities. Collectively, it turned the focus both inward toward multiple, previously overlooked aspects of their integration into the local (non-Jewish) surrounding societies, and outward, toward their involvement in broader historical transformations that reshaped the region or even the global economy, for example by looking at Sephardim and Mizrahim as agents in the trade of global commodities.

At the same time, it should be noted that much of this recent expansion of research, especially in Europe and North America, has not necessarily penetrated public awareness in Israel, and vice versa. Because of language barriers (Hebrew, French, and English), the scholarly activity in each of these three centers of scholarship has not yet been fully integrated. Furthermore, the role of Mizrahi/Sephardi scholarship is quite different in the Israeli public sphere where it is more organically connected to contemporary social questions, given Israel's large Mizrahi population, most of whose members read primarily or exclusively in Hebrew. As such, the scholarship based in each of these regions—emanating mainly from Israel, France, and the United States—seems to be developing on parallel tracks with partial connections.

Most of the English-language studies conducted after 2010 are dedicated to a single nation-state, city, or regional cluster of cities, such as Beirut, Baghdad, Salonica, Algeria, or mandatory Palestine. Only a few studies adopt a transnational approach; two notable examples are important source-text anthologies, *Sephardi Lives: A Documentary History, 1700–1950*[18] and *Modern Middle Eastern Jewish Thought: Writings on Identity, Politics, and Culture, 1893–1958.*[19] Except for a few edited volumes that cover multiple regions, scholarship has not integrated research on the three main geographic and cultural subareas covered by Sephardi/Mizrahi studies—the "Ottoman heartland" (present-day Greece and Turkey), the Levant (Mashreq), and North Africa (the Maghreb). Studies of Sephardi Ladino-speaking communities tend to be clustered separately from scholarship on the Arabic (and French)-based Levantine and North African communities, which lean more heavily toward French, in addition to Arabic and Amazigh (Berber). Additionally, most of the scholarship to date deals with intellectual and social history rather than religious studies, with some exceptions.[20] *A History of Jewish and Muslim Relations: From the Origins to the Present Day*—an encyclopedic, comprehensive edited volume organized chronologically and thematically—may be the most fully integrated history involving Sephardi/Mizrahi life: It approaches its subject matter from all angles, including religious practice and belief, and traverses the full geographic range of Jewish life in the Islamic world.[21]

The post-2000s scholarship can be grouped into regional clusters, as follows: North Africa; Ottoman and mandatory Palestine; Iraq; Iran; Yemen; Egypt; Syria and Lebanon; Greece and the Ottoman Turkish heartland; Bukharan, Georgian, and Central Asian Jews; and Sephardi Jews in the Americas and the global diaspora, including the Caribbean. From a disciplinary standpoint, the subfield of Sephardi/Mizrahi studies leans heavily toward history but also includes publications in the fields of anthropology, sociology, literature and culture (including film), and ethnomusicology. Much of the newer work focuses on pre-1948 Jewish involvement in local political movements (e.g., Ottomanism, Zionism, local nationalisms), within internal or local debates (in the Jewish community or broader society), and within transnational or international movements, organizations, and trade. Other recent work delves into questions of poverty and social class, legal history, citizenship, and urban space. Jointly, the scholarship has convincingly shown that Jews throughout the Islamic world—as well as emigrés and descendants in the Americas—pursued multiple avenues of modern affiliation and belonging. In political movements these ranged from Zionism to Ottomanism to communism to anticolonial independence movements; in other cases, these avenues of belonging were less overtly ideological and more a function of class, business interests, and artistic pursuits. Scholarship now demonstrates that Sephardi and Mizrahi Jews were not merely passive witnesses to broader historical forces beyond their control. Instead, in a variety of ways, the scholarship portrays them as movers and shakers in culture, politics, and economics. The following section outlines some of the scholarly nodes or clusters within the field; due to space limitations, this overview does not include sections on the Jews of Yemen, India, or Central Asia.[22]

Pre-1948 Palestine

Palestine in the Ottoman and mandatory periods has inspired several recent studies in Hebrew and English; their two major focal points are the social dynamics of a "mixed" society of Muslims, Christians and Jews and the intellectual lives of Palestinian Sephardim. Among the range of historical actors subsumed by the "Sephardi/ Mizrahi" label, Sephardi Jews in Palestine exhibited exceptional multilingualism and mobility. Often fluent in Arabic, Hebrew, and Ladino and sometimes also in Turkish, these figures blur the lines between "Sephardi," "Mizrahi," and "Arab Jew." They were also distinguished by their unique location at the heart of the Zionist project, which positioned them directly in the middle ground between European Jewish newcomers and Palestinian Arabs.[23] The scholarship has explored topics such as Ottoman identity among Sephardi Jews, as well as Muslims and Christians, in post-1908 Palestine (Campos); the relations of Palestinian Sephardim with their Arab neighbors in mandatory Palestine (Jacobson and Naor); and the roles of Sephardi intellectuals as social, political, and cultural mediators between European Jews and Palestinian Arabs (Eyal). Menachem Klein's *Lives in Common* follows relationships in daily life between Jews and Arabs in Jerusalem, Jaffa, and Hebron, with an emphasis on the texture of everyday interactions. In intellectual history, studies cover Sephardi and Arab Jewish intellectuals in Palestine at the turn of the twentieth century (Evri) and the intellectual and literary lives of Sephardim in Jerusalem from the late nineteenth century through the 1930s (Noy).

The Levant

A rich scholarship on the Jews of Iraq in the first half of the twentieth century demonstrates the social, political, economic, and cultural dimensions of Jewish involvement in the Iraqi national project from the 1920s through the 1940s, as well as Iraqi Jewish interest in the Zionist movement.[24] Nancy Berg's and Reuven Snir's books on Iraqi Jewish writers contribute a literary perspective to Jews in Iraq and their aftermath after emigration to the State of Israel. The case of Iraqi Jews stands apart for two reasons: the depth of Jewish identification with an Arab nationalism and the deep and enduring identification of a Jewish population with classical Arabic. The contributions of Iraqi Jews to Iraqi Arabic literature and Iraq's classical music tradition (the *maqam*) are often characterized in the scholarship as exceptional or qualified as one of two exceptional cases, the other being Egyptian Jewish participation in Egypt's cinema and musical industries during the same period (more on this later). Iraqi Jewish identification with the Iraqi homeland, in particular Baghdad, famously withstood emigration to Israel and the West, sparking an unusual number of memoirs, novels, and films by Iraqi Jewish emigrés and their descendants. Several documentary films also explore Jewish attachment to Baghdad through questions of diaspora, cultural memory, and family history.

Studies of Egyptian Jewish history and literature present a vision that is partly analogous to the Iraqi case, with added complexities. Scholars have investigated the modern histories of Egyptian Jews in the nineteenth and twentieth centuries, as well as their diasporic afterlives after widespread emigration from Egypt.[25] Before the mass emigrations of Egyptian Jewry from the 1950s to the 1970s, Egyptian Jews were a heterogenous population that included "native"

Jewish populations (notably, a strong Karaite community), Sephardi Jews from Greece and Italy who emigrated to Egypt in the nineteenth century, and Ashkenazi Jews drawn by economic opportunity. Many twentieth-century Jewish Egyptians were primarily Francophone, whereas others embraced Arabic in a manner parallel to the Jews of Iraq. The cosmopolitan character of Egypt's Jews, as explored by Deborah Starr and others, played an important role both in the community's self-perception and its perception by non-Jews. Jewish stars of Egyptian cinema and music such as the director Togo Mizrahi, the actress and singer Layla Murad, and the musical composer Dawud Husni have fascinated the Egyptian public, but their legacies have been complicated by the political tensions between Egypt and Israel.

Studies of Syrian and Lebanese Jews also follow the transformations of those communities from the late Ottoman period to the French period and beyond. Yaron Harel's multiple books on Syrian Jewry delve into the economic and social effects of European interventions on Syrian Jewish life and take a closer look at Zionist activity in Damascus and the colorful history of chief rabbis of Damscus, Aleppo, and Baghdad. Tomer Levi focuses on Beirut's Jewish community during the transition to French rule in the context of port cities, and Kirsten Schulze follows the history of Lebanese Jews over the course of the twentieth century. Other studies have examined the Lebanese Jewish press and eighteenth-century Syrian and Egyptian Jewish history.[26]

The Ottoman Sephardic World

Turning to the Ladino-speaking worlds of Anatolia, Greece, and the Balkans, recent publications explore Ottoman Jewish modernity and trace the transformations besetting Jewish populations after the collapse of the Ottoman Empire, Greco-Turkish partitions, and the formation of the modern Greek and Turkish nation-states.[27] For example, Julia Phillips Cohen's book on southeastern Europe and Anatolia (mainly Salonica, Istanbul, and Izmir) follows Ottoman Jewry's attempts to negotiate its path to modernity within the framework of Ottoman imperial citizenship; it offers examples of intercommunal cooperation between the Jewish and Armenian and between Jewish and Greek Orthodox religious and lay leaders, a counterpoint to the intercommunal rivalry more commonly discussed in modern histories of Sephardi and Mizrahi Jewries. Devin Naar's research carries the narrative forward into the context of the Greek state, telling the story of Salonican Jews as they grappled with their new status as citizens of a nation and sought to find their place within Greek society. Dina Danon's earlier mentioned book focuses on the politics of class. In religious studies and literature, Matthias Lehmann explores parallel questions of modernization among Ottoman Sephardi Jewry through the lens of rabbinic writings in Ladino, whereas Olga Borovaya reconstructs the history of Ladino literature from its sixteenth-century origins to its flourishing in the nineteenth and early twentieth centuries. Marc Baer's book on the Dönme, the Sabbatean crypto-Jews, follows their history from the seventeenth-century into their involvement in twentieth-century Turkish politics.

The Maghreb

Scholarship on Maghrebi Jews has enjoyed a robust scholarly trajectory, with self-study by Maghrebi Jews as well as French research on colonial history reaching back to the late nineteenth century. The broad range of scholarship in Hebrew, French, and English includes the histories of Moroccan, Tunisian, Algerian, and Libyan Jewish communities from the colonial period to independence; Jewish involvement in modern political movements in these countries; studies of Jewish space (e.g., the mellah); and the particular vagaries of Algerian Jewish history.[28] Aomar Boum's ethnography *Memories of Absence: How Muslims Remember Jews in Morocco* examines the impact of Jewish emigration from Morocco on those who remain[29]: How have Moroccan Muslims grappled with the past histories and the present absence of their former Jewish neighbors? Jessica Marglin's *Across Legal Lines: Jews and Muslims in Modern Morocco* opens the field to legal history, approaching the Moroccan legal system as a lens onto the social and economic integration of Jews into precolonial Moroccan society.[30] Finally, in an important addition to the field, scholars including Susan Miller, Aomar Boum, and Sarah Stein have recently drawn attention to the understudied stories of the Holocaust and Jewish resistance in North Africa.

Sephardi/Mizrahi Transnationalism and Diasporas

Scholarship on Sephardi/Mizrahi modernity in transnational and diasporic perspectives is expanding the field beyond its regional limits toward a more global orientation. One cluster concerns Sephardi migration to Latin America: Sephardi Jews in Argentina (Adriana Brodsky); histories of legal documentation and citizenship among Ottoman Sephardi migrants in Mexico, who were part of an extensive Sephardi diaspora extending to France, Cuba, and the United States (Devi Mays); and Moroccan Jews in Latin America (Aviad

Moreno). Studies of Sephardi migration to the Americas invite discussion of the intersectional dimension of Sephardi experience; the Latin American collective ethnicization of Sephardim as "Turcos" (Turks) links Sephardi history to questions of race and racialization in the context of the Americas. Other scholars follow the trajectories of North African Jews into France (Ethan Katz, Maud Mandel), whereas Aviva Ben-Ur and Devin Naar follow the stories of Ladino-speaking Sephardi communities in the United States. Transnationalism is also a feature of Sephardi involvement in global trade and social practices, such as the international commitments of Baghdadi Jewry in nineteenth-century global Jewish philanthropy (Sasha Goldstein-Sabbah), Ashkenazi and Sephardi Jews in the global trade in ostrich feathers (Sarah Stein), the Baghdadi Sassoon family's Asian trade network, which stretched from colonial India to Shanghai (Joseph Sassoon), or citizenship and inheritance law across the Mediterranean (Jessica Marglin). The movement of Sephardi and Mizrahi studies from local to transnational and global contexts opens new dimensions in the study of integration, shifting the focus from questions of how Sephardi and Mizrahi individuals were integrated into the multiethnic fabric of their local societies at the everyday level, or how intellectuals and community leaders pursued the collective integration of their Jewish community into national communities in formation, to larger forms of integration—those of Sephardi integration into the global economy or transnational social and economic networks. These transnational studies also move their subjects out of the Muslim-majority context, thereby presenting different questions concerning Jewish and non-Jewish relations beyond the familiar questions of Jews and Muslims. Future scholarship will likely build on such work to produce new transnational perspectives on the MENA Jewish experience.

The Arab Jew

The generative question of the "Arab-Jew" (or Arab Jew, unhyphenated) is the focal point of a dynamic conversation within Sephardi/Mizrahi studies. It has provided the conceptual framework for the field's most interdisciplinary work, including numerous contributions in literary and cultural studies. The term "Arab Jew" refers to Jews from Arabic-speaking countries. Varieties of the term had long circulated in the backdrop of discussions on Sephardim and Mizrahim, but Ella Shohat moved it to the forefront with her 1992 essay, "Reflections of an Arab Jew," sparking an extensive scholarly debate for and against the term.[31] Initially, the term was taken up by scholars of comparative literature and cultural studies, but historians and sociologists soon entered into the conversation. In its current incarnation, the term "Arab Jew" is meant to reclaim the cultural, linguistic, and historical "Arabness" of Jews with origins in the Arab world in the face of widespread cultural and linguistic erasure. This erasure resulted from the bidirectional pressures of Zionism and post-1948 Arab nationalisms, each of which insisted that Jews could not be Arab, and vice versa.

The term "Arab-Jew" has been widely contested by scholars who see it as anachronistically imposing an Arab identity on a Jewish population that had not historically seen or generally referred to itself as "Arab"; many point out that "Arab" itself was not a widespread identity even for non-Jews until well into the twentieth century. The term is also rejected by many contemporary Mizrahim in Israel who do not see themselves as "Arab." Conversely, the term has been embraced by numerous scholars, intellectuals, artists, and activists and has inspired a wide range of responses ranging from poetry to memoir to spoken word and scholarly work. Scholarship invoking the "Arab Jew" includes literary and historical studies pertaining to Jewish life in Arab countries both before and after emigration to Israel. Some cultural invocations of the term "Arab-Jew" include the late Iraqi Israel writer Sasson Somekh's *Baghdad, Yesterday: The Making of an Arab Jew*,[32] poetry by Sami Shalom Chetrit and members of the Israeli collective Ars Poetika, and stories by the Israeli Canadian writer Ayelet Tsabari, among many other examples from popular culture. Sociologists Yehouda Shenhav and Gil Eyal also explore Arab Jewish history and identity both before 1948 and in the State of Israel.

Mizrahim in Israel (History and Sociology)

Complementing the many historical studies of MENA Jews in their countries of origin and building on foundational studies of Mizrahim in Israel by sociologists Shlomo Swirski and Sami Smooha, another significant area of Sephardi/Mizrahi studies concerns the story of Mizrahim in Israeli society. Much of the post-2000 scholarship in this area covers the history of the Mizrahi political struggle and activism from the 1950s to 1990s (Sami Shalom Chetrit), ethnic-based inequality in the Israel labor market in early statehood (Aziza Khazzoom), Iraqi immigrants in the *ma'abarot* (transit camps; Orit Bashkin and Esther Meir-Glitzenstein), relations between the Israeli police and Mizrahi transit camp residents and activists (Bryan Roby), and the rise of the SHAS political party, among other topics. Currently, scholars are delving into the racialization of Mizrahim in Israel (also mentioned later).[33]

Music, Cinema, Literature, and Cultural Studies

Cinema and music are both topics of wide interest as they relate to Mizrahim in Israel and to their cultural involvement in their pre-emigration homelands. Ella Shohat's pioneering 1989 study of the representation of Sephardim and Mizrahim in Israeli cinema paved the way for scholarship on Israeli cinema in general, and especially for work on Mizrahim and Israeli film (Yaron Shemer, Rami Kimchi, and Raz Yosef). More recently, Mizrahi music, a major facet of Israeli popular culture, has begun to attract serious scholarly interest (Amy Horowitz, Nadeem Karkabi, and Oded Erez). These two cultural forms had colorful histories among Jews before their emigration to Israel. In the first half of the twentieth century, Iraqi, Egyptian, and North African Jews were prominently involved in the musical industries of their countries (Inbal Perlson, Hanan Hammad, Chris Silver), and Egyptian Jews also played a leading role in Egypt's storied cinema history (Deborah Starr). Going back further in time and place, Ottoman Jews and, later, Turkish Jews created special instrumental and vocal musical forms related to Ottoman court music and/or Sabbatean traditions (Edwin Seroussi, Maureen Jackson, Hadar Feldman Samet, Maureen Jackson). Work on Mizrahi literature exploring questions of language politics, identity, cosmopolitanism, Hebrew-Arabic bilingualism, and other topics is another vigorous and rapidly expanding area within Sephardi/Mizrahi studies, with numerous contributions from scholars based in and outside Israel.[34] Foodways are an additional area of cultural studies with special resonance in Sephardi and Mizrahi culture: Multiple scholars have not only charted the cultural importance of food but have also explored the function of cookbooks as vehicles of communal identity for displaced communities.

Future Directions

As Sephardi/Mizrahi studies continues its twenty-first-century development, non-Jewish artists and scholars throughout the MENA region, in parallel, have revived the exploration of questions of their own nations' Jewish pasts. Notably, Muslim scholars in the region, especially in Morocco, have been working on the history of their erstwhile Jewish communities since at least the 1990s. This resurgence of interest takes multiple forms: From Saudia Arabia to Morocco to Egypt, Turkey, and Iraq, films, soap operas, novels, museums, and academic works are all working through the open questions left by the departure of their Jewish neighbors and fellow citizens. At the time of this writing, the Moroccan state is investing resources in the expansion of Jewish Studies in Morocco, and Morocco-based scholars are collaborating with U.S.-based scholars to disseminate historical studies of MENA Jewry in Arabic.[35] With time, this engagement with the Sephardi/ Mizrahi past from the "other end" is bound to enrich the scholarly discourse.

The field is also reckoning with its own internal blind spots. Recently, Sephardi/Mizrahi studies has begun grappling with questions of race and racialization, both in terms of the racialization of Mizrahim in Israel and the aforementioned questions of race in other transnational contexts, such as Sephardim in the Americas.[36] Gender is a second area of future growth; only a handful of books dedicated to MENA Jewish women's issues—both in historical and present-day contexts—have appeared in Hebrew or English since the 1990s,[37] but multiple gender-focused doctoral dissertations are underway. Additionally, scholars are demonstrating growing interest in the question of how Muslim-majority states are remembering their lost Jewish populations, largely through representation of the Arab-Jewish past in fiction, television, and film—a phenomenon with expressions in Saudi Arabia, Iraq, Egypt, Morocco, and elsewhere.[38]

Current historical scholarship is abetted by the steadily expanding digitization of sources, such as the Historical Jewish Press project—an important digital, multilingual collection of Jewish periodicals hosted by the National Library of Israel—and Diarna, the Geo-Museum of North African and Middle Eastern Jewish Life. Diarna, meaning "our homes," is a virtual museum of Jewish heritage sites primarily in the Maghreb and Middle East with more than a dozen virtual exhibits searchable by country. The University of Washington hosts an extensive Sephardic Studies Digital Collection, and Stanford University has initiated a Digitized Ladino Library project.

Sephardi/Mizrahi scholarship challenges Jewish Studies to reconceptualize the narrative of Jewish modernity and its underlying beliefs. Scholars of Sephardi and Mizrahi history and culture have demonstrated that the Jewish encounter with modernity had a multitude of drivers and forms and that Middle Eastern and North African Jews were not only subjects but also agents of change who participated in and influenced global economic structures and cultural trends. Far from being the members of hermetic, tradition-bound, and static communities that MENA Jews had once been made out to be, they were active participants in society on all levels, from the legal rulings of rabbis to the creation of Jewish periodicals in Arabic, Ladino, and Persian to involvement in international political movements. In Israel, Mizrahi culture and politics and the Arab Jew debates continue to generate discussion in the public sphere and inspire new research. A dynamic, quickly evolving field, Sephardi/Mizrahi studies stands to reshape Jewish Studies while connecting it to other scholarly disciplines such as Middle Eastern, Islamic, and Latin American studies, as well as global studies of race and ethnicity.

Recommended Readings

Alcalay, Ammiel. *After Jews and Arabs: Remaking Levantine Culture* (University of Minnesota Press, 1993).

Behar, Moshe, and Zvi Ben Dor Benite. *Modern Middle Eastern Jewish Thought: Writings on Identity, Politics, and Culture, 1893–1958* (Brandeis University Press, 2013).

Cohen, Julia Phillips, and Sarah Stein, eds. *Sephardi Lives: A Documentary History, 1700–1950* (Stanford University Press, 2014).

Goldberg, Harvey E., ed. *Sephardi and Middle Eastern Jewries: History and Culture in the Modern Era* (Indiana University Press, 1996).

Meddeb, Abdelwahab, and Benjamin Stora. *A History of Jewish and Muslim Relations: From the Origins to the Present Day*, trans. Jane Marie Todd and Michael B. Smith (Princeton University Press, 2013).

Rodrigue, Aron. *Jews and Muslims: Images of Sephardi and Eastern Jewries in Modern Times* (University of Washington Press, 2003).

Simon, Reeva Spector, Michael Menahem Laskier, and Sara Regeur, eds. *The Jews of the Middle East and North Africa in Modern Times* (Columbia University Press, 2003).

Somekh, Sasson. *Baghdad, Yesterday: The Making of an Arab Jew* (Jerusalem: Ibis, 2007).

Stillman, Norman. *The Jews of Arab Lands in Modern Times* (Jewish Publication Society, 1991).

Tsur, Yaron. "Israeli Historiography and the Ethnic Problem" [Hebrew] *Pe'amim* 94–95 (2003): 7–56.

Notes

1. Clémence Boulouque, *Another Modernity: Elia Benamozegh's Jewish Universalism* (Stanford University Press, 2020).

2. Rami Kimchi, *Israeli Borekas Films: Their Origins and Legacy* (Indiana University Press, 2023)

3. Lior B. Sternfeld, *Between Iran and Zion: Jewish Histories of Twentieth-Century Iran* (Stanford University Press, 2018).

4. Kay Kaufman Shelemay, *Let Jasmine Rain Down: Song and Remembrance among Syrian Jews* (University of Chicago Press, 1998).

5. Olga Borovaya, *Modern Ladino Culture: Press, Belles Lettres, and Theatre in the Late Ottoman Empire* (Indiana University Press, 2012).

6. Usiel Oscar Schmelz and Sergio DellaPergola, "Demography," in *Encyclopaedia Judaica*, ed. Michael Berenbaum and Fred Skolnik, 553.

538   CHAPTER 25

7. Cohen, "The Neo-Lachrymose Conception of Jewish-Arab History," in *Tikkun* 6 (1991): 55–60. See also Bernard Lewis, *The Jews of Islam* (Princeton University Press, 1984).

8. Abitbol, "Jews of Muslim Lands in the Modern Period: History and Historiography," in *Sephardic Jewry and Mizrahi Jews*, ed. Peter Y. Medding (Oxford University Press, 2007), 44–65; citation 55.

9. Schroeter and Chetrit, "The Transformation of the Jewish Community of Essaouria (Mogador) in the Nineteenth and Twentieth Centuries," in *Sephardi and Middle Eastern Jewries: History and Culture in the Modern Era*, ed. H. E. Goldberg (Indiana University Press, 1996), 99–116; citations 99–100.

10. Shohat, "Rupture and Return: Zionist Discourse and the Study of Arab Jews," *Social Text* 21, no. 2 (2003): 49–74.

11. Danon, *The Jews of Ottoman Izmir: A Modern History* (Stanford University Press, 2020).

12. Leading scholars from this wave include Ammiel Alcalay, Tamar Alexander, Robert Attal, Joëlle Bahloul, Esther Benbassa, Joseph Chetrit, Harvey Goldberg, Mohammed Kenbib, Aron Rodrigue, Daniel Schroeter, Ella Habiba Shohat, Norman Stillman, Yaron Tsur, and Yosef Tobi.

13. Stanford Shaw, *The Jews of the Ottoman Empire and the Turkish Republic* (Macmillan, 1991), and *The Jews of the Ottoman Empire*, ed. Avigdor Levy (Darwin, 1994).

14. Jewish Publication Society, 1991.

15. *French Jews, Turkish Jews: The Alliance Israélite Universelle and the Politics of Jewish Schooling in Turkey, 1860–1925* (Indiana University Press, 1990) and *Images of Sephardi and Eastern Jewries in Transition: The Teachers of the Alliance Israélite Universelle, 1860–1939* (University of Washington Pres, 1993).

16. Editions Métailié, 1992; Engl. (Cambridge University Press, 1996).

17. University of Minnesota Press, 1993.

18. Ed. J. Phillips Cohen and S. Abrevaya Stein (Stanford University Press, 2014).

19. Ed. M. Behar and Z. B. Benite (Brandeis University Press, 2013).

20. Zvi Zohar's *Rabbinic Creativity in the Middle East* (Bloomsbury Academic, 2013), one of a few important exceptions, deals directly with Middle Eastern Jewish responses to question of modernity (in Iraq, Egypt, and Syria) from the standpoint of rabbinic writings, rather than from the perspectives of laypeople based on secular archival sources and the press. See also Matthias Lehmann, *Ladino Rabbinic Literature and Ottoman Sephardic Culture* (Indiana University Press, 2005), and Marc D. Angel, *Voices in Exile: A Study in Sephardic Intellectual History* (KTAV, 1991).

21. Abdelwahab Meddeb and Benjamin Stora, eds., *A History of Jewish and Muslim Relations: From the Origins to the Present Day* (Princeton University Press, 2013).

22. For representative titles on Yemen, see Noah Gerber, *Ourselves or Our Holy Books? The Cultural Discovery of Yemenite Jewry* [Hebrew] (Ben Zvi Institute, 2013); Ari Ariel, *Jewish-Muslim Relations and Migration from Yemen to Palestine in the Late Nineteenth and Twentieth Centuries* (Brill, 2014); and Mark S. Wagner, *Jews and Islamic Law in Early 20th-Century Yemen* (Indiana University Press, 2014). For Iran, see Daniel Tsadik, *Between Foreigners and Shi'is: Nineteenth Century Iran and Its Jewish Minority* (Stanford University Press, 2007); David Yeroushalmi, *The Jews of Iran in the Nineteenth Century: Aspects of History, Community, and Culture* (Brill, 2009), and Lior B. Sternfeld, *Between Iran and Zion: Jewish Histories of*

Twentieth-Century Iran. On India, see Nathan Katz, *Who Are the Jews of India?* (University of California Press, 2000); Yulia Egorova, *Jews and India: Perceptions and Image* (Routledge, 2006); and *The Baghdadi Jews in India: Maintaining Communities, Negotiating Identities, and Creating Super-Diversity,* ed. Shalva Weil (Routledge, 2019); on Burma, see Ruth Cernea, *Almost Englishmen: Baghdadi Jews in British Burma* (Lexington, 2006). For Central Asia, see Alanna E. Cooper, *Bukharan Jews and the Dynamics of Global Judaism* (Indiana University Press, 2012), and Bram Chen, *The Jews of the Caucus in Dagestan: Collective Identity and Communal Survival* [Hebrew] (Bar Ilan University, 2006).

23. Works on these "Sephardi notables" include Michelle Campos, *Ottoman Brothers: Muslims, Christians and Jews in Early 20th-Century Palestine* (Stanford University Press, 2011); Abigail Jacobson and Moshe Naor, *Oriental Neighbors: Middle Eastern Jews and Arabs in Mandatory Palestine* (Brandeis University Press, 2016); Menachem Klein, *Lives in Common: Arabs and Jews in Jerusalem, Jaffa, and Hebron* (Hurst, 2014); Amos Noy, *Experts or Witnesses* [Hebrew] (Rosling, 2017), and Yuval Evri, *The Return to Al-Andalus* [Hebrew] (Magnes, 2020).

24. On Iraq, see Yitzhak Avishur, Orit Bashkin, Moshe Gat, Nissim Kazzaz, Esther Meir-Glitzenstein, Nissim Rejwan, Jonathan Sciarcon, Aline Schlaepfer, Reuven Snir, and Zvi Yehuda.

25. See Deborah Starr, *Togo Mizrahi and the Making of Egyptian Cinema* (University of California Press, 2020); on Leila Murad, see Hanan Hammad, *Unknown Past: Leila Murad, the Jewish-Muslim Star of Egypt* (Stanford University Press, 2022). On Egyptian Jews, see Jacob Landau, Joel Beinin, Hagar Hillel, Gudrun Krämer, Dario Miccoli, and Alon Tam.

26. See the work of Guy Bracha, Jacob Landau, and Thomas Philipp.

27. See historical scholarship by Julia Phillips Cohen, Dina Danon, Marc Mazower, Devin Naar, and Sarah Stein; on Ladino literature, see Olga Borovaya and Michael Alpert.

28. See, for example, works by Michel Abitbol, Robert Attal, Joelle Bahloul, Aomar Boum, Josef Chetrit, Brahim El Guabli, Oren Kosansky, Susan Gilson Miller, Harvey Goldberg, Emily Benichou Gottreich, Alma Heckman, Mohammed Kenbib, Joshua Schreier, Sarah Abrevaya Stein, Benjamin Stora, Yosef Tobi, Yaron Tsur, and Lucette Valensi.

29. Stanford University Press, 2013.

30. Yale University Press, 2016.

31. See Shohat, "Dislocated Identities: Reflections of an Arab Jew," *Movement Research: Performance Journal* 5 (Fall–Winter 1992): Ch. 8; and Lital Levy, "The Arab Jew Debates: Media, Culture, Politics, History," *Journal of Levantine Studies* 7 (2017): 79–103.

32. Ibis, 2007.

33. See work by Orit Bashkin, Sami Shalom Chetrit, Aziza Khazoom, Smadar Lavie, Bryan Roby, and Rachel Shabi.

34. See, for example, literary scholarship by Ammiel Alcalay, Ketsia Alon, Almog Behar, Gil Anidjar, Nancy Berg, Yuval Evri, Gil Hochberg, Lital Levy, Kfir Cohen Lustig, Yochai Oppenheimer, Batya Shimony, Reuven Snir, and Deborah Starr. Monique Balbuena and Dalia Kandiyoti have written on modern Sephardic writers.

35. For example, Aomar Boum and his Morocco-based colleague Khalid Ben Srhir's series, Morocco and Its Mediterranean Surroundings: Jewish Texts and Translations.

36. See Bryan Roby, "How Race Travels: Navigating Global Blackness in J. Ida Jiggetts's Study of Afro-Asian Israeli Jewry," *Jewish Social Studies* 27 (2022): 1–42.

37. See Rachel Simon, *Change within Tradition among Jewish Women in Libya* (University of Washington Press, 1992); Margalit Shilo, *Princess or Prisoner? Jewish Women in Jerusalem, 1840–1914* (Brandeis University Press, 2005); Jonathan Sciarcon, *Educational Oases in the Desert: The Alliance Israélite Universelle's Girls' Schools in Ottoman Iraq, 1895–1915* (SUNY Press, 2017); and Yali Hashash, *Whose Daughter Are You? Ways of Speaking Mizrahi Feminism* [Hebrew] (Ha-kibutz Ha-me'had, 2022). These books are accompanied by a larger number of scholarly articles on MENA Jewish women; see the many articles and edited books by Henriette Dahan Kalev. See also Shir Alon, "Gendering the Arab Jew: Feminism and Jewish Studies after Ella Shohat," *Jewish Social Studies* 24 (2019): 57–73, and Lital Levy, "Partitioned Pasts: Arab Jewish Intellectuals and the Case of Esther Azhari Moyal (1873–1948)," in *The Making of the Arab Intellectual (1880–1960): Empire, Public Sphere, and the Colonial Coordinates of Selfhood*, ed. D. Hamza (Routledge, 2012), 128–63. See also Levy, *A Jewish Woman in Arabic Letters: The Life and Works of Esther Azhari Moyal* (forthcoming)

38. See Brahim El Guabli and Mostafa Hossein, eds., *Remembering Jews in Maghrebi and Middle Eastern Media* (Penn State University Press, 2024).

26

Israel Studies

Jonathan Marc Gribetz, Princeton University

FLIP BACK to the table of contents of this companion volume and notice that there are no chapters on Poland studies, Iraq studies, U.S. studies, or studies of any other contemporary country, no matter how many Jews lived there in the modern period—except for this one on Israel studies. What is Israel studies, and in what sense is it a part of and yet distinctive within Jewish Studies? This chapter explores the definition and history of the field of Israel studies with a particular focus on the ways in which it fits and does not fit within the framework of Jewish Studies.

If we understand Israel studies to be the academic field that encompasses scholarship about Zionism and its consequences in Palestine, Israel, and beyond, the field is nearly as old as the phenomena it studies. In 1899, for instance, just two years after the first Zionist Congress met in Basel, Switzerland, and called for "a publicly recognized, legally assured homeland in Palestine" for "the Jewish people," Columbia University professor Richard Gottheil had already published an article on the "various stages" through which the Zionist movement had passed.[1]

If, however, a field is defined not by the research questions individual scholars ask but by a collective self-consciousness and by institutions, we might look instead to the creation of academic journals and associations as we attempt to trace the history of Israel studies.[2] An academic journal focused on the study of Zionism was founded in Israel just a year after armistice agreements ended the state's founding war. In 1950 the first issue of the Hebrew-language *Shivat Zion: A Yearbook for the Study of Zionism and the Revival of Israel* was published; this journal, however, was short-lived, with only four volumes printed before its

541

demise in 1956. In 1970 a new Hebrew-language journal, *Ha-Tsiyonut: Journal for the History of the Zionist Movement and the Jewish Yishuv in the Land of Israel*, was established by the Haim Weizmann Institute for the Study of Zionism at Tel Aviv University (TAU). *Ha-Tsiyonut*'s founding editor Daniel Carpi described the journal as "the first compilation of research articles on the history of the Zionist movement and the Jewish Yishuv in the Land of Israel in modern times."[3] *Ha-Tsiyonut*'s last issue was published in 2001. The following year, a new Hebrew-language journal, under the same editorial leadership, took its place: *Yisrael: A Journal for the Study of Zionism and the State of Israel—History, Culture, Society*. Nominally at least, the study of Zionism had been replaced by the study of Israel.

This transformation—from "Zionism studies" to "Israel studies"—had already occurred several years earlier in an English-language journal published by the same TAU institute where *Ha-Tsiyonut* and *Yisrael* were based. In 1980 the institute inaugurated a journal called *Zionism: An International Journal of Social, Political, and Intellectual History*. This journal's founding coeditor Anita Shapira explained that "although Zionism as a movement is approaching the first centenary of its birth, no adequate journal in English has yet appeared which concerns itself exclusively with the subject in all its complexity: as an ideology, as a political movement and as a Jewish colonizing force in Palestine which during one hundred years produced notable new forms of social organization."[4] (The political implications of the phrase "a Jewish colonizing force in Palestine" have no doubt changed since 1980.)

In 1994 *Zionism* was renamed the *Journal of Israeli History: Studies in Zionism and Statehood*. The coeditors Ronald Zweig and Michael Oren explained that the journal would continue to publish "the latest research and the best scholarship on the history of the Zionist movement and thought; on the Jewish community in Palestine; and the relations between that community and the Jewish world, and between the Jews of Palestine and their Arab neighbors," just as *Zionism* had. However, because Israeli archives from the post-1948 period had recently been opened to researchers, the editors changed the journal's name "to reflect the broadening of the subjects it addresses," now not only the movement that sought to create a state but also the state itself.[5]

In 1996, during the still heady, if increasingly violent and uncertain, period of the Oslo process, two years after *Zionism* became *Israeli*, yet another English-language journal emerged, this time simply bearing the name of the new field, *Israel Studies*. As its founding editorial board wrote in its inaugural issue, the journal "welcomes contributions from students of Israeli history, literature, political science, economics, sociology, anthropology, and historical geography," and the "temporal boundaries include the pre-state period," even as "emphasis is on the State of Israel." In addition, the board asserted that "attention will be given to the study of the different groups that constitute Israeli society" while "due recognition is also given to events and phenomena in Israel's diaspora communities as they affect the state."[6] *Israel Studies* was affiliated with the Association for Israel Studies (AIS), the professional academic organization created in 1985 by "a group of scholars from many disciplines" who believed "that an organizational framework for the exchange of ideas about all aspects of Israeli society was needed," as Ian Lustick, one of the AIS's founders, put it a few years later.[7]

The preceding narrative of the rise of Israel studies starts in Israel and in Hebrew, and its practitioners were, in the main, Jews. This is the conventional origin story of Israel studies, and it is perfectly reasonable and compelling, but it is not exhaustive. There is an alternative, parallel narrative of Israel studies that begins in Beirut and in Arabic (although, like its Israeli-Hebrew counterpart, it quickly expands into English), and its practitioners were largely Arabs. Just a few months after *Ha-Tsiyonut* was founded in Tel Aviv in 1970, the first issue of a journal called *Shu'un Filastiniyya* (Palestinian Affairs) was published in March 1971 about 135 miles north in Beirut by the Palestine Liberation Organization Research Center. The founding editor Anis Sayegh explained that the journal would specialize in "the affairs of the Palestinian people; of the Palestinian issue; of the Palestinian struggle; of the land of Palestine, the society of Palestine, and the culture of Palestine—past, present, and future."[8] Lacking the words "Zionism" and "Israel," this list of research topics may appear different from those of *Yisrael* or *Israel Studies*, but *Shu'un Filastiniyya* was deeply interested in understanding Jewish nationalism and the State of Israel. Indeed, the very first article it published was titled "'Hawks and Doves' in Israel." Also in the first issue were articles titled "Israel and Global Imperialism" and "Israeli Policy in the Occupied Territories," along with sections on "Israeli Policy" and the "Israeli Economy."

The very same year, 1971, the nearby independent Institute for Palestine Studies (founded in 1963) printed the first issue of its *Journal of Palestine Studies* (*JPS*). Published in English, *JPS* was explicitly aimed at a foreign audience of "students, intellectuals, academics specialists, diplomats, [and] government officials . . . in Western Europe, in North America, in the socialist countries and in the countries of the Third World."[9] Like the first issue of *Shu'un Filastiniyya*, the inaugural issue of *JPS* included articles focused on Israel, such as "Israel's Nuclear Options" and "Recent Knesset Legislation and the Arabs in Israel."

Some might object to giving pride of place to or even including these Beirut-based journals in the story of Israel studies. The PLO Research Center (whose long-time director Anis Sayegh frequently characterized its studies of Israel as a project of "knowing the enemy") and the Institute for Palestine Studies could not be viewed as "truly academic," the argument would go, because both institutions were officially committed to supporting "the Palestinian cause."[10] There is no doubt that these institutions and the journals they produced preferred certain approaches to and positions on the Palestine–Israel conflict over others. The same, however, might be said of the journals produced by the Haim Weizmann Institute for the Study of Zionism at Tel Aviv University or by the sponsorship of the Ben-Gurion Research Center in affiliation with the AIS. The goal of "knowing the self" is not necessarily more neutral or academic than that of "knowing the enemy." Both, taught Sun Tzu, were essential for winning the war.[11]

In any case, both *Shu'un Filastiniyya* and *JPS* promised their readers intellectual openness and diversity (though the former acknowledged certain political limits and a baseline standard for inclusion in the debate, whereas the latter claimed the only criteria would be intellectual honesty). Sayegh, introducing *Shu'un Filastiniyya*, promised "multiple opinions, positions, and voices," all "united in the belief in the complete right to all of Palestine."[12] By contrast, Hisham Sharabi, the founding editor of *JPS*, asserted that his journal would "not ask our contributors to take any one position or view: we do not require them to be partisans of the Palestinian cause." *JPS* would rather provide "an international forum where all aspects of the Palestine question and the Arab-Zionist conflict may be freely discussed." Sharabi further pledged that the journal would not "engage in polemics or become a propaganda vehicle." "Commitment," he wrote, "does not preclude fairness or objectivity. Indeed, we believe that the cause of peace and justice in Palestine—as well as all over the world—is best served by adhering to the facts and their unbiased analysis."[13] In all, these approaches to the study of Israel (and Palestine) do not seem categorically distinct from those of the journals and institutes that populate the Israel-Hebrew-Jewish narrative of Israel studies.

Although these may appear to be two distinct, if contemporaneous, origin stories of the rise of Israel studies, presenting them as though they are merely parallel to one another would be misleading. Israel studies as founded in Tel Aviv and Israel studies as established in Beirut were never entirely separate from one another. Scholars in Israel were avidly reading the publications of Palestinian and Arab scholars at the PLO Research Center, IPS, and elsewhere—publications that were filled with references to the work of those same Israeli and Jewish scholars. In other words, although there may be two origin stories, there are not two entirely discrete fields in an intellectual sense.

That said, institutionally and sociologically, it was the field founded in Tel Aviv, rather than the one established in Beirut, that more directly evolved into the field of Israel studies as we know it today in the United States, represented, say, by the membership of the AIS. But although the AIS is formally affiliated with the Association for Jewish Studies (AJS) and the PLO Research Center, now based in Ramallah, is not, it is worth noting that many of the research interests of those early scholars in Beirut would have fit just as well within a Jewish Studies framework as the research interests of those based in Tel Aviv. Consider the fact that the PLO Research Center commissioned and issued Arabic books on *State and Religion in Israel* (1968), *Israel and World Jewry* (1969), *Zionism and the Talmud* (1970), *The American Council for Judaism* (1970), and *Jews of the Arab Countries* (1971) and published the journal article "Hasidism and Zionism" in *Shu'un Filastiniyya* (1976). In its early years the Israel studies movement founded in Beirut was, for its own reasons, especially interested in exploring the relationship and tension between Jewish religion and Jewish nationalism, whereas the Israel studies of Tel Aviv was, also for its own reasons, often more interested in politics and statecraft. In other words, at least in the fields' formative decades, the Israel studies of Beirut might be said to have fit more comfortably under a Jewish Studies umbrella than its counterpart in Tel Aviv, in the sense that the former was more concerned with understanding Israel's place in the broader context of Jewish history, culture, and values. Many of the topics that occupied the PLO Research Center during its time in Beirut (1965–83)—the role and treatment of Mizrahim, women, and Palestinians in Israel and the tensions between religion and nationalism—have, over the years, risen to the top of the research agenda of Israel studies scholarship broadly.

If we cannot draw a line, institutionally and sociologically, between the institutes in Beirut and Israel studies in the United States as represented by the AIS, we might more persuasively draw that line between the work done in Beirut beginning in the 1960s and that now being done both there and elsewhere in the Arab world. After all, the study of Israel among Arab scholars did not end when the PLO Research Center was expelled from Lebanon in 1983. Even as the PLO's center was forced to shut in Beirut, the IPS remained there—as it does to the present day. Since 2000 the Palestinian Center for Israeli Studies in Ramallah, known by the acronym Madar, has been analyzing Israeli affairs and publishing reports. In 2014 a Center for Israel Studies was founded in Jordan. In addition to independent think tanks, Arab universities have established

546   CHAPTER 26

programs in Israel studies. Since 2015 the premier Palestinian university, Birzeit, for instance, offers an MA program in Israeli Studies that aims to "train scholars for researching and writing about the various (political, security, economic, social, cultural) aspects of Israeli society and its settler-colonial structure, and understanding its international and regional contexts, and its impact on the Palestinians and the Arab region."[14]

Is Israel studies today part of Jewish Studies? At Birzeit there is no department of Jewish Studies, but students who pursue the Israeli Studies master's degree are expected not only to learn about Zionism and Israel and be able to use Hebrew for research but also to gain a solid understanding of "Judaism and Jewish history at large." The course "Judaism and Jewish History" is one of six required of Birzeit's Israeli Studies students. This course offers an introduction to Israelite and Jewish history and religion from the Canaanite period through the rise and development of Reform Judaism, Orthodoxy, Zionism, and anti-Zionism: "From the Tanakh to the Palmach," some might say.

Institutionally, in U.S, and European universities, Israel studies is often (though not always) part of Jewish Studies. At Brandeis University and New York University, the homes of the two largest centers for Israel studies in the United States, the Israel studies faculty chairs are based in the Department of Near Eastern and Judaic Studies and the Department of Hebrew and Judaic Studies, respectively. At Columbia University, where the towering Jewish historian Salo Baron founded a Center for Israeli Studies as early as 1948 and that is now home to the Institute for Israel and Jewish Studies, the formal link between Jewish Studies and Israel studies is evident.[15] At the University of Washington, the Israel Studies Program is housed in the Center for Jewish Studies. The University of California, Berkeley, is home to an Institute for Jewish Law and Israel Studies, and Harvard Law School hosts the Julis-Rabinowitz Program on Jewish and Israeli Law. Is it only natural that those who study the Zionist movement and the state it created—"the nation-state of the Jewish people" as per the state's Basic Law since 2018—should do so in the context of others who study Judaism and Jewish history?

Not all scholars of Israel studies see it that way. There are those who argue that even though this placement of Israel studies within Jewish Studies may seem natural, the arrangement is unhelpful for actually understanding the contemporary state of Israel. Johannes Becke, for instance, calls for "a systematic rupture between the research fields of Jewish Studies and Israel Studies" because "the field of Jewish Studies is unequipped to explore the reality of Israeli politics, culture, and society."[16] Instead, Becke champions what he dubs "methodological

Canaanism," which would explore "the rise of a Jewish-Israeli nation as an integral element of nation-building and state formation in the Middle East and North Africa" (199). Such an approach demands that Israel studies be integrated not into Jewish Studies but into "the broader field of Middle Eastern Studies" (200).

I am unpersuaded by the assertion that Jewish Studies lacks the methodological tools to study Israel, not least because this claim assumes that Jewish Studies is a discipline with a particular methodology. As this volume demonstrates, Jewish Studies is not itself a discipline but rather a multidisciplinary field of study that focuses on Jewish communities and their political, social, economic, cultural, textual, and religious lives in the context of the non-Jewish communities among which Jews have lived over the course of history. There is no a priori reason why Jewish Studies as a field is expansive enough to include "scripture" and "solonialism" (two other chapters in this volume) but too narrow to include "Israel studies."

Derek Penslar, an eminent scholar of modern Jewish, Zionist, and Israeli history, argues that even though "the Zionist project cannot be understood outside of the context of Jewish civilization," Jewish Studies as an academic field "is not well-suited to the study of modern Israel."[17] Penslar explains that Jewish Studies includes both textualists (who study Judaism, Jewish thought, and Jewish literature) and contextualists (mainly historians, along with some political scientists and cultural studies scholars). Israel studies, he contends, "clearly lies in the contextualist camp," though even in that camp of Jewish Studies, Israel studies is not truly at home. Jewish Studies' contextualists "think mainly about identity, community, and the mutual dynamic of Jewish and non-Jewish culture" and are acutely interested in "anti-Semitism and its effects on the Jewish world." By contrast, Israel studies scholars "are concerned with the accumulation and exercise by Jews of sovereign power, state formation and practice, diplomatic affairs, and ethnic conflict within the Israeli polity" (178–79). Especially in the respective formative years of Jewish Studies and Israel studies, their practitioners had very distinct concerns.

Gauging from the programs of recent annual conferences of the AIS, the interests and methods of the field of Israel studies seem to have expanded beyond the early ideal type. The field now includes textualists, and many of its contextualists are also investigating "identity, community, and the mutual dynamic of Jewish and non-Jewish culture"; that is, subjects that are traditionally the domain of Jewish Studies. At the 2023 AIS conference, for instance, one could hear papers on a variety of identity-focused subjects, such as "Cemeteries as Representing National Identity," "Tracing Jewish Identity Construction

548 CHAPTER 26

beyond the Typologies of Mainstream Groups in Israel among Native-Born Israeli Jews," "Beith Chabad: Preserving Israeli Identity in Brussels," "Muzika Mizrahit, Queer Identity, and Intersectionality in Israel's LGBTQ Scene," "Constructing Identity and Belonging through Israeli Reform Conversion," and "What Converts Can Teach us about Issues in Modern Jewish-Israeli Identity."[18] None of these topics has much to do with sovereignty, state formation, or diplomacy, and only some bear on ethnic conflict.

This widening of the scope of concern within Israel studies has been endorsed by the AIS leadership, as evidenced by the books that the association has awarded its highest monograph prize: the Yonathan Shapiro Award for Best Book in Israel Studies. In the last decade, winners of this prize have included Liora Halperin's *Babel in Zion: Jews, Nationalism, and Language Diversity in Palestine, 1920–1948*,[19] Noam Zadoff's *Gershom Scholem: From Berlin to Jerusalem and Back*,[20] Abigail Jacobson and Moshe Naor's *Oriental Neighbors: Middle Eastern Jews and Arabs in Mandatory Palestine*,[21] Diego Rotman's *The Yiddish Stage as a Temporary Home—On Dzigan and Shumacher's Theater, 1927–1980*,[22] Sarah Willen's *Fighting For Dignity: Migrant Lives at Israel's Margins*,[23] Gali Druker Bar-Am's *I am Your Dust: Representations of the Israeli Experience in Israeli Yiddish Prose, 1948–1967*,[24] and Giora Goodman and Tony Shaw's *Hollywood and Israel*.[25] Culture, language, literature, and identity are all now regarded as legitimate subjects of research in the field such that the distinctions of yesteryear between the major themes that occupy Israel studies and those that concern Jewish Studies no longer appear so stark.

There is a more obvious reason, however, why Israel studies may be an awkward fit in Jewish Studies. Although Israel was meant to be a "Jewish state" when the UN General Assembly voted to partition Palestine in 1947 and though it was proclaimed a "Jewish state" in its declaration of independence the following year, Israel was never a state consisting only of Jews. Today, it is a state with some two million citizens who do not identify as Jewish (not to mention the millions of non-Jewish noncitizens who live under some degree or another of Israeli rule). If, as I proposed provisionally , Jewish Studies focuses on Jewish communities in a (generally non-Jewish) context, does the inverse—namely, research on non-Jewish communities in a Jewish context—fit within the scope of Jewish Studies? Consider, for example, the following three research topics: folk songs and poetry among Palestinian Muslim citizens of Israel, mutual aid networks among non-Jewish African refugees in Tel Aviv, and American evangelical Christian pilgrimages to Jerusalem. Each of these topics would fit comfortably within an Israel studies framework as the field is currently configured. Should these topics and others like them—in which Jews and the Jewish state serve as the background and context but not as the primary focus of analysis—also be regarded as Jewish Studies?

Or consider a different question that emerges from academic and political debates in recent years: What would happen if the field of Israel studies were structurally conjoined with that of Palestine studies? At present, there is a growing community of scholars who study Palestine and especially Palestine's Arabic-speaking communities who see their work within the frame of Palestine studies. As a field in the United States, Palestine studies is less developed institutionally than Israel studies, but it is gradually expanding. In 2010 Columbia University established the Center for Palestine Studies, the first of its kind on an U.S. university campus. Penslar argues that "because scholars of Israel and of Palestine scrutinize the same small bit of land, the same events, and often the same people," the two currently separate fields of Israel studies and Palestine studies could be reorganized into a more capacious field called "Israel/Palestine Studies."[26] Nominally, such a field would be a very natural home for—and could even encourage—say, studies of Hebrew literature written by Palestinians or studies of political collaboration between Palestinians and Israelis during the British Mandate era or today. The term "Israel/Palestine Studies" also better suits scholarship on the Jewish community in Late Ottoman or Mandate Palestine for which the term "Israel Studies" is anachronistic, if not also teleological. Indeed, as early as 2015, the University of Colorado Boulder created an endowed professorship in Israel/Palestine Studies. If Palestine studies and Israel studies, as they currently exist, were folded into a single field of Israel/Palestine Studies, the new field would presumably encompass not only the areas of encounter between Palestine and Israel's Jews and Arabs but also the study of each community on its own: each community's nationalisms, politics, cultures, religions, and so on. Would the entire new field of Israel/Palestine Studies fit under the Jewish Studies umbrella or only the research conducted within it that focuses squarely on Jews?

Although such questions are debated among scholars in these fields, they will be answered not in theory but in practice—by the gatekeepers who decide what gets published in Jewish Studies book series and journals and who get jobs in Jewish Studies departments and programs. Time will tell.

In the meantime, for a sense of the state of the field, consider some of the questions American, Israeli, and Europe-based scholars of Israel (whether they tend to identify as an Israel studies scholar or not) have been investigating in recent years. If religion was ever truly imagined to be on the verge of disappearance, the reality in Israel, as elsewhere in the Middle East and beyond, has proven otherwise. Given the ever-increasing prominence of religion in the Israeli public sphere, Israel studies scholars have undertaken important research in analyzing the history of religion in Zionism and Israel. Alexander Kaye, in *The Invention of Jewish Theocracy: The Struggle for Legal Authority in Modern Israel*, argues that the idea that Jewish religious law ought to be the sole legal authority of the state is not an ancient one that Religious Zionists finally found the opportunity to implement in the new State of Israel.[27] Instead, it is thoroughly modern, developed by a small group of Religious Zionists led by Isaac Herzog, former chief rabbi of Dublin and, from 1937, the Ashkenazic chief rabbi in Palestine. Kaye shows how, whereas premodern Jewish thought assumed a legally pluralistic landscape, it was only in the twentieth century that the assumption emerged that legal centralism was a necessity. Daniel Mahla's *Orthodox Judaism and the Politics of Religion: From Prewar Europe to the State of Israel* shows us how two distinct forms of Jewish Orthodoxy—emphatically Zionist national-religious Orthodoxy and formally anti-Zionist ultra-Orthodoxy—emerged organizationally in Europe and Palestine in the first half of the twentieth century.[28] Mahla focuses not merely on the ideological positions that divided these communities but also and especially on the "mechanisms of contentious politics and mutual impacts and enmeshments" between and among the respective organizations. Yaacov Yadgar's *Israel's Jewish Identity Crisis: State and Politics in the Middle East* explores contemporary debates in Israel over the Jewishness of the state by studying the controversies concerning authority over conversion to Judaism, the 2018 Basic Law declaring Israel the "nation-state of the Jewish people," the "religionization" of the state, and proposals for non-Jewish or even anti-Jewish Israeli nationalism.[29]

The central physical and symbolic locus of the Palestinian–Israeli conflict was and remains Jerusalem's iconic Temple Mount/Noble Sanctuary, a constant tangible reminder that the century-old struggle is not merely territorial. Yitzhak Reiter and Dvir Dimant's *Islam, Jews, and the Temple Mount: The Rock of Our/Their Existence* aims to show that contemporary Palestinian denial of a Jewish history to this site reverses a long-standing Islamic acceptance of the Jews' connection to it.[30] In two important studies—first, *Righteous Transgressions: Women's Activism on the Israeli and Palestinian Religious Right*,[31] and then, *Women and the Holy City: The Struggle over Jerusalem's Sacred Space*,[32] political scientist Lihi Ben Shitrit draws our attention to the central and unique role of women in current fights over holy sites in Jerusalem. In *Women and the Holy City*, Ben Shitrit considers three case studies—Women for the Temple, Women of the Wall, and the Murabitat—to show how Jewish and Muslim women have participated in shaping both the religio-national conflict over the esplanade and the internal Jewish debate over who controls the nature of prayer at the Western Wall. Ben Shitrit brings these cases into conversation with recent theoretical scholarship on the question of religious freedom, modeling how insights from Israel studies can contribute to larger debates among scholars of religion and politics.

Israeli Jewish religious women's claims to authority extend beyond the confines of Jerusalem's sacred shrines and into the homes and families of Israel's ultra-Orthodox communities. Michal Raucher's *Conceiving Agency: Reproductive Authority among Haredi Women* shows how ultra-Orthodox women claim autonomy from the male religious and medical authorities they encounter during their pregnancies.[33] Disregarding these men's dictates, ultra-Orthodox women decide on their own about contraceptives, prenatal testing, fetal ultrasounds, and the like. Raucher contends, however, that this indifference to male authority "should not be regarded as freedom from religious life" but instead should be understood as women "draw[ing] on their embodied experience of pregnancy, cultural norms of reproduction, and theological beliefs in their relationship to divine activity during reproduction" (3). Raucher engages with work not only in Jewish Studies and Israel studies but also with women's history and feminist theoretical scholarship based in other societies elsewhere in the Middle East and beyond.

Israel studies scholars have productively explored questions of gender and sexuality in numerous contexts, both historical and contemporary. Viola Alianov-Rautenberg's *No Longer Ladies and Gentlemen: Gender and German-Jewish Migration to Mandatory Palestine* considers how gender informed the distinct experiences of women and men who fled Nazi Germany to Palestine in the 1930s.[34] The gendered nature of this story, Alianov-Rautenberg argues, was recognizable even before the immigrants left Germany, including whether and under what status a Jew would be permitted by the British to enter Palestine; it persisted in the immigrants' first experiences in Palestine, their encounters with their new neighbors, their employment opportunities and expectations, their housework, and their family lives. The book ultimately contends that "looking at migration through a gendered lens enables us to understand the category of gender in the process of its very construction and reconstruction" (250). In *Queer Judaism: LGBT Activism and the Remaking of Jewish Orthodoxy in Israel*, the sociologist Orit Avishai shows how twenty-first-century LGBT Israeli Orthodox Jews have created communities and transformed others as they have sought "livable lives."[35] Avishai argues that, although others have focused on "identity conflict" that LGBT Orthodox Jews experience, this framing "fails to capture how in the process of coming out of the shadows, LGBT persons did not merely reconcile religiosity and sexuality—they produced new Orthodox identities" (13). Avishai thus challenges the "intellectual secularist bias" she sees among gender and sexuality scholars and calls instead for taking religion seriously as one of a "long list of identity attributes considered through the lens of intersectionality" (11). Israel studies scholarship thus attempts to intervene in historiographic and theoretical questions of relevance far beyond the particularities of the case of Palestine and Israel.

One of the areas in which Israel studies scholarship has been most engaged and influential is in the study of national collective memory, because Zionism and Israel proved to be illuminating case studies for the construction of national stories, symbols, and myths. Inspired by Yael Zerubavel's pioneering *Recovered Roots: Collective Memory and the Making of Israeli National Tradition*,[36] Liora Halperin's *The Oldest Guard: Forging the Zionist Settler Past* explores the construction of the concept of the "First Aliya" and the evolving memory and memorialization of that period and the personalities and political practices associated with it.[37] Engaging with scholarship on other settler-colonial contexts, Halperin argues that the First Aliya came to be remembered as a community and period in which Zionists lived alongside Arabs not in conflict and indeed sometimes quite amicably; yet they lived on clearly unequal terms, with Arabs serving Jewish employers and Jewish interests, a condition Halperin terms "hierarchical coexistence."

The triangular relationship—hierarchical or otherwise—between Middle Eastern/Mizrahi Jews, Ashkenazi Jews, and Christian and Muslim Arabs in British-era Palestine is the primary focus of Abigail Jacobson and Moshe Naor's *Oriental Neighbors*. Jacobson and Naor argue that, because of Mizrahi Jews' cultural knowledge and linguistic abilities, they crossed "both geographical borders and boundaries of identity" and thus "maintained cultural, educational, economic, religious, political, and social links with their peers in the Arab world." As a result, "Sephardi and Oriental Jews served as mediators not only between the old and new Yishuv" (9); that is, not only among Jews of different political and geographical backgrounds in Palestine but also between Jews and Arabs. Hillel Cohen's *Haters, A Love Story: On Mizrahim, Arabs (and Ashkenazim, too) from the Beginning of Zionism through the Events of 2021* explores this triangle over a more expansive timeframe, showing the complexities and contradictions in these relations and their transformations over time.[38] These books are exemplars of a wave of scholarship in recent years focused on the encounters between European Jews, Middle Eastern Jews, Muslim Arabs, and Christian Arabs since the Late Ottoman period in Palestine.

The 1948 War—in which the State of Israel was founded while nearly three-quarters of a million Palestinian Arabs fled or were expelled—has been a topic of scholarly interest ever since. When, in the 1980s, Israel began opening the archives associated with this war, researchers sought to challenge what they regarded as myths that had been propagated by Israel and its advocates to justify Israeli forces' actions during the war and the resulting exile of most of the Palestinians who had lived in the territory that became Israel. These "New Historians" used the records of leaders within the military to demonstrate, among other things, that the "Palestinian refugee problem" was not created by accident or against the will of Zionist and Israeli military and political leaders. Shay Hazkani's *Dear Palestine: A Social History of the 1948 War* breaks new ground in the historiography of this war by exploring the experiences of regular soldiers—Arab and Israeli—through a careful study of letters they wrote during the war.[39] Using these personal letters written by soldiers in the Arab Liberation Army and the Israel Defense Forces, Hazkani shows that the 1948 War was far more complicated than the New Historians portrayed it. In fact, the distinct experiences of various demographic groups among the soldiers—Ashkenazi and Mizrahi (especially Moroccan) Jews, as well as Arabs from around the region— suggest that the traditionally assumed binary of "Jew" versus "Arab" was as much an effect as it was a cause of the war, constructed, at times rather uncomfortably, in the course of the violence.

Relations between Jews and Arabs in the Holy Land changed dramatically, of course, after the 1948 War. Adel Manna's *Nakba and Survival: The Story of Palestinians Who Remained in Haifa and the Galilee, 1948–1956* argues that the story of the 1948 war and that of the Palestinians who remained inside Israel ought not be told separately from one another but rather are essentially linked.[40] Manna also explores the different experiences of Druze, Muslim, and Christian Palestinians during the war and afterward as citizens of Israel. Shira Robinson's earlier *Citizen Strangers: Palestinians and the Birth of Israel's Liberal Settler State* focuses on the place of Palestinian citizens of Israel during the state's first two decades.[41] Studying the system of military rule under which most of Israel's Palestinian citizens lived until 1966, Robinson deems their status "paradoxical" because they were both "citizens of a formally liberal state and subjects of a colonial regime." Arguing that Israel's conquests in 1967 and the subsequent debates over the occupation have obscured our understanding and memory of Israel's history before the Six-Day War, Robinson aims to "restore empire to the history of post-1948 Israel, and post-1948 Israel to the history of imperialism" (3).

Seeing Israel in comparative context is also a main objective of Johannes Becke's *The Land beyond the Border: State Formation and Territorial Expansion in Syria, Morocco, and Israel.*[42] Becke's focus is the period at which Robinson stopped: Israel's conquest of and rule over the territories it seized in the course of the 1967 War. Becke considers post-1967 Israel to be a case of "third wave irridentism" and "state expansion" that is best understood in comparison to two other contemporary cases in the Middle East and North Africa: Syria's domination of Lebanon (1976–2005) and Morocco's annexation of Western Sahara (since 1975). Becke's argument is that these three phenomena, each with its "capture of contested territory, military occupations, and demographic engineering," are not "ghostly recurrences of a bygone colonial era" or "contradictory to the era of decolonization" but rather "a constitutive feature of postcolonial state formation" (2).

Each side in the Palestinian–Israeli conflict has, from the start, appealed to principles of international law. Two recent books have studied this history with conflicting conclusions. Steven E. Zipperstein's *Law and the Arab-Israeli Conflict: The Trials of Palestine* studies what the author views as "trials" before the Shaw Commission of 1929, the Lofgren Commission of 1930, and the Peel Commission of 1937.[43] The Zionist and Arab presentations before these commissions were an "opportunity to litigate the two most important issues dividing the parties during the early years of the conflict" (364): whether the Balfour Declaration was legal (and, if so, over what portions of Palestine it ought to be imposed) and who had legal rights to the Western Wall. Zipperstein aims to demonstrate that employing international law as a tool in the conflict ("lawfare") is not a new approach. Rather, "the parties began using the law and legal procedure more than a century ago to advance their positions and influence international opinion" (xiv). Lori Allen's *A History of False Hope: Investigative Commissions in Palestine* takes a more skeptical approach to this topic.[44] Allen studies the history of international commissions sent to analyze violent episodes in the Palestinian–Israeli conflict, focusing on the relationship especially of Palestinians to the King-Crane Commission of 1919, the Peel Commission of 1937, the Anglo-American Committee of Inquiry in 1946, the UN Special Committee to Investigate Israeli Practices Affecting the Human Rights of the Population of the Occupied Territories since 1967, and the Mitchell Committee of 2009. Allen argues that these commissions, and the liberal assumptions and "international law" discourse they demand of their participants, have deeply informed the way in which Palestinians conceive of and articulate their struggle. "The legal approach," writes Allen, "has become part of a Palestinian political tradition" (4). Allen ultimately argues that these commissions have done more to distract from than to resolve the conflict they have ostensibly come to assess.

Scholars of Palestine and Israel studies have published more sweeping studies that highlight particular themes in the broader history of Zionism and the Palestinian–Israeli encounter. Rashid Khalidi's *The Hundred Years' War on Palestine: A History of Settler Colonialism and Resistance, 1917–2017* argues that "the modern history of Palestine can best be understood . . . as a colonial war waged against the indigenous population, by a variety of parties, to force them to relinquish their homeland to another people against their will."[45] Although Khalidi sees this war, in certain respects, as a typical case of colonialism, he also notes features that distinguish it, including that it eventually morphed into a national conflict between Palestinians and Israelis. Another unique feature of the Zionist colonial project is that it "expertly" wove the Jews' "biblical connection to the historic land of Israel" into its ideological structure such that "a late-nineteenth-century colonial-national movement adorned itself with a biblical coat that was powerfully attractive to Bible-reading Protestants in Great Britain and the United States, blinding them to the modernity of Zionism and its colonial nature" (9).

Derek Penslar has encouraged the field of Israel studies to take more seriously psychology and emotions. In *Theodor Herzl: The Charismatic Leader*, he explores in subtle and sensitive detail Herzl's psychological instability, particularly his disturbed and disturbing inner world that affected not only his personal and familial relationships but also his public and professional ambitions and ultimately his leadership of the Zionist movement.[46] *Zionism: An Emotional State* even more explicitly brings the emotional turn to Israel studies.[47] If academic scholarship on Zionism had tended to focus on elite ideology and political institutions, Penslar shifts the field's attention to "the role emotion has played in the realization of the Zionist project to create and maintain a Jewish national home." This theoretically sophisticated and historically rich work helps us understand why "people the world over," Jews and non-Jews alike, have such "strong feelings about Israel" (4).

To be sure, many of the topics that Israel studies scholars research could be studied elsewhere, whether in other subfields of Jewish Studies, in Middle Eastern studies, or in the various methodological disciplines. Because of the advent of the academic field of Israel studies, however, these topics increasingly are seen as its domain. The result is that Israel studies, still a small field with a small community of scholars, bears the outsized academic burden of studying half the contemporary world's Jews (along with their many non-Jewish neighbors). Moreover, university courses on topics related to Israel tend to be among the most highly enrolled courses in any Jewish Studies roster. In these ways, Israel studies is an absolutely crucial component of Jewish Studies today. Thus, despite the political pressures that the field faces from all corners—its practitioners are regularly accused of being either pro-Israeli apologists, anti-Israeli propagandists, and sometimes of being both—the field will likely continue to expand in the coming years.

If current scholarly trends persist, one imagines that Israel studies scholars will continue probing the continuities and ruptures between diasporic and sovereign Jewish history; digging deeper into the Israeli state's archives and those of its many institutions to better understand the state's domestic and foreign politics; studying the multiple languages of the country's natives and immigrants so as to read their texts and engage with their oral histories; and analyzing Israel's diverse cultural production of literature, film, music, art, and dance in Middle Eastern and global perspectives. A radically interdisciplinary field whose scholars are encouraged to take seriously Jews' social, textual, and religious histories and cultures and who acknowledge the diversity of the experiences of Jews and their neighbors in an always complex and ever-transforming world, Israel studies may be considered not only to fit within but also to offer a model for Jewish Studies more broadly.

Recommended Readings

Alianov-Rautenberg, Viola. *No Longer Ladies and Gentlemen: Gender and the German-Jewish Migration to Mandatory Palestine* (Stanford University Press, 2023).

Becke, Johannes. *The Land beyond the Border: State Formation and Territorial Expansion in Syria, Morocco, and Israel* (SUNY Press, 2021).

Ben Shitrit, Lihi. *Women and the Holy City: The Struggle over Jerusalem's Sacred Space* (Cambridge University Press, 2021).

Cohen, Hillel. *Enemies, A Love Story: Mizrahi Jews, Palestinian Arabs, and Ashkenazi Jews from the Rise of Zionism to the Present* (Hebrew; Ivrit, 2022).

Halperin, Liora. *The Oldest Guard: Forging the Zionist Settler Past* (Stanford University Press, 2021).

Hazkani, Shay. *Dear Palestine: A Social History of the 1948 War* (Stanford University Press, 2021).

Jacobson, Abigail, and Moshe Naor. *Oriental Neighbors: Middle Eastern Jews and Arabs in Mandatory Palestine* (Brandeis University Press, 2016).

Kaye, Alexander. *The Invention of Jewish Theocracy: The Struggle for Legal Authority in Modern Israel* (Oxford University Press, 2020).

Khalidi, Rashid. *The Hundred Years' War on Palestine: A History of Settler Colonialism and Resistance, 1917–2017* (Metropolitan, 2019).

Manna, Adel. *Nakba and Survival: The Story of Palestinians Who Remained in Haifa and the Galilee, 1948–1956* (University of California Press, 2022).

Penslar, Derek J. *Zionism: An Emotional State* (Rutgers University Press, 2023).

Rabineau, Shay. *Walking the Land: A History of Israeli Hiking Trails* (Indiana University Press, 2023).

Notes

1. "The Zionist Movement," *North American Review* 169, no. 513 (August 1899): 227.

2. For a different and more extensive examination of the history of the field, see Nahum Karlinsky, "Reflections on the Development of Israel Studies" [Hebrew], in *'Am ve-'Olam* (Nation and World), ed. Dimitry Shumsky, Yonatan Meir, and Gershon David Hundert (Merkaz Zalman Shazar, 2019), 271–300.

3. *Ha-Tsiyonut* 1 (1970): 7.

4. *Zionism* 1 (1980): 2.

5. "Note from the Editors," *Journal of Israeli History* 15 (1994): 2.

6. *Israel Studies* 1 (Spring 1996): 1.

7. "Preface," in *Books on Israel*, Vol. 1 (SUNY Press, 1988), vii.

8. "Palestinian Affairs" (Arabic), *Shu'un Filastiniyya* 1 (1971): 4.

9. Hisham Sharabi, "This Journal . . . ," *Journal of Palestine Studies* 1 (1971): 1.

10. See Jonathan Marc Gribetz, *Reading Herzl in Beirut: The PLO Effort to Know the Enemy* (Princeton University Press, 2024), 14–20, 65.

11. *Sun Tzu on the Art of War*, trans. by Lionel Giles (Routledge, 2013), 24–25.

12. "Palestinian Affairs," 4.

13. "This Journal . . . ," 1.

14. See https://www.birzeit.edu/en/study/programs/MA-Israeli-studies. On this program, see Rebecca Stein's "How One Palestinian University Is Remaking Israel Studies," *Mondoweiss*, online at mondoweiss.net.

15. See Solomon Wiener, "A Home for Israel and Jewish Studies at Columbia: On the History and Mission of the IIJS," *The Current*, Spring 2019, online at columbia-current.org.

16. "Methodological Canaanism: The Case for a Rupture between Jewish Studies and Israel Studies," in *Jewish Studies and Israel Studies in the Twenty-First Century: Intersections and Prospects*, ed. C. Schapkow and K. Hödl (Lexington, 2019), 199–214.

17. "Toward a Field of Israel/Palestine Studies," in *The Arab and Jewish Questions: Geographies of Engagement in Palestine and Beyond*, ed. Bashir Bashir and Leila Farsakh (Columbia University Press, 2020), 173–200.

18. For the full program of the 2023 Association for Israel Studies annual conference, see https://ws.eventact.com/Conference2023/Program.

19. Yale University Press, 2014.

20. Brandeis University Press, 2015.

21. Brandeis University Press, 2016; Hebrew, 2021.

22. Hebrew, 2018; Engl., Magnes, 2021.

23. University of Pennsylvania Press, 2019.

24. Hebrew, Yad Yitshak Ben Zvi, 2021.

25. Columbia University Press, 2022. For the full list of Shapiro Prize winners since 2004, see AIS Israel Studies Awards, online at aisisraelstudies.org.

26. "Toward a Field," 192.

27. Oxford University Press, 2020.

28. Cambridge University Press, 2020.

29. Cambridge University Press, 2020.

30. Routledge, 2020.

31. Princeton University Press, 2016.

32. Cambridge University Press, 2021.

33. Indiana University Press, 2020.

34. Stanford University Press, 2023.

35. New York University Press, 2023.

36. University of Chicago Press, 1995.

37. Stanford University Press, 2021.

38. Hebrew; Ivrit Hotsaah Laor, 2022.

39. Stanford University Press, 2021.

40. University of California Press, 2022.

41. Stanford University Press, 2013.

42. SUNY Press, 2021.

43. Routledge, 2020.

44. Stanford University Press, 2021.

45. Metropolitan, 2020.

46. Yale University Press, 2020.

47. Rutgers University Press, 2023.

ACKNOWLEDGMENTS

WE WOULD like to express our deep gratitude to our editor Fred Appel at Princeton University Press, who has shown extraordinary patience and care in helping this book reach publication. We thank James Collier of PUP who helped shepherd the project along from its earliest stages. We are grateful to Melody Negron at Westchester Publishing Services and to Gail Naron Chalew for her expert copyediting.

We commissioned Sally Freedman as an editorial assistant, and her hard work at multiple junctures was crucial to the development and completion of the volume. We also thank the Program in Judaic Studies at Princeton University for its financial support of this project.

Most of all, we would like to thank the contributors to this volume. They not only wrote great essays but also helped shape the volume by providing feedback to each other as well as to us. This volume is truly a collaborative project.

With gratitude, this volume is our small tribute to all the scholars in Jewish Studies who have kept the field alive for two centuries, sometimes doing so in the face of very daunting circumstances.

INDEX

Abbasid caliphate, 71, 88
Abitbol, Michel, 525
Abraham, Karl, 400
Abrahams, Israel, 122, 214
Abram/Abraham, 21, 27, 286
Abramovich, Sholem Yankev (S.Y.)
(Mendele Mocher Sfoim), 260–61,
357–58, 417–18
Abrams, Daniel, 165
Abu El-Haj, Nadia, 463
Abuhav, Orit, 459
Abulafia, R. Abraham, 166, 167
Adler, Michael, 214
Adler, Nathan, 214
Adler, Rachel, 483
Adorno, Theodor, 240–41
Adret, Shelomo Ibn, 108
Aegean culture, 19
Aelia Capitolina, 53
African American Jews, 498
African Hebrew Israelites, 299
Agnon, Shmuel Yosef (S. Y.), 265, 357, 359
Ahasuerus (king), 32
Ahuvia, Mika, 287
Akiba, 68
Alcalay, Ammiel, 527
Aleichem, Sholem, 264–65, 358, 361
Alexander, Michael Scott, 500
Alexander Jannaeus, 46, 48
Alexander the Great, 37, 40
Alexandria, Egypt, 18, 41, 43–44, 52, 84, 87,
91, 344
Algeria, 211–14
Alianov-Rautenberg, Viola, 551
Allen, Lori, 554–55
Allen, Theodore W., 494

Allgemeine Zeitung des Judentums (AZdJ),
220–22
Alliance Israélite Universelle (AIU), 211
Alterman, Natan, 358
Altshuler, Mordechai, 422
Amenemope, 19
American Jewish sociology: attention
to diversity in, 445–47; big data in,
448–49; longitudinal data in, 447–48;
methods in, 437–42; survey research of,
437–38
American Jews, 206, 319, 320–22, 324, 325,
461, 488–93. *See also* American Jewish
sociology
Amichai, Yehuda, 356
Amidah Prayer, 73–74, 288, 374
Ammerman, Nancy, 314
Amsterdam, Netherlands, 96, 186,
187, 407
Anderson, Benedict, 83
angels, 44–45, 72, 282–83, 285, 287
Annales School, 122, 124
anthropology, culture in, 463–65. *See also*
Jewish ethnography
Antiochus III (king), 45
Antiochus IV (king), 40, 45
antisemitism, 4, 9, 139–43, 191, 204, 213–14,
225, 239–46, 441
Antler, Joyce, 512
apocalyptic literature, 51, 282
Appiah, Kwame Anthony, 306–7
Aquinas, Thomas, 167
Arab nationalism, 530, 534
Arabs/Arab Jews, 533–34, 553
Aragonese Crown, 95
Aramaic language, 18, 333, 335–38

Arendt, Hannah, 185, 203–5, 222, 233, 239
Aristobulus, 44
Aristophanes, 70
Arkin, Kimberly, 469
Arye Maimon Institute, 126
Ashkenaz, 103, 165, 174
Ashkenazi Hasidim, 167
Ashkenazi Jews: of Amsterdam, 96; Christian influences to, 149–50; civil rights struggles and, 492; defined, 521; legal definition of, 92–93; population of, 522; religious practice of, 135–36
Ashlag, Rabbi Yehuda Leib, 171
Ashton, Dianne, 321
Assan, Valerie, 212
Association for Israel Studies (AIS), 543, 545, 547–48
Association for Jewish Studies, 3, 8
Assyrian Empire, 26, 39
Astronomical Book and Book of the Watchers, 45
Athalia (queen), 26
Atler, Robert, 357
Auerbach, Berthold, 353
Auschwitz, 237, 240
Austin, John, 476
authoritarian personality, 240–41
Avishai, Orit, 467, 551–52
Avni, Sharon, 324, 440
Ayyubid sultanate, 87, 89, 109
Azulai, Rabbi Chaim Yosef David, 174

Babel, Isaac, 265, 358, 410
Baboy, Pirqoy ben, 71
Babylonian Empire, 20, 26, 39
Babylonian Talmud (Bavli), 60, 70–71, 72, 73, 74, 163, 480
Bacharach, Rabbi Naftali, 171
Bacher, Wilhelm, 353
Baer, Marc, 532
Baer, Yitzhak, 102–5, 106, 107, 108–9, 122, 148, 151–52
Baghdad, 71, 87, 88, 152, 217, 334, 340, 525, 528, 530, 531
Bahloul, Joëlle, 524, 527
Baker, Cynthia, 296, 300, 301, 470
Balfour Declaration, 224

Band, Arnold, 357
Bankier-Karp, Adina, 437
Bar-Am, Gali Druker, 548
Baron, Salo Wittmayer: diasporic social history and, 99–102; diversifying emancipation and, 195–96, 202; on the Holocaust, 145; influence of, 204; on Islam, 152; on Jewish communal autonomy, 108; on Jewish legal position, 154; "Nationalism and Intolerance" of, 193–94; on political templates, 193; on regimes, 203; studies of, 122, 123, 143–44; viewpoint of, 155–56
Barrès, Maurice, 214
Barthes, Roland, 359
Bartov, Omer, 243
Barzilay, Tzafrir, 154–55
Bashkin, Orit, 534
Baskin, April, 500
Batnitzky, Leora, 484
Bauer, Yehuda, 234, 241
Baum, Bruce, 494
Baumgarten, Elisheva, 107, 512
Baumgarten, Jean, 423
Be'chol Lashon, 498–99
Becke, Johannes, 546–47, 554
Behar, Ruth, 466
Beider, Chaim, 419
Beit Yosef (Caro), 172, 173
Bell, Derrick, 494
Bellow, Saul, 358
Bemporad, Elissa, 422
Benghazi, Libya, 218
Benor, Sara Bunin, 440
Bentham, Jeremy, 476
Ben-Ur, Aviva, 533
Benveniste, Rabbi Haim, 174
Beregovsky, Moisei, 415
Berg, Nancy, 530
Berger, David, 148
Berger, Shlomo, 423
Berliner, Adolf, 121, 122
Berlinger, Gabrielle Anna, 321
Bernstein, Abraham Moshe, 375
Best, Werner, 244
Bezalel Art Institute, 405–6
Bhabha, Homi, 223
Biale, David, 493, 499

Bialik, H. N., 265, 358
Bildung, 255, 258–59, 260
Bindewald, Friedrich, 221
Birnbaum, Pierre, 196–97
Bitton, Mijal, 439
Bloch, Isaac, 212–13
Block, Rabbi Irving J., 499
Blough, Karen, 150
Blumenkranz, Berhard, 126, 403
Boas, Franz, 458
Bock, Jerry, 263
Boer War, 214
Book of Enoch, 44, 45
Borokhov, Ber, 420
Borovaya, Olga, 532
Boum, Aomar, 532
Boyarin, Daniel, 506
Boyarin, Jonathan, 455
Brafman, Yonatan, 484
Braude, Benjamin, 524
Braun, Robert, 441, 443–44
Brettschneider, Marla, 500
Brink-Danan, Marcy, 469
Britain, colonialism and, 214–18
Brodsky, Adriana, 532
Brougham, Lord, 215
Browning, Christopher, 244
Brumberg-Kraus, Jonathan, 322–23
Buber, Martin, 405, 425
Budick, Sanford, 359
Bunzl, Matti, 469
Burckhardt, Jacob, 399
Burgess, Ernest W., 490
burial practices, 130
Bush, Andrew, 300–301

Cairo Geniza, documents from, 61, 84, 86, 88, 89–90, 103, 105–6, 107, 135, 523
calendar, 50, 51, 168, 278–80, 282
Calvinist Church, 96
Cammy, Justin, 425
Canpanton, Rabbi Isaac, 174
cantors, 382–83
Capitoline Jupiter temple, 52, 53
Capri, Daniel, 542
Carlebach, Shlomo, 386
Caro, Rabbi Joseph, 171, 172–74, 178
Caro, Rabbi Yosef, 178

Case, Holly, 210
Catholic Church, 94, 147, 148
Celan, Paul, 359
Centralverein, 441
Chad, Jordan, 425–26
Chagall, Marc, 263, 411, 415
Chaldeans, 29
Charney, Daniel, 418–19
Charney, Shmuel, 355, 418–19
Chayei Adam societies, 177
Chazan, Robert, 148, 155
Chetrit, Joseph, 525
Chetrit, Sami Shalom, 534
Christians/Christianity/Christian world: churches of, 129–30; development of, 104; gender and, 134; idiom of, 151; Islamic world as compared to, 104; Jewish communities in, 93; Jewish conversion to, 140; Jewish views of, 146; Jews and, 167–68; from Judeans to, 53; material culture and, 133–34; rituals of, 132–33; space of, 131–34
Chronicles (Hebrew Bible), 33–34, 43
circumcision, 45, 47, 53, 130, 277
citizenship: as catalyst for transformation, 193; defined, 186, 200; denial of, 490; extraterritorial, 199–200, 201; legal belonging and, 200; political rights and, 200–201
citizenship of Jews: case study for political theory and, 186–90; as central category for Jewish studies, 190–95; defined, 186; in modern era, 144; musical communities and, 386; revoking of, 198; types of states and, 196–97; in World War II, 203. *See also specific locations*
civil rights movement, 491–92
Claudius (emperor), 52
Clermont-Tonnerre, Stanislas de, 97–98
Cohen, Hillel, 552
Cohen, Jeremy, 151, 153
Cohen, Julia Phillips, 199, 531
Cohen, Marc, 152, 153
Cohen, Rabbi Shabtai, 175
Cohen, Richard, 256
Cohen, Stephen M., 498
Cohn-Wiener, Ernst, 401

colonialism: emancipation and, 222; France and Britain and, 210–18; imperial policy and, 238; Italy and, 218–22; Kaiserreich and, 220–22; summary of, 226–27; terminology and typology of, 208–10; Zionism and, 223–26

commerce, 131, 132, 201, 316

commercial printing industry, 172

common Jewish narrative, 299

communes, 102–5

Communities of Violence (Nirenberg), 153–54

Community Rules, 50

Confino, Alon, 242, 245

Constantinople, 95

Conversation, The, 451

conversion, 47–48, 151

convivencia, 153

Cordovero, Rabbi Moses, 169

Council of Four Lands (Poland and Ukraine), 94

Council of Lithuania, 94

Council of Trent, 172

covenant, 19

Cover, Robert, 478, 480–81

COVID-19 pandemic, 437

Crasnow, S. J., 326

creation narrative, 69–70, 276, 278, 283, 285

Crémieux, Adolphe, 211, 212, 215

Crenshaw, Kimberle, 493, 494

Crete, 93

critical race theory (CRT), 494

Crusades, 142, 151

cultural pluralism, 488, 489, 499–500

Cyprus, 52

Cyrenaica (Libya), 52, 219

Damascus Affair, 215–16

Daniel (Hebrew Bible), 33, 51

Danon, Abraham, 379

Danon, Dina, 531–32

Darmstadt Haggadah, 150

Darwin, Helana, 438, 446

Dashefsky, Arnold, 498

David, 21, 26, 27, 34, 46, 275

Dawidowicz, Lucy, 234

Day of Atonement (Yom Kippur), 277, 279

Dead Sea Scrolls, 18, 29, 43, 44, 49–50, 282–83

Delamere, Lord, 217

Delgado, Richard, 494

Demetrius the Chronographer, 44

Derrida, Jacques, 351, 510–11

Diadochi period, 40–41

Diarna, 536

diasporas, 37, 52, 122, 337, 363, 422, 529, 532–34

Dik, Ayzik Meyer, 428

Diner, Dan, 234

Dinur, Ben Zion, 122, 241

dispersion, 512–13

Dobrushin, Yeheskel, 418

Documentary Hypothesis, 24, 25–26

Dominguez, Virginia, 455

Dorin, Rowan, 155

Dropkin, Celia, 424

Drumont, Edouard, 213

Dubnow, Simon, 99–102, 141–43, 148, 192–93, 194, 223, 317

Du Bois, W. E. B., 488, 490, 492, 493

Dura Europos, 410

Durkheim, Émile, 99, 444

Dworkin, Ronald, 304–5, 306, 478–81, 482

Early Hellenistic Times, 40–45

Early Modern Period, 81, 131, 135, 144, 168–72, 193, 346, 364n3, 474, 483–84

East Africa, 216–17

Easter, 149

Eckhart, Meister, 167

Efros, Abram, 405

Egypt, 19, 41, 52, 88, 89–91, 135–36

Egyptian Jews, 41, 84, 86, 89–90, 522, 530–31, 535

Eichler-Levine, Jodi, 320, 323–24

Einstein, Albert, 425

Ein Yaakov societies, 177

Eisenberg, Jewlia, 427

Elephantine, 40, 276

Eliashev, Isidor [Yisroel] (Bal Makhshoves), 418

Eliezer, Rabbi, 57, 66, 72

El-Or, Tamar, 467

emancipation: colonialism and, 222; conceptual claims of, 203; conditional models of, 197; critique of, 192, 194–95; dating of, 197; defined, 192; diversifying, 195–98; emigration following, 192; equivocality of, 204; external and internal, 191; forms of, 197; historiography of, 190–95, 204–5; in liberal state, 189; nationalist view of, 191; in the Ottoman Empire, 198–202; revoking of, 198, 202; unconditional models of, 197; Zionism and, 224–25. *See also* citizenship; citizenship of Jews; specific locations

emigration, 192, 522

empire, cultural impact of, 50–51. *See also specific empires*

Engel, David, 231

Enlightenment, 2, 241–42, 351

Epstein, Marc Michael, 150

Erez, Oded, 535

Eric, Max, 418

eschatology, 29, 51

Essenes, 44, 48, 49–50, 284

Esther, Book of (Hebrew Bible), 32

Estraikh, Gennady, 422

Ethiopia/Ethiopian Jews, 218, 219, 342

ethnic identity, 489–90, 491–92

Ettinger, Shmuel, 241

Europe/European Jews: background of, 119; citizenship and, 184, 192–93, 194, 197, 206, 319; nationhood of, 371; overview of, 128–34. *See also specific locations*

Even-Zohar, Itamar, 356, 357

everyday Judaism: allies in, 131; beginnings of, 119–20; Christians and, 125–28; Christian space and, 131–34; church of, 129–30; communal organization of, 123; defined, 119–20; elites and non-elites in, 130–31; entanglement, appropriation, and adaptation in, 128–29; gender and, 134; halakhah and, 125; history of the Jews and, 120–24; homes in, 131; Jewish space and, 131–34; in Jews of Europe, 128–34; language in, 124; material culture and, 133–34; methods of, 124–25; overview of, 119; periodization of,

124–25; Protestant Reformation and, 135; rituals in, 124, 130, 132–33; social and cultural distinctions of, 130–31; synagogue of, 122, 129–30

Exclusiveness and Tolerance (Katz), 146–47

expulsions, Jewish, 155

extraterritoriality, 199–200, 201

Eyal, Gil, 534

Eybeschutz, Rabbi Jonathan, 175

Ezra, Abraham ibn, 142

Ezra, David, 217–18

Ezra-Nehemiah (Hebrew Bible), 34

Fader, Ayala, 323, 439, 467, 512

Falk, Rabbi Joshua, 175

Fanon, Frantz, 492

Fascist Revolution, 218–19

fasting, 279

Fatimid caliphate, 86, 90, 109

Fayum, 41

Feldman, David, 215

Feldman, Jackie, 466

Feldman, Rachel Z., 323, 460

Feldman, Zeev, 427

feminist movement, 507–9

Fernheimer, Janice W., 499

festivals, 277–78, 279. *See also* Hanukkah; Passover; Rosh Hashanah (Festival of Trumpets); Shavuot (Festival of Weeks); Sukkot; specific festivals

Fétis, François-Joseph, 377

Fifth Zionist Congress, 405, 409

Final Solution, 235

Finch, Martha, 322

Finkelstein, Louis, 104

Finkin, Jordan, 424

First Millenium, heritage of, 162–63

Fishbane, Michael, 294–95

flood narrative, 19, 24

folk songs, 378–79, 385–86

food studies, 322–23

Forman, Frieda, 424

formation of character, 255–56

Fox, Nicole, 439–40

Frakes, Gerold, 423

France, 93, 142, 192, 210–14

Franchetti, Leopoldo, 218

Frankenberg, Ruth, 494
Frankl, Ludwig August, 375
French Revolution, 139, 192, 197, 212
Frenkel, Michal, 445–46
Freud, Sigmund, 400
Friedländer, Saul, 234, 241, 242
Friedman, Joshua, 464
Funnye, Rabbi Capers C. Jr., 498–99
Fusṭāṭ, 88–89, 91, 103–4

Gabirol, Solomon ibn, 142
Galilee, 169–70
Gallagher, Charles, 493
Gamaliel, Rabbi, 66, 72
Gandhi, Mahatma, 222
Gans, Eduard, 140, 416
Gaulle, Charles De, 213
gefilte fish, 312
Geiger, Abraham, 67
Geiger, Ludwig, 220
Gemeinschaft (community), 98–99
gender studies: addition and transformation in, 509–12; introduction to, 505–6; since the 1970s, 507–9; since the 1990s, 509
Genesis Rabbah, 67, 69, 70
Gentiles, 144, 242
Gerlach, Christian, 247
Germanic law, 104–5
German Jews, 186, 398–99
German South West Africa (SWA), 220–21
Germany, 93, 98, 142, 188, 192, 220–22, 246–47. See also Holocaust
Gesellschaft (society), 98–99
ghettos, 142, 193–94, 402, 416, 424–25
Gibbon, Edward, 152
Gierke, Otto, 98, 104
Ginsburg, Shaul, 379
Ginzburg, David, 405
Gitelman, Zvi, 422
Gladstone, Yaakov, 499
Glaser, Amelia, 422
Glazer, Nathan, 491
Glenn, Hermann, 222
Globocnik, Odilo, 238
Glückel of Hameln, 423
Gobineau, Arthur, 399
God, 22, 23, 276, 282–88
Goitein, Shelomo Dov, 105–6, 134, 153

Goldhagen, Daniel, 244
Goldmann, Nahum, 198
Goldschmidt, Henry, 326
Gollance, Sonia, 427
Gombrich, Ernst, 401, 402–3
Goodenough, Ernst, 401
Goodman, Giora, 548
Gordon, Lewis R., 499, 500
Gordon, Milton, 491, 492
Gorshman, Shira, 424
Gottheil, Richard, 541
Graetz, Heinrich, 98, 101, 120–21, 123, 141, 143, 155
Great Revolt, 37, 49, 57
Greco-Macedonian dynasties, 50
Greek philosophy, 44
Greenberg, Uri Zvi, 265
Grinberg, Marat, 362
Gross, Jan, 242
Güdemann, Moritz, 121–22
Gui, Bernard, 148
Guide for the Perplexed, 166

Ha'am, Ahad, 223, 255, 406
Hachaim, 177
Hackett, Conrad, 446
Hadrian, 53
Hagaddah, 149
Hahn Tapper, Aaron J., 297–99
halakhah (Jewish law): changes to, 483; comparison of, 154; defined, 477; everyday Judaism and, 125–26; influence of, 106; introduction to, 474–75; in Israel, 483–84; of Jewish community, 87, 91–92; Jews and Christians in, 132; local courts, Jews and Christians in, 132; overview of, 61–64, 174–76; paideic model of law and, 481; philosophy and, 309; return of common law mind in, 478–81; of the Zohar, 165
halakhic literature, 177
Halbertal, Moshe, 482
Halevi, Judah, 142
Halkin, Shimon, 355
Hall, David D., 314
Halperin, Liora, 548, 552
Hammad, Hanan, 535
Hanukkah, 46, 51, 321

Harel, Yaron, 531
Harnick, Sheldon, 263
Harris, Cheryl, 494
Hart, H. L. A., 476
Hartman, Geoffrey, 359
Hartman, Harriet, 438
Hasan-Rokem, Galit, 408
Hasidic Jews, 428, 440, 465–66
Hasidic movement, 76, 171
Hasidism, 166, 171, 192, 194
Hasmonean Dynasty, 44, 46–48
Ha-Tsiyonut (journal), 542
Hatzaad Harishon, 499
Haverkamp, Alfred, 126
Hayes, Christine, 482
Haynes, Bruce, 460
Hazkani, Shay, 553
heavenly realm, God and, 282–88
hebraica veritas, 167–68
Hebrew Bible: alterations to, 18; biblical
    interpretation of, 34–35; Book of Psalms
    in, 30–31; composition of, 21–34;
    contents of, 21–34; historical contexts
    of, 19–20; as history, 20–21; introduction
    to, 15–17; Masoretic text of, 17–18;
    monolatry and, 20; monotheism and,
    20; *Nevi'im Aharonim* (Latter Prophets)
    in, 27–29; *Nevi'im Rishonim* (Former
    Prophets) in, 26–27; Pentateuch of, 16,
    21–22; Prophets of, 26–29; Tanakh of, 15,
    22; texts of, 17–18; Torah of, 21–26;
    wisdom literature in, 31; Writings in,
    29–34
Hebrew language, 18, 335–38, 345–47,
    355, 356
Heilman, Samuel, 459
Heine, Heinrich, 264, 353
Hekhalot literature, 167
Hellenization, 37, 398
Heller, Rabbi Aryeh Leib, 176
Hellerstein, Kathryn, 424
HEP HEP riots, 139–40
Herbert, Ulrich, 244
Herero peoples, 221
Herod the Great (king), 48, 275
Hertzberg, Arthur, 209
Herzl, Theodor, 191, 216, 223–24, 555
Herzog, Elizabeth, 458

Herzog, Isaac, 550
Hevrat Mishniot, 177
Hevrat Tehilim (psalm societies), 176–77
Hezekiah (king), 23
high priest, 41, 46, 57
Hilberg, Raul, 239
Hildebrand, Klaus, 241
Hilgruber, Andreas, 237
Hillel, House of, 67–68
History of the Jews (Graetz), 141
Hitler, Adolf, 237–38, 240, 241, 246
Hittite culture, 19
Hiyya, Rabbi, 72
Hoberman, J., 428
Hok LeYisrael, 177
Hollinger, David, 470
Holocaust: antisemitism and, 239–46;
    approach toward, 123; artistic-literary
    account of, 145; deaths of others and,
    236–39; defining catastrophe of, 235–36;
    introduction to, 231–32; Jewish history
    and, 239–46; in Jewish Studies, 231–32,
    249; language changes from, 345; other
    genocides and, 246–48; resistance
    during, 441; as unprecedented, 233;
    Yiddish and, 424–25
home, 281, 320
Horkheimer, Max, 241
Horowitz, Amy, 444, 535
House of Hillel, 67–68
House of Orange, 97
House of Shammai, 67–68
Howard M. Metzbaum Multiethnic
    Placement Act of 1994, 496
Howe, Irving, 358
Hrushovski, Binyamin (Benjamin
    Harshav), 356, 357
Human Genome project, 8
Husni, Dawud, 531
Hyde, Allen, 442

Iberia, 93, 107
Idel, Moshe, 165, 166
Idelsohn, Abraham Z., 378
identity, 8, 38, 53, 120, 293, 295, 306–8, 407,
    444. *See also* Jewish identity
Idumeans, 47–48
Ignatiev, Noel, 494

Imhoff, Sarah, 319, 326, 463, 506
imperial model of law, 481
imperial policy, 237–38
Improperia (Christian prayer), 149
Indian Arms Act of 1878, 217
intermarriage, 34, 37, 324–25, 437, 465, 491, 492, 500, 512
international law, 554–55
interpretive theory of law, 304–6
interwar period, 143–45, 242, 425
inward acculturation, 93, 107, 128, 150
Iran, 88, 89
Iraq, 88, 89, 103, 530
Isaac, 83
Ishamel, 68
Islam/Islamicate lands/Islamic world: Arabic terms in, 86; Ashkenaz in, 103–4; attacks on Jews in, 525; cultures of petition in, 212; examination of, 132; history of Jews in, 88–93, 145, 520, 524; Jewish affiliation and belonging in, 134–36, 142, 529; Jewish ancestry in, 521; Jewish community governance in, 105–6; Jewish music in, 370, 389; Jewish myths and counter-myths in, 151–53; monuments of, 399; multinational empires in, 201; postmodernity and, 469; premodern, 519; religious law in, 110; rise of, 124; Sephardi/Mizrahi life in, 220, 528; Temple in, 276
Israel (biblical): conquests by, 554; destruction of Northern Kingdom of, 26–27; Israelites/Israelite cultures, 19, 22, 82
Israel (modern state): creation of departments of Jewish history in, 124; creation of State of, 148; immigration to, 522; Jewish citizenship in, 195–96, 198, 206; Jewish community in, 103; in Jewish ethnography, 459; Jewish law in, 483–84; Jewish music in, 387; Jewish-ness of, 550; Jewish Studies research in, 3; Mizrahim in, 534; 1948 War and, 553; significance of, 296; Six-Day War and, 225–26, 553–54
Israel studies: burden of, 555–56; colonial war and, 555; defined, 541; gender and sexuality in, 551–52; institutionalization

of, 545–46; international law and, 554–55; in Jewish Studies, 546–47, 548–49; national collective memory in, 552; origin of, 545; Palestine studies and, 549; psychology and emotions in, 555; publications in, 542–44; questions in, 549–50; scope of concern in, 548; Zionism and, 555
Israel Studies (journal), 542–43
Isserles, Rabbi Moses, 173–74
Italy, 135, 198, 218–22
Itureans, 47

Jäckel, Eberhard, 241
Jackson, John L., Jr., 460
Jackson, Maureen, 535
Jacob, 83
Jacobs, Janet L., 460
Jacobson, Abigail, 548, 552
Jacobson, Matthew Frye, 491, 494
Jaldati, Lin, 427
Jason, 45
Jehoiachin (king), 27
Jeremiah (Hebrew Bible), 18
Jeremiah, Rabbi, 69–70
Jerome, 168
Jerusalem, 39, 42, 45, 46, 53, 88, 91, 550–51. *See also* Israel
Jerusalem School of history, 122–23
Jerusalem Talmud (Yerushalmi), 163
Jerusalem Temple: calendar of, 50, 278–79; centrality of, 37; desecration of, 45; destruction of, 23, 51–52, 56, 283–84; festivals in, 277–78, 279; Judean recovery of, 45–46; pilgrimages to, 46–47; rebuilding of, 39; rituals in, 276–77; sacredness of, 276; sacrificial cult in, 40; significance of, 275–76; sources regarding, 276–77
Jesus, 55, 149, 168
Jewish art, 256–57, 263, 264–66, 397–403, 404–11
Jewish Buddhists, 325, 438–39
Jewish centers, 164
Jewish community: alternate words for, 86–87; authority of, 81; autonomy in, 81, 94–95, 102; breaking paradigm of communal autonomy in, 107–10;

business and, 91; centrality of, 81; centralized structure of, 90; charities of, 91; in Christian world, 93; citizenship and, 98; community and commune in, 102–5; conflicts in, 91–92; court system of, 91–92; demographics of, 82; diasporic social history and, 99–102; disruption to, 93; early modern centralization of, 94–97; education in, 90; in Egypt, 89–91; forced resettlement and, 95; governance in, 81, 92, 93, 94, 97, 106; halakhah (Jewish law) of, 87, 91–92; in historiography, 97–110; internalist approach to, 106; introduction to, 80–82; inward acculturation in, 93; in Islamic world, 88–93; Israelite assembly in, 82; *kehila* (communal organization) and, 116–17n91; legal status of, 87; locations of, 84, 96 (*see also specific locations*); loyalties in, 89–90; micro-communities of, 95; multilevel administration of, in Islamic world, 88–93; musical, 383–88; as oligarchy, 96; organizational persistence of, 101; *qahal* and, 83–85, 86, 87, 93; *qehilla* and, 85–87, 102–3, 117n92; recordkeeping by, 94; relief to the poor by, 91; segregation and, 116n91; in the sources, 82–97; state support for, 92; as state within a state, 80; *taqqanot* (statutes) in, 93; taxation and, 108; voluntary membership in, 101; women in, 109. *See also specific locations*
Jewish digital culture, 7
Jewish economic history, 117n98
Jewish *embourgeoisement,* 254, 256, 262
Jewish ethnography: contemporary contours of, 460–61; introduction to, 317–18, 455–57; Jewish pieties and religiosities in, 466–67; Jewish Question in, 468–69; Jewish relatedness in, 460–61; Jewish travels in time and space in, 465–66; past trajectories of, 458–60; production of Jewish culture in, 463–65; summary of, 469–71; vernacularized engagements with Jewishness and, 462–63
Jewish folklore studies, 7
Jewish genetics, 462–63, 496–97

Jewish identity/Jewishness: acceptance of, 299; characteristics of, 296, 299; citizenship and, 191, 193; defined, 298, 300–301; dual, 439; engagements with, 462; as ethnicity, 319; expressions of, 320; genetics and, 496; hybridity of, 301; inward acculturation of, 128, 149–50, 151; from Judeanness to, 47–48, 53; meaning-making and, 438; melting pot metaphor and, 488; nationalism of, 206; political parties and, 307–8; as race, 487; recognition of, 307; refractions of, 461; as relational phenomenon, 438–39; retainment of, 149; state and, 187; transformation of, 191; whiteness and, 500–501. *See also* race
Jewish language: archaic features of, 341; distinctive features of, 334–35; Hebrew and Aramaic influences to, 335–37; history of, 333–34; innovative features of, 341–42; introduction to, 331–32; in Jewish literature, 363; migrated regionalisms in, 340; naming, 332–33; new research directions for, 347–48; non-Jews' use of, 344; other contact languages in, 338–40; shift, endangerment, and post-vernacularity of, 344–45; summary of, 348–49; textual influence in writing of, 337–38; variation of, 342–43. *See also specific languages*
Jewish law. *See* halakhah (Jewish law)
Jewish learning, 300, 301–2
Jewish literature: audience of, 362; character of, 352; complex of, 360; conceptualization of, 353–54; contiguity of, 360–61; debate regarding, 353; defined, 350–51, 352; developments in study of, 363; gender and sexuality in, 361–62; languages in, 363; midrash in, 359; polysystem theory of, 356–57; positivist methodologies regarding, 354; transnationalism and, 361; in the United States, 355–56, 357–58; unity of, 355; Wissenschaft approach to, 352–53; Zionist-Hebraist approach to, 354–55
Jewish modernity, 192
Jewish Museum (New York), 401

Jewish music: categories of, 383; institutionalizing, 381–83, 386–87; introduction to, 368–70; in Jewish Studies, 388–90; liturgical, 377–78, 385–86; musical communities in, 383–88; possibility of, 370–72; recording technologies for, 371–72; repositories of, 392n14; sound archive of, 380–81; in state of Israel, 387; tracing, 372–73; written archive regarding, 373–80; Yiddish, 426–28
Jewish nationalism, 100–101, 102, 193, 294, 354, 378, 545. *See also* nationalism
Jewish philosophy, 164–68
Jewish Question, 203–4, 468–69
Jewish revolts, 52–53
Jewish Studies: challenges of, 3; citizenship as central category for, 190–95; as counter to anti-Jewish hostility and discrimination, 9–10; diversity of, 3–4; focus of, 548–49; humility in, 10; importance of, 9–10; integration of, 10; introduction to, 294–300; Jewish art in, 410–11; Jewish learning and, 301–2; Jewish music in, 388–90; knowledge explosion in, 4; locations for, 3–4; normativity and, 302–8; origin of, 2–3; overview of, 1, 2; politics in, 9; pride in, 10; self-validating identity in, 308; subjects in, 2; theoretical reflections on, 300–302; whiteness studies and, 493–95
Jewish tax, 52
Jews: animosity toward, 123; characterization of, 301; Christians and, 167–68; commonalities of, 122–23; conversion of, 140; as *dhimmi,* 134; education of, 256; intellectual accomplishments of, 141; from Judeans to, 53; legal positions of, 154; loss of security of, 202; multiple allegiances of, 331; persecution of, 127; perseverance of, 146; polity of, 205; as religious minority, 52; resilience of, 143; as scapegoat, 145; survival of, 146; term meaning of, 37–38; unity of, 140
Jews of color, 495–502
Jews of Islam (Lewis), 152
John Hyrcanus, 47
Jonathan, 46
Jones, Faith, 424

Joseph, Shoa Menachem, 219
Josephus Flavius, 44, 48, 283–84
Josiah (king), 23, 27
Journal of Palestine Studies (JPS) (journal), 543–44
Jubilees, 43
Judah the Patriarch, 62
Judaism: abolition of, 189; academic study of, 295; authenticity of, 148; Conservative, 297; defined, 16, 294; as family of tradition, 296; origin of, 37, 38; persistence of, 189; polythetic chart of, 296; Rabbinic transformation of, 56–70; Reform, 297; scientific approach to study of, 140. *See also* everyday Judaism
Judea/Judeans: destruction in, 40–41; establishment of, 26; forms of worship of, 51–52; incorporation of, 38; to Jews and Christians, 53; loss of political autonomy of, 45; massacre of, 52; Mizpah capital of, 39; resettlement of, 39; Samaria and, 40; settlements of, 40; society of, 49; to Syria Palestine, 53; term meaning of, 38
Judeo-Bolshevism, 243

Kabbalah: characterizations of, 141, 166–67; Christian, 167–68; ecstatic, 167; emergence of, 164–68; *Guide for the Perplexed* and, 166; halakhah and, 477; Jewish, 167–68; language of, 170; Lurianic, 169–71, 177; Safed, 169
Kabbalah Centre (Los Angeles, California), 325
Kabbalistic unification *(yihudim),* 172
Kaell, Hillary, 463
Kafka, Franz, 265, 359, 361
Kahn, Susan, 462–63
Kaiserreich, 220–22
Kallen, Horace M., 488
Kallenbach, Hermann, 222
Kant, Immanuel, 254
Kaplan, Yosef, 96
Karetot, 64
Karkabi, Nadeem, 535
Karpeles, Gustav, 352–53
Kasstan, Ben, 463

INDEX 571

Katz, Dana E., 403
Katz, Dovid, 428
Katz, Ethan, 533
Katz, Jacob, 106, 123–24, 146–47, 194–96, 204, 241, 477–78
Katznelson, Ira, 196–97
Kaufmann, Yehezkel, 17
Kaye, Alexander, 550
Kaye/Kantrowitz, Melanie, 500
kehila (communal organization). See qehilla
Kelman, Ari, 438, 445
Khalidi, Rashid, 555
Khazzoom, Aziza, 534
Khmelmytsky pogroms, 96
Kilcher, Andreas, 458
Kim, Helen Kiyong, 500
Kimchi, Rami, 535
Kinderschreck, 441
kinot, 151
Kirschnblatt-Gimblett, Barbara, 458
Kishinev pogrom, 156
Kiyong, Helen, 326
Klaley Hagmara (Caro), 173
Klapper, Melissa, 512
Klausner, Joseph, 354
Klausner, Yosef, 355
Klein, Elka, 104, 108
Klein, Menachem, 530
Klein, Shira, 218
kloyzen, 171, 172
Knesset Hagedolah (Benveniste), 174
Kolleg, Abraham Geiger, 382
Kompert, Leopold, 258–59
Kook, Lenin, 425
Kook, Rabbi, 425
Kornfeld, Moshe, 464
Kotler-Berkowitz, Laurence, 447
Krakowski, Eve, 512
Kramer, Michael, 360
Krasner, Jonathan, 440
Kravel-Tovi, Michal, 444
Kreitman, Ester, 424
Kremer, Rabbi Eliyahu, 176
Krieger, Leonard, 235
Kristol, Irving, 492
Krone, Adrienne, 323
Krutikov, Mikhail, 421, 422, 425
Kugelmass, Jack, 459, 466

Kuhn, Thomas, 513
Kurzweil, Baruch, 355

Lacan, Jacques, 359
lachrymose narrative, 122
Ladino, 334, 339, 341, 345, 346
Lamarck, Jean Baptiste, 489
Lamentations (Hebrew Bible), 32
Landau, Rabbi Yechezkel, 176
Landsberger, Franz, 401
Lansky, Aaron, 429
Lascar, Sascha, 447
Lasker, Daniel, 148
Last Supper, 149, 168
Leavitt, Noah Samuel, 500
Lebanon, 554
legal belonging, 200
legal canon, 172–74
legal pluralism, 483–84
Lehmann, Marcus, 353, 532
Lehrer, Erica, 465
Leibman, Laura, 511–12
Leipzig Maḥzor, 150
Leite, Naomi, 460, 466
Leman, Judah, 425
Leon, Nissim, 467
Leon, R. Moses de, 164
Lester, Julius, 496
Letter of Aristeas, 43
Levant, 530–31
Levene, Mark, 247
Levi, Tomer, 531
Levin, Rivka, 424
Lévi-Strauss, Claude, 469–70
Levita, Elia, 86
Leviticus Rabbah, 67
Levitt, Kim, 326
Levitt, Noah Samuel, 326
Levy, André, 466
Levy, Avigdor, 524
Levy, Lital, 359
Levy, S., 353
Lewis, Bernard, 152, 524
Lewis, Thomas A., 302, 303
LGBTQ Jews, 446, 551–52
liberalism, 186, 189, 191, 508
Libya, 220
Lichtenstein, Matty, 440, 443

Liebes, Yehuda, 164–65, 168
Limonic, Laura, 445
Lipshitz, Shifra, 415
Lipsitz, George, 494
Lipton, Sara, 403
Lisek, Joanna, 424
Lissitzky, El, 263, 415
literature, defined, 351. *See also* Jewish
  literature
Lithuania, 240
Littman, Lynn, 318
lived religion: expanding boundaries and
  further directions in, 324–27; food
  studies in, 322–23; introduction to,
  312–14; Jewish ethnography and, 317–18;
  material religion and, 316, 320–21; media
  studies in, 323–24; ritual studies in,
  321–22; in the United States, 314–16; U.S.
  Jewish, 318–24. *See also* religion
Lofton, Kathryn, 315–16
longitudinal data, 447–48
Lorberbaum, Yair, 482
Love of Zion (Mapu), 259–60
Loving v. Virginia, 496
Lubavitch, Chabad, 326
Lukacs, Georg, 425
Luria, Rabbi Isaac (Ari), 169–70
Lurianic Kabbalah, 169–71, 177
Lustick, Ian, 543
Luzzatto, Rabbi Moshe Chaim/Haim, 171, 354

Maccabean crisis, 45–46
Maghrebi Jews, 532
magic, 287
Mahla, Daniel, 550
Maimon, Arye, 126
Maimon, Solomon, 259
Maimonides, Moses, 142, 152, 164, 165, 167,
  176, 295
Makhshoves, Ba'al (Isidor Elyashev), 355
Mandel, Maud, 533
Mann, Michael, 247
Manna, Adel, 553
Mapu, Abraham, 259–60
Marcello, Benedetto, 376
Marcus, Ivan, 93, 107, 128, 149–50, 151, 153
Marek, Peysekh, 379
Marglin, Jessica, 199–200, 532
Margolin, Anna, 424

Margolis, Rebecca, 428
Marian imagery, 150
marriage, 130
Marx, Karl, 185, 186–90, 194, 202, 492
Marxism, 124
Mary (mother of Jesus), 151
Masoretic text (Hebrew Bible), 17–18
Mass, 150
material culture, 41–42, 133–34
material religion, 316, 320–21. *See also*
  religion
Maupassant, Guy de, 214
Mays, Devi, 532
McClendon, David, 446
McDannell, Colleen, 316, 406
media studies, 323–24
Mediterranean diasporas, 39
Mehta, Samira, 325, 326, 511–12
Meir, Rabbi, 60
Meir-Glitzenstein, Esther, 534
Mekhilta de- Rabbi Ishmael, 68
Mellinkoff, Ruth, 403
Memmi, Albert, 222
Mendelssohn, Moses, 191, 192, 353
Mendes-Flohr, Paul, 187
Meroz, Ronit, 165
Mesopotamia, 19, 39
Messianism, 29
Mevorach, Katya Gibel, 499
Meyer, Carol, 507
Middle Ages, 124–25, 164–72
Middle Eastern and North African
  (MENA) Jews, 525–26, 534, 536
midrash, 67–70, 359
migration, 88, 89
Miller, Susan, 532
Mills, C. Wright, 435
Mintz, Alan, 357, 358–59
Miriam, 150
Miron, Dan, 257–58, 357–58, 360–61, 421
Mishnah, 61–64, 65–67, 71–72; *mishnayot,*
  163; order of Nashim, 62
Mishpat Ivri (Hebrew law) movement, 477
Mizrahi Jews, 518–23, 524. *See also*
  Sephardi/Mizrahi studies
Molodowsky, Kadia, 424
moneylending, 155
monolatry, 20
monotheism, 20

Monsterscu, Daniel, 467
Montefiore, Sir Moses, 215
Moreno, Aviad, 532–33
Morgan, David, 406
Morinaud Law, 228n15
Morocco, 216, 228n15, 532, 535–36, 554
Moses, 21, 56, 82
Moses, Dirk, 232, 247–48
Moss, Kenneth, 422
Mount Gerizim, 40, 47, 276
Moynihan, Daniel Patrick, 491
Murad, Layla, 531
music, 264, 369–70, 371, 535. *See also*
    Jewish music
Mussolini, Benito, 218–19
Myerhoff, Barbara, 318, 459, 470–71
Myers, Davin N., 147
Myers, Jody, 323, 325
mysticism, 164–68, 287

Naar, Devin, 531, 533
Nachman, Rav, 428
Nahmanides, Moses, 148
Nahon, Gerard, 126
Najara, R. Israel, 375
Nalewajko-Kulikov, Joanna, 414
Naor, Moshe, 548, 552
Nathan of Gaza, 171
nationalism, 100, 104, 124, 140, 191, 224,
    351, 387, 545. *See also* Jewish nationalism
National Study of Youth and Religion
    (NSYR), 448, 449
Naumbourg, Samuel, 377
Nazism, 3, 146, 235–36, 237, 245, 247.
    See also Holocaust
Nebuchadnezzar (king), 27
neoconservativism, 492
Neumann, Boaz, 245
Newman, Barnett, 263
niggun, 374–75
1948 War, 553
Nirenberg, David, 153–54, 155
Noah, 24
Nolte, Ernst, 237
non-elites, in everyday Judaism, 130–31
Nordau, Max, 406
Norich, Anita, 359–60
normativity, 293, 296, 302–8
Northern Kingdom, 26

nostalgia, 256–58
Nostra Aetate ("Declaration on the
    Relation of the Church to Non-
    Christian Religions"), 147, 148
Nove, Chaya, 428
Nuremberg Laws, 235, 489–90

obrazovanie (education), 255
Ochs, Vanessa L., 320, 321–22, 464
O'Connell, Daniel, 215
Odessa, Pinchas (Pinkhes) Minkowsky,
    371–72
Ofer, Dalia, 512
Omi, Michael, 493
Onias III (High Priest), 45
orality, of rabbinic literature, 59–60, 65
Oren, Michael, 542
Or Hachaim (Atar), 177
Orientalism, 409
Orientals, Jews as, 140, 209, 409
Origins of Totalitarianism, The (Arendt),
    203–4
Orsi, Robert A., 315, 327
Orthodox Jews: on annihilation, 233;
    anthropological works regarding, 467;
    blame from, 239; as called into being,
    444; food practices of, 323; forms of,
    550; LGBTQ, 446, 551–52; mental health
    of, 437–38; on ritual practice, 297; on
    staying by us, 343
Ottoman Empire, 94, 95–96, 135, 172, 197,
    198–202, 524, 531–32
Ottoman Palestine, 215
Oven of Akhnai, 57
Ozick, Cynthia, 358

paideic model of law, 481
Pale of Settlement (Russia), 317, 458
Palestine, 3, 88, 103, 224, 225–26, 529–30
Palestine studies, 549, 555
Palestinian-Israeli conflict, 550, 554
Palestinian Talmud (Yerushalmi), 70, 71,
    72, 74
Paley, Grace, 358
Pan-German League, 221
Panofsky, Erwin, 401, 402
Paris Treaties, 243
Park, Robert Ezra, 490
Passover, 46, 149, 277, 279

574 INDEX

Paths of Emancipation (Birnbaum and
  Katznelson), 196
Patriarchate, 58–59
Penslar, Derek, 547, 555
Pentateuch, 16, 21–22, 23–24, 25, 43, 44
Peretz, Y. L., 418, 421
Perl, Joseph, 260
Perlson, Inbal, 535
Perry, Menakhem, 357
persecution, 127, 142, 144–46, 154–56, 216,
  240, 245–46. *See also* Holocaust
Persian Empire, 37, 39, 42
Persian Era, 39–40
Peskowitz, Miriam, 507
Pharisees, 44, 48, 284
Philippson, Ludwig, 140, 353, 404
Philippson Bible, 404
Philips, Bruce, 497–98
Philo of Alexandria, 44, 70, 283
philosophy: halakhah and, 477; interpreta-
  tion types in, 305, 306; introduction to,
  293–300; of religion, 302–3; state of field
  of, 294–302; summary of, 309
piety, 75, 85, 107, 167, 258, 280–81, 457,
  466–67
pilgrimages, 46–47, 275–76
pilpul, 174
Pinchas-Mizrachi, Ronit, 449
Pines, Meir, 354
Pinsker, Leo, 223
Pirenne, Henri, 103
Pissarro, Camille, 411
piyyut, 375, 386
Plate, S. Brent, 406
Plato, 70
PLO Research Center, 544, 545
Podhoretz, Norman, 492
poetry, 375. *See also piyyut*
Polak, Henry, 222
Poland, 94, 95, 173, 238
Polish-Lithuanian Commonwealth,
  94–95, 96
political science, 190
political theory, 185, 186–90
population genetics, 8. *See also* Jewish
  genetics
Portnoy's Complaint (Roth), 266
positivism, in Jewish law, 475–78
Postel, Guillaume, 168

Postema, Gerald, 480
Practica inquisitionis heretice pravitatis
  (Gui), 148
prayer, 74–75, 374–75
Prell, Riv-Ellen, 459
Priestly (P) document, 24–25
prisca theologia, 167–68
Promey, Sally M., 406
prophecy: *navi,* 28; *Nevi'im Aharonim*
  (Latter Prophets), 27–29; *Nevi'im*
  Rishonim (Former Prophets), 26–27
Prophets (Hebrew Bible), 26–29, 42–44
Protestantism, 491–92
Protestant Reformation, 135
psalms, 30
Psalms, Book of (Hebrew Bible), 30–31
pseudepigraphy, 44
psychoanalysis, 400–401
Ptolemaic Egypt, 41
Ptolemy II (king), 43–44
Ptolemy III (king), 41
Purim, 279

qahal, 83–85, 86, 87, 93
Qaraites, 89, 90, 91
qehilla, 85–87, 102–3, 116–17n91, 117n92
Qumran, 50, 282

Rabbanites, 89, 90, 91
rabbinical courts, women in, 109
rabbinic responsa, 125–26
rabbinic sources, God in, 284–86, 288
rabbinic study houses, 280–81
rabbis: elites and, 130–31; halakhah and,
  61–64, 125–26; introduction to, 55–56;
  midrash and, 67–70; Mishnaic literature
  and, 61–64; overivew of, 75–76; pluralism
  of, 57; Rabbinic literature and, 59–61, 73,
  125–26; Rabbinic transformation of
  Judaism and, 56–70; Shema and, 65–67;
  Talmuds and, 70–75. *See also* sages
Rabin, Shari, 319
Rabinovich, S. N., 260
Rabinowitch, Sholem (Sholem Aleichem),
  417–18
race, 326, 444, 487, 488–502
Rachel of Mainz, 151
racialization, 213, 225
radical ethnonationalism, 244

INDEX 575

Rapoport, Shloyme Zanvil (S. An-sky), 317, 404–5
Raucher, Michal, 467, 551
Ray, Jonathan, 107–8
Reed, Anette Yoshiko, 287
Reform Jews, 299
Reider, Joseph, 403
religion, 38, 273, 295, 306–8, 315, 316, 326, 409. *See also* lived religion
religious studies, 273–82
Renanot-Institute of Jewish Music, 382
repentance, 29
responsa, 125–26
Reuchlin, Johannes, 376
Revealer of Secrets (Perl), 260
re-vernacularization, 346
Rewritten Bible, 43
Reyzen, Zalman, 354, 419
Rich, Adrienne, 505
Ringelblum, Emmanuel, 425
ritual/Jewish rituals: Christian metaphors and, 150; in everyday Judaism, 124, 130, 132–33; God's place in, 285; of initiation, 150; in the Jerusalem Temple, 276–77; language of, 171; in music, 377; overview of, 275–82; studies of, 321–22
Roberman, Sveta, 469
Robinson, Shira, 553–54
Roby, Bryan, 534
Rock-Singer, Cara, 326
Rodrigue, Aron, 199, 526
Roediger, David, 494
Rojanski, Rachel, 414
Roma, 237
Roman Empire, 51–53
Roman law, 104–5
romanticism, 104, 224
Rosenfarb, Chava, 424
Rosensweig, Claudia, 423
Rosh Hashanah (Festival of Trumpets), 277, 279
Roskies, David, 358–59, 424–25
Ross, Tamar, 483
Roth, Cecil, 144–45, 146, 265–66
Roth, Guenther, 104
Roth, Henry, 358
Roth, Philip, 358
Rothko, Mark, 263
Rotman, Diego, 548

Rubin, Joel, 427
Rubin, Ruth, 427
Russia, 243, 317, 415, 418
Russian Jews, 192, 422
Ruth (Hebrew Bible), 34

Sabbath, 277, 278
Sack, Daniel, 322
Sacks, Karen (Brodkin), 494
sacrifice, 23, 24
Sadan, Dov, 355
Sadducees, 44, 48, 284
Safedian revolutions, 168–72
Safed Kabbalah, 169
Safran, Gabriella, 458
sages, 55, 56, 57, 58, 59–60, 64. *See also* rabbis
Said, Edward, 409
Salome Alexandra, 46
Samaria, 40, 47
Samaritans, 299
Samet, Hadar Feldman, 535
Sampter, Jessie, 319, 326
Samuel, Rabbi, 70
Saperstein, Aliya, 445
Sapoznik, Henry, 427
Sasson, Haim Hillel Ben, 106, 122
Satlow, Michael, 295–98
Sayegh, Anis, 543, 544
Schachter, Allison, 359, 424
Schapiro, Meyer, 402
Schatz, Boris, 406
Schhwarz, Karl, 401
Schilbrack, Kevin, 294, 302, 303
Schlesin, Sonja, 222
Schnabel, Landon, 446
Schneerson, Menachem Mendel, 322
Scholem, Gershom, 164, 190, 370, 425, 485
Schönberg, Arnold, 263–64
Schreckenberg, Heinz, 403
Schroeter, Daniel, 525
Schulze, Kirsten, 531
Schwartz, Delmore, 358
Scott, Joan, 509–11, 513
Second Commandment, 400
Second Temple, 52, 277
Second Temple Period, 37
Second Vatican Council, 147
sectarianism, 49–50
seder, Passover, 149

576 INDEX

Seeman, Don, 460
Sefer Hasidism (Book of the Pious), 374–75
segregation, 116n91, 146, 490
Seidman, Naomi, 361, 423–24, 427
Seleucids, 47, 51
selihot, 151
Semyonov, Moshe, 442
Senderovich, Sasha, 422
Sephardi Jews, 98, 169, 199, 200, 467,
    521–23
Sephardi/Mizrahi studies: decline
    narrative in, 523–26; future directions
    in, 535–37; introduction to, 518–21;
    Levant and, 530–31; music, cinema,
    literature, and cultural studies in, 535;
    Ottoman Sephardic world and, 531–32;
    post-1990s expansion and scholarship
    by area in, 526–32; pre-1948 Palestine
    and, 529–30; Sephardi and Mizrahi Jews
    in, 521–23; transnationalism and
    diasporas in, 532–34
Seroussi, Edwin, 535
Sfard, Dovid, 414
Shabbes Goy (Katz), 147
Shaikevitsh, N. M. (Shomer), 263
Shain, Michelle, 437
Shammai, House of, 67–68
Shandler, Jeffrey, 324
Shapira, Anita, 542
Shapiro, Efraim, 449
Shavuot (Festival of Weeks), 277, 279
Shaw, Tony, 548
Shaykh al-Islam, 172
Shema, 65–67, 72, 73, 74–75
Shemer, Yaron, 535
Shemini Atzeret, 279
Shenhav, Yehouda, 534
Sheskin, Ira, 438, 447, 498
Shitrit, Lihi Ben, 512, 550–51
Shneer, David, 422, 427
Shoham-Steiner, Ephraim, 150, 151
Shohat, Ella, 526, 533, 535
Shtok, Fradl, 424
Shulchan Arukh, 169, 172, 173, 174, 175–76
Shu 'un Filastiniyya (Palestinian Affairs)
    (journal), 543
Sigalow, Emily, 325, 439–40
Silver, Chris, 535

Simeon, Rabbi, 75
Simon, 46
Simon Bar Kochba, 53
Simon-Shoshan, Moshe, 482
Simonsohn, Uriel, 109
Singer, Isaac Bashevis, 358, 421
Sinti, 237
Sirat, René, 222
Six-Day War, 225–26, 553–54
Sklare, Marshall, 436
Slouschz, Nahum, 354
Smith, Jonathan Z., 315
Smith, J. Z., 296
Snir, Reuven, 530
Social Darwinism, 488, 490
Sokol, Yosef, 446
Solomon, 21, 26, 32, 46, 275
Soloveitchik, Rabbi Chaim, 176
Solveitchik, Haym, 477–78
Somekh, Sasson, 534
Song of Songs (Hebrew Bible), 32
"Songs of the Sabbath Sacrifice," 282–83
songsters, 379–80
Sorkin, David, 197–98, 202
Soviet Union. *See* Russia
Spain, 135
Spanish-Portuguese communities, 384–85
Spencer, Herbert, 490
Sperber, Daniel, 404
Spinoza, Baruch, 25, 185, 186–90, 194, 196,
    202, 353
Stadler, Nurit, 467
Starr, Deborah, 535
Stasov, Vladimir, 405
Stein, Sarah Abrevaya, 199–201, 532
Steinberg, Leo, 400
Steinschneider, Moritz, 352
Stern, David, 359
Stern, Zehavit, 428
Sternberg, Meir, 357
Stillman, Norman, 526
Stolow, Jeremy, 324
Stora, Benjamin, 524
Strassfeld, Max, 507
Sukkot (Festival of Tabernacles), 46, 48,
    277, 279, 321
summer camp, 440
Surnow, Rose, 312

INDEX 577

Sutzkever, Avrom, 425
synagogue: of everyday Judaism, 122, 129–30; floor mosaics of, 286; function of, 280; music in, 371; origins of, 41; rest from tribulations in, 142; significance of, 122; voluntary membership to, 101
Syria, 45, 112n29, 554
Syrian Sephardic community, 439
Syria Palestine, 53
Szendroi, Kriszta Eszter, 428
Szwarcman-Czarnota, Bella, 424
Szymaniak, Karolina, 424

tabernacle, 275–76
Talmon, Jacob, 234
Talmud, 70–75, 162, 163–64, 165
Tamarkin, Noah, 463
Tanakh, 15, 22
Tanzimat reforms, 199
Tapper, Aaron Hahn, 445, 498
taqqanot (statutes), 93
Ta-Shma, Israel, 165
Tavory, Iddo, 444
Taylor, Charles, 298
Tay-Sachs disease, 496–97
Teif, Moisei, 415
Tel Aviv School, 356
Temple Scroll, 43
Testaments of the Twelve Patriarchs, 44
Theologico-Political Treatise (Spinoza), 186–87
Thomas, Laurence, 499
Thompson, Jennifer A., 325, 465
Titus, 52
Tobin, Diane, 498–99
Tobin, Gary, 498–99
Tönnies, Ferdinand, 98
Torah, 21–26, 42–44, 74–76, 150, 162–63, 295
Tosafists, 173
Tosefta, 63
Tov, Israel Ba'al Shem, 167, 171
Trajan, 52
transnationalism, 361, 532–34
Traverso, Enzo, 240
Trismegistus, Hermes, 168
Tsabari, Ayelet, 534
Tunisia, 211, 228n15
Turkish Jews, 199

Turniansky, Chava, 423
Tweed, Thomas, 315
Twine, France Winddance, 493
Twitty, Michael W., 496
Tyshler, Alexander, 415

Udel, Miriam, 424
Ugarit language, 19
Ukraine, 4, 240
ultra-Orthodox (Haredi) Jews, 239, 439, 466, 467, 550, 551; mortality rates, 449
United States: antisemitism in, 9; civil rights movement in, 491–92; identity politics in, 500; Jewish citizenship in, 195, 198, 206; Jewish literature in, 355–56, 357–58; Jewish loss of security in, 202; Jewish Studies in, 4–5; laws of, 478, 480–81; literature rise in, 355–56; lived religion in, 314–16, 318–27; race in, 489–93; socioeconomic diversity in, 446–47, 491. See also American Jewish sociology; American Jews
Uris, Leon, 263
US Holocaust Museum, 236

Valensi, Lucette, 524
Veidlinger, Jeffrey, 317, 422
Veiner, Meir, 418
Vermel, Solomon, 405
Vespasian, 52
Vindicta Salvatoris (The Vengeance of the Savior), 149
violence, 139–43, 144, 153–56
Vital, David, 231
Vital, Rabbi Hayyim, 170
Viterbo, Egidio da, 168
von Goethe, Johann Wolfgang, 351
von Herder, Johann Gottfried, 351
von Hofmannsthal, Hugo, 425
von Treitschke, Heinrich, 140

Wagner, Richard, 399
Waligorska, Magdalena, 465
Wallace, Michael, 442
Wannsee conference, 236
Warburg, Aby, 401, 402
Washington, Booker T., 490
Washington, Robin, 498

Wasserman, Varda, 445–46
Waxman, Meyer, 353
Webber, Jonathan, 455
Weber, Max, 99, 399, 492
Wehler, Hans Ulrich, 240
Weiman Kelman, Zohar, 424
Weinrich, Max, 354, 355, 416
Weinrich, Uriel, 357, 419
Weiss, Dov, 286
Weiss, Judith, 168
Weitzman, Lenore, 512
Wellek, René, 356
Wellhausen, Julius, 16, 24
Werczberger, Rachel, 467
White, Hayden, 236–37
whiteness, 488
whiteness studies, 493–95, 500
Wiesel, Eli, 233
Wildt, Michael, 244
Wilhelm II (kaiser of Germany), 220
Winant, Howard, 493
Winckelmann, Johann Joachim, 398
Winfield, Taylor Paige, 444
Wirth, Louis, 491
Wirth-Nesher, Hana, 350, 361
wisdom literature, 31
Wisdom of Ben Sira, 44
Wisse, Ruth, 360, 421
Wissenschaft (science), 3
Wissenschaft des Judentums (Verein für
   Cultur und Wissenschaft der Juden),
   140, 165, 190, 205, 317, 368, 399–400, 416
Wittgenstein, Ludwig, 296, 297
women: citizenship and, 187; feminist
   movement and, 507–9; in Jerusalem
   fights, 550–51 (*See also* gender studies);
   legal strategies of, 109; societies of, 177;
   Yiddish and, 423–24
Woolf, Virginia, 510
World War I, 242–43
World War II, 203. *See also* Holocaust
worship, 23, 51–52, 129–30, 280, 287–88
Wright, Bradley, 442
Writings (Hebrew Bible), 29–34

Yahwistic (J) document, 24
Yahwistic religion, 16–17
Yares, Laura, 319, 320, 324
Yehudim/Ioudaioi, 37–38

Yerushalmi, Yosef Hayim, 148
Yiddish: digital humanities and, 426;
   disincentivized use of, 346; German as
   compared to, 341, 348; Hasidic, 428;
   Holocaust and, 424–25; influences from,
   342–43; introduction to, 414–15; Jewish
   literature in, 354, 355, 356; literature,
   417–21; music, dance, summer programs,
   and communities of, 426–28; old, 423;
   origin of, 415–16; as post-coterritorial,
   334, 339; post-vernacular, 345; pushing
   boundaries of imagination in, 424–28; as
   real language, 415–17; resistance and,
   257–58; Russian/Soviet Jewish experience
   regarding, 422; summary of, 429;
   systems/features of, 338, 339, 341; today's
   questions regarding, 421–24; women/
   gender studies and, 423–24
Yochai, Rabbi Shimon bar, 171
Yohanan, Rabbi, 69, 74–75
Yom Kippur, 279
Yose, Rabbi, 72
Yosef, Rabbi Ovadia, 174
Yosef, Raz, 535
Yuval, Israel, 128–29, 148–49, 151, 153

Zabbalat Shabbat service, 170
Zach, Natan, 356
Zack, Naomi, 499
Zadoff, Noam, 548
Zakai, Sivan, 448
Zakkai, Rabban Yohanen ben, 57
Zalcman, Beth, 449
Zangwill, Israel, 216, 488
Zborowski, Mark, 458
Zerubavel, Yael, 552
Zilbercweig, Zalmen, 419
Zinberg, Israel, 353–54, 418
Zinger, Oded, 109
Zionism, 101, 191, 209, 223–27, 354, 508,
   541–42, 555
Zionism (journal), 542
Zionist historiography, 151–52
Zipperstein, Steven E., 554
Zohar, 164–66, 169, 170–72
Zola, Émile, 214
Zucker, Sheva, 424
Zunz, Leopold, 190–91, 350–51, 352
Zweig, Ronald, 542